WOMEN'S HUMAN RIGHTS

As an instrument that addresses the circumstances that affect women's lives and enjoyment of rights in a diverse world, the Convention on the Elimination of All Forms of Discrimination against Women is slowly but surely making its mark on the development of international and national law. Using national case studies from South Asia, Eastern and Southern Africa, Australia, Canada and Northern Europe, *Women's Human Rights* examines the potential and actual added value of the CEDAW in comparison and interaction with other equality and anti-discrimination mechanisms. The studies demonstrate how state and non-state actors have invoked, adopted or resisted the CEDAW and related instruments in different legal, political, economic and socio-cultural contexts, and how the various international, regional and national regimes have drawn inspiration and learned from each other.

ANNE HELLUM is a professor at the Faculty of Law, Department of Public and International Law, University of Oslo, Norway.

HENRIETTE SINDING AASEN is a professor at the Faculty of Law, University of Bergen, Norway.

WOMEN'S HUMAN RIGHTS

CEDAW in International, Regional and National Law

Edited by

ANNE HELLUM

AND

HENRIETTE SINDING AASEN

CAMBRIDGE
UNIVERSITY PRESS

CAMBRIDGE
UNIVERSITY PRESS

University Printing House, Cambridge CB2 8BS, United Kingdom

Cambridge University Press is part of the University of Cambridge.

It furthers the University's mission by disseminating knowledge in the pursuit of education, learning and research at the highest international levels of excellence.

www.cambridge.org
Information on this title: www.cambridge.org/9781107034624

First published 2013

A catalogue record for this publication is available from the British Library

Library of Congress Cataloguing in Publication data
Women's human rights : CEDAW in international, regional, and national law /
[edited by] Anne Hellum, Henriette Sinding Aasen.
pages cm. – (Studies on human rights conventions ; 3)
Includes bibliographical references and index.
ISBN 978-1-107-03462-4 (hardback)
1. Women (International law) 2. Women's rights. 3. United Nations.
Committee on the Elimination of Discrimination Against Women.
I. Hellum, Anne. II. Aasen, Henriette Sinding.
K644.W6445 2013
342.08'78–dc23
2013000791 CIP

ISBN 978-1-107-03462-4 Hardback

Additional resources for this publication at www.cambridge.org/hellum

CONTENTS

Notes on contributors *page* viii
Preface and acknowledgements xvii
List of abbreviations xix

Introduction 1
ANNE HELLUM AND HENRIETTE SINDING AASEN

PART I **Potential added value of the CEDAW** 25

1 The Committee on the Elimination of Discrimination against Women 27
ANDREW BYRNES

2 The United Nations Working Group on the Issue of Discrimination against Women in Law and Practice 62
FAREDA BANDA

3 The CEDAW: a holistic approach to women's equality and freedom 95
RIKKI HOLTMAAT

4 The CEDAW as a legal framework for transnational discourses on gender stereotyping 124
SIMONE CUSACK

5 From the CEDAW to the American Convention: elucidation of women's right to a life's project and protection of maternal identity within Inter-American human rights jurisprudence 158
CECILIA M. BAILLIET

6 Pulling apart? Treatment of pluralism in the CEDAW and the Maputo Protocol 183
CELESTINE NYAMU MUSEMBI

PART II **Actual added value of the CEDAW: socio-economic rights 215**

7 Engendering socio-economic rights 217
SANDRA FREDMAN

8 'Women's rights are human rights!': the practice of the United Nations Human Rights Committee and the Committee on Economic, Social and Cultural Rights 242
FLEUR VAN LEEUWEN

9 Property and security: articulating women's rights to their homes 268
INGUNN IKDAHL

10 Maternal mortality and women's right to health 292
HENRIETTE SINDING AASEN

PART III **The CEDAW in national law 321**

11 The implementation of the CEDAW in Australia: success, trials, tribulations and continuing struggle 323
ANDREW BYRNES

12 The Canadian experience with the CEDAW: all women's rights are human rights – a case of treaties synergy 358
LUCIE LAMARCHE

13 India's CEDAW story 385
MADHU MEHRA

14 Judicial education on the Convention on Elimination of Discrimination against Women in Nepal 410
KABITA PANDEY

15 From ratification to implementation: 'domesticating' the CEDAW in state, government and society. A case study of Pakistan 430
SHAHEEN SARDAR ALI

16 Zimbabwe and CEDAW compliance: pursuing women's equality in fits and starts 454
CHOICE DAMISO AND JULIE STEWART

17 The CEDAW after all these years: firmly rooted in Dutch clay? 482

MARJOLEIN VAN DEN BRINK

18 The CEDAW in the UK 511

SANDRA FREDMAN

19 Domestication of the CEDAW in France: from paradoxes to ambivalences and back again 531

HÉLÈNE RUIZ FABRI AND ANDREA HAMANN

20 Rise and fall of the CEDAW in Finland: time to reclaim its impetus 557

KEVÄT NOUSIAINEN AND MERJA PENTIKÄINEN

21 Making space and giving voice: the CEDAW in Norwegian law 588

ANNE HELLUM

Conclusions 625

ANNE HELLUM AND HENRIETTE SINDING AASEN

Index 656

CONTRIBUTORS

HENRIETTE SINDING AASEN (dr. juris) is a professor at the Faculty of Law, University of Bergen, Norway. She headed the University of Bergen Democracy and Rule of Law programme from 2008 to 2012, and is the leader of three interdisciplinary research projects funded by the Norwegian Research Council: Juridification and Social Citizenship in the Welfare State; Constitution, Welfare State and Social Citizenship; Health Promotion, Dignity and Human Rights: Improvement of Maternal Health in Tanzania (this project will be expanded to other African countries in 2013). All the projects have an interdisciplinary approach and address the role of socio-economic rights in democratic welfare states or in developing countries, and with a particular focus on vulnerable groups whose social citizenship and basic rights are threatened. Her latest publications address the right to health from the perspective of women, children, illegal immigrants and old persons, as well as the role of law and human rights in securing basic values of the welfare state. She provides courses for international students in human rights law, healthcare law and welfare state law, and has participated in several law commissions in the areas of health, medical research, human rights and education.

SHAHEEN SARDAR ALI BA, LLB, MA, LLM, PhD is Professor of Law at the University of Warwick in the United Kingdom, and Vice-chair of the UN Working Group on Arbitrary Detention. She was formerly Professor II at the University of Oslo, Norway, Professor of Law at the University of Peshawar, Pakistan, and Director of the Women's Study Centre at the same university. She has published extensively in the areas of Islamic law and jurisprudence, international law of human rights, women's and children's rights, and gender, law and development. Her most recent selected publications include *From Transnational Relations to Transnational Laws: Northern European Law at the Crossroads* (2010) co-edited with A. Hellum and A. Griffiths; 'Cyberspace as emerging Muslim discursive space? Online *fatawa* on women and gender relations and its impact on Muslim family law norms' (2010); 'A comparative perspective of the United Nations Convention on the Rights of the Child and the principles of Islamic law: law reform and children's rights in Muslim jurisdictions' (2007) in S. Goonesekere (ed.), *Protecting the World's Children: Impact of the UN Convention on the Rights of the Child in Diverse Legal Systems* (2007); *Human Rights, Plural Legalities and Gendered Realities. Paths Are Made by Walking* (2007) co-edited with A. Hellum, J. Stewart and A. Tsanga; *Conceptualising Islamic Law, CEDAW and Women's Human Rights in Plural Legal Settings: A Comparative Analysis of Application of CEDAW in Bangladesh, India and Pakistan* (2006); *Gender and Human Rights in Islam and International Law. Equal before Allah, Unequal before Man?* (2000).

CECILIA M. BAILLIET is Professor, Deputy Director of the Department of Public and International Law and Director of the Master's Programme in Public International Law at the University of Oslo. She has a doctoral degree in Law from the University of Oslo and a combined JD/MA (honours) degree from the George Washington University Law School and Elliott School of International Affairs. Her publications address the vulnerability of humanity, examining the cross-fields of international public law, human rights, women's law, refugee law and counter-terrorism. She is currently researching and teaching the right to peace. Among her publications are *Security: A Multidisciplinary Normative Approach* (2009) and *Cosmopolitan Justice and its Discontents* (2011) co-edited with Katja Franko Aas.

FAREDA BANDA is Professor of the Laws of Africa at the University of London, School of Oriental and African Studies. She holds a doctorate in Law from the University of Oxford. Her areas of interest/expertise include the human rights of women, family law, and issues pertaining to law and society in Africa. She co-edits the Journal of African Law, is an Associate Editor (Africa) of the International Survey of Family Law while also sitting on the editorial board of the International Journal of Law, Policy and the Family. She is on the international advisory boards of three other publications. Her publications include a book entitled *Women, Law and Human Rights: An African Perspective*. She has worked as a consultant for the United Nations OHCHR writing a report on laws that discriminate against women.

MARJOLEIN VAN DEN BRINK is a lecturer in law at the Utrecht University Law School, the Netherlands. Between 2001 and 2012 she combined this position with membership of the Dutch national equal opportunities body (Commissie gelijke behandeling). She undertakes research in the field of international law, especially human rights law, with particular reference to gender and non-discrimination perspectives.

ANDREW BYRNES is Professor of Law at the University of New South Wales and Chair of the Australian Human Rights Centre. He writes on international law (in particular human rights law), and has written on CEDAW and the human rights of women, among other topics. He was involved in the drafting of anti-discrimination legislation, has advised equality commissioners in Australia and Hong Kong, and was closely involved in the drafting of the OP-CEDAW and of the Convention on the Rights of Persons with Disabilities. He is a member of the advisory committee of the International Women's Rights Action Watch (Asia-Pacific), and was a member of the Asian Development Bank's External Forum on Gender and Development from 2000 to 2009. He has acted as a consultant on gender and other human rights issues to the OHCHR, the UN Division for the Advancement of Women, the ILO, UNESCAP, the Commonwealth Secretariat and other bodies. He was President of the Australian and New Zealand Society of International Law from 2009 to 2013 and external legal adviser to the Australian Parliamentary Joint Committee on Human Rights (2012–2013). Further details at www.law.unsw.edu.au/staff/ByrnesA/Publications.asp.

SIMONE CUSACK is an Australian lawyer and works as a Senior Policy/Research Officer at the Australian Human Rights Commission. She has published and lectured widely on women's rights issues, including the CEDAW and its Optional Protocol, and is co-author (with Professor Rebecca J. Cook) of *Gender Stereotyping: Transnational Legal Perspectives* (2010). She is also the founding editor of the Optional Protocol to CEDAW wesbite (http://opcedaw.wordpress.com/), which provides information about developments related to the Optional Protocol. Simone holds a BA/LLB (Hons) from Monash University, Australia, and an LLM from the University of Toronto, Canada.

CHOICE DAMISO is a lawyer. She was Counsel to the Zimbabwe Parliament and now works with UNFPA.

SANDRA FREDMAN is the Rhodes Professor of the Laws of the British Commonwealth and the USA at the University of Oxford, a Fellow of the British Academy and an Honorary Professor at the University of Cape Town. She is South African, a graduate of the University of the Witwatersrand

and Oxford University. She was made a Queen's Counsel (honoris causa) in 2012. She has published widely in the fields of equality, labour law and human rights. Her published books include *Human Rights Transformed* (2008); *Discrimination Law* (2nd edn 2011); *Women and the Law* (1997); *The State as Employer* (1988) with Gillian Morris; and *Labour Law and Industrial Relations in Great Britain* (2nd edn 1992) with Bob Hepple. She has also edited two books: *Age as an Equality Issue* (2003) with Sarah Spencer, and *Discrimination and Human Rights: The Case of Racism* (2001). She was a scientific director of the EU Network of Legal Experts in the Non-Discrimination Field, and she has been an expert adviser to the proposed Single Equality Bill in Northern Ireland, the Equalities Review in the UK, the Canadian Review of Federal Labour Law, the UN Human Rights Commission working group on national action plans against racism, the UN Working Group on Women's Rights, the World Development Report 2013 and Indian gender discrimination legislation. She is a Fellow of Gray's Inn and holds an academic tenancy at Old Square Chambers.

ANDREA HAMANN holds a PhD in Public International Law from the Sorbonne Law School (University of Paris 1 Panthéon-Sorbonne), on the subject 'Adjudicating compliance in the WTO dispute settlement system'. Her research and publications focus on international dispute settlement, compliance with international law, women's human rights and the CEDAW.

ANNE HELLUM is a professor at the Department of Public and International Law at the University of Oslo. She is Director of the Institute of Women's Law, Child Law, Discrimination and Equality Law, and Director of the Faculty of Law's interdisciplinary research centre Rights, Individuals, Culture and Society (RICS). She is a guest professor at the Southern and Eastern Africa Regional Centre for Women's Law (SEARCWL) at the University of Zimbabwe. She is leader of the international research projects 'Gender, human rights and water governance: actors, norms and institutions (South Africa, Malawi, Kenya and Zimbabwe)' and 'Gender identity and sexual orientation in international and national (Norwegian) law'. Among her most recent international publications are *Human Rights, Plural Legalities and Gendered Realities: Paths Are Made by Walking* (2007) with Julie Stewart and Amy Tsanga; *From Transnational Relations to Transnational Laws: Northern European Law at the Crossroads* (2011) with Anne Griffiths and Shaheen S. Ali; and *Worlds of Human Rights: Ambiguities of Rights Claiming in Africa* (2013) with Bill Derman and Kristin Sandvik.

RIKKI HOLTMAAT has been a professor of International Non-Discrimination Law at Leiden Law School since 2003. She graduated *cum laude* in Law at Utrecht University in 1983 and worked as a member of the academic staff of the Dutch Emancipation Council from 1982 to 1985. From 1985 to 2001 she lectured on Women and Law at the University of Leiden. Her PhD thesis (1992) investigated the construction of unequal gender relations in social security law in the Netherlands. Publications concern the fields of labour law, social security law, EU equality law, the CEDAW and feminist legal theory. Besides this, she has also worked as an independent consultant and researcher in the area of gender, law and non-discrimination since 1998. Since 2005 she has been a member of the European Commission's Network of Legal Experts in the Non-Discrimination Field; since 2008 she has also been a member of the European Commission's Network of Legal Experts in the Field of Gender. She has carried out research projects for the Dutch government and for Dutch NGOs, and for several international organisations, among others UNICEF, the International Commission of Jurists, the OHCHR, ILO, OSCE/ODIHR and the European Commission.

INGUNN IKDAHL is a postdoctoral fellow at the Institute of Public and International Law, Faculty of Law, University of Oslo. She obtained her PhD in Jurisprudence in 2010 on the dissertation 'Securing women's homes. The dynamics of women's human rights at the international level and in Tanzania'. She also teaches at the Southern and Eastern Africa Regional Centre for Women's Law (SEARCWL) based in Harare. Her research on women's human rights focuses on themes at the intersection of development, livelihood, access to and management of natural resources, care work and discrimination.

LUCIE LAMARCHE is the Gordon F. Henderson Chair in Human Rights at University of Ottawa, Canada, where she also is the Research Director of the Human Rights Research and Education Centre. Lucie Lamarche is Associate Professor at the Faculty of Law and Political Science of Université du Québec à Montréal, Canada. Her fields of interest and publications mainly concern economic and social rights, women's rights, social security and social protection, and human rights institutions.

FLEUR VAN LEEUWEN, LLM, PhD is an assistant professor at Bogazici University in Istanbul, Turkey, and owner of Havva Human Rights

Projects (havvahumanrights.com). She conducts research and publishes articles on women's human rights, reproductive rights, and the rights of lesbians, gays, bi- and transsexuals, in various languages, books and journals. In 2009 she obtained her PhD in Human Rights Law at Utrecht University, the Netherlands. In that same year she published the book *Women's Rights are Human Rights – The Practice of the UN Human Rights Committee and the Committee on Economic, Social and Cultural Rights.*

MADHU MEHRA is a lawyer, a founding member and Executive Director of Partners for Law in Development, a legal resource group on women's rights in India. She undertakes action research, production of knowledge resources, training and advocacy on the CEDAW and international human rights law, and feminist legal perspectives relating to women's rights in respect of family, culture, sexuality and violence against women. She has written on the above themes and, notably, has researched and drafted the review of fifteen years of the mandate of the UN Special Rapporteur on Violence Against Women (1994–2009).

KEVÄT NOUSIAINEN, LLD is Professor of Comparative Law and Legal Theory at Turku University, Finland. She has carried out a number of studies and conducted various national and Nordic research projects on rights of women and discrimination, and has lately published articles on intersectional discrimination.

CELESTINE NYAMU MUSEMBI is a lawyer with interdisciplinary training in Legal Anthropology. She earned her LLB degree from the University of Nairobi in 1993, and her LLM and SJD degrees from Harvard Law School in 1995 and 2000 respectively. She is currently a senior lecturer at the University of Nairobi School of Law. She previously served as Fellow of the Institute of Development Studies, Sussex (UK) for six years. She teaches and researches in the areas of human rights and development, gender and politics, citizen participation in governance, family law and property relations. She recently co-authored *Ours by Right: Law, Politics and Realities of Community Property in Kenya* (2013).

KABITA PANDEY, Advocate, LLM in Gender and Human Rights and Master in Political Science, is a public interest lawyer in Pro Public and Women for Human Rights, Single Women Group in Nepal. She has filed and represented several public interest litigations on behalf of her organizations and on her own behalf in the Supreme Court of

Nepal, for the protection and promotion of women's human rights and rights of children. She is also coordinating a community mediation programme aimed to promote access to justice and societal harmony at the local level especially for women and other marginalized communities of Nepal. She worked as Task Force member of Women's Political Participation (WPP) at the Asia Pacific Forum on Women, Law and Development, Chang Mai, Thailand, 2006, and worked as an expert member of a team that prepared a model constitution from the gender perspective on behalf of Pro Public and UNIFEM and submitted it to the then Constituent Assembly.

MERJA PENTIKÄINEN, LLD, DES, is a senior researcher in international law. Her fields of expertise cover, in particular, various human rights questions, including minority and indigenous peoples' issues, women and human rights, violence against women, discrimination, racism and other forms of intolerance, human rights aspects of international migration and integration within society, international and national security and human rights, and human rights aspects of responsible business and sustainable development. She has published numerous monographs and articles on these questions.

HÉLÈNE RUIZ FABRI has degrees in Law and Political Science, and a Doctorate from the University of Bordeaux. She is currently Dean of the Sorbonne Law School (University of Paris 1 Panthéon-Sorbonne), Director of the Joint Institute of Comparative Law of Paris (UMR de droit comparé – Paris I/CNRS) and Director of the Master 2 Degree Programme in International Economic Law. She teaches and researches International Law, WTO Law and International Dispute Settlement. She has published extensively in the fields of WTO Law and Dispute Settlement, and also in Constitutional Law. She taught at the Academy of European Law (Florence) and at the Academy of International Law (The Hague). She also has experience at the Council of Europe (as a legal consultant on the ratification and the implementation of the European Convention on Human Rights in East European countries), at the French administration and at the Organisation internationale de la Francophonie (as a legal consultant on cultural diversity).

JULIE STEWART is Professor of Law and Director of the Southern and Eastern Africa Regional Centre for Women's Law (SEARCWL), University of Zimbabwe. SEARCWL runs a regional Masters Programme in Women's Law. She has published extensively in the fields of women and law, and on the intersections between state laws, customary laws and human rights in Southern Africa. In 2011 SEARCWL published *Women and Law: Innovative Approaches to Research and Analysis*, which is a documentation and discussion of the evolution of the courses on the Masters in Women's Law Programme.

PREFACE AND ACKNOWLEDGEMENTS

The international human rights regime consists of a broad range of instruments and monitoring bodies that all contribute to uphold respect for human rights. This book situates the Convention on the Elimination of All Forms of Discrimination against Women (CEDAW) in a legal landscape where states are under multiple international, regional and national obligations to respect, protect and fulfil women's civil, political, social and economic rights.

The idea of this book grew out of the research project 'Should states ratify human rights conventions?' headed by Professor Andreas Føllesdal and Professor Geir Ulfstein at the Center for Advanced Studies (CAS), Norway, in 2009 and 2010. The book is the outcome of the international conference *From Ratification to Implementation: CEDAW in International and National Law*, held in Oslo on 11–12 March 2009. This conference provided an arena for exchange of ideas between human rights scholars and practitioners from Northern Europe, South Asia, Australia, Canada and Southern Africa.

The conference was organized and funded by CAS and the research group Rights, Individuals, Culture and Society (RIKS) at the Department of Public and International Law at the Faculty of Law, University of Oslo. We are particularly grateful to the Norwegian Agency for Development Cooperation (NORAD), which funded the participation of scholars and practitioners from the Global South. We are also very grateful to Elisabeth Wenger Hagene from the Department of Public and International Law for her excellent administrative support before and during the conference.

A number of people have commented on the papers presented at the conference and reviewed the draft chapters in this book. In addition to two anonymous reviewers from Cambridge University Press, we would like to thank Kirsten Ketscher, Hege Skjeie, Malcolm Langford, Cees Flinterman, Rebecca Cook, Helen Keller, Andrew Byrnes, Mads Andenæs, Ingunn Ikdahl, Geir Ulfstein and Andreas Føllesdal for valuable comments on the conference papers and the draft chapters. We are particularly grateful to Geir Ulfstein and Andreas Føllesdal for stimulating discussions throughout the process.

We would also like to thank the Faculty of Law, University of Bergen, for providing funding for editorial assistance and proofreading. Special thanks to Padmaja Barua for her meticulous technical assistance.

Last but not least we thank Cambridge University Press for making this edited volume on the CEDAW part of the new series, Studies on Human Rights Conventions.

ABBREVIATIONS

AAAQ	Available, Accessible, Acceptable Services of Good Quality
ACHR	American Convention on Human Rights
ADA	Anti-Discrimination Act 1977 (New South Wales, Australia)
African Women's Protocol	Protocol to the African Charter on Human and People's Rights on the Rights of Women in Africa
AIPPA	Access to Information and Protection of Privacy Act (Zimbabwe)
ALRC	Australian Law Reform Commission
APAFEJE	Asia Pacific Advisory Forum on Judicial Education on Equality
APWA	All Pakistan Women's Association
CAT	Convention against Torture and Other Cruel, Inhuman or Degrading Treatment or Punishment
CEDAW	Convention on the Elimination of All Forms of Discrimination against Women
CERD	Committee on the Elimination of Racial Discrimination
CESCR	Committee on Economic, Social and Cultural Rights
CHR	Commission on Human Rights
CIDA	Canadian International Development Agency
CMW	International Convention on the Protection of the Rights of All Migrant Workers and the Members of Their Families
CNCDH	Commission nationale consultative des droits de l'homme/National Advisory Commission on Human Rights (France)
COC	Federation of Dutch Associations for the Integration of Homosexuality
COs	Concluding Observations
CRC	Convention on the Rights of the Child
CRPD	Convention on the Rights of Persons with Disabilities

CSCE	Conference on Security and Cooperation in Europe
CSOs	Civil Society Organizations
CSW	Commission on the Status of Women
DAW	Division for the Advancement of Women
EC	European Community
ECHR	European Convention for the Protection of Human Rights and Fundamental Freedoms
ECJ	European Court of Justice
ECtHR	European Court of Human Rights
EEA	European Economic Area
EEC	European Economic Communities
EFTA	European Free Trade Association
EHRC	Equality and Human Rights Commission
EOC	Equal Opportunities Commission
Equality Act	Act on Equality between Women and Men (Finland)
ESA	East and Southern African
ESCR	economic, social and cultural rights
FAFIA	The Canadian Feminist Alliance for International Action
FGM	female genital mutilation
GCs	General Comments
GNU	Government of National Unity (Zimbabwe)
GPA	Global Political Agreement (Zimbabwe)
HALDE	Haute autorité de lutte contre les discriminations et pour l'égalité/ High Authority to Combat Discrimination and Promote Equality (France)
HRC	Human Rights Committee
HRCP	Human Rights Commission of Pakistan
ICCPR	International Covenant on Civil and Political Rights
ICERD	International Convention on the Elimination of All Forms of Racial Discrimination
ICESCR	International Covenant on Economic, Social and Cultural Rights
ICJ	International Court of Justice
ICPD	International Conference on Population and Development
ICTR	International Criminal Tribunal for Rwanda
ICTY	International Criminal Tribunal for the former Yugoslavia
ILO	International Labour Organization
INSTRAW	International Research and Training Institute for the Advancement of Women
IOM	International Organization for Migration
IRS	Individual Rights Strategy
IWRAW-AP	International Women's Rights Action Watch – Asia Pacific
JORF	Journal officiel de la République française

JSCOT	Commonwealth Parliamentary Joint Standing Committee on Treaties (Australia)
JURK	Free Legal Advice for Women (Norway)
LAMA	Legal Age of Majority Act 1982 (Zimbabwe)
LGBT	lesbian, gay, bisexual and transgender
Maputo Protocol	Protocol to the African Charter on Human and People's Rights on the Rights of Women in Africa
MDGs	Millennium Development Goals
MMR	maternal mortality ratio
MWD	Ministry of Women's Development (Pakistan)
NAWO	National Alliance of Women's Organisations (India)
NCHR	Norwegian Centre for Human Rights
NCs	Native Commissioners
NCSW	National Commission on the Status of Women (Pakistan)
NGOs	non-governmental organizations
NHRIs	National Human Rights Institutions
OAS	Organization of American States
OHCHR	Office of the United Nations High Commissioner for Human Rights
OP-CEDAW	Optional Protocol to the Convention on the Elimination of All Forms of Discrimination against Women
OSAGI	Office of the Special Adviser on Gender Issues and Advancement of Women
OSCE	Organization for Security and Co-operation in Europe
POSA	Public Order and Security Act (Zimbabwe)
RDA	Racial Discrimination Act 1975 (Cth) (Australia)
SADC Protocol	Southern African Development Community Protocol on Gender and Development
SDA	Sex Discrimination Act 1984 (Cth) (Australia)
SGP	Staatkundig Gereformeerde Partij/The Reformed Political Party (Netherlands)
SSCC	Strategy of Social and Cultural Change
SSS	Social Support Strategy
UDHR	Universal Declaration of Human Rights
UN	United Nations
UN Women	UN Entity for Gender Equality and the Empowerment of Women
UNCHR	United Nations Commission on Human Rights
UNFPA	United Nations Fund for Population Activities
UNGA	United Nations General Assembly
UNICEF	United Nations International Children's Emergency Fund
UNIFEM	United Nations Development Fund for Women

UPR	Universal Periodic Review
VAW	violence against women
VWL	Victorian Women Lawyers' Association (Australia)
WEL	Women's Electoral Lobby (Australia)
WG	Working Group on Laws that Discriminate against Women
WHO	World Health Organization
WLSA	Women and Law in Southern Africa Research Trust
WNC	Women's National Commission (UK)
WOZA	Women of Zimbabwe Arise
WWWW	Women Who Want to be Women (Australia)
ZLR	Zimbabwe Law Reports
ZWLA	Zimbabwe Women Lawyers' Association

Introduction

ANNE HELLUM AND HENRIETTE SINDING AASEN

1 Background and overall perspectives

For most of human history, men have been assigned a superior status in law. In the twentieth century, however, with the drafting of international and regional human rights conventions and with the emerging women's movement, the political and legal atmosphere changed, and discrimination based on sex and gender became a human rights concern.[1] Following the Universal Declaration of Human Rights (UDHR) of 1948, the International Covenant on Civil and Political Rights (ICCPR) and the International Covenant on Economic, Social and Cultural Rights (ICESCR) in 1966 explicitly affirmed the obligation of States Parties to ensure the equal rights of men and women to enjoy all civil, political, social and economic rights set forth in the two Covenants.[2] The United Nations (UN) Convention on the Elimination of All Forms of Discrimination against Women (CEDAW) was adopted on 18 December 1979, reaffirming

The editors would like to thank Geir Ulfstein, Andreas Føllesdal and the authors for their inputs to the introduction.

[1] The CEDAW, like the UN Charter, the UDHR, ICCPR and ICESCR, uses the term sex and sex-based discrimination. At the time of the enactment of these instruments, the term sex was understood as a biological category. The term gender, which in the social sciences is understood as a social category, does not appear in international human rights discourse until the 1990s. Today the term gender is used by all human rights treaty bodies without any clear definition. In General Recommendation 28, the CEDAW Committee uses the following definition: 'The term gender refers to socially constructed identities, attributes and roles for women and men and society's social and cultural meaning for these biological differences resulting in hierarchical relationships between women and men and in the distribution of power and rights favoring men and disadvantaging women' (para. 5). A comprehensive account of the use of the terms women, sex and gender in the CEDAW and UN treaties and documents is found in C. Chinkin and M. A. Freeman, 'Introduction' in M. Freeman, C. Chinkin and B. Rudolf (eds.), *The UN Convention on the Elimination of All Forms of Discrimination against Women: A Commentary* [hereinafter *CEDAW Commentary*] (Oxford University Press, 2012) 14–15.

[2] Article 3 of the ICCPR, Article 3 of the ICESCR.

in the preamble faith in fundamental human rights, dignity and worth of the human person and in the equal rights of men and women.

The framers of the Convention concluded that the gender-neutral symmetrical approach that covered discrimination on the basis of sex in other international treaties did not sufficiently recognize the pervasive discrimination against women on the basis of their sex, and that a convention and a treaty body with an asymmetric and gender-specific approach was needed.[3] The preamble to the CEDAW expresses concern for continued discrimination against women despite the existing international covenants on human rights that promote non-discrimination and equality of rights of men and women. Concerned that 'in situations of poverty women have the least access to food, health, education, training and opportunities for employment and other needs', the preamble emphasizes the importance of a holistic approach that includes civil, political, social and economic rights, in order to improve the situation of women. Recognizing 'a change in the traditional role of men as well as the role of women in society', 'the great contribution of women to the welfare of the family and to the development of society' and 'the social significance of maternity and the role of both parents in the family and in the upbringing of children', the preamble envisions a transformative approach to women's rights and gender equality. The preamble forms the backdrop for the three overarching themes of this book:

- the CEDAW's *transformative* approach, linking equal rights, social support and socio-cultural elements;
- the CEDAW's *holistic* approach, linking civil, political, social and economic rights;
- the CEDAW's *gender-specific* approach to equality and non-discrimination.

The CEDAW as a gender-specific instrument, acknowledging the shortcomings of other human rights regimes and the indivisibility of all human rights, is applicable to both the private and public domains, and is seen by optimist and constructivist feminist legal scholars as the equality and non-discrimination regime with the greatest potential to ensure substantive gender equality for women.[4] In a situation where women's protection

[3] The main view of the framers of the Women's Convention is described in A. Byrnes, 'Article 1' in M. Freeman, C. Chinkin and B. Rudolf (eds.), *CEDAW Commentary* 51–70 at 52.

[4] L. Farha, 'Committee on the Elimination of Discrimination against Women: women claiming economic, social and cultural rights – the CEDAW potential' in M. Langford (ed.), *Social Rights Jurisprudence: Emerging Trends in International and Comparative Law*

against discrimination based on sex and gender is embedded in a rapidly increasing body of international, regional and national hard and soft law instruments, this perspective calls for research that addresses the CEDAW regime's actual added value in comparison to and in interaction with other mechanisms. To this end, this book seeks to situate the CEDAW and its Committee in a legal landscape where states are under multiple interacting international, regional and national obligations to respect, protect and fulfil women's right to equality and non-discrimination. The overall aim is to provide an understanding of the CEDAW regime's potential and actual added value in relation and comparison to coexisting and overlapping international, regional and domestic equality and non-discrimination regimes.

The authors in this book address three interrelated theoretical assumptions regarding the contribution of the CEDAW in international, regional and national law. The first is that the Convention's transformative approach, which combines an equal rights element, a social support element and a socio-cultural element, makes it better equipped than other treaties to address existing legal, social and cultural barriers to substantive equality.[5] The second assumption is that the CEDAW's recognition of the interdependence and indivisibility of civil, political, social and economic rights makes it the instrument with the greatest potential to address the close relationship between women's marginalization, social rights and inequality.[6] The third assumption is that the establishment of a gender-specific treaty with a specialized treaty body is a measure that will strengthen the capacity of individual women and women's organizations to make States Parties accountable for their obligation to respect, protect and fulfil the human rights of women.[7]

These three assumptions form the overall point of reference for the authors in this book. In combination with the notion of added value, they

(Cambridge University Press, 2008) 553–68; R. Cook and S. Cusack, *Gender Stereotyping: Transnational Legal Perspectives* (Philadelphia: University of Pennsylvania Press, 2010); R. Holtmaat and J. Naber, *Women's Human Rights and Culture* (Cambridge: Intersentia, 2011); C. A. MacKinnon, 'Creating international law: gender as a new paradigm' in C. M. Bailliet (ed.), *Non-State Actors, Soft Law and Protective Regimes* (Cambridge University Press, 2012) 17–32.

[5] Cook and Cusack, *Gender Stereotyping*; Holtmaat and Naber, *Women's Human Rights and Culture*.

[6] Farha, 'Committee on the Elimination of Discrimination against Women'.

[7] K. Knop, 'Why rethinking the sovereign state is important for women's international human rights law' in R. Cook (ed.), *Human Rights of Women. National and International Perspectives* (University of Pennsylvania Press, 1995) 153–64.

frame the key research questions that are dealt with in the different sections of the book. A distinction between potential and actual added value of the CEDAW is used in order to distinguish the future potential of the CEDAW from current and past achievements, and to separate normative content from empirical realities.

Part I of the book deals mainly with the CEDAW's *potential* added value with regard to legal and social reform, due to its transformative, holistic and gender-specific approach. Part II examines mainly the *actual* added value of the CEDAW, in particular with regard to social and economic rights. There are, however, overlapping analyses of potential and actual added value of the CEDAW in both these parts, since these normative and empirical aspects are interrelated and intertwined. Part III presents national case studies that explore the actual and potential domestic impact of the CEDAW from Northern Europe, Southern Asia, Canada and Southern Africa.

Posing critical questions and providing analysis of the CEDAW, the role and work of the CEDAW Committee, the implementation and domestication of the CEDAW, as well as the interplay between the CEDAW and other international and regional human rights regimes, the chapters in this volume constitute a critical assessment of the CEDAW's potential and actual contribution to international, regional and national legal developments.

2 Potential added value of the transformative approach (Part I)

The first part of the book addresses the potential added value of the CEDAW and the work of the CEDAW Committee. As pointed out by Rikki Holtmaat, the *transformative* approach is a crucial aspect of the CEDAW. One objective of the Convention is to alter the existing patriarchal and discriminatory structures and patterns embedded in law, society and culture.[8] In line with the demand for substantive equality, the object and purpose of the Convention is threefold: (1) to ensure full equality of women before the law, and protection against discrimination in the public and the private spheres; (2) to improve the de facto position of women; and (3) to address gender-based stereotypes that uphold unequal gender relations.[9]

[8] See R. Holtmaat, 'Article 5' in M. Freeman, C. Chinkin and B. Rudolf (eds.), *CEDAW Commentary* 141–67; R. Holtmaat, Chapter 3, this volume.

[9] General Recommendation No. 25.

This three-pronged approach sets the CEDAW apart from other gender-neutral and symmetric human rights regimes, such as the ICCPR, the ICESCR, the European Convention for the Protection of Human Rights and Fundamental Freedoms (ECHR) and the European Union Directive on Gender Equality. Unlike these other international and regional instruments, the Protocol to the African Charter on Human and People's Rights on the Rights of Women in Africa (the Maputo Protocol) is by and large based on the same model as the CEDAW.

The gender-specific three-pronged transformative approach of the CEDAW, which to a large extent has served as a model for the Maputo Protocol, has been viewed as a more fruitful and promising approach than the approach of formal gender-neutral equality.[10] Due to its emphasis on the need for social support systems that address the legal, social and cultural obstacles to substantive equality, including the needs and vulnerabilities particular to women, the CEDAW is regarded as the human rights instrument with the greatest potential to address and combat women's socio-economic marginalization, dependency and inequality.[11]

The assumptions of significant potential added value related to the CEDAW's transformative approach raise a series of interrelated research questions dealt with by the authors in Part I of the book. The question of how the transformative approach of the CEDAW and the CEDAW Committee supplements other international and regional conventions and treaty bodies is an overarching theme. A key concern in this regard is how the CEDAW and regional instruments strike a balance between equality and difference in order to achieve substantive equality in different political, social and cultural contexts. A related question regarding the legitimacy and the effectiveness of the CEDAW as a tool for change is how a balance is struck by the CEDAW and other regional instruments between effective implementation of women's protection against gender stereotypes embedded in social and cultural beliefs on the one hand, and respect for national values, sovereignty and democracy on the other hand. A critical concern regarding the CEDAW regime as a tool for social and cultural change is its conception of culture. In particular, it is important to address the relationship between static and homogenous approaches to culture, which see culture as a barrier to change, in contrast to culture

[10] Cook and Cusack, *Gender Stereotyping*; Holtmaat and Naber, *Women's Human Rights and Culture*.

[11] Farha, 'Committee on the Elimination of Discrimination against Women'.

understood as dynamic, contested and changing, and as such a tool for change.[12]

The authors in this part of the book rely on various methods and sources to address these research themes. Andrew Byrnes, Rikki Holtmaat and Simone Cusack use a textual legal approach to describe and analyze the development of the norms and procedures associated with the transformative approach, focusing on the General Recommendations, individual communications and Concluding Comments of the CEDAW Committee. Fareda Banda takes stock of the actual achievements of the CEDAW regime thus far by addressing the potential synergies between the CEDAW and the Working Group on Laws that Discriminate against Women (WG) from 2010. Through comparative Latin American and African perspectives, Cecilia Bailliet and Celestine Nyamu Musembi explore the CEDAW's potential added value as well as current limitations in different legal, social and cultural contexts. Bailliet uses narratives in order to give voice to individual women's experiences of human rights violations. Nyamu Musembi situates her comparison between the CEDAW and the Maputo Protocol in the context of local court cases and the lives of individual women.

2.1 *Overview of the chapters in Part I*

Andrew Byrnes (Chapter 1) introduces the CEDAW and its Committee. He provides a detailed presentation and analysis of the Committee, including fresh and critical assessments of its composition, reporting procedures, work (and workload), and the role and potential for international and domestic impact. Although the main focus is on the Committee, the special nature of the CEDAW, with its particular transformative and holistic approach, is integrated into the discussion of the role and function of the Committee. The analysis of how the CEDAW is advancing equality in a world of social and cultural diversity and sovereign states gives insight into the many and significant challenges facing this particular human rights body. A key question is how to strike a balance between the concern for effective implementation and the legal, political and social legitimacy of the Committee in situations where women's rights issues are deeply related to interpretations of culture.

[12] S. E. Merry, 'Constructing a global law – violence against women and the human rights system', *Law & Social Inquiry* 28:4 (2003) 941–77.

Fareda Banda (Chapter 2) follows up the question of effectiveness and added value of the CEDAW with a timely discussion of the need and function of the newly appointed UN Working Group on Laws that Discriminate against Women. The Working Group was established by the Human Rights Council in 2010 due to failure of states to revoke and amend laws that discriminate against women. An important question is whether or not there is a need for this body, and what role it should have, in addition to the existing CEDAW regime. Considering the process leading up to the establishment of the Working Group, and the discussion of its mandate (which is more limited than that of the CEDAW), challenges and opportunities, Banda provides valuable and critical reflections not only on this new body, but also on the role, potential and limitations of the CEDAW and its Committee in fighting discrimination against women.

Rikki Holtmaat (Chapter 3) divides the overarching goal of the CEDAW into three sub-aims: to ensure full equality of women before the law; to improve the de facto position of women; and to modify gender-based stereotypes. She deals mainly with the third sub-aim and the corresponding legal and political methods envisioned in Article 5(a) of the CEDAW, which include transformative equality as a distinct aspect. The potential added value of the CEDAW's transformative jurisprudence, which combines an equal rights element, a social support element and a socio-cultural element, raises a series of questions about its democratic and socio-cultural legitimacy. Entering a realm where cultural, religious and national norms and values often conflict, Holtmaat explores how the CEDAW Committee strikes a balance in its jurisprudence between effective implementation of women's protection against gender stereotypes embedded in social and cultural beliefs and practices, and national sovereignty and democracy. A related question is how the Committee strikes a balance between equality and difference in order to ensure substantive equality in different historical, social and cultural contexts.

Simone Cusack (Chapter 4) states that, during its first thirty years of operation, the CEDAW has proved to be a catalyst for legal and policy reform, an effective tool in domestic litigation, advocacy and activism, and an important means of holding States Parties accountable for violations of women's human rights. However, much of the potential of the CEDAW for advancing women's human rights has yet to be realized. According to Cusack, one area of considerable untapped potential incorporates the obligations of States Parties in Articles 2(f) and 5(a) of the CEDAW to modify or transform gender stereotypes and eliminate wrongful gender stereotyping. Cusack provides in-depth analysis of the term 'gender stereotyping' and explains why stereotyping is a human rights issue. She argues that the CEDAW provides a powerful yet largely unexplored legal framework for addressing gender stereotyping. In addition, she identifies some of the limitations of using the CEDAW as a framework for addressing stereotyping, and considers how those limitations might be overcome or minimized.

Cecilia M. Bailliet (Chapter 5) contributes to the discussion on elimination of all forms of discrimination against women by giving important input to one of the most challenging dilemmas within the field of women's rights: the balance between equality and difference. She argues that maternity is a valuable life project of women, and that motherhood should be viewed as a type of agency to be protected by the state. While the aim of Article 5(b) of the CEDAW is to combat prejudice or inferior conceptions of women and lift the social perception of maternity, this provision has been overshadowed by Article 5(a) in CEDAW jurisprudence and the academic literature. In contrast, the regional Inter-American Court of Human Rights has adopted a difference-oriented perspective in order to protect maternal identity as part of women's human dignity. The Court uses narratives or individual testimonies to give voice and recognition to the experiences of individual women, and to elucidate the scope of women's right to a life project. The case of *Miguel Castro-Castro Prison* v. *Peru* (2006) serves to define the content and scope of the protection of maternity as a life project. This enables the protection discussion to move beyond the traditional focus on sexual autonomy in order to address maternal identity. Bailliet contrasts the approach of the regional court with academic criticism, which seeks to underscore the duty to avoid wrongful gender stereotypes according to Article 5(a) of the CEDAW. The chapter concludes that the Inter-American Human Rights System complements the CEDAW by precisely addressing the protection interests framed in Article 5(b).

Celestine Nyamu Musembi (Chapter 6) provides comparative perspectives from countries in Southern and Eastern Africa concerning the complex relationship between gender, human rights and legal pluralism. She addresses the CEDAW Committee's view that, under the circumstances, elimination of discrimination against women necessitates wholesale displacement of other moral codes. While recognizing the need for cultural and social reform as prescribed by the CEDAW (Articles 2(f) and 5(a)), the author problematizes the CEDAW Committee's abolitionist approach to the plural legal regimes of African countries as expressed mainly in General Recommendation No. 21, and Concluding Observations on periodic reports submitted by selected East and Southern African (ESA) States Parties. The position of the CEDAW Committee is compared with the approach of the Maputo Protocol and selected ESA countries. For example, while the CEDAW Committee makes it clear that nothing short of elimination of polygamy will suffice, the Kenyan and Ugandan governments appear to have taken an approach aimed at a gradual phasing-out of polygamy (by providing for conversion of polygamous into monogamous marriages but not the reverse) and extending equal protection of the law to all women. The Maputo Protocol provides for women's right to live in a 'positive cultural context' (Article 17), and unlike the CEDAW calls on states to enact legislation signalling that monogamy is the *encouraged* and *preferred* form of marriage, while at the same time ensuring that the rights of all women in marriage and family are promoted and protected.

3 Actual added value of the holistic approach: socio-economic rights (Part II)

Due in part to the schism between civil and political rights on the one hand and economic, social and cultural rights on the other, the capacity of international human rights law to respond to the concerns of socially and economically marginalized women was for a long time seen as limited. As the principal forms of oppression against large groups of women operate in the socio-economic domain, critical feminist scholars in the 1990s argued that international law, by according priority to civil and political rights, had little to offer women.[13] In light of recent developments in international social rights theory and practice, particularly the recognition of the indivisibility of civil, political, social and economic rights, the question is no longer whether or not international human rights law has something to offer women, but where in the human rights system women's social and economic rights are best protected.[14] Optimist feminist legal scholars argue today that the CEDAW's recognition of the interdependence and indivisibility of civil, political, social and economic

[13] H. Charlesworth, C. Chinkin and S. Wright, 'Feminist approaches to international law', *American Journal of International Law* 85:4 (1991) 613–45.

[14] D. Otto, 'Defending women's economic and social rights: some thoughts on indivisibility and a new standard of equality' in I. Merali and V. Oosterveld (eds.), *Giving Meaning to Economic, Social and Cultural Rights* (University of Pennsylvania Press, 2001) 52–62; U. Khliq and R. Churchill, 'The protection of economic and social rights: a particular challenge?' in H. Keller and G. Ulfstein (eds.), *UN Human Rights Treaty Bodies: Law and Legitimacy* (Cambridge University Press, 2012) 199–261.

rights makes it the instrument with the greatest potential to address the close relationship between women's marginalization, social rights and inequality.[15]

With a focus on social and economic rights, particularly reproductive rights and the right to safe housing, the second part of the book addresses the *actual* added value of the CEDAW and the work of the CEDAW Committee. Two research questions involving the intertwined analytical dimensions of the potential and actual added value of the CEDAW are dealt with. The first is whether and to what extent the CEDAW has simply extended existing social and economic rights to women, or whether the Convention has contributed to transforming these rights in the light of women's lived experiences, constraints and social realities. The concept of *engenderment*, developed by Sandra Fredman in Chapter 7, is used as an analytical tool for the assessment of the CEDAW's actual and potential added value to the international human rights regime. In Part II, the authors explore whether or not existing human rights, such as the rights to life, health and housing, have been transformed, engendered and implemented in a way that accommodates the specific needs of women in various contexts and social realities.

The second question is whether the jurisprudence of the CEDAW Committee has made its mark on other sub-systems or whether it has operated in isolation and as such has contributed to fragmentation and marginalization. A closely related issue is how the proliferation of sub-systems of international law, such as the CEDAW and the CEDAW Committee, has affected the development of international law. Recent studies of normative developments within international law point to the actual normative synergies between different sub-systems and international law in general, and between the CEDAW and other international and regional protective regimes in particular.[16] Critics have, however, feared that the proliferation of specialized human rights agencies will

[15] Farha, 'Committee on the Elimination of Discrimination against Women'.

[16] B. Simma, 'Universality of international law from the perspective of a practitioner', *European Journal of International Law* 20:2 (2009) 265–97; C. M. Bailliet, 'Introduction' in C. M. Bailliet (ed.), *Non-State Actors, Soft Law and Protective Regimes* 1–7; MacKinnon, 'Creating international law'; V. B. Strand, *Diskrimineringsvern og religionsutøvelse* (Protection against Discrimination and Religious Freedom) (Oslo: Gyldendal, 2012); V. B. Strand, 'Balancing an individual and a structural approach towards gender equality, the question of the police hijab' in R. Nielsen and C. D. Tvarnø (eds.), *Scandinavian Women's Law in the 21st century* (Copenhagen: DJØF Publishing, 2012) 219–48.

result in fragmentation and marginalization of human rights in general and the rights of women in particular.[17]

These overarching research themes are explored by Sandra Fredman, Fleur van Leeuwen, Ingunn Ikdahl and Henriette Sinding Aasen by means of a textual and comparative legal analysis of convention texts, General Recommendations, individual communications and Concluding Observations of the CEDAW Committee, the ICESCR Committee and the Human Rights Committee. To determine whether or not and to what extent the CEDAW and the work of its Committee provide additional actual value with regard to the engenderment of social and economic rights, all the authors compare the approaches taken by various human rights regimes. To give voice to women's experiences and concerns, Ikdahl extends her analysis to the lived realities of women on the ground in an urban settlement in Dar es Salaam in Tanzania.

3.1 Overview of the chapters in Part II of the volume

Sandra Fredman (Chapter 7) introduces the concept of *engenderment*, which is the underlying analytical tool for the analysis of the CEDAW in the following chapters. She starts out with a verdict from the 1995 Human Development Report devoted to gender, which states that '[h]uman development if not engendered, is endangered'.[18] Moving beyond an equal rights approach, which is limited to extending existing socio-economic rights to women, the engenderment approach asks whether or not the rights themselves have been transformed in light of women's lived experiences, constraints and social realities. Most human rights treaties prohibit discrimination on grounds of sex. Fredman argues that this approach to equality does not change the gendered nature of social institutions and structures, and that substantive equality requires that the rights themselves are recast in light of women's needs. First, she considers the distinctive nature of women's experiences of poverty and disadvantage in terms of gendered barriers to economic participation, gender-based

[17] International Law Commission/Martti Koskenniemi, *Fragmentation of International Law: Difficulties Arising from the Diversification and Expansion of International Law*, A/CN.4/L.682, 13 April 2006; D. Buss and A. Manji, *International Law. Modern Feminist Approaches* (Oxford: Hart, 2005); H. Charlesworth and C. Chinkin, *The Boundaries of International Law: A Feminist Analysis* (Melland Schill Studies in International Law) (Manchester University Press, 2000) 218–20.

[18] United Nations Development Programme (UNDP), *Gender Development* (Oxford University Press, 1995) 1. Available at http://hdr.undp.org/en/reports/global/hdr1995/chapters (last accessed 22 January 2013).

violence, limited agency and restricted access to socio-economic goods. Second, she examines the meaning of equality in the context of gender, and the limits of formal equality are clearly spelled out. Furthermore, she discusses what engendering socio-economic rights means in theory and practice. Third, through textual analysis of convention text and General Recommendations, she compares and contrasts the extent to which socio-economic rights are engendered in the ICESCR and the CEDAW.

Fleur van Leeuwen (Chapter 8) discusses the role of the CEDAW more indirectly by focusing on how women's rights are protected in the mainstream human rights system. She opens her chapter with this famous slogan from the women's rights movement at the World Conference on Human Rights in Vienna in 1993: 'Women's rights are human rights!' The statement reflects the fact that much of what women experience as everyday abuse in their lives was largely kept outside the realm of mainstream (malestream) international human rights. This deficiency was recognized in Vienna in 1993, and the states represented at the Conference agreed that the status and experiences of women should be systematically addressed and integrated into the UN mainstream human rights system and mechanisms, including the work of the monitoring bodies. The author identifies the traditional critique of the CEDAW: that mainstream monitoring bodies did not address blatant violations of women's dignity as violations of human rights, but instead left these issues to be dealt with by the specialized CEDAW Committee. Furthermore, she explores how and to what extent the HRC and the ICESCR Committee have now mainstreamed gender into their comments, observations and recommendations.

Ingunn Ikdahl (Chapter 9) starts out with a case describing the insecure housing of a widow living in an informal settlement in Dar es Salaam, Tanzania. She addresses the double vulnerability of women in informal settlements: they experience insecurity due to in-laws refusing to see them as owners upon widowhood, but are also subject to the same vulnerability as men at the hands of a state that does not recognize the legitimacy of the settlement. The situation illustrates both the gender bias in the distribution of property rights between spouses and the urgency of the right to housing. At the local level, a mixture of norms comes into play: state law, norms of fairness, religious norms and customary norms. At the international level, the housing theme illustrates current dynamics in the development of international human rights law. Despite the inclusion of equal rights for women and the principle of non-discrimination in the human rights conventions, women's experiences of insecure housing have been marginalized in human rights discourses. Since the early 1990s several UN institutions and mechanisms have, however, engaged in developing more detailed human rights analyses of women's rights and access to land, property and housing. By contrasting and comparing the General Recommendations and reports of the CEDAW Committee, the ICESCR Committee and the Special Rapporteur on the Right to Adequate Housing, Ikdahl identifies two different paths for approaching women's rights to their homes in international law, focusing on the lack of equality in the distribution of *property* rights between husband and wife, and the gendered nature of *security* of tenure for one's home.

Henriette Sinding Aasen (Chapter 10) addresses the high maternal mortality rate in many developing countries, and conceptualizes preventable maternal deaths as violations of women's rights to life and health. This constitutes a particular form of gender-based discrimination and structural disadvantage suffered by poor women in particular. Although high-level international campaigns by the UN and the World Health Organization (WHO) have focused on strategies to reduce the alarmingly high maternal mortality rate in the most-affected areas, it still constitutes a major challenge for women's right to health. While both Article 12 of the ICESCR and Article 12 of the CEDAW contain provisions concerning the right to health, Article 12 of the CEDAW is formulated in more specific and women-oriented terms, granting women adequate maternal healthcare services. The author examines the interplay and jurisprudence of both the ICESCR Committee and the CEDAW Committee with regard to their responsiveness to women's particular experiences and needs related to maternal healthcare. Of particular interest concerning state obligations is the Available, Accessible, Acceptable Services of Good Quality (AAAQ) framework developed by the ICESCR Committee, which is also utilized by the CEDAW Committee in its communications with States Parties. *Accessibility* of services is a highly relevant theme with regard to maternal mortality, and includes the right to adequate information as well as to physical and economic access to appropriate services.

4 The CEDAW in national law (Part III)

The CEDAW and the CEDAW Committee were welcomed by African, Asian and Northern feminist scholars who regarded the CEDAW regime as a space in which women's different voices, interests and claims in international law could be represented.[19] More pessimistic feminist scholars feared, however, that the CEDAW, because it lacked an adequate system of supervision, would have very limited instrumental value.[20] In this part of the book, the transformative capacity of the CEDAW and the CEDAW Committee are described and discussed in light of domestic case studies from Northern Europe, Canada, South Asian and Southern African countries.[21]

The aim of these studies is to explore whether or not and with what outcome the CEDAW has been invoked, adopted or resisted by state and non-state actors in various legal, political, economic, social and cultural contexts. Maintaining a focus on the CEDAW and the CEDAW Committee, the chapters in Part III situate the CEDAW in national legal landscapes where states are under multiple interacting international, regional and national obligations to respect, protect and fulfil women's right to equality and non-discrimination. Each case study explores whether or not and to what extent the Convention and the Committee have provided additional avenues of intervention in comparison to or in synergy with other national, regional and international treaties. Exploring the political, legal, social and economic context in which the CEDAW is domesticated, the authors provide qualitative insights that supplement empirical macro-studies identifying factors that are assumed to have a bearing on the effects of ratifying human rights conventions.[22] Whether actual changes in national law are taking effect at the local level are critical questions only marginally dealt with by the chapters in this part of the book, whose main focus is on legal and political contestations taking place at the national level.[23]

[19] R. Cook (ed.), *Human Rights of Women. National and International Perspectives.*

[20] See Charlesworth and Chinkin, *The Boundaries of International Law* 21; S. Kouvo, *Making Just Rights? Mainstreaming Women's Human Rights and a Gender Perspective* (Uppsala: Iustus, 2004).

[21] The CEDAW case study project, which is part of the project 'Should states ratify human rights conventions', has been carried out by Anne Hellum.

[22] See generally B. A Simmons, *Mobilizing for Human Rights: International Law in Domestic Politics* (Cambridge University Press, 2009). All these factors with the exception of the availability of other international and regional mechanisms are dealt with by B. A. Simmons.

[23] A growing body of legal and anthropological literature is focusing on women's human rights from a local bottom-up perspective. S. E. Merry, *Human Rights and Gender Violence: Translating International Law into Local Justice* (University of Chicago Press, 2006); A. Hellum, J. E. Stewart, A. Tsanga and S. S. Ali (eds.), *Human Rights, Plural Legalities and Gendered Realities: Paths Are Made by Walking* (Harare: Weaver Press, 2007); R. Sieder and J. McNeish (eds.), *Gender Justice and Legal Pluralities: Latin American and African*

To describe and understand the process whereby the CEDAW is domesticated at the national level, the authors, who are all highly qualified legal scholars or lawyers, focus on legal changes that have taken place through legislation and judicial review. Through a textual legal approach, they examine legislative debates and judicial review with a view to determining whether or not, by whom and to what effect the Convention and the Committee's General Recommendations and Concluding Observations have been invoked. To better understand the outcomes of these processes, the authors extend their perspective to the historical and political contexts of the legal texts. Drawing on insider knowledge, acquired through provision of expert advice to governments or non-governmental organizations, the authors provide fresh insights into the complex and uneven processes through which international law is domesticated.

The studies have been selected on the basis of a combination of availability and assumed variations regarding the domestication of the CEDAW.[24] Influential factors are the availability of other international and regional mechanisms, the degree of democracy, the nature of the legal system and the dominant legal culture, the states' motivations for ratification, the democratic elements in the process of ratification and monitoring, the extent of legal education of duty bearers and rights holders, and the strength of civil society and its national, regional and international networks.[25]

In the presentation below we have grouped the studies in two main categories that show the most striking difference regarding the CEDAW's effect on national law: states that have acceded regional mechanisms providing protection against gender discrimination and states that have not or have acceded regional instruments with weak enforcement mechanisms. The South Asian and Canadian studies represent states that have not acceded to regional instruments. In Southern Africa, Zimbabwe has acceded the Protocol to the African Charter on Human and People's Rights on the Rights of Women in Africa (the Maputo Protocol). The Maputo Protocol has the same international framework as other treaties,

Perspectives (London: Routledge, 2012); A. Hellum. 'Introduction: human rights in a gendered, relational and plural legal landscape' in B. Derman, A. Hellum and K. B. Sandvik (eds.), *Worlds of Human Rights: Ambiguities of Rights Claiming in Africa* (Leiden: Brill, 2013) 131–42.

24 Regrettably we did not have resources to include case studies from Latin America. Furthermore, the South African case study fell out along the way.

25 With the exception of availability of regional mechanisms, most of these factors are addressed in Simmons, *Mobilizing for Human Rights*.

yet the African Commission, which is tasked with the monitoring of the Protocol, has not developed its gender analysis of human rights violations on the continent, making the enforcement ineffectual. The Northern European case studies represent a legal scenario where the CEDAW coexists with two regional treaty regimes that include protection against sex discrimination: the European Convention on Human Rights (ECHR) and EU law. The studies are presented country by country within these categories. There are, however, significant variations between and within these broad categories as to whether or not and to what extent the CEDAW makes its mark on law reform and judicial review.

4.1 Lacking or weak regional mechanisms: South Asia, Southern Africa and Canada

Australia, Canada, India, Nepal and Pakistan are states that have not acceded to regional human rights mechanisms. Canada is a member of the Organization of American States (OAS) but has not ratified the American Convention on Human Rights. Zimbabwe has acceded the Maputo Protocol. Australia and the South Asian states mentioned have no regional or sub-regional human rights mechanisms available to which they can submit themselves. All of these states are characterized by ethnic diversity, normative pluralism and, with the exception of Nepal, a common law heritage as former British colonies. With the exception of Zimbabwe, they are all federal states. The struggle for women's human rights, however, takes place in differing political contexts, ranging from relatively democratic states such as Australia, Canada and India, post-conflict states such as Nepal, and autocratic states such as Pakistan and Zimbabwe.

The Australian case study (Chapter 11) carried out by Andrew Byrnes shows how, in an endeavour to promote gender equality, both state and non-state actors have used the CEDAW as a vehicle of legal change in a federal state with a legal system that has no general constitutional guarantee of equality, or of sex or gender equality. Unlike the CEDAW, which takes a gender-specific approach, the Sex Discrimination Act 1984 (SDA) prohibits discrimination on the grounds of sex and marital status against both women and men in many of the areas it covers. The study describes how the Convention has provided a policy framework and specific equality standards for a number of inquiries into law and policy reform, including a major review of laws by the Australian Law Reform Commission (ALRC), which recommended that the SDA contain a general prohibition of discrimination as defined in Article 1 of the

CEDAW. According to Byrnes, women's rights advocates have found the broad-ranging and detailed stipulations of the CEDAW substantively more useful both for legal action and political solidarity compared with the brief and general non-discrimination guarantees of the ICCPR and the ICESCR (none of which are incorporated into domestic law). This reflects the fact that the CEDAW and the SDA both emerged from the women's movement in which the advocates of legislative reform in the 1970s and 1980s in Australia also participated. Byrnes demonstrates how the SDA of 1984 was motivated primarily by a desire to address discrimination against women and to give effect to the provisions of the CEDAW, which Australia ratified in 1983. As shown by Byrnes, Australian courts have drawn on the Convention and CEDAW Committee output to give CEDAW-consistent interpretations of the SDA in a number of cases.

In Chapter 12, Lucie Lamarche explores the domestication of the CEDAW in the context of Canada as a dualist federal state of the Americas. Canada ratified the CEDAW in 1981 without reservations. A year later the Canadian feminist campaign for an effective constitutional equality standard resulted in the inclusion of two new sex equality provisions in the Canadian Charter of Rights and Freedoms (the Charter). The Supreme Court of Canada has dealt with a number of cases where the equality provisions in the Charter have been invoked, but has only referred to the CEDAW in two of these cases. The Canadian Charter has in recent years been criticized by feminist activists and scholars because of its inadequate protection of social and economic rights and as such the equality of the most marginalized women in society. Lamarche describes how women's organizations have turned to the international human rights arena in order to make the conservative government accountable for the growth of women's poverty and inequality resulting from its neo-liberal policies. The case study examines the process of shadow reporting by the Canadian women's movement to the CEDAW Committee and the ICESCR Committee during the decade 1998–2008.

The Indian case study is authored by Madhu Mehra (Chapter 13). When India signed the CEDAW in 1981, the Indian Constitution already guaranteed gender equality and mandated affirmative action for women. The study describes how in the 1990s India aligned its economy with the global market, positioned itself as a significant member of the international community and ratified the CEDAW in 1993. The ratification followed the completion of an extensive law reform exercise aimed at closing the gap between the constitutional promise of equality and the statutory law. With the presence of international donor aid, regional alliances and NGOs flushed with the experience of the run-up and follow-up to the Beijing Conference in 1995, the CEDAW became an important tool for many Indian women's organizations. According to Mehra, the country review processes have provided an arena for convergence between women's groups at the local, state and national levels, for the collective production of shadow reports, as well as for simultaneous engagement with the government. India's reservations to Articles 5(a), 16(1) and 16(2) in the Convention have been a barrier to implementation of the CEDAW in family law, particularly the community-specific family and marriage laws for Muslims, Christians, Parsis and Hindus. Through review of cases where the CEDAW has been invoked by the Indian Supreme Court, the study shows how the judiciary, in the context of a volatile political terrain marked by identity politics, has played a leadership role in domesticating the CEDAW. The political nature of the terrain related to incorporation of the CEDAW is brought out through illustration of the judicial navigation of the various challenges with which the Supreme Court is confronted.

The CEDAW was ratified by Nepal in 1991 without reservations. Despite political and constitutional reform, Nepalese law and society are strongly influenced by the Hindu religion and customary norms that define the status of women in terms of their sex and marital status. In Chapter 14, Kabita Pandey describes how the civic organization Pro Public, through a combination of legal literacy, judicial education and public-interest litigation, has used the CEDAW as a tool for legal change. In spite of the Interim Constitution and the Nepalese Treaty Act implying that ratified conventions take precedence when coming into conflict with other Nepalese laws, the pace of legislative and administrative change was slow in the first ten years after ratification of the CEDAW. Pandey's study describes how the Nepalese civic organization Pro Public, in cooperation with the Asia Pacific Forum for Judicial Education on Equality Issues, embarked in 1997 on a judicial education programme focusing on the CEDAW. Comparing cases decided by the same Supreme Court judges before and after the judicial education programme, Pandey explores whether or not and to what extent the legal education of the judges prompted a more dynamic jurisprudence. She also explores how the range of directive orders issued by the Supreme Court, and how requiring the enactment and amendment of discriminatory laws concerning widows' allowances, women's property rights, marital rape, sexual harassment and discrimination, have been implemented by the executive branch of government.

Pakistan acceded to the CEDAW in 1996. Shaheen Sardar Ali's study (Chapter 15) shows how demands for accession to the CEDAW were initiated and strongly articulated by civil society as well as in some governmental and political quarters. Her research situates the fifteen-year journey toward final accession in 1996 and the subsequent struggle for domestication in the context of visible, invisible and hidden power relations that underlie the prevailing dissonance between formal laws and governmental policy on the one hand, and religious practices and beliefs on the other. According to Ali, the accession process opened up spaces for advancing women's rights and the CEDAW at a national level, such as the National Commission on the Status of Women and the Women Ministers Forum. In the post-accession period, the CEDAW became part of training programmes run by governmental and non-governmental bodies. Despite this, no steps to incorporate the CEDAW into national legislation through an Act of Parliament, as required by the Convention and the Constitution, have thus far been taken. A series of laws that are discriminatory to women, such as the Citizenship Act of 1951, the Law of Evidence Act of 1984 and the Hudood Ordinance of 1979 remain in force. In the reported case law of Pakistan's superior judiciary, there are four judgments in which the court specifically alluded to the CEDAW, most of them by the same judge.

Zimbabwe signed the CEDAW in 1991 and ratified it without reservations in 1998. Julie Stewart and Choice Damiso's longitudinal study (Chapter 16) shows how the CEDAW has been invoked by state and non-state actors under different governments. They address the situation under the de facto one-party ZANU PF rule, associated with rampant economic mismanagement and human rights abuses, and under the Government of National Unity (GNU), which was put in place due to strong regional and international pressure after violent elections in 2008. The overarching theme is how proponents of women's rights and gender equality have navigated in a contested political and legal terrain, where the Constitution privileges customary law when it conflicts with the principle of gender equality in areas of personal and family law. Through a comprehensive analysis of judicial review and law reform, the study shows how, in the context of a highly nationalist and undemocratic political and legal terrain, the judiciary, women's rights organizations and independent experts have achieved piecemeal legal change through mobilization of national sources of law, mainly statutory and customary law. The CEDAW has been referred to in two Supreme Court decisions, one concerning inheritance (the *Magaya* case) and one concerning pregnancy discrimination (the *Mandividza* case). Focusing on the present situation, where the Unity government seeks to appear in the best possible light internationally, the authors discuss the options and limits of using the CEDAW as a lobbying tool for constitutional reform.

4.2 Strong regional mechanisms: the Northern European studies

The Northern European states included in this book are the Netherlands, France, the UK, Finland and Norway. They have all acceded to the European Convention on Human Rights and are EU or European Free Trade Association (EFTA) members. All of these states are characterized by increasing ethnic diversity, normative pluralism, declining economies (with the exception of Norway), and accumulating regional and international legal obligations. The legal systems represent different European legal cultures in the throes of change, ranging from Roman Dutch law, common law, French civil law and Nordic civil law. While the struggle for women's human rights takes place in relatively democratic states, there are significant differences regarding the status of human rights and gender equality in national law.

The Netherlands ratified the CEDAW in 1991 with a unique provision included in the Act approving ratification. The provision required that the government periodically report to Parliament on the implementation of the Convention (Chapter 17). This, according to Marjolein van den Brink, led the Dutch Parliament to adopt the holistic three-dimensional approach implying that direct discrimination and legal inequalities must be eliminated, the position of women must be improved and the dominant gender ideology must be combated.[26] The study shows how the CEDAW Committee's requirement that women's NGOs be involved in the reporting procedures has since 1995 been followed up through the government's financial support for the preparation of shadow reports. Over the years, shadow reporting has become an arena where different majority and minority women's organizations coordinate and frame their claims with the assistance of experts on women's rights and gender equality. Due to budget cuts, many of the established study centres for gender and the law have lost their funding in recent years. In spite of the high degree of involvement of parliamentarians, women's organizations and academic

[26] See Holtmaat's chapter on the CEDAW's three-dimensional approach in this volume (Chapter 3).

scholars, the CEDAW is, according to van den Brink, largely absent in political and legislative debates. Van den Brink also notes that the absence of the CEDAW in Dutch courts is striking, in particular when compared to the Convention on the Rights of the Child (CRC), the ECHR and the EU gender equality directives. A prominent case that was decided recently by the European Court of Human Rights (ECtHR) with reference to the CEDAW is that concerning the male-dominated religious Staatkundig Gereformeerde Partij/The Reformed Political Party's (SGP) refusal to accept women as (full) members.

The UK signed the CEDAW in 1981. It was ratified in 1986 with comprehensive reservations, including in relation to legislation and rules governing pension schemes and certain social security benefits. Sandra Fredman's study (Chapter 18) describes how successive Conservative and Labour governments have consistently refused to incorporate the CEDAW into the Human Rights Act in spite of repeated criticism from the CEDAW Committee. The Committee argues that incorporation of the ECHR is not sufficient, since it does not provide for the full range of women's human rights in the CEDAW or cater to temporary special measures. The study demonstrates the potential added value of the work of the CEDAW Committee, particularly its criticism that the principle of equality used in the UK focuses to too great a degree on gender neutrality, same treatment and equal opportunity. Although many women's organizations regard the CEDAW as a valuable lobbying tool drawing ministerial attention to women's rights issues, according to Fredman there is little evidence of real change as a result of the Committee's interventions. This is explained by the strong influence of EU law, the Convention's lack of visibility in society at large and the lack of recognition in the dominant legal culture due to the vague character of the Committee's Concluding Observations. There have, however, been two cases against the UK since it acceded to the Optional Protocol in 2004, both of which were declared inadmissible by the CEDAW Committee. Increasing attention has been paid in recent years to the CEDAW as an interpretative aid in cases before the courts. One example is the *Yemshaw* case, where the CEDAW Committee's definition of gender-based violence in General Recommendation 19 was invoked.

France signed the Convention in 1980 and ratified it through an Act of Parliament in 1983 with a number of reservations. To perceive the ambiguous reception of a gendered instrument in the context of the universal French legal tradition, Hélène Ruiz Fabri and Andrea Hamann begin by reflecting on the dominant French political and legal culture that marginalizes specificity by privileging universalism (Chapter 19). While most reservations were withdrawn very shortly after the ratification of the Convention, reservations to Articles 14.2(h), embodying rural women's social and economic rights such as water and sanitation, and 16(1)(g), guaranteeing equality between men and women in marriage and family relations, have prevailed. In spite of significant amendments, the law on family still establishes that without an explicit declaration by both parents, a child will automatically be given only the name of the father. This rule was challenged in a case against France under the Optional Protocol, but the complaint was considered inadmissible by the CEDAW Committee. The principle of gender equality is guaranteed by the Constitution in its Preamble and in twenty-two new laws relating to women's rights adopted between 2002 and 2007. These were, according to the authors, mainly adopted to ensure conformity of French law with EU law. Case law relating to the CEDAW is either non-existent or minimalistic and inconsistent. The Conseil d'État, the highest French administrative court, is the only higher jurisdiction whose case law exhibits traces of the CEDAW.

Finland ratified the CEDAW in 1986. In Chapter 20 Kevät Nousiainen and Merja Pentikäinen show how the ratification prompted reform of Finnish legislation held to be contrary to the CEDAW. The Act on Equality between Women and Men 1986 (the Equality Act) was the most visible legislative outcome of the ratification. The study shows that in spite of constitutional reform and making human rights instruments a part of national law, references to the CEDAW in law reform and judicial review have been few in comparison to EU law, the ECHR and the ICCPR. By engaging major women's organizations in close cooperation with the government, the authors argue that Finnish 'state feminism' has diminished the interest of these organizations in making use of the Convention's reporting and communications procedure. They point to the mixed character of Finland's state reporting method, which does not clearly separate the activities and the views of NGOs from those of the state. In recent years the CEDAW Committee's call for increased civil society participation in the state reporting procedure has been commended by Finnish NGOs, which presented separate reports in 2004 and 2008. Finland's recent decision not to enact a new unified and gender-neutral discrimination act but to uphold the Equality Act indicates, however, that women's organizations and the CEDAW Committee's views are gaining ground.

As described in Anne Hellum's study (Chapter 21), gender-equality legislation was already in place when Norway ratified the CEDAW without reservations in 1981. In light of the Gender Equality Act of 1978, which prohibits gender discrimination and aims to improve the position of women, it was assumed that Norwegian law was in conformity with the CEDAW. In 2009, after fierce debate, the CEDAW was incorporated into the Human Rights Act and put on an equal footing with the gender-neutral prohibitions against sex discrimination embedded in the ICCPR, the ICESCR and the ECHR, which were all incorporated in the Act in 1999. The study shows how the EU Gender Equality Directive, which through the European Economic Agreement is directly binding in Norwegian law, works in synergy with the CEDAW, and has prompted a series of reforms that strengthen women's protection against direct and indirect discrimination. The study shows that the CEDAW has been of particular importance in relation to laws that provide protection against structural discrimination and discrimination on religious grounds. It has also served as a safeguard against gender-neutral laws that overlook the specific situations of different groups of women. No individual cases have been lodged under the Optional Protocol (lodged by Norway in 2002), and there are very few court cases. The overwhelming majority of discrimination cases are handled by the Equality and Anti-Discrimination Ombud and the Equality and Anti-Discrimination Tribunal, which in a number of cases have interpreted the Gender Equality Act in light of the CEDAW.

PART I

Potential added value of the CEDAW

1

The Committee on the Elimination of Discrimination against Women

ANDREW BYRNES

1 Introduction

When the Convention on the Elimination of All Forms of Discrimination against Women (CEDAW) was drafted during the 1970s, there was considerable discussion about whether an international monitoring procedure was needed and, if so, what form it should take. Eventually, the decision was taken to establish a body of independent experts, modelled on the existing committees established under the International Convention on the Elimination of All Forms of Racial Discrimination (ICERD) (the Committee on the Elimination of Racial Discrimination – CERD) and the International Covenant on Civil and Political Rights (ICCPR) (the Human Rights Committee – HRC).[1]

The Committee on the Elimination of Discrimination against Women was thus established, '[f]or the purpose of considering the progress made in the implementation of the … Convention'.[2] The primary method envisaged in the Convention for the Committee to carry out this task was its consideration of reports to be submitted regularly by States Parties on the steps that they had taken to implement the Convention. As with the other

[1] See Ineke Boerefijn, 'Article 17' in Marsha Freeman, Christine Chinkin and Beate Rudolf (eds.), *The UN Convention on the Elimination of All Forms of Discrimination against Women: A Commentary* (Oxford University Press, 2012) [hereinafter *CEDAW Commentary*] 475–8; Lars Rehof, *Guide to the Travaux Préparatoires of the United Nations Convention on the Elimination of All Forms of Discrimination against Women* (Dordrecht: Martinus Nijhoff, 1993) 187–98; Kiku Fukuda, 'Article 17: The Committee on the Elimination of All Forms of Discrimination against Women' in Japanese Association of International Women's Rights, *Commentary on the Convention on the Elimination of All Forms of Discrimination against Women* (1995) 307–22; Noreen Burrows, 'The 1979 Convention on the Elimination of All Forms of Discrimination against Women', *Netherlands International Law Review* 32 (1985) 419–60.

[2] Article 17(1).

UN human rights treaty bodies, the way in which the Committee has carried out this work has taken the form of what is described in United Nations jargon as engaging in a 'constructive dialogue' with States Parties. While the CERD and the HRC were given the additional functions of considering individual complaints of violations of their respective treaties by States Parties that had accepted the procedures and of considering complaints by one State against another alleging violation of the treaty, the CEDAW Committee was not given any such additional roles; these were to come twenty years later, when the Optional Protocol to the CEDAW conferred on the Committee the competence to receive individual complaints against States Parties and also to undertake inquiries into grave or systematic violations of the Convention alleged to exist in a State Party.

This chapter provides a general overview of the composition and functioning of the Committee. It does not explore these issues in great depth, as there are recent scholarly studies on this topic,[3] but provides this material by way of a springboard to reflect on the broader significance of the Committee and its contribution. The chapter examines the role of the Committee as a forum for holding governments accountable for their international undertakings, for the engagement of civil society as part of national and transnational struggles to achieve women's equality, and as a site for the generation and interpretation of legal norms.

2 Composition of the Committee

The Committee comprises twenty-three members, who are nominated and elected by the States Parties to the Convention. Article 17(1) provides that the members should be 'of high moral standing and competence in the field covered by the Convention', and also requires that 'consideration [be] given to equitable geographical distribution and to the representation of the different forms of civilization as well as the principal legal systems'. Members are elected to serve four-year terms on the Committee (and may be re-elected); approximately half the members of the Committee are elected every two years. There is no limit on the number of terms a member may serve, and some members have been re-elected multiple times (with a small number having served for almost twenty years).

[3] See in particular the chapters on Articles 17 to 22 of the Convention by Ineke Boerefijn in *CEDAW Commentary* 475–530; and Suzanne Egan, *The United Nations Human Rights Treaty System: Law and Procedure* (Haywards Heath: Bloomsbury Professional, 2011) 159–64.

The membership of the Committee has been overwhelmingly female, though four men have served on the Committee (and a number of other men have been nominated but not elected). The range of disciplinary backgrounds of members has been diverse, including law, politics, international diplomacy, medicine, public health, education, dentistry – although between a third and a half of members have regularly had a legal background, frequently in combination with another field of expertise. The stipulation in the Convention that the membership reflect the diversity of different legal systems and different civilisations, and the standard UN practice of seeking regional diversity and representation has meant that members have come from all regions, though some regions have been overrepresented at different times (Eastern Europe was overrepresented in the early days of the Committee; currently, the Western Europe and Others Group is slightly overrepresented).[4]

Members are elected to serve in their personal capacity as independent experts; they are not government representatives and are not to be subject to the instructions of the government that nominates them. What nearly all the members of the Committee have shared is a demonstrated expertise in advancing the rights and interests of women in different ways, generally over a sustained period of many years. Nevertheless, as with a number of the other treaty bodies, there has been concern among civil society and commentators about the number of persons elected to the Committee who simultaneously hold positions in the executive government. This is seen by many as potentially incompatible with the independence required of committee members (though many such members have been highly experienced in the subject matter of the Convention and activists for women's rights themselves). The issue is most sharply in focus when the members in question are serving diplomats or senior foreign affairs officials. Despite criticism of this practice in the context of the CEDAW and other treaty bodies, States Parties continue to nominate and elect such candidates.[5] A cynical reading of this would be that it is one way in which States Parties seek to restrain the exercise by committees of critical and expansive approaches to the conduct of their mandate.

[4] *Background Information on Enhancing and Strengthening the Expertise and Independence of Treaty Body Members, Note by the Secretariat* [hereinafter *Strengthening Expertise Paper*], HRI/MC/2012/2, p. 4, Table 5 (showing that 15% of States Parties but 31% of members of the Committee came from this group, with Africa and Eastern Europe underrepresented on the basis of this calculation).

[5] The UN High Commissioner for Human Rights reported in mid 2012 that 31 of 172 members of the UN human rights treaty bodies (18%) were 'Diplomat/Government officials' and another 11 (6%) were 'Retired diplomat/Government officials'. Navanethem Pillay,

The CEDAW Committee spent most of its first two decades as a body that was part of, but also apart from, the 'mainstream' UN human rights system.[6] This was reflected in the institutional location of the responsibility for servicing the Committee in the Branch (and subsequently Division) for the Advancement of Women (DAW) that was located in Vienna and then in the Department of Economic and Social Affairs in New York. This was the part of the UN Secretariat responsible for dealing with issues relating to the advancement of women and that also serviced the Commission on the Status of Women (CSW), which was the body from whence the Convention had originated. This arrangement reflected the separation of women's (rights) issues from the human rights system and their pursuit largely as matters of development and social affairs rather than as human rights issues (notwithstanding the contribution of the CSW to the body of human rights instruments). The other human rights treaty bodies were serviced by the Centre for Human Rights (which was consolidated with the Office of the High Commissioner for Human Rights in 1997), based in Geneva. The evolution of the CEDAW saw an increasing engagement of the CEDAW with the other human rights bodies, especially from the early 1990s, an engagement not always reciprocated by other treaty bodies.

The increasing self-awareness of the CEDAW Committee that the Convention and its own supervisory role were critical components of the UN human rights system was reflected in the increasing convergence of many of the procedures adopted by the CEDAW and the other treaty bodies (sometimes as a result of innovations pioneered by the CEDAW,

Strengthening the United Nations Human Rights Treaty Body System, A Report by the United Nations High Commissioner for Human Rights, June 2012 [hereinafter *Pillay Report* 2012]. In the case of the CEDAW Committee, the OHCHR indicated that there were 5 (22%) and 3 (13%) of members who fell into these categories: *Strengthening Expertise Paper*, p. 4, Table 5. Following the 2010 elections there were 4 diplomats on the Committee (one of them on leave), and 5 members who were government officials or recently retired government officials, generally in the area of equal opportunities or women's equality. Thus, about a third of the Committee membership fell consistently into this category (leaving judges out of account), and that proportion has been roughly the same at least since 2002.

6 See Andrew Byrnes, *The Convention and the Committee: Reflections on their Role in the Development of International Human Rights Law and as a Catalyst for National Legislative and Policy Reform* [hereinafter *Byrnes CSW Paper*], paper presented at UN Commission on the Status of Women, 54th session, New York, 1–12 March 2010, Interactive Panel III, 'Commemorating 30 years of CEDAW', available at: http://law.bepress.com/unswwps/flrps10/art17/ (last accessed 23 January 2013) and Andrew Byrnes, 'The Committee on the Elimination of Discrimination against Women' in Frédéric Mégret and Philip Alston (eds.), *The United Nations and Human Rights: A Critical Appraisal* (Oxford: Clarendon Press, 2nd edn, forthcoming).

at other times with the CEDAW adapting its practice in the interests of harmonisation). CEDAW members also participated in the regular meetings of the chairpersons of treaty bodies and the subsequently instituted inter-committee meetings, which have been an important venue for sharing information and working toward improvement and harmonisation of the different procedures of the various treaty bodies. The growing importance of the CEDAW as a source of human rights knowledge is also to be seen in the increasing volume of its jurisprudential output, in particular in its General Recommendations and, more recently, in its case law under the Optional Protocol. Thus, the CEDAW Committee has gradually become an integrated member of the UN human rights treaty body family, a development underlined by the institutional shift of responsibility for servicing the Committee from the DAW in New York to the Office of the High Commissioner for Human Rights (OHCHR) in Geneva from the beginning of 2008. At the same time, the CEDAW has sought to maintain its distinctiveness and the distinctiveness of the premise on which the Convention is based, namely the gendered and patriarchal nature of many societies and of the international order.

3 The reporting procedure

Under Article 18 of the Convention, States Parties are obliged to submit an initial report within one year of the entry into force of the Convention for the individual State Party and every four years thereafter.[7] For its first decade the CEDAW's major tasks were the development of procedures for the review of State Party reports and the commencement of that process as States Parties began to submit their initial reports. That role has

[7] For descriptions of the working methods of the Committee, see *Overview of the Working Methods of the Committee on the Elimination of Discrimination against Women in Relation to the Reporting Process* [hereinafter *CEDAW Working Methods Overview* 2009], CEDAW/C/2009/II/4, Annex III. An analysis of the CEDAW Committee's working methods in comparison with those of other treaty bodies can be found in *Report on the Working Methods of the Human Rights Treaty Bodies Relating to the State Party Reporting Process, Note by the Secretariat* [hereinafter *Treaty Body Working Methods Report* 2011], Inter-Committee Meeting of the Human Rights Treaty Bodies Twelfth Meeting, Geneva, 27–29 June 2011, HRI/ICM/2011/4. The CEDAW also has the power to request reports from States on an exceptional basis, a power it has exercised in relation to the Federal Republic of Yugoslavia (Serbia and Montenegro) (CEDAW/C/YUG/SP.1 (1994)), India (following the systemic violations in Gujarat) (CEDAW/C/IND/SP.1 (2009)), Guinea (due 2009) and the Democratic Republic of the Congo (due 2010).

continued to form the bulk of the Committee's work, although carrying out its other functions has increasingly consumed more time.

Ideally, the submission and review of a report provides an opportunity for a State Party to assess progress made in implementing the Convention, to benefit from an external expert and objective assessment of the situation in the country, and to be held accountable by its citizenry for its failures to ensure effective enjoyment of the rights guaranteed in the Convention. Many States tend in their reports – especially their initial reports – to overemphasise their achievements (especially legislative changes), while giving far less attention to their failures to act, the de facto situation or the difficulties they have faced in seeking to achieve equality for women.

The CEDAW Committee's goal in considering a report is to identify the actual situation in the country, including not only the progress made, but also the obstacles and reverses that need to be addressed. The Committee draws on its own expertise, the State Party's report, the material provided by the Secretariat and other agencies. However, a critical source of further information that enables it to evaluate the government account is material provided by civil society organisations, especially those working on women's human rights issues at the national level. The Committee also receives information from other UN human rights treaty bodies, human rights procedures and various specialised agencies and programmes of the UN, but it is the NGO material that is of particular importance.

Equally, the point of the submission and review of a report by the CEDAW Committee is not simply an event in a far-off northern city, but it is only when the process of preparation, consideration and evaluation of a report by the Committee is linked into domestic process – of policy-making in government and of advocacy in the case of civil society organisations – that the procedure is likely to have any significant impact at the domestic level.

As with the other treaty bodies, the overall record of submission of reports has been patchy, both in terms of timeliness of submission and in quality of reports.[8] Most States Parties have submitted initial reports, though frequently not on time, and many States Parties have submitted

[8] According to the OHCHR, only 16% of the reports due to be submitted to the treaty bodies in 2010 and 2011 were submitted on time; even allowing a year's grace period after the deadline, only one-third of the reports due were submitted within that time: *Pillay Report* 2012 at 21.

one or more subsequent periodic reports.[9] There are still a few countries that have not submitted initial reports, some of them delinquent for extended periods.[10] The Committee has on a number of occasions permitted States Parties to submit combined reports in order to bring themselves up to date in the discharge of their reporting obligations. The Committee has decided that it has the power to undertake a review of the situation in a country without a report, preferably with a delegation present. Dominica was the first State Party to be reviewed in this manner, in 2009.[11] As at the end of 2011 there were four States Parties that had not submitted reports but which were scheduled to be considered in the absence of a report.[12]

Almost from the time when it began to review State Party reports, the Committee has faced difficulties in dealing with its workload in the time allocated to it. The Convention provides for the Committee to meet normally for a period of two weeks each year, and this is what the Committee did in the first few years of its existence. Even though some States Parties did not submit initial reports or did so late, the rapid ratification of the Convention in its early years meant that the Committee was unable to review the reports it had received in a timely fashion and a backlog developed. For much of its life the Committee has regularly requested additional meeting time to permit it to discharge its functions, which have expanded beyond the core function of consideration of reports. That additional meeting time has been granted on many occasions by the UN General Assembly, normally on an exceptional basis, until a backlog of reports awaiting consideration has been cleared. However, the exception has become the norm, first so that the Committee met for two two-week sessions a year (which expanded to three-week sessions, with additional meeting time for a pre-sessional working group), and in recent years, to three three-week sessions per year (with additional time allowed for pre-sessional working groups).[13]

As of 2012 the Committee was meeting for three three-week sessions per year, along with pre-sessional working groups. At each session the Committee normally reviews seven or eight reports (it considered

[9] According to the OHCHR, as of April 2012, there were 10 overdue initial reports under the Convention and 30 overdue periodic reports. *Ibid.* at 23.

[10] See *Status of Submission of Overdue Reports by States Parties under Article 18 of the Convention, Report of the Secretariat of the Committee* [hereinafter *Status of Submission* 2012], A/67/38, part III, Annex I (2012).

[11] See *List of Issues and Questions in the Absence of Initial and Periodic Reports: Dominica*, CEDAW/C/DMA/Q/7 (2008) and CEDAW/C/SR.870 and SR.871 (2009).

[12] *Status of Submission* 2012, para. 3.

[13] An amendment to article 20, though adopted by States Parties in 1995, has yet to enter into force.

twenty-two reports in 2010 and twenty-three reports in 2011). As of late June 2012, the Committee had forty-five States Parties scheduled for its next six sessions (52nd to 57th sessions), which meant an already full programme until mid 2014; there were a further seven reports submitted but yet to be scheduled. Thus, States Parties may be waiting up to two years for their reports to be considered in the normal course of events. In 2011 thirty reports were received and twenty-three were considered.[14] Thus, if the present practice were to continue, at the average rate of considering reports, and accepting that there was already in mid 2012 a delay of two years, it seems that a small backlog is likely to continue to accumulate, at a rate of roughly five reports per year, despite the failure of some States Parties to report at all or on time.

The CEDAW Committee has drawn up or endorsed a number of sets of guidelines for States Parties on the form and content of their reports. Currently, the Committee requires States Parties to comply with the *Harmonized Guidelines on Reporting to the International Human Rights Treaty Monitoring Bodies* adopted in 2006,[15] and the revised CEDAW-specific reporting guidelines adopted by the Committee at its 40th session (2008).[16] Together these require States Parties to submit a common core document that is of relevance to all treaties, as well as a treaty-specific report; this is the result of efforts to harmonise the reporting process and to make it less burdensome for States Parties.

Once a State Party has submitted its report, a pre-sessional working group of the Committee draws up a list of up to thirty questions, based on preliminary work by the country rapporteurs and the Secretariat. This list is sent to the State Party, generally two sessions ahead of the session at which the report is scheduled to be considered, with a request that the State Party respond within six weeks.[17] The list of issues for initial reports proceeds article by article, while for second and subsequent periodic reports the lists of issues are arranged in clusters[18] and focus in particular on the implementation of previous recommendations made by the Committee.[19]

[14] *Status of Submission* 2012, para. 5.

[15] See HRI/MC/2006/3; HRI/GEN/2/Rev.4, at paras. 1–59 (2007).

[16] Decision 40/I, *Convention-specific Reporting Guidelines of the Committee on the Elimination of Discrimination against Women*, A/63/38, part I, Annex I (2008).

[17] A/59/38, paras. 418–40.

[18] *Treaty Body Working Methods Report* 2011, para. 43.

[19] *Ibid.* para. 44.

Actors other than States Parties also have the opportunity to have input into the preparation by the Committee of lists of issues and in its substantive consideration of State Party reports. Article 22 of the Convention provides explicitly for participation by the specialised agencies of the United Nations in the work of the Committee and empowers the Committee to invite them to contribute reports on 'the implementation of the Convention in areas falling within the scope of their activities'. A number of the specialised agencies have regularly contributed written reports to the Committee, initially focusing more generally on the work of the agency relevant to the implementation of the Convention, but for some time now these have also provided country-specific information in response to the Committee's current guidelines on the issue.[20] In addition, these agencies are invited to participate in closed meetings of the pre-sessional working group of the Committee, to provide briefings to the Committee on the situation in particular States Parties.

Equally, civil society organisations have the opportunity to contribute formally and informally to the work of the Committee.[21] Since the Committee's early days, civil society organisations, especially those concerned with women's human rights at the national and international level, have provided written and informal oral briefings to Committee members. The Committee invites NGOs to make written or oral submissions to its pre-sessional working group to inform the drafting of the list of issues,[22] as well as to provide material at the session at which the State Party report is considered. The CEDAW sets aside time at the beginning of the first and second weeks of each session for NGOs to address the Committee in public session. Informal briefings of the Committee and of individual members are also held.[23]

Specific provision has also been made for National Human Rights Institutions (NHRIs) to contribute formally to the work of the Committee. The first formal oral intervention by an NHRI was permitted in July 2005,[24] and there have been a number since that time. The

20 *Report of the Committee on the Elimination of Discrimination against Women on its Thirty-fourth, Thirty-fifth and Thirty-sixth Sessions*, A/61/38, part I, annex II, 79–80 (2006).

21 See generally Shanthi Dairiam, 'From global to local: the involvement of NGOs' in Hanna Beate Schöpp-Schilling and Cees Flinterman (eds.), *The Circle of Empowerment: Twenty-Five Years of the UN Committee on the Elimination of Discrimination against Women* [hereinafter *The Circle of Empowerment*] (New York: Feminist Press, 2007) 313.

22 *CEDAW Rules of Procedure*, rule 47.

23 See *Treaty Body Working Methods Report* 2011, para. 125.

24 *Ibid.* para. 113.

Committee adopted a statement on NHRIs in 2008, in which it underlined the importance of NHRIs to the domestic implementation of the Convention and welcomed the submission of written information for the pre-sessional working groups and the session, and undertook to make time available for oral interventions by NHRIs at the public sessions of the Committee.[25]

The Committee considers the reports of States Parties in public sessions, in the presence of State Party representatives,[26] normally devoting two meetings to the consideration of each report. Following a formal introduction by the delegation (ideally no more than thirty minutes in length), the Committee poses questions to the delegation,[27] led by the country rapporteurs,[28] with other members permitted to put additional questions and with time limits imposed on all members.[29] The Committee has adopted the practice, as have other treaty bodies, that a member of the Committee from a State Party whose report is being considered does not participate in any aspect of the consideration of the report.

Following the conclusion of the 'dialogue', the Committee considers and adopts Concluding Observations on the report (previously called Concluding Comments), which have been drafted by the country rapporteurs, generally with the assistance of the Secretariat.[30] The Concluding Observations provide an evaluation of the State Party's achievements and challenges, identifying both progress and shortfalls; they provide recommendations specifically tailored to the country in question, as well as a number of more general recommendations that the Committee includes in its Concluding Observations on most countries.

The form of the Concluding Observations has evolved. The Committee has adopted a structure with a list of relevant headings[31] to be used in the document ('flexibly and as appropriate for the State party concerned'[32]), and there are a number of standard paragraphs that appear in virtually

[25] *Statement by the Committee on the Elimination of Discrimination against Women on its Relationship with National Human Rights Institutions*, Decision 40/II, A/63/38, part I, Annex II, para. 7 (2008).

[26] *Treaty Body Working Methods Report* 2011, para. 73.

[27] A/59/38, part II, paras. 418–440 and *Treaty Body Working Methods Report* 2011, para. 61.

[28] *Treaty Body Working Methods Report* 2011, paras. 65 and 66.

[29] *Ibid.* para. 61.

[30] *Ibid.* para. 76.

[31] Decision 41/II, *Report of the Committee on the Elimination of Discrimination against Women on its Fortieth and Forty-first Sessions*, A/63/38, part II, Annex X, 261 (2008).

[32] Decision 41/II, A/63/38, part II, 88.

all Concluding Observations,[33] as well as comments that are focused specifically on the situation in individual States Parties.[34] The Concluding Observations include an introduction, a section that sets out positive developments, and a final section setting out concerns and specific recommendations as to the actions the State Party should take. This last section is normally the longest and sets out, area by area, the issues to be addressed that the Committee considers are the most important. The Committee now also regularly specifies the date for submission of the next report in the Concluding Observations.[35]

Under its new follow-up procedure the Committee identifies a number of priority recommendations in the Concluding Observations and requests the State Party to report back to it within one to two years on the steps it has taken to respond to those recommendations. So far as other recommendations are considered, the Committee will only follow up on their implementation when it next reviews the situation in a country, which will normally be when the next report is considered.

Following the transmission of the Concluding Observations to the States Parties concerned, it is open to States Parties to submit their comments on them. While there is no formal procedure for receiving and dealing with these comments,[36] they are circulated to Committee members and acknowledged in the annual report,[37] with the more recent comments being posted on the website of the OHCHR.[38] Prior to the adoption

[33] These include a standard reminder of 'the obligation of the State party to systematically and continuously implement all the provisions of the Convention' and 'urges the State party to give priority attention to the implementation of the present Concluding Observations between now and the submission of the next periodic report'; references to the role of Parliaments in implementing the Convention, the need to disseminate information about the Convention, the Optional Protocol and Concluding Observations; the need to ratify the Optional Protocol and the Amendment to Article 20 of the Convention (where this has not been done); and the implementation of the Beijing Platform for Action.

[34] See *CEDAW Working Methods Overview* 2009, para. 21.

[35] *Treaty Body Working Methods Report* 2011, para. 75.

[36] It is not clear that Article 21 of the Convention – which provides that 'suggestions and general recommendations based on the examination of reports and information received from the States Parties … shall be included in the report of the Committee together with comments, if any, from States Parties' – applies to Concluding Observations (rather than general suggestions and general recommendations).

[37] Decision 21/II, A/54/38/Rev.1, p. 45. See *Treaty Body Working Methods Report* 2011, at para. 79.

[38] See, e.g., *Comments from the Republic of Belarus Concerning the Concluding Observations Issued by the Committee on the Elimination of Discrimination against Women* (CEDAW/C/BLR/CO/7), Diplomatic Note, 22 February 2011, available at: www2.ohchr.org/english/bodies/cedaw/docs/Noteverbale22-02-11_Belarus_CEDAW48.pdf (last accessed 23

in 2008 of the new follow-up procedure,[39] relatively few States Parties had taken the opportunity to provide comments directly in response to the Concluding Observations.[40] The new follow-up procedure provides the opportunity for a State Party to respond to the specific Concluding Observations on which a response is requested (the response being circulated as an official document), but also presumably on other matters, though to date the responses do not appear to have gone beyond the recommendations specified. The government responses and any further exchanges between the Committee and the State Party are made public on the Committee's website.[41] The Committee's follow-up procedure has provided an opportunity for the dialogue between the Committee and the State Party to continue beyond the one-off engagement that otherwise culminates in the public hearings; and the Committee's Rapporteur on Follow-up has been detailed and insistent in her assessment of the extent to which recommendations have or have not been implemented.[42]

January 2013). Belarus had asked these to be circulated as an official document as well as to have them placed on the website; only the latter request appears to have been acceded to. See Decision 49/V, *Exchange of Notes Verbales between the Permanent Mission of Belarus to the United Nations Office at Geneva and the Secretariat Regarding Comments To Concluding Observations of the Committee on the Elimination of Discrimination against Women, Note Verbale Dated 23 May 2011 from the Permanent Mission of Belarus Addressed to the Secretariat* and *Note Verbale Dated 22 July 2011 from the Secretariat Addressed to the Permanent Mission of Belarus*, A/67/38, part I, Annex III.

39 *Treaty Body Working Methods Report* 2011, para. 85.

40 See, e.g., three States in 1999 (Greece, Mexico and China: see A/54/38/rev.1, Annex VII (1999)) and three States in 2007 (Chile, China and Mauritania: see A/62/38, Annex XI), two from the thirty-ninth to forty-first sessions (Republic of Korea and Lebanon: A/63/38, part II, Annex VII (2008)); Bahrain and Rwanda (A/64/38, part II, Annex IX (2009)); six at the end of the forty-fourth session: Azerbaijan, Denmark, Japan, Switzerland, Timor-Leste and Tuvalu) and three at the end of the forty-fifth session: Netherlands, Ukraine and the United Arab Emirates (A/65/38, part I, Annex X). Belarus also submitted comments in 2011 (A/67/38, part I, Annex III (2012)): see *supra* note 39.

41 Committee on the Elimination of Discrimination against Women, Follow-up Reports, available at: www2.ohchr.org/english/bodies/cedaw/followup.htm (last accessed 23 January 2013).

42 See, e.g., the letters sent by the Rapporteur for Follow-up of 19 February 2010 and 4 November 2011 to Kyrgyzstan and the additional information provided by Kyrgyzstan (CEDAW/C/KGZ/CO/3/Add.1 (2011)), available in the Follow-up section for the CEDAW Committee on the OHCHR website: www2.ohchr.org/english/bodies/cedaw/followup.htm (last accessed 23 January 2013). In 2012, in an assessment of its follow-up procedure to date, the Committee concluded that it was 'achieving its stated goal of acting as a tool of implementation of the Convention and more specifically the recommendations set out in selected Concluding Observations. This procedure is therefore proving to be an effective reporting procedure under Article 18 of the Convention that enables the Committee to monitor progress achieved between reporting cycles (A/67/38, part II, para. 18 (2012)).

4 General Recommendations and other contributions of policy/interpretive nature

Article 21(1) of the Convention confers on the Committee the power to 'make suggestions and general recommendations based on the examination of reports and information received from the States Parties'. These suggestions are to be included in the Committee's annual report, 'together with comments, if any, from States Parties'. The Committee has drawn on this power to develop a substantial body of interpretive material on specific articles of the Convention as well as cross-cutting themes (such as violence against women, the rights of older women and the rights of female migrant workers).

In 1997 the Committee outlined a procedure[43] for the development of General Recommendations that has provided the framework for the elaboration of General Recommendations since that time. That process involved the following stages:

(a) 'an open dialogue between the Committee, non-governmental organizations and others on the topic of the general recommendation' (sometimes involving a day of discussion on the topic), in which all interested parties are invited to participate and make submissions;
(b) preparation of a draft General Recommendation by the designated Committee member, considered by the Committee; and
(c) final adoption of the General Recommendation by the Committee.[44]

The process has also involved the informal solicitation of expert advice or circulation of drafts among interested parties, and on occasion academic institutions and non-governmental organisations have organised seminars at which CEDAW members and other experts have explored the issues and possible content of a General Recommendation.

As of early 2013 the Committee had adopted twenty-nine General Recommendations.[45] The early General Recommendations were a mix of brief, resolution-style documents, some addressing substantive matters and some dealing with organisational or other matters. The first major breakthrough in this regard came in 1992 with the Committee's General Recommendation 19 on violence against women, which analysed violence against women as a form of discrimination covered by the Convention

[43] A/52/38/Rev.1, para. 480.

[44] *CEDAW Working Methods Overview* 2009, para. 35.

[45] For the text of the General Recommendations, see www2.ohchr.org/english/bodies/cedaw/comments.htm (last accessed 23 January 2013).

and articulated the obligations of the State in relation to violence both by the State and also by non-State actors (including violence in the home).[46] Since that time, nearly all of the General Recommendations adopted have been even more expansive and detailed. The Committee has been concerned to set out in these documents not just an analysis of the legal and policy measures that the Convention requires, but also to explain the context in which the Convention's provisions are to be interpreted and to develop the conceptual underpinnings of equality theory and the content of State obligation in that context.

The most detailed General Recommendations adopted as of mid 2012 have addressed a number of issues of general obligation under the Convention – most importantly the concepts of equality and discrimination and temporary special measures (General Recommendation 25 (2004)), and the nature of States Parties' obligations under Article 2 (General Recommendation 28 (2010)). They have also engaged with a range of specific thematic issues including both specific articles of the Convention – General Recommendation 21 (1994) dealing with equality in marriage and the family; General Recommendation 23 (1997) dealing with women in political and public life; General Recommendation 24 (1999) dealing with women and health – and cross-cutting themes (General Recommendation 19 (1992) dealing with violence against women; General Recommendation 26 (2008) dealing with women migrant workers; and General Recommendation 27 (2010) dealing with older women and protection of their human rights).

The General Recommendations are a rich resource of legal and policy guidance, and it is hard to select highlights. However, among the most important jurisprudential contributions made by the General Recommendations are:

- the conceptualisation of violence against women as a form of 'discrimination against women' within the meaning of the Convention – most importantly in General Recommendation 19;
- the development under the Convention of the States Parties' obligation of 'due diligence', namely to take all reasonable measures to ensure that women are not subject to discrimination by non-State actors – initially articulated by the Committee in the context of violence against women, but of more general application;

[46] See Elizabeth Evatt, 'Finding a voice for women's rights: the early days of CEDAW', *George Washington International Law Review* 34 (2002) 515–53.

- the elaboration of the notion of non-discrimination and substantive equality that underpins the Convention – in a number of General Recommendations but perhaps most importantly in General Recommendation 25 on temporary special measures under the Convention;
- the development of the implications of the concept of discrimination in the form of stereotyping;[47]
- an exploration of the impact of multiple forms of discrimination (intersectionality); and
- the articulation of the relevance of discrimination based on sexuality to the definition of discrimination against women.[48]

In addition to these General Recommendations, in 2011 the Committee adopted a 'General Statement' on rural women[49] – a rather curious designation likely to confuse, because the statement is discursive and could equally well have been issued as a General Recommendation (especially as the Committee stated its intention to continue drafting a General Recommendation on the subject).[50] The same would appear to apply to the Committee's Statement in relation to gender equality in situations of displacement, asylum and statelessness, adopted in 2011,[51] on which topic the Committee is also currently drafting a General Recommendation.[52] In the same way the Committee could well have issued a General Recommendation on reservations instead of its 1994 Statement that was subsequently incorporated into reporting guidelines.

As of mid 2012 the Committee had on its agenda the preparation of General Recommendations on four topics: the economic consequences of marriage and its dissolution (in fact adopted in early 2013); on harmful

[47] See generally Rebecca J. Cook and Simone Cusack, *Gender Stereotyping: Transnational Legal Perspectives* (Philadelphia: University of Pennsylvania Press, 2010).

[48] Though there has been some dissent within the Committee on this issue: see the disagreement over terminology in the voting on General Recommendation 27 (older women) and General Recommendation 28 (Article 2), both of which referred to discrimination on the basis of 'sexual orientation and gender identity': A/66/38, part II, pp. 102–3 (2010), paras. 23–29 (2011).

[49] Decision 50/VI, *General Statement of the Committee on the Elimination of Discrimination against Women on Rural Women*, adopted on 19 October 2011, 50th session, A/67/38, part II, Annex II, 55 (2012).

[50] A/67/38, part II, para. 43 (2012); A/67/38, part III, para. 40 (2012).

[51] Decision 50/V, *Statement of the Committee on the Elimination of Discrimination against Women on the Anniversaries of the Adoption of the 1951 Convention Relating to the Status of Refugees and the 1961 Convention on the Reduction of Statelessness*, A/67/38, part II, Annex I (2012).

[52] A/67/38, part II, para. 42 (2012); A/67/38, part III, para. 39 (2012).

practices (the CEDAW/Convention on the Rights of the Child (CRC) joint General Recommendation); on the human rights of women in conflict and post-conflict situations; and on access to justice.

The stimulus for the development of individual General Recommendations has varied. In some cases external events have triggered a sense that the Committee needs to articulate how the Convention applies to a particular issue or practice;[53] in other cases individual members of the Committee have had a special interest in a particular Article or issue and have urged the adoption of a General Recommendation on the theme.[54] In yet other cases civil society groups have engaged in advocacy to persuade the Committee that it should address a particular topic in a General Recommendation. In any case the proponents of the development of a General Recommendation on a specific topic must persuade the Committee as a whole that this is something that should be taken up as part of the Committee's already significant workload.

Overall, the process of drafting General Recommendations has become increasingly transparent and open to contributions from a wide range of interested parties. The Committee issues public calls for input from interested parties on the subjects it has chosen for General Recommendations. For example, as part of its preparation for the elaboration of a General Recommendation on women in conflict and post-conflict situations, the Committee issued a call for submissions[55] and subsequently a concept

[53] For example, the attention given to the issue of violence against women in the early 1990s and the proposed elaboration of a new international instrument on violence against women (which resulted in the adoption of the United Nations Declaration on the Elimination of Violence against Women) moved the Committee to develop General Recommendation 19. Among other motivations, the Committee was concerned to underline that States Parties were already obliged to eliminate public and private violence against women under the Convention, and that a new normative instrument would merely reiterate or give detailed content to these obligations rather than fill a normative gap. Evatt, 'Finding a voice for women's rights'.

[54] For example, Hanna Beate Schöpp-Schilling, member of the Committee from Germany for many years, had a particular interest in the question of temporary special measures dealt with by Article 4, and devoted considerable energy to the development of General Recommendation 25, which is an extended discussion of the concepts of discrimination and equality under the Convention and the obligations of States Parties to adopt temporary special measures. Ruth Halperin-Kaddari, member from Israel, played a similar role in relation to the development of the General Recommendation 29 on the economic consequences of marriage, family relations and their dissolution, and there are other examples.

[55] General Discussion on 'women in conflict and post-conflict situations', available at: www2.ohchr.org/english/bodies/cedaw/discussion2011.htm (last accessed 23 January 2013).

note[56] to provide a basis for a public general discussion on the theme held at its 49th session in July 2011;[57] the note looked very much like the first draft of a General Recommendation. In a move reflecting this greater transparency the Committee published submissions from civil society and some intergovernmental organisations on the OHCHR website.[58] This approach is also seen in the Committee's innovative exercise of seeking to elaborate with the Committee on the Rights of the Child a Joint General Recommendation/General Comment on Harmful Practices. A general call for submissions on the theme was issued in 2011,[59] with submissions from civil society made available on the website.[60]

On a number of occasions expert meetings held by academic institutions or non-governmental organisations have been organised to contribute analysis and material for consideration by the Committee in its deliberations, and these have been influential in the approach that the Committee has adopted.[61]

[56] *Concept Note: General Discussion on the Protection of Women's Human Rights in Conflict and Post-conflict Contexts*, 2011, available at: www2.ohchr.org/english/bodies/cedaw/docs/GRConceptNote.pdf (last accessed 23 January 2013).

[57] Committee on Elimination of Discrimination against Women, Day of General Discussion – 'Women in conflict and post-conflict situations', 18 July 2011, New York, available at: www2.ohchr.org/english/bodies/cedaw/docs/Discussion2011/SummaryReportCEDAWWomenInConflict.pdf (last accessed 23 January 2013).

[58] If governments have made any submissions, however, these do not appear on the website. Other committees do not always post government submissions, either – see, e.g., CAT's website, which posted submissions by civil society organisations in relation to its draft General Comment on Article 14, but did not post those made by governments.

[59] Joint CEDAW–CRC General Recommendation/Comment on Harmful Practices, Call for submissions, available at: www2.ohchr.org/english/bodies/cedaw/JointCEDAW-CRC-GeneralRecommendation.htm (last accessed 23 January 2013).

[60] *Ibid.*

[61] For example, the New York-based International League for Human Rights, in collaboration with the International Women's Rights Action Watch, organised a seminar on violence against women a few days prior to the Committee's 1992 session in New York, at which the question of violence against women and the adoption of a General Recommendation on the subject were on the agenda. See International League for Human Rights, *Combatting Violence Against Women* (New York: ILHR, 1993).

In October 2002 the Universities of Maastricht, Utrecht and Leiden organised an expert seminar in Maastricht focused on the issue of temporary special measures under the Convention with the purpose of contributing to the Committee's deliberations in preparing a General Recommendation on that topic. The report of this meeting, including papers presented and commentaries, was published as Ineke Boerefijn *et al.* (eds.), *Temporary Special Measures: Accelerating de facto Equality of Women under Article 4(1) UN Convention on the Elimination of All Forms of Discrimination against Women* (Antwerp: Intersentia, 2003). The CEDAW Committee adopted General Recommendation 25 on temporary special measures at its January 2004 session.

The CEDAW has also made a number of other statements both on general issues as well as in relation to the situation of women in specific countries. The former have sometimes been occasioned by significant anniversaries or international conferences, or in response to invitations from other bodies for the CEDAW's contributions on specific issues. The Committee has stated that the purpose of these pronouncements is 'to clarify and confirm its position with respect to major international developments and issues that bear upon the implementation of the Convention'.[62] For example, the Committee has issued statements on such topics as reservations (1998); gender and racial discrimination (2001); gender and sustainable development (2002); discrimination against older women (2002); the occasion of the ten-year review and appraisal of the Beijing Declaration and Platform for Action (2005); gender aspects of the tsunami disaster that took place in South-East Asia in December 2004 (2005); the international financial crisis (2009); gender and climate change (2009); and on the anniversaries of the adoption of the 1951 Convention relating to the Status of Refugees and the 1961 Convention on the Reduction of Statelessness (2011).[63] The Committee has also issued statements in relation to specific countries, expressing solidarity with Afghan women (2002), and expressing concern about the situation of women in Iraq (2004) and Gaza (2009).[64] The latter, which have involved both statements to the international community at large and communications direct to the governments of particular countries (for example,

In February 2007 the International Women's Rights Action Watch (Asia Pacific), in collaboration with the Australian Human Rights Centre of the Faculty of Law, University of New South Wales, organised an expert seminar in Kuala Lumpur for the purpose of contributing to discussion of the proposed General Recommendation on Article 2 of the Convention. Participants included women's human rights activists and advocates, international law experts, academics, and past and present members of the CEDAW Committee. The outcome document of the meeting put forward many ideas that were ultimately reflected in CEDAW's General Recommendation 28 adopted in 2010. See International Women's Rights Action Watch Asia Pacific, *Possible Elements for Inclusion in a General Recommendation on to Article 2 of CEDAW, Outcome Document of the Expert Group Meeting on CEDAW Article 2: National and International Dimensions of State Obligation* (Kuala Lumpur: IWRAW Asia Pacific, 2007), available at: www.iwraw-ap.org/aboutus/pdf/Elements_paper_final_version_Jan9.pdf (last accessed 23 January 2013).

[62] *Ways and Means of Expediting the Work of the Committee on the Elimination of Discrimination against Women, Note by the Secretariat* [hereinafter *Ways and Means* 2009], Committee on the Elimination of Discrimination against Women, Forty-fourth session, 20 July to 7 August 2009, Item 6 of the provisional agenda, CEDAW/C/2009/II/4, para. 40.

[63] *Treaty Body Working Methods Report* 2011, para. 137.

[64] *Ways and Means* 2009, para. 40.

Libya and Egypt)[65] have manifested the CEDAW Committee's desire to respond to situations of conflict or transition in which the human rights of women might be at risk or which offer opportunities to improve or embed the rights of women in new constitutions or laws.

The output of the Committee – in particular its General Recommendations (most prominently its General Recommendation 19 on violence against women, but others as well) – has also begun to have an influence on the work of national courts and tribunals, having been cited in a number of important cases.[66]

5 The Committee's work under the Optional Protocol to the Convention

An emerging area of importance, likely to increase in significance, is the jurisprudence of the Committee under the Optional Protocol,[67] in particular under the individual communications procedure. The inquiry procedure is still in its early days, with the report of only one inquiry completed by the Committee published so far,[68] although the Committee had at least two other inquiries underway as of mid 2012 – the Philippines and Canada.[69] The number of individual cases lodged and decided under the Optional Protocol

[65] Decision 49/III. Letters from the Chair of the Committee to the Governments of Egypt and Tunisia, Identical letters dated 31 March 2011 from the Chair of the Committee to the Prime Minister and the Minister for Foreign Affairs of Egypt [and Tunisia], 49th session, A/67/38, part I, Annex II, 18 (2012).

[66] See the cases referred to in *Byrnes CSW Paper*, and the International Law Association Committee on International Human Rights Law and Practice, *Interim Report on the Impact of the United Nations Treaty Bodies on the Work of National Courts and Tribunals*, in International Law Association, *Report of the Seventieth Conference*, New Delhi (London: ILA, 2002) 507–55; *Final Report on the Impact of the United Nations Treaty Bodies on the Work of National Courts and Tribunals* [*ILA Final Report* 2004], in International Law Association, *Report of the Seventy-First Conference, Berlin* (London: ILA, 2004) 621–87. See also Robyn Emerton *et al.*, *International Women's Rights Cases* (London: Cavendish, 2005).

[67] As of 27 June 2012 there were 104 States Parties to the Optional Protocol. See generally Jane Connors, 'Optional Protocol' in *CEDAW Commentary*, 607–79; UN Division for the Advancement of Women, Department of Economic and Social Affairs, *The Optional Protocol: Text and Materials* (New York: United Nations, 2000); Egan, *The United Nations Human Rights Treaty System* at 371–89. For a comprehensive listing of resource materials, and information and commentary on recent developments, see *Optional Protocol to CEDAW* blog, available at: http://opcedaw.wordpress.com (last accessed 23 January 2013).

[68] CEDAW/C/2005/OP.8/Mexico.

[69] Domini M. Torrevillas, 'CEDAW to look at Manila women's violations', *The Philippine Star*, 20 October 2009, available at: http://www.philstar.com/opinion/515498/cedaw-look-manila-womens-violations (last accessed 23 January 2013).

is relatively modest, given that the Optional Protocol entered into force over a decade ago. Roughly forty cases had been registered by mid 2012 and nearly all of those had been cases against members of the Council of Europe or Canada (with one case each against Peru, Brazil and the Philippines).

The Committee has made important contributions to international human rights law and the jurisprudence of the Convention in a number of cases involving violence against women that have involved the death of women at the hands of partners or former partners. These cases have built on the analysis set out by the Committee in its General Recommendation 19 on violence against women, and have given content to the so-called obligation of 'due diligence', that is the obligation of the State Party to take all reasonable measures to prevent the violation of the rights of a woman by a non-State actor. These cases have set a high bar in terms of the level of legislative protection and the practical implementation of the legal standards required, though the facts in these cases showed a consistent and sustained pattern of actual and threatened violence against the women concerned to which the State Party should clearly have responded before rather than after the women's deaths.[70]

The Committee has also found violations of the Convention in cases in which the domestic courts relied on gender stereotypes in conducting a rape trial in which the defendant was ultimately acquitted;[71] where a young woman ended up dead because of a failure to diagnose her condition and provide available and adequate obstetric care;[72] by denying a minor who had been sexually abused access to therapeutic abortion and delaying surgery that contributed to her subsequent paralysis;[73] and where a woman was held in a prison with an all-male staff and was subjected to sexual humiliation and harassment over a period of five days.[74]

[70] See generally Bonita Meyersfeld, *Domestic Violence and International Law* (London and Portland, OR: Hart Publishing, 2010) at 42–52, 232–5.

[71] *Karen Tayag Vertido* v. *The Philippines*, Communication No. 18/2008, CEDAW/C/46/D/18/2008 (2010). See Simone Cusack and Alexandra S. H. Timmer, 'Gender stereotyping in rape cases: the CEDAW Committee's decision in *Vertido* v. *The Philippines*', *Human Rights Law Review* 11:2 (2011) 329–42.

[72] *Alyne da Silva Pimentel Teixeira (deceased)* v. *Brazil*, Communication No. 17/2008, CEDAW/C/49/D/17/2008 (2011). See Judith Bueno de Mesquita and Eszter Kismödi, 'Maternal mortality and human rights: landmark decision by United Nations human rights body', *Bulletin of the World Health Organization* 90 (2012) 79–79A; and Rebecca J. Cook and Bernard Dickens, 'Upholding pregnant women's right to life', *International Journal of Gynaecology and Obstetrics* 117 (2012) 90–4.

[73] *L.C.*v. *Peru*, Communication No. 22/2009, CEDAW/C/50/D/22/2009 (2011).

[74] *Inga Abramova* v. *Belarus*, Communication No. 23/2009, CEDAW/C/49/D/20/2008 (2011).

The violence cases have also led to important progress at the domestic level in terms of law, policy and administrative change, and in the development of the follow-up procedures of the Committee. Follow-up to decided cases finding violations is a critical element of the process and has given rise to some difficulties under other treaties. The Committee has had some success with its follow-up procedures, due in part at least to the willingness of States Parties to cooperate. For example, in relation to Austria the process has involved a continuing discussion with the State Party (and the author/representative), which it seems will not be formally closed until the Committee is satisfied that the appropriate measures have been taken.[75]

As the Committee's body of case law grows,[76] and more decisions are adopted in which the Committee finds violations, the question of domestic implementation will assume greater importance. While much responsibility in this respect lies with the executive government and legislature, often the courts may need to be involved, if, for example, a court decision needs to be reviewed or reversed. Similar issues have arisen in relation to the implementation of the views of other human rights treaty bodies, as in many countries the decision of the treaty bodies have no formal legal status, and the successful complainant may therefore not be able to rely directly on the decision of the CEDAW Committee to make or reopen a case under domestic law.[77] An instance of this can be seen in one of the cases against Austria, in which the Austrian Supreme Court stated in the context of a civil claim for compensation brought as a result of the case of *Şahide Goekce (deceased)* v. *Austria*[78] that the decision and recommendations of the CEDAW Committee were not relevant to the domestic court's decision, as the establishment of the facts and their legal assessment was solely a matter for the Austrian courts.[79]

[75] See, e.g., *Report of the Committee on the Elimination of Discrimination against Women on its Forty-second and Forty-third sessions*, A/64/38, at 150 (*Yildirim* v. *Austria*). See also the discussion in Rosa Lugar, 'Die UNO-Frauenrechtskonvention CEDAW als Instrument zur Bekämpfung der Gewalt an Frauen: zwei Beispiele aus Österreich", *Frauen Fragen* 1 (2009) 22–38, at 34–6.

[76] For a compilation of summaries of all of the Committee's decisions up to June 2012, see Open Society Justice Initiative, *Case Digests: UN Committee on Elimination of Discrimination against Women (CEDAW) 2004–12* (2012), available at: www.soros.org/briefing-papers/case-digests-un-committee-elimination-discrimination-against-women-cedaw-2004-12 (last accessed 23 January 2013).

[77] *ILA Final Report* 2004, paras. 29–43.

[78] Communication No. 5/2005.

[79] Decision of 29 November 2007, para. 2 (referred to in Lugar, 'Die UNO-Frauenrechtskonvention CEDAW' at 35 n. 64).

The Committee has so far published the results of only one inquiry conducted under Article 8 of the Optional Protocol, in relation to Mexico,[80] and has announced that it is engaged in two others (the Philippines and Canada (2011)),[81] though a number of requests have been made (five in 2011,[82] including one in relation to the United Kingdom).[83]

6 The Committee's role – advancing equality in a world of diversity and sovereign States

The Committee's role requires that it assess the extent of implementation of the Convention in nearly all the countries of the world. It thus has had to seek to apply a universal standard of equality and non-discrimination to societies that are enormously diverse – from tiny island nations to the world's largest countries located in all regions, representing different levels of development and legal systems; manifesting a variety of religious, traditional and cultural systems; and with political systems ranging from advanced liberal democracies through socialist States to countries in turmoil or seeking to find a transition from internal conflict and social disruption (including genocidal killings and civil wars) to a stable, just and ordered society. This diversity, and the fact that the Committee is carrying out an international supervisory function that involves making judgements (albeit not legal ones) on the extent to which sovereign States have given effect to their international obligations, poses significant challenges of competence, legitimacy, diplomacy and effectiveness.

Under the Convention, States Parties assume obligations of different levels of generality, stringency and immediacy.[84] These range from quite general obligations to take 'appropriate' or 'necessary' measures

[80] CEDAW/C/2005/OP.8/Mexico. See Andrew Byrnes and Maria Herminia Graterol, 'Violence against women: private actors and the obligation of due diligence', *Interights Bulletin* 15 (2006) 156–7; Maria Regina Tavares da Silva and Yolanda Ferrer Gómez, 'The Juárez Murders and the inquiry procedure' in *The Circle of Empowerment* at 298.

[81] Press Release by the Committee on the Elimination of Discrimination against Women concerning the inquiry regarding disappearances and murders of Aboriginal women and girls in Canada, 16 December 2011, available at: http://web.archive.org/web/20120412020217/http://www2.ohchr.org/english/bodies/cedaw/docs/CanadaInquiry_Press_Release.pdf (last accessed 8 February 2013).

[82] CEDAW/C/52/2, para. 61 (2012).

[83] For information and documentation relating to the Mexico, Philippines and Canadian inquiries, and the request in relation to the United Kingdom, see http://opcedaw.wordpress.com/inquiries/all-inquiries/ (last accessed 23 January 2013).

[84] See generally Andrew Byrnes, 'Article 2' in *CEDAW Commentary*, 71–99, and CEDAW Committee, General Comment 28 (2010) on Article 2 of the Convention.

to eliminate discrimination generally, to making specific obligations in specific areas, such as obligations to replace discriminatory penal laws or to ensure that women enjoy equality before the law or the right to vote in elections. In some cases the obligations can be given effect to immediately, and there are objective indicators that can be used to determine whether the State Party has done so (for example, whether a marital rape exception exists under domestic law, or whether there is legislation in force that protects against discrimination in employment). In other cases, while there may be a clear obligation to act immediately, there may be a range of options available to the State Party to achieve the goal of eliminating discrimination, and much may depend on local political and social conditions as to which is the most effective or the most feasible.

The Committee thus faces the challenging task of assessing whether the steps a State Party has taken (or its failure to act) are consistent with its Convention obligations. This can be a challenging task for an external body – especially where the assessment of what is appropriate depends on a detailed knowledge and understanding of local conditions. It depends in part on the specificity of the standards it is applying, the information available to the Committee, the nature of the process of interaction with the State Party in consideration of the report and follow-up, and the quality of analysis and judgement of the Committee. The challenges the Committee faces in carrying out its supervisory role are not unique: the other treaty bodies face similar challenges, and many international bodies with external review, evaluation or adjudicative functions are frequently confronted with similar issues when assessing whether complex situations in a State are in conformity with that State's international obligations.

The effectiveness of the Committee's assessments and recommendations – and advocacy based on them – will depend in significant part on the legitimacy and persuasiveness of the Committee's output, though the political will of government is also critical to actual progress.

It is an easy response to a critical assessment or evaluation by an external body for States to argue that the body simply does not have all the relevant facts, especially if the body, as inevitably happens on occasion, gets some facts wrong, does not understand the full national context or has been overly influenced by NGOs with a particular agenda that skews the overall picture of progress in the country. Such responses can also be bolstered by the invocation of the democratic mandate of a government, where there is a democratic political system and a government policy is justified by reference to their status as such a government or by reference to majoritarian opinion (or even by a reference to an asserted constitutional duty to respect the views of minority communities).

Of course, one rather formal response to these sorts of criticism is that the legitimacy of the assessment and recommendations made by the Committee derives in part from the very fact of its creation and the acceptance of its monitoring functions by States Parties. The CEDAW Committee, like the other treaty bodies, was created by the drafters of the treaty to carry out specific functions (later supplemented by the functions conferred on it by the Optional Protocol). States that become parties to the treaty thus accept the role of the Committee as set forth in the Convention (and the Optional Protocol, if they also become parties to that instrument). That, of course, is a statement of the formal position (and one that carries little weight in the eyes of many States Parties that find themselves the subject of criticism). States Parties that may in theory have accepted the role of the Committee to monitor and review their performance will not feel constrained to accept without question or criticism its assessment of the acts of a State Party. In practice, the legitimacy and stature of Committee's pronouncements are dynamic, and depend on the substance and manner of its work over sustained periods. The influence of the Committee and its pronouncements is thus necessarily a work in progress, built up over time by continued interactions with individual States Parties and the States Parties collectively, as well as with the other communities that have expectations of and monitor the work of the Committee (such as civil society groups and scholars).

In some cases the Committee can be quite direct and specific in identifying legislation, policies or practices that are inconsistent with the Convention and recommending steps to remedy the situation both under the reporting procedure and especially under the Optional Protocol procedures. At the same time, many of the Committee's pronouncements and recommendations are more general, offering a series of possible steps that the State Party may wish to consider, rather than prescribing every step in detail. This is, of course, the case with General Recommendations, which tend to list a range of possible issues and actions that States Parties should consider taking. Concluding Observations tend to be more focused and specific, though not always – the contribution of the Committee is frequently to challenge the State Party to identify the measures that it thinks will be most effective in the national context in addressing identified failures to guarantee equality, and ensuring that the State Party addresses those problems through the adoption of concrete steps that will bring measurable progress. While not all 'constructive dialogues' between the Committee and States Parties have been free of tension (much of which is lost in the accounts contained in the Committee's summary records), on the whole the approach of the Committee and most governments is a positive one, intent on taking those steps that reasonably can be taken to advance the goals of the Convention.

The Committee recognises that States Parties may be in a better position to make an assessment of the situation and needs at the domestic level; an important aspect of the Convention's obligations of implementation (and reporting) is to ensure that the State Party undertakes the required data collection and monitoring as a necessary basis for the identification and addressing of problems (as part of the obligation to adopt a policy, and general aspect of the obligation to implement the Convention de facto). For example, in General Recommendation 24 (1999) on the right to health, the Committee comments:

> 9. States parties are in the best position to report on the most critical health issues affecting women in that country. Therefore, in order to enable the Committee to evaluate whether measures to eliminate discrimination against women in the field of health care are appropriate, States parties must report on their health legislation, plans and policies for women with reliable data disaggregated by sex on the incidence and severity of diseases and conditions hazardous to women's health and nutrition and on the availability and cost-effectiveness of preventive and curative measures. Reports to the Committee must demonstrate that health legislation, plans and policies are based on scientific and ethical research and assessment of the health status and needs of women in that country and take into account any ethnic, regional or community variations or practices based on religion, tradition or culture.[85]

This is not to say that the Committee will allow a State Party unlimited and unreviewable discretion – its role is after all to undertake an assessment of consistency with the Convention and to provide analysis and recommendations to the State Party.

Of course, in any case neither recommendations by the Committee in the form of Concluding Observations nor views and reports under the Optional Protocol procedures are legally binding as a matter of international law, though plainly they are to be given weight. The minimum obligation of the State Party should be to consider seriously the

[85] General Recommendation 24 (1999), para. 9.

recommendations and whether and how they should be implemented, and to articulate their position in response to a recommendation.[86] A response is arguably even more important when a State Party decides not to follow or to explicitly reject a recommendation of the Committee. Sometimes States Parties do this on an ad hoc basis, submitting comments in response to Concluding Observations,[87] and sometimes they take the matter up in a subsequent report. Often, however, if a State Party does not agree with a Committee recommendation, it might not articulate its disagreement, but no action will be taken and the matter will be taken up by the Committee or NGOs in the next reporting cycle or at the domestic level.

The follow-up procedure adopted in 2008 may change this, at least in relation to those priority recommendations in respect of which the Committee asks the State Party to report. For example, in 2009 the Committee recommended, inter alia, to the United Kingdom that, as part of its development of a single Equality Act, it should take the opportunity to incorporate other provisions of the Convention into domestic law. This recommendation was one of those identified by the Committee for priority follow-up, requiring a response from the UK within a specified period. The United Kingdom responded:

> The UK rejects this recommendation on the basis that such an approach would create a separate, parallel regime within the Equality Bill that incorporates all the elements of the Convention that are, to the extent that the UK is obliged to comply with them, already covered by or present in other areas of UK law.[88]

It also provided further information about what was involved in the development of the single Equality Act. The Committee responded to this, stating that it 'would appreciate receiving further information on the incorporation of the provisions of the Convention in the appropriate legislation',[89] though one would have thought that much of that material

[86] Article 7(4) of the Optional Protocol requires States Parties to 'give due consideration to the views of the Committee, together with its recommendations' in individual cases and to respond within twelve months.

[87] See the discussion above relating to the comments made by States Parties in response to Concluding Observations.

[88] *Information Provided by the Government of the United Kingdom of Great Britain and Northern Ireland under the Follow-up Procedure to the Concluding Observations of the Committee*, CEDAW/C/UK/CO/6/Add.1, para. 5 (2009).

[89] Letter of 19 February 2012 from the Rapporteur on Follow-Up to the Ambassador of the United Kingdom, available at: www2.ohchr.org/english/bodies/cedaw/docs/followup/UnitedKingdom.pdf (last accessed 23 January 2013).

was contained in the documents submitted earlier by the United Kingdom under the reporting procedure.

In general, though, there appear to be relatively few instances in which States Parties have rejected a Committee recommendation outright, either because the State Party does not share the Committee's legal analysis or because it disputes the factual basis or policy suitability of the proposal. Constitutional or political difficulties may be alluded to as a reason for not adopting the exact steps recommended by the Committee, for example where constitutional amendments are recommended or the use of temporary special measures where that may cause legal difficulties.

There also appears to have been little resort by States Parties to direct challenges to the Committee's recommendations and decisions by invoking the democratic legitimacy of the government (where it exists) or arguments of nationalism or principles of subsidiarity. The more direct challenges or excuses for inaction have tended to come in the areas of religion, traditions, custom and 'culture', and often involve States Parties invoking the unwillingness of others to act, especially particular religious communities or the community at large, issues that often arise in the discussions about the coverage, validity and acceptability of reservations referring to or based on such beliefs and practices.

So far as the political organisation of individual States Parties is concerned, it does not appear that the Convention itself is premised upon the desirability of a particular political system either as a matter of general principle or because such a system might be more conducive to achieving the goals of the treaty.[90] This could hardly have been otherwise, given the diversity of States involved in the drafting of the treaty, and the prominent role played both by Western liberal democratic States and socialist States (the latter priding themselves particularly on their achievements in the field of women's equality and the visibility of women in many traditionally male-dominated sectors and the social support given to women so far as maternity and childcare went).

Nevertheless, despite the absence of an explicit statement of preference in the Convention for particular forms of political organisation, the

[90] See Sarah Wittkopp, 'Article 7' in *CEDAW Commentary*, 197–231 at 202. One might compare in this context the statement of the Committee on Economic, Social and Cultural Rights that the ICESCR is not premised on a particular political system for the achievement of its goals – a reflection of the Cold War origins of the two Covenants and the view of many that ESC rights were goals that were a particular concern of socialist States and that they were not especially appropriate as 'rights' for inclusion in the agendas of liberal democratic Western States). CESCR, General Comment 3, para. 8 (1990).

Committee has drawn from the Convention the inference that the treaty requires the realisation of the equality of women and men in political and public life (Article 7 of the Convention) within the framework of a democratic society.[91] On this reading, the Convention requires more than just ensuring that women enjoy the same rights and opportunities, *de jure* and de facto, as men in the spheres of political and public life – though that is obviously a step that must be taken.

How does the Committee then deal with the range of different political regimes, in some of which men may be denied political opportunities (sometimes on the basis of equality with women – that is, no one has meaningful political rights)? The Committee has been pragmatic in this respect. It looks for the possibilities of advancing women's human rights within individual systems of government – even those run by hereditary monarchies or autocratic governments (in which ironically the concentration of power can sometimes make the repeal of discriminatory laws and practices a faster and easier process than in more democratic systems). It calls for the available steps toward equality to be taken, all the while arguing for women's full participation in all aspects of political and public decision-making (whether or not men are already engaged there as well).

The question of a democratic mandate to discriminate can also arise where a popularly elected government endorses an approach to political and social organisation that is not based on equality of women and men, whether that philosophy be drawn from religion, tradition, custom or some other source – a situation that often seems to follow on from popular uprisings against autocratic or oppressive governments. In these contexts, while accepting the desirability of democratic government, the Committee nonetheless sees itself as legally and morally justified in asserting that women's equality cannot be subordinated to national laws and practices, even if these are the result of a government elected by a majoritarian or other democratic process. For the CEDAW the norm of equality of women and men is the overriding international norm, one

[91] In General Recommendation 23 (1997), para. 6, the Committee states: '[T]he Convention envisages that, to be effective, this equality [of women and men in political and public life] must be achieved within the framework of a political system in which each citizen enjoys the right to vote and be elected at genuine periodic elections held on the basis of universal suffrage and by secret ballot, in such a way as to guarantee the free expression of the will of the electorate, as provided for under international human rights instruments', referring to Article 21 of the UDHR and Article 25 of the ICCPR (from which some of the language of Article 7 of the Convention is drawn).

that cannot be displaced by other norms, and the international legal obligation of the State is to promote that norm and provide protection against encroachments on it, even in pursuit of decisions that claim to have a democratic mandate.

Nor is the Committee is prepared to accept attempts by States Parties to wash their hands of obligations accepted under the Convention by claims that the responsibility for (in)action lies with other political entities under constitutional systems that allocate power to federal and state authorities or under other devolution arrangements.[92] This reflects both the standard international law position that a State cannot rely on its internal constitutional or political arrangements to justify a failure to carry out its treaty obligations and the provisions of the Convention.

The Committee has also been unwilling to accept that the fact that a State Party has limited power to control, influence or change the attitudes and beliefs of non-State actors exempts it from all responsibility in relation to discrimination practised by those actors, insisting on a high level of due diligence to take all reasonable measures to address that conduct and underlying discriminatory attitudes, as required by Article 2 and Article 5(a) in particular.[93]

In its practice the Committee has been consistent in urging fundamental changes to domestic constitutional and legislative arrangements, holding States Parties accountable for the discrimination that may result from devolved political arrangements (formally within a federal system or more informally),[94] and urging States Parties to ensure that they carry out their obligations in relation to discrimination by non-State actors (obligations made explicit by Articles 2 and 5(a), but also covered by many other provisions of the Convention).

7 The Committee, States Parties and resistance justified by reference to religious, customary or traditional practices

The Committee operates in a world of competing international and national norms that have their origins in international law instruments and customary international law, national legislation, and other systems of law and binding social norms. From the perspective of States Parties, relevant norms include not just international treaties – some of which

[92] See Andrew Byrnes, 'Article 2' at 93.

[93] See generally Rikki Holtmaat, 'Article 5' in *CEDAW Commentary*.

[94] Byrnes, 'Article 2' at 93 n. 178.

may appear to compete with or complement the Convention – but also national norms, including constitutional and legislative rules, and other systems of applicable law recognised or endorsed by the State, such as religious or customary laws.

In much of its work the Committee engages with national, religious cultural laws or other practices that appear inconsistent with the Convention, so as a result there will always be questions of the legitimacy and effectiveness of its views. The Committee appears to see its position and vantage point as normatively unproblematic – the norms of the Convention are its starting point; to the extent that they have been accepted by States Parties, then the Committee is able to further bolster its normative claims by reliance on the clear principles of international law (reflected in the treaty's provisions) that a State is obliged to bring law and practice in its territory into line with its Convention obligations, and that systems of law and practice that conflict with that obligation provide no justification for refusing or failing to do so.

The nature of the CEDAW, which seeks to transform patriarchal structures and society in order to ensure women enjoy full equality in all fields of life,[95] has posed particular challenges in relation to some religious practices and interpretations, as well as traditional and customary practices. These have been particularly acute in the context of law, practices and customs relating to marriage and family relations, but have extended beyond that field. The Committee has taken the view that the obligations contained in the Convention are far-reaching, and were intended to be so, and that States Parties that have accepted the obligations under the Convention cannot interpose custom, religion or tradition to justify a failure to do so. Thus, there is an assertion of a universal value of equality (albeit realisable in specific contexts in different ways).

The tension has frequently been seen in the context of reservations to the Convention, especially the significant number of general reservations or reservations to central Articles of the Convention such as Articles 2 and 16.[96] Many of these have been explained or justified by reference to the asserted incompatibility of certain provisions of the Convention with religious law (most prominently Islam, but others as well), traditions or customary practices or law, or the Constitution or general law of the State. The Committee's objections to some of these general reservations

[95] Holtmaat, 'Article 5', and Frances Raday, 'Culture, Religion and CEDAW's Article 5(a)' in *The Circle of Empowerment*, 68–85.

[96] See Jane Connors, 'Article 28' in *CEDAW Commentary*, 565–95.

have included the concern that they do not specify exactly what the purported inconsistencies are, so that it is difficult to assess the coverage of the Convention and the extent of the obligation assumed by the State in question.

Furthermore, the Committee has expressed the view on a number of occasions that it considers reservations to core provisions of the Convention such as Articles 2 and 16 to be incompatible with the object and purpose of the Convention, and thus impermissible under Article 18 of the Convention (as well as under the general law of treaties). The legal implications of this – and the similar objections and comments made by some States Parties in response to the reservations entered by other States Parties – are unclear. While maintaining its position on incompatibility, the Committee has adopted a fairly pragmatic approach to dealing with States Parties – it would not want States Parties to remove themselves from the treaty regime, and sees the potential for progress in continuing dialogue and pressure in the context of consideration of successive reports.

The Committee has also sought to engage on substance, challenging States to identify the discrepancies, and in the case of Islam pointing to the experience of other Muslim countries that have been able to ratify the Convention with less extensive or no reservations.

It has been suggested that the approach taken to 'culture' in the Convention and in the Committee's practice unduly emphasises a limited, out-of-date and impoverished understanding of 'culture', and that this focus on culture as a primary barrier to the realisation of human rights also neglects other causes of oppression of and denial of rights to women such as economic and political arrangements. Anthropologist Sally Engle Merry has made this argument generally in relation to the international human rights system, as well as with specific reference to the CEDAW context.[97] She writes:

> Culture often appears as a relatively static and homogenous system, bounded, isolated, and stubbornly resistant. The convention and, to some extent, the committee members rely on a vision of culture that imagines it as integrated, consensual, and sustained by habitual compliance with its rules.[98]

[97] Sally Engle Merry, 'Constructing a global law – violence against women and the human rights system', *Law & Social Inquiry* 28:4 (2003) 941–77.

[98] Merry, 'Constructing a global law' at 946; and Sally Engle Merry, 'Gender justice and CEDAW: the Convention on the Elimination of All Forms of Discrimination against Women', *Hawwa* 9 (2011) 49–75 at 55 (largely drawing on arguments and evidence set out in Merry, 'Constructing a global law').

She contrasts this with more recent models of culture developed in anthropology:[99]

> Rather than operating as an isolated and smoothly humming machine, a cultural system is in constant and creative interaction with other societies and with transnational forces. When the drafters of the convention thought about culture, they used the former meaning. Further, they used culture to describe other worlds, not their own.[100]
>
> The convention and the questions of the experts suggest that certain features of cultural belief and institutional arrangements, such as patterns of marriage, divorce, and inheritance, can serve as barriers to women's progress. The committee and other human rights groups identify and seek to change 'harmful traditional practices' rooted in custom and tradition, of which female genital mutilation is the prototype. Many who write about women's rights to protection from violence see culture as a problem rather than as a resource.[101]

She further argues:

> In other words, there is an old vision of culture as fixed, static, bounded, and adhered to by rote juxtaposed to a more modern understanding of culture as a process of continually creating new meanings and practices that are products of power relationships and open to contestation among members of the group and by outsiders. In CEDAW discussions, when culture is raised as a problem, its old meaning is invoked. This is, of course, the way the term is used in the convention itself, which explicitly condemns cultural practices that discriminate against women in Articles 2 and 5 (see below). When culture is discussed as a resource, or when there is recognition that the goal of the CEDAW process is cultural reformulation, the second meaning is implied. Needless to say, the coexistence of these two quite different understandings of culture in the same forum is confusing. I think it obscures the creative cultural work that the CEDAW process accomplishes.[102]

While it is certainly the case that much of the discussion around matters of culture and tradition in the CEDAW context focuses on the negative impact on women's enjoyment of human rights, that is hardly surprising, given that the purpose of the Convention is to respond to violations of women's human rights, and a goal of the reporting procedure is to identify

[99] Merry, 'Gender justice and CEDAW' at 55.

[100] One might reasonably ask whether this adequately reflects the significant participation of women from non-Western countries in the drafting and the importance to them of addressing the issues of culture and its relationship to the equality of women.

[101] Merry, 'Gender justice and CEDAW' at 55 (citations omitted).

[102] *Ibid.* at 56. See also Merry, 'Constructing a global law' at 947 (making the same argument in similar terms).

shortfalls and difficulties with a view to addressing them. While this may mean that there is little discussion of the positive aspects of culture and tradition and their potential as a resource for achieving women's human rights, to conclude that the Convention and the Committee see culture and tradition as something integrated, static and backward, and solely as detrimental to women's equality, seems to go too far. The CEDAW Committee certainly sees the tensions that can exist between particular interpretations of culture and the Convention, and rejects those aspects of cultural practices that mean that women are discriminated against. The adherence to static and stubbornly resistant notions of culture appears to be more characteristic of those opposing the implementation of the CEDAW than of the CEDAW members, who see culture as a dynamic resource.

There is some merit in the claim that there may be a tendency to adopt an approach of 'exoticising' culture – that is, seeing culture as primarily located in non-Western societies and communities. As Rikki Holtmaat writes:

> Article 5 does not address only 'exotic', 'backward', 'traditionalist' or 'oppressive cultures', but all human relations and institutions or structures in which gender stereotypes and fixed parental gender roles are used in a way that is detrimental to the full realisation of women's human rights.[103]

While much of the CEDAW Committee's concern has been with cultural and religious practices in non-Western countries,[104] its increased focus on stereotypes that reflect subordinate and unequal roles for women has been an explicit and consistent focus of the Committee's attention for many years, in relation to countries from all regions and all cultural and religious traditions.

8 Conclusion

The Committee provides an important site for the implementation of the Convention's goals, and are a forum where the efforts of governments, civil society, intergovernmental organisations and an external expert evaluator intersect. It provides a point where national and transnational advocacy

[103] Holtmaat, 'Article 5' at 150.

[104] For example, the Committee's criticism of polygamy as inconsistent with equality: General Recommendation 21 (1994) (equality in marriage and family relations), para. 14; General Recommendation 27 (older women), para. 28.

networks come together with a body that has an institutional legitimacy conferred on it by the States on whose records it opines. This chapter has argued that the Committee has been a vigorous actor in the cause of universal standards of human rights, and has engaged in advocacy for a norm of equality that transcends and prevails over national laws, practices, religions, customs and traditions that are inconsistent with that norm. This is not to say that the Committee (or the Convention) is antagonistic to religion or traditional cultures and customary laws and practices as such – indeed, it sees the centrality of these to women's sense of themselves and their place in the world[105] – but that it is resolute in being critical of those harmful practices that deny women's agency, violate their dignity or their persons, and exclude them from full participation in the life of their communities and societies. In some cases the Committee sees the way to equality for women in a more equal role for them as participants in the generation and transmission of cultural meaning and value by women, recognising that religion, tradition and culture are not unchanging but dynamic, not self-explanatory but interpreted by authoritative gatekeepers.

Although there are significant methodological challenges in isolating the impact of any one factor in bringing about change,[106] overall the reporting procedure under the Convention appears to have contributed in many cases to changes in law and practice at the national level to bring these into conformity with the Convention. Of course, ratification of the Convention and even effective use of the reporting procedure do not always lead to change, and on occasion States Parties may take little or no action in response to Committee recommendations and may not be scheduled to appear again before the Committee for a number of years, and even then may simply engage in passive resistance rather than active resistance to renewed Committee recommendations.

But there are many encouraging accounts of the contribution of the Convention and the Committee's work. In a review of the impact of the Convention and the reporting procedure, Shanthi Dairiam, a human rights advocate and former CEDAW Committee member, cites cases in which the interaction of the Committee's review of a State Party report and the national NGOs' use of the Concluding Comments has contributed to reform – for example, the 1992 reform of more than twenty discriminatory provisions in the Country Code (*Muluki Ain*) of Nepal,

[105] Holtmaat, 'Article 5' at 150.

[106] See generally Beth A. Simmons, *Mobilizing for Human Rights: International Law in Domestic Politics* (Cambridge University Press, 2009).

changes to provisions of the Hindu Succession Act in India relating to inheritance, amendments to the Personal Status Code of Morocco in 2004 and amendments to laws in Kyrgyzstan on land rights in 2004.[107] Savitri Goonesekere, emeritus professor of law and former CEDAW Committee member, refers to the impact of the Committee's Concluding Comments on promoting the removal of discriminatory provisions in nationality laws in Fiji, Jamaica, Liechtenstein, Thailand, Burundi, India and Sri Lanka, as well as influencing reforms to family law in Fiji and the Maldives.[108] She concludes that 'the Committee's Concluding Comments on the need for a holistic review of family law, and its critique of discrimination, have clearly provided an impetus for many countries to repeal received colonial laws, transform customary laws, and initiate a process of local law reform based on commitments to CEDAW'.[109] There are many other cases in which civil society and other domestic actors such as National Human Rights Institutions have engaged with the reporting procedure and taken up CEDAW Concluding Observations or General Recommendations to support their own domestic advocacy, frequently bringing about change.[110] The Committee's jurisprudence under the Optional Protocol has begun to provide an additional resource in individual cases, but also more generally for advocates who wish to draw on the Convention in their domestic advocacy.

[107] Dairiam, 'From global to local' at 320–3.

[108] Savitri Goonesekere, 'Universalizing women's human rights through CEDAW' in *The Circle of Empowerment* at 52, 58.

[109] *Ibid.* at 60.

[110] See Ilana Landsberg-Lewis (ed.), *Bringing Equality Home: Implementing the Convention on the Elimination of All Forms of Discrimination against Women* (New York: UNIFEM, 1998) and Marilou McPhedran *et al.* (eds.), *The First CEDAW Impact Study: Final Report* (2000). For further instances, see the examples from twelve different countries and a review of the literature assessing impact in Andrew Byrnes and Marsha Freeman, *The Impact of the CEDAW Convention: Paths to Equality*, background paper prepared for the World Development Report 2012 (2011), available at: http://law.bepress.com/unswwps/flrps12/art7/ and http://papers.ssrn.com/sol3/papers.cfm?abstract_id=2011655 (last accessed 23 January 2013).

2

The United Nations Working Group on the Issue of Discrimination against Women in Law and Practice

FAREDA BANDA

1 Introduction

In 1995, at the Fourth World Conference on Women in Beijing, governments undertook to 'revoke any remaining laws that discriminate on the basis of sex'.[1] This chapter looks at how the failure by states to meet that challenge led to the decision by the Human Rights Council in 2010 to appoint a United Nations Working Group on Laws that Discriminate against Women (hereafter WG). It retraces the steps that led to the appointment of the group, including the important input of non-governmental organizations (NGOs) whose persistence drove the process along.[2] I also consider my own involvement as a consultant hired by the Women and Gender Unit of the Office for the High Commissioner for Human Rights (OHCHR) to conduct a study on the desirability or otherwise of having a special mechanism within the Special Procedures Framework[3] to address

My thanks to Anne Hellum for her helpful insights. Thanks are also due to the anonymous reviewer(s).

[1] *Beijing Declaration and Platform for Action* 1995, A/CONF.177/20/Rev.1 [hereinafter the *Beijing Declaration*].

[2] Equality Now was the organization that initiated discussions on the failure of states to meet the Beijing goals and that, working in coalition with other NGOs, acted as the lead advocate for the Special Rapporteur project. Equality Now, 'NGO coalition in support of the creation of a Special Rapporteur on Laws that Discriminate against Women', available at: www.equalitynow.org/sites/default/files/annualreport_2005.pdf (last accessed 14 February 2013); J. Neuwirth, 'Inequality before the law: holding states accountable for sex discriminatory laws under the Convention on the Elimination of All Forms of Discrimination against Women through the Beijing Platform for Action', *Harvard Human Rights Journal* 18 (2005) 19–54, at 20.

[3] Special Procedure mechanisms that fall under the auspices of the High Commission for Human Rights generally fall into two categories – country situation or thematic studies.

discriminatory laws.[4] The chapter then considers the mandate of the WG and identifies challenges and opportunities for the work of the group.

The chapter observes the interaction between international NGO's, different UN bodies such as the Human Rights Council, the Commission on the Status of Women (CSW), the Committee on the Elimination of All Forms of Discrimination against Women (CEDAW Committee) and different states. In doing so, the chapter provides a window into the multiple negotiations and power struggles that take place within the UN system: power struggles between (1) NGO's setting out to strengthen women's protection against discrimination and UN bodies; (2) power struggles within and between different UN bodies competing for scarce resources; and (3) power relations between States Parties and UN bodies in the context of a political climate with intensifying conflicts.

2 History

The Beijing pledge to eliminate discriminatory laws seemed simple and straightforward, requiring states to:

> Review national laws, including customary laws and legal practices in the areas of family, civil, penal, labour and commercial law in order to ensure the implementation of the principles and procedures of all relevant international human rights instruments by means of national legislation, and revoke any remaining laws that discriminate on the basis of sex and remove gender bias in the administration of justice.[5]

The principle of non-discrimination, including on grounds of sex, is at the heart of human rights law and embedded in international customary

It is the latter that was envisaged and discussed in this chapter. Thematic mandates have four functions: the preparation of reports on issues pertaining to their area of expertise, visiting states to investigate issues arising, receiving individual complaints from victims of human rights violations within their area, and finally offering support to the Office of the United Nations High Commissioner for Human Rights (OHCHR) in promoting and protecting human rights. ECOSOC, Commission on the Status of Women: *Advisability of the Appointment of a Special Rapporteur on Laws that Discriminate against Women*, 13 December 2005, UN Doc. E/CN.6/2006/8, paras. 23 and 24 [hereinafter *CSW Advisability Report* 2005].

[4] F. Banda, *Mechanism for Addressing Laws that Discriminate against Women* (Geneva: United Nations OHCHR publication, 6 March 2008) [hereinafter the *Banda Report*], available at: www.ohchr.org/Documents/Publications/laws_that_discriminate_against_women.pdf (last accessed 24 January 2013).

[5] *Beijing Declaration*, para. 232(d).

law.[6] Despite this, by the time of the 2000 Beijing +5 General Assembly Special Review of the conference, little progress had been made. In the year preceding the review, Equality Now, a US-based NGO, had issued a report that highlighted discrimination in forty-five countries. By the time of the +5 Review in 2000, only three of the states had moved to change their laws.[7]

At the Beijing +5 Review, states acknowledged the persistence of discrimination, including in law. They agreed that discriminatory laws created a barrier to the realization of the *Platform for Action*, hence the call to:

> Create and maintain a non-discriminatory and gender-sensitive legal environment by reviewing legislation with a view to striving to remove discriminatory provisions as soon as possible, preferably by 2005, and eliminating legislative gaps that leave women and girls without protection of their rights and without effective recourse against gender-based discrimination.[8]

[6] UN General Assembly, *Universal Declaration of Human Rights*, 10 December 1948, 217 A (III), available at: www.unhcr.org/refworld/docid/3ae6b3712c.html (last accessed 23 June 2012), Articles 2, 7.

The International Covenant on Civil and Political Rights, 1966 (ICCPR), 999 UNTS 171, entered into force 23 March 1976, Articles 2, 3 and 26; The International Covenant on Economic, Social and Cultural Rights, 1966 (ICESCR), 993 UNTS 3, entered into force 3 January 1976, Articles 2 and 3; Convention on the Rights of the Child, 1577 UNTS 3, entered into force 2 September 1990, Article 2; International Convention on the Protection of all Migrant Workers and Members of their Families, 2220 UNTS 3, entered into force 1 July 2003, Article 7. Convention on the Rights of Persons with Disabilities, 2515 UNTS 3, entered into force 3 May 2008, preamble paras. a, h and p, and Articles 2, 3(b) and (g), 5 and 6. See also CEDAW General Recommendation No. 25, UN Doc., E/CN.6/2004/CRP.3, Annex 1. Available at: www.un.org/womenwatch/daw/cedaw/recommendations/General%20recommendation%2025%20%28English%29.pdf (last accessed 23 June 2012).

CCPR General Comment 18, 10 November 1989, UN Doc. HRI/GEN/1/Rev.6 at 146 (2003); CCPR General Comment 28, 29 March 2000, UN Doc. CCPR/C/21/Rev.1/Add.10.

CESCR, General Comment No. 16, 11 August 2005, UN Doc. E/C.12/2005/4, para. 16; CESCR General Comment No. 20 on Non-discrimination, 2 July 2009, UN Doc. E/C.12/GC/20; see also Legal Status and Rights of Undocumented Workers, Inter-American Court of Human Rights, Advisory Opinion, OC-18/03, 17 September 2003, Inter-Am. Ct HR, (Ser. A) No. 18, 2003, paras. 82–110.

[7] Equality Now, 'Words and deeds: holding governments accountable in the Beijing +5 Review process', Women's Action 16:4, 1 July 2000.

[8] UNGA, *Further Actions and Initiatives to Implement the Beijing Declaration and Platform for Action*, 16 November 2000, UN Doc. Assembly Res. S-23/3, para. 68(b). See also para. 68(f). Available at: www.un.org/womenwatch/daw/followup/ress233e.pdf (last accessed 24 January 2013).

States were also encouraged to ratify the Convention on the Elimination of All Forms of Discrimination against Women (CEDAW) and to limit reservations that undermined the Convention's object and purpose.[9] The Beijing +5 Outcome document also highlighted the importance of introducing legislation to tackle violence against women including marital rape and laws to eradicate harmful practices including female genital mutilation.[10]

Following the 2000 Review, civil society and academics kept up the pressure, highlighting the continued discrimination against women and urging action.[11] Equality Now filed three communications under the little-used complaints mechanism of the Commission on the Status of Women (CSW). The first communication, in 2004, identified a selection of forty states chosen for 'geographical and subject matter diversity' to highlight the problem. Only three of the forty states amended their laws. In 2005 Equality Now filed another communication identifying thirty-six remaining recalcitrant states.[12] The final communication made by Equality Now singled out Saudi Arabia for multiple breaches including a recently enacted law that allowed men to vote in municipal elections but not women.[13] While the CSW found that the communications had indeed 'revealed a consistent pattern of reliably attested injustice and discriminatory practices against women', it did not make any recommendations for action.[14] Noting that only fourteen of the forty states originally identified had responded to the communication, Equality Now urged the Commission to continue to pursue states, reminding them of their international law obligations to guarantee equality.[15] While acknowledging the

[9] *Ibid.* at para. 68.

[10] *Ibid.* at para. 69.

[11] C. Meillon and C. Bunch (eds.), *Holding on to the Promise: Women's Human Rights and the Beijing +5 Review* (New Jersey: Centre for Women's Global Leadership, 2001); Equality Now, 'Words and deeds: holding governments accountable in the Beijing +10 Review process', Women's Action 16.5, Update March 2004; Equality Now, 'Words and deeds: holding governments accountable in the Beijing +10 Review process', Women's Action 16.9, Update February 2007; Equality Now, 'Words and deeds: holding governments accountable in the Beijing +15 Review process', Update: Women's Action 16.10, February 2010; Equality Now, 'Words and deeds: holding governments accountable in the Beijing +15 Review process', Women's Action 16.11, 24 August 2010.

[12] Letter from Equality Now (C. Mackinnon and J. Neuwirth) to the Commission on the Status of Women (CSW) on A Communication on the Status of Women, 19 August 2004.

[13] Letter from Equality Now (J. Neuwirth) to the CSW on Denial of Women's Suffrage in Saudi Arabia, 31 August 2005 (on file with the author).

[14] *Ibid.* at 2.

[15] *Ibid.* at 3. See also *CSW Advisability Report* 2005, para. 36.

limited scope of the CSW's mandate, whose primary aim is 'to identify global trends and patterns concerning women's rights, but not to afford direct redress to victims of human rights violations',[16] Equality Now criticised the CSW for not taking a more robust approach to the communications that had pinpointed the existence of a plethora of laws that discriminated against women. Specifically, the CSW was challenged on its failure to make concrete proposals for remedying the problem.[17] Equality Now pressed for the appointment of a Special Rapporteur who would report annually to the CSW and whose role would include ongoing dialogue with governments as well as highlighting and sharing examples of good practice. Equality Now argued: 'A special rapporteur could address these issues on a thematic basis, cross-cutting national boundaries in a way that CEDAW is not able to do.'[18] The NGO pressure for the creation of a Special Rapporteur continued to build with more than 300 of the participants from 42 countries in the Economic Commission for Europe, which took part in the European Beijing +10 NGO Forum preparatory to the main government meeting, agreeing by consensus, to the creation of a Special Rapporteur on national laws and practices that discriminate against women.[19]

In the interim, in 2004 the CEDAW Committee marked the 25th anniversary of the adoption of the Convention by issuing a statement in which it noted the failure to achieve universal ratification of the Convention as recommended by the Beijing +5 Review. The Committee further noted that while there had been progress in the realisation of women's human rights, still:

> It must, however, also be pointed out that in no country in the world has women's full *de jure* and de facto equality been achieved. Discriminatory laws are still on the statute books of many States parties. The co-existence of multiple legal systems, with customary and religious laws governing personal status and private life and prevailing over positive law and even constitutional provisions of equality, remains a source of great concern.[20]

16 OHCHR, 'Human Rights Treaty Bodies – Petitions', available at: www2.ohchr.org/english/bodies/petitions/CSW.htm#women (last accessed 13 February 2012).

17 Equality Now, 'Annual Report 2005: Take a stand, make a difference' at 7.

18 *Ibid.* at 4.

19 Equality Now, 'Campaign for a Special Rapporteur on Laws that Discriminate against Women (Beijing +10)', 2004 at 4.

20 UN Statement to commemorate the twenty-fifth anniversary of the adoption of the Convention on the Elimination of All Forms of Discrimination against Women, 13 October 2004, available at: www.un.org/womenwatch/daw/cedaw/anniversary25.htm (last accessed 9 June 2012).

The statement also addressed the negative impact of gender stereotyping on women, and their limited access to power and decision-making as well as resources. The Committee addressed the lack of political will to bring about gender equality as a key problem.[21]

The following year (2005), to mark Beijing +10, the CEDAW Committee issued a statement in which it acknowledged the 'synergies' between the Beijing *Platform for Action* and the CEDAW and noted that the two complemented each other with the Platform drawing attention to women's rights and the Convention acting as the 'primary instrument for the promotion of equality between women and men and the elimination of all forms of discrimination against women'.[22]

At its 49th session in 2005, the CSW, the body tasked with keeping conference pledges under review (in this case Beijing +10), identified the continuation of both *de jure* and de facto discrimination and, shockingly, that rather than eliminating discriminatory laws, some states had actually introduced them. In a resolution the CSW asked the OHCHR to advise on the implications of appointing a Special Rapporteur on laws that discriminate against women, paying attention to avoiding duplication with existing mandates.[23] At the invitation of the CSW, the OHCHR consulted the CEDAW Committee about its views on the need for a new mechanism.[24] Not surprisingly the CEDAW Committee did not 'see the necessity' for establishing the mandate because its remit was to tackle discrimination against women in both law and practice. However, the Committee did go on to make proposals for the form that any mandate should take in the event that the Commission decided to proceed.[25] These included a

[21] *Ibid.*

[22] UN Report of the Committee on the Elimination of Discrimination against Women, 32nd Session, *Statement of the Committee on the Elimination of Discrimination against Women on the Occasion of the 10 Year Review and Appraisal of the Beijing Declaration and Platform for Action* (General Assembly Official Records, 60th session, Supplement No. 38 (A/60/38).

[23] Commission on the Status of Women, *Final Report of the 49th Session of the CSW, Resolution 49/3 on the Advisability of the Appointment of a Special Rapporteur on Laws that Discriminate against Women*, E/CN.6/2005/11. See also Equality Now, 'Statement in support of a Special Rapporteur on Laws that Discriminate against Women', August 2005.

[24] It is interesting to note that the while supportive of CSW Resolution 49, the United States objected to the suggestion that the CEDAW Committee be consulted about the creation of a Special Rapporteur, noting that it was inappropriate as: 'that is beyond the mandate of that Committee'. *US Statement: Special Rapporteur on Laws that Discriminate against Women*, 49th Session, UN CSW, available at: http://2001–2009.state.gov/p/io/uncnf/43762.htm (last accessed June 2012).

[25] *CSW Advisability Report* 2005, para. 40.

focus on: a requirement to address various types of discriminatory laws; customary and other forms of law (common and codified law); and *de jure* and de facto discrimination against women. The mandate should clearly spell out the scope of the discriminatory legislation to be covered and should also include indirect discrimination. Lastly, the Commission should consider the ways in which a mandate holder could have a significant political impact at the national level.

Two reports were prepared by the Secretary General in 2005 and 2006.[26] I will focus on the first, which provided an overview of the work of various treaty bodies and Special Procedures. It identified the CEDAW Committee as the body that: 'takes the most consistent and systematic approach to reviewing the persistence and impact of sex-discriminatory laws'.[27] The report found that most of the Special Procedure mandates did not focus on sex.[28] However, the report did note that most of the new mandates now required the mandate holder to apply a gender perspective.[29] The 2005 report considered the advisability of appointing a Special Rapporteur and suggested that such a mechanism would be an important tool in the implementation of Beijing, and also that it could complement the work of existing human rights bodies and Special Procedure mechanisms provided that there was not duplication. Such a mechanism would accelerate the realization of equality by providing the necessary momentum.[30]

The CSW took note of the report containing the OHCHR's and other views and asked for further 'views on ways and means that could best complement the work of the existing mechanisms and enhance the Commission's capacity with respect to discriminatory laws' for consideration at its 51st (2007) session.

In any event, the decision on whether or not to appoint a Special Rapporteur was postponed, yet again, in part due to the review of the Special Procedure mandates at the OHCHR[31] (also under consideration

[26] *CSW Advisability Report* 2005. See also ECOSOC, Commission on the Status of Women, (on the *Advisability of the Appointment of a Special Rapporteur on Laws that Discriminate against Women*, 13 December 2006, E/CN.6/2007/8) [hereinafter *CSW Advisability Report* 2006]. The 2006 report complemented the previous report (*CSW Advisability Report* 2005 E/CN.6/2006/8), and 'should therefore be read in conjunction with it'.

[27] *CSW Advisability Report* 2005, para. 16.

[28] *Ibid.* at para. 25. [29] *Ibid.* at para. 27. [30] *Ibid.* at para. 50.

[31] *CSW Advisability Report* 2007, E/CN.6/2007/8, para. 31, available at: http://daccess-dds-ny.un.org/doc/UNDOC/GEN/N06/661/63/PDF/N0666163.pdf?OpenElement (last

was the consolidation of the UN mechanisms working on 'women-related' issues).[32] This review of the gender architecture ultimately led to the creation of the UN Entity for Gender Equality and the Empowerment of Women (UN Women) in 2010.[33] The OHCHR suggested that a decision on the usefulness and viability of a Special Rapporteur be deferred to the CSW 52nd session (2008) in order to incorporate and build on the review's outcome. For its part, the OHCHR offered to prepare a report on the compatibility of the proposed mandate with the existing mechanisms. I was hired as the consultant to undertake this review and to prepare a report.

3 *The Banda Report on Laws that Discriminate against Women*

Commissioned in January 2007, the terms of reference of *The Banda Report on Laws that Discriminate against Women*[34] required the consultant to review UN human rights mechanisms[35] and the work of UN agencies working on women's rights. The aim was to ascertain to what extent the issue of laws that discriminate against women was being considered and whether a new mechanism was indeed necessary. The terms of reference also required the consultant to try to identify whether laws that discriminate against women continued to exist and the areas in which such laws were to be found. In light of the information gathered, the consultant was required to answer the question of whether a new special procedure mechanism was needed.

Meeting the objectives of the project necessitated the use of three data collection techniques. To address the issue of the work currently being undertaken within the UN required collecting and analyzing treaty body general comments, state reports, Concluding Observations and, where relevant, communications. Time constraints limited the consideration

accessed 14 February 2013). Equality Now 'Words and deeds: holding governments accountable in the Beijing +10 Review process' Women's Action 16.9, February 2007.

32 These were the Division for the Advancement of Women (DAW), International Research and Training Institute for the Advancement of Women (INSTRAW), Office of the Special Adviser on Gender Issues and Advancement of Women (OSAGI), United Nations Development Fund for Women (UNIFEM).

33 UNGA, *System-wide Coherence*, 21 July 2010, UN Doc. Assembly Res 64/289.

34 This is the name by which the report became known within the UN. CSW, 56th Session, Oral Statement by Kamala Chandrikirana, Chairperson of the Working Group on Discrimination against Women in Law and in Practice, New York, 5 March 2012. Available at: www.un.org/womenwatch/daw/csw/csw56/statements/Ch-P-working-group.pdf (last accessed 24 January 2013).

35 The terms of reference can be found in Appendix A in the *Banda Report* at 140–2.

of state reports to the preceding five years. It also required examining the mandates of Special Rapporteurs. Reports of the Special Rapporteurs were further analyzed for their gender content.[36] UN documents on mainstreaming were also analyzed. Moreover, initiatives undertaken by UN agencies in the field of women's rights (including the girl child) were considered, and interviews held with UN officials in UNICEF (United Nations International Children's Emergency Fund), UNIFEM (United Nations Development Fund for Women), UNFPA (United Nations Fund for Population Activities), OSAGI (Office of the Special Adviser on Gender Issues and Advancement of Women) and IOM (International Organization for Migration) and DAW. A second data-collecting mechanism involved conducting interviews with UN officials and NGOs. This was to try to get the views of those charged with administering the system – did they consider a new mechanism necessary? What did their work involve? The NGOs provided the civil society perspective. I gave guarantees of anonymity to all UN personnel interviewed. I conducted interviews with UN human rights personnel at both the OHCHR in Geneva and also the human rights section and other agencies mentioned above at the UN headquarters in New York.

Finally, given that the focus of the project was on laws that discriminate against women, it was necessary to try to ascertain the extent to which such laws were still in existence. While the campaigning NGO Equality Now had already done excellent work producing a sample list of states with discriminatory laws and reproducing the offending provisions, it was still important to design and send out a questionnaire to ascertain the current position.[37] The questionnaire was divided into seven parts (A–G) as follows:

> Part (A) The Constitution and National Laws – provisions on equality and information on laws that discriminate against women.
>
> Part (B) Responses to Discriminatory Laws – by governments, courts and civil society.
>
> Part (C) Omissions and the Use of Temporary Special Measures
>
> Part (D) The International and Regional Human Rights Systems – ratifications by state, participation by NGOs by way of shadow reports and dissemination of concluding observations of human rights committees nationally.

[36] *Banda Report* at 52.

[37] Equality Now (2004), 'Words and deeds: holding governments accountable in the Beijing +10 Review process', Women's Action 16.6, Update March 2004.

Part (E) Special Procedures – testing awareness of special procedure mechanisms. Had there been any engagement with special procedure mandate holders, and if there had been, the form of that engagement and the outcome.

Part (F) Advisability of Special Mechanism on Laws that Discriminate against Women – respondent's views on whether one was needed and reasons for this.

Part (G) Anything else – inviting respondents to comment on issues of interest, including regional perspectives on the issue of laws that discriminate against women and also the challenges of operating within plural legal systems.[38]

While *de jure* discrimination was the focus, the questionnaire made clear that information on de facto discrimination would also be welcome. In many states the law is complex, comprising plural normative systems including statute law, common law, customary laws and religious laws. These coexist, sometimes harmoniously, but often not. Indeed the adoption of the definition of discrimination found in Article 1 of the CEDAW, which encompasses *de jure* as well as de facto discrimination, made this a *sine qua non*.[39] Moreover, evidence from state reports and general comments all pointed to the fact that de facto discrimination was a key factor in women's lack of enjoyment of their rights.[40] The preamble to the questionnaire that went out said:

> The project covers State sanctioned laws and regulations 'in all areas affecting women's civil, cultural, economic, political and social rights'. By State sanctioned is meant those laws that receive official recognition within the formal legal system.

[38] The full questionnaire and covering letter can be found in Appendix C of the *Banda Report* at 147.

[39] A. Byrnes, 'Article 1', in M. Freeman, C. Chinkin and B. Rudolph (eds.), *The UN Convention on the Elimination of All Forms of Discrimination against Women: A Commentary* (Oxford University Press, 2012) 51–70 [hereinafter M. Freeman *et al.*, *CEDAW*]. See also CEDAW General Recommendation 28 on the core obligations of States Parties under Article 2 of the Convention on the Elimination of All Forms of Discrimination against Women, UN Doc. CEDAW/AC/GC/28, 2010.

[40] See also CEDAW General Recommendation 21 on Marriage and Family Relations, UN Doc. HRI/GEN/1/Rev.9 (Vol. II), paras. 3, 12, 15, 24, 28, 33, 45, 46; CEDAW General Recommendation 23 on Women in Public Life, UN Doc. a/52/38/Rev. 1, paras. 9, 10; CEDAW Committee, Concluding Observations: Peru, 10 July 1998, UN Doc. CEDAW/C/PER/3–4, paras. 313 and 317; CEDAW Committee, Concluding Observations: Mauritania, 11 June 2007, UN Doc. CEDAW/C/MRT/CO/1, paras. 15, 21 and 22; CEDAW Committee, Concluding Observations: Russian Federation, 30 July 2010, UN Doc. CEDAW/C/USR/CO/7, para. 20.

The questionnaire was sent to a wide variety of people in governments, UN agencies, academics and NGOs.[41] In the introduction to the questionnaire, I encouraged the recipient to share the questionnaire. This snowballing technique is much used in social survey research. As with all questionnaire surveys including those administered, as in this case, by email, the response rate was at first slow. I had to follow up several times. The responses were variable. Some were comprehensive, sending in over twenty-five pages of cases, laws and views, while others only answered part of the questionnaire – largely to do with their views about whether there should be a mechanism.

I asked the OHCHR to have the questionnaire, which was in English, translated into at least three of the official UN languages (Arabic, French and Spanish), but only received the French version and this after two months of waiting. I think language was a barrier to some, particularly in the South and Central American region. One enterprising group in Francophone West Africa arranged for their own translation and were able to submit a response in a mixture of French and English (Franglais).

While chasing up questionnaires, I began going through all the documents that I had been given in Geneva and New York and of course all the treaty body material. From these, I learnt that a great deal had been done within the UN on women's rights. Initiatives included the institution-wide mainstreaming initiative, which required all institutions to take account of the need to integrate a gender perspective into their work.[42] In Special Procedures, this saw more mandates being created with a specific gender focus. Most impressive in their focus on women's rights were Special Rapporteurs on indigenous people, minorities, health and superlatively the Special Rapporteur on Housing, who had written a series of reports that had included consultation with the CEDAW Committee about the possibility of a General Recommendation on women and the right to housing.[43] However, the statistics on the number of communications sent to Special Procedures were, when disaggregated by sex, unedifying. Specifically, in 2005 only 13 per cent were sent by women. Men accounted for 76 per cent, with 7 per cent not having the sex of the applicant recorded. The paper

[41] A list of respondents to whom the questionnaire was sent or from whom responses were received is listed in Appendix D of the *Banda Report* at 152.

[42] *Report of the Secretary General on the Question of Integrating the Human Rights of Women Throughout the United Nations System*, 25 March 1998, E/CN.4.1998/49. UN, *Integrating a Gender Perspective into the Work of the United Nations Treaty Bodies*, 3 September 1998 HRI/MC/1998/6. See generally the *Banda Report* at 41–53.

[43] See also Ikdahl in this volume.

trail also showed that treaty bodies were more directed in their questioning of States Parties on issues pertaining to the enjoyment or otherwise by women of their rights. There was greater cross-pollination between Committees, which often referred to Concluding Observations made by their peers on other Committees in dialogue with states. Moreover, the General Comments of treaty bodies showed greater attention being paid to the ways in which women experienced discrimination.[44] Again, not surprisingly, the CEDAW Committee emerged as the committee that was most focused in the attention it paid to women's lives and rights.

I started interviews in Geneva, where I spoke to the research and support personnel for a number of Special Rapporteurs,[45] people in both the regional human rights offices as well as those working directly with the main treaty bodies and finally with the Secretariat in the Special Procedures sections. I got the impression from the Geneva leg that many staff were reticent about the creation of a new mechanism, using words like 'duplication' and 'wasteful' while also citing (human) resource shortage, which they linked to their own exhaustion. Some seemed jaded by the whole process, with one asking:

> If there are 41 Special Rapporteurs, do we need another? It is not about numbers but about whether the need is there. It may be political – will the Council approve it? Let's look at what we have in all parts of the house, especially when CEDAW comes here (to Geneva), see what our strengths are and what we can do together. We need to know what we have.[46]

This reticence, I must hasten to add, was not universal – some did speak out in favour of a new mechanism, with one observing that one person's duplication was another's focus, and another noting:

> Why do we have a Special Rapporteur on Torture and also a Torture Committee? Maybe it is seen as immediate and also that it matters. I guess they just don't rate women very highly or maybe they are afraid of the reaction in the (Human Rights) Council.[47]

It is also worth noting that the idea of a having a Working Group rather than just one Special Rapporteur came from a UN official in Geneva. The

[44] *Banda Report* at 41–55.

[45] They assist the Special Rapporteur who are part-time appointees having full-time jobs elsewhere.

[46] *Banda Report* at 118.

[47] Cited in the *Banda Report* at 123. See also N. Rodley, 'United Nations human rights treaty bodies and special procedures of the Commission on Human Rights – complementarity or competition?', *Human Rights Quarterly* 25:4 (2003) 882–908.

NGOs that I met with in New York including the Centre for Reproductive Rights, Human Rights Watch Women's Division and Equality Now, were unilaterally positive and supportive of the idea and in the case of Equality Now, not surprisingly so.

4 Questionnaire responses

An analysis of the questionnaire responses focusing on the laws identified as discriminating against women showed that even (the majority of) those states that had constitutions guaranteeing equality before the law had laws that discriminate against women. Personal status laws were identified as the most problematic. Discriminatory provisions were found in laws enshrining a lower age of marriage for girls than boys and, in some cases, sanctioning child marriage, paternal power vis-à-vis decisions concerning the child that was often linked to marital power over the wife, discrimination in nationality and citizenship laws, different grounds for divorce, and discriminatory property division on death and divorce. Even procedural laws were sometimes found to be discriminatory, privileging male witnesses over female ones. Discriminatory practices and provisions were also identified in employment law and criminal law. The discriminatory laws echoed the state reservations to the CEDAW.[48] Disturbingly the directly legally discriminatory laws came primarily, though not exclusively, from southern states (northern states had discriminatory laws on succession to monarchies).[49]

4.1 To have a mechanism or not

Those who were opposed or sceptical about the need for the creation of a new mechanism argued the following in outline:

(i) that the creation of a new mechanism would result in duplication and it would take away from the work of the CEDAW Committee;
(ii) other committees would stop focusing on women's rights issues;
(iii) that there was already a Special Rapporteur dealing with violence against women; and
(iv) that a focus on *de jure* discrimination was not helpful.

[48] See also J. Connors, 'Article 28', in M. Freeman *et al.*, *CEDAW*, 565–95.
[49] *Banda Report* at 56–115.

These arguments were considered in turn.[50] Of these four, the first on duplication was the most often repeated. The duplication was said to be with the CEDAW Committee and the rest of the human rights treaty bodies and with the Special Rapporteurs on Violence against Women and Trafficking.[51]

Those in favour of the creation of a separate mechanism argued that the CEDAW Committee and a new Special Rapporteur on laws that discriminate against women should be seen as complementary mechanisms. They identified shortcomings in the treaty-based system, highlighting the problems of missing and incomplete reports. Indeed the CEDAW Committee itself identified thirteen states that had not reported for more than ten years; thus there could be no dialogue or engagement with them.[52] Further, proponents of a new special mechanism noted that human rights committees had limited resources for follow-up, which led to Concluding Observations being ignored and thus no state accountability. While some committees had complaints mechanisms, these had not been ratified by all the states that were parties to the main convention or treaty, thus highlighting their limitations. Moreover, the low usage by women of the complaints mechanisms of both Special Procedure and treaty bodies did not bode well for systematically tackling discriminatory laws. It was argued that a new Special Rapporteur could assist the CEDAW Committee by following up on its (and indeed other committees') Concluding Observations vis-à-vis laws that discriminate against women. Indeed, it was noted that the CEDAW Committee could issue instructions to the Special Rapporteur about states that needed following up and that the two would have a symbiotic, cooperative relationship.

The Special Rapporteur could maintain an ongoing dialogue with States Parties and undertake thematic surveys as well as sharing data on good practice. It was also noted that there were examples of other treaty bodies having 'duplicated' Special Procedure mechanisms, and that these

[50] The arguments echoed those articulated by states and other consultees in *CSW Advisability Report* 2006, paras. 10–29.

[51] I personally found this argument frustrating, suggesting as it does that violence against women is the only violation that women face. There was also a hint of 'we have "given them" two mechanisms already (plus CEDAW), what more do they want?' See also R. Kapur, 'The tragedy of victimisation rhetoric: resurrecting the "native" subject in international post-colonial feminist legal politics', *Harvard Journal of Human Rights* 15 (2002) 19–54.

[52] CEDAW, 'Ways and means of expediting the work of the Committee on the Elimination of All Forms of Discrimination against Women: Note by the Secretariat', CEDAW/C/2007/1/4, Annex III.

operated without undue overlap. NGOs working on women's rights were particularly keen on the appointment of a new Special Rapporteur, seeing him or her as enhancing their lobbying and educational work within their home jurisdictions.[53] Additionally, a Special Rapporteur was said to be important in strengthening mainstreaming across all the entities of the United Nations.

Acknowledging the work of the human rights treaty mechanisms on women's rights issues, but still arguing for a new mechanism, was law professor Catherine Mackinnon:

> Discriminatory laws pervasively continue to exist, present mechanisms having barely begun to scratch their surface, far less to solve the problems they pose. A special mechanism would build upon and support the work of CEDAW and others in this area, including by generating the on-going continuous (rather than periodic) dialogue with countries that no current mechanism can. It would also heighten the visibility of discriminatory laws internationally, including by reporting directly to the Human Rights Council, highlighting the issue as a priority in the human rights field. Further, while some features of discrimination against women by law are simple and blatant, others interface in more subtle and complex ways with women's inequality as a whole. All the dimensions of *de jure* discrimination are more likely to emerge when investigated together in mutual comparative light. Current international mechanisms by design can only address these issues one country at a time. A complementary mechanism like a Special Rapporteur would offer the unique resources and mandate to approach the problem systematically on the global scale on which it exists. From the cumulative interconnections, patterns, and themes that can only be discerned in an overarching cross-cutting transnational inquiry, fresh and effective approaches to legal equality for women could emerge.[54]

On balance, the consensus came down in favour of the appointment of a special mechanism that should expand beyond *de jure* to also look at discrimination in practice. Furthermore, it was suggested that consideration be given to issues pertaining to implementation, access to justice and enforcement. Also included in a proposed mandate was the identification of examples of good practice. Cooperation with regional mandates, especially the Inter-American and African Special Rapporteurs on women's

[53] Supporters included the Malaysian-based Sisters in Islam, Zambian-based WILDAF (Women in Law and Development in Africa), Jerusalem-based Women's Centre for Legal Aid and Counselling, Nepal-based Foundation for Women, Law and Development, and a Tanzanian-based organization. See the *Banda Report* at 127–31.

[54] Professor Catherine Mackinnon as cited in the *Banda Report* at 124–5.

rights, was mooted. Clearly a mapping exercise of existing laws would need to be done, both by looking at Concluding Observations of all the human rights treaty bodies as well as by means of independent research.

Published in March 2008, the report received a great deal of support from the then High Commissioner for Human Rights, Louise Arbour. The High Commissioner used the report as the basis for her 2008 Women's Day statement in which she asked for states to review and repeal any discriminatory laws.[55] The report also formed the basis of the annual Inter-Parliamentary Union conference held later that year.[56] Parliamentarians from around the globe discussed and brought examples of progressive laws passed, while also acknowledging legislative gaps that remained.

5 Negotiations for a mandate on laws that discriminate against women

The Human Rights Council considered the matter of whether to have a Special Rapporteur in 2009. A Council resolution sponsored by thirty-eight States Parties from Africa, Europe, North and South America, and the Middle East (Israel)[57] identified why dealing with laws that discriminate was important:

> The Human Rights Council recognises that women's inequality before the law has resulted in the lack of equal opportunities for women in education, access to health, economic participation, access to labour and disparities in salaries and compensation, public and political participation, access to decision making processes, inheritance, ownership of land, financial services, including loans and nationality and legal capacity among others, as well as increased vulnerability to discrimination and violence and that all countries face challenges in these areas.[58]

The resolution welcomed the work done by the CEDAW Committee on women's equality. It also recognized the work done by the Human Rights

[55] OHCHR, 'Women are still discriminated against in all countries, says UN Human rights chief' 7 March 2008, available at: http://reliefweb.int/node/259520 (last accessed 9 June 2012).

[56] Inter-Parliamentary Union with the Office of the High Commissioner for Human Rights, *Sixth Information Seminar on Parliaments and CEDAW: Addressing Laws that Discriminate against Women*, Geneva, 16 October 2008. See www.ipu.org/splz-e/cedaw08.htm (last accessed 23 March 2012).

[57] Human Rights Council, 'Elimination of discrimination against women', 1 October 2009, A/HRC/12/L.3/Rev.1.

[58] *Ibid.* at para. 6.

Council in 'addressing the issue of discrimination against women in both law and practice' and called for half a day to be set aside to discuss the issue of discrimination against women.[59] This duly took place with panellists including one CEDAW Committee member as well as an academic, a representative from UNIFEM and the Special Rapporteur on violence against women.[60]

Further, the Council decided to ask for a report to be prepared on the need for a mechanism.[61] This was done in house by the OHCHR and, like most UN documents, merely reiterated the litany of existing documents that had gone before on the matter.[62] It recalled the international human rights framework on non-discrimination, highlighting the CEDAW Committee's call for the use of substantive equality, which covered direct and indirect discrimination as well as that grounded in gender stereotypes. This in turn called for 'systemic and structural transformation of institutions and attitudes that reflect and entrench discrimination against women'.[63] The *Thematic Study* made the link between equality and the attainment of the Millennium Development Goals (MDGs), especially MDG 3 Gender Equality.[64]

Recommendations included making a consideration of laws that discriminate against women a standing item on the list of questions that states have to address in the Universal Peer Review process. Moreover, it was suggested working with UN Women to ensure that the focus of its new work plan included equality before the law. The new mechanism could also perform a consolidating function, drawing and building on the findings of the CEDAW Committee and other treaty bodies.

The *OHCHR Thematic Study* 2010 concluded that, notwithstanding existing treaty bodies and Special Procedure mechanisms, there was still scope for a new mechanism and recommended that the

59 *Ibid.* at paras. 10 and 11. See also para. 16 on the half-day.

60 15th Session of the HRC, Panel Discussion on elimination of discrimination against women, Room XX, Palais des Nations, Geneva, Monday 20 September 2010.

61 HRC, 'Elimination of discrimination against women', paras. 15 and 16.

62 Human Rights Council, *Thematic Study of the Office of the United Nations High Commissioner for Human Rights on Discrimination against Women, in Law and Practice, and How the Issue is Addressed Throughout the United Nations Human Rights System*, 30 August 2010, A/HRC/15/40, paras. 3 and 51 [hereinafter *OHCHR Thematic Study* 2010].

63 *Ibid.* at para. 10. See also para. 11. CEDAW General Recommendation 25 on Temporary Special Measures, para. 8 and CEDAW General Recommendation No. 28 on State Obligations.

64 *OHCHR Thematic Study* 2010.

Council follow it up. Recommendations included working with the International Parliamentary Union to lobby states to amend laws. The new mechanism should also have the ability to investigate and suggest model laws.

Finally in October 2010, the matter was again considered by the Human Rights Council. A resolution was proposed by Mexico with Columbia to set up a working group of five independent experts who were to have three years to conduct their work in the first instance. Worthy of note is the last-minute attempt by Saudi Arabia to include an amendment:

> ABDULWAHAB ATTAR (Saudi Arabia), speaking in a general comment, said Saudi Arabia suggested a small amendment of the Operational Paragraph 1 to the draft resolution L.15. 'We call upon States to take all appropriate measures in accordance with their international commitments under international human rights law to eliminate discrimination against women by any person, organization, or enterprise.' The paragraph had been approved in many past resolutions and Saudi Arabia was merely requesting an addition that had been approved by the Council on earlier occasions.

In effect, Saudi Arabia was seeking to add the words: 'We call upon States to take appropriate *measures in accordance with their international commitments*' [65] to the Human Rights Council's 2009 resolution, which, echoing CEDAW Article 2(d), reads: 'reaffirms the obligations of States to take all appropriate measures to eliminate discrimination against women by any person, organization or enterprise'.[66] The Saudi position is notable for its remarkable consistency in arguing that respect for municipal cultural–religious frameworks should prevail over international human rights norms.[67] Indeed, the Saudi reservation to Article 2 of the CEDAW on state obligations explains that it is ratifying on the understanding that the Convention is to be interpreted according to Saudi laws including religion (Shariah), a stance objected to by European states as being in violation of

[65] OHCHR, 'Human Rights Council establishes Working Group on Discrimination against Women in Law and Practice', Human Rights Council, Morning, 1 October 2010. A disclaimer attached to this document notes 'for use of media, not an official record', available at: www.ohchr.org/en/NewsEvents/Pages/DisplayNews.aspx?NewsID=10405&LangID=E (last accessed 9 June 2012) [hereinafter *OHCHR News* 2010]. Emphasis added.

[66] A/HRC/12/L.3/Rev.1, 1 October 2009, para. 1.

[67] Saudi Arabia had tried the same during the drafting of the UDHR. S. Waltz, 'Universal human rights: the contribution of Muslim states', *Human Rights Quarterly* 26:4 (2004) 799–844, at 819–25. See also K. Hashemi, 'Religious legal traditions, Muslim states and the Convention on the Right of the Child: an essay on the relevant UN documentation', *Human Rights Quarterly* 29:1 (2007) 194–227, at 202, 207–15.

both the object and purpose of the CEDAW under Article 28(2) and the Vienna Convention on the Law of Treaties 1968.[68]

Debate raged about both the aim of the Saudi proposed amendment and also whether it should be permitted to seek to amend a resolution at that (late) stage in the proceedings. States including Bahrain, Djibouti, Libya, Jordan and Pakistan argued in favour of the right of Saudi Arabia to seek to make a last-minute amendment and said that it could be incorporated without adverse effect on the general tenor of the resolution. China noted that it:

> [F]ully agreed with … and supported the amendment put forward by Saudi Arabia, as China believed that the protection and promotion of human rights was ultimately the task of national Governments, in accordance with their commitments under international law to protect and promote women's rights and eliminate discrimination. Governments should not only act in line with international agreements, but also in line with the consensus agreed upon in the international community to protect and support the rights of women.[69]

Similarly, Libya argued that it:

> [B]elieved that under all religions women enjoyed their rights and were respected and valued. Libya would fully support the amendment and said that everyone should understand the relativism of some concepts; there might be divergences in cultures and religions and it was the diversity that made the world what it was. No country should have anything imposed on them without that country being a party to a particular international instrument.[70]

There were many rejoinders including from the United States and the United Kingdom, together with representatives speaking on behalf of the Africa group and the European Union. The culmination came when co-resolution sponsor Mexico noted that there had been extensive consultation enabling comments and amendments to be incorporated before the resolution had been tabled. It noted that in addition to Colombia, there were sixty co-sponsors of the resolution and that while there had

[68] Reservations to CEDAW and objections, available at: www.un.org/womenwatch/daw/cedaw/reservations-country.htm (last accessed 23 March 2012). Vienna Convention on the Law of Treaties, 1155 UNTS 331, entered into force 27 January 1980, Article 19. See CEDAW Committee, *List of Issues and Questions with regard to Consideration of Periodic Reports: Saudi Arabia*, 16 August 2007, UN Doc. CEDAW/C/SAU/Q2, para. 2. See also CEDAW Committee, *Concluding Observations: Saudi Arabia*, 8 April 2008, UN Doc. CEDAW/C/SAU/CO/2, paras. 9 and 12.

[69] *OHCHR News* 2010.

[70] *Ibid.*

in the past been 'caveats to the application of certain rights that were not absolute rights', it further noted:

> The problem was that in this specific paragraph, the subject was discrimination against women, full stop. It was not a discussion of norms or of distinct ways of implementing laws. The Council could not accept a caveat or a reservation along the proposed lines when what it was talking about was discrimination against women. For reasons of principle, the proposed forms of words could not be accepted. There was no single law that could prevent discrimination against women, and this was why there could be no weakening of the rights of women by using the form proposed. The Human Rights Council could not accept reservations, limitations or caveats which would mean that it was questioning the absolute right women had to not be discriminated against, be it under the law or in any other fashion. The concerns of those supporting the resolution were fully reflected in the resolution and in the mandate of the Working Group.[71]

The argument that the principle of non-discrimination was non-derogable won the day. The proposed amendment was voted on, with 18 in favour, 22 against and 4 abstentions.[72] The amendment was therefore rejected. However, the closeness of the figures for and against (which become equal if one factors in the abstentions) suggests the points of resistance and challenge that will face the Group of five going forward. The resolution was adopted without a vote.[73] Against all hope and expectation, a new mechanism was approved.[74]

6 The new Working Group

On 8 October 2010 the UN Human Rights Council decided to establish, for a period of three years, a new Working Group of five independent experts, of balanced geographical representation, on the issue of discrimination against women in law and in practice.[75] While a single

[71] *Ibid.*

[72] OHCHR, 'Human Rights Council establishes Working Group on Discrimination against Women in Law and Practice', Human Rights Council, 1 October 2010.

[73] See generally, Human Rights Council, *Report of the Working Group on the Issue of Discrimination against Women in Law and in Practice*, 5 April 2012, A/HRC/20/28, para. 8 [hereinafter *Working Group Report* 2012].

[74] Asked publicly about my own assessment of the likelihood of a new mechanism being created, I was sceptical, noting 'Turkeys don't vote for Christmas.' I am pleased to have been proved wrong.

[75] *Human Rights Council Resolution, 15/23 on the Elimination of Discrimination against Women*, 8 October 2010 A/HRC/RES/15/23 [hereinafter *HRC, Elimination of Discrimination*].

Special Rapporteur had been mooted for a long time, the appointment of a Working Group seems to be the right decision. A subject as broad, complex and fraught as discrimination against women in law and practice is best addressed by a group of people from all the major regions and legal systems of the world. Each member will have specialist knowledge not only of the law, but of the areas of controversy and of current practice and trends. Moreover, given the tendency to label issues of equality as 'emanating from the West' and calling women from the global South who work for equal rights 'westoxified', it seems wise to have included a global balance in the membership of the group.[76] They can give each other cover and support when the name-calling inevitably begins. Equally important is the expansion of the mandate beyond formal laws to include practice.

The mandate of the Working Group required it:

(a) to develop a dialogue with states, the relevant UN entities, national human rights institutions, experts on different legal systems and civil society organizations to identify, promote and exchange views on best practices related to the elimination of laws that discriminate against women in terms of implementation or impact and, in that regard, to prepare a compendium of best practices;
(b) to undertake studies in cooperation with and reflecting the views of states and relevant UN entities on ways and means in which the Working Group can cooperate with and fulfil its mandate;
(c) to make recommendations on the improvement of legislation and implementation of law to contribute to the realization of Millennium Development Goal number three on gender equality;
(d) to work with other Special Procedure mechanisms and CEDAW together with UN Women with a view to avoiding duplication;
(e) to consult relevant stakeholders including regional and national human rights mechanisms; and
(f) to compile a report on good practices in eliminating discrimination against women.[77]

[76] 'Westoxification' is a term coined by Uma Narayan to describe the phenomenon of silencing outspoken 'local women' by discrediting them as a-cultural and 'brainwashed' by the 'West'. U. Narayan, *Dis/locating Cultures/Identities, Traditions, and Third World Feminism* (New York: Routledge, 1997).

[77] *HRC, Elimination of Discrimination*, para. 18, available at: www2.ohchr.org/english/bodies/hrcouncil/docs/15session/A.HRC.RES.15.23_En.pdf (last accessed 14 February 2013).

The Resolution also called on agencies within the United Nations and other groups including NGOs to cooperate fully with the Working Group in the fulfilment of its mandate.[78] The CSW was explicitly mentioned as one of the entities to which the Working Group had to submit its reports.[79]

The call for nominations for the five Working Group members duly went out.[80] Out of a total of 245 names put forward, a shortlist of 15 was drawn up.[81] Final selection took place at the Human Rights Council meeting in March 2011. The five members of the Working Group, all women, who were appointed by the Human Rights Council in March 2011 and assumed their functions on 1 May 2011, are Kamala Chandrakirana (Indonesia); Emna Aouij (Tunisia); Mercedes Barguet (Mexico); Frances Raday (Israel/United Kingdom); and Eleonora Zielinska (Poland).[82] Of these two, Emna Aouij and Frances Raday have served as CEDAW Committee members. All have extensive expertise in women's rights.[83]

In formulating its work plan, the Working Group decided to have one member take the position of Chairperson on an annual basis.[84] The founding Chairperson is Kamala Chandrakirana. Initially the Working Group identified four thematic areas falling under four broad categories:

(1) public life and citizenship including nationality and citizenship laws and political representation for women;
(2) economic life including employment laws, wage gaps, access to goods and services, economic exploitation of women's sexuality in trafficking and pornography, policies, practices and codes related to business, transnational corporations and natural resource management;
(3) family life including religious and customary personal law, forced marriage, child marriages; and

[78] *Ibid.* at para. 20. [79] *Ibid.* at para. 21.

[80] Action Canada for Population Development and others, 'Proposed criteria for the selection of candidates for the UN Working Group on Discrimination against Women', 11 November 2010.

[81] Human Rights Council, Letter from Sihasak Phuangkethkeow, President of the Human Rights Council to All Permanent Representatives to the Human Rights Council, Geneva, 1 February 2011.

[82] 'OHCHR Working Group on the issue of discrimination against women in law and in practice'. See: www.ohchr.org/EN/Issues/Women/WGWomen/Pages/WGWomenIndex.aspx (last accessed 23 March 2012).

[83] *Ibid.*

[84] *Working Group Report* 2012.

(4) health and safety including reproductive rights, violence against women, women in detention and maternal mortality.[85]

Thereafter a fifth, violence against women, was added as a cross-cutting category.

In its first work plan covering 2012–2013, the WG has elected to focus on public and political life and social and economic life. It is the first issue that is the current subject of research with the WG looking at efforts undertaken in times of political transition, particularly transitions that involve fundamental changes of political regime and/or of the legal system. In gathering data, the WG has written letters and devised a simple one-page questionnaire requesting information from governments and other interested stakeholders. It is interested in discriminatory constitutional and legislative provisions, including on violence against women as well as information on women's access to justice within societies in transition. The second theme on social and economic life is to be tackled in 2013.[86] Parallel to this process is the Working Group's compilation of a compendium of what it has decided to term 'good or promising practice'[87] for presentation to the Human Rights Council.[88]

Although still in its infancy, the WG has shown itself to be remarkably astute in its chosen areas of focus, which are both topical in light of the multiple ongoing political revolutions as well as in light of the severe economic climate that has had a huge impact on women's lives and access to social and economic rights.[89] Moreover, the concentration on economic and social life in 2013 will help to draw attention to Millennium Development Goal 3 on Gender Equality, just as the 2015 deadline for the culmination of progress towards meeting the goals comes into view. The two topics have, of course, the added advantage of being far less contentious than other possible areas of focus including health and safety (if

[85] OHCHR Briefing note, 1st session of the Working Group on Discrimination against Women in Law and Practice – Geneva, 6–10 June 2011. Available at: www.ohchr.org/EN/Issues/Women/WGWomen/Pages/FirstsessionWG.aspx (last accessed 20 March 2012).

[86] OHCHR Working Group on Discrimination against Women in Law and Practice, 'Methods of work', available at: www.ohchr.org/EN/Issues/Women/WGWomen/Pages/MethodsOfWork.aspx (last accessed 4 April 2012). See also *Working Group Report* 2012.

[87] *Working Group Report* 2012, para. 18.

[88] The Resolution mandates that the group uses good practice and best practice interchangeably. Compare *HRC, Elimination of Discrimination*, para. 18(a) and (f). A discussion of the use of 'good, best or promising practice' is beyond the scope of this chapter.

[89] *Working Group Report* 2012, paras. 32–5.

this covers abortion law). This long-term strategic approach augurs well for a renewal of the WG mandate, which will then, hopefully, lead to a bolder approach to women's rights by engaging with controversial issues. Equally important will be its relationship with the CEDAW Committee and UN Women. Contacts have been made with both bodies and, given the shared objective of ending discrimination against women in law and practice, good working relationships seem assured. At its first session the WG undertook 'to firstly build an information base from the concluding observations of CEDAW and other treaty bodies'[90] and to 'explore the availability of statistical data 30 years after CEDAW to show in a dynamic way progress in women's situation particularly in public and economic life'.[91] The WG also undertook to develop 'a qualitative mapping of available sources of information'.[92] The Human Rights Council Resolution setting up the Working Group decreed that the WG should report to both the CSW and the Council. In her first address to the CSW, the Chairperson of the Working Group noted that she saw the CSW annual meeting as an important place to raise issues of equality of women and to engage with governments, NGOs and other stakeholders. In conclusion, she hoped for 'continuous and effective coordination between the Human Rights Council and its Special Procedures and CSW in the spirit of promoting a coherent approach in overcoming the remaining obstacles to full equality and women's human rights by the various bodies and mechanisms within the United Nations'.[93]

Going forward, there is room for optimism.[94]

[90] To mark the establishment of the Working Group, Equality Now prepared a report: 'Discrimination against women in law: a report drawing from the Concluding Observations of the Committee on the Elimination of Discrimination against Women', May 2011. See also, J. Hunt, 'UN Working Group on Discrimination against Women in Law and Practice', prepared for Advocates for International Development, 3 August 2011.

[91] OHCHR Briefing note – 1st session of the Working Group on Discrimination against Women in Law and Practice, Geneva, 6–10 June 2011. In its first report the Working Group cited the CEDAW Committee and Human Rights Committee general comments as guides to its work. See *Working Group Report* 2012, paras. 25 and 26.

[92] Useful may be M. Freeman *et al.*, *CEDAW*. See also UNIFEM, *Translating CEDAW into Law: CEDAW Legislative Compliance in Nine Pacific Island Countries* (Suva: UNIFEM, 2007); UNIFEM, *Gender Equality Laws: Global Good Practice and a Review of Five South East Asian Countries* (Bangkok: UNIFEM, 2009).

[93] K. Chandrakirana Oral Statement at 3.

[94] *Ibid.* at 2–3.

7 Opportunities

Equality Now started its February 2010 update on the laws that discriminate by highlighting that it was 'pleased to report that more than half of a total of 52 countries highlighted in both previous reports have fully or partially repealed or amended the discriminatory laws indicated'.[95] The integration of a gender perspective into the work of all UN human rights committees and agencies, while not perfect, is a cause for further optimism, not least because it will mean that the Working Group is being assisted in its work on many fronts, which can only be good for meeting the challenging objective of eliminating discrimination against women in law and practice.[96] The CEDAW Committee and indeed the human rights treaty bodies have considerably extended the understanding of equality beyond a formal model requiring legal change. Substantive equality requires closer attention to be paid to the factual situation of women including historical inequalities and deploying, if necessary, the use of temporary special measures. An intersectional analysis of discrimination is key.[97] Also worthy of note is the adoption by the CEDAW Committee and others of transformative equality, which involves engaging with structural discrimination grounded in culture, which augurs well for the Working Group as its performs its mandate.[98] Moreover, the CEDAW Committee, with which the Working Group will work closely and with which it has already held consultative meetings, has ramped up its consideration of legal discrimination, and one can now see in Committee reports subsections specifically addressing laws that discriminate against women.[99] The Committee now also has follow-up procedures for engaging States

[95] Equality Now, 'Words and deeds: holding governments accountable in the Beijing +15 Review process' Update: Women's Action 16.10, February 2010 at 1.

[96] UN Women, *In Pursuit of Justice: 2011–2012 Progress of the World's Women* (New York: UN Women, 2011).

[97] CEDAW General Recommendations 25 and 28. See also CEDAW Committee, *Concluding Observations: Norway*, 2 March 2012, UN Doc. CEDAW/C/NOR/CO/8, paras. 9–10, 18, 21–23.

[98] The jurisprudence of the Committee under the Optional Protocol to CEDAW has been impressive. Some examples include *A.T.* v. *Hungary*, CEDAW/C/36/D/2/2003; *A.S.* v. *Hungary*, CEDAW/C/36/D/4/2004; *Fatma Yildirim (deceased)* v. *Austria*, CEDAW/C/39/D/6/2005; *Vertido* v. *The Philippines*, CEDAW/C/46/D/18/2008; and *R.K.B.* v. *Turkey*, CEDAW, Comm. No. 28/2010, UN Doc. CEDAW/C/51/D/28/2010. See also, R. Holtmaat 'Article 5' in M. Freeman *et al.*, *CEDAW*, 122–67.

[99] CEDAW Committee, *Concluding Observations: Uganda*, 5 November 2010, UN Doc. CEDAW/C/UGA/CO/7 (2010), paras. 11 and 12.

Parties.[100] Crucially the Working Group intends to receive information from a range of sources and to use communications 'with Governments and other actors in a spirit of soliciting dialogue on issues falling within its mandate'. Hopefully the 'appropriate action' that it promises to take will yield cooperation and positive results.[101] At the regional and national levels there are many positive developments in norm making, including new protocols, policies and constitutions.[102] Moreover, national courts have proved adept at progressing the equality and women's human rights agenda.[103]

Given the historical resistance to the idea of women's rights, these positive elements have to be tempered with a dose of realism. The last section looks briefly at some of the challenges that will face the Working Group.

8 Challenges

The breadth and scope of the Working Group's mandate requires it to traverse legal, economic, socio-religious and cultural terrain. In engaging states, the Working Group will be faced with the 'who are you to tell us how to order our societies?' phenomenon. The resistance of states to change can be seen in the difficulties faced by human rights committees in getting states to lift reservations, particularly those related to the CEDAW.[104] If states fail to comply with voluntarily entered into agreements, then what are the chances that they will listen to the Working Group? There is a direct correlation between those states that were resistant to the setting-up

[100] CEDAW Committee, *Concluding Observations: India*, 22 October 2010, UN Doc. CEDAW/C/IND/CO/SP.1 (2010).

[101] *Working Group Report* 2012, para. 40.

[102] See for example Council of Europe Convention on Preventing Violence against Women and Domestic Violence, ETS 210, not yet in force. See also African Union Decade for Women, AU Assembly Dec. 487 (XIX) declaring 2010–2020 as African Women's Decade. Articles 27(3) and 27(4) of the Constitution of Kenya, 27 August 2010.

[103] M. Ssenyonjo, 'Women's right to equality and non discrimination: discriminatory family legislation in Uganda and the role of Uganda's constitutional court', *International Journal of Law Family and Policy* 21:3 (2007) 341–72. *Rono* v. *Rono* (2005) AHRLR 107 (KeCA 2005); *In Re Estate of Lerionka Ole Ntutu*, Succession Cause No. 1263 OF 2000, 2008 Eklr 1; *Noorfadilla Binti Ahmed Saikin* v. *Chayed Bin Basirun*, Originating Summons No. 21–248–210, Malaysian High Court at Shah Alam; *Fornah* v. *Secretary of State for the Home* Department [2006] UKHL 46; *Shilubana and Others* v. *Nawmitwa* 2008 (9) BCLR 914 (SA CC); *Law & Advocacy for Women in Uganda* v. *Attorney General (Constitutional Petition No. 8 of 2007)*, [2010] UGCC 4. IACtHR; *González et al. ('Cotton Field')* v. *Mexico*, Judgment, 16 November 2009.

[104] Connors, 'Article 28' at 573–5.

of a Working Group and those with the most problematic reservations, including to provisions relating to state obligations under Article 2 of the CEDAW. Challenging religious laws, even with the benefit of different interpretations preferred by academics and religious progressives, will remain controversial and difficult. Moreover, given the existence of plural normative orders in many jurisdictions, saying states are responsible for violations of rights by non-state actors (including discriminatory laws outside the state's direct control) is legally accurate and indeed taken for granted in academic discourse, but much harder to monitor, evaluate and change in practice.

There is of course the gap between law and practice in all states. There are many states that do not have laws that are facially discriminatory, but still discrimination persists. The discrepancy in pay between men and women is such an example. In the United Kingdom the pay gap between men and women has persisted and 'progress towards the eradication of the wage gap between men and women has stalled, especially in the private sector and for persons employed in part-time work'.[105] The figures are even worse for migrant women and men. How should this be dealt with? Linked to this are challenges in quantifying women's domestic labour on the ending of marital contracts when women's unpaid work is taken for granted and as comprising part of the gendered bargain of marriage.[106]

Given the seeming intractability of gender stereotyping, there is the ongoing question about how to tackle its pervasive and often negative impact on institutional frameworks that exist to protect women.[107] A pressing example is the low conviction rate in rape cases in some states, which can be explained in part by institutional (police and prosecutorial) failure to rise above and indeed challenge pervasive gender stereotyping of the 'kind of woman who gets raped' and who may thus have 'deserved

[105] CESCR Committee, *Concluding Observations: United Kingdom of Great Britain and Northern Ireland, the Crown Dependencies and the Overseas Dependent Territories*, 12 June 2009, UN Doc. E/C.12/GBR/CO/5, para. 18.

[106] See in particular the dissenting opinions in *B.J.* v. *Germany*, CEDAW Communication 1 of 2003, Decision of 14 July 2004 (inadmissible) appendix. See also dissenting opinion of Hale, LJ in the UK Supreme Court decision of *Radmacher* v. *Granantino* [2010] UKSC 42.

[107] See also R. Holtmaat, 'CEDAW: a holistic approach to women's equality and freedom' in this volume. See also S. Cusack, 'CEDAW as a legal framework for transnational discourses on gender stereotyping' in this volume; C. Nyamu Musembi, 'Pulling apart? Treatment of pluralism in CEDAW and the Maputo Protocol' in this volume; R. Cook and S. Cusack, *Gender Stereotyping: Transnational Legal Perspectives* (Philadelphia: University of Pennsylvania Press, 2011); R. Holtmaat and J. Naber, *Women's Human Rights and Culture: From Deadlock to Dialogue* (Antwerp: Intersentia, 2010).

it', who is to be distinguished from the 'kind of woman who did not ask for it'.[108] Engaging with this issue in a meaningful and measurable, or at least results-indicative way, will prove challenging for the Working Group.

Implementation is also an issue. Zimbabwe has one of the most progressive laws on violence against women, but it is worth noting that it was drafted at one of the most violent times in the country's post-independence history.[109] There seems to be a disconnect between outlawing private violence while the state both condones and perpetuates public violence.[110] Intransigent judges may also pose a problem. This is exemplified by the gratuitously offensive comments made by Kenyan judges in a case challenging the non-implementation of a provision in the 2010 constitution, which called for the appointment of Supreme Court justices to reflect a sex balance of one-third women and a maximum of two-thirds men.[111]

Compliance will be a problem for the Working Group. It is very much based on state cooperation. While it has been suggested that states that are compliant tend to have good laws and policies already, even those states can be stubborn and resistant. If an issue is controversial at the local level, governments may choose, for political gain, to defy the legal obligation to end discrimination, preferring the political gains to be had at the national level from open defiance. A recent example is the intransigence of Poland over abortion rulings made by the European Court of Human Rights in the *Tysiac* v. *Poland* case, which led to the State Party being requested by the CEDAW Committee to fulfil its obligations to women in this regard.[112] The fact that Poland is yet to comply hints at the limits of law anticipated by Allott.[113] Another example of a deliberate rolling back of gains made is the cynical passage of the 2009 Shia Personal Status law in Afghanistan by the Karzai Government, which

[108] Amnesty International, *Case Closed: Rape and Human Rights in the Nordic Countries: Summary Report* (London: Amnesty International, 8 March 2010); CEDAW Committee, *Concluding Observations: Norway*, para. 23; Amnesty International, *Breaking the Silence: Sexual Violence in Cambodia* (London: Amnesty International, 8 March 2010).

[109] A. Hellum *et al.*, 'Rights claiming and rights making in Zimbabwe: a study of three human rights NGOs', in B. A. Andreassen and G. Crawford (eds.), *Human Rights, Power and Non-Governmental Action: Comparative Analyses of Rights-Based Approaches and Civic Struggles in Development Contexts* (London: Routledge, 2012).

[110] F. Banda, 'Recent developments in Zimbabwe', in B. Atkins (ed.), *International Survey of Family Law* (London: Jordans, 2007) 333–51.

[111] *FIDA and Five Others* v. *Attorney General and Another* [2011] Eklr (Petition 102 of 2011).

[112] *Tysiac* v. *Poland*, ECHR Application no. 5410/03, 20 March 2007. See also *L.C.* v. *Peru*, UN Doc. CEDAW/C/50/D/22/2009 (4 November 2011).

[113] A. Allott, *The Limits of Law* (London: Butterworth, 1980).

was afraid of losing power in the election that was pending. Neither the complaints of local women's NGOs pointing out the discriminatory effects of the legislation on Shia women, nor the blandishments of the US-dominated coalition would convince the government to alter its position. Here the human rights of Shia women were sacrificed at the altar of political expedience.

A major problem facing the Working Group is that there may be differences in both understanding and interpretation of the idea of equality, not least within the regional human rights frameworks. The Protocol to the African Charter on the Rights of Women 2003 starts with the CEDAW-based definition of non-discrimination in Article 1, but rapidly changes, in the provisions on the division of property on divorce and death, to the more problematic entitlement to an 'equitable' rather than equal right to property. The effect is to create a lack of clarity.[114] Equity, if understood as fairness, can yield a range of results from equal to unfair. Moreover, the choice of the word equitable in the property division sections reflects the reservations made by some states, not least Egypt, to Article 16 of the CEDAW, which cites as its justification for differential treatment of men and women in divorce:

> Islamic *Sharia's* provisions whereby women are accorded rights equivalent to those of their spouses so as to ensure a just balance between them. This is out of respect for the sacrosanct nature of the firm religious beliefs which govern marital relations in Egypt and which may not be called in question and in view of the fact that one of the most important bases of these relations is an equivalency of rights and duties so as to ensure complementary which guarantees true equality between the spouses.[115]

The inconsistency between international and regional considerations on equality can also be found in the Revised Arab Charter 2004. Like its African counterpart, the Arab Charter appears to embrace, in Articles 11 and 3(1), the standard equal protection before the law and non-discrimination provisions found in the international system. However, it also invokes a model of equality grounded within a religious framework in Article 3(3), which provides:

[114] See also the chapter by Nyamu Musembi in this volume.

[115] Reservation of the Arab Republic of Egypt in respect of Article 16 of the CEDAW, available at: www.un.org/womenwatch/daw/cedaw/reservations-country.htm (last accessed 23 June 2012); see CEDAW General Recommendation No. 21 on Marriage and Family Relations, paras. 26, 34, 35.

> Men and women are equal in respect of human dignity, rights and obligations within the framework of the positive discrimination established in favour of women by the Islamic Shariah, other divine laws and by applicable laws and legal instruments. Accordingly, each State party pledges to take all the requisite measures to guarantee equal opportunities and effective equality between men and women in the enjoyment of all the rights set out in this Charter.[116]

Other points of difference between the regional and international include provisions on polygyny. The Human Rights and CEDAW Committees have both said that polygyny constitutes discrimination against women and is a breach of the principle of non-discrimination on grounds of sex.[117] However, the African Protocol allows polygyny as a means of protecting women in existing (de facto) polygynous marriages. Moreover, in *Hassam* v. *Jacobs N.O.* the South African High Court preferred the African Protocol interpretation over that of the CEDAW, reasoning that denying widows of polygynous Muslim marriages from inheriting property and receiving maintenance under statutory law 'would be unfairly discriminatory against them and in be in conflict with the provisions of section 9 (non-discrimination) of the Constitution'.[118] Which of these two interpretations will the Working Group choose: the strict reading of polygyny as discrimination, or the more nuanced one that perceives the banning of polygyny as being contrary to the interests of women who may be cast aside without access to property or maintenance?

Related to this is the changing understanding of discrimination over the decades.[119] In the *Banda Report* some respondents cited labour laws based on old International Labour Organization Conventions proscribing

[116] The interpretive provision, Article 43, is unhelpful in that it invokes both domestic and international law as guides to interpretation without specifying what is to happen in the event of a conflict between the 'protective' provisions of domestic law and the requirements of international human rights law. Other provisions making the rights subject to national law have the problem of breaching Article 27 of the Vienna Convention on the Law on Treaties, which provides that the national law cannot trump international provisions; but what of regional ones? See also CEDAW Committee, *Concluding Observations: Saudi Arabia*, paras. 13 and 14.

[117] CEDAW General Recommendation No. 21, para. 14, Human Rights Committee, General Comment 28, Equality of rights between men and women (article 3), UN Doc. CCPR/C/21/Rev.1/Add.10 (2000), para. 24.

[118] *Hassam* v. *Jacobs N.O. and Ors* Case No. 5704/2004, High Court (CPD), Judgment 18 July 2008, para. 19. See also para. 22. See also *Ngwenyama* v. *Mayelane and Minister of Home Affairs* (474/2011) [2012] ZASCA 94.

[119] N. Hevener, 'An analysis of gender based treaty law: contemporary developments in historical perspective', *Human Rights Quarterly* 8:1 (1986) 70–88.

women from working in the mines or the military as protective and thus positive, while others construed these as discriminatory.[120]

If the Working Group is to consider intersectional discrimination, then what is it to do about both legal and factual discrimination against minorities[121] who are considered controversial in some regions? This could include the impact on lesbian women of laws that prohibit them from adopting children, or which deny or put additional barriers to them accessing reproductive technologies that are given to heterosexual women as of right.[122] Increasingly, family provisions on the right to marry are drafted specifying that the marriage is between people of the opposite sex, rather than the more neutral drafting found in the International Bill of Rights.[123] Should the Working Group engage with this issue given existing sensitivities? The experience of the Special Rapporteur on the promotion of rights while countering terrorism is telling. His report on terrorism and gender, which included a wide definition of gender identity and sexual orientation, was heavily criticized by states who said he had strayed from his remit. This points, some might argue, to a need for caution.[124] Would intervening in issues pertaining to sexual orientation discrimination lead, as some have claimed, to a discrediting of the entirety of the Working Group's human rights work? Put simply – should lesbian women 'be sacrificed for the greater good'? Can a Working Group on laws that discriminate based on a human rights mandate take such an approach? What about non-discrimination being a binding norm of immediate enforceability *without exception?* The clear answer is a resounding 'No!'

120 *Banda Report* at 109–11.

121 The mandate of the Working Group includes a consideration of minorities – *HRC, Elimination of Discrimination*, para. 17.

122 See generally *Du Toit and Another* v. *Minister of Welfare and Population Development and Others* [2003] SA 198 (CC) on adoption; *J and B* v. *Director General, Department of Home Affairs and Others* [2003] (5) BCLR 463 (CC) on parental rights for a child conceived artificially; *V.* v. *V* [1998] (4) SA 169 (HC) on custody.

123 See for example Revised Arab Charter, 2004 Article 33(1) and Constitution of the Republic of Kenya, 2010 Article 45(2). Cf Article 16(1) UDHR, Article 23(2) ICCPR, Article 10(1) ICESCR on the right to marry and found a family. While arguably the drafters anticipated marriage as being between two people of the opposite sex, it is possible to argue that, not having specified that marriage must be between men and women, leaves open the development of national laws to incorporate marriage between people of the same sex. This reading might be buttressed by factoring in developments in discrimination law that now incorporates sexual orientation as a protected ground. CESCR General Comment 20 on Non-discrimination, para. 34, CEDAW General Recommendation 28, para. 18.

124 *Report of the Special Rapporteur on the Promotion and Protection of Human Rights and Fundamental Freedoms while Countering Terrorism*, 3 August 2009, A/64/211, para. 20.

If, as proclaimed in Vienna, 'human rights are women's rights', then there can be no equivocation on the part of the Working Group in tackling the often hate-filled and violent campaigns against lesbian women.[125] Strengthening and buttressing the Working Group in its work should be the jurisprudence of human rights committees, which point to sexual orientation as a protected category.[126] Furthermore, in 2011 the Human Rights Council itself adopted a Resolution on sexual orientation.[127] Finally, it is worth noting that there has been enormous progress made at the national level, not least the Indian decision in the *Naz Foundation* case that led to the repeal of a section of the Penal Code that criminalized sexual activity between two people of the same sex.[128] The Court highlighted that the ban had been based on British colonial laws and did not reflect Indian traditions and values, thus laying to rest the 'western imposition of perversion' theories that often dominate discussions on sexual orientation in Africa and beyond.[129] The Indian example could be used by the Working Group as an example of good practice in its engagement with other states. Moreover, the Working Group could use positive examples from within a region in its engagement with recalcitrant states.[130]

In practice, the issue for the Working Group will be how to engage states with difficulties in a way that is not seen as antagonistic and judgemental.

[125] See for example CEDAW Committee, *Concluding Observations: Russian Federation*, 16 August 2010, UN Doc. CEDAW/C/USR/CO/7, paras. 40 and 41. CEDAW Committee, *Concluding Observations: Uganda*, para. 44.

[126] M. O'Flaherty and J. Fisher, 'Sexual orientation, gender identity and human rights law: contextualising the Yogyakarta Principles', *Human Rights Law Review* 8 (2008) 207–48.

[127] Human Rights Council Resolution on Human Rights, Sexual Orientation and Gender Identity, 15 June 2011 A/HRC/17/L.9/Rev.1; *Report of the United Nations High Commissioner for Human Rights,* Discriminatory laws and practices and acts of violence against individuals based on their sexual orientation and gender identity, 17 November 2011, A//HRC/19/41.

[128] *Naz Foundation* v. *Government of NCT of Delhi and Others* WP(C) No.7455/2001. See also, *Atala Riffo and daughters* v. *Chile*, Judgment of 24 February 2012, Series C No. 239 (Inter-American Court of Human Rights) (Spanish only), English translation of official summary issued by the IACtHR available at: http://williamsinstitute.law.ucla.edu/wp-content/uploads/Summary-AtalaDecision-English-Mar-2012.pdf (last accessed 4 May 2012).

Human Rights Watch, *This Alien Legacy: The Origins of 'Sodomy' Laws in British Colonialism*, 17 December 2008.

[129] See generally S. Tamale (ed.), *African Sexualities* (Oxford: Pambazuka, 2011). See also M. Mutua, 'Sexual orientation and human rights' in Tamale, *African Sexualities*, 452–62.

[130] R. Murray and F. Viljoen, 'Towards non discrimination on the basis of sexual orientation: the normative basis and procedural possibilities before the African Commission on Human and Peoples' Rights and the African Union', *Human Rights Quarterly* 29 (2007) 86–111.

This will be particularly important in light of that part of the mandate requesting states to give 'serious consideration to responding favourably to the requests of the working group to visit their countries to enable it to fulfil its mandate effectively'.[131] The *Banda Report* highlighted the importance of visits of Special Rapporteurs, especially to NGOs working in the field. NGOs reported that the engagement with state officials had helped to open up avenues of communication, and that following the visit of the Special Rapporteur, the NGOs had been able to press home the advantage by advancing their agenda on law reform.[132] This reinforces the need for states to:

> Provide gender-sensitive human rights education and training to public officials, including, inter alia, police and military personnel, corrections officers, health and medical personnel, and social workers, including people who deal with migration and refugee issues, and teachers at all levels of the educational system, and make available such education and training also to the judiciary and members of parliament in order to enable them to better exercise their public responsibilities.[133]

It is noteworthy that in the Beijing *Platform for Action* the strategic objective that follows that on equality and the need to eliminate discriminatory laws is on legal literacy, with states being required to translate human rights instruments into indigenous languages to facilitate learning and usage. Moreover, states are also required to: '(c) Disseminate information on national legislation and its impact on women, including easily accessible guidelines on how to use a justice system to exercise one's rights' and also to make known information on the international human rights complaint mechanisms and ways of accessing them.[134]

[131] *HRC, Elimination of Discrimination*, para. 19.

[132] *Banda Report* at 54–5. See also *HRC, Elimination of Discrimination*, para. 20 inviting NGOs to 'cooperate fully with the working group in the fulfilment of its mandate'.

[133] *Beijing Declaration*, para. 232(i).

[134] *Ibid.* Strategic Objective 1:3, paras. 233(a), (c), (e). See also Rights of Women, *Women's Access to Justice: A Research Report* (London: Rights of Women, 4 February 2011). Available at: www.rightsofwomen.org.uk/pdfs/Policy/Womens_access_to_Justice-a_research_report.pdf (last accessed 8 June 2012).

3

The CEDAW: a holistic approach to women's equality and freedom

RIKKI HOLTMAAT

[Thus], regardless of a universal sex-equality norm, women's reality is one of gross inequality.[1]

The abolition of gender norms ... would be the abolition of gender and the radical reformulation – perhaps beyond human recognition – of sexuality. But their reform could begin to make it less true that our society constructs women as inferior to men.[2]

1 Introduction

From its title, it appears that the overall object and purpose of the Convention on the Elimination of All Forms of Discrimination against Women (CEDAW, further: the Women's Convention or the Convention) is *the elimination of all forms of discrimination against women*. In this chapter I will explain that this aim may be divided into three sub-aims: to ensure full equality of women before the law; to improve the de facto position of women; and to modify gender-based stereotypes. In turn, these sub-aims relate to three possible political and legal methods to enhance women's equality and freedom: i.e. through (1) guaranteeing women's individual rights, (2) giving social support to women and (3) enhancing social and cultural change. Most of my attention will go to the third sub-aim and the corresponding third method and to the provision on which this sub-aim/method is based, that is to Article 5 CEDAW (further:

This chapter builds on various research projects and derives some texts from earlier publications that I have written in this area.

[1] B. E. Hernández-Truyol, 'Out of the shadows: traversing the imaginary of sameness, difference, and relationalism – a human rights proposal', *Wisconsin Women's Law Journal* 17 (2002) 111–62 at 145.

[2] K. Anthony Appiah, 'Stereotypes and the shaping of identity', *Californian Law Review* 88:41 (2000) 41–53 at 52.

Article 5). This provision lays the basis for an approach to enhancing women's human rights that goes beyond the well-known distinction between formal and substantive equality,[3] and includes transformative equality.[4] It opens up possibilities to read the Women's Convention as not only prohibiting direct and indirect discrimination against women as compared to men, but as also putting an obligation on States Parties to combat systemic or structural gender discrimination.

This interpretation of the meaning and scope of the Convention is based on (the drafting of) its text,[5] and on an in-depth analysis of the CEDAW Committee's General Recommendations, its Concluding Observations and its decisions under the Optional Protocol.[6] Contrary to pessimistic voices in the academic literature about the potential of the Women's Convention, this analysis shows that, compared to a standard sex-equality norm, it has considerable additional value. That is, the Convention requires fundamental changes in society in order to create more room for diversity and freedom for women (and men) to decide for themselves what it means to be a woman (or a man).[7] On the grounds of

[3] This distinction has dominated discussions within feminism and feminist legal theory for several decades. See, for example, R. Hunter, *Rethinking Equality Projects in Law. Feminist Challenges* (Oxford/Portland: Hart Publishing, 2008) and R. Holtmaat, 'Van gelijke behandeling naar Ander Recht' in E. Brems and L. Stevens (eds.), *Recht en gender in België* (Bruges: Die Keure, 2011) 237–61.

[4] This term has been coined by Sandra Fredman. See S. Fredman, 'Beyond the dichotomy of formal and substantive equality. Towards new definitions of equal rights' in I. Boerefijn *et al.* (eds.), *Temporary Special Measures: Accelerating de facto Equality of Women Under Article 4(1) UN Convention on the Elimination of All Forms of Discrimination against Women* (Antwerp/Oxford/New York: Intersentia, 2003) 111–18.

[5] As far as the drafting process is concerned, I relied on L. A. Rehof, *Guide to the Travaux Préparatoires of the United Nations Convention on the Elimination of All Forms of Discrimination against Women* (Dordrecht/Boston/London: Martin Nijhoff Publishers, 1993).

[6] The documents that are produced by the CEDAW Committee may be found at www.un.org/womenwatch/daw/cedaw/sessions.htm (up to the 41st Session) and at www2.ohchr.org/english/bodies/cedaw/ (from 42nd Session onwards) (last accessed 8 February 2013). I have studied all General Recommendations, all Concluding Observations from the 1st to the 44th session, and all Decisions under the Optional Protocol until the year 2010. My main objective was to reveal how the Committee interprets the States Parties' obligations under the Convention, most specifically under Articles 2(f), 5(a) and 5(b), and 10(c), which all cover the issue of (parental) gender roles and gender stereotyping.

[7] See also Simone Cusack's chapter about the CEDAW's significant role in combating gender stereotypes in this volume. The argument is that the right to equality is very much linked to the right to freedom to choose one's own identity, instead of being forced to adopt stereotyped and gendered self-images and roles. This affects men in a similar way as women. See J. M. Kang, 'The burdens of manliness', *Harvard Journal of Law and Gender* 33 (2010) 477–507.

this analysis, it will be argued that the Convention is not only dedicated to the fundamental principle of human equality, but also to the idea(l)s of human autonomy, freedom and diversity.

A difficult question that arises in this context is whether international human rights law can effectively impose an obligation on States Parties to modify gender stereotypes[8] and fixed parental gender roles.[9] The implementation of this obligation very much depends on their willingness to give up part of their sovereign powers to 'govern' the content and nature of gender relations (for example, through family law and inheritance law). In many countries the way gender relations are structured is closely linked to how States Parties see and experience their national identities. States are most hesitant to implement international law, and are especially inclined to openly contest its legitimacy, when such presumed identity factors are at stake. Before exploring these issues further, I will start out with some observations about the underlying human rights values that colour the interpretation of the Women's Convention as a whole.

2 The human rights values that are incorporated in the Women's Convention

The general object and purpose of the Convention must be interpreted in light of its fundamental principles and values, as declared in the Convention's Preamble. These point back to the Charter of the United Nations, which firmly declares that all human beings are equal in rights and in dignity.[10] This principle was elaborated in the 1948 United Nation's Universal Declaration of Human Rights, stating in the Preamble that 'recognition of the inherent dignity and of the equal and inalienable rights of all members of the human family is the foundation of freedom, justice and peace in the world', and in Article 1 stating that '[A]ll human beings are born free and equal in dignity and rights. They are endowed with reason and conscience and should act towards one another in a spirit of brotherhood.' These most fundamental principles of human rights are

[8] This expression summarises the content of Article 5(a) of the CEDAW, discussed below in this chapter.

[9] This expression summarises the content of Article 5(b) of the CEDAW, discussed below in this chapter.

[10] In a similar vein, see the Preambles of the International Covenant on Civil and Political Rights (ICCPR), the International Covenant on Economic, Social and Cultural Rights (ICESCR), the International Convention on the Elimination of All Forms of Racial Discrimination (ICERD) and the International Convention on the Rights of the Child (CRC), which all refer to the Preamble of the UN Charter.

based on the presumption that *all* human beings – irrespective of time and place of birth, national or ethnic origin, race, language, class or caste, sex, sexual orientation, disability or any other classification that human beings can possibly construct between themselves and regardless of their actual differences– are potentially rational and responsible beings who have a genuine desire to be in control of their own lives.[11] *Equality* and *dignity* mean that not subjugation but participation, not dependency but autonomy, not slavery but freedom are the key notions in this human rights value orientation.[12] It means that neither destiny nor fate, neither cultural inheritance nor religious prescriptions, but the autonomy and capacity of each human being to make one's own life plan come true is the foundational idea(l) behind human rights.[13] Even to the present day, such freedom and autonomy are most often denied to women through a great variety of discriminatory laws and practices, beliefs, customs and traditions all over the world, which are based on gender stereotypes and fixed parental gender roles.[14] The Convention's Preamble recognises this, as it

[11] This expresses the fundamental value of the inherent equality of all human beings, which forms the basis for the principle of formal equality in and before the law. Besides this, the principle of substantive equality has also received recognition in international law. In that principle, it is recognised that in fact all human beings are differently situated, that is, they occupy different social, geographic, economic or other positions. At the core of the principle of substantive equality is the recognition of these de facto differences, and the idea of distributive justice, which requires that human beings should have equal opportunities to make something of their lives.

[12] H. Bielefeldt, ' "Western" versus "Islamic" human rights conceptions? A critique of cultural essentialism in the discussion on human rights', *Political Theory* 28:1 (2000) 90–121 and M. Winston, 'Human rights as moral rebellion and social construction', *Journal of Human Rights* 6 (2007) 279–305.

[13] Although autonomy and freedom are most often interpreted in an individualistic way, it must be remembered that human rights protection also includes the protection of family life and national and cultural rights. The individual, in other words, can only become a human person within the context of family, culture and nation. See R. Holtmaat and J. Naber, *Women's Human Rights and Culture: From Deadlock to Dialogue* (Antwerp: Intersentia, 2011) at 96.

[14] In Holtmaat and Naber, *Women's Human Rights and Culture* and in R. Holtmaat, 'Article 5' in M. A. Freeman, C. Chinkin and B. Rudolf (eds.), *The Convention on the Elimination of All Forms of Discrimination against Women: A Commentary* [hereinafter *CEDAW Commentary*](Oxford University Press, 2012), I discuss the concepts of gender stereotypes and fixed parental gender roles (in relation to Article 5 of the CEDAW) in more detail. See also R. J. Cook and S. Cusack, *Gender Stereotyping: Transnational Legal Perspectives* (Philadelphia: University of Pennsylvania Press, 2009), and Cusack, this volume. Men who do not conform to the culturally defined male gender role and identity also encounter discrimination on the grounds of their gender. See, for example, D. S. Cohen, 'Keeping men "men" and women down: sex segregation, anti-essentialism and masculinity', *Harvard Journal of Law and Gender* 33 (2010) 509–53.

expressly states that discrimination against women violates the principles of equality of rights and respect for human dignity.[15]

3 The Convention's definition of discrimination and its scope

Article 1 of the Convention defines discrimination against women as:

> Any distinction, exclusion or restriction made on the basis of sex which has the effect or purpose of impairing or nullifying the recognition, enjoyment or exercise by women, irrespective of their marital status, on a basis of equality of men and women, of human rights and fundamental freedoms in the political, economic, social, cultural, and civil or any other field.

Most importantly, the Convention incorporates the standard that *all forms* of discrimination against women that lead to an infringement of their human rights should be eliminated. The words 'distinction, exclusion or restriction' are interpreted in an extensive way by the Committee and by academic commentators.[16] Such a broad interpretation of the non-discrimination principle indicates a human rights approach to combating discrimination,[17] as opposed to a formal legal approach, in which a (symmetrical) sex equality or *equal treatment* norm prevails.[18] In such a human rights approach, discrimination against women is seen as an instance of their oppression,[19] which, according to Iris Marion Young, can take at least five different forms. According to her, women experience a mixture of exploitation, marginalisation, powerlessness, cultural imperialism and violence.[20] This means that not only factual unequal treatment on the grounds of sex and legal discrimination,[21] but also (sexual)

15 CEDAW Preamble, paras. 1–3.

16 See A. Byrnes, 'Article 1' in Freeman *et al.*, *CEDAW Commentary*.

17 Winston, 'Human rights as moral rebellion'.

18 The CEDAW definition is very different from the formal equal treatment definitions of discrimination that are dominant in the context of (inter alia) European sex equality law. See R. Holtmaat, 'European women and the CEDAW Convention. The way forward' in *L'égalité entre femmes et hommes et la vie profesionnelle. Le point sur les développements actuels en Europe* (Paris: Dalloz, 2003) 153–74 and R. Holtmaat and C. Tobler, 'CEDAW and the European Union's policy in the field of combating gender discrimination', *Maastricht Journal of European and Comparative Law* 12:4 (2005) 399–425.

19 See Winston, 'Human rights as moral rebellion', who states that one should keep in mind that all human rights law is meant to put an end to the oppression of certain people or groups of people by their government or by other people.

20 I. M. Young, *Justice and the Politics of Difference* (Princeton University Press: 1990) 40ff.

21 See Article 2 and many of the substantive Articles of the Convention.

harassment, sexist hate speech or violence against women[22] should be ruled out. 'Oppression' includes hidden or indirect forms of sex discrimination and structural or systemic gender stereotypes and gendered structures that are deeply rooted in the religion, culture or tradition of a particular society as well as in its laws and public policies.[23] The drafters of the Convention recognised this and stressed in the Preamble that a change in the traditional roles of both men and women in society and in the family is a prerequisite for achieving full equality between men and women.[24]

The Convention explicitly recognises the disadvantaged position of *women* and (at least at first sight)[25] awards protection to women exclusively. This differs from so-called sex neutral or symmetrical anti-discrimination provisions in many international conventions, in national constitutions and in European Union law, for example, where *unequal treatment on the ground of* (either male or female) *sex* is prohibited.[26] The Convention acknowledges that in present day conditions it is mostly women who suffer from discrimination on the ground of their sex, as well as from a range of other discrimination grounds (i.e. they suffer from intersectional discrimination)[27]. Recently in the USA, a discussion has been started by Darren Rosenblum as to whether the Women's Convention should be 'unisexed', that is whether it would be better to prohibit all discrimination on the ground of sex and/or gender, instead of discrimination against

[22] See in particular CEDAW General Recommendations 12 and 19.

[23] This means that all laws and legal constructs must be subjected to an in-depth gender analysis. See R. Holtmaat, 'The power of legal concepts: the development of a feminist theory of law', *International Journal of the Sociology of Law* 5 (1989) 481–502 and R. Holtmaat, 'Gender, the analytical concept that tackles the hidden structural bias of law' in *Recht Richtung Frauen: Beitrage zur feministischen Rechtswisschenschaft* (Lachen/St Gallen: Dike Verlag, 2001) 159–82. A methodology for such an analysis has been developed in R. Holtmaat, *Towards Different Law and Public Policy: The Significance of Article 5a CEDAW for the Elimination of Structural Gender Discrimination* (Doetinchem: Reed Business Information, 2004).

[24] CEDAW Preamble, paras. 13 and 14.

[25] Below in this chapter I will argue that a wide interpretation of Article 5 of the CEDAW allows us to include men as well as intersexual and LGBT (lesbian, gay, bisexual and transgender) people who suffer from gender stereotypes and strict masculinity codes, under the protection against discrimination on the basis of this Convention.

[26] Holtmaat, 'European Women and the CEDAW Convention', and Holtmaat and Tobler, 'CEDAW and the European Union's policy'.

[27] K. Crenshaw, 'Demarginalizing the intersection of race and sex, a black feminist critique of antidiscrimination doctrine, feminist theory, and antiracist politics', *University of Chicago Legal Forum* (1989) 139–67.

women.[28] Rosenblum presents an important argument in an attempt to answer this question positively: the word 'sex' might be understood to include not only the male and female sex but all kinds of sexes, including transgendered, intersexed, and other differently sexed and gendered people.[29] To me, this is not a convincing reason to change the scope of the Convention. A prohibition of discrimination on the grounds of sex is commonly interpreted in a binary or bipolar scheme in which the (presumably essential) male and female sexes are compared to one another, and where only one of the two sexes suffers a certain disadvantage, the non-discrimination norm becomes applicable. The vast (feminist) literature shows the strong tendency toward assimilation to the male norm that is inherent in sex discrimination law as it has been constructed since the 1970s.[30] Changing the understanding of sex to include 'other' sexes as well might appear to be as difficult and controversial as acknowledging that differences between men and women are culturally and socially constructed instead of 'natural' or 'God-given'. The Dutch (male) professor of Constitutional Law, Henc van Maarseveen, in an early comment on the Women's Convention, congratulated the drafters for the fact that it prohibits discrimination of *women*. Transforming the demand for women's equality into a demand for sex equality, in his view, takes the sting out of the prohibition of discrimination because it soon will be used mainly by dominant, well-positioned men to demand whatever small 'advantage' women might have over them: 'The person who has the power of definition, who succeeds at defining discrimination against women as sex discrimination, takes the sting out of the matter and at the same time does not have to fear much from it anymore.'[31] The Convention is rightfully directed at the elimination of discrimination against women, because to the present day it is mostly men who set the standards of behaviour for women in many areas of life, [32] most notably in respect to family relations

[28] D. Rosenblum, 'Unisex CEDAW, or what's wrong with women's rights', *Columbia Journal of Gender and Law* 20:2 (2011) 98–194 and B. E. Hernández-Truyol, 'Unsex CEDAW? No! Super-sex it!', *Columbia Journal of Gender and Law* 20 (2011) 195–223.

[29] Rosenblum, 'Unisex CEDAW' at 125.

[30] A summary of these discussions may be found in Fredman, 'Beyond the dichotomy of formal and substantive equality'.

[31] H. van Maarseveen, 'Internationaal vrouwenrecht. Een afzonderlijk rechtsgebied?' in H. van Maarseveen *et al.* (eds.), *Internationaal recht en vrouwen (Deel 1 Commentaren)* (Zwolle: Tjeenk-Willink, 1987) 69–81 at 74–5. (Quote translated from Dutch by the author). See also C. Smart, *Feminism and the Power of Law* (London: Routledge, 1989) at 2.

[32] Although gender stereotypes and (separate) gendered roles for women and men also lead to 'harnessed' ideas about masculinity and to men being imprisoned in male roles and tasks, men at the same time make use of gender differences to dominate women. See

and child rearing, through firmly entrenched laws and practices that precisely describe women's inferior (and men's superior) roles and opportunities in life. But men, to a great extent, also determine the culture of workplace relations,[33] the ways people operate in economic or financial affairs,[34] and the 'culture of politics'.[35]

4 The additional value of the Women's Convention

In early feminist legal literature on international human rights law, the Women's Convention was not welcomed as an important contribution for the advancement of the human rights of women. On the contrary, it was often heavily criticised for having very limited instrumental value, because it lacks an adequate system of supervision and because there are ample possibilities for States Parties to make reservations.[36] Further points of critique were that the Convention only requires States Parties to take appropriate measures and does not impose clearly defined obligations backed up by effective deterrent sanctions,[37] and that it does not

Cohen, 'Keeping men "men" and women down' at 523, who distinguishes between 'hegemonic masculinity' and 'hegemony by men'. 'Hegemonic masculinity ... works to subordinate both women and non-hegemonically masculine men. It subordinates women by definition, as hegemonic masculinity is associated with characteristics that allow men to subordinate women; it subordinates other men, non-hegemonically masculine men, by labelling their expressions of personhood as inferior to "true" manhood.'

33 Sexual harassment very often being part of the culture at the workplace and on that ground being presented as 'normal' behaviour. See for example, A. McKinnon and T. I. Emerson, *Sexual Harassment of Working Women: A Case of Discrimination* (New Haven: Yale University Press, 1979).

34 According to feminist critiques, thereby causing financial and economic crises and unsustainable economic development. See, for example, J. K. Gibson-Graham, *The End of Capitalism (As We Knew It): A Feminist Critique of Political Economy – 10 Years On* (Minneapolis: University of Minnesota Press, 2006).

35 See, for example, D. Alexander and K. Andersen, 'Gender as a factor in the attribution of leadership traits', *Political Research Quarterly* 46 (1993) 527.

36 See H. Charlesworth and C. Chinkin, *The Boundaries of International Law: A Feminist Analysis* (Manchester University Press, 2000) at 21. See also C. I. Nyamu, 'How should human rights and development respond to cultural legitimization of gender hierarchy in developing countries?', *Harvard International Law Journal* 41:2 (2000) 381–418 at 391. Nyamu discusses the fact that attempts by human rights activists to find a legal basis for State responsibility for discrimination against women often fail because many (mainly Islamic) States have made reservations to Articles 2 and 16 of the Convention.

37 See, for example, A. X. Felmeth, 'Feminism and international law. Theory, methodology and substantive reform', *Human Rights Quarterly* 22:3 (2000) 658–733 at 710 and H. Charlesworth, C. Chinkin and S. Wright, 'Feminist approaches to international law', *American Journal of International Law* 85:4 (1991) 613–45 at 634.

oblige States Parties to take positive measures. Charlesworth and Chinkin conclude that: 'For these reasons, even the comparatively broad definition of discrimination contained in the Women's Convention may not have much cutting edge against the problems women face worldwide.'[38] More importantly, the Convention was blamed for using a definition of equality in terms of 'equal to men': 'equality is defined as being like a man'.[39] On the basis of a textual analysis, it was stated that the Convention requires a comparison to be made with a male standard, which means in order to get equal rights, women must assimilate to the male norm.[40] This (supposed) emphasis on formal equality misjudges the underlying structures and power relations that contribute to the oppression of women.[41] Summing up the critique, Charlesworth, Chinkin and Wright conclude that 'the Women's Convention ... is an ambiguous offer. It recognizes discrimination against women as a legal issue but is premised on the notion of progress through good will, education and changing attitudes and does not promise any form of structural, social or economic change for women'.[42] Other commentators, such as Lijnzaad and Burrows, did acknowledge that the Convention covers a broad area and that it goes further than the elimination of (formal) discrimination as it also requires the elimination of gender stereotypes. Nevertheless, these authors also conclude that it is an 'instrument without teeth'.[43]

It is very regrettable and damaging that such outdated opinions about the limited value of the Women's Convention are still echoed in contemporary academic literature, where authors repeat the view that the Convention might do more harm than good. These opinions have arguably been expressed[44] without any apparent knowledge of the practice

[38] Charlesworth and Chinkin, *The Boundaries of International Law* at 230.

[39] Charlesworth *et al.*, 'Feminist approaches to international law' at 631.

[40] *Ibid.*

[41] Charlesworth and Chinkin, *The Boundaries of International Law* at 229.

[42] Charlesworth *et al.*, 'Feminist approaches to international law' at 634.

[43] See, for example, L. Lijnzaad, 'Over rollenpatronen en de rol van het Verdrag' in A. W. Heringa, J. Hes and L. Lijnzaad (eds.), *Het Vrouwenverdrag. Een beeld van een verdrag* (Antwerp/Apeldoorn: Maklu, 1994) 43–57 and N. Burrows, 'The 1979 Convention on the Elimination of All Forms of Discrimination against Women', *Netherlands International Law Review* 32 (1985) 419–60. An extensive discussion of the literature up to 2004 may be found in Holtmaat, *Towards Different Law and Public Policy.*

[44] See, for example, S. E. Merry, 'Gender justice and CEDAW: the Convention on the Elimination of All Forms of Discrimination against Women', *Journal of Women of the Middle East and the Islamic World* 9 (2011) 49–75 at 53 and 58, who argues, for example, that the Convention focuses primarily on equalising women's status with that of men, and Rosenblum, 'Unisex CEDAW', who (inter alia) takes it that the Convention

of the last decades of the CEDAW Committee's work, including the Committee's dynamic interpretation of the Convention,[45] nor of the ways in which the Convention is sometimes used by the judiciary,[46] nor using any recent studies on the subject.[47]

It has been thoroughly analysed and well documented for some time now that the Women's Convention in fact offers important additional value as compared to the (formal) sex equality approach that is predominant in many national, supranational (for example, the EU) and international legal systems.[48] This development of the interpretation of the Convention has been stimulated inter alia by a series of studies that were conducted in the Netherlands,[49] which in turn have inspired the CEDAW

'provides a first step, but not a workable solution to inequality' (at 113) and that 'most of the CEDAW provisions follow a formal equality yardstick' (at 137).

45 Which was extensively documented in Holtmaat, *Towards Different Law and Public Policy*; Holtmaat and Tobler, 'CEDAW and the European Union's policy'; F. Raday, 'Culture, Religion, and CEDAW's Article 5(a)' in H. B. Schöpp-Schilling and C. Flinterman (eds.), *The Circle of Empowerment* (New York: The Feminist Press, 2007) 68–85; R. Holtmaat, 'Preventing violence against women: the Due Diligence Standard and Article 5(a) CEDAW' in C. Benninger-Budel (ed.), *Due Diligence and its Application to Protect Women from Violence* (Leiden/Boston: Martinus Nijhoff Publishers, 2008) 225–39; and Cook and Cusack, *Gender Stereotyping*.

46 See for example, the important study of Cook and Cusack on gender stereotyping and the way in which judges deal with that issue, sometimes with a call on CEDAW. Cook and Cusack, *Gender Stereotyping*. A recent example of 'good judiciary practice' is the landmark decision of the Shah Alam High Court in Malaysia in the case of Noorfadilla where this Court deemed CEDAW directly applicable in a pregnancy discrimination case (Decision of 12 July 2011; on file with the author).

47 Although her article was published in 2011, Merry ('Gender justice and CEDAW') calls Bayefsky's study (*The UN Human Rights Treaty System: Universality at the Crossroads* (Ardsley, NY: Transnational Publishers, 2001)) 'recent' (at 52). Her most recent literature reference on CEDAW concerns Schöpp-Schilling and Flinterman's 2007 book *Circle of Empowerment*; she does not quote any other material between 2001 and 2010. She therefore misses out on many other relevant publications in terms of the topic of her article (see, for example, the publications mentioned in this chapter). Rosenblum, according to his footnotes, hardly read any documents from the CEDAW Committee and sticks to a quite literal interpretation of the Convention, based on the text as it was adopted in 1979 – as he himself acknowledges in footnote 24 of his article 'Unisex CEDAW'.

48 Christine Chinkin, who has taken part in the project to put together the *CEDAW Commentary*, has now fully acknowledged the Convention's great potential in contributing to the enhancement of women's human rights. Chinkin wrote the chapter on violence against women (VAW) in that commentary and was one of the editors of that book. See also E. Sepper, 'Confronting the "sacred and unchangeable": the obligation to modify cultural patterns under the Women's Discrimination Treaty', *University of Pennsylvania Journal of International Law* 30:2 (2008), 585–639.

49 The Dutch government actively stimulated legal research in the area of CEDAW. See van den Brink's chapter on the implementation of CEDAW in the Netherlands in this volume.

Committee to elaborate on a broader interpretation of the Convention's object and purpose. In these studies it was recognised that the Women's Convention not only addresses unequal treatment of women (as compared to men) in laws and public policies or in policies of employers, for example, but also addresses other forms of gender-specific discrimination such as violence against women, polygamy and the failure to provide adequate healthcare to women, both in public and private life.[50] It was found that the Convention admits to the existence of the unequal power relations between the sexes by taking an asymmetrical approach to discrimination, that it is quite unique in its recognition of the persistently damaging role of gender stereotypes, and that it entails a broad, encompassing approach to the principle of equality between the sexes, not only requiring formal and substantive equality but also striving for transformative equality. In the remaining part of this chapter I will concentrate on the Convention's role in combating gender stereotypes and in enhancing transformative equality.

5 The triple approach to equality in the Women's Convention

On the basis of an analysis of the nature and structure of the Convention by an independent commission of experts,[51] in 1998 the Dutch government adopted the view that the Convention's overall aim to eliminate all forms of discrimination against women can be divided into three sub-aims.[52] The CEDAW Committee, in its Concluding Observations on the second and third Country Reports of the Netherlands, stated in 2001 that it appreciated this work and in the same document subscribed

[50] See the CEDAW Committee's General Recommendations 12, 19, 21 and 24.

[51] See L. S. Groenman *et al.*, *Het vrouwenverdrag in Nederland anno 1997* (The Hague: Ministerie van SZW, 1997). The Groenman Commission (named after its chair) was installed by the Dutch government to write a report about the implementation of the Convention in the Netherlands. The present author was a member of this Commission. Their report was submitted to the Second Chamber of Parliament in 1998. A translation in English of the main chapters of this report is included as an appendix in Holtmaat, *Towards Different Law and Public Policy*. The Commission based itself on the historical background and a textual analysis of the Convention, on the General Recommendations and Concluding Comments of the Committee, and on the relevant legal literature up to the year 1996.

[52] This position was confirmed in the second and third Country Reports of the Netherlands to the CEDAW Committee (submitted in 2000, discussed by the CEDAW Committee in 2001).

to the Dutch analysis of the Convention's threefold aims.[53] In its General Recommendation No. 25 on temporary special measures on the ground of Article 4(1), adopted in January 2004,[54] the Committee confirmed that the object and purpose of the Convention is threefold:

1. to ensure full equality of women before the law and protection against discrimination in the public as well as the private sphere;
2. to improve the de facto position of women; and
3. to address prevailing gender relations and the persistence of gender-based stereotypes.

These three purposes reflect a threefold interpretation of the fundamental principle of equality. *Full equality between men and women*, a principle to which the Convention refers in many of its Articles, means much more than equality before and in the law. Of course, Article 2 makes it unambiguously clear that women have equal rights under the law and should not be treated differently purely *because* they are women. Women have the *right to formal equality*. In addition, the Convention in its Articles 3, 4 and 24 makes it clear that all appropriate measures need to be taken in order to achieve women's de facto equality with men. This means that sometimes (in the language of Article 4) temporary special measures are necessary. With the inclusion of the right to *substantive equality*, the Convention acknowledges that individual human beings, through place of birth, mental and physical capacities, wealth, development of the country, discrimination and a whole range of other factors, in fact have very different positions and possibilities in life. Women, in many cultures around the world, are in a position of inequality and oppression not only because of physical or biological differences, but also because of persistent political, social, economic and cultural discrimination against them.

The third mentioned objective of the Convention, that is addressing prevailing gender relations and the persistence of gender-based stereotypes, is laid down in Article 5, which provides that:

States Parties shall take all appropriate measures:

(a) to modify the social and cultural patterns of conduct of men and women, with a view to achieving the elimination of prejudices and

[53] 25th Session of the CEDAW Committee, July 2001, A/56/38, CEDAW/C/SR. 512 and 513, para. 196.

[54] CEDAW Committee, General Recommendation 25 on Article 4, para. 1, of the Convention on the Elimination of All Forms of Discrimination against Women, on temporary special measures (Thirteenth Session, 2004), paras. 6 and 7.

customary and all other practices that are based on the idea of the inferiority or the superiority of either of the sexes or on stereotyped roles for men and women; and

(b) to ensure that family education includes a proper understanding of maternity as a social function and the recognition of the common responsibility of men and women in the upbringing and development of their children, it being understood that the interest of the children is the primordial consideration in all cases.[55]

In short, the Article, in its two parts, calls for the modification of gender stereotypes and fixed parental gender roles.[56] It should be read in conjunction with Article 2(f), which requires that States Parties 'take all appropriate measures, including legislation, to modify or abolish existing laws, regulations, customs and practices which constitute discrimination against women'. Rebecca Cook writes that these Articles combined mean that States Parties are obliged to:

> reform personal status laws and to confront practices, for instance of religious institutions, that, while claiming to regard the sexes as different but equal, in effect preclude women from senior levels of authority and influence. These articles strongly reinforce the commitment to eliminate all forms of discrimination, since many pervasive forms of discrimination against women rest not on law as such but on legally tolerated customs and practices of national institutions.[57]

According to the CEDAW Committee, Article 5 means that the Convention acknowledges that gender stereotypes and fixed parental gender roles 'affect women not only through individual acts by individuals but also in law, and legal and societal structures and institutions'.[58] Therefore, the Convention not only addresses *personal convictions*, *cultural practices* and *traditional values*, but also addresses the *systemic and structural discrimination against women* that is embedded in the country's laws and

[55] The Article is part of the first section of the Convention, which contains the general obligations for the States Parties. These norms are to be regarded on their own merits, but they are also indicative for the interpretation of all other Articles of the Convention.

[56] See Holtmaat, 'Article 5' for a more extensive analysis of the content and scope of this Article.

[57] R. J. Cook, 'State accountability under the Convention on the Elimination of All Forms of Discrimination against Women' in R. J. Cook (ed.), *Human Rights of Women. National and International Perspectives* (Philadelphia: University of Pennsylvania Press, 1994) 228–56, at 239–40.

[58] CEDAW Committee, General Recommendation No. 25, para. 7. See also e.g. CEDAW Committee, Luxembourg (2000), A/55/38, CEDAW/C/SR.446 and 447, para. 404.

policies, and – in order to overcome the structural discrimination that results from that inequality – calls for *transformative equality* or 'equality as transformation'.[59]

It should be noted that, in this regard, the Women's Convention has taken the lead. After its adoption, similar provisions were included in many other international documents.[60] Some international documents use wording similar to that of Article 5.[61] A wide range of documents express the recognition of maternity as a positive social function and the sharing of responsibilities of parents as important values and approaches.[62] A very clear example may be found in the Committee on Economic, Social and Cultural Rights (CESCR) General Comment 16, where it is fully acknowledged that gender stereotypes and fixed parental gender roles stand in the way of the fulfilment of all of women's human rights.[63] The CESCR defines gender stereotyping as a form of discrimination against women,[64] thereby reflecting a wide acceptance of the CEDAW Committee's analysis of the causes and consequences of discrimination against women. Traditional gender roles, prejudices and stereotypes are seen by the CESCR and also by the Human Rights Committee (HRC) as important obstacles to the full enjoyment of women's social and economic rights.[65]

6 Article 5 and discrimination against women

Although Article 5 does not contain the word discrimination, and Article 1, in which discrimination is defined, does not mention gender stereotypes and fixed parental gender roles, these phenomena can be related to discrimination against women in two ways. A first line of reasoning is that, through the inclusion of Article 5, especially when read in combination with the Convention's Preamble, the Convention acknowledges that

59 Fredman, 'Beyond the dichotomy of formal and substantive equality' at 116. See also further below in this chapter.

60 See Cook and Cusack, *Gender Stereotyping* at 145–6 and 174.

61 For example, the Convention of Belém do Para: Articles 7(e) and 8(b); the Protocol to the Banjul Charter on the Rights of Women in Africa, Articles 2(2) and 4(d), and Articles 6 and 13.

62 For example, the Preamble and Article 18(1) of the CRC; Article 17 American Convention on Human Rights (ACHR); UN CCPR 'General Comment 19' (1990) UN Doc. HRI/GEN/1/Rev.1 para. 8.

63 UN CESCR General Comment 16 (2005) UN Doc. E/C.12/2005/4, para. 14.

64 UN CESCR General Comment 20 (2009) UN Doc. E/C.12/GC/20, para. 20.

65 For example, UN CESCR General Comment 16 (2005) UN Doc. E/C.12/2005/4, para. 14; UN CCPR General Comment 28 (2000) UN Doc. CCPR/C/21/Rev.1/Add.10, paras. 5 and 25.

gender stereotypes and fixed parental gender roles *lie at the base* or are a *root cause* of discrimination against women.[66] In that way, it looks as if Article 5 is not an integral part of the prohibition of discrimination under the Convention, but that it merely tells us something about the ultimate causes of discrimination.[67] Secondly, in some views, the inclusion of this provision in the Convention, especially when read in conjunction with Article 2(f), means that discrimination, as defined in Article 1, also covers *prejudices* and all *customs and practices that are based on the inferiority of women and on stereotyped roles for men and women*. This means that these phenomena should be seen as discriminatory in themselves.[68]

The CEDAW Committee sometimes points to stereotypes as *causing* discrimination and sometimes calls stereotypes *discriminatory per se*. Sometimes, both views are present in one text. An example thereof can be found in a Concluding Observation about Burundi:

> The Committee continues to be concerned about the persistence of patriarchal attitudes and deep-rooted stereotypes regarding the role and responsibilities of men and women in society, *which discriminate against women*. The Committee is also concerned that the preservation of negative cultural practices and traditional attitudes *serves to perpetuate women's subordination* in the family and society and constitutes a serious obstacle to women's enjoyment of their fundamental rights.[69]

It would be most helpful if the Committee, in a new General Recommendation on Article 5, would be more explicit and specific about the discriminatory nature of gender stereotyping and fixed parental gender roles.[70]

[66] This is also reflected in the Committee's appeal of 1986, where it remarks that it is necessary 'to overcome obstacles to equality *arising from* prejudices, customs or practices'. UN Doc. A/41/45, para. 365, as cited by M. Wadstein, 'Implementation of the UN Convention on the Elimination of All Forms of Discrimination against Women', *Human Rights Quarterly* 10 (1988) 5–21 at 13.

[67] For example, Wadstein, 'Implementation of the UN CEDAW', and Lijnzaad, 'Over rollenpatronen'.

[68] ECOSOC General Comment No. 20, E/C.12/GC/20, 25 May 2009, para. 20. S. Cusack and R. J. Cook, 'Combating discrimination on sex and gender' in C. Krause and M. Scheinin (eds.), *International Protection of Human Rights: A Textbook* (Åbo: Institute for Human Rights, Åbo Akademi University, 2008) at 222. See also R. J. Cook and S. Howard, 'Accommodating women's differences under the Women's Anti-Discrimination Convention', *Emory Law Journal* 56:4 (2007) 1039–91 at 1043.

[69] CEDAW Committee, *Concluding Observation: Burundi* (2008), CEDAW/C/BDI/CO/4, para. 17 (emphasis added).

[70] The CEDAW Committee issued General Recommendation No. 3 on Article 5 in its Sixth Session in 1987. See UN Doc. A/42/38. See also Cook and Cusack, *Gender Stereotyping* at 13 and 137ff., and Cusack's chapter in this volume.

7 Three strategies to eliminate discrimination against women

The three approaches to equality that were adopted by the CEDAW Committee should not be seen as competing ways of conceptualising this basic principle of human rights,[71] but should be seen as complementary to each other. The first five Articles of the Convention make clear that formal, substantive and transformative equality lie at the basis of a simultaneously applied (holistic) approach to combating discrimination against women. For that purpose, three different strategies could and should be applied by the States Parties to the Convention:

(1) a strategy of giving individuals a legal right (entitlement) to equal treatment before and in the law (an *Individual Rights Strategy*; *IRS*);
(2) a strategy of providing social support to those persons or groups of persons who have least opportunities to lead a meaningful life as a human being, for example to those who are disabled or poor, and/or who are discriminated against on the grounds of (inter alia) sex (a *Social Support Strategy*; *SSS*); and
(3) a strategy to take away the structural causes of such discrimination through a process of social and cultural change (*Strategy of Social and Cultural Change*; *SSCC*).[72]

This three-dimensional empowering approach may be illustrated with the example of violence against women (VAW).[73] When one examines the CEDAW Committee's Concluding Observations with respect to this issue, it is clear that the Committee discusses the necessity of measures in all three areas. It pleads for legal reform, especially in terms of prohibiting all kinds of VAW; for putting in place protective and preventive measures; and for putting an end to all gender stereotypes and cultural and religious practices that sustain the idea of women's inferiority to men or that in some way or another make VAW appear as an acceptable social or cultural practice.[74]

[71] Like the formal and substantive approach, which have been seen as competing interpretations of (legal) equality by many feminist legal scholars. See Fredman, 'Beyond the dichotomy of formal and substantive equality'.

[72] See for example, Groenman *et al.*, *Het vrouwenverdrag in Nederland anno 1997*, and Holtmaat, *Towards Different Law and Public Policy*.

[73] See Holtmaat, 'Preventing violence against women'.

[74] The 'case law' of the Committee on the issue of VAW has been analysed in great depth in Chinkin's contribution to the *CEDAW Commentary*.

8 Article 5 of the Women's Convention: the international legal basis for enhancing transformative equality

Articles 2–5 of the Convention, read together, instruct States Parties to adopt a comprehensive or holistic strategy to combat discrimination against women, aiming at formal, substantive *and* transformative equality.[75] Transformative equality, or 'equality as transformation',[76] aims at changing society in such a way that those features of existing cultures, religions or traditions, and of legal, social and economic structures that obstruct the equality and human dignity of women are subjected to fundamental change. This means that 'States parties are required to undertake a social re-ordering of their political economy, and the cultural valuations ascribed to men and women.'[77] This requirement has been adopted as an international legal obligation, where Article 5 'requires a modification of social and cultural patterns of conduct'.[78] In other words, it calls for 'a possible feminisation of culture, at least of the culture that is represented in the legal order'. [79] In this view, Article 5 embodies what could also be phrased as the *vehicle for cultural change*.[80]

This analysis of Article 5 was first elaborated in the work of the already mentioned Dutch Commission of independent experts who carried out an in-depth study into the nature and scope of the Women's Convention at the end of the 1990s.[81] On the basis of an analysis of the Committee's General Recommendations and Concluding Observations on Article 5, the Commission held that besides addressing individual beliefs and conduct of men and women, this provision calls for eradicating gender differences that have become an intrinsic part of a society's social and legal structures and systems.[82] As a consequence of this, States Parties not only have to put an end to direct and indirect discrimination against women,

[75] Groenman *et al.*, *Het vrouwenverdrag in Nederland anno 1997*; Holtmaat, *Towards Different Law and Public Policy*; Holtmaat and Tobler, 'CEDAW and the European Union's policy'; and Cook and Cusack, *Gender Stereotyping*.

[76] Fredman, 'Beyond the dichotomy of formal and substantive equality' at 116.

[77] Cusack and Cook, 'Combating discrimination on sex and gender' at 207. See also Cook and Cusack, *Gender Stereotyping* at 5.

[78] Fredman, 'Beyond the dichotomy of formal and substantive equality' at 116.

[79] Van Maarseveen, 'Internationaal vrouwenrecht' at 75.

[80] *Ibid.*; Groenman *et al.*, *Het vrouwenverdrag in Nederland anno 1997.*

[81] Groenman *et al.*, *Het vrouwenverdrag in Nederland anno 1997.*

[82] *Ibid.* at 27. After the publication of the Groenman report, the Dutch government ordered a follow-up study in which the content and scope of Article 5(a) of the CEDAW was investigated in more depth. See Holtmaat, *Towards Different Law and Public Policy.*

but they also have to reveal and replace the gender stereotypes that *underlie* existing laws and public policies.[83] The Commission argued that:

> [I]f this does not happen, the implementation of full equality before the law and a policy to improve the position of women could sometimes have contrary effects. The concepts and assumptions that are currently being used in law and public policies are often coloured by gender stereotypical relationships and expectations. If these concepts and assumptions are included in new legislation or new policies, this will lead to unwitting and unintentional reproduction of gender differences.[84]

The Commission concluded that on the basis of Article 5, States Parties are obliged to question the content of existing legal rights and duties from a gender perspective. This method or strategy 'creates the possibility that dominant (male) norms are not assumed to be self-evident. In a number of areas, this can mean that it is not *equal* rights or *equal* opportunities that must have priority, but that *other* rights must be developed or *other* opportunities must be offered'.[85]

The CEDAW Committee adopted the principle of transformative equality in 2004, when in General Recommendation No. 25 it acknowledged that measures must be taken 'towards a real transformation of opportunities, institutions and systems so that they are no longer grounded in historically determined male paradigms of power and life patterns'. [86]

9 Article 5 of the Women's Convention: freedom, autonomy and diversity

Article 5 not only subscribes to the principle of women's equality, but also expresses the principle of human autonomy or freedom, sometimes also phrased as the principle of diversity. Combating gender stereotypes and fixed parental gender roles is not only required in order to achieve full equality of women, but also – and perhaps foremost – these cultural transformations are required in order to achieve more freedom, autonomy and space for diversity for women.

[83] This methodology is further developed in Holtmaat, *Towards Different Law and Public Policy*, Chapters 15 and 16.
[84] Groenman *et al.*, *Het vrouwenverdrag in Nederland anno 1997* at 27.
[85] *Ibid.* Italics in original. See also Holtmaat, 'The power of legal concepts'.
[86] General Recommendation No. 25, para. 10.

Above, it was stated that the underlying presumption of the principles of human equality and dignity[87] is that *all* human beings in principle have an authentic desire to control their own lives and are deemed capable of making rational choices for what it means to be living a dignified and worthy life as a human being. Constructing firm ('closed') categories of human beings, and attributing a set of fixed (often negative) characteristics to those who are placed within a particular category, results in a deprivation of people's control over their own lives. The gendered categories of 'man' and 'woman' or 'male' and 'female' are examples of such fixed social and cultural constructions.[88] The *social and cultural patterns of conduct* and *stereotyped roles* that are addressed in Article 5, which are based on *prejudice* and on *traditional or customary ideas about the inferiority of women*, deny the individual woman the possibility to be a person in her own right and to utilise all of her human capacities and capabilities in order to lead a meaningful life according to her own interests and convictions.[89] Gender stereotypes and fixed parental gender roles therefore not only deny women the right to be treated respectfully as equal and dignified human beings, they also deny women the autonomy to live their lives according to their own interests and convictions about their personal and unique contributions to sustaining and developing humanity. Women (and men!) have a fundamental right not to be confined to constructed (essentialist) understandings of femininity or masculinity, or to prefixed (and fixated) female and male parental roles that are entrenched in their culture, tradition or religion, as well as in the main social and legal institutions or organisations of their society. In the words of Cook and Cusack: 'Any law, policy or practice that aims to promote substantive equality and non-discrimination must … honour the basic choices

87 The fact that the Preambles of the main Human Rights Covenants all mention equality and dignity in one breath already indicates that equality is not the sole foundational principle of human rights.

88 Gendered categories are often presented as 'natural', 'essential' or 'God-given', that is, as *eternal* and *unchangeable*. I have discussed the role of gender-essentialism in Holtmaat and Naber, *Women's Human Rights and Culture*.

89 M. Nussbaum, *Women and Human Development. The Capabilities Approach* (Cambridge University Press, 2000). See also Kang, 'The burdens of manliness' at 478, who argues that guaranteeing the right to self-definition is the main objective of (US) constitutional equality clauses: 'By the right to self definition, I mean the right not to be overly dominated by government in how I structure and give meaning to my identity.' The right to be free from gender stereotypes, in that sense, should also stretch to men, according to Kang.

women make (or would like to make) about their own lives, and enable them to shape or carve out their own identities.'[90]

The CEDAW Committee has made it clear that a correct implementation of the Convention requires 'the recognition that women can have various roles in society, not only the important role of mother and wife, exclusively responsible for children and the family, but also as an individual person and actor in her community and in the society in general'.[91] In this way, the Convention recognises that all human being are equal, have equal rights and deserve respect for their human dignity, but at the same time they may have very *diverse* ideas and wishes about what they actually want to do with their lives.[92] Therefore, the concepts of individual autonomy, freedom and diversity are crucial for a correct understanding of the content and scope of Article 5 and of the Convention as a whole.

A similar 'diversity principle' lies at the basis of all anti-discrimination clauses in international human rights law and in national constitutions, which ban unequal and undignified treatment on the basis of an individual belonging to a certain 'category' or 'class' of human beings. Some categorisations, like those on the basis of race or sex, are deemed to be so invidious that they are subjected to a 'strict scrutiny test' by the judiciary. As South African Supreme Court Justice Sachs clarified:

> [w]hat the Constitution requires is that the law and public institutions acknowledge the variability of human beings and affirm the equal respect and concern that should be shown to all as they are. At the very least, what is statistically normal ceases to be the basis for establishing what is legally normative ... What becomes normal in an open society, then, is not an imposed and standardised form of behaviour that refuses to acknowledge difference, but the acceptance of the principle of difference itself.[93]

For *all* women and men this 'diversity principle' is as important as the principle of equality per se. But it is important first and foremost for women and men who do not conform to dominant legal, social and cultural standards about what it means to be a female or male person. Women's

[90] Cook and Cusack, *Gender Stereotyping* at 68.

[91] CEDAW Committee, *Concluding Observations: Suriname* (2002), A/57/38 (part II), CEDAW/C/SR. 557, 558 and 566, para. 48. See also CEDAW Committee, *Concluding Observations: Uzbekistan* (2001), A/56/38, CEDAW/C/SR.500, 501 and 507, para. 169.

[92] Lijnzaad, 'Over rollenpatronen' at 57.

[93] Judgment in *National Coalition for Gay and Lesbian Equality* v. *Ministry of Justice*, South African Supreme Court 1999 1 SA 6 (CC), para. 143, as quoted by E. Bonthuys and C. Albertyn (eds.), *Gender, Law and Justice* (Cape Town: Juta, 2007) at 28.

sexuality and their reproductive capacity are crucial for the construction of gender stereotypes and fixed parental gender roles in all traditions and cultures and in all periods of human history up to the present time. This means that the construction of human sexuality as (exclusively) *heterosexual* forms part of the construction of patriarchal gender relations.[94] The most blatant transgression of the patriarchal female gender identity and her fixed gender (motherly) role is the lesbian woman who chooses to renounce a male sexual partner and thereby also rejects the protection of the male head of household, and all other forms of male supervision and control of her life.[95] As was discussed above,[96] the obligation to modify gender stereotypes and fixed parental gender roles is also of great importance to men who do not want to conform to their assigned 'masculine' identity and gender role. Beyond that, this obligation is equally important for all 'differently sexed' (intersex, transsexual) people and people with a 'different sexuality' (gay, lesbian and bisexual people).[97] Gender stereotypes and fixed parental gender roles directly affect the lives of all persons who renounce traditional heterosexual and patriarchal feminine and masculine gender identities and gender roles.[98] Through a wide interpretation of Article 5, all of these situations may be brought under the

[94] See J. Butler, *Gender Trouble: Feminism and the Subversion of Identity*, 1st edn (London/New York: Routledge, 1990) at 1–34 and 110–28 and J. Butler, 'Imitation and gender subordination' in D. Fuss (ed.), *Inside/Out: Lesbian Theories, Gay Theories* (New York: Routledge, 1991) at 13. See A. M. Gross, 'Sex, love, and marriage: questioning gender and sexuality rights in international law', *Leiden Journal of International Law* 21 (2008) 235–53. At 251, Gross summarises Butler's position as follows: 'the division in two genders as part of the institution of compulsory heterosexuality, (which) requires a binary polarised gender system since patriarchy and compulsory heterosexuality are only possible in a world built on such a hierarchised division'. Real liberation or emancipation of women and gay and lesbian people, according to this author, requires 'undoing gender', instead of accepting the thus prefixed gender categories and identities (as either being male/female or heterosexual/homosexual). Another way of expressing the same principle is saying that a *transformation* of gender and sexuality needs to take place. See also Gross, 'Sex, love, and marriage' at 252.

[95] Lesbian women being gang raped in order 'to cure them' from their outrageous 'abnormal' sexual preference, is an example of this kind of 'correction'. See for example, *Report of the UN Special Rapporteur on the Question of Torture and Other Cruel, Inhuman or Degrading Treatment or Punishment*, Commission on Human Rights, March 2006, UN Doc. E/CN.4/2006/6/Add.1, paras. 180 and 183.

[96] See text in footnotes 14 and 32.

[97] That is, different from the heterosexual norm and other than the binary male–female scheme.

[98] Cook and Cusack, *Gender Stereotyping* at 2.

scope of the Convention.[99] It seems that the Committee, although still in a careful way, is now willing to do so.[100]

10 States Parties' obligations to modify gender stereotypes and State sovereignty

The existence of gender stereotypes and fixed parental gender roles is linked to cultural patterns, customary rules, religious prescriptions or beliefs and traditions in a particular society or country.[101] This means that the international obligation to modify gender stereotypes and fixed parental gender roles runs against the vested interests of many stakeholders in *keeping women in their 'proper' (traditional) place.*[102] Often they justify or defend women's inequality or women's 'different' roles with the argument for the freedom of religion or the right to maintain or preserve a particular culture.[103] Yakin Ertürk, the former UN Special Rapporteur on violence against women, has observed that: 'despite the fact that the international community has recognised the universality of rights, identity politics and cultural relativist paradigms are increasingly employed to constrain in particular the rights of women'.[104] And in the words of

[99] It is therefore not necessary to 'unisex' CEDAW, as is argued by Rosenblum in 'Unisex CEDAW'. This author does discuss Article 5 of the CEDAW, but does not give much attention to its relevance for intersex and LGBT people.

[100] In 2009 the Committee recognised that women may be discriminated against on the grounds of their sexuality, thereby possibly including their homosexuality. However, it seems to be hesitant to use that word or to use the word lesbianism. See, for example, CEDAW Committee, *Concluding Observations: Guatemala*, CEDAW/C/GUA/CO7 (2009) para. 19, where it speaks of sexuality in general. It has mentioned sexual orientation and gender identity in CEDAW Committee, *Concluding Observations: Panama*, CEDAW/C/PAN/CO/7 (2010) para. 22. In its General Recommendations on older women (GR 27) and on Article 2 (GR 28), adopted in October 2010, the CEDAW Committee has explicitly mentioned sexual orientation and gender identity. See www.iglhrc.org/cgi-bin/iowa/article/takeaction/resourcecenter/1235.html (last accessed 11 January 2012).

[101] In the following, I will capture all of these phenomena under the word 'culture' or 'cultural' (without the quotation marks).

[102] See Holtmaat and Naber, *Women's Human Rights and Culture*, Chapter 3 for the description of various stakeholders.

[103] There is extensive international legal and academic debate about the 'clash' between women's human rights and the right to culture. See Holtmaat and Naber, *Women's Human Rights and Culture*, Chapter 3 para. 2.5. It is especially contested whether the right to culture prevails over women's human rights or vice versa.

[104] UN Special Rapporteur on Violence Against Women (VAW), *Report on Intersections between Culture and Violence against Women*, 17 January 2007, UN Doc. A/HRC/4/34, para. 68.

the Independent Expert in the Field of Cultural Rights, Farida Shaheed: '[T]he challenge is to ensure that the right to pursue, develop and preserve culture in all its manifestations is in consonance with and serves to uphold the universality, indivisibility and interdependence of all human rights.'[105]

Apart from individual men and women, heads of families and traditional or religious leadership, the State itself may be an important stakeholder in maintaining the status quo of unequal gender relations.[106] This is because the construction of a particular cultural specificity as regards 'true' gender relations may influence to a high degree a State's perception of its (presumed) essential national identity through which it distinguishes itself from other States.[107] The construction of particular gender identities and parental gender roles very much lies at the basis of the claimed identity of many (traditionalist) cultures, which are adopted and presented by political leaders or national governments as the one and only national culture.[108] National identities often coalesce around women's bodies and incorporate racial or ethnic judgements.[109] Therefore, States may have a great interest in maintaining or sustaining the existing gendered social and cultural order because this may (so to say) 'keep the country together'. Often, such culture is expressed in rules and practices that deny women's equality and curtail women's freedoms. These rules or practices are not just expressions of oppression or hatred of women, but serve to preserve and sustain the group's or nation's particular cultural or religious identity or even its very existence. Sometimes, a government goes as far as proclaiming that the prevailing gender relations within the family form 'the

105 Quote by Farida Shaheed, Independent United Nations Expert in the Field of Cultural Rights, in her first press Statement on 23 November 2009. See: www.ohchr.org/en/NewsEvents/Pages/DisplayNews.aspx?NewsID=9619&LangID=e (last accessed 20 July 2010).

106 As becomes apparent from the work of Ann Hellum, State resistance to women's equality does not only come from the side of (religious) dictatorships in the south. See Hellum's chapter in this volume and A. Hellum, 'The Global Equality Standard meets Norwegian sameness' in A. Hellum, S. Ali and A. Griffiths (eds.), *From Transnational Relations to Transnational Laws: Northern European Laws at the Crossroads* (London: Ashgate, 2010). An example of the ambivalent responses of States (and their organs) to the CEDAW is given in Ali's chapter in this volume.

107 Gross, 'Sex, love, and marriage'.

108 Most famous in this respect are two crucial symbols of cultural unity in France, consisting of the positive symbolic images of two women: Jeanne D'Arc and 'Marianne'.

109 L. Vollp, 'Blaming culture for bad behaviour', *Yale Journal of the Humanities* 12 (2000) 89–115 at 90.

foundation of the State'.[110] A particular construction of gender relations is often embedded in the State's constitution, in order for the State to distinguish itself from other States (e.g. from a State from which it has become independent, after a long duration of colonisation). An example is Article 41(2) of the Irish Constitution, which reads as follows:

> 1° In particular, the State recognises that by her life within the home, woman gives to the State a support without which the common good cannot be achieved.
> 2° The State shall, therefore, endeavour to ensure that mothers shall not be obliged by economic necessity to engage in labour to the neglect of their duties in the home.

This provision, according to the CEDAW Committee, reflects a stereotyped image of the roles of women 'in the home and as mothers'.[111] Demanding that a State Party modify gender stereotypes and fixed parental gender roles, as Article 5 does, in such cases strikes at the heart of the State's fundamental understanding of its own identity.

From this perspective, it will come as no surprise that there is strong (most often implicit) resistance by States to implement international provisions that oblige them to promote gender equality. This observation links up with important research findings from which it appears that 'States apparently are more willing to negotiate, in other words seem less attached to their sovereignty, when material issues are at stake, as opposed to normative questions'.[112] The conclusion from this research is that 'all States shared their reluctance to part with social and cultural practices', and that 'social values, more so than economic or military power, are the strongest aspects of global civil society's challenges to autonomy and legitimacy'.[113] This is even more so when the construction of fixed gender

[110] CEDAW Committee, *Concluding Observations: Guatemala* (1994), A/49/38, CEDAW/C/SR. 242 and 246, para. 70.

[111] CEDAW Committee, *Concluding Observations: Ireland* (1999), A/54/38, CEDAW/C/SR. 440 and 441, paras. 193–194. Catholic Ireland thus wanted to distinguish itself from Protestant Britain. See M. van den Brink, 'Gendered sovereignty? In search of gender bias in the international law concept of state sovereignty' in I. Boerefijn and J. Goldschmidt (eds.), *Changing Perceptions of Sovereignty and Human Rights. Essays in Honour of Cees Flinterman* (Antwerp: Intersentia, 2008) 65–83.

[112] See van den Brink, 'Gendered sovereignty?' at 73, who discusses the research of E. Friedman, K. Hochstetler and A. M. Clark, 'Sovereignty challenges and bargains on the environment, human rights, and women', *International Studies Quarterly* 44:4 (2000) 591–614.

[113] Van den Brink, 'Gendered sovereignty?' at 75, quoting Friedman *et al.*, 'Sovereignty challenges and bargains on the environment' at 611–12.

identities and parental gender roles lies at the basis of the national identity of a country, which is the case with many post-colonial and traditionalist countries that have strong links with certain religious beliefs or religious institutions.

From the very beginning the CEDAW Committee has acknowledged that a change of culture requires the strong political will of States Parties to do so effectively: '[M]embers emphasised that attitudes and behaviour could be changed if there was political will and broad support.'[114] Even if a State is willing to bow its head under international pressure or is voluntarily willing to accept international human rights standards, it may be very difficult for it to effectively implement these norms in the internal legal order as well as at the horizontal level (i.e. between private parties or citizens among themselves). This is particularly so when an international norm requires a change of well-established patterns of conduct that are based on tradition, religion, custom or culture of many of its inhabitants, as is the case with Article 5. In order to be able to implement this norm, it is necessary that the State is *legally* and *culturally* legitimised to enforce or even promote such change.[115] The necessary formal legal legitimisation for the implementation of Article 5 can be found in the fact that the State has ratified this Convention.[116] After ratification of a human rights convention, a national government – be it monistic or dualistic with respect to the effects of international law on its own legal system – may argue (for example in its Parliament, answering political opposition) that it is *obliged* to implement the norms that are included in it. However, cultural legitimisation, especially when it concerns equality between men and women, is far more difficult to achieve because it requires modifying or overcoming very deeply rooted gender stereotypes and fixed parental gender roles.

The effectiveness of programmes to modify gender stereotypes and fixed parental gender roles will most probably be very limited if the State Party internally lacks cultural legitimisation or symbolic validation to do so;[117] that is, if there is no connection with norms and values that

[114] CEDAW Committee, *Concluding Observations: Ecuador*, UN Doc.A/49/38, 13th Session (1994) para. 524.

[115] See C. Packer, *Using Human Rights to Change Tradition* (Antwerp/Oxford/New York: Intersentia, 2002) at 15.

[116] States Parties are obliged to implement international norms in good faith, and so on. See Cook, 'State accountability under the CEDAW' at 229ff. See also CEDAW Committee, *Concluding Observations: Portugal*, CEDAW/C/PRT/CO/7 (2008) para. 29.

[117] Hernández-Truyol, 'Out of the shadows'148ff.

(also) exist in its society, in particular with norms and values that women themselves consider to be of crucial importance for their lives and for the realisation of their human rights. States will certainly have difficulty finding this (internal) cultural legitimisation when there are important cultural majorities or even minorities that oppose women's equality. In such situations women's (equal) rights are often constructed as opposite to a nation's culture or to particular (minority or majority) religious rights. This makes implementation, even by governments who are highly committed to women's human rights, a very difficult issue. One of the strategies of advocates of women's human rights could be to help the State Party to enhance or broaden this necessary cultural legitimisation by way of an intercultural or cross-cultural dialogue about women's rights.

11 Enhancing a dialogue to avoid a clash between women's human rights and culture

In order to achieve a higher level of cultural acceptance of the norm of women's equality, it is important to stimulate a dialogue between the State and international actors (for instance the CEDAW Committee), but also to promote and enhance a dialogue between the State and the main internal stakeholders, that is, religious leaders, community leaders and (women's) NGOs.[118] Many academic commentators acknowledge that the only way out of a deadlock between opposite and fixed positions about women's human rights and culture is to engage in an intercultural or cross-cultural dialogue.[119] When one has to choose between, on the one hand, forcing some cultures to eradicate or abolish traditional practices that are deemed to violate women's human rights (and will thereby most likely generate even more resistance), and on the other hand the position of cultural relativism, in which moral or ethical values, including the values of women's equality and dignity, no longer seem to have any

[118] See the recommendations made by the CEDAW Committee in its Concluding Observations, as cited below in notes 123 and 124.

[119] For example, A. Shachar, *Multicultural Jurisdictions: Cultural Differences and Women's Rights* (Cambridge University Press, 2001); A. Phillips, *Multiculturalism without Culture*, (Princeton University Press, 2007); Nyamu, 'How should human rights and development respond to cultural legitimization'; and A. A. An-Na'im, 'Problems of universal cultural legitimacy' in A. A. An-Na'im and Francis M. Deng (eds.), *Human Rights in Africa. Cross Cultural Perspectives* (New York: Brookings Institution, 1990) 331–67.

weight, the most effective and safe middle way seems to be to try to start understanding each other and speaking with each other. In the words of Celestine Nyamu: 'The non-abolitionist approach, therefore, calls for a non-hegemonic human rights practice that incorporates the two simultaneous processes of internal discourse and cross-cultural dialogue, in order to find legitimacy for human rights principles within all cultures.'[120] Engaging in such a dialogue is also seen as the only way to guarantee that women's voices are heard in the process of the implementation of human rights standards.[121]

In its Concluding Observations, the CEDAW Committee often stresses the necessity of engaging in a dialogue with civil society about cultural changes that need to take place in order to put an end to discrimination against women. It 'urges the State party to intensify co-operation in this regard with civil society organisations, women's groups and community leaders, traditional and religious leaders, as well as teachers and the media'.[122] And it urges the State Party 'to undertake such efforts in co-ordination with a wide range of stakeholders, and involving all sectors of society, so as to facilitate social and cultural change and the creation of an enabling environment that is supportive of gender equality'.[123]

In order to do so, States Parties need to interpret their culture and traditions in a non-essentialist and dynamic manner. In the words of a General Comment of the ESCR Committee: 'The expression "cultural life" is an explicit reference to culture as a living process, historical, dynamic and evolving, with a past, a present and a future.'[124] This has also been acknowledged by the CEDAW Committee,[125] who

[120] Nyamu, 'How should human rights and development respond to cultural legitimization' at 393.

[121] Currently, this strategy is attracting more and more political and scholarly attention in all areas of legal pluralism or multilayered jurisdictions. See, for example, F. Fontanelli, G. Martinico and P. Carrozza, *Shaping Rule of Law Through Dialogue. International and Supranational Experiences* (Groningen: European Law Publishing, 2009).

[122] CEDAW Committee, *Concluding Observations: Nigeria*, CEDAW/C/NGA/6 (2008) para. 323.

[123] CEDAW Committee, *Concluding Observations: Nicaragua*, CEDAW/C/NIC/CO/6 (2007) para. 12.

[124] UN CESCR General Comment 21, 20 November 2009, UN DOC. E/C. 12/GC/21, para. 11.

[125] Here again I disagree with Merry ('Gender justice and CEDAW'), who states that the Convention and the Committee adhere to a static and essentialist view of culture and also use culture to describe other worlds, not their own. For a more detailed discussion on this issue, see Holtmaat and Naber, *Women's Human Rights and Culture* at para. 3.1.

in many Concluding Observations encourage States Parties to see culture as something that can be changed and that can (also) incorporate the human rights standards that are embodied in the Convention. An example of this stance can be found in a Concluding Observation on Jordan of 2007, where the Committee 'urges the State party to view culture as a dynamic aspect of the country's social fabric and life and therefore subject to change'.[126]

12 Concluding remarks

This chapter argues that the Women's Convention contains a holistic understanding of equality and that it includes the principle of freedom or diversity. On this basis, the Convention aims at eliminating all forms of discrimination against women by means of various strategies of legal, social and cultural reform. Especially in the last part of the chapter, it becomes clear that such reform meets with a lot of (often silent) resistance, and sometimes even with a vehement call upon other values and rights, such as the right to sustain and support cultures, traditions and religions, however oppressive these may be for women. It is not enough that Article 5 offers the legal legitimacy for the necessary changes in this respect; it is also required that States Parties and other stakeholders find the roads to broaden and strengthen the necessary cultural legitimisation for the process of modifying gender stereotypes and fixed parental gender roles. Thanks to the existence of Article 5, the Women's Convention is a revolutionary instrument that addresses the root causes of discrimination against women. However, in order for this instrument to become

[126] CEDAW Committee, *Concluding Observations: Jordan* (2007), CEDAW/C/EST/JOR/CO/4, para. 20. See also CEDAW Committee, *Concluding Observations: Mozambique* (2007), CEDAW/C/MOZ/CO/2, paras. 20 and 21 and CEDAW Committee, *Concluding Observations: Cook Islands* (2007), CEDAW/C/COK/CO/1, para. 23. We found a similar consideration for the first time in CEDAW Committee, *Concluding Observations: Angola* (2004), A/59/38/CEDAW/C/SR. 655 and 661, para. 147. The Committee in its earlier days at some points went rather far in suggesting that a particular culture or religious practice or conviction can and should be changed. See, for example, CEDAW Committee, *Concluding Observations: Libyan Arab Jamahiriya* (1974), A/49/38, CEDAW/C/SR.237 and 240, para. 130 and CEDAW Committee, *Concluding Observations: Pakistan* (2007), CEDAW/C/PAK/CO/3, para. 29. In the latter Concluding Observation the Committee 'calls on the State party to take prompt action to counteract the influence of non-State actors, which, through the misinterpretation of Islam and the use of intimidation and violence, are undermining the enjoyment by women and girls of their human rights'.

effective, all stakeholders in the advancement of women's human rights need to take steps in order to enhance the necessary cultural, social and legal changes. Improving the quality and effectiveness of transnational and local dialogues about women's human rights and culture is an important step in that direction.

4

The CEDAW as a legal framework for transnational discourses on gender stereotyping

SIMONE CUSACK

1 Introduction

The thirtieth anniversary of the adoption of the Convention on the Elimination of All Forms of Discrimination against Women (CEDAW) in 2009 provided an important opportunity to reflect on the contributions of this instrument to the advancement of women's human rights. It also provided a timely opportunity to consider how the CEDAW might be utilised more effectively in pursuit of this goal over the coming decades. During its first thirty years in operation, the CEDAW proved to be a catalyst for legal and policy reform, an effective tool in domestic litigation, advocacy and activism, and an important means of holding States Parties accountable for violations of women's human rights.[1] Yet much of the potential of the CEDAW for advancing women's human rights has yet to be realised. One area of considerable untapped potential is the obligations of States Parties in Articles 2(f)[2] and 5[3] of the CEDAW to modify or transform

The author would like to thank Rebecca J. Cook, Alexandra Timmer and the editors for their thoughtful comments on earlier drafts of this chapter. Thanks is also due to the participants of the *From Ratification to Implementation: CEDAW in International and National Law* Conference held in Oslo in 2010, for their helpful comments. Any errors are the responsibility of the author alone. While the author works as a Senior Policy/Research Officer at the Australian Human Rights Commission, this chapter does not necessarily reflect the views of the Commission.

[1] See generally A. Byrnes, 'The Convention on the Elimination of All Forms of Discrimination against Women and the Committee on the Elimination of Discrimination against Women: reflections on their role in the development of international human rights law and as a catalyst for national legislative and policy reform' [hereinafter 'The CEDAW and the CEDAW Committee'], UNSW Law Research Paper No. 2010–17 (2010).

[2] Article 2(f) requires States Parties to 'take all appropriate measures, including legislation, to modify or abolish existing laws, regulations, customs and practices which constitute discrimination against women'.

[3] Article 5(a) requires States Parties to 'take all appropriate measures' to 'modify the social and cultural patterns of conduct of men and women, with a view to achieving the

gender stereotypes and eliminate wrongful gender stereotyping. States Parties have made little progress in the implementation of these obligations, even though the 'persistence of stereotypical attitudes' has repeatedly been labelled a 'significant challenge to the practical realization of women's human rights', and there have been numerous calls to make the elimination of wrongful gender stereotyping 'a key element in all efforts to achieve the realization'[4] of those rights. This chapter argues that the CEDAW provides a powerful, yet largely unexplored, legal framework for addressing gender stereotyping. On the basis of that view, it seeks to bring the potential of Articles 2(f) and 5 to the fore, so that they might be capitalised on to the fullest extent possible.

The chapter begins in section 2 by briefly examining the concepts of gender stereotypes and gender stereotyping and outlining why stereotyping is a human rights issue. Section 3 outlines some of the reasons why the CEDAW has such potential as a framework for addressing gender stereotyping. It also identifies some of the limitations of using the CEDAW as a framework for addressing stereotyping and considers how those limitations might be overcome or, at the very least, their effects minimised. Responding to one of the limitations of the CEDAW framework identified in section 3, namely the lack of clarity surrounding States Parties' obligations in respect of gender stereotyping, section 4 offers a possible interpretation of the content and meaning of the obligations in Articles 2(f) and 5, applying the widely accepted tripartite framework of state obligations – the obligations to respect, protect and fulfil. Section 5 posits that the question of if and when gender stereotyping can be justified under the CEDAW will be one of the biggest interpretative challenges facing the Committee on the Elimination of Discrimination against Women (CEDAW Committee or Committee) moving forward. Assuming that stereotyping can sometimes be justified, section 5 briefly outlines some of the issues that the Committee will need to take into account when determining the circumstances in which stereotyping is a permissible

elimination of prejudices and customary and all other practices which are based on the idea of the inferiority or the superiority of either of the sexes or on stereotyped roles for men and women'. Article 5(b) requires States Parties to 'take all appropriate measures' to 'ensure that family education includes a proper understanding of maternity as a social function and the recognition of the common responsibility of men and women in the upbringing and development of their children'.

[4] Commission on the Status of Women, 54th Session, *Commemorating 30 Years of the Convention on the Elimination of All Forms of Discrimination against Women: Moderator's Summary*, 29 March 2010, UN Doc. E/CN.6/2010/CRP.12, paras. 10–11.

limitation of rights guaranteed by the CEDAW. Section 6 concludes by arguing that there are encouraging signs that indicate that States Parties' obligations to modify or transform gender stereotypes and eliminate wrongful gender stereotyping will be a central theme of the Committee's work over the coming decades. It suggests that strong leadership from the Committee, as well as other international and regional human rights treaty bodies, will ensure that the threat of stereotyping is taken seriously. It is argued that this will, in turn, likely produce measureable gains in the advancement of women's human rights and the achievement of substantive equality.

2 Defining and conceptualising gender stereotyping

Gender stereotyping was one of the key issues singled out by the framers of the CEDAW, along with such other issues as equality in marriage and family relations and equality in political and public life, as requiring the attention of States Parties. It is an issue that continues to be singled out today as a 'significant challenge to the practical realization of women's human rights'.[5] There remains much confusion, however, about the meaning of the terms 'gender stereotype' and 'gender stereotyping'. Moreover, there has been limited discussion of the reasons why gender stereotyping is problematic from a human rights perspective. In an attempt to disrupt the status quo, section 2.1 offers a possible interpretation of the meaning of the terms gender stereotype and gender stereotyping. Section 2.2 then provides an explanation of why gender stereotyping is a human rights issue.

2.1 Understanding gender stereotypes and gender stereotyping

Almost all of us, if asked, could provide examples of gender stereotypes. The responses elicited to such a request would invariably include common gender stereotypes such as 'women are nurturing' and 'men are breadwinners'. Not all of us, however, would be able to articulate clearly what the terms 'gender stereotype' or 'gender stereotyping' actually mean. If pressed further, many of us would also struggle to distinguish plainly between the meaning of those terms and that of related but distinct concepts, such as social and cultural norms, myths, prejudices, stigma and generalisations. While the inability to pinpoint a definition or definitions of these terms may be of little consequence in our day-to-day lives,

[5] *Ibid.*

certainty of meaning becomes increasingly important where legal obligations are involved. It is curious, then, that little attention has been paid by international human rights treaties and treaty bodies to elucidating the meaning of the terms that form the essence of States Parties' obligations to modify gender stereotypes and eliminate wrongful gender stereotyping. What, for example, are the 'gender stereotypes' that States Parties are expected to modify or transform?

One approach, followed in this chapter, is to define a gender stereotype as a generalised view or preconception about the attributes or characteristics that are or ought to be possessed by, or the roles that are or should be performed by, women and men (e.g. women are empathetic, men are athletic).[6] Understood in this way, a gender stereotype operates to create assumptions about the attributes or characteristics possessed by individuals and the roles that they perform, based on their membership in a particular sex or gender group; all of the dimensions of personality that make individuals unique are filtered through the lens of a stereotypical belief about their sex or gender.[7] If the term gender stereotype refers to a generalised view or preconception based on sex or gender, the term gender stereotyping refers to the practice of ascribing a stereotypical belief to an individual, by reason only of her or his membership in the social group of women or men.[8] It is the practice of applying 'gender stereotypic knowledge in forming an impression of an individual man or woman'.[9] Where the stereotypes of women as mothers and carers are at play, for example, it is presumed that an individual woman strives to be and will become a mother and a carer, irrespective of her distinctive reproductive health capacity, physical and emotional circumstances, and individual priorities.[10]

[6] See R. J. Cook and S. Cusack, *Gender Stereotyping: Transnational Legal Perspectives* (Philadelphia: University of Pennsylvania Press, 2010) at 1, 9, 20, 25–31. Gender stereotypes come in varied and overlapping forms, including sex stereotypes, sexual stereotypes, sex-role stereotypes and compounded stereotypes. Sex stereotypes are preconceptions concerning the physical, including biological, emotional and cognitive, attributes or characteristics that are or should be possessed by women and men (e.g. women are physically and mentally weak). Sexual stereotypes are preconceptions about the sexual characteristics or qualities that women and men are believed or expected to possess (e.g. men have strong libidos). Sex-role stereotypes are preconceptions concerning the roles that women and men perform or are expected to perform, and the types of behaviours to which they are expected to conform (e.g. women should be mothers and caregivers). Compounded gender stereotypes are preconceptions about different subgroups of women and men that result from the ascription of attributes, characteristics or roles based on sex or gender and one or more other traits, such as disability or sexual orientation (e.g. women with a disability are asexual).

[7] See *ibid.* at 9. [8] See *ibid.* at 12, 20. [9] *Ibid.* at 20. [10] See *ibid.* at 11.

Gender stereotypes often embody dominant social and cultural norms, meaning the formal and informal rules that govern the values, beliefs, attitudes and behaviours that a particular community or culture deems acceptable (e.g. dress codes, rules of etiquette, beauty standards). However, social and cultural norms can underpin laws, regulations, customs and practices that discriminate against women, independent of gender stereotypes. Examples include social and cultural norms that operate to deny women access to property or inheritance, sanction the unlawful killing of women accused of witchcraft, encourage women (but not men) to undergo plastic surgery to meet dominant beauty standards, or condone forced marriage. Article 2(f) requires States Parties to take steps to address all violations that are based on discriminatory social and cultural norms and not just those norms that give rise to harmful gender stereotypes and/or the practice of wrongful gender stereotyping. Where a gender stereotype is based on or embodies a social and cultural norm and the stereotype is applied to a woman in ways that violate her rights under the CEDAW, States Parties are required to eliminate the practice of wrongful gender stereotyping and modify or transform the operative norm and the operative gender stereotype.

2.2 *Gender stereotyping as a human rights concern*

The goal of addressing gender stereotyping is not the construction of a world free of all gender stereotypes, since stereotypes can, and do, perform important social functions. One such function is to maximise simplicity and predictability.[11] It was Walter Lippmann who, in 1922, first suggested that:

> the real environment is altogether too big, too complex, and too fleeting for direct acquaintance. We are not equipped to deal with so much subtlety, so much variety, so many permutations and combinations. And although we have to act in that environment, we have to reconstruct it on a simpler model before we can manage it.[12]

The goal, instead, is modification or transformation of stereotypical beliefs that are *harmful* (for example, stereotypes 'based on the idea of the inferiority or the superiority of either of the sexes'[13]) and elimination of the practice of *wrongful gender stereotyping*, meaning those forms of gender

[11] See *ibid.* at 14–16.
[12] See W. Lippmann, *Public Opinion* (1922; rep. New York: Macmillan, 1957) at 16.
[13] Article 5(a) CEDAW.

stereotyping that result in discrimination or violations of other rights and freedoms, such as the right to a fair trial or the freedom from gender-based violence against women. As the CEDAW Committee recently explained, the elimination of all forms of discrimination against women and the achievement of substantive equality requires States Parties 'to modify and transform gender stereotypes and eliminate wrongful gender stereotyping, a root cause and consequence of discrimination against women'.[14]

Refraining from wrongful gender stereotyping enables states to treat individuals with dignity and respect and honour the choices that they make (or would like to make) about their own lives, including what it means for them to be a woman or a man or a person of another gender.[15] The harm of failing to abstain from wrongful gender stereotyping lies in using the power of the state to prescribe certain attributes, characteristics or roles to individuals based on their sex or gender, and in exercising that power in ways that regulate, penalise or stigmatise non-conforming individuals. An example is a law enforcement officer who fails to properly investigate a reported abduction and dismisses the significance of the alleged crime because the female victim was wearing a short skirt at the time of her disappearance, in defiance of stereotypical norms that women should be modest.[16] States might have particular views about the nature of the sexes or preferences for how they should behave or the roles they should perform in society. However, they must not unreasonably impose their stereotypical views or preferences on individual women and men[17] or infringe the rights of non-conforming individuals.[18]

[14] CEDAW Committee, *R.K.B.* v. *Turkey*, Communication No. 28/2010, 13 April 2012, UN Doc. CEDAW/C/51/D/28/2010 (2012), at para. 8.8.

[15] See R. Holtmaat, *Towards Different Law and Public Policy: The Significance of Article 5a CEDAW for the Elimination of Structural Gender Discrimination* (The Hague: Reed Business Information, 2004) at xii. See also Cook and Cusack, *Gender Stereotyping* at 112.

[16] See CEDAW Committee, *Report on Mexico Produced by the Committee on the Elimination of Discrimination against Women Under Article 8 of the Optional Protocol to the Convention, and Reply from the Government of Mexico*, 27 January 2005, UN Doc. CEDAW/C/2005/OP.8/MEXICO [hereinafter *Ciudad Juárez Inquiry*], paras. 57, 67; IACtHR, *González et al. ('Cotton Field')* v. *Mexico*, Judgment, 16 Nov. 2009, Series C No. 205, paras. 152–154, 196–208, 398–402.

[17] The CEDAW Committee has, for instance, criticised Ireland for institutionalising stereotypes of women as mothers and homemakers in its Constitution, and strongly urged it to stop perpetuating those stereotypes, including through its supreme law: CEDAW Committee, *Concluding Observations: Ireland*, UN Doc. CEDAW/C/IRL/CO/4–5, 22 July 2005, paras. 24–25.

[18] See Cook and Cusack, *Gender Stereotyping* at 111–112. See also D. A. Widiss, E. L. Rosenblatt and D. NeJaime, 'Exposing sex stereotypes in recent same-sex marriage jurisprudence', *Harv. J.L. and Gender* 30 (2007) 461–505 at 464, 469, 488; R. B. Siegel, 'The new

Failure to take reasonable steps to protect women against wrongful gender stereotyping by private actors (for example, employers, religious organisations, media) makes states complicit in the resultant harms to women and the perpetuation of this harmful practice, more generally. Whether through omissions of action or condoning wrongful gender stereotyping by private actors, states' failure to protect legitimises gender stereotypes and creates a culture of impunity around their use, further strengthening their resilience across different social sectors and over time. For instance, repeated failings on the part of many states to work with the media to promote positive and non-stereotypical portrayals of women has helped to fuel an industry already rife with invidious stereotyping of women.[19] Another example is the failure of some states to address gender stereotypes that facilitate polygyny[20] and fuel the spread of HIV/AIDS.[21]

States must ensure that individuals are free to make their own choices about what it means for them to be a woman or a man and to have those choices respected and honoured – they must ensure that 'all human beings, regardless of sex, are free to develop their personal abilities, pursue their professional careers and make choices without the limitations set by stereotypes, rigid gender roles and prejudices'.[22] Law policies, programmes and practices need to be restructured and reformulated in order to ensure that they do not perpetuate women's oppression, including by devaluing women, limiting their life plans or reflecting patriarchal attitudes that attribute subservient characteristics and roles to women through gender stereotypes. There also needs to be a transformation of stereotypical views of men and women in the political economy (i.e. the division of labour and resources) and in the cultural valuations ascribed to men and women (i.e. the privileging of masculinity and devaluing of femininity). This will require the adoption of measures to ensure that,

politics of abortion: an equality analysis of woman-protective abortion restrictions', *U. Ill. L. Rev.* (2007) 991–1053 at 1042–3, 1048.

[19] See for example, CEDAW Committee, *Concluding Observations: Albania*, 16 September 2010, UN Doc. CEDAW/C/ALB/CO/3, para. 25; CEDAW Committee, *Concluding Observations: Russia*, 16 August 2010, UN Doc. CEDAW/C/USR/CO/7, para. 21.

[20] See CEDAW Committee, General Recommendation No. 21, UN Doc. A/49/38 (Supp) at 1 (1994), para. 14. See generally L. M. Kelly, 'Polygyny and HIV/AIDS: a health and human rights approach', *Journal for Juridical Science* 31:1 (2006) 1–38; R. J. Cook and L. M. Kelly, *Polygyny and Canada's Obligations Under International Human Rights Law* (Ottawa: Department of Justice, Canada, 2006).

[21] See generally Kelly, 'Polygyny and HIV/AIDS'.

[22] CEDAW Committee, General Recommendation No. 28, 16 December 2010, UN Doc. CEDAW/GC/28, para. 22.

among others things, women's individual worth, talents and capabilities are recognised, and those activities and roles traditionally associated with women are valued.

3 The added value of the CEDAW in addressing wrongful gender stereotyping

Before writing *Gender Stereotyping: Transnational Legal Perspectives*,[23] Professor Rebecca J. Cook and I undertook extensive research on gender stereotyping. Our research showed that legal discourses on gender stereotyping had been limited mainly to national concerns and were concentrated in a small handful of countries (e.g. America, Canada, South Africa). While we learnt, and continue to learn, much from the depth and richness of domestic-centred debates, we found that the global reach of gender stereotypes demands a broader and more inclusive conversation about the practice and its consequent social and legal harms. We hypothesised that discourses on gender stereotyping would benefit immeasurably from insights gained from transnational legal perspectives.[24] In this hypothesis we were guided by the wisdom of the former Canadian Supreme Court Justice Claire L'Heureux-Dubé, who observed that a debate that encompasses international and comparative perspectives on wrongful gender stereotyping may 'provide a much-needed external perspective on the myths and stereotypes that may continue to permeate the values and laws of our own communities and cultures'.[25]

Proceeding on the basis of our belief about the importance and value of transnational perspectives, Professor Cook and I argued that the CEDAW provides a leading framework for debates about gender stereotyping.[26] In view of the fact that the current volume explores the added value of the CEDAW, it is perhaps timely to return to the decision we made in writing *Gender Stereotyping* to use the CEDAW. In so doing, I hope to articulate the reasons why we concluded that the CEDAW provides a sound legal framework for transnational discourses on gender stereotyping. How, in

[23] Cook and Cusack, *Gender Stereotyping* (outlining a methodology for addressing wrongful gender stereotyping).

[24] *Ibid.* at 7–8.

[25] The Honourable Madame Justice C. L'Heureux-Dubé, 'Beyond the myths: equality, impartiality, and justice', *Journal of Social Distress and the Homeless* 10:1 (2001) 87–104 at 101. See also J. Nedelsky, 'Embodied diversity and the challenges to law', *McGill L. J.* 42 (1997) 91–117 at 107.

[26] Cook and Cusack, *Gender Stereotyping* at 3–4.

other words, at least in our view, does the legal framework articulated in the CEDAW add value to transnational discourses on gender stereotyping? And what, if any, limitations need to be overcome to ensure the future integrity of this framework?

3.1 *A robust legal framework*

3.1.1 Express obligations to address gender stereotyping

The CEDAW is one of few legal instruments to expressly require states to address gender stereotyping and that provides a set of binding international legal standards against which the acts and omissions of states in relation to stereotyping can be measured.[27] In general terms, the Preamble[28] and Articles 2(f) and 5 of the CEDAW expressly require States Parties to modify or transform gender stereotypes (for example, through public education campaigns) and eliminate wrongful gender stereotyping (for example, by amending a law that enforces a gender stereotype). Article 10(c) of the CEDAW contains express obligations to address gender stereotyping in the field of education.[29] In addition to these express obligations, the CEDAW Committee has applied Articles 2(f) and 5(a) to the fields covered in Articles 6 to 16 of the CEDAW (for example, health, employment, marriage and family relations). In so doing, it has sent a clear message that it views the obligations in Articles 2(f) and 5(a) not only as freestanding obligations but also as 'overarching, cross-cutting obligations that need to be read in conjunction with other human rights

[27] For examples of other human rights treaties that require the elimination of wrongful stereotyping, see Protocol to the African Charter on Human and Peoples' Rights on the Rights of Women in Africa, OAU Doc. CAB/LEG/66.6, entered into force 25 November 2005, Articles 2(2), 4(2)(d), 12(1)(b); Inter-American Convention on the Prevention, Punishment and Eradication of Violence against Women, OAS/Ser.L/V/1.4 rev., entered into force 5 March 1995, Articles 6(b), 8(b). In the absence of express obligations, some courts and treaties bodies have interpreted the rights to non-discrimination and equality as requiring the elimination of wrongful stereotyping: see, for example, Committee on Economic, Social and Cultural Rights, General Comment No. 16, 11 August 2005, UN Doc. E/C.12/2005/4, paras. 11, 14, 19.

[28] CEDAW, Preamble para. 14 (providing 'that a change in the traditional role of men as well as the role of women in society and in the family is needed to achieve full equality between men and women').

[29] Article 10(c) CEDAW (providing that States Parties shall take all appropriate measures to eliminate 'any stereotyped concept of the roles of men and women at all levels and in all forms of education by encouraging coeducation and other types of education which will help to achieve this aim and, in particular, by the revision of textbooks and school programmes and the adaptation of teaching methods').

and fundamental freedoms, because gender stereotyping does not exist in isolation'.[30]

The obligations in Articles 2(f) and 5(a) extend further still, to rights not expressly guaranteed under the CEDAW but which are recognised under other treaties or customary international law and have an impact on the elimination of all forms of discrimination against women and the achievement of substantive equality.[31] In *Karen Tayag Vertido* v. *The Philippines*, for example, the Committee held the Philippines legally accountable for wrongful gender stereotyping that affected, inter alia, the victim's ability to access a fair and just trial.[32] In reaching its finding, the Committee observed that 'stereotyping affects women's right to a fair and just trial and … the judiciary must take caution not to create inflexible standards of what women or girls should be or what they should have done … based merely on preconceived notions'.[33] The Committee made this finding even though the right to a fair trial is not expressly guaranteed in the CEDAW.[34]

3.1.2 Obligations to address gender stereotyping are central to the achievement of substantive equality

Another reason that the CEDAW adds value to transnational discourses on gender stereotyping is that the Committee has made it clear that the obligations in Articles 2(f) and 5 to 'address prevailing gender relations and the persistence of gender-based stereotypes' are *central* to the elimination of all forms of discrimination against women and the achievement of substantive equality.[35] The immediate consequence of the Committee's

[30] Cook and Cusack, *Gender Stereotyping* at 75. See for example, CEDAW Committee, General Recommendation No. 27, 16 December 2010, UN Doc. CEDAW/C/GC/27, para. 16.

[31] See generally CEDAW Committee, General Recommendation No. 28 at para. 7. See also Andrew Byrnes, 'Article 1' in M. A. Freeman, C. Chinkin and B. Rudolf (eds.), *The UN Convention on the Elimination of All Forms of Discrimination against Women: A Commentary* (Oxford University Press, 2012) 51–70 at 62.

[32] CEDAW Committee, *Karen Tayag Vertido* v. *The Philippines*, Communication No. 18/2008, 22 September 2010, UN Doc. CEDAW/C/46/D/18/2008 (2010), paras. 8.2–8.8. See also *R.K.B.* v. *Turkey* at paras. 8.7–8.8; CEDAW Committee, *V.K.* v. *Bulgaria*, Communication No. 20/2008, 27 September 2011, UN Doc. CEDAW/C/49/D/20/2008 (2011), paras. 9.11–9.12.

[33] *Karen Tayag Vertido* v. *The Philippines* at para. 8.4.

[34] Elements of the right to a fair trial are protected in Article 15(1) of the CEDAW, which provides that 'States Parties shall accord to women equality with men before the law'.

[35] See CEDAW Committee, General Recommendation No. 25, 30 January 2004, UN Doc. A/59/38, para. 7. The centrality of States Parties' obligations in respect of wrongful

characterisation of these obligations is acknowledgment of the significance of the obligations and States Parties' compliance with them, for the recognition, exercise and enjoyment of women's human rights. Such acknowledgment emphasises that efforts to eliminate direct and indirect discrimination and improve women's de facto position in society will only go so far toward achieving substantive equality, unless they are also accompanied by measures to transform structural inequality that stems from, inter alia, wrongful gender stereotyping.[36] A further consequence of the Committee's characterisation is that reservations that seek to limit or qualify the obligations of States Parties to address gender stereotyping are likely to be declared incompatible with the object and purpose of the treaty and, thus, impermissible pursuant to Article 28(2) of the CEDAW.[37]

3.1.3 Widespread recognition of obligations to address gender stereotyping

The obligations in the CEDAW to modify or transform gender stereotypes and eliminate wrongful gender stereotyping are recognised by, and binding on, almost all Member States of the United Nations.[38] The corollary of widespread international support for the CEDAW is that it provides a foundation for transnational discourses that is already recognised by the overwhelming majority of states around the world. By ratifying or acceding to the CEDAW, States Parties effectively agreed to a common framework for discussions about gender stereotyping (among other issues) that is not limited by any one domestic legal system but, rather, supports the

gender stereotyping is reinforced in the Preamble of the CEDAW, which acknowledges 'that a change in the traditional role of men as well as the role of women in society and the family is needed to achieve full equality' and was echoed recently by the Committee when it affirmed that Article 2 of the CEDAW, including Article 2(f), is 'the very essence of the obligations of States parties under the Convention'. See also CEDAW Committee, General Recommendation No. 28 at para. 41.

36 See generally R. Holtmaat, this volume; S. Fredman, this volume; S. Fredman, 'Beyond the dichotomy of formal and substantive equality: towards a new definition of equal rights' in I. Boerefijn *et al.* (eds.), *Temporary Special Measures: Accelerating de facto Equality of Women Under Article 4(1) UN Convention on the Elimination of All Forms of Discrimination against Women* (Antwerp, Oxford, New York: Intersentia, 2003) 111–18.

37 Article 28(2) CEDAW (providing that '[a] reservation incompatible with the object and purpose of the present Convention shall not be permitted').

38 As at the time of writing, 187 states had ratified or acceded to the CEDAW, 104 of which had also ratified or acceded to the Optional Protocol to the Convention on the Elimination of All Forms of Discrimination against Women 2131 UNTS 83, entered into force 22 December 2000.

sharing of external perspectives on gender stereotyping. That is not to suggest, however, that the CEDAW Committee assumes that there is only one correct approach to addressing gender stereotyping. An advantage of using the CEDAW as a framework for transnational discourses is that it allows for the adoption by States Parties of nuanced and flexible solutions to the varied individual and structural experiences of wrongful gender stereotyping. And it does this while still raising awareness of women's collective experiences of gender stereotyping, including through the reporting procedure.

While support for, and the perceived legitimacy of, the CEDAW have come under attack due to high numbers of reservations and declarations, these critiques unravel, even if only in relation to Articles 2(f) and 5, in the face of indications from the Committee that States Parties' attempts to evade their obligations to address gender stereotyping are unlikely to be tolerated due to their central role in the achievement of substantive equality.[39] Moreover, while general reservations to Article 2, including Article 2(f), may be high, States Parties seem less attached to their sovereignty where Article 5 is concerned, as evidenced in the comparatively low number of reservations made by States Parties to this provision.[40] It is also noteworthy that no other international or regional human rights treaty that expressly requires States Parties to address gender and/or other forms of stereotyping enjoys the same level of support or recognition as the CEDAW.[41]

3.1.4 Beyond stereotypes of women

A further reason that the CEDAW adds value to transnational debates about gender stereotyping is that it requires States Parties to address gender stereotypes of men, in addition to gender stereotypes of women.[42] The

[39] See section 3.1.2.

[40] See United Nations Treaty Collection, available at: http://treaties.un.org/ (last accessed 1 February 2013).

[41] *Ibid.*

[42] In a departure from other provisions in the CEDAW that focus almost exclusively on women (e.g. 'suppress all forms of traffic in women') or on men only in relation to women or as a yardstick for equality (e.g. 'equality between men and women'), Article 5(a) requires the modification or transformation of gender stereotypes, and the elimination of wrongful gender stereotyping, of both women and men. The obligations in Article 5(a) to address gender stereotyping of both sexes/genders are echoed in the Preamble to the CEDAW, which stresses that 'a change in the traditional role of men as well as the role of women in society and in the family is needed to achieve full equality'. The obligations of States Parties to address the full spectrum of gender stereotypes were affirmed implicitly in the *Vertido* Case, when the Committee held the Philippines accountable for the decision of a

framers of the CEDAW appear to have understood that gender stereotypes are relational in nature (i.e. they tend to assign women and men distinct yet mutually reinforcing attributes, characteristics and roles) and that stereotypes of women and men therefore need to be examined concurrently. The framers also appear to have understood that wrongful gender stereotyping not only disadvantages women, but also men[43] and society in general and that focusing exclusively on gender stereotypes of women would, to paraphrase Nancy Levit, leave umbilical parts of the problem of wrongful gender stereotyping unresolved.[44] The focus of the CEDAW on gender stereotypes of women and men is to be welcomed, therefore, as it requires States Parties to take the relational quality of gender stereotypes into account, examine how the construction of masculinities (in addition to the construction of femininities) fosters gender hierarchies and male dominance, and address the full range of harms caused by wrongful gender stereotyping.

3.1.5 State accountability for wrongful gender stereotyping

States Parties can be held legally accountable for their failures to comply with the obligations in Articles 2(f) and 5, either through the periodic reporting procedure in Article 18 of the CEDAW[45] or the

trial court judge to acquit the accused of rape based on gender stereotypes of women and men, rather than law or fact. See *Karen Tayag Vertido* v. *The Philippines*.

[43] The hidden price men may pay for being stereotyped on the basis of their sex and/or gender includes: marginalisation of men who are battered, raped or sexually harassed; overrepresentation of men (especially certain subgroups of men) in the criminal justice system; impaired access to caring and nurturing roles, both in private and professional settings; physical and psychological harms of warfare; and physical harm resulting from high-risk behaviour engaged in to prove one's so-called 'manliness'. See generally N. E. Dowd, N. Levit and A. McGinley, 'Feminist Legal Theory meets Masculinities Theory' in F. R. Cooper and A. C. McGinley (eds.), *Masculinities and Law: A Multidimensional Approach* (New York University Press, 2012); N. E. Dowd, *The Man Question: Male Privilege and Subordination* (New York University Press, 2010); J. M. Kang, 'The burdens of manliness', *Harv. J.L. and Gender* 33 (2010) 477–507; D. S. Cohen, 'Keeping men "men" and women down: sex segregation, anti-essentialism and masculinity', *Harv. J.L. and Gender* 33 (2010) 509–53; R. Collier, 'Masculinities, law, and personal life: towards a new framework for understanding men, law, and gender', *Harv. J.L. and Gender* 33 (2010) 431–75; N. E. Dowd, 'Asking the man question: masculinities analysis and feminist theory', *Harv. J.L. and Gender* 33 (2010) 415–30; J. C. Williams and S. Bornstein, 'The evolution of "FReD": family responsibilities discrimination and developments in the law of stereotyping and implicit bias', *Hastings L.J.* 59 (2008) 1311–58.

[44] N. Levit, 'Feminism for men: legal ideology and the construction of maleness', *UCLA L. Rev.* 43 (1995–6) 1037–116 at 1054.

[45] Article 18 CEDAW (providing that 'States Parties undertake to submit … for consideration by the Committee, a report on the legislative, judicial, administrative or

Communication[46] or Inquiry[47] procedures of the Optional Protocol to the Convention on the Elimination of All Forms of Discrimination against Women (Optional Protocol). Attempts to hold States Parties accountable for wrongful gender stereotyping have been successful in the majority of Communications decided on the merits in which stereotyping was raised as an issue for the Committee's consideration,[48] as well as in the Committee's first Inquiry.[49] For example, in *L.C.* v. *Peru* the Committee found that the State Party, through the actions of medical staff at a public hospital, had engaged in wrongful gender stereotyping (among other things), in violation of Article 5 of the CEDAW. In the Committee's expert view, the decision of medical staff to delay necessary spinal surgery and refusal to perform an abortion on L.C., a

other measures which they have adopted to give effect to the provisions of the present Convention and on the progress made in this respect'). Because use of the periodic reporting procedure to address wrongful gender stereotyping has been examined elsewhere, this chapter focuses mainly on relevant Optional Protocol jurisprudence. See Holtmaat, this volume; R. Holtmaat, 'Article 5' in M. A. Freeman, C. Chinkin and B. Rudolf (eds.), *The Convention on the Elimination of All Forms of Discrimination against Women: A Commentary* (Oxford University Press, 2012) 141–68.

[46] Article 2 Optional Protocol (providing 'Communications may be submitted by or on behalf of individuals or groups of individuals, under the jurisdiction of a State Party, claiming to be victims of a violation of any of the rights set forth in the Convention by that State Party').

[47] Article 8(1) Optional Protocol (providing '[i]f the Committee receives reliable information indicating grave or systematic violations by a State Party of rights set forth in the Convention, the Committee shall invite that State Party to cooperate in the examination of the information and to this end to submit observations with regard to the information concerned').

[48] For Communications in which allegations of wrongful gender stereotyping have been considered on the merits, see CEDAW Committee, *A.T.* v. *Hungary*, Communication No. 2/2003, 26 January 2005, UN Doc. CEDAW/C/32/D/2/2003 (2005); CEDAW Committee, *Fatma Yildirim* v. *Austria*, Communication No. 6/2005, 1 October 2007, UN Doc. CEDAW/C/39/D/6/2005 (2007); CEDAW Committee, *Şahide Goekce* v. *Austria*, Communication No. 5/2005, 6 August 2007, UN Doc. CEDAW/C/39/D/5/2005 (2007); *Karen Tayag Vertido* v. *The Philippines*; CEDAW Committee, *Inga Abramova* v. *Belarus*, Communication No. 23/2009, 27 September 2011, UN Doc. CEDAW/C/49/D/23/2009 (2011); *V.K.* v. *Bulgaria*; CEDAW Committee, *L.C.* v. *Peru*, Communication No. 22/2009, 25 November 2011, UN Doc. CEDAW/C/50/D/22/2009 (2011); *R.K.B.* v. *Turkey*. Several dissenting Committee members considered allegations of wrongful gender stereotyping in Communications that have been declared inadmissible. See CEDAW Committee, *Cristina Muñoz-Vargas y Sainz de Vicuña* v. *Spain*, Communication No. 7/2005, 9 August 2007, UN Doc. CEDAW/C/39/D/7/2005 (2007); CEDAW Committee, *Michéle Drayas et al.* v. *France*, Communication No. 13/2007, 4 August 2009, UN Doc. CEDAW/C/44/D/13/2007 (2009); CEDAW Committee, *G.D. and S.F.* v. *France*, Communication No. 12/2007, 4 August 2009, UN Doc. CEDAW/C/44/D/12/2007 (2009).

[49] See *Ciudad Juárez Inquiry*.

pregnant minor who had been repeatedly sexually assaulted and who subsequently attempted suicide, was based on the prescriptive sex-role stereotype that women should be mothers. The Committee reasoned that reliance on this stereotype had the effect of prioritising protection of the foetus over the life, health and dignity of L.C., and ultimately contributed to her becoming a paraplegic.[50] In another Communication, *A.T.* v. *Hungary*, the Committee condemned widespread gender stereotyping in Hungary that had the effect of positioning women as subordinate to men. The Committee linked that stereotyping to the author's experiences of domestic violence and the failure of the state to take adequate steps to put an end to it and, on that basis, found Hungary in violation of its obligations under Article 5(a) of the CEDAW, read in conjunction with Article 16 on marriage and family relations.[51]

With only a small number of Communications decided and one Inquiry completed, it is perhaps too soon to draw any concrete conclusions regarding the effectiveness of the CEDAW and its Optional Protocol as a tool to hold States Parties accountable for wrongful gender stereotyping. Nevertheless, several encouraging developments are worthy of brief consideration here. Perhaps one of the most exciting developments is the growing leadership of the CEDAW Committee and, in particular, individual members of the Committee, on the issue of gender stereotyping. Nowhere is this leadership clearer than in the readiness of several Committee members to raise gender stereotyping in two separate Communications concerning the ability of women in France to change their surname, even though the authors themselves had not identified stereotyping as an issue for consideration.[52] Just as exciting is the Committee's increasingly sophisticated analysis of gender stereotyping, as evidenced in the *Vertido* Case, where the Committee named and examined operative gender stereotypes and analysed at length how the trial judge's reliance on them impaired the rights of the victim, Karen Tayag Vertido, in violation of the CEDAW.[53] Also welcome is the recognition in the Committee's views in the *Vertido* Case that the obligations of States Parties in respect of harmful gender stereotyping are not limited to the rights and freedoms expressly enumerated in the CEDAW, but extend also to those rights and freedoms guaranteed by other treaties.[54] The approach adopted by the

[50] *L.C.* v. *Peru* at para. 8.15.

[51] *A.T.* v. *Hungary* at para. 9.4.

[52] See *G.D. and S.F.* v. *France* at para. 8; *Michéle Drayas et al.* v. *France* at para. 7.

[53] *Karen Tayag Vertido* v. *The Philippines* at paras. 8.4–8.6.

[54] *Ibid.* at para. 8.4.

Committee ensures that individual women can submit Communications under the Optional Protocol alleging wrongful gender stereotyping that has violated such rights and freedoms as the right to life, the right to an adequate standard of living and the freedom of expression.

There are, however, several areas of concern worthy of brief consideration here. One concern is that the CEDAW Committee has failed to take advantage of several important opportunities to consider how gender stereotypes are implicated on the facts. For example, in *Cristina Muñoz-Vargas y Sainz de Vicuña* v. *Spain* one Committee member, in a dissenting opinion, condemned a Spanish law that entrenched male primacy in the order of succession on the basis that it perpetuated discrimination and institutionalised stereotypes, in violation of the CEDAW.[55] Yet the remaining Committee members either were unable to discern or chose not to address the institutionalisation of gender stereotypes in the relevant law. Had they done so, they might, as the dissenting Committee member did, have seen fit to declare the Communication admissible. Missed opportunities, such as that in the Spanish Communication, seem at odds with the Committee's own recognition that addressing gender stereotyping is central to the elimination of all forms of discrimination against women, which would seem to include discriminatory forms of succession to hereditary titles of honour that are based on gender stereotypes.[56]

A further concern, which materialises in two domestic violence Communications against Austria, relates to the consistency of the Committee's approach to stereotyping. In the Communications against Austria, the Committee noted 'linkages between traditional attitudes by which women are regarded as subordinate to men and domestic violence', but found that the submissions did not warrant further findings in relation to Article 5(a).[57] It is unclear on what basis the Committee reached this conclusion and how these Communications differed from *A.T.* v. *Hungary*, where the Committee earlier found a violation of the state's obligations to address gender stereotyping related to domestic violence. As the Committee develops its jurisprudence on gender stereotyping, it is imperative that these concerns are addressed so as to ensure that States Parties are held fully accountable for their violations of Articles 2(f) and 5.

[55] *Cristina Muñoz-Vargas y Sainz de Vicuña* v. *Spain* (individual opinion by Committee member Mary Shanthi Dairiam, dissenting) at paras. 13.1–13.13.

[56] See Cook and Cusack, *Gender Stereotyping* at 149.

[57] *Goekce* v. *Austria* at para. 12.2; *Yildirim* v. *Austria* at para. 12.2.

3.2 *Limitations of the CEDAW framework*

Section 3.1 pointed to some of the ways that the CEDAW adds value to transnational discourses on gender stereotyping. Nevertheless, there are limits to the CEDAW's framework for addressing gender stereotyping that, although by no means fatal, need to be examined so that they can be overcome or, at the very least, their effects minimised.

3.2.1 Limited understanding of state obligations

A potential limitation of the CEDAW as a framework for transnational discourses on gender stereotyping is that the obligations in Articles 2(f) and 5 have been formulated in sweeping and ambiguous terms.[58] Consider, for example, Article 5(a), which requires States Parties to 'take all appropriate measures to modify the social and cultural patterns of conduct of men and women'. What it means for a State Party to 'modify' social and cultural 'patterns of conduct' is not defined in Article 5(a) or any other provision of the CEDAW. Addressing the breadth and ambiguity of Article 5(a), Noreen Burrows has argued that '[t]he obligation on the State is to modify behaviour patterns using all appropriate measures. The measures themselves are not defined nor is the extent of the behaviour patterns which are to be changed. Presumably each State must decide for itself the extent of sex-role stereotyping in its cultural and social practices and then attempt to change these patterns'.[59]

While it is true that the language used in Articles 2(f) and 5 to articulate the obligations of States Parties with respect to gender stereotyping is broad in scope, there is a tendency to overstate the significance of this potential limitation of the CEDAW framework. The constant need to determine the content and meaning of human rights is not unique to Articles 2(f) and 5 or to the CEDAW in general, but is common to all human rights protected in international treaties, which have been described by one commentator as 'invariably vague and ambiguous'.[60] Rather than seeing the language of

[58] See H. J. Steiner and P. Alston, *International Human Rights in Context: Law, Politics, Morals*, 2nd edn (New York: Oxford University Press, 2000) at 179; B. R. Roth, 'The CEDAW as a collective approach to women's rights', *Mich. J. Int'l J.* 24 (2002–3) 187–225 at 192; E. Sepper, 'Confronting the "sacred and unchangeable": the obligation to modify cultural patterns under the women's discrimination treaty', *U. Pa. J. Int'l. L.* 30:2 (2008) 585–639 at 589.

[59] Noreen Burrows, 'The 1979 Convention on the Elimination of All Forms of Discrimination against Women', *Netherlands International Law Review* 32 (1985) 419–60 at 428.

[60] See John Tobin, 'Seeking to persuade: a constructive approach to human rights', *Harv. Hum. Rts. J.* 23 (2010) 1–50 at 1.

the CEDAW as a limitation, its breadth should be welcomed, as Andrew Byrnes suggests, as allowing 'flexibility in its interpretation and its adaptability to new issues and understandings'.[61]

The relatively modest and incremental attention given by the Committee, at least initially, to elucidating the content and meaning of the obligations in Articles 2(f) and 5, rather than the broad terminology used therein, is a more pressing concern for transnational discourses on gender stereotyping. It is not just that the Committee has given modest attention to states' obligations in Articles 2(f) and 5, but that it has also failed to seize opportunities to lay down clear guidance on the content and meaning of those obligations. In the *Vertido* Case, for example, the Committee failed to take the opportunity to elucidate states' obligations to address systemic stereotyping by members of the judiciary. Had the Committee addressed these obligations, it might have recommended that the Philippines establish continued education and training programmes for judges, prosecutors and lawyers that aim to foster impartial and independent legal proceedings conducted free of wrongful gender stereotyping. The Committee might have encouraged the Philippines government to take steps to ensure that a central focus of such training was educating judges to identify wrongful gender stereotyping, name operative gender stereotypes, and understand if and when gender stereotyping violates human rights.[62] That the Committee has been slow or reluctant to provide clear and detailed guidance on the obligations in Articles 2(f) and 5 could be seen to undermine its characterisation of them as central to efforts to achieve substantive equality.

Some feminist legal scholars have sought to elucidate the general and specific obligations in Articles 2(f) and 5,[63] and some guidance can be found in the CEDAW Committee's existing body of jurisprudence on stereotyping. Yet there is no substitute for a clear statement from the Committee – ideally in the form of a General Recommendation – that gives content and clarity to the obligations of States Parties to modify or transform gender stereotypes and eliminate wrongful gender stereotyping.[64] In addition

[61] Byrnes, 'The CEDAW and the CEDAW Committee' at 6.

[62] See generally UN General Assembly, 66th Session, *Interim Report of the Special Rapporteur on the Independence of Judges and Lawyers*, 10 August 2011, UN Doc. A/66/289, paras. 34–40, 94–96.

[63] See Holtmaat, 'Article 5'; Cook and Cusack, *Gender Stereotyping*.

[64] See F. Raday, 'Culture, Religion, and CEDAW's Article 5(a)' in H. Beate Schöpp-Schilling and C. Flinterman (eds.), *The Circle of Empowerment: Twenty-Five Years of the UN Committee on the Elimination of Discrimination against Women* (New York: Feminist Press, 2007) 68–85 at 81; Cook and Cusack, *Gender Stereotyping* at 137.

to defining and guiding States Parties on their obligations in relation to gender stereotyping, a General Recommendation from the Committee has the potential to stimulate and enrich transnational discourses about gender stereotyping. A commitment from the Committee to elucidate States Parties' obligations in this area must also involve ensuring 'that, where appropriate, new General Recommendations on other issue-specific provisions of the Convention, such as Article 10 on education, articulate States Parties' obligations to eliminate wrongful gender stereotyping as they pertain to those provisions'.[65] In this regard, the Committee could build on the approach adopted in General Recommendation No. 19 on violence against women (as well as in other General Recommendations), in which it recognised that wrongful gender stereotyping perpetuates and justifies gender-based violence against women, and urged States Parties to adopt measures to address such stereotyping.[66] The Committee must also be vigilant in ensuring that, where relevant, States Parties' obligations to address wrongful gender stereotyping are articulated in its decisions and reports under the Optional Protocol and in its Concluding Observations issued under the reporting procedure.

3.2.2 Modest recognition of compounded stereotyping

A second potential limitation of the CEDAW is the absence of any express recognition that there is no monolithic experience of gender stereotyping, but varied experiences that result from compounded stereotyping. When addressing gender stereotyping, the CEDAW refers to stereotypes of 'men and women'[67] and, in so doing, glosses over the myriad stereotypes of different subgroups of men and women. Contrast this approach with that adopted in the Convention on the Rights of Persons with Disabilities, which expressly obligates States Parties to 'undertake to adopt immediate, effective and appropriate measures to combat stereotypes, prejudices and harmful practices relating to persons with disabilities, including those based on sex and age, in all areas of life'.[68] The lack of any express recognition in the CEDAW of compounded stereotyping is echoed in many of the Committee's Concluding Observations and its Optional Protocol jurisprudence, which often fail to identify operative stereotypes of different

[65] Cook and Cusack, *Gender Stereotyping*.

[66] See CEDAW Committee, General Recommendation No. 19, January 1992, UN Doc. A/47/38 at 1 (1994), paras. 11, 24(t)(ii).

[67] Article 5(a) CEDAW.

[68] Convention on the Rights of Persons with Disabilities, 993 UNTS 3, entered into force 3 May 2008, Article 8(1)(b).

subgroups of women and men. An example is the Committee's report on in its inquiry into the systematic abduction, rape and murder of women in Ciudad Juárez, Mexico, which failed to address compounded stereotyping of poor, young, migrant women and, instead, treated Mexican women as a homogeneous group that shares the same experiences of gender stereotyping.[69]

If the CEDAW is truly to be a leading framework for debates about gender stereotyping, the Committee must ensure that varied experiences of gender stereotyping are taken into account, and States Parties are held accountable not only for wrongful gender stereotyping of women (and men) but also different subgroups thereof. It is encouraging, therefore, that the Committee's jurisprudence on stereotyping is already becoming more nuanced, reflecting, at least in part, growing understanding of compounded stereotyping and its implications for the achievement of substantive equality.[70] This emergent approach is reflected, among other places, in the 2010 Concluding Observations on the Netherlands, in which the Committee noted its concern regarding the persistence of compounded stereotypes of immigrant and migrant men and women, and called for the development of 'additional programmes to address gender stereotypes related to discrimination on other grounds, such as race, age, sexual orientation and disability'.[71] Increased attentiveness to compounded stereotypes, as in the case of the Netherlands' Concluding Observations, will allow for more constructive dialogue with States Parties and more targeted responses to stereotyping. Consideration of compounded stereotypes of poor, young, migrant women in the *Ciudad Juárez Inquiry* might, for instance, have led to more critical analysis of how to tackle the view of this particular subgroup of women as 'waste' that can be disposed of once their value has been used up.[72] Just as important is the need to work collaboratively with other human rights treaty bodies, especially those bodies monitoring treaties that impose express obligations related to stereotyping, to ensure a considered and consistent approach to compounded stereotyping across the entire international human rights system.

[69] See *Ciudad Juárez Inquiry*. See also Cook and Cusack, *Gender Stereotyping* at 165–72.

[70] Growing awareness of compounded stereotyping is commensurate with growing awareness of the broader concept of compounded discrimination (also known as intersectional or multiple discrimination). See generally CEDAW Committee, General Recommendation No. 28 at para. 18.

[71] CEDAW Committee, *Concluding Observations: The Netherlands*, February 2010, UN Doc. CEDAW/C/NLD/C0/5, para. 25.

[72] See Cook and Cusack, *Gender Stereotyping* at 167–72, citing M. W. Wright, 'The dialectics of still life: murder, women, and maquiladoras', *Public Culture* 11 (1999) 453–73,

3.2.3 Institutionalisation of gender stereotypes

A third potential limitation of the CEDAW is that certain of its provisions institutionalise gender stereotypes, in blatant disregard for the goals of Articles 2(f) and 5 and, more broadly, the CEDAW's overarching object and purpose of achieving substantive equality. Dianne Otto has argued persuasively that Article 6, which requires States Parties to 'suppress all forms of traffic in women and exploitation of prostitution of women', perpetuates the stereotype of women as (sexually) weak and vulnerable (among other stereotypes) and, thus, in need of protection. She writes:

> The protected woman can ... be discerned in the ambiguous provision requiring 'the suppression ... of the exploitation of prostitution of women' (Article 6), which clearly does not recognise the rights of women as workers in the sex industry. Instead it seems to cast all prostitution as 'exploitation' and, therefore, all sex workers as needing protection from their 'exploiters'. Such over-simplification of the complexity of women's economic decision-making not only denies women agency, but also reflects gendered anxieties about women's sexuality, as did the earlier anti-trafficking instruments.[73]

An alternative approach, modelled on New Zealand's Prostitution Reform Act 2003, might have been for the CEDAW to distinguish more clearly between those forms of prostitution that constitute exploitation and those that do not, and to establish a framework that explicitly safeguards the welfare and human rights of trafficked victims and sex workers.

The institutionalisation of gender stereotypes in Article 6 is, in part, a reflection of understandings of female sexuality and the sex and trafficking industries in the period during which the CEDAW was drafted. Even so, the stereotypes implicit within the text of Article 6 serve as a reminder of the part that feminists and women's rights-centred instruments, including the CEDAW, have played, and continue to play, in reproducing gender stereotypes and related mythologies.[74] Gender stereotyping is not just something that is done *to* women; it is done by and to all of us, and is a consequence of our living in a world that is structured around,

reprinted in J. Comaroff and J. L. Comaroff (eds.), *Millennial Capitalism and the Culture of Neoliberalism* (Durham, NC: Duke University Press, 2001) 125–46 (discussing the 'disposable' women concept).

[73] D. Otto, 'Disconcerting "masculinities": reinventing the gendered subject(s) of international human rights law' in D. Buss and A. Manji (eds.), *International Law: Modern Feminist Approaches* (Oxford; Portland, OR: Hart, 2005) 105–29 at 118–19.

[74] See *ibid.* at 118.

indeed saturated with, gender stereotypes.[75] That certain provisions of the CEDAW institutionalise gender stereotypes does not preclude its use as a legal framework for debates about gender stereotyping, provided that those stereotypes are contested and transnational discourses are framed in ways that ensure that embedded stereotypes are not perpetuated. To use the example of Article 6 of the CEDAW, the challenge is how to recognise the vulnerable situation of many (but not all) individuals within the sex industry, without perpetuating the stereotype of women as (sexually) weak and vulnerable.

3.2.4 Gender stereotypes versus stereotypes of men and women

Another potential limitation of the CEDAW, which is addressed only briefly here, is its codification of the male/female binary of gender stereotyping. Consider again Article 5(a) of CEDAW, which addresses 'stereotyped roles for men and women', and the Preamble, which deals with 'the traditional role of men as well as the role of women in society and in the family'.[76] Both Article 5(a) and the Preamble reify diametrically opposed and heteronormative categories of gender stereotypes. By focusing on stereotypes related to men and women, rather than the broader concept of 'gender' stereotypes, the CEDAW and the Committee in its jurisprudence overlook the gradations and complexities of gender and, more specifically, gender stereotyping. A consequence of this framing is the creation of false and polarising categories of gender stereotypes that expressly exclude from debates those individuals who do not fit neatly into either category, including transgender and intersex persons. To borrow the powerful words of Darren Rosenblum, the use in the CEDAW of categories of stereotypes of men and stereotypes of women 'truncate[s] the diversity of gender identity'.[77] Such truncation is harmful not only to those persons excluded from debates, or who are included only to the extent that they are characterised as 'non-conforming', but also to the CEDAW's broader goal of substantive gender equality. It is important, therefore, that transnational discourses focus on gender stereotypes, rather than the narrower categories of stereotypes of women and stereotypes of men.

[75] See Cook and Cusack, *Gender Stereotyping* at 14–16.

[76] CEDAW, Preamble. para. 14.

[77] See Darren Rosenblum, 'Unisex CEDAW, or what's wrong with women's rights', *Colum. J. Gender and L.* 20:2 (2011) 98–194 at 135.

4 Defining state obligations to address gender stereotyping

Understanding of the potency of the CEDAW as a framework for transnational legal discourses on gender stereotyping is in its embryonic stages. Feminist legal scholars have begun to explore the value and limits of the CEDAW in relation to gender stereotyping, as section 3 shows. Further strengths and weaknesses of the CEDAW will undoubtedly emerge as closer scrutiny is brought to bear on Articles 2(f) and 5, and as understanding of gender stereotypes and gender stereotyping evolves. For now, at least, it is clear that there is value in utilising the CEDAW to propel discourses on gender stereotyping beyond the domestic and into the transnational sphere. And while the limitations of the CEDAW cannot be ignored, and nor should they be, there are steps that can be taken to help minimise, even overcome, many of them.

Fashioning the limitations outlined in section 3.2 into an agenda for strengthening the CEDAW and transnational discourses on gender stereotyping is one way to move forward. Any such agenda must prioritise articulation of States Parties' obligations in Articles 2(f) and 5 to modify or transform gender stereotypes and eliminate wrongful gender stereotyping. Section 4 outlines a possible approach to the interpretation of those obligations.[78] In order to do this, it draws on the text of the CEDAW, particularly Articles 2(f) and 5, as well as the jurisprudence of the CEDAW Committee on gender stereotyping. Section 4 uses as its primary interpretative tool the widely accepted tripartite framework of state obligations – namely, the obligations to respect, protect and fulfil human rights and fundamental freedoms.

4.1 Obligation to respect

The obligation to respect requires States Parties to refrain from arbitrarily interfering with women's human rights and fundamental freedoms.[79] The CEDAW Committee has explained that the first limb of the tripartite framework requires States Parties to abstain 'from making laws, policies, regulations, programmes, administrative procedures and institutional structures that directly or indirectly result in the denial of the equal enjoyment by women of their civil, political, economic, social and cultural

[78] Section 4 builds on and updates the discussion of state obligations in Cook and Cusack, *Gender Stereotyping* at 71–103.

[79] See CEDAW Committee, General Recommendation No. 28 at paras. 9–10, 37(a).

rights'.[80] According to the Committee, the obligation to respect also requires States Parties to refrain from 'performing, sponsoring or condoning any practice, policy or measure that violates the Convention'.[81]

Applied to Articles 2(f) and 5 of CEDAW, read in conjunction with Articles 1 and 2(d), the obligation to respect requires States Parties to refrain from wrongful gender stereotyping. It also prohibits States Parties from exercising state powers in ways that regulate, penalise, stigmatise or otherwise marginalise individuals who do not conform to gender stereotypes. Legislative branches must not enact laws that institutionalise gender stereotypes in ways that violate women's human rights and fundamental freedoms. The executive branch of States Parties must ensure that policies, regulations, programmes, administrative procedures and institutional structures are not based on gender stereotypes. State agents and officials, including politicians, must refrain from making public statements or decisions that are based on gender stereotypes.[82] States Parties must ensure that all legal structures and processes, rules of evidence, criminal investigations and legal proceedings are impartial and fair, and not affected by gender stereotyping.[83] Members of the judiciary must not enforce laws based on gender stereotypes, but rather must invalidate them and/or recommend their repeal or amendment. Members of the judiciary must also be careful not to apply, enforce or perpetuate gender stereotypes through their behaviour, reasoning or decisions, including, for example, by reinforcing sex-role stereotypes about marriage during divorce proceedings.[84] Related to this, gender stereotypes should not be a determining factor in deciding the extent of women's legal rights and protections.[85]

The leading authority on the application of the obligation to respect to Articles 2(f) and 5(a) of the CEDAW is the *Vertido* Case.[86] In April 2005, the Regional Trial Court of Davao City in the Philippines acquitted Jose B. Custodio of raping Karen Vertido.[87] In support of her ruling, Judge

[80] *Ibid.* at para. 9. [81] *Ibid.* at para. 37(a).

[82] See Articles 2(d), 2(f) and 5(a) CEDAW. See also *Ciudad Juárez Inquiry* at paras. 50, 54, 56, 67.

[83] See generally UNGA, *Interim Report of the Special Rapporteur on the Independence of Judges and Lawyers*; *Karen Tayag Vertido* v. *The Philippines*.

[84] See *V.K.* v. *Bulgaria* at para. 9.12.

[85] Human Rights Committee, General Comment No. 28, 29 March 2000, UN Doc. CCPR/C/21/Rev.1/Add.10 (2000), para. 20.

[86] *Karen Tayag Vertido* v. *The Philippines*.

[87] *The People of the Philippines* v. *Jose B. Custodio*, Crim. Case No. 37,921–96, 11 April 2005 (Philipp., Regional Trial Court Davao City).

Virginia Hofileña-Europa cited insufficient evidence to prove beyond all reasonable doubt that the accused was guilty of the crime of rape. Her Honour also emphasised her unfavourable assessment of the victim's credibility based (among other things) on her failure to take advantage of perceived opportunities to escape from the accused. Following judgment, the author (i.e. Vertido) submitted a Communication to the CEDAW Committee claiming that the decision to acquit infringed her rights under the CEDAW.[88] Of particular relevance here is the author's claim that the decision had no basis in law or fact but, rather, 'was grounded in gender-based myths and misconceptions about rape and rape victims ... without which the accused would have been convicted'.[89] What is significant about this claim is that the author sought to hold the Philippines accountable for the failure of Judge Europa to refrain from arbitrarily interfering with her rights in the CEDAW, including Articles 2(f) and 5(a).

In its decision, the CEDAW Committee affirmed that States Parties can be held accountable under the CEDAW where judges fail to refrain from wrongful gender stereotyping, in violation of Articles 2(f) and/or 5(a) (the obligation to respect). Acknowledging that gender stereotyping can impede women's access to a fair trial, the Committee stressed that 'the judiciary must take caution not to create inflexible standards of what women or girls should be or ... have done when confronted with ... rape based merely on preconceived notions of what defines a rape victim or a victim of gender-based violence, in general'.[90] The majority concluded that, on the facts, Judge Europa had evaluated the victim's behaviour against gender stereotypes, and formed a negative view of her creditability because she had not responded as a rational and ideal victim was expected to in a rape situation.[91] It further concluded that the trial decision contained 'several references to stereotypes about ... sexuality being more supportive for the credibility of the alleged perpetrator than the creditability of the victim'.[92]

The Committee affirmed the application of the obligation to respect to Articles 2(f) and 5(a) of the CEDAW in *V.K.* v. *Bulgaria*, in which it held the State Party accountable for its failure to provide V.K. effective protection against domestic violence. Recalling its decision in the *Vertido* Case, the Committee noted that States Parties are accountable under the CEDAW

[88] *Karen Tayag Vertido* v. *The Philippines* at paras. 3.1–3.17.

[89] *Ibid.* at paras. 3.4–3.5.

[90] *Ibid.* at para. 8.4. [91] *Ibid.* at para. 8.5.

[92] *Ibid.* at para. 8.6.

for judicial decisions that are based on gender stereotypes, rather than law and fact. '[S]tereotyping', the Committee said, 'affects women's right to a fair trial and … the judiciary must be careful not to create inflexible standards based on preconceived notions of what constitutes domestic or gender-based violence.'[93] Considering the facts, the Committee found that the refusal of Bulgaria's courts to grant a permanent protection order was based on gender stereotypes related to domestic violence and that the divorce proceedings had been influenced by gender stereotypes related to the roles and behaviours expected of men and women within marriage and family relations. According to the Committee, reliance by the judiciary on these gender stereotypes resulted in discrimination and the revictimisation of V.K, in violation of the CEDAW.[94]

4.2 Obligation to protect

The obligation to protect requires States Parties to take all appropriate measures to ensure that state and private actors do not unlawfully infringe rights.[95] This means that States Parties must '[t]ake steps to prevent, prohibit and punish violations of the Convention by [state actors] third parties … and to provide reparation to the victims of such violations'.[96]

Interpreted in light of Articles 2(f) and 5, as well as Articles 2(a)–(c) and 2(e), the obligation to protect requires States Parties to take positive steps to ensure that appropriate laws, policies and plans of action are in place and properly administered and implemented to address wrongful gender stereotyping. States Parties should also implement education and training programmes to educate the public about gender stereotypes and wrongful gender stereotyping.[97] Such programmes should name gender stereotypes, identify the consequent harms of wrongful gender stereotyping for all and provide guidance on the steps that can be taken to eliminate the practice of wrongful gender stereotyping. They should also promote tolerance of, and respect for, the multiple and varied expressions of sex and gender, in an effort to debunk the erroneous

93 *V.K.* v. *Bulgaria* at para. 9.11.

94 *Ibid.* at para. 9.12.

95 See CEDAW Committee, General Recommendation No. 28 at paras. 9–10, 37(a).

96 *Ibid.* at para. 37(b).

97 See CEDAW Committee, General Recommendation No. 3, April 1987, UN Doc. A/42/38 at 78 (1987); CEDAW Committee, General Recommendation No. 19 at paras. 24(f), 24(t)(ii); CEDAW Committee, General Recommendation No. 24, 1999, UN Doc. A/54/38 at 5 (1999), at para. 28.

notion that there is a singular and correct expression of femininity and/or masculinity to which individuals are obliged to conform. Education and training programmes should further aim to dismantle androcentric norms and replace sexism with positive valuations of those characteristics, roles and behaviours that are coded as feminine.

States Parties are required to put legal structures into place to ensure that complaints of wrongful gender stereotyping are investigated promptly, impartially and independently. Courts and other relevant decision-making bodies should also hold actors legally accountable for wrongful gender stereotyping and provide effective remedies to those who have been harmed by gender stereotyping. States Parties that fail to protect women against wrongful gender stereotyping can be held accountable under the CEDAW, in accordance with the due diligence obligation.[98] For example, in *R.K.B.* v. *Turkey* the Committee held the State Party accountable for the failure of its courts to challenge and reject evidence submitted by an employer in an unfair dismissal case that relied on sexual stereotypes that condoned extramarital affairs by men, but not women (obligation to protect).[99]

4.3 Obligation to fulfil

The obligation to fulfil – the last limb of the tripartite framework – enjoins states to ensure the full realisation of rights in law and in practice.[100] The CEDAW Committee has explained that this obligation requires States Parties to 'take a wide variety of steps to ensure that women and men enjoy equal rights de jure and de facto, including, where appropriate, the adoption of temporary special measures'.[101] The Committee has further explained that 'States parties should consider that they have to fulfil their legal obligations to all women through designing public policies, programmes and institutional frameworks that are aimed at fulfilling the specific needs of women leading to the full development of their potential on an equal basis with men'.[102]

[98] See CEDAW Committee, General Recommendation No. 28 at para. 13. See also R. Holtmaat, 'Preventing violence against women: the Due Diligence Standard with respect to the obligation to banish gender stereotypes on the grounds of Article 5(a) of the CEDAW Convention' in C. Benninger-Budel (ed.), *Due Diligence and its Application to Protect Women from Violence* (Leiden, Boston: Martinus Nijhoff, 2009) 63–90.

[99] *R.K.B.* v. *Turkey* at paras. 8.7–8.8.

[100] See CEDAW Committee, General Recommendation No. 28 at para. 20.

[101] *Ibid.* at para. 9. [102] *Ibid.*

Applied to Articles 2(f) and 5 of the CEDAW, the obligation to fulfil requires States Parties to adopt all appropriate measures to ensure that women can exercise and enjoy the right to be free from wrongful gender stereotyping. Pursuant to the obligation to fulfil, States Parties should conduct an audit of national laws and policies, and reform or repeal those that apply, enforce or perpetuate gender stereotypes. Executive branches should adopt a comprehensive national strategy on wrongful gender stereotyping,[103] either as part of a national plan of action to achieve gender equality or as a stand-alone plan of action on stereotyping. The plan should identify the structures put in place to monitor the implementation of measures to ensure that the right to be free from wrongful gender stereotyping is realised in practice (for example, the adoption and independent monitoring of gender equality guidelines for media). Executive branches should work closely with heads of government departments and peak bodies to facilitate the elimination of wrongful gender stereotyping in different sectors, by naming the gender stereotypes that operate in those sectors and revealing how they harm women and men, and identifying concrete steps to bring an end to wrongful gender stereotyping in those sectors. Executive branches should also adopt measures designed to break gender stereotypes, such as ensuring access to paid parental leave for men to encourage them to assume equal responsibility for caring or permitting women to serve in armed combat roles. The Committee has explained that 'temporary special measures should be adopted to accelerate the modification and elimination of cultural practices and stereotypical attitudes and behaviour that discriminate against or are disadvantageous for women'.[104]

States Parties should also establish effective remedies for wrongful gender stereotyping and ensure that women and men can access those remedies. The obligation to fulfil requires the establishment of institutionalised and continuing education and training programmes for judges, prosecutors and lawyers that aim to foster impartial and independent legal proceedings conducted free of wrongful gender stereotyping.[105] A central focus of such training should be educating judges

[103] See for example, CEDAW Committee, *Concluding Observations: Russia*, 16 August 2010, UN Doc. CEDAW/C/USR/CO/7, para. 21; CEDAW Committee, *Concluding Observations: Albania*, 16 September 2010, UN Doc. CEDAW/C/ALB/CO/3, para. 25; CEDAW Committee, *Concluding Observations: United Arab Emirates*, 5 February 2010, UN Doc. CEDAW/C/ARE/CO/1, para. 25.

[104] CEDAW Committee, General Recommendation No. 25 at para. 38.

[105] *Karen Tayag Vertido* v. *The Philippines* at para. 8.9(b). See also UNGA, *Interim Report of the Special Rapporteur on the Independence of Judges and Lawyers*.

to name gender stereotypes, identify their harms and hold public and private actors accountable for wrongful gender stereotyping. Such training should also urge judges to invalidate and/or recommend the repeal or amendment of laws that are found to unlawfully apply, enforce or perpetuate gender stereotypes.

In the *Vertido* Case the Committee paid close attention to the Philippines' non-compliance with the obligation to respect the right to be free of wrongful gender stereotyping. Yet it remained largely silent as to the failure of the state to comply with the obligation to fulfil that same right. This is somewhat surprising given the information submitted by the author regarding the pervasiveness of wrongful gender stereotyping in the Philippines judiciary.[106] Had the Committee scrutinised this information more closely, it might also have held the Philippines liable for its failure to educate its judiciary properly about the obligations incumbent upon them to not only abstain from stereotyping but also to name, contest and dismantle harmful gender stereotypes, including those related to rape. It appears, however, that the Committee was conscious of this breach when it recommended that the Philippines '[e]nsure that all legal procedures in cases involving crimes of rape and other sexual offenses are impartial and fair, and not affected by prejudices or stereotypical gender notions'.[107] 'To achieve this', the Committee explained, 'a wide range of measures are needed, targeted at the legal system, to improve the judicial handling of rape cases, as well as training and education to change discriminatory attitudes towards women.'[108]

5 The 'good' gender stereotype: is gender stereotyping ever justified?

The CEDAW does not contain a general limitations provision,[109] nor do Articles 2(f) or 5 contain internal limitations,[110] similar to those found in some other human rights instruments. One of the biggest interpretative challenges facing the CEDAW Committee in future is how to resolve the difficult and contested question of when it is permissible for States Parties to limit rights guaranteed by the CEDAW, including in particular those in

106 *Karen Tayag Vertido* v. *The Philippines* at para. 3.8.

107 *Ibid.* at para. 8.9(b). 108 *Ibid.*

109 See for example, Canadian Charter of Rights and Freedoms of 1982 (Can.), section 1.

110 See for example, International Covenant on Civil and Political Rights, 999 UNTS 171, entered into force 23 March 1976, Articles 12, 19.

Articles 2(f) and 5. Alexandra Timmer captured this challenge succinctly when she said: 'stereotypes often serve a legitimate social function; how do we determine which stereotypes are legitimate and which stereotypes should be actionable by law?'[111]

The limitations question that the Committee needs to determine can be divided into two parts, the first concerning stereotypical *beliefs*, specifically: when is it permissible for States Parties not to modify or transform gender stereotypes? States Parties are compelled by Articles 2(f) and 5 to adopt all appropriate measures to modify or transform the gender stereotypes that are characterised as harmful to women. The absence of harm may, however, be justification for States Parties not adopting measures to modify or transform a gender stereotype.[112] The central question for determination then becomes: what is the measure of whether or not a stereotypical belief based on sex/gender is harmful? The answer to this question will require careful case-by-case analysis by the CEDAW Committee of the attributes, characteristics or roles attributed to women and men through gender stereotypes and what they say about the worth, talents and capabilities of individual women and men. It is important to note, however, that it is not just hostile or negative gender stereotypes that can be harmful to women. Seemingly benign, protective or benevolent stereotypes can also be harmful, including when they confine women to specific roles, keep them in their place or deny their ability to make autonomous decisions about their life plans.

The second part of the limitations question that the Committee needs to determine concerns the *practice* of gender stereotyping, specifically: when is gender stereotyping permissible? Gender stereotyping might constitute a permissible limitation of rights if the limitation serves a legitimate purpose and the means chosen to attain that purpose are both reasonable and proportionate.[113] It has been argued that a legitimate purpose is one that has an objective and reasonable goal and, on that basis:

111 See A. Timmer, 'Book review, Gender Stereotyping: Transnational Legal Perspectives (Rebecca J. Cook and Simone Cusack), Philadelphia: University of Pennsylvania Press, 2010', *H.R.L.R.* 10:3 (2010) 583–6 at 585.

112 See R. Holtmaat and J. Naber, *Women's Human Rights and Culture: From Deadlock to Dialogue* (Antwerp: Intersentia, 2011) at 33, 49, 59–60; Cook and Cusack, *Gender Stereotyping* at 17–18, 23.

113 See, for example, Committee on Economic, Social and Cultural Rights, General Comment No. 20, 25 May 2009, UN Doc. E/C.12/C/20 (2009), para. 13 (providing that '[d]ifferential treatment based on prohibited grounds will be viewed as discriminatory unless the justification for differentiation is reasonable and objective. This will include an assessment as to whether the aim and effects of the measures or omissions are legitimate,

> that gender stereotyping that seeks to alleviate women's immediate disadvantage is in pursuit of a legitimate purpose, since it aims to address the consequences of past discrimination against women. However, gender stereotyping that seeks to create or maintain existing gender hierarchies is not a legitimate purpose; it is not legitimate as it is antithetical to the Women's Convention's overarching object and purpose of eliminating all forms of discrimination against women and ensuring substantive equality.[114]

It has been further argued that a reasonable and proportionate response:

> requires that the means chosen to achieve the legitimate purpose not be excessive. Gender stereotyping that results in the impairment or nullification of the recognition, enjoyment, or exercise by women, on a basis of equality of men and women, of human rights and fundamental freedoms, will be characterized as excessive (i.e. not proportionate) and, therefore cannot be justified under ... the Women's Convention.[115]

The purposes of gender stereotyping that will be characterised by the CEDAW Committee 'as legitimate, and the means chosen to achieve those purposes that will be deemed proportionate, will vary depending on the context within which such stereotyping occurs'.[116] For that reason, the question of which justifications for wrongful gender stereotyping will withstand scrutiny under the CEDAW will ultimately need to be determined by the Committee on a case-by-case basis.[117]

The question of whether gender stereotyping is a permissible limitation under the CEDAW will sometimes be clear-cut. It is exceedingly unlikely, for example, that a State Party could ever successfully claim that a member of its judiciary was justified in basing its decision to acquit an accused of rape on gender stereotypes rather than law or fact.[118] The challenge for the CEDAW Committee will be to provide guidance on permissible limitations in circumstances that are substantially more complex than this. Consider, for instance, the situation where there are short-term benefits for women but negative long-term consequences, if a state agent stereotypes on the basis of sex/gender.[119] Is a presidential pardon that seeks to

compatible with the nature of the Covenant rights and solely for the purpose of promoting the general welfare in a democratic society. In addition, there must be a clear and reasonable relationship of proportionality between the aim sought to be realised and the measures or omissions and their effects').

114 Cook and Cusack, *Gender Stereotyping* at 128.

115 *Ibid.* 116 *Ibid.* 117 *Ibid.* at 123.

118 See *Karen Tayag Vertido* v. *The Philippines*.

119 See also Nyamu Musembi in this volume; A. Hellum, 'Transnational challenges to international and national law: Norwegian–Pakistani women at the interface' in C. M. Bailliet (ed.), *Non-State Actors, Soft Law and Protective Regimes* (Cambridge University Press, 2012).

alleviate immediate disadvantage to women by authorising the early release of female (but not male) prisoners so that they can care for dependent children justified even if it entrenches the sex-role stereotype of women as carers, a fundamental cause of women's disadvantage?[120] Is a state policy that seeks to increase women's access to education[121] or participation in other areas of public life (e.g. sport) by requiring separate education, facilities or, for example, transport for women justified even if it institutionalises gender stereotypes related to women's vulnerability or capabilities?[122] Consider, also, the situation where a gender stereotype reflects a statistical reality but, by putting its stamp of approval on that stereotype, the state entrenches the stereotype and stigmatises or excludes non-conforming individuals. Does the fact that the stereotype reflects a statistical reality make its incorporation into law a permissible limitation of the right to be free of wrongful gender stereotyping? What about situations where a state agent or official seeks to justify gender stereotyping by making broad appeals to culture, religion or tradition?[123] And what about situations where intervention by a State Party to protect against wrongful gender stereotyping by private actors would unjustifiably limit the exercise and enjoyment of other human rights?[124] How should States Parties seek to

[120] See, for example, *President of the Republic of South Africa* v. *Hugo* 1997 (4) SA 1 (CC) (S. Afr., Constitutional Court). See also J. Elvin, 'The continuing use of problematic sexual stereotypes in judicial decision-making', *Fem. Leg. Stud.* 18 (2010) 275–97 at 281.

[121] On gender stereotyping in the education sector, see generally J. Jha and E. Page, *Exploring the Bias: Gender and Stereotyping in Secondary Schools* (London: Commonwealth Secretariat, 2009).

[122] The author acknowledges Shaheen Sardar Ali, who raised this example during the *From Ratification to Implementation: CEDAW in International and National Law* Conference held at the University of Oslo Faculty of Law on 11–12 March 2010.

[123] See generally Holtmaat and Naber, *Women's Human Rights and Culture*; A. Timmer, 'Toward an anti-stereotyping approach for the European Court of Human Rights', *H.R.L.R.* 11:4 (2011) 707–38.

[124] See L. A. Rehof, *Guide to the Travaux Préparatoires of the United Nations Convention on the Elimination of All Forms of Discrimination against Women* (Dordrecht, Boston, London: M. Nijhoff Publishers, 1993) at 80 (noting concerns raised during the drafting process regarding potential conflicts with other human rights, including the freedom of expression); T. Meron, *Human Rights Law-Making in the United Nations: A Critique of Instruments and Process* (Oxford: Clarendon Press, 1986) at 66, quoted in Roth, 'The CEDAW as a collective approach to women's rights' at 193 (worrying that the breadth of Article 5(a) 'might permit States to curtail to an undefined extent privacy and associational interests and the freedom of opinion and expression. Moreover, since social and cultural behavior may be patterned according to factors such as ethnicity or religion, state action authorized by [paragraph] (a) … may conflict with the principles of forbidding discrimination [on those bases]. The danger of intrusive state action and possible violation of the rights of ethnic or religious groups might have been mitigated by limiting state action to education measures').

balance the right to be free of wrongful gender stereotyping against potentially competing human rights, including the freedom from arbitrary interference in private life and cultural rights? (See also Nyamu Musembi in this volume.)

6 Conclusion

The CEDAW Committee showed great leadership and vision when, in its General Recommendation No. 25, it characterised the obligation to modify or transform gender stereotypes and eliminate wrongful gender stereotyping as one of three categories of obligations central to the achievement of substantive equality. Yet, with few exceptions, the significance of this authoritative statement and the potential of Articles 2(f) and 5 of the CEDAW to help realise the goal of substantive equality have been largely overlooked. One reason for this is the failure of the CEDAW Committee to seize opportunities to give content and meaning to the broadly defined obligations in Articles 2(f) and 5 of the CEDAW. Another is the failure of women's rights advocates to realise and take full advantage of their potential. The recent decisions of the Committee in cases such as *Vertido* and *R.K.B.* are, therefore, encouraging. They show that Articles 2(f) and 5 can produce measureable gains in the protection of the rights of women, and put States Parties on notice that the Committee will hold accountable those states that do not meet their obligations to modify or transform gender stereotypes and eliminate wrongful gender stereotyping. Moreover, these decisions have the potential to focus attention on wrongful gender stereotyping and cause the Committee's visionary statement in General Recommendation No. 25, in which it called on States Parties to address prevailing gender relations and gender stereotypes, to be revisited.

While these recent cases may serve as a catalyst for reinvigorating transnational legal discourses on gender stereotyping, these discourses are unlikely to move beyond their embryonic stages if the CEDAW Committee does not make articulation of States Parties' obligations to modify or transform gender stereotypes and eliminate wrongful gender stereotyping a priority. Key issues that need to be addressed include States Parties' obligations to address compounded stereotypes and the question of if and when wrongful gender stereotyping is a justifiable limitation of the rights in Articles 2(f) and 5 of the CEDAW. Strong leadership from the CEDAW Committee on these issues will not only help to guide States

Parties in the implementation of their obligations under the CEDAW, but will also influence the thinking and decision-making of other human rights treaty bodies as well as domestic courts. If the Committee is successful in this endeavour, it may change forever – and for the better – the way we think about discrimination and inequality.

5

From the CEDAW to the American Convention: elucidation of women's right to a life's project and protection of maternal identity within Inter-American human rights jurisprudence

CECILIA M. BAILLIET

1 Introduction

One of the most challenging dilemmas within the field of women's rights is how to balance equality and difference approaches. Within the Convention on the Elimination of All Forms of Discrimination against Women (CEDAW), the expression of recognition of maternity as a social function within the Preamble and Article 5(b) was intended to combat prejudice or inferior conceptions of women, lifting the social perception of the mother's role to one of active worth. Thus far within its jurisprudence, the CEDAW Committee has approached maternal rights from the perspective of non-discrimination and equality. Cases addressing maternity leave and workplace protection during pregnancy have been analyzed pursuant to Article 11 (non-discrimination in the field of employment), maternity care according to Article 12 (non-discrimination in healthcare), and cases involving family planning and child rearing within the context of marriage have been pursued according to Article 16 (non-discrimination in the family), instead of Article 5(b).[1] In contrast, at the regional level the Inter-American

[1] See *Alymeda da Silva Pimentel Teixeira* v. *Brazil*, CEDAW/C/49/D/17/2008, 10 August 2011, establishing violations of Articles 12 and 2(c) and (e) due to discriminatory denial of access to maternity care resulting in the death of the infant; *Dung Thi Thy Nguyen* v. *The Netherlands*, CEDAW/C/361/D/3/2004, 29 August 2006, addressing maternity leave benefits, Article 11 (2, 2(b)) no violation established; *A.T.* v. *Hungary*, Comm. No. 2/2003, CEDAW, 26 January 2005, involving domestic violence, finding violations of Articles 2(a)(b)(e), 5(a) and 16; and *Szijiharto* v. *Hungary*, CEDAW Comm. No. 4/2004 A/61/38 (2006), 14 August 2006, addressing enforced sterilization of a Roma woman, finding violations of Articles 10(h), 12 and 16(1e). See also UN Declaration on the Elimination of

Court of Human Rights adopted a difference-oriented perspective when addressing the claims related to violation of maternal identity in the case of *Miguel Castro-Castro Prison* v. *Peru* (2006).[2] This chapter suggests that the approach of the regional court reflects a higher level of legitimacy as it offers an interpretation of human rights that is more inclusive of the women actually concerned.

Exploration of the continuing relevance of difference valuation over formal equality as an important vehicle for achieving a holistic protection of women's rights is pursued. Maternal identity is examined as an important manifestation of human dignity.[3] Martha Fineman specifically called for attention to be placed on the family (defined as the Mother/Child paradigm):

> I assert that the family is typically considered as an afterthought (if at all) by feminist legal theories whose attention remains focused on equality in the workplace and on issues surrounding sexuality and violence against women. When it is addressed, the family is considered more of an anomaly to be corrected than an institution so pivotal to the maintenance of societal structure and operation that it seems impervious to reform … much of feminist legal theory fails to place the family and the role of mother as central institutions for the development of theory … legal theory must recognize the reality of existing systemic and persistent inequality and move beyond the simplistic equality paradigm, establishing an affirmative feminist theory of difference.[4]

She highlighted the connection between mother and child as an important value when discussing equality between the sexes – describing a vertical, inter-generational, biological tie of intimacy between people.[5] As described by Robin West:

> Indeed, perhaps the central insight of feminist theory of the last decade has been that women are 'essentially connected', not 'essentially separate', from the rest of human life, both materially, through pregnancy,

Discrimination against Women (1967), Article 10(2) addressing maternity leave, and the International Covenant on Economic, Social and Cultural Rights (1966), Article 10(2) on protection of mothers and maternity leave. The ILO has also been active in promoting maternity leave.

[2] IACtHR, *Case of the Miguel Castro-Castro Prison* v. *Peru* (Merits, Reparations and Costs), Judgment, Ser. C No. 160, 25 November 2006.

[3] N. Levit and R. R. M. Verchick, *Feminist Legal Theory: A Primer* (New York University Press, 2006) at 18.

[4] M. A. Fineman, *The Neutered Mother, the Sexual Family and other Twentieth-Century Tragedies* (New York: Routledge, 1995) at 12.

[5] *Ibid.* at 5 and 41.

intercourse, and breast-feeding, and existentially, through the moral and practical life.[6]

The second section of this chapter reviews the debate regarding the concept of maternity within the *Travaux Préparatoires* of the CEDAW, culminating in normative recognition of its social significance. This is followed by a presentation of the Inter-American Court of Human Rights' use of narratives within its jurisprudence to elucidate the scope of women's right to a life's project, including maternity rights, as a means to guarantee human dignity. This chapter argues that motherhood should be viewed as a type of agency to be protected by the state. I juxtapose the approach of the regional court towards acknowledgement of violations affecting maternal identity with academic criticism that seeks to underscore the duty to avoid wrongful gender stereotypes according to Article 5(a) of the CEDAW. My main argument is that the academic criticism is precarious as it ignores the reclamation by women of recognition of their rights from the perspective of difference. In my opinion, there is a tension between Article 5(a) and (b) that merits exploration.[7] Hence, this chapter complements Cusack's chapter in this volume by addressing dilemmas presented by mischaracterization of wrongful gender stereotyping. The conclusion suggests that the Inter-American human rights system contextualizes the CEDAW's value within the region through its support for holistic recognition of maternity rights.

[6] R. West, 'Jurisprudence and gender', *U. Chi. L. Rev.* 55:1 (1998) 1–72 at 3.

[7] M. McCarthy, '"Something not to be grasped": notes on equality on the occasion of the twentieth anniversary of mulieris dignitatem', *Ave Maria L. Rev.* 8:1 (2009) 121–52 at 123: '(W)hen it comes to the equality of women and men, the unique differences that can be found at the most basic level of the "division of labor" between them, such as the fact that only men can "beget" and only women can ovulate, carry, give birth to, and nurse a child, must be played down. For to possess "more of something" (unequally in the case of commonly held traits, such as physical strength or empathy, for example, or exclusively in the case of certain anatomical features and processes) necessarily suggests diminishment of the other or that something has been "taken away from" the other, thus putting into question his or her equal dignity and worth and unleashing the various envies and fears. Freud's envious female comes to mind, but also the more recently discovered male, driven as he is by "womb envy" and fear. It was not for nothing that the Grand Dame of postmodern "difference feminism," Luce Irigaray, dumped the language of equality altogether when she asked insubordinately, "Equal to whom?"'

2 Recognition of the social significance of maternity within the CEDAW

According to the *Travaux Préparatoires*, the USSR supported the creation of a preamble to underscore the relation between development and women's participation in all areas, from employment to maternity.[8] With respect to the preamble, Sweden had proposed using the word 'parenthood' instead of 'maternity'. Denmark, Finland, the Netherlands and Norway proposed replacing the 'social significance of maternity' with the 'social significance of child-bearing'.[9] The final text included both aspects (emphasis added):
Preamble, para. 13:

> Bearing in mind the great contribution of women to the welfare of the family and to the development of society, so far not fully recognized, *the social significance of maternity* and the role of both parents in the family and in the upbringing of children, and aware that the role of women in procreation should not be a basis for discrimination but that the upbringing of children requires a sharing of responsibility between men and women and society as a whole.

As pertaining to Article 5(b), the USSR provided a draft that contained the principles adopted in the final treaty text:

> States parties shall adopt all necessary measures with a view to preparing public opinion for the complete eradication of prejudices, customs and all other practices based on the concept of inferiority of women and for recognition of motherhood as a social function.[10]

[8] The UN Declaration on Social Progress and Development (1969), Article 11(b) links protection of mothers to social evolution: 'Social progress and development shall aim at the continuous raising of the material and spiritual standards of living of all members of society, with respect for and in compliance with human rights and fundamental freedoms, through the attainment of the following main goals: the protection of the rights of the mother and the child.' This perspective is upheld by scholars who link the nurture of children to the development of civic participants. L. C. McClain, 'Care as a public value: linking responsibility, resources, and republicanism', *Chi.-Kent L. Rev.* 76 (2000–2001) 1673–732; M. A. Fineman, 'Contract and care', *Chi.-Kent L. Rev.* 76 (2001) 1403–40 at 1408, cited by L. T. Kessler, 'Transgressive caregiving', *Fla. St. U. L. Rev.* 33 (2005) 1–88 at 61.

[9] L. A. Rehof, *Guide to the Travaux Préparatoires of the United Nations Convention on the Elimination of All Forms of Discrimination against Women* (Dordrecht: Martinus Nijhoff, 1993) at 40. See also T. S. Dahl, 'Equal status and birth law' in A. Hellum (ed.), *Birth Law* (Oslo: Scandinavian University Press, 1993) 1–29 at 11, discussing the purpose of birth law as a separate legal field and distinct area of women's law.

[10] Rehof, *supra* note 9 at 79.

It then joined the Philippines with another draft that stated:

> The States parties shall adopt all necessary measures with a view to educating public opinion for the complete eradication of prejudices, customs and all other practices based on the concept of women and for the recognition that the protection of motherhood is a common interest of the entire society which should bear responsibility for it.[11]

There were diverging opinions, as the Federal Republic of Germany and Portugal supported the mention of society's interest in protecting motherhood, while Norway was concerned that this wording would bind women to that role too closely. The UK found this language to be vague and that it might relate to social policy beyond the Convention. The World Health Organization (WHO) preferred wording that expressed motherhood to be of common interest to the entire society (rather than referring to protection). Denmark found the language to be outmoded, while Mexico was of the view that governments should recognize that protection of motherhood was a common obligation of society. The USA objected to the term 'motherhood' as it was discriminatory against men and contrary to US law. Finally, the Working Group replaced it by consensus with the term 'maternity'.[12] The final language of Article 5(b) in the CEDAW is reflective of cultural feminism that seeks positive valuation of feminine roles:[13]

> The States parties shall take all appropriate measures:
>
> (b) To ensure that family education includes a proper understanding of *maternity as a social function* and the recognition of the common responsibility of men and women in the upbringing and development of their children, it being understood that the interest of the children is the primordial consideration in all cases [emphasis added].

R. C. Preston and R. Z. Ahrens highlight the key components of cultural feminism on normative development:

> While the male conception of self is that of an autonomous individual, female self-conception is largely connected to the world and others.

[11] *Ibid.*

[12] However, Morocco did not consider maternity to have a social function.

[13] For an example of cultural feminism, see C. Gilligan, *In A Different Voice: Psychological Theory and Women's Development* (Cambridge, MA: Harvard University Press, 1982). 'Women's concept of value revolves not around the axis of autonomy, individuality, justice and rights, as does men's, but instead around the axis of intimacy, nurturance, community, responsibility and care': West, *supra* note 6 at 2.

> Cultural Feminism's goal does not lie in merely identifying the unique traits of women – traditional patriarchy has already done that – but in celebrating them and recognizing them as strengths. Cultural Feminists argue that these traits and characteristics are not only important but must be taken into account in order for women to enjoy full equality. Further, they recognize that true equality may entail the recognition of human rights that are directed solely at women. They are concerned with protecting and fostering the female experience.[14]

In spite of the incorporation of specific language affirming the value of maternity within the CEDAW, it may be argued that the concept of maternity as a fulfilling experience for women has received insufficient attention within parts of feminist literature. In contrast, within Africa, Asia and Latin America perceptions of motherhood as a guarantor of status within society prompt feminist voices from these regions to value recognition of difference over notions of equality:

> The importance of motherhood and the valuation of the childbearing capacity by African women is probably the most fundamental difference between the African woman and her Western counterpart in their struggle to end discrimination against women. For African women, the role of mother is often central and has intrinsic value.[15]
>
> Unlike feminist movements in the US and Europe, women's activism in Latin America never fully and enthusiastically embraced 'equality feminism'. This may be the result of identification of women with their family responsibilities and motherhood as a still essential female role.[16]

In this chapter 'maternity' is used interchangeably with 'motherhood' and 'maternal identity', as these terms all focus on the state of being a mother, as well as the characteristics, feelings and qualities associated with this connective experience. One of the most promising vehicles for recognizing difference is the use of narratives, which is discussed in the next section.

[14] R. C. Preston and Ronald Z. Ahrens, 'United Nations Convention documents in light of feminist theory', *Mich. J. Gender and L.* 8 (2001) 1–44 at 9.

[15] F. Chioma Steady, 'The Black Woman cross-culturally: an overview' in F. Chioma Steady (ed.), *The Black Woman Cross-Culturally* (Rochester, VT: Schenkman Books, 1981) 7–41 at 34–5.

[16] See J. P. Bruno, 'Third-world critiques of Western feminist theory in the post development era', paper posted 2006.

3 The use of narrative in human rights

As noted by J. S. Peters, narrative can serve as a form of redress and has an independent legal–political function.[17] As 'narrative truth' it gives voice to individual subjective experience as a legitimate source of truth with claims to rights and justice, restoring dignity and providing closure to the victim and community. L. Goodmark also states:

> Proponents of narrative legal scholarship also stress how narratives bring the voices of those traditionally deprived of power within the legal system to the forefront. Arguing that while it may appear neutral, the law itself is a story, structured around narratives developed by the powerful, proponents of narrative theory offer alternative narratives to illustrate the ways that the law excludes these voices and advocate for the need to reform the law to address 'outsider' voices. Narratives help to create common ground, allowing individuals to understand and empathize with the experiences of individuals and groups who are, or seem to be, different. Narratives can bridge the gap between the abstractions of the law and the individual experiences of the humans involved in legal proceedings.[18]

Narratives evolved within the customary traditions of all peoples, and have been recognized in Africa and the Americas as forms of conflict resolution and peace building. In the modern period they have been used in the context of claims rooted in oppression based on race and/or gender.[19] They appear in reports addressing domestic violence, detention, war crimes and so on, in order to promote law reform and as *amici curiae* in national and international forums. In particular, they have been instrumental in international criminal tribunals and formed part of national healing processes conducted via truth commissions. Additionally, they form a central part of refugee status determination. Feminist legal critics have used narrative to highlight institutionalized injustice, and intersectional feminists and third-wave feminist legal theorists use narrative as a form of discourse.[20] The narrative seeks to dismantle exclusionary,

[17] J. S. Peters '"Literature", the "rights of man" and narratives of atrocity: historical backgrounds to the culture of testimony', *Yale J.L. and Human.* 17 (2005) 253–84 at 253–4.

[18] L. Goodmark, 'Telling stories, saving lives: the Battered Mothers' Testimony Project, women's narratives, and court reform', Bepress Legal Series, paper nr. 517 (2005), available at: http://law.bepress.com/cgi/viewcontent.cgi?article=2578&context=expresso (last accessed 5 February 2013).

[19] See J. C. Murphy, 'Lawyering for social change: the power of the narrative in domestic violence law reform', *Hofstra L. Rev.* 21:4 (1993) 1243–93.

[20] See D. L. Rhode, 'Feminist critical theories', *Stan. L. Rev.* 42 (1989–1990) 617–38 at 621. On intersectional feminist theory, see P. J. Williams, *The Alchemy of Race and Rights* (Cambridge, MA: Harvard University Press, 1991); E. V. Spelman, *Inessential Woman:*

hierarchical tendencies within law and promote holistic recognition of protection rights of persons subject to discrimination by relating personal experiences. Its use in forums addressing human rights serves to develop our understanding of norms within contextual situations, thereby constituting an important component in the emancipative aspiration of identifying new protection dimensions. In short, it is a mechanism to provide restorative justice through recognition. Berta Hernández-Truyol advocates participation of women's voices in inquiry processes in order to ensure that their rights are respected:

> The common thread of each inquiry, of course, is to make women visible and raise their voices so that their needs are met and their rights are respected and fulfilled worldwide. In this regard, there has to be an acceptance that in order to raise women's voices a discursive process of communication that includes women is necessary. Regardless of who the ultimate decision-maker is, the process must include and integrate the views of those who are the subjects and the objects of the process, from whom expectations are being generated by the process.[21]

Foster, Haupt and de Beer describe narrative as providing 'inter-subjective understanding' as opposed to prediction and control provided by delineating facts.[22]

The victims in the cases I will discuss include women held within detention centres in Peru and identified by the state as being linked to the Shining Path, who have been silenced by their isolation from general society. It may be argued that the state's classification of them as linked to terrorism renders them particularly vulnerable, indicating an increased need for empathy from those determining their claims of reparation in the event of violations.[23]

The Inter-American Court of Human Rights utilizes quasi-narrative or third-person narrative, along with narrative to enable holistic analysis of the protection interest of human rights victims. The Court has sought to

Problems of Exclusion in Feminist Thought (Boston, MA: Beacon Press, 1988) at 133–59. On third-wave feminist theory see R. Dicker and A. Piepmeier (eds.), *Catching A Wave: Reclaiming Feminism for the 21st Century* (Boston, MA: Northeastern University Press, 2003), which calls for recognition of feminine roles such as motherhood.

21 B. E. Hernández-Truyol, 'Out of the shadows: traversing the imaginary of sameness, difference, and relationalism – a human rights proposal', *Wis. Women's L.J.* 17 (2002) 111–62.

22 D. Foster, P. Haupt and M. de Beer, *Theatre of Violence: Narratives of Protagonists in the South African Conflict* (Cape Town: HSRC Press, 2005).

23 K. Schaffer and S. Smith, *Human Rights and Narrated Lives: The Ethics of Recognition* (New York: Palgrave MacMillan, 2004) at 1.

develop normatively the scope of non-discrimination, which it declared to be a *jus cogens* norm in its *Advisory Opinion on Undocumented Migrants*.[24] It uses narratives to flesh out our understanding of non-discrimination and the scope of harm to marginalized groups, such as indigenous people and women.[25] In the case of victims asserting violations against maternal identity, this methodology may be considered to enable a progressive discussion of how to approach this issue from the perspective of human rights recognition and reparation. As we shall explore, by using the narrative the Inter-American Court of Human Rights is able to expand our understanding of human dignity and maternity.

4 Recognition of violation of a woman's life plan

Cook and Cusack define harm as 'denial of recognition of individual dignity and worth ("recognition effects")'.[26] They cite the Inter-American Commission on Human Rights' view in the *Morales de Sierra* case.[27] The Commission notes that the right to honour and dignity (as guaranteed in the American Convention on Human Rights (ACHR)) embodies a number of elements related to the dignity of the individual, 'including for example, the ability to pursue the development of one's personality and aspirations, determine one's identity, and define one's personal relationships'.[28] The Inter-American Court is at the forefront in enunciating recognition of a violation of one's 'life plan' as regards human rights victims, in particular women.

The case of *Loayza Tamayo* v. *Peru* involved a female university professor who was detained, raped and tortured by state agents. Her life was radically changed after the abuse: she gave up her studies, moved abroad, suffered deep depression and chronic post-traumatic stress disorder. Her ability to fulfil her ambitions was devastated and her options in life were severely limited. From a transcendental perspective, her personal aspirations were destroyed and in this manner her very sense of self was

[24] IACtHR, *Advisory Opinion on Juridical Condition and Rights of the Undocumented Migrants*, OC-18/03, 17 September 2003.

[25] IACtHR, *Awas Tingi* v. *Nicaragua*, Judgment 31 August 2001, Series C No. 79.

[26] Rebecca J. Cook and Simone Cusack, *Gender Stereotyping: Transnational Legal Perspectives*, (Philadelphia: University of Pennsylvania, 2010) at 59.

[27] IACommHR, *Maria Eugenia Morales de Sierra*, Case 11.625, Report no. 4/01, Guatemala (19 January 2001).

[28] *Ibid.* at 66.

permanently altered. The Court summarized the narrative she provided in testimony, noting:

> In this sense, the victim's testimony has unique import, as she is the one who can provide the most information concerning the consequences of the wrongful acts of which she was the victim.[29]

The victim petitioned the Court for compensation on account of damage to the life plan. Judges Cançado Trindade and Abreu-Burelli highlighted the concept of providing reparation from the *perspective of the victim*, in light of his or her needs, aspirations and claims. The Court determined that these actions had long-term effects in that they inhibited the fulfilment of the woman's potential and goals (personal and professional), which could be considered an important manifestation of freedom. The Court held the state responsible for failing to prevent the violations, and in that manner highlighted a breach of the social contract of which the natural consequence is the 'self-imposed' exile of the victim. The narrative is thus a third-person narrative, in which the Court expresses recognition of the violation (adopting the language offered by the victim's lawyer in terms of elucidating the components of the life's plan):

> 152. It is obvious that the violations committed against the victim in the instant Case prevented her from achieving her goals for personal and professional growth, goals that would have been feasible under normal circumstances. Those violations caused irreparable damage to her life, forcing her to interrupt her studies and to take up life in a foreign country far from the context in which her life had been evolving, in a state of solitude, poverty, and severe physical and psychological distress. Obviously this combination of circumstances, directly attributable to the violations that this Court examined, has seriously and probably irreparably altered the life of Ms. Loayza-Tamayo, and has prevented her from achieving the personal, family and professional goals that she had reasonably set for herself.

What is important to recognize is that the Court is very clear in highlighting the individual harm suffered and personal experience, hence avoiding essentialist argumentation. The next section reviews the relationship between maternal identity and one's life plan.

[29] IACtHR, *Loayza Tamayo*, Reparations, Judgment 27 November 1998, Series C. No. 42, para. 73.

5 Recognition of maternity rights and life plan

The Inter-American Court of Human Rights developed its recognition of an individual's life plan as intrinsic to maintenance of human dignity within the context of maternal identity in the case of *Miguel Castro-Castro Prison* v. *Peru*.[30] This case involved a military attack on a prison, resulting in injury of 175 inmates, the death of 42 persons, and cruel, inhuman treatment of 322 inmates. The Court found violations of the American Convention concerning rights to life (Article 4), humane treatment (Article 5), fair trial (Article 8), judicial protection (Article 25 ACHR, and Article 7b of the Belém Convention), and of the Inter-American Convention to Prevent and Punish Torture (Articles 1, 6 and 8). The decision contains a rich collection of narratives of victims, witnesses, and experts on torture and psychology, all highlighting maternal dimensions related to harm experienced.

One may suggest that although the concept of maternity appears intertwined with human rights, our understanding of its protection dimensions have been limited. Consider the following definition:

> *Maternity or motherhood* is the social and legal acknowledgment of the parental relationship between a mother and her child. It is specially related with the protection of the baby and the mother within and after childbirth.[31]

Although this definition appears to focus on the bond between a woman and her infant, the Inter-American human rights system has developed a more expansive view of maternity, one in which the bond extends throughout the child's maturation and death.

The Court cited the CEDAW Committee's General Recommendation No. 19 on 'violence against women' in order to ground its analysis of the violation of sexual rape (in the form of vaginal examinations) amounting to torture, and forced nudity amounting to sexual violence in violation of the right to humane treatment.[32] In addition, the Court highlighted violations against mothers, specifically:

[30] IACtHR, Merits, Reparations and Costs, Judgment 25 November 2006, Ser. C. No. 160.

[31] See: www.absoluteastronomy.com/topics/Maternity (last accessed 22 October 2010) (emphasis in original).

[32] Paras. 303–313.

1. Denial of prenatal and postnatal care for pregnant women in the detention centre,
2. Violations against next of kin and solitary confinement of inmates that rendered communication with their children impossible and caused psychological suffering.[33]

Judge Cancado Trindade highlighted particular harm imposed related to maternal identity:

1. Timing of the attack so that the search for the bodies in the morgue by the next of kin coincided with Mother's Day imposed additional suffering,
2. Denial of life plans as some women were unable to become mothers due to the lengthy pursuit of justice.

This decision received criticism in the form of an academic article authored by P. P. Zuloga. Her core argument was that the Inter-American Court of Human Rights reinforced Latin American social stereotypes of women by recognizing violations of maternal identity.[34] She approved of the Court's recognition of sexual violence and rape as violations meriting compensation.[35] Indeed, recognition of sexual violence and rape as violations of international law meriting prosecution has been a primary focus of the Northern/Western feminist movement, culminating in case law within the International Criminal Tribunal for the Former Yugoslavia (ICTY) and the International Criminal Tribunal for Rwanda (ICTR), as well as adoption of UN Security Council Resolutions 1325 and 1820.[36] In some respects it may be suggested that the focus on attaining prosecution of rape may have resulted in less attention being paid to other protection aspects relevant to women, including those linked to maternal identity. Zuloga recognized that the attack deliberately intended to demoralize the Shining Path by targeting the women's wing of the

[33] Paras. 330, 333 and 342.

[34] P. P. Zuloga, 'The path to gender justice in the Inter-American Court of Human Rights', 17 *Tex. J. Women and L.* 17 (2007–2008) 227–96.

[35] The Inter-American Court issued three decisions afterwards addressing sexual violence: *Case of González et al. ('Cotton Field')* v. *Mexico*, Judgment, Series C No. 205 (16 November 2009) (addressing gender stereotyping as well); *Case of Fernández Ortega and Others* v. *Mexico* (Preliminary Objections, Merits, Reparations and Costs), Judgment, Series C No. 215 (20 August 2010); *Case of Rosendo Cantú and Others* (Preliminary Objections, Merits, Reparations and Costs), Judgment, Series C No. 216 (31 August 2010).

[36] See: www.un.org/Docs/sc/unsc_resolutions08.htm (last accessed 5 February 2013). See C. MacKinnon, 'Defining rape internationally: a comment on Akayasu', *Colum. J. Transnat'l L.* 44:3 (2006) at 940.

prison on women's visiting day, with the search for bodies occuring on Mother's Day. Moreover, she admitted that the victims specifically requested the Court to find the violations against mothers to be particularly severe. Nevertheless, she was suspect of Judge Cançado Trindade's characterization of maternity as being sacred and requiring special care, respect and acknowledgement. Zuloga's scepticism is in keeping with the classic equality feminist criticism against typology of the mother as one who 'needs "protection" during times of both war and peace and is more an object than a subject of international law'.[37] This depiction prompted many feminists to reject maternity as a value, given the consequences of marginalization.[38]

It is of concern that the perception of the protection accorded to women is deemed to be related to a lack of agency, or passivity, instead of considering that protection may be accorded in reward of agency, a duty owed by the state or society towards individuals who have imparted a benefit via care and formation of future generations. Otto cites with concern the protective representation of mothers in Article 25 of the Universal Declaration of Human Rights: 'Motherhood and childhood are entitled to special care and assistance.'[39] She further calls for replacing the 'injured subjectivities produced by human rights law with subjects who have agency to struggle for rights. Such a reinvention also requires fully accepting the constructed and fluid nature of gender differences.'[40]

I argue that there is a need to revise this rhetorical description and its underlying assumptions. Motherhood must be recharacterized as a form of agency, and the provision of protection is a duty by the state owed to mothers, not on account of their passivity/helplessness, but rather precisely on account of their actions as mothers. As pointed out by Martha Fineman:

[37] D. Otto, 'Disconcerting "masculinities": reinventing the gendered subject(s) of international human rights law' in D. Buss and A. Manji (eds.), *International Law: Modern Feminist Approaches* (Oxford and Portland, OR: Hart, 2005) 105–30 at 106.

[38] See M. Chamallas, *Introduction to Feminist Legal Theory* (New York: Aspen, 2003) at 16: 'Equality theorists argued that protection through the law was harmful to women because it served to restrict women's lives to the home and family.'

[39] *Ibid.* at 113. The UN Declaration on Human Rights (1948), Article 25(2) on care and assistance to mothers (this was proposed by India's delegate and met with no opposition). See A. Eide, 'Article 25' in A. Eide, G. Alfredsson, G. Melander, L. Adam Rehof and A. Rosas (eds.), *The Universal Declaration of Human Rights: A Commentary* (Oslo: Scandinavian University Press, 1992). See also the International Covenant on Economic, Social and Cultural Rights, Article 10(2): special protection should be accorded to mothers during a reasonable period before and after childbirth. During such period working mothers should be accorded paid leave or leave with adequate social security benefits.

[40] Otto, *supra* note 37 at 128.

> most mothers do not experience motherhood as 'oppressive' ... Mother has been neutered in several senses. She is taken out of contexts. In policy discussions, just as she is de-gendered, Mother is also de-raced and de-classed. Mother is treated as though she has no ethnic or cultural community that helps to define her. Equality makes Mother an empty legal category, robbing real-life mothers of the protection of their specificity. This neutering happens in the context of a racist and misogynist culture that paradoxically fills the neutered Mother with idealized and demonized contents.[41]

Indeed, human rights have been defined as protections of minimal aspects of agency or autonomy, and it is in this light that the concept of maternity, which implies human action, responsibility and intimacy, needs to be interpreted.[42]

Judge Cançado Trindade invoked the narrative of one of the victims in order to ground the finding of a violation, thereby confirming Schaffer and Smith's observation that this methodology is 'one of the most potent vehicles for advancing human rights claims'.[43] This process creates an international space for personal testimony that highlights the maternal dimensions of the violation. It is important to note that the victim herself chooses to present this perception of violation; it was not imposed upon her by the Court. Because narratives may be used to identify 'disjunction between the values espoused by the community and the actual practices that occur',[44] the testimony of violations related to maternal rights is particularly significant within a Latin American culture that traditionally sanctifies the role of the mother.

Zuloga criticized the cultural dimensions of the maternal role as being linked to gender stereotypes that should not be promoted within the international human rights regime. In contrast, I argue that this perspective inappropriately negates protection rights linked to biological/social difference. Social norms oriented towards protection and honour of mothers need not only be viewed as a negative, but rather may also

[41] Fineman, *supra* note 4 at 53 and 67. She adds: 'There is a need for the development of theoretical language to express women's experiences so as not to alienate women who live some aspects of traditional lives.'

[42] In comparison, within the field of international humanitarian law, medical and religious personnel are granted special protection on account of their agency, as are soldiers placed *hors de combat* or taken as prisoners of war. The crucial consideration is that the identification of a duty of care towards them is not considered to objectify the soldiers.

[43] Schaffer and Smith, *Human Rights and Narrated Lives* at 1.

[44] Fineman, *supra* note 4 at 72.

indicate positive protection elements that seek to uphold human dignity, instead of repressing it.

Judge Cançado Trindade argued that his approach pursues precisely a gender analysis and includes the narrative of a mother to highlight the importance of recognition of violation related to maternal identity. In his view, non-discrimination requires recognition of difference in order to provide protection:

> 58. The present case cannot be adequately examined without a gender analysis. Remember that, as a first step, the United Nations Convention of the Elimination of All Forms of Discrimination against Women (CEDAW, 1979) advanced on a holistic vision of the matter, tackling women's rights in all areas of life and in all situations (in fact, I would even add in the light of the cas d'espèce, in the deprivation of freedom); the Convention cries out for the modification of socio-cultural patterns of behavior (Article 5) and highlights the principle of equality and non-discrimination.
>
> 62. There was then the extreme violence in the experience itself of maternity, when facing the brutality perpetrated against their children. In the aforementioned public hearing before this Court in the present case of the Castro Castro Prison, a mother (Mrs. Julia Peña Castillo), a witness in the case, described it with eloquence:
>
> (...) On June 06, 1992, who speaks is the mother of many children (...), (...) my mother's instinct was more than for the house, for more than just cooking, I left everything behind (...). When I arrived there [at Castro Castro] there was more than just the press, (...) there were many soldiers, there were trucks going in and others coming out, (...) there I started screaming, (...) screaming and saying: – 'what are you doing, my children my children'! It was the first thing reflected in my words, my children. (...)
>
> (...) There many of us mothers hugged, we hugged strongly because the roars of the cannon reached out hearts. Each roar represented a very strong pain because you could see the splinters flying from the pavilions. (...) There was a mother next to me, I hugged her and she told me 'my daughter is alive, my daughter is alive' (...). Hearing her got me very excited. Later that day the situation was worse, you could no longer hear voices, just shots fired from what sounded like a machine gun or a long weapon (...), you could hear it and then it would stop, and then on the other side again. (...) The gunshots continued. We stayed there all night, we did not know anything, who was dead, who was injured, how many had died, nothing because they did not give us any information. Even the police officers that came out (...). They did not give us any type of information (...). (...) They were not interested.

> 63. In even another dimension, many of the women who survived the bombing of the Prison of Castro Castro – as has been stated in this Concurring Opinion (para. 13, *supra*) – have not been able to be mothers yet, since, as stated in the public hearing in the cas d'espèce before this Court, they have since then used all their existential time in searching for truth and justice. Thus, we are facing here a maternity that has been denied or postponed (a damage to a life project), forced upon them by the cruel circumstances, as claimed with all pertinence by the common intervener of the representatives of the victims and their next of kin (*supra*) [internal citations omitted].

It is essential to note that the claim of denial of the possibility to become mothers is raised by the applicants in the hearing, not imposed upon them by the Court. The Court recognized their claim, in keeping with prior case law addressing the life project as an element of reparation. The applicants' request for recognition of violation of fulfilment of an aspect of their personal life's project (motherhood) should not be invalidated because the concept of motherhood as a woman's natural role and destiny may be considered a stereotype.[45] Whereas the *Loayza Tamayo* case addressed the combined violation of personal and professional goals of a female university professor, in this case the applicants specifically identify the personal goal of motherhood as the goal interfered with. It is a reflexive recognition that provides equal protection through its recognition of difference.

6 Misdiagnosis of wrongful gender stereotypes

Cook and Cusack provide us with a definition of wrongful gender stereotypes and explain their scope, with arguments that mirror the Inter-American Court's identification of the right to a life plan:

> A gender stereotype can harm women when it diminishes their dignity as human beings … A gender stereotype infringes women's dignity when it fails to recognize their intrinsic and equal worth as human beings or when, for example, it treats them in ways that do not take into account their actual situations … When a gender stereotype fails to respect the basic choices women have made (or would like to make) about their own lives, when it interferes with their ability to shape, or carve out, their own identities, when it lowers expectations of them, or, for example, negatively impacts their sense of self, goals, and/or life plans, it degrades them. The

[45] On the notion of motherhood as a stereotype, see Cook and Cusack *supra* note 26 at 11.

> gender stereotype constricts women's identities, meaning that it prevents women from defining and presenting themselves as they would like. Instead, women have been publicly defined or presented in the manner of another's choosing, and their ability to shape their own identities and direct their lives according to their own values, priorities, and aspirations has been denied.[46]

Cook and Cusack call for treating women according to their diverse individual needs, abilities, priorities and circumstances.[47] Nevertheless, they caution against the assignation of difference for 'benign purposes/benevolent paternalism' and the prescription of roles. This confirms a bias towards traditional equality values over difference perspectives. The Inter-American Court sought to provide reparation for violation of life plans and addressed gender-related violations by the state. It sought to restore human dignity and thus justified its recognition of maternal identity as meriting protection and reparation. The Court's identification of harms related to maternal identity appears legitimate, proportionate and reasonable as it seeks to redress targeting of mothers/women. It appears that the Court sought to pursue recognition of the victims according to individual circumstances. In *Miguel Castro-Castro Prison* v. *Peru* the recognition of motherhood as an aspiration (life plan/personal goal/life choice/shaping of identity one would like to make) meriting recognition grants the benefit of compensation, and does not impose a burden on women. It seeks to uphold dignity, not to degrade or marginalize them or prescribe an identity that is contrary to their life plans. It should be noted that this case appears to build upon the Court's prior jurisprudence setting forth the state's duty to guarantee human dignity in life involving indigenous people and minors.[48]

Judge Cançado Trindade explicitly noted that the victims and their families made normative reference to the Convention of Belém do Pará, rather than the Commission, thereby enabling the Court to make a gender analysis of the violations:

> 68. In the legal proceedings (in both the written and oral stages) before this Court, it was the representation of the victims and their next of kin, and not the Commission, who insisted on relating the protection norms of the Convention of Belém do Pará (specifically its Articles 4

[46] Cook and Cusack, *supra* note 26 at 64–5. See also Cusack's chapter in this volume, describing wrongful gender stereotyping as resulting in discrimination or leading to violations of other rights and freedoms.

[47] Cook and Cusack *supra* note 26 at 173.

[48] IACtHR, *Sawhoyamaxa Case* v. *Paraguay* (2006), *Villagran Morales/the Street Children Case* v. *Guatemala* (1999), and the *Juvenile Reeducation Case* v. *Paraguay* (2004).

> and 7) with the violations to the American Convention on Human Rights. This exercise comes to attend the necessary gender analysis in the present case. Article 4 of the Convention of Belém do Pará states that 'every woman' has the right to 'recognition, enjoyment, exercise, and protection' of all the human rights enshrined in international instruments on the matter, among which it expressly mentioned the rights to life, humane treatment, to not be submitted to tortures, to respect to 'the inherent dignity of her person'.
>
> 69. And, through Article 7 of the Convention of 1994, the States Parties agree to pursue a series of measures to 'prevent, investigate, punish, and eradicate' the different forms of violence against women. In the present case of the Castro Castro Prison, where, for the first time in the history of this Court, the gender analysis is set forth – to my satisfaction as a Judge – by the representatives of the victims themselves and their next of kin (and not by the Commission) as the true plaintiff before the Court and as subjects of International Law, the human rights of women have been violated with special cruelty, constituting the aggravated international responsibility of the Respondent government [internal citations omitted].

It is hard to reconcile Zuloga's demand that the Court explicitly recognize gender-specific forms of violations in the form of rape and sexual violence but negate its explicit recognition of gender-related violations that relate to maternal identity. It may be contended that Zuloga has a 'carnal bias' within her interpretation of human rights, one which prioritizes sexual autonomy over maternal identity. Article 1 of the UN Declaration on the Elimination of Violence against Women (1993) defines violence against women as going beyond physical elements: 'any act of gender-based violence that results in, or is likely to result in, physical, sexual or psychological harm or suffering to women, including threats of such acts, coercion or arbitrary deprivation of liberty, whether occurring in public or in private life'. In like manner, the definition contained in Article 1 of the Inter-American Convention on the Prevention, Punishment and Eradication of Violence against Women also recognizes mental harm:

> For the purposes of this Convention, violence against women shall be understood as any act or conduct, based on gender, which causes death or physical, sexual or psychological harm or suffering to women, whether in the public or the private sphere.

The danger of accepting Zuloga's argument is that it pursues a singular approach to protection, the consequence of which is contempt or denial of recognition of a particular experience of harm, which in this case was claimed by a distinct group of women. In effect, this position calls upon us to silence, ignore or render invisible the voices of mothers because their perceptions of harm are misconceived as falling outside of the accepted paradigm of gender protection. There is a need to reconceive the gendered identity of mother in a positive manner. Zuloga concludes by advocating the espousal of a sex discrimination approach as opposed to a particular, gender-based approach:

> the Court made enormous strides when it took on the issue of gendered violence in Plan de Sanchez and in Castro Castro, but [that] it erred when it endorsed the same stereotype used to victimize women and men in this cases. There are enough objective facts in this case to conclude that there was enhanced suffering of certain victims in the Castro Castro case because of their undeniably close relationship to other victims, especially those who were parents of the victims. It is not only reasonable but also necessary for a human rights court to recognize that the victims of the Castro Castro massacre, men and women, were maliciously targeted with a social stereotype that heightened their suffering based on their sex. This approach entails necessarily finding that the state also violated the right to equality of the victims. To rule that sex discrimination was the basis of the treatment that the victims received is very different from an essentialist ruling that a mother's pain or a woman's pain is worse because they are mothers and women. This finding was entirely possible in Castro Castro without jeopardizing the examination of the case with a gendered lens; to see women and men as such, recognizing their particular circumstances without reducing them to their social stereotypes would have made this case the remarkable, positive precedent that it deserves to be.[49]

This rhetoric establishes distinct constructs of categories for protection, under the guise of pursuing a 'universal' theory, which in effect neglects difference in variation within the experience of harm.[50]

In my opinion, maternal identity can be as important as sexual autonomy in the definition of a woman's life. To emphasize one aspect of female experience as legitimate for human rights protection but not the other appears unsound, biased and fallacious. One may turn to Refugee Law for relevant elucidation of this point. Consider this case from the Immigration and Refugee Board of Canada addressing whether asylum should be granted to the mother of an illegitimate child in China:

> The panel referred to a decision of the German Federal Administrative Court where that Court found that '[i]n general, a threat to life, limb

[49] Zuloga, *supra* note 34.

[50] See M. Malik, 'Feminism and its "other": female autonomy in an age of "difference"', *Cardozo L. Rev.* 30 (2008–2009) 2613–28 at 2616.

> or freedom of one spouse also poses a threat to the marriage and thus ... a hardship for the other spouse'. The Canadian Refugee Board panel member concluded: In my opinion, the principle which the German administrative court enunciated in respect to spouses, is more persuasive in respect to a relationship between a mother and a child, particularly a child of tender years. The hardship for the parent of a child being persecuted may be even more poignantly felt by a mother than would the hardship which is felt by one spouse when the other spouse is persecuted ... The panel found the claimant to be a Convention refugee.[51]

In fact, infliction of severe pain or suffering upon a family member as means of extracting information, intimidating or punishing a person is also specifically recognized as a form of torture. Returning to the Inter-American Court case, although one may argue that a father's pain over the loss of a child may be equivalent to that of a mother, it is undeniable that the strategic decision to launch an attack so that the parents would have to search for the bodies on Mother's Day would have a particular impact on mothers. This concept is derived directly from the victims' testimonies:

> 64. And, in the dimension of the after-life, the experience of maternity has also been seriously affected. It has been well illustrated in the desperate search, in the morgues, by the victims' next of kin, of the remains of the inmates who died in the armed attack against the Prison of Castro Castro, and the indifference of the state authorities. As stated by the Court in the present Judgment,
>
> (...) The testimonies included in the body of evidence coincide when they state that an additional element of suffering was the fact of being [the mothers and next of kin] in that situation of uncertainty and despair on 'Mother's Day' (Sunday May 10, 1992) (para. 338).

Judge Cançado Trindade seeks to expand the range of apperception of harm into the transcendental realm of human experience. Relationships between family members are recognized as composing a fundamental aspect of human identity. They have a distinct value and merit reparation when violation is pursued with the intention of exploiting the relationship to magnify the scope of harm. Maternal identity is formed *within* the intimate connection between mother and child, and when that attachment is brutally violated, mothers may demand recognition of this particular form of harm.[52] Indeed, Robin West suggests:

[51] CRDD V91-00998, Groos, Robles, 15 November 1991.

[52] Gilligan, *supra* note 13 at 159, cited by West, *supra* note 6 at 18. West characterizes separation as the official harm of cultural feminism (at 19, 28, 60–6, 65): 'Women's concept of harm revolves not around a fear of annihilation by the other but around a fear of

> Put phenomenologically, instead of narratively, feminist legal theorists need to show through stories the value of intimacy – not just to women, but to the community – and the damage done – again, not just to women, but to the community – by the law's refusal to reflect that value.[53]

Within its jurisprudence, the Court has developed various dimensions of what may be considered to fall within a scope of harm to maternal identity akin to West's 'connection thesis'. For example, one may consider the *Case of Cantoral Huamaní and García Santa Cruz* v. *Peru* (2007), in which the Inter-American Court cites the psychologist's report noting the impact of the loss of the father of the family, which meant that the mother had to work on Christmas Day and Mother's Day, leaving the children alone. One may also consider the *Case of González et al. ('Cotton Field')* v. *Mexico* (2009) in which the Court cites the narratives of mothers reflecting on their need for the truth after the disappearance of their daughters in Ciudad Juárez, Mexico, and the psychological damage experienced as a result of the lack of response by the authorities.[54] Similarly, the UN Human Rights Committee recognized the liability of the state for violation of Article 7's prohibition of torture and cruel, inhuman or degrading treatment or punishment with respect to the anguish and stress caused to the mother of a woman who was disappeared and the uncertainty concerning her fate and whereabouts.[55] It found violation of the same Article in two other cases in which mothers were denied information regarding the date of execution of their sons, access to the body for burial and location of the burial site, thereby subjecting them to a state of uncertainty and mental distress amounting to inhuman treatment.[56] The identification of maternal identity as a central element of a particular woman's life project is intended to uphold her human dignity rather than diminish it,

separation and isolation from the human community on which she depends, and which is dependent upon her … Women have, from law's inception, lacked the power to make law protect, value, or seriously regard our experience … a legal system which fails to value intimacy, fails to protect against separation … feminist legal theorists need to show through stories the value of intimacy – not just to women, but to the community – and the damage done – again, not just to women, but to the community – by the law's refusal to reflect that value.'

[53] West, *supra* note 6 at 65.

[54] Paras. 413–24. See also IACtHR, *La Cantuta* v. *Peru*, Judgment, Series C No. 162, 29 November 2006, para. 125.

[55] UN Human Rights Committee, *Quinteros* v. *Uruguay*, Communication No. 107/1981 (21 July 1983) para. 14.

[56] UN Human Rights Committee, *Banderenko* v. *Belarus*, Comm. No. 886/1999 para. 10, CCPR/C/77/D/886/1999 (3 April 2003) and *Lyashkevich* v. *Belarus*, Comm. No. 887/1999 para. 9.2 CCPR/C/77/D/887/1999 (3 April 2003). See also *Sarma* v. *Sri Lanka*, Comm.

and hence should not be considered a harmful gender stereotype. By recognizing narratives elucidating the scope of maternal identity and harm, the Inter-American Court supports the phenomenological evolution of human rights protection towards holistic protection of women. Failure to place sufficient emphasis on narrative evidence may result in denial of protection.[57]

7 Conclusion: in pursuit of international and regional harmonization

In this chapter it is suggested that the Inter-American Court's use of narratives expands upon the foundation established by the CEDAW's recognition of maternity, as a form of agency according to Article 5b, in order to provide more holistic, reflexive protection of related rights meriting recognition and reparation. It may be argued that a finding of violation, accompanied by a narrative in which the victim is permitted to voice in his/her own words his/her personal experience of the scope of harm may be more in keeping with the notion of having a judgment serve as part of reparation. The narrative serves to avoid generalizations or gender stereotypes, as the story is about an individual. This permits recognition that not all persons belonging to a particular category may identify with a scope of harm that is defined by the expression of personal experience. The benefits of recognition of maternal identity are made evident by consideration of consequences related to non-recognition of maternal violations, for example the risk of radicalization and further oppression, such as the prosecution of the mothers of the victims of the massacre at Beslan.[58] They were prosecuted as extremists in Russia due to their attempt to pursue assignation of state responsibility within the court system. It

No. 950/2000, CCPR/C/78/D/950/2000 (16 July 2003) in which the state is found to have violated Article 7 in relation to both the father and the mother of a man who was disappeared. One may consider that it is recognized that torture or inhuman or degrading treatment may be the consequence of psychological harm (not only physical harm).

57 One may consider the dissent in the case of *Zhen Zhen Zheng* v. *The Netherlands*, Communication No. 15/2007, CEDAW/C/42/D/15/2007 (26 October 2009). CEDAW Committee members Mary Shanti Dairiam, Violeta Neubauer and Silvia Pimental highlighted interviews and reports in which the woman described being subjected to forced sex, rape, detention, as well as previous hardship endured as an illiterate, poor orphan. They utilized this material to contradict the majority's dismissal of the claim. Their conclusion indicated that the narratives revealed that she had been a victim of trafficking, thereby meriting protection from the state.

58 See http://siberianlight.net/mothers-of-beslan-victims-charged-with-extremism/ (last accessed 5 February 2013).

is important to recognize that the enunciation of maternal demands for the right to truth and justice with respect to the disappearance of their children by the Mothers of the Plaza de Mayo in Argentina was considered to form part of the foundation of the modern human rights era, as it launched transnational response networks. It would be ironic if recognition of harm related to motherhood was later described as inappropriate within the context of human rights and mischaracterized as a wrongful gender stereotype.

Because the CEDAW Committee has yet to address a case involving Article 5(b), there is imbalance within the jurisprudence, which places emphasis on equality rather than difference. The relevance of the use of narratives by the Inter-American Court is that it highlights the way in which the CEDAW may be further interpreted in order to achieve its aspiration of attaining respect for the dignity of all women, including mothers. This chapter highlights the potential for using narratives as a vehicle by which to achieve harmony between the language in Articles 5(a) and (b) of the CEDAW. The Inter-American Court of Human Rights supports recognition of difference as a central element of protection of women's rights. It may be argued that the Court seeks to expand interpretation of the CEDAW in order to apply its standards directly in the regional context.

The majority of Latin American states have ratified the CEDAW and its Protocol. The CEDAW Committee's review of country reports within the Americas primarily focuses on the following issues: harmonization of national legislation with the Convention, monitoring functions, education of the judiciary, implementation of the Convention in federal systems and enforcement in provinces, employment legislation and maternity leave, the situation of indigenous women, discriminatory culture, gender stereotyping within the judiciary, media, educational systems and society, and the importance of reducing maternal mortality, as well as provision of prenatal and postnatal care in urban and rural areas.

Within the Inter-American human rights system, both the Inter-American Court and Commission of Human Rights have produced case law in which women's rights are addressed via reference to substantive and procedural guarantees relating to a state's due diligence duty to prevent, investigate, punish and redress cases in which women have been subjected to violations within the American Convention (or in the alternative, the American Declaration), inter alia: the right to humane treatment (Article 5, ACHR), the right to fair trial (Article 8, ACHR) and the right to due process (Article 25, ACHR).[59]

Moreover, the Inter-American Convention on the Prevention, Punishment and Eradication of Violence against Women (Convention of Belém do Pará) serves as an additional source for holding states accountable for failing to investigate cases in which women have been subjected to harm (Article 7b).[60] This Convention has been ratified by more states than any other convention in the Inter-American system. Nonetheless, the Inter-American Commission has noted that 'Most cases of violence against women are never formally investigated, prosecuted and punished by the administration of justice systems in the hemisphere.'[61]

The CEDAW Committee follows up implementation of regional norms: for example during discussion of Nicaragua's report, it queried the implementation of the Convention of Belém do Pará; and with respect to Brazil the Committee inquired as to enforcement of an Inter-American

[59] The Inter-American Court's cases addressing the protection of women include: *Case of Fernández Ortega and Others* v. *Mexico* (Preliminary Objections, Merits, Reparations and Costs), Judgment, Series C No. 215 (20 August 2010); *Case of Rosendo Cantú and Others* (Preliminary Objections, Merits, Reparations and Costs), Judgment, Series C No. 216 (31 August 2010); *Case of González et al. ('Cotton Field')* v. *Mexico*, Judgment, Series C No. 205 (2009); *Cantoral-Humaní and García-Santa Cruz* v. *Peru*, Judgment, Series C No. 167 (10 July 2007); *Miguel Castro-Castro Prison* v. *Peru*, Judgment, Series C No. 160 (25 November 2006); *Sawhoyamaxa Indigenous Community* v. *Paraguay*, Judgment, Series C No. 146 (29 March 2006); *Girls Yean and Bosico* v. *Dominican Republic*, Judgment, Series C No.130 (8 September 2005); *Molina-Theissen* v. *Guatemala*, Judgment, Series C No. 106 (4 May 2004); *Plan de Sanchez Massacre* v. *Guatemala*, Judgment, Series C No. 105 (29 April 2004); *De La Cruz-Flores* v. *Peru*, Judgment, Series C No. 115 (18 November 2004); *Lori Berenson-Mejia* v. *Peru*, Judgment, Series C. No. 119 (25 November 2004); and *Maria Elena Loayza-Tamayo* v. *Peru*, Judgment, Series C No. 33 (17 September 1997). Further the *Yakye Axa Indigenous Community Case* v. *Paraguay*, Judgment, Series C No. 125 (17 June 2005) highlighted the state's duty of care to pregnant women. The Inter-American Commission has had several important cases, including: *Maria Merciadri de Morini*, Case 11.307 Report No. 103/01, Argentina (11 October 2001); *Maria Eugenia Morales de Sierra*, Case 11.625, Report No. 4/01, Guatemala (19 January 2001); *Ana, Beatriz, and Celia Gonzalez Perez*, Case 11.565, Report No. 129/99, Mexico (19 November 1999); *Maria Da Penha Maia Fernandes*, Case 12.051 Report No. 54/01, Brazil (16 April 2001); *Jessica Lenahan et al.*, Case 12.626, Report No. 80/11, United States (21 July 2011).

[60] IACtHR, *Case of the Miguel Castro-Castro Prison* v. *Peru* (Merits, Reparations and Costs), Judgment, Ser. C No. 160 (25 November 2006); *Case of Fernández Ortega and Others* v. *Mexico* (Preliminary Objections, Merits, Reparations and Costs), Judgment, Series C No. 215 (20 August 2010); *Case of Rosendo Cantú and Others* (Preliminary Objections, Merits, Reparations and Costs), Judgment, Series C No. 216 (31 August 2010).

[61] Inter-American Commission of Human Rights, *Access to Justice for Women Victims of Violence in the Americas*, OEA/Ser.L/V/II p. viii (20 January 2007).

Commission of Human Rights view, in the case of Maria da Penha Maia Fernandes, calling for prosecution of a perpetrator of domestic violence.[62] Finally, the Committee conducted an inquiry on gender violence in Ciudad Juárez, Mexico. This produced specific recommendations addressing the state's duty to investigate and punish the perpetrators, complementing recommendations by the Special Rapporteur of the Inter-American Commission on Human Rights.[63] The CEDAW Committee supports the Inter-American Human Rights System as a partner in the protection of women's rights. We may be witnessing symbiosis of the systems in providing protection for women's rights.

[62] UN Committee on the Elimination of Discrimination against Women, *Summary Record: Consideration of Combined Reports Submitted by Brazil*, CEDAW/C/SR.611 (11 July 2003); UN Committee on the Elimination of Discrimination against Women, *Summary Record: Consideration of Sixth Periodic Report of Nicaragua*, CEDAW/C/SR.761 (13 February 2007).

[63] UN Committee on the Elimination of Discrimination against Women, *Report on Mexico under Article 8 of the Optional Protocol*, CEDAW/C/2005/OP.8/Mexico (27 January 2005); Inter-American Commission on Human Rights, *The Situation of the Rights of Women in Ciudad Juárez, Mexico: The Right to be Free from Violence and Discrimination*, OEA/Ser.L/V/II.117 (7 March 2003).

6

Pulling apart? Treatment of pluralism in the CEDAW and the Maputo Protocol

CELESTINE NYAMU MUSEMBI

1 Introduction

The United Nations (UN) Convention on the Elimination of All Forms of Discrimination against Women (CEDAW) recognizes that discrimination against women does not arise only from formal laws; from 'state action' narrowly defined. Discrimination against women is also produced and sustained by stereotypes and beliefs contained in other moral codes such as community customs and religious norms. Hence Articles 2(f) and 5(a) place obligations on states to take legislative and other measures to 'modify' or 'abolish' such stereotypes or ideas of inferiority or superiority of men and women so as to achieve the CEDAW's objective of eliminating all forms of discrimination against women. But does the text of the CEDAW suggest that elimination of discrimination against women necessitates wholesale displacement of these other moral codes? Or does it suggest that the convention recognizes that in some instances achievement of substantive equality for women may require recognition and upholding of some principles and practices embodied in those other moral codes?[1]

The author wishes to thank the reviewers for their comments, and Bonface Omondi and Maureen Elavisa for research assistance.

[1] A number of scholars studying the lived realities of different groups of women against the background of international legal protection against gender discrimination have emphasized the need for research that puts gendered understandings about people's local experiences, problems and practices in a continuous dialogue with evolving human rights principles so as to find a way out of the seemingly contentious relationship between women's human rights and legal pluralism. See A. Hellum, S. S. Ali and A. Griffiths (eds.), *From Transnational Relations to Transnational Laws: Northern European Law at the Crossroads* (Farnham: Ashgate, 2011). See also A. Hellum, J. Stewart, S. S. Ali and A. Tsanga (eds.), *Human Rights, Plural Legalities and Gendered Realities: Paths Are Made by Walking*

This chapter explores this question by examining in detail the position that the CEDAW Committee has taken in instances that have brought this question to the surface. Following this introduction, section 2 will examine what has emerged as the CEDAW Committee's preferred approach. This will be contrasted in section 3 to the approach taken in the framing of the Protocol to the African Charter on Human and Peoples' Rights on the Rights of Women in Africa (Maputo Protocol). Section 4 will explore the manner in which selected East and Southern African (ESA) states have approached the issue of legal pluralism,[2] in particular the striking of a balance between sanctioning the operation of customary and religious laws and ensuring protection against gender-based discrimination in recent constitutional reforms. Section 5 examines cases in which women have, in essence, asked the courts to affirm their entitlements under customary laws and practice, sometimes in circumstances that require the courts to affirm customary norms or practices that raise questions as to their compatibility with human rights.

The concluding section reflects on the appropriate feminist response when confronted with the difficult choice of when to affirm plural normative orders as securing justice for women on terms that they value, and when to reject such a path on account of its potential negative long-term effect in sustaining a context in which meaningful choice is structurally constrained. Which of the paths helps us to ask the right questions: the CEDAW Committee's approach, the Maputo Protocol approach or neither?

2 Pluralism under the CEDAW

Articles 2 and 5 of the CEDAW (particularly 2(f) and 5(a)) have been variously identified as the provisions that get to the heart of what must be done

(Harare: Weaver Press, 2007) [hereinafter Hellum *et al.*, *Human Rights*]; C. Nyamu, 'How should human rights and development respond to cultural legitimization of gender hierarchy in developing countries?', *Harvard International Law Journal* 41:2 (2000) 381–417.

[2] The term 'legal pluralism' has been understood at two levels. At the first level it refers to the coexistence of two or more legal orders, as in post-colonial contexts where the same subject matter may be governed by various laws drawing from different sources. For instance, statutory laws on family law coexist with family laws drawn from custom or from religion, and all of these multiple sources are recognized as law. At the second level 'legal pluralism' is understood as a phenomenon that goes beyond post-colonial settings. It is simply a broadened understanding of the category 'law' as encompassing norms emanating from multiple norm-generating sites, the state being simply one of those sites, as opposed to a state-centric view of law. See J. Griffiths, 'What is legal pluralism', *Journal of Legal Pluralism and Unofficial Law* 24 (1986) 1–56.

in order for the object and purpose of the CEDAW to be realized, namely the elimination of all forms of discrimination against women.[3] Arguably, all the measures spelled out in Article 2(a) through to 2(e) are measures that states already had an obligation to undertake prior to the CEDAW by virtue of non-discrimination and 'equal right of men and women to the enjoyment of rights' clauses in previous international human rights documents.[4]

The hallmark of the CEDAW comes with Article 2(f) moving state obligation beyond the comfort zone of availing individual rights to redress for individual discrimination, to requiring transformative cultural change that deals with systemic discrimination.[5] This is no doubt in recognition of the fact that without such deep-reaching cultural transformation, there can be no genuine equality between the sexes.[6] Any gains secured through legal change could unravel or have effects contrary to what was envisaged.[7] This call for transformative cultural change is reinforced through Article 5(a), which places on States Parties an obligation to 'take all appropriate measures' to 'modify the social and cultural patterns of conduct of men and women, with a view to achieving the elimination of prejudices and customary and all other practices which are based on the idea of the inferiority or the superiority of either of the sexes or on stereotyped roles for men and women'.

The text of Article 5(a) is clear that:

(1) the goal is the elimination of prejudices (wrongful stereotypes) and customary practices premised on subordination of either sex, or on stereotyped gender roles; and
(2) the state is to take *all appropriate measures*, meaning that no limit is placed on the range of options available to the state as it works toward that goal.

The framing of Article 5(a) has earned both criticism for being broad and ambiguous, and acclaim for allowing flexibility and adaptability to new

[3] See Holtmaat, this volume; Cusack, this volume; CEDAW General Recommendation No. 20, *Reservations to the Convention* (11th Session, 1992); CEDAW General Recommendation No. 25, *On temporary special measures* (30th Session, 2004). See also R. Cook, 'Reservations to the Convention on the Elimination of All Forms of Discrimination against Women', *Virginia Journal of International Law* 30 (1990) 643–712.

[4] See, for instance, Article 3 of the International Covenant on Civil and Political Rights and Article 3 of the International Covenant on Economic, Social and Cultural Rights.

[5] See Holtmaat, this volume.

[6] See Cusack, this volume.

[7] See Holtmaat, this volume.

situations.[8] In my view, the bottom line is that whichever option (or range of options) the state chooses must be shown to be progressive, in the sense of making progress toward – not away from – the goal.

It would not be inaccurate to say that religious and customary laws and practices on family relations have been regarded as the primary address for ideas of superiority or inferiority of women and men (read the subordination of women), and for stereotyped gender roles. The legal systems of most post-colonial African states give explicit recognition to these plural normative orders, and therefore they operate not as parallel informal legal systems, but are officially sanctioned by the state's legal system. The CEDAW Committee in several instances gives the impression that the very fact that these normative orders are officially sanctioned to operate is in itself a violation of the CEDAW. Notwithstanding the broad language of Article 5(a) and the apparent flexibility given to states in choice of tools, the CEDAW Committee's interpretation suggests that the Committee's preferred approach when confronted with practices that it considers to be inconsistent with gender equality but which are sanctioned by religious or customary norms is one of:

(a) legislation as the predominant intervention; and
(b) legislation that is prohibitory in nature; and
(c) prohibitory legislation that is immediate rather than gradual.

This is essentially an abolitionist approach.[9] The main body of this section proceeds to substantiate the claim that the CEDAW Committee has taken an abolitionist approach, by referring to specific CEDAW Committee documents, mainly General Recommendation No. 21 and Concluding Observations on periodic reports submitted by selected ESA States Parties.

2.1 General Recommendation No. 21

General Recommendation No. 21 was issued in 1994 and it focused on elaborating states' obligations with respect to ensuring equality in marriage and family relations. The CEDAW Committee identifies three Articles as central to equality in marriage and family relations: Article 9 on nationality, Article 15 on equality before the law and Article 16 on marriage.

[8] See Cusack, this volume.

[9] See Nyamu, 'How should human rights and development respond'.

The Committee noted the prominent role of personal or customary law in the area of marriage and family relations. Throughout the General Recommendation, these personal or customary law systems are spoken of largely as a negative force. What is emphasized is their tendency to restrict women's rights to equal status and responsibility within marriage.[10] There is no suggestion that these norms and practices can play any role in achieving the objectives of the CEDAW.

In commenting specifically on Article 16, the Committee notes that there are a variety of family forms, but all of these, whether based on formal law, custom or religion, must accord women equality 'both at law and in private'.[11] The Committee then takes on the issue of polygamy. Even though the text of the CEDAW does not refer to polygamy, the Committee is unequivocal in holding that polygamous marriage 'contravenes a woman's right to equality with men and can have such serious emotional and financial consequences for her and her dependants that such marriages ought to be discouraged or prohibited'.[12] The Committee goes on to castigate states whose constitutions guarantee equal rights and yet those same states 'permit polygamous marriages in accordance with personal or customary law'. The Committee takes the view that such states violate the constitutional rights of women, and are also in violation of Article 5(a) of the CEDAW.

This position was echoed in a General Comment by the Human Rights Committee in 2000.[13] The Committee starts by noting that 'the enjoyment of rights by women throughout the world is deeply embedded in tradition, history and culture, including religious attitudes'.[14] The Committee then notes that equal exercise of the right to marry implies that polygamy is incompatible with the principle of equality of rights between men and women.[15] The Committee underlines this conclusion as follows: 'Polygamy violates the dignity of women. It is an inadmissible discrimination against women. Consequently, *it should be definitely abolished wherever it continues to exist*.'[16] Both Committees assume, first, that polygamy is always non-consensual and, secondly, that the only appropriate response is to legislate against it.

[10] See, for example, General Recommendation No. 21, paras. 14, 15 and 17.

[11] *Ibid.*, para. 13. [12] *Ibid.*, para. 14.

[13] UN Human Rights Committee, General Comment No. 28, *Equality of Rights Between Men and Women* (2000), available at: www.unhchr.ch/tbs/doc.nsf/(Symbol)/13b0277612 2d4838802568b900360e80?Opendocument (last accessed 28 March 2012).

[14] *Ibid.*, para. 5. [15] *Ibid.*, para. 24.

[16] *Ibid.*, para. 24. Author's emphasis.

There is an apparent change of tone one year later. As a follow-up to General Recommendation No. 21, the CEDAW Committee commissioned its Secretariat in 1995 to prepare analysis of Article 2 of the Convention. In the Secretariat's opinion, Article 2(f) read together with Article 5(a) implies that the state must employ public means to address discriminatory customs and practices.[17] The Secretariat notes that some of these discriminatory practices are deeply rooted, but nonetheless emphasizes the state's duty to exercise due diligence to prevent them and deal with them. The Secretariat also notes that although the Convention specifically mentions legislation as one of the means to be employed in achieving such change in customary and religious practices, legislation is not the only means. Other administrative, policy and educational measures can be employed. The Secretariat rightly understood that it can prove futile to use legislation as the only or the predominant strategy with respect to some practices such as polygamy.[18]

However, this change of tone appears not to have taken root, because a review of the CEDAW Committee's Concluding Observations on states' reports from the East and Southern African region suggests a retreat to the 'immediate legislative abolition' approach.

2.2 *Review of the CEDAW Concluding Observations on polygamy in East and Southern African states' reports*

A review of Concluding Observations made concerning seven East and Southern African states' reports shows that the Committee expresses serious concern that the states allow continued existence of laws (customary and religious) that allow polygamy.[19] States that have taken no steps at all

[17] See CEDAW/C/1995/4, available at: www.un.org/esa/gopher-data/ga/cedaw/14/1995–4.en (last accessed 13 February 2013).

[18] Kenya's criminal law, as well as formal legislation on marriage, creates the offence of 'bigamy'. The offence is committed when a person who has been married under statutory law enters into a customary or religious marriage during the subsistence of the statutory marriage, or vice versa. The law prescribes a prison sentence of five years with or without hard labour (see section 43, Marriage Act; section 171, Penal Code). Despite these provisions, there is no record of anyone ever having been charged with the crime of bigamy. Even when it becomes evident to a court during divorce proceedings that one of the parties is already in a customary marriage, the court simply makes note of this and does not invoke section 43 to punish the offence. See, for instance, *Ann Njogu* v. *John Warui Weru*, High Court of Kenya at Nairobi, Divorce Cause No. 129 of 2005, available at: www.kenyalaw.org (the official website of the Kenya National Council for Law Reporting) as 2007 eKLR (electronic Kenya Law Reports).

[19] This overall approach taken in CEDAW's Concluding Observations finds resonance with that taken in the UN Human Rights Committee's Concluding Observations on the

to address the issue, as well as states that have made some attempts – legislative, administrative or aimed at social education – are equally rebuked in stylized language contained in a standard stern paragraph that is administered to all with the slightest variation. Nothing in this stylized language suggests appreciation of the differentiated circumstances of each state, nor the varying levels of effort at reform. It only reinforces the conclusion that, in the view of the CEDAW Committee, nothing short of immediate legislative prohibition will do, an attitude that narrows the scope of possible actions envisioned in Article 5(a). This attitude also discloses a lack of appreciation of the fact that in dealing with practices that are defended as cultural (whether the defence has deep-seated widely shared justification or is merely rhetorical), social education and mobilization may often be 'a better initial mechanism for change than starting out with the pursuit of legislative reform'.[20]

At the CEDAW Committee's 39th session in 2007, and at the 48th session in 2011, the Committee took issue with the treatment of polygamy in Kenya's draft legislation on marriage and marital property, in particular that the Draft Marriage Bill provides that two forms of marriage will be recognized in Kenya – monogamous and polygamous – and proceeds to provide for a procedure for conversion of polygamous or potentially polygamous marriages into monogamous marriage, provided certain conditions are met.[21]

The Committee also took issue with the draft legislation on matrimonial property which, if enacted, will be the first time that the Kenyan Parliament has taken action to clarify spouses' rights to property.[22] The draft

issue of polygamy and other marriage practices deemed inconsistent with Article 3 of the International Covenant on Civil and Political Rights. See, for example, UN Human Rights Committee, Concluding Observations with respect to the following African countries: Gambia, 12/08/2004 CCPR/CO/75/GMB, para. 18; Cameroon, UN Doc. CCPR/C/79/Add 116 (1999) para. 10; Algeria, UN Doc. CCPR/C/79/Add95 (1998) para. 13; Libya UN Doc. CCPR/C/79/Add 101 (1998), para. 17; Senegal UN Doc. CCPR/C/79/Add 82 (1997) para. 12; Nigeria UN Doc. CCPR/C/79/Add 65 (1996), para. 25.

20 A. M. Tripp, *The Politics of Women's Rights and Cultural Diversity in Uganda* (Geneva: United Nations Research Institute for Social Development, 2000) at 3.

21 Sections 4 and 5 of Draft Marriage Bill (2007). Polygamous or potentially polygamous marriages may be converted into monogamous ones provided at the time of conversion there is only one wife. The fact that no provision is made for conversion of a monogamous marriage into a polygamous one indicates that the state is signalling a preference for monogamous unions, which would be consistent with Article 6 of the Maputo Protocol.

22 The draft legislation secures each spouse's matrimonial property by requiring spousal consent for any transaction involving property designated as matrimonial. Each spouse is presumed to have an equal interest in the matrimonial home, regardless of the respective contributions made by each spouse. A spouse is protected from eviction from

law addresses marital property rights in both monogamous and polygamous marriages. With respect to polygamous marriages, it makes elaborate provisions, spelling out the rights of each wife by order of seniority as follows:[23]

(a) matrimonial property acquired by the man and the first wife shall be owned equally by the man and the first wife only, if the property was acquired before the man married the second wife;
(b) matrimonial property acquired by the man after the man marries a second wife shall be regarded as owned equally by the man, the first wife and the second wife, and the same principle shall be applied to any subsequent wife or wives.

The section goes on to clarify that where it is clear by agreement or by conduct that certain property is exclusive to a particular wife, then the other wives will not be presumed to have an interest in it.

The Committee took the view that the approach taken in this draft legislation did not send a signal that the government was discouraging polygamy. Instead, it was creating a legal framework for it, which amounts to facilitating it. The Committee therefore urged the Kenyan government to 'address harmful cultural and traditional customs and practices, such as the use of the bride price and polygamy, more vigorously'.[24] The Committee called on the Kenyan government to 'implement measures aimed at eliminating polygamy, as called for in the committee's General Recommendation No. 21 on equality in marriage and family relations'.[25]

Four years later, at its 48th Session (January/February 2011), the CEDAW Committee reiterated its concerns in much the same words, decrying the persistence of 'harmful practices including … polygamy' and that the State Party had not taken 'sustained and systemic action' to

the matrimonial home. Non-monetary contribution is expressly recognized. These basic principles are a major leap forward from the current state of the law. In resolving marital property disputes courts currently resort to the English Married Women's Property Act of 1882, which is applicable to Kenya by virtue of section 3 of the Judicature Act 1967, the law that spells out the sources of law that Kenyan courts may apply. For a detailed discussion of trends in judicial decision-making in this contentious and highly discretionary area of law see C. Nyamu Musembi, '"Sitting on her husband's back with her hands in his pockets": commentary on judicial decision-making in marital property cases in Kenya' in A. Bainham (ed.), *The International Survey of Family Law* (Bristol: Jordan Publishing, 2002) 229–42.

23 Section 11, Draft Matrimonial Property Bill (2007).

24 CEDAW 39th Session, 2007, CEDAW/C/KEN/CO/6, para. 22.

25 *Ibid.* at para. 43.

modify or eliminate such stereotypes and negative cultural values and harmful practices'.[26] Specifically, the Committee expressed concern that the Draft Marriage Bill did not prohibit polygamy.[27]

Uganda's Draft Domestic Relations Bill approaches the issue of polygamy in exactly the same manner as Kenya's draft bill.[28] The only notable difference is that Uganda's draft legislation spells out conditions that a husband must fulfil before he is legally permitted to marry an additional wife, and a procedure for verifying compliance with those conditions.[29] The Committee's Concluding Observations with respect to Uganda express concern about persistence of 'harmful practices, including polygamy, early marriages and the bride price'. The Committee concludes that the Ugandan government has not taken 'effective and comprehensive action' to modify or eliminate these negative traditional values and practices.[30]

While the CEDAW Committee makes it clear that nothing short of elimination of polygamy will suffice, the Kenyan and Ugandan governments appear to have taken an approach aimed at gradual phasing out of polygamy (by providing for conversion of polygamous into monogamous marriages but not the reverse), and more importantly at extending equal protection of the law to all women,[31] not just those who are in a position to opt for a monogamous relationship.

[26] CEDAW 48th Session, 2011, CEDAW/C/KEN/CO/7, para. 17.

[27] *Ibid.*, para. 45.

[28] See sections 19, 64 and 70 of Uganda's Draft Domestic Relations Bill.

[29] See section 31. A husband's application for a marriage licence for a subsequent marriage under Islamic or customary law must attach a declaration stating that he has the economic means to ensure that the current level of maintenance to his wives and children will not drop; that he has made provision for a separate matrimonial home for the subsequent wife (except where the wives have agreed to live together); and that he is able to give the same treatment to all the wives. Section 32 requires full disclosure of his property ownership, indicating individual and matrimonial. Third parties are allowed to object to the grant of the licence (section 37), and he may appeal to the court if the marriage registrar declines approval.

[30] CEDAW/C/UGA/CO/7, para. 19.

[31] At the same time the approach taken by the Kenyan and Ugandan governments challenges the narrow construction of the 'equality before the law' provision in the CEDAW (Article 15). The Article only speaks of 'equality with men before the law'. The male standard limits the understanding of unequal protection before the law to mean only those instances where men receive protection to the exclusion of women, or better protection than women. Yet there are situations where only certain categories of women will be denied protection or accorded inadequate protection relative to other categories of women, as is the case with women in polygamous unions in contexts where the formal law currently pretends that those unions do not exist.

With respect to Malawi, the Committee expresses concern about the existence of multiple marriage regimes and the discriminatory provisions that persist in the laws governing marriage and family relations. The Committee is 'particularly concerned that customary law allows polygamy'.[32] The Committee does not mention that out of all the states reviewed, Malawi comes closest to the Committee's preferred approach: Malawi is the only African state whose draft legislation explicitly outlaws polygamy.[33] Instead the Committee only expresses concern about delay in enacting the draft legislation in question, then subjects Malawi to the same assessment as the other states, in the standard phrase about lack of a 'systemic and sustained' strategy by the state to modify or eliminate harmful traditional practices, patriarchal attitudes and stereotypes.

The CEDAW Committee's Concluding Observations with respect to Tanzania similarly express concern about the persistence of harmful traditional and cultural practices, listing polygamy alongside practices such as female genital mutilation and bride price. The Committee is particularly concerned that not only customary law, but also section 10 of the Law of Marriage Act of 1971, allow polygamy while the same Act prohibits women from having more than one husband, and that 'proposed amendments to the Law of Marriage Act will not criminalize polygamy'.[34] The Committee urges the state to take 'sustained and systemic action' to modify or eliminate these harmful traditional and cultural practices in accordance with Article 2(f).[35]

Zambia is issued with a similarly worded call for 'sustained and systemic action' to eliminate stereotypes and harmful practices, which include polygamy and other discriminatory customary and religious practices that are permitted by virtue of Article 23(4) of the Zambian Constitution.[36]

[32] CEDAW/C/MWI/CO/6, para. 42.

[33] See Malawi Law Reform Commission's Draft Marriage, Divorce and Family Relations Bill (2005). Section 17 states: 'No person shall be married to more than one spouse.' However, the proposed ban on polygamy will not apply retrospectively to existing polygamous marriages. The government introduced the Bill into parliament in 2010 and then withdrew it, citing concerns expressed by Parliamentarians and promising to reintroduce it after revisions. It has not been reintroduced. See Centre for Human Rights and Rehabilitation, *Alternative Report for the Review of Republic of Malawi by the Human Rights Committee* (January, 2011), available at: http://chrr.ultinets.net/wp-content/uploads/2011/01/CHRR-submission-to-the-Human-Rights-Commitee.pdf (last accessed 19 June 2012).

[34] CEDAW/C/MWI/CO/6, para. 146.

[35] CEDAW/C/TZA/CO/6, paras. 117 and 118.

[36] CEDAW/C/ZMB/CO/5–6, para. 13.

Lesotho's report asserts that polygamy is an acceptable customary practice, but that it is on the decline. The government then goes on to argue that nonetheless, customary law contains safeguards against potentially negative financial and emotional consequences for wives and children, for instance by requiring that existing spouses be consulted and that separate property be designated for each household.[37] The government indicates that it only needs expanded capacity and increased financial resources to monitor adherence to these customary safeguards. In response, the Committee expresses 'serious concern' about the 'persistence of harmful norms, practices and traditions, patriarchal attitudes and deep-rooted stereotypes' and 'the state party's limited efforts to address such discriminatory practices directly ... in particular polygamy and bride price'.[38] In paragraph 39(c) the Committee makes explicit what, in its view, would amount to addressing such practices 'directly': 'prohibit polygamy in accordance with the Committee's General Recommendation No. 21'.

There is no indication that the Committee is willing to engage Lesotho on the measures it proposes to employ in order to show why the Committee regards those measures as limited. Rather, the Committee makes it clear that nothing short of immediate prohibition will suffice.

In Botswana's report the government itself decried the subordinate status imposed on wives under customary and religious law, citing several practices, and lamenting that although polygamy was abolished under the Common Law, it was still sanctioned by some religions.[39] In response to this, the Committee demanded to know whether the government had any comprehensive plan to deal with the obstacles identified and attributed to customary and religious laws. The CEDAW Committee's engagement with the government of Botswana departs from the script, in the sense that rather than take on individual issues such as polygamy, the Committee takes on Botswana's Parliament for its failure to repeal a constitutional clause that accords customary and religious laws a special status that ensures they cannot be challenged as being discriminatory, despite court rulings that the clause in question is inconsistent with the equality clause. Exemption clauses will be the subject of discussion in section 4, so we will not dwell on them here.

To conclude this section, it is accurate to observe that the CEDAW Committee appears to be taking the position that unless a state has

[37] CEDAW/C/LSO/1–4, paras. 94 and 95.

[38] See CEDAW, Concluding Observations, CEDAW/C/LSO/CO/1–4, at para. 20.

[39] CEDAW/C/BOT/3, para. 118.

legislated against polygamy and other practices that are viewed as embodying negative gender stereotypes, any other measures taken fall short of Articles 2(f) and 5(a), which amounts to interpretive narrowing of the scope for state action anticipated by the two Articles. The fact that states that have made attempts to address the practices are condemned in equal measure and in almost identical language with those that have made no attempt, suggests lack of genuine effort at constructive engagement on the part of the CEDAW Committee. The very existence of pluralism is in and of itself viewed as inconsistent with Articles 2(f) and 5(a) of the CEDAW, suggesting that in the view of the Committee, unless moral codes premised on religious and cultural norms are displaced, it is impossible to secure equality for women.

The next section contrasts this approach to that adopted in the text of the Maputo Protocol.

3 Pluralism in the Maputo Protocol

The Protocol to the African Charter on Human and Peoples' Rights on the Rights of Women in Africa (the Maputo Protocol) was adopted by the African Union in 2003, and came into force in 2005. As of the end of 2011 it had been ratified by 30 Member States of the African Union, and signed by 46 of the total membership of 53.[40] The Protocol was the result of about a decade and a half of work by women's human rights advocates. The Protocol supplements the African Charter's limited provisions on gender equality and women's rights.[41] It requires states to take measures to outlaw gender discrimination in all spheres and take corrective action against such discrimination through measures such as laws and development plans.

In terms of subject matter, the Protocol has coverage similar to that of the CEDAW, but there are distinct ways in which it frames rights within an

[40] For ratification status, see www.achpr.org/instruments/women-protocol/ratification/ (last accessed 14 February 2013).

[41] The Charter only mentioned women in one clause of one Article (18(3)), lumping women's rights together with protection of family and upholding of culture, which, according to gender equality advocates, 'has its ambivalences toward women's rights'. See, for example, M. Munalula, 'Changing the customary law standard of gender justice: the additional Protocol to the African Charter on Human and Peoples' Rights on the Rights of Women in Africa' in M. O. Hinz and H. K. Patemann, *The Shade of New Leaves: Governance in Traditional Authority: A Southern African Perspective* (Berlin: Lit, 2006) 167–82.

understanding of the specific socio-cultural context of Africa.[42] Examples include the following:[43]

- The Protocol goes beyond the CEDAW to expressly provide for a right to be free from violence, including unwanted or forced sex (Articles 3 and 4). Among other measures, the Protocol calls upon states to undertake peace education and social communication aimed at eradicating 'elements in traditional and cultural beliefs, practices and stereotypes which legitimize and exacerbate the persistence and tolerance of violence against women'. This is particularly relevant to practices of non-consensual (often under-age) marriages justified as part of culture.
- A call on states to prohibit and condemn harmful practices that have a negative effect on the human rights of women, including (but not restricted to) practices justified on culture, such as female genital mutilation and scarification (Article 5).
- Protection of widows from inhuman, degrading or humiliating treatment, as well as guaranteeing their right to consensual remarriage, their right to inherit and remain in the matrimonial home, and their automatic right to custody and guardianship of their children subject to the principle of the best interests of the child (Articles 20 and 21). This provision is attentive to past and current research exposing widowhood practices across sub-Saharan Africa, such as routine eviction from the matrimonial home, which practices contravene women's human rights.[44]

[42] I find little to persuade me in critiques that have accused the Protocol of taking no account of African realities, such as D. M. Chirwa, 'Reclaiming (wo)manity: the merits and demerits of the African Protocol on Women's Rights', *Netherlands International Law Review* 53:1 (2006) 63–96. For articles analyzing the Protocol in relation to the CEDAW and the African Charter, see D. Olowu, 'A critique of the rhetoric, ambivalence and promise in the Protocol to the African Charter on Human and Peoples' Rights on the Rights of Women in Africa', *Human Rights Review* 8:1 (2006) 78–101; M. Ssenyonjo, 'Culture and the human rights of women in Africa: between light and shadow', *Journal of African Law* 51:1 (2007) 39–67; F. Banda, 'Women, law and human rights in Southern Africa', *Journal of Southern African Studies* 32:1 (2006) 13–27.

[43] The examples highlighted here have a bias toward family relations. There are other provisions that illustrate the Protocol's wider coverage of issues, dictated by its particular attention to past and current issues that have defined the specificities of the African context, such as provisions on 'a right to peace' and rights of women connected to armed conflict and post-conflict reconstruction (Articles 10 and 11).

[44] See, for example, Women and Law in Southern Africa Research Trust (WLSA – Zimbabwe), *Inheritance in Zimbabwe: Laws, Customs and Practices* (Harare: SAPES Press, 1994); WLSA Research Trust, *Picking up the Pieces: Widowhood in Southern*

- Special protection of elderly women (Article 22), in view of recent worrying trends of violence targeted at elderly women in the pretext of ending witchcraft, which cuts against the celebrated African ethic of respect for the elderly.[45] Related to this is the special protection of women with disabilities (Article 23) who are similarly vulnerable to structural discrimination and violence that readily finds an excuse in misinformed attitudes justified on a vague reference to culture.[46]

The examples above speak to instances in which the Protocol's coverage goes beyond the CEDAW's express provisions on account of contextualization of contemporary African realities. However, there are some provisions that go beyond differences in coverage and contextualization to suggest lack of congruence between the CEDAW and the Protocol.

The first example concerns the approach to culture in the two documents. While the Protocol calls on states to take measures against practices and attitudes defended as culture that go against the rights of women, the Protocol also provides for women's right to live in a 'positive cultural context' (Article 17). The provision places a duty on the state to ensure enhanced participation of women in the formulation of cultural policies at all levels (Article 17). In this respect, the Protocol differs radically from the CEDAW because the latter only refers to 'culture' with negative connotations: as an impediment to the full realization of equality for women, and as something that the state needs to take measures to eliminate.

Another example is the Article on marriage, specifically the approach that the Protocol takes to the issue of polygamy. Article 6 of the Protocol is similar to Article 16 of the CEDAW in placing emphasis on full and free consent, and on equal rights of spouses. However, unlike the CEDAW,

Africa (Harare: WLSA Research Trust, 1995); Okech-Owiti, N. Karuru, W. Mitullah and K. Mubuu (eds.), *Research Report on Inheritance Laws and Practices in Kenya* (Nairobi: Women and Law in East Africa WLEA, 1995); U. Ewelukwa, 'Post-colonialism, gender, customary injustice: widows in African societies', *Human Rights Quarterly* 24 (2002) 424–86. See also Ikdahl, this volume.

45 See, for example, HelpAge International, 'No country for old women' (2012), available at: www.helpage.org/newsroom/features/no-country-for-old-women/ (last accessed 8 June 2012).

46 See, for example, the myths and practices surrounding albinism. Campaign organizations have taken up the issue. For information on these see www.underthesamesun.com; http://sas.albinism.org; and www.albinismfoundationea.com (last accessed 8 June 2012).

the Protocol chooses not to remain silent on the issue of polygamy. The Protocol does not follow the path charted by the CEDAW Committee's General Recommendation No. 21, nor in the Concluding Observations discussed above, by calling for measures that legislate against polygamy. Rather, the Protocol simply calls on states to enact legislation signalling that monogamy is the *encouraged* and *preferred* form of marriage, while at the same time ensuring that 'the rights of women in marriage and family, including in polygamous marital relationships are promoted and protected'.

In General Recommendation No. 21 and in the Concluding Observations discussed above, the CEDAW Committee takes the position that polygamy contravenes a woman's right to equality and urges States Parties to *discourage and prohibit* such marriages on account of the serious emotional and financial consequences they entail for women and their dependants. On this issue the CEDAW and the African Protocol appear to be at loggerheads, the latter apparently taking the pragmatic position that whether or not polygamy sits comfortably with gender equality, the women already in these relationships should not be denied protection of the law in their family relations.[47]

As the discussion of the Concluding Observations shows, it appears that the ESA countries that have attempted any reform at all are reading from the Protocol's script rather than the CEDAW's. The following section examines the direction that the recent wave of constitutional reform in the region has taken, with respect to the question of establishing a legal framework for legal pluralism. In other words, how has the question of balance between equality (specifically gender equality) and recognition of religious and cultural diversity been answered in the recently enacted constitutions of the East and Southern African states?

4 Pluralism in recent constitutional reforms in the ESA region

Pluralism defines most post-colonial legal systems, particularly in the areas of marriage and family relations. Post-independence constitutions in all of the ESA countries contained a standard clause exempting 'personal law systems'[48] from constitutional prohibition of discrimination,

[47] For a similar conclusion as to pragmatism in the Protocol's chosen approach, see Ssenyonjo, 'Culture and the human rights of women in Africa' at 57.

[48] A term used to refer collectively to customary and religious laws relating to matters of personal status such as marriage, divorce, adoption, burial and succession to property.

effectively sanctioning conduct that would otherwise be regarded as discriminatory for the sole reason that it was justified on personal law. The standard post-independence constitution model was, therefore, that personal law enjoyed 'supra-constitutional' status.

The historical context that explains these exemption clauses has been well documented,[49] and it relates to the independence bargain in the various states. The imminence of independence spawned factionalism among the several national groups, each seeking special constitutional entrenchment of its specific group interests as a precondition to agreeing to any post-independence constitutional arrangements.

In Kenya the pluralism clause can be attributed largely to the demands of the Sultan of Zanzibar on behalf of the Muslim minority who inhabited the ten-mile coastal strip. The strip was part of the Sultan's territory and jurisdiction prior to British colonial rule in East Africa. The British then negotiated with the Sultan in 1895 for a lease of the ten-mile coastal strip. At the dawn of independence in the early 1960s, the incoming post-colonial government wished to have the strip officially annexed as part of the territory of post-independent Kenya. The Sultan was in a strong bargaining position because he could well have refused to renounce his sovereignty, thereby withdrawing his participation in the constitution-making process and precipitating a political crisis by precluding a merger of the coast with the rest of mainland Kenya.[50] His only demand was that his former subjects be guaranteed freedom to practise their religion as well as the continued operation of the Kadhi's courts that apply Muslim law with respect to personal law matters such as marriage, divorce and inheritance.[51]

The final language of the constitutional clause that was negotiated to accommodate the Sultan's demands was not, however, restricted to Muslim personal law. It was framed broadly so as to cover all systems of personal law – religious and customary – already operating

[49] Y. Ghai, 'Independence and safeguards in Kenya', *East African Law Journal* 3 (1967) 177–217; Y. Ghai and P. McAuslan, *Public Law and Political Change in Kenya: A Study of the Legal Framework of Government from Colonial Times to the Present* (Nairobi and New York: Oxford University Press, 1970).

[50] Ghai, 'Independence and safeguards in Kenya' at 184–7.

[51] *Ibid.* at 185. The agreement also enumerated other guarantees such as the right to teach Arabic in Muslim primary schools, the continued legal validity of land titles issued to coastal inhabitants (mostly Arabs) by the British Crown under the 1908 Land Titles Ordinance, and a guarantee that all administrative officers in predominantly Muslim areas would be Muslims.

in the country. The clause was seen as important in enabling minority groups to preserve their identity, customs and traditions in the face of a government dominated by the two largest ethnic groups (Luo and Kikuyu) and that was perceived as being centralist and 'impatient with diversity'.[52]

As further safeguard, the pluralism clause was placed in the fundamental rights chapter of the Constitution, making it an entrenched provision. This meant that it could only be amended by a special majority in Parliament – three-fourths of the votes of all the Members of Parliament.[53] Thus, Kenya's independence Constitution contained section 82(1), which defined and prohibited discrimination; but this was followed by two qualifications that are relevant to the issue of personal laws. The first qualification was contained in section 82(4)(b), which provided that the anti-discrimination clause would not apply 'with respect to adoption, marriage, divorce, burial, devolution of property on death or other matters of personal law'. The second qualification was contained in section 82(4)(c), which provided that any law that was enacted to be applied to persons of a particular race or 'tribe of customary law' would not be held to be discriminatory.

Across English-speaking sub-Saharan Africa the specific history of personal law exemption clauses may vary, but the language is very similar to that used in Kenya's independence Constitution.

Recent constitutional reforms have seen the demise of personal law exemption clauses from the constitutions of Uganda,[54] Ghana,[55] Malawi

[52] *Ibid.* at 195.

[53] *Ibid.* at 214.

[54] The 1967 Constitution contained exceptions similar to Kenya's section 82(4). See Ministry of Gender and Community Development, *Women and the 1995 Constitution of Uganda* (Kampala: Government of Uganda, 1995). See also H. F. Morris and J. S. Read, *Uganda: The Development of its Laws and Constitution* (London: Stevens, 1966) at 174. These were removed in the 1995 Constitution.

[55] Article 17(4)(b), Constitution of the Republic of Ghana (1992). While the provisions of the Zambian and Zimbabwean Constitutions contain terminology that is virtually identical to the Kenyan Constitution's section 82(4), the Ghanaian Constitution provision is different. It does not expressly provide constitutional immunity to the operation of personal laws. It simply reserves to Parliament the power to enact legislation for 'matters relating to adoption, marriage, divorce, burial, devolution of property on death or other matters of personal law', which power when exercised shall not be regarded as discriminatory.

and Kenya, but the clause remains in the constitutions of other countries such as Botswana,[56] Zambia,[57] Zimbabwe[58] and Lesotho.[59]

I have argued elsewhere that through these exemption clauses the state, though seemingly adopting a 'hands-off' approach, actually sanctions negative discrimination by denying access to constitutional remedies to those aggrieved by treatment that is justified as having a basis in personal law.[60] By according supra-constitutional status to personal law, the state privileges the views of those able to assert private power to define customary or religious norms in ways that disadvantage weaker social groups. By closing the avenue of constitutional challenge, the state is overtly endorsing, or at the very least acquiescing in, the establishment and preservation of asymmetrical social arrangements by denying some people within a community or sub-group a voice in shaping social norms.

It is this constitutional model, and not the mere existence of multiple family law systems, that the CEDAW Committee ought to be concerned about. This is because through this constitutional exemption of personal law from scrutiny, states have availed themselves of a ready excuse for doing nothing to redress the discriminatory impacts of the application of religious and customary law.[61]

[56] Section 15(4), paragraphs (c) and (d), Constitution of Botswana (1966). At the 45th Session of the CEDAW Committee (2010) the Botswanan government maintained that it saw no need to review (let alone repeal) the exemption clause as some court cases had interpreted that clause in conjunction with section 3 of the Constitution to conclude that only customary and religious norms that are consistent with the Constitution would be upheld. If that is truly the case, then what purpose is served by retaining the clause? Should legislation not simply encode that judicial interpretation by removing the clause altogether?

[57] Section 25(4) paragraphs (b) and (c), The Constitution of Zambia (1971). Zambia has made unsuccessful attempts at constitutional review. The latest draft of the proposed constitution, however, proposed to retain the exemption clause intact. The CEDAW Committee took issue with this in its Concluding Observations at its 49th Session (July 2011). See CEDAW/C/ZMB/CO/5–6, para. 14.

[58] Article 23(3) paragraphs (a) and (b), The Constitution of Zimbabwe (Revised, 1996). See also discussion of these constitutional provisions in W. Ncube, 'Defending and protecting gender equality and the family under a decidedly undecided Constitution in Zimbabwe' in J. Eekelaar and T. Nhlapo (eds.), *The Changing Family: International Perspectives on the Family and Family Law* (Oxford: Hart Publishing, 1998) 509–28 at 516.

[59] Article 18(4) paragraphs (b) and (c), The Constitution of Lesotho (1993, Revised 2000).

[60] See Nyamu, 'How should human rights and development respond'; Nyamu Musembi, 'Sitting on her husband's back'.

[61] There are examples across the region of courts invoking personal law exemption clauses to make decisions that are manifestly against the idea of equality in the CEDAW. In these cases, the judges acknowledge the discriminatory nature and impact of a customary or religious practice, but proceed to rule that the exemption clause means that the court can

The 1990s' wind of democratic change and its accompanying constitutional and legal reforms made it clear that this was no longer tenable; hence the shift in a significant number of countries to a model that attempts to balance recognition of personal law systems with the upholding of constitutional principles of equality and non-discrimination. It is important to note that in none of the ESA countries has the pendulum swung to the extreme position of elimination of personal law systems altogether. Rather, provision is made for retaining and promoting those aspects of personal law/cultural systems that are seen as compatible with democratic principles, primarily equality, while filtering out aspects perceived as negative.

Uganda's 1995 Constitution, for instance, strikes a balance that is explicitly between women's rights (Article 33) and the right to practise culture (Article 37). Article 33(6) prohibits 'laws, cultures, customs and traditions which are against the dignity, welfare or interest of a woman or which undermine their status'.

Ghana's 1992 Constitution provides through Article 26 the right to practise one's culture, but also prohibits 'all customary practices which dehumanize or are injurious to the physical and mental well-being of a person'.

Malawi's 1994 Constitution requires Parliament to enact legislation 'to eliminate customs and practices that discriminate against women'.[62] However, some analysts have pointed out that the Constitution may have limited its own ability to achieve this aim by virtue of Article 26, which provides for the right to 'participate in the cultural life of his or her choice'. This is because the framing of Article 26 gives it an absolute quality, without indicating that the right to practise one's culture may be limited, for instance if certain aspects of the practice of culture are found to constitute discrimination.[63] However, it could also be argued plausibly that such an absolutist reading of Article 26 is pre-empted by Article 44,

do nothing about the discrimination. For examples of such cases see the Zimbabwean case of *Venia Magaya* v. *Nakayi Magaya*, Civil Appeal No. 635/92, Judgment No. S.C. 210/98 (delivered on 16 February 1999). See also the Kenyan case of *Virginia Edith Wambui Otieno* v. *Joash Ougo & Omolo Siranga*, *Kenyan Appeal Reports*, 1 (1982–88) at 1049. For further discussion of the case, see Nation Newspapers, *S.M. Otieno: Kenya's Unique Burial Saga* (Nairobi: Nation Newspapers, 1987). See also D. W. Cohen and E. S. Atieno Odhiambo, *Burying S.M.: The Politics of Knowledge and the Sociology of Power in Africa* (London: James Currey, 1992).

62 Article 24(a), Constitution of the Republic of Malawi (1994).

63 L. Mwambene, 'Reconciling African customary law with women's rights in Malawi: the Proposed Marriage, Divorce and Family Relations Bill', *Malawi Law Journal* 1 (2007) 113–22.

which lists among the rights to which there is to be no derogation, restriction or limitation the right to equality and the right to freedom of conscience. In addition, Article 44(2) is a general clause to the effect that the only limitations on rights that will be recognized are 'those prescribed by law, which are reasonable, recognized by international human rights standards and necessary in an open and democratic society'.

It is therefore accurate to conclude that the Malawi Constitution is among the constitutions that attempt to provide for a balance between recognition of cultural rights and the right to equality, including gender equality.

Similarly, Kenya's 2010 Constitution marks a clear departure from the exemption contained in section 82(4). Article 2 on the supremacy of the Constitution makes this absolutely clear by adding clause 2(4): 'Any law, including customary law, that is inconsistent with this Constitution is void to the extent of the inconsistency.'

Article 45(4) gives Parliament the power to enact legislation that retains the recognition of 'marriages concluded under any tradition, or system of religious, personal or family law', and non-statutory norms and institutions for regulating family relations. However, in the 2010 Constitution these non-statutory norms and institutions are only given recognition 'to the extent that any such marriages or systems of law are consistent with this constitution'. The 'supra-constitutional' status that personal law systems enjoyed under the old Constitution has been stripped away.

This means that any application of such non-statutory norms and the operation of any institution under these systems must be consistent with the Constitution, including the Bill of Rights with its strong provisions on equality and non-discrimination (Article 27). Parliament cannot enact a law whose effect would be to exempt them from constitutional scrutiny. The legislative power given by Article 45(4) is by no means a door to the return of section 82(4).

However, an exemption in modified form does remain for Muslim personal law, but it is much more narrowly tailored than the blank cheque that was section 82(4). Article 24(4) of the 2010 Constitution provides as follows:

> The provisions of this Chapter on equality shall be qualified to the extent strictly necessary for the application of Muslim law before the Kadhi's courts, to persons who profess the Muslim religion, in matters relating to personal status, marriage, divorce and inheritance.

The phrase 'to the extent strictly necessary' anticipates a process of scrutiny to determine whether an exemption is warranted in each specific situation. Secondly, the exemption can only relate to a specific case before the Kadhi's court. It is not a blanket exemption of all Muslim personal law in all forums. When read together with Article 170(5), which requires that in order for the Kadhi's court to have jurisdiction over a case, the parties must be people who profess the Muslim faith and who also *submit to the jurisdiction of the Kadhi's courts*, it can be concluded that the Constitution of 2010 goes a long way to remedy the gagging of dissent that was contained in the previous section 82(4).

The formulation of Article 170(5) gives the possibility of opting out of the Kadhi's courts' jurisdiction altogether, while Article 24(4) makes it clear that discrimination is not an automatic corollary of the application of Muslim personal law. This is potentially empowering for Muslim women: they could opt out of the Kadhi's courts, or they could seize upon the opportunity presented by Article 24(4) to challenge discriminatory approaches to the application of Muslim personal law, thereby working for gradual transformation of the institutions that apply Muslim personal law.

But for the narrow exemption with regard to application of Muslim personal law, Kenya's constitutional framework for accommodating pluralism now closely resembles the South African model. In South Africa's post-apartheid Constitution, customary laws and the exercise of traditional authority are accorded constitutional recognition, but they are expressly subjected to scrutiny for compatibility with constitutional principles.[64]

This review of recent constitutional reforms in ESA countries establishes that the dominant practice is consistent with the approach taken by the Maputo Protocol, namely the recognition of a right to culture, alongside the opening up of possibilities to challenge and weed out negative norms and practices that are justified on culture. None of the reforms take the direction suggested by the CEDAW Committee, namely that the very existence of pluralism is itself an impediment to gender equality, or

[64] See Article 211(1), Constitution of the Republic of South Africa (as adopted by the Constitutional Assembly on 8 May 1996): 'The institution, status and role of traditional leadership, according to customary law, are recognized subject to the constitution.' Section 211(3) states: 'The courts must apply customary law when that law is applicable, subject to the constitution and any legislation that specifically deals with customary law.'

that reform is only possible through immediate legislative prohibition of specific practices sanctioned by personal law systems. By striking the kind of balance envisioned in these constitutional provisions, it is possible for a gradual sifting to occur: those aspects seen as enhancing rights and equality will be safeguarded, while those seen as inimical to rights and equality will be challenged.[65]

5 Pluralism in the courts: women's agency in defining culture and rights

> Imagine that a man slaps a woman in rural KwaZulu-Natal, South Africa. At the same time, another man slaps a woman in a popular neighbourhood in Khartoum, and yet a third does the same in a classroom at the Sorbonne in Paris. All three women protest: the woman in Paris that her rights have been violated, the woman in Khartoum that her dignity has been violated, and the woman in KwaZulu-Natal that custom has been violated. Every victim protests. But the language of protest is different in each case. How is one to understand this difference? Is not the starting point of protest to take power at face value, and to question its claim and thus legitimacy?[66]

The approach taken by the CEDAW Committee is one that positions 'culture' and 'rights' as polar opposites, the former being conceived of largely as a negative force that impedes realization of rights. Such an

[65] These constitutional provisions have been tested in litigation by individual women, often assisted by women's rights organizations. See, for example, cases discussed in M. Ndulo, 'African customary law, customs, and women's rights', *Indiana Journal of Global Legal Studies* 18:1 (2011) 87–120. However, the focus in such litigation tends to be on challenging specific cultural practices as contrary to women's human rights, giving the impression that culture is always on the opposing side to rights. There is little reference to instances in which women have employed the medium of culture to claim their rights. This is the case in other contexts as well, beyond the African context. See, for example, cases discussed in F. Raday, 'Traditionalist religious and cultural challengers – international and constitutional human rights responses', *Israeli Law Review* 41 (2008) 596–634. For discussion of cases in both categories (i.e. those in which women are challenging negative deployment of culture, as well as cases in which women are relying on culture to articulate their claims), see R. Odgaard and A. W. Bentzon, 'Rural women's access to landed property: unearthing the realities within an East African setting' in Hellum *et al.*, *Human Rights*; J. Stewart and A. Tsanga, 'The widow's and female child's portion: the twisted path to partial equality for widows and daughters under customary law in Zimbabwe' in Hellum *et al.*, *Human Rights* 407–36.

[66] M. Mamdani, 'Introduction' in M. Mamdani (ed.), *Beyond Rights Talk and Culture Talk: Comparative Essays on the Politics of Rights and Culture* (Cape Town: David Philip Publishers, 2000) 1–13.

approach leaves no possibility of common ground, and has been questioned.[67] Such an approach effectively suggests that in order for women to access rights, the moral codes that they live by have to be displaced first. As another commentator has put it, 'African women would have to first strip themselves of culture before enjoying their rights.'[68]

But the Maputo Protocol and the approaches taken in recent ESA constitutional reforms suggest that culture can be a resource that enhances the claiming of rights, and possibly the expansion of the domain of rights. This last section explores the question: have women made use of culture as a resource in their claim-making? Or, to draw from Mamdani's scenarios in the quote above, have women employed custom as their chosen language of protest? Framing the question in this manner marks a deliberate departure from the more common approach where litigation around women's rights and culture focuses on challenging specific cultural practices as inconsistent with gender equality.

In exploring this question in the context of formal litigation in courts, this section of the chapter will examine selected cases in which women have asserted rights, drawing directly or indirectly from constitutional protection of the right to practise one's culture. In the context of Kenya, this right was not expressly provided for until the 2010 Constitution came into force.

So far, in only one case has a woman relied on the constitutional protection of the right to culture to make a claim: in the 2011 case of *Monica Jesang Katam* v. *Jackson Chepkwony & another*.[69] The case involved the practice colloquially labelled in legal texts as 'woman to woman' marriage.

Some background on the practice is necessary for understanding the case and the analysis that follows. The practice is found in several communities across the African continent.[70]

[67] See, for example, A. An-Na'im and J. Hammond (eds.), *Cultural Transformation and Human Rights in Africa* (London: Zed Books, 2002); C. Nyamu Musembi, 'Are local norms and practices fences or pathways? The example of women's property rights' in A. An-Na'im and J. Hammond (eds.), *Cultural Transformation and Human Rights in Africa* 126–50; T. Nhlapo, 'The African customary law of marriage and the rights conundrum' in M. Mamdani (ed.), *Beyond Rights Talk and Culture Talk* 136–48.

[68] S. Tamale, 'The right to culture and the culture of rights: a critical perspective on women's sexual rights in Africa', *Feminist Legal Studies* 16:1 (2008) 47–69 at 55.

[69] High Court of Kenya at Mombasa, Succession Cause No. 212 of 2010. Available at www.kenyalaw.org (as eKLR, 2011).

[70] In Kenya the practice has been documented in the following communities: Kamba, Kikuyu, Kisii, Kuria and various Kalenjin sub-tribes such as Nandi and Kipsigis. See

The typical scenario is that an older woman finds herself unable to have biological children or has only daughters, which disadvantages her in a context where property is handed down through male descendants, and women's own position in relation to property is dependent on their position in relation to male kin. Custom allows the childless or 'sonless' woman to enter into an arrangement with a younger woman, upon an exchange of gifts with her family, who then bears children for her. In some communities the older woman, if married, needs her husband's approval, and in others it is her autonomous decision.

In some situations the practice is prompted not by inability to bear children, but on account of an older single woman having independently acquired wealth. Woman-to-woman marriage is the route that custom offers such a woman toward relative autonomy in deciding who inherits her wealth. This was more common in trading societies such as the Ibo and Dahomey, where such women would thereby establish their own lineage, and their property and social status would be transmitted through that lineage.[71]

Children born to the younger woman are regarded as belonging either to the lineage of the older woman's husband (where the older woman is married), or to the older woman's lineage of birth, where the older woman is single, or to her own independent lineage, in societies that made provision for that. Any children born to the younger woman prior to the marriage (and she will often have had children as this serves as a guarantee of her fertility) will also belong to her new family, if the necessary compensation is paid to her parents in order for the children to be transferred to the new lineage.

In some communities it is the older woman who decides with whom the younger woman will have sexual relations. In other communities

E. Cotran, *Casebook on Kenya Customary Law* (Milton Park: Professional Books, 1987). Various Kenyan court cases are also discussed here. See note 74. See also J. Kenyatta, *Facing Mount Kenya: The Traditional Life of the Gikuyu* (New York: Vintage Books, 1965); R. S. Oboler, 'Is the female husband a man? Woman/woman marriage among the Nandi of Kenya', *Ethnology* 19:1 (1980) 69–88. The practice has been documented in about forty pre-colonial African societies, with some continuing to the present era. See J. Cadigan, 'Woman-to-woman marriage: practices and benefits in Sub-Saharan Africa', *Journal of Comparative Family Studies* 29 (1998) 89–98; B. Greene, 'The institution of woman-marriage in Africa: A cross-cultural analysis', *Ethnology* 37:4 (1998) 395–412. See also I. Amadiume, *Male Daughters, Female Husbands: Gender and Sex in an African Society* (London: Zed Books, 1987), discussing woman-to-woman marriage with respect to Ibo society in Nigeria.

[71] Greene, 'The institution of woman-marriage in Africa'.

the younger woman has a free hand in deciding. In some communities a specific man from the lineage of the older woman's husband (where she is married) or her own lineage (where she is single), or any man among her acquaintances, is designated to biologically beget children with the younger woman. In any case the man in question acquires no rights over the children. His role is purely biological. The children bear the name of the new family's lineage. Thus the label 'woman-to-woman' is not altogether accurate as no sexual relations take place between the two female parties.

The practice has historically received the expected condemnation from religious quarters.[72] Beyond religious quarters it is generally criticized as retrogressive and out of step with modernity. Organizations working on women's rights have had nothing to say about this practice and will rarely include it on their lists of 'harmful cultural practices'. This is either because they do not consider it as serious enough compared to other abuses, or for reason of not wanting to be on the same side of the issue as religious bodies, who often take positions opposed to gender equality.

The relative decisional autonomy accorded to the older woman in some communities robs the narrative of the simplicity of one-dimensional sexual subordination of women by men. No doubt sexual subordination sets the background context for the practice, but it certainly is not the only dimension of the narrative.

Although I have encountered one case of a young woman fleeing from such a relationship,[73] the majority of cases involving this practice are brought by younger women petitioning the court to affirm the validity of the custom, give recognition to the relationship and affirm their entitlements flowing from the relationship. The cases all involve disputes with the older woman's kin over property. Invariably, such relatives seek to displace the younger woman's claim either by arguing that the practice of woman-to-woman marriage no longer exists in their culture, or that it was not carried out in strict adherence to tradition, or that the

[72] The church constitutions are silent on this, as are the by-laws that I could find, yet it is common knowledge that the mainstream denominations (Anglican, Presbyterian and Baptist) have consistently opposed the practice, and various denominations have excommunicated women (and any husbands involved) who were found to have engaged in the practice. Informal discussion with Dr. Henry Mutua, Theologian, Africa International University (Nairobi, Kenya), 10 June 2012.

[73] *Maria Angoi* v. *Marcella Nyomenda*, High Court of Kenya at Kisii (Aganyanya Ag. J.), Civil Appeal No.1 of 1981 (reproduced in Cotran, *Casebook on Kenya Customary Law*).

younger woman was only taken in as a servant and that there was really no marriage.[74]

Such cases have been reported since the 1990s. What is unique about the *Monica Katam* (2011) case is that it is the only one decided after the 2010 Constitution was adopted, and thus the only one that invokes the constitutional recognition of 'culture' as part of the national values and principles laid out in Article 11(1) as the basis for her claim. An 85-year-old unmarried woman died, leaving a substantial estate (valued at over 2 million Kenya Shillings, which is roughly 25,000 USD). Monica Katam, a 35-year-old mother of two teenage sons, had been living with her and taking care of her for over three years. She applied for letters of administration over the estate, describing herself as the 'widow' of the deceased, having been married to her according to Nandi customary law, which permitted woman-to-woman marriage. The older woman's nephew and niece (brother and sister, the children of her sister) sought to defeat Monica's claim by producing a will allegedly written by the deceased, which the court ruled was a forgery. The relatives further denied that a woman-to-woman marriage had existed between the two women, arguing that Monica was 'only a servant'. They also tried to discredit her claim by arguing that the custom of woman-to-woman marriage was no longer practised among the Nandi. The younger woman and her family were, however, able to prove with clear witness testimony,[75] written agreements signed and thumb-printed publicly between Monica's family and the older woman's family, as well as photographs, that the requisite customary ceremonies had taken place, both for her betrothal and marriage, as well as for the 'adoption' of her two sons by the older woman.

[74] For examples of cases falling along this spectrum of counter-arguments see *Millicent Njeri Mbugua* v. *Alice Wambui Wainaina*, High Court of Kenya, Civil Appeal No. 50 of 2003 (Nyeri) (eKLR 2008); *Maroa Wambura Gatimwa* v. *Sabina Nyanokwe Gatimwa and five others*, Kenya Court of Appeal, Civil Appeal No. 331 of 2003 (Kisumu) (eKLR 2010); *Mule Ndeti* v. *Ngonyo Sila*, Kenya Court of Appeal, Civil Appeal No. 128 of 1997 (Nairobi); *In the Matter of the Estate of the late Tapkigen Mase, & Philip Biegon & Emmy Chemutai* v. *Joseph Kipngeno Chepkwony*, High Court of Kenya, Succession Cause No. 23 of 2002 (Kericho) (eKLR 2006); *Serah Muthee Munyao* v. *Ruth Mueni Kitundu*, High Court, Probate and Administration Cause No. 42 of 2002 (Machakos); *In re Estate of Ngetich*, High Court, Probate and Administration Cause No. 29 of 1996, *Kenya Law Reports* 2003:84. All cases are available at: www.kenyalaw.org, the official website of the Kenyan National Council for Law Reporting.

[75] Including testimony of the objectors' maternal cousin, who testified to the first objector's (nephew's) presence at the ceremonies, which was also proven by production of photographs.

In recognizing her claim to the estate, the judge went into great detail to understand the custom in practice, citing previous court decisions that have recognized the practice, as well as ethnographic material on the community in question – the Nandi.[76] The judge then observed:

> Indeed, contemporary social systems, for instance, in the shape of current practices in the domain of family among the Nandi, are, I think, to be regarded as aspects of culture which will rightly claim protection under Article 11(1) of the Constitution of Kenya, 2010.

Even though the language of Article 11(1) is not framed so as to directly confer a 'right to culture', the judge interpreted it to mean that it embodied the principles that should guide the court 'in considering the implications of the woman-to-woman marriage in this case'.

So is this customary marriage practice contrary to gender equality? In the words of General Recommendation No. 21 of the CEDAW, does it have 'serious emotional and financial consequences'? Such a negative consequence is not self-evident in every case. Indeed, in some cases – certainly in the *Monica Katam* case and others cited above – the financial consequences at least favoured her and her sons. For the older woman who gets to decide to whom to bequeath her property, this appears to be an expression of relative autonomy. However, it cannot escape notice that the whole institution is premised on valuing women only for their reproductive capacity. The older woman is forced to resort to this customary practice in order to secure her own position in a male-defined inheritance system, as well as escape the stigma of childlessness or 'sonlessness'.[77] The younger woman has been sought out only on the basis of her demonstrated ability to bear children and provide labour, and she enters into it to aid her own and her children's escape from poverty and the stigma of illegitimacy.

In accounts that portray the practice as empowering for women,[78] the practice is cited as one way in which women get to occupy gender positions

[76] Among the material cited extensively in the judgment are Oboler, 'Is the female husband a man?' and Cotran, *Casebook on Kenya Customary Law*.

[77] Arguably, relative to other options for dealing with childlessness or 'sonlessness' in customary settings, this one at least gives the older woman a voice in the decision. For discussion of this topic, see A. Hellum, *Women's Human Rights and Pluralism in Africa: Mixed Norms and Identities in Infertility Management in Zimbabwe* (Harare and Oslo: Mond Books, 1999).

[78] Greene, 'The institution of woman-marriage in Africa'; Amadiume, *Male Daughters, Female Husbands*.

that are otherwise conceived of as male (e.g. 'husband'). The practice is therefore a deconstruction of the socially constructed notion of gender, and illustrates the potentially empowering flexibility of gender roles in traditional African societies.[79] A less optimistic reading of the practice, however, is that it affirms power as having a male gender,[80] but only carves out exceptional circumstances in which those who are biologically female are allowed to access power. Even this reading is only from the perspective of the older woman. From the perspective of the younger woman, it is difficult to read power (in the sense of her empowerment) into the relationship. Indeed, in some communities the terminology for woman-to-woman marriage translates as buying a slave.[81] Typically the younger woman is drawn from categories of socially disadvantaged women, for instance those widowed or divorced at a young age,[82] or single mothers, invariably from poor backgrounds.

In view of this double-edged effect or interpretation of the practice, what stance should (African) feminists take in relation to disadvantaged women's invocation of their rights under such a custom? These women are able to secure their own and their children's customary entitlement to family property, but by virtue of relying on an institution that values them only for their productive and reproductive labour, while perpetuating the maleness of power. This kind of case offers more opportunity for engagement than an issue such as polygamy, which probably oversimplifies the issue for feminists by accentuating the sexual subordination angle. Woman-to-woman marriage foregrounds an intergenerational and class-based subordination as well, permitting an intersectional analysis that is closer to social reality.

A similar dilemma is raised by cases in which daughters rely on customary recognition of entitlement in order to claim a share of family resources. These claims are not made in the language of equal entitlement with their brothers. Rather, they tend to be made in the restricted language of 'use rights' (as opposed to outright ownership), implicitly accepting a lesser category relative to the outright ownership presumed to be conferred on their brothers. These claims tend to be made in the language

[79] Greene, 'The institution of woman-marriage in Africa'; Amadiume, *Male Daughters, Female Husbands*.

[80] See Greene, 'The institution of woman-marriage in Africa'. See also D. O'Brien, 'Female husbands in southern Bantu societies' in A. Schlegel (ed.), *Sexual Stratification: A Cross-Cultural View* (New York: Columbia University Press, 1977) 99–108.

[81] Greene, 'The institution of woman-marriage in Africa'.

[82] *Ibid.*

of the dutiful or caring daughter who therefore deserves to benefit from the elderly parents' property (or estate, in the case of inheritance claims). This language contrasts with the automatic entitlements of sons that vest as a matter of right and need not be earned through duty.

Such scenarios are documented in several writings that have engaged with the issue of women's property rights in a context of pluralism. Although some of these documented claims have been made in court,[83] the vast majority are presented in informal dispute resolution forums and are therefore recorded in empirical research.[84] Odgaard and Bentzon[85] profile some such claims in village-level forums in two districts in Tanzania inhabited by members of the Hehe ethnic group. The authors found that among fathers there was strong recognition of daughters' (including married daughters') claims to land in their natal (birth) villages. The authors 'uncovered numerous examples of daughters' who had successfully relied on informal intra-family and other village-level forums to enforce land rights granted to them by their fathers in their natal villages.[86]

Stewart and Tsanga also refer to research conducted by Women and Law in Southern Africa Research Trust (WLSA) in the 1980s and 1990s in Zimbabwe, which documents a strong customary basis for a 'right of return' for married daughters, entitling them to support from their natal families, which invariably meant a right to occupy, build on and use land.[87] Empirical research in Eastern Kenya also found a level of support for daughters' customary entitlement to land and livestock in their natal

[83] See for example *Chihowa* v. *Mangwende*, 1987 (1) ZLR 228 SC (Zimbabwe Supreme Court). In this case the daughter in question insisted on her right to be appointed heir under customary law, and to be held to the same obligations as any customary heir. See also *Ephraim* v. *Pastory* (High Court of Tanzania, 1990, available at 87 *Int. L. Rep.* 106 (1992)). In this case a daughter had inherited land from her father and then sold it outside the clan. A relative challenged her right to sell the land outside the clan, arguing that as a woman she had no right to dispose of the land. She successfully asserted her customary right to do so subject to the same restriction as any male clan member: the customary right of redemption by any of her kinsmen.

[84] Examples include Odgaard and Bentzon, 'Rural women's access to landed property'; Stewart and Tsanga, 'The widow's and female child's portion'; C. Nyamu, 'Gender, culture and property relations in a pluralistic social setting' Doctor of Juridical Studies (SJD) Dissertation, Harvard Law School (2000); C. Nyamu Musembi, 'Why engage with local norms and institutions? The case of women's property rights in rural Kenya', *East African Journal of Peace and Human Rights* 9:2 (2003) 255–89.

[85] Odgaard and Bentzon, 'Rural women's access to landed property'.

[86] *Ibid.* at 221.

[87] Stewart and Tsanga, 'The widow's and female child's portion'. Also addressed in Damiso and Stewart's chapter in this book.

families.[88] Empirical research among the Taita of Kenya's coastal region also documents a well-established custom of 'gifting' land to a daughter, which guarantees her user rights for the lifetime of her parents, regardless of her marital status. The user rights might even survive after her parents' death if she is able to negotiate successfully with her brothers.[89]

All these scenarios present a double bind similar to that presented by woman-to-woman marriage. On the one hand, without the customary basis for their claim, these women would be at the mercy of arbitrary actions of male kin, depriving them of access to resources crucial to their livelihoods. On the other hand, the custom in question rests on an underlying status differentiation between the entitlements of daughters and those of sons: between those perceived as having permanent membership in the family and those whose membership is transient and their claims therefore contingent; between those in whom property rights vest automatically and those whose property rights must be negotiated and justified; between those who are entitled and those who are pitied.[90]

Is the making of claims in this bounded context an endorsement or reinforcement of the underlying status differentiation? Some feminists would most likely argue that it is. Yet wholesale rejection of customary norms and practice on property for this reason spells the very real possibility of destitution (both economic and social) for some women for whom this is the only basis for entitlement. Which path should an African feminist take in these contexts? We reflect further on this issue in the conclusion.

6 Conclusion: what course of action for African feminists?

The dilemma posed by the cases discussed above is parallel to the one posed by Cusack in her chapter in this volume concerning gender stereotyping: what is the appropriate feminist response in situations where measures are undertaken that confer tangible and immediate benefits on

[88] Nyamu, 'Gender, culture and property relations'; Nyamu Musembi, 'Why engage with local norms and institutions?'

[89] See G. C. Mkangi, *The Social Cost of Small Families and Land Reform: A Case Study of the Wataita of Kenya* (Oxford: Pergamon Press, 1983); M. M. Mwachofi, 'Land reform in Taita: a study of socio-economic underdevelopment in a Kenya district', Bachelor of Arts Dissertation, University of Nairobi (1977).

[90] Nyamu, 'How should human rights and development respond'.

women, but that rest on a stereotyped understanding of gender roles and therefore pose long-term negative consequences?[91]

It falls upon African feminists to discern the potential for expansion of the spaces for women's agency, even when (especially when) those spaces appear to be constrained by an ideology of gendered subordination. Ideology can be contested and eroded, albeit gradually, sometimes through overt protest, and sometimes through subtle but deliberate institutionalization of divergent social practices.[92] This path is more likely to enable 'enhanced participation of women in the formulation of cultural policies at all levels' and help realize African women's right to live 'in a positive cultural context'.[93]

It is not too late for the CEDAW Committee to get involved and help steer a global component of this project. However, this will only be possible if the CEDAW Committee gets back on the briefly trodden path charted by its Secretariat's 1995 report. That report, as discussed above, interpreted the combined effect of Articles 2(f) and 5(a) to mean that the state had diverse means at its disposal in fulfilling its obligation of positive transformation of customary and religious practices to align with gender equality. The Secretariat rightly understood that the two clauses did not dictate a narrow focus on legislation, let alone simply prohibitory legislation. The CEDAW Committee can draw inspiration from the Maputo Protocol's approach in order to engage African states in a less stylized and more productive dialogue on legal pluralism: one that reflects an in-depth understanding of each country's context and each country's milestones along the path toward transformed gender relations.

[91] To illustrate this dilemma, Cusack cites the South African Constitutional case of *President of the Republic of South Africa* v. *Hugo*, 1997(4) SA 1 (CC). The president issued a pardon to female but not male prisoners, justifying such action on the need for women prisoners to be available to care for their children. The benefit to female prisoners is obvious, but so is the stereotyping of the childcare role as belonging to women and not to men.

[92] See S. Hirsch and M. Lazarus-Black, 'Introduction – Performance and paradox: exploring law's role in hegemony and resistance' in S. F. Hirsch and M. Lazarus-Black (eds.), *Contested States: Law, Hegemony and Resistance* (London: Routledge, 1994) 1–31; S. E. Merry, *Human Rights and Gender Violence: Translating International Law into Local Justice* (University of Chicago Press, 2006); A. Hunt, 'Rights and social movements: counter-hegemonic strategies', *Journal of Law and Society* 17:3 (1990) 309–28; S. F. Moore, 'Uncertainties in situations, indeterminacies in culture' in S. F. Moore, *Law as Process: An Anthropological Approach* (London: Routledge and Kegan Paul, 1978).

[93] Article 17, Maputo Protocol.

PART II

Actual added value of the CEDAW: socio-economic rights

7

Engendering socio-economic rights

SANDRA FREDMAN

1 Introduction

'Human development if not engendered, is endangered.'[1] This was the verdict of *Gender Development*, the 1995 Human Development Report devoted to gender. In this chapter I examine whether the Convention on the Elimination of All Forms of Discrimination against Women (CEDAW) can make a unique contribution to international human rights law by 'engendering' human rights. In most human rights documents there is a provision prohibiting discrimination on grounds of sex in the enjoyment of the rights therein.[2] The implicit assumption is that the rights are given, and should simply be extended to women. But, it is argued here, this does little to address the gendered nature of social institutions and structures. Instead, human rights should be 'engendered' or infused with substantive gender equality. The CEDAW, by contrast, through its express focus on women, goes a long way towards engendering human rights. But it still does not go far enough. As a point of reference for women in all societies and contexts, it is of great importance that we continue to develop the CEDAW in the direction of engendered human rights, particularly

This chapter is an adaptation of a paper written for the Women and Poverty Workshop run by the Centre for Advanced Legal Studies in Johannesburg, South Africa in April 2009. See S. Fredman, 'Engendering socio-economic rights' *South African J. of Human Rights* 25:3 (2009) 410–41. The author would like to thank the editors of this volume for their valuable comments on earlier versions of this chapter and Chris McConnachie for his research assistance in finalising the draft.

[1] United Nations Development Programme (UNDP), *Gender Development* (Oxford University Press, 1995) at 1, available at: http://hdr.undp.org/en/reports/global/hdr1995/chapter (last accessed 8 February 2013).

[2] See, for example, Article 14 of the European Convention for the Protection of Human Rights and Fundamental Freedoms (ECHR); Articles 2(2) and 3 of the International Covenant on Economic, Social and Cultural Rights (ICESCR); Article 3 of the International Covenant on Civil and Political Rights (ICCPR).

through the medium of General Recommendations and the developing jurisprudence under the Optional Protocol.

What then does the concept of 'engendered socio-economic rights' entail? As a start, it is necessary to recognise the distinctive nature of women's experience of poverty and disadvantage. This suggests that it is not sufficient simply to extend human rights to women. Instead, rights need to be recast in the light of the demands of substantive gender equality. Substantive equality goes beyond treating women in the same way as men and requires transformative measures. This in turn entails reconceptualising the rights themselves. This chapter begins by considering the gendered nature of women's disadvantage. The second part examines the meaning of equality in the context of gender and argues that a substantive notion of equality requires a recharacterisation of the rights themselves. The capabilities approach of Amartya Sen and Martha Nussbaum is helpful in this process because it requires attention to be paid to the extent to which women are able to be and do what they value. But the capabilities approach needs to be tempered by valuing caring and responsibility together with agency and choice. In the third part I compare and contrast the extent to which socio-economic rights are engendered in the International Covenant on Economic, Social and Cultural Rights (ICESCR) and the CEDAW respectively. It is concluded that the CEDAW's unique contribution to international human rights law lies in its potential to engender human rights, a potential which has thus far been only partially realised.

2 Gendered disadvantage

2.1 Gendered barriers to economic participation

For men, the risk of poverty is predominantly connected to exclusion from the labour market, whether due to low skills, previous unemployment or lack of regional job opportunities. For women, however, there are other, gender-based factors leading them into poverty and keeping them there. In particular, women's poverty is closely linked to their role in the family, particularly their caring roles. Unpaid caring roles can significantly limit women's access to decent paid work, leaving many women with no choice but to accept precarious and low-paid work.[3] Part-time

[3] G. Rosenblatt and K. Rake, 'Gender and poverty', Fawcett Society 1, available at: www.fawcettsociety.org.uk/index.asp?PageID=759 (last accessed 6 March 2013).

work is particularly at risk of offering low pay; yet women predominate in part-time work. In the EU most of the increase in women's employment over the past decade has been through part-time and precarious work.[4] Women also predominate in the informal sector. In sub-Saharan Africa 84 per cent of non-agricultural workers who are women are informally employed compared to 63 per cent of men. Moreover, the informal economy is segmented by employment status and by sex. The highest-paid segment – micro-entrepreneurs who hire others – is predominantly male, while women are overrepresented in the lowest-paid segment of the informal economy – as homeworkers or industrial outworkers.[5] Furthermore, divorce, widowhood, separation and teenage parenthood are major triggers of women's poverty in a way that they are not for men.[6]

Women's continuing primary responsibility for home work and childcare also affects the value attached to women's market work. Because domestic work and childcare can in principle be done for free at home, much of women's paid work is seriously undervalued. This includes catering, cleaning, caring work and subsistence agricultural work. Thus while women's participation in paid work has increased worldwide, occupations remain highly segregated, with women clustering in low-paid, low-status jobs.[7] In addition, women predominate in agricultural work, particularly in sub-Saharan Africa.

The result is that although women's participation in paid work has increased, this has not necessarily improved their economic status.[8] As Floro and Meurs demonstrate, '[w]orking conditions, such as job security, health and occupational safety and pay do not automatically improve for women as employment increases; indeed, these conditions may deteriorate under the pressure of global competition'.[9] In all countries, women's

4 European Commission, *Equality between Women and Men – 2009*, Report submitted to the European Parliament, the Council, the European Economic and Social Committee, and the Committee of the Regions; International Labour Organization (ILO), *Global Employment Trends for Women: 2009* (Geneva: ILO, 2009).

5 WIEGO, *Women and Men in Informal Employment*, available at: http://wiego.org/sites/wiego.org/files/resources/files/Women-Men-in-Informal-Employment.pdf (last accessed 6 March 2013).

6 G. Rosenblatt and K. Rake, *Gender and Poverty* (London: Fawcett Society, 2003) 1–5 at 3.

7 F. Bettio and A. Verashchagina, *Gender Segregation in the Labour Market: Root Causes, Implications and Policy Responses in the EU* (European Commission, 2009).

8 International Labour Organization, *Global Employment Trends*, *supra* note 4.

9 M. S. Floro and M. Meurs, 'Global trends in women's access to "decent work"', Occasional Paper No. 43, ILO (2009) at 13.

average earnings lag considerably behind that of men's,[10] and the pay gap is particularly large in the informal sector. Thus while paid work can bring with it a modicum of agency and independence, women are often in a position where they have no option but to accept precarious and exploitative pay and other working conditions. With no economic value given to unpaid activities, women's contribution remains invisible,[11] as does their role in facilitating men's ability to access work.[12] This affects not just their actual income but also their ability to act as equal partners in most economic transactions, such as property ownership or their ability to offer collateral for bank loans. Moreover, because women are for the most part engaged in low-paid work in the small-scale retail sector, informal sector or small farming, they are particularly vulnerable to economic downturns, public spending cuts and privatisation of public utilities such as water and electricity.[13]

The fact that the traditional household division of labour has remained intact despite women's increased participation in paid work means that women work longer hours than men in nearly every country,[14] and a significantly larger proportion of their working time than that of men is spent on unpaid activities.[15] As a recent study put it: '[i]nstead of replacing time in reproductive work with time in paid work, and shifting compensating amounts of reproductive work to men, it has been found that women tend to increase their total work time'.[16] However, the solution is complex. For example, one way to release women from time-consuming

[10] B. Rodenberg, 'Gender and poverty reduction', Working Paper 4, German Development Institute (2004) at 2; European Commission, *Equality between Women and Men – 2009*.

[11] UNDP, *Gender Development* at 93.

[12] *Ibid.* at 97. The UNDP estimates that if the value of unpaid work performed by women and men were seen as market transactions at prevailing wages, and the value of underpayment of women's work was included, a further 70 per cent or $16 trillion would be added on to the officially estimated $23 trillion of global output. This figure demonstrates the extent of the undervaluation of women's contribution.

[13] Rodenberg, 'Gender and poverty reduction' at 5.

[14] The UNDP (in *Gender Development* at 88) reported in 1995 that women carry 53 per cent of the burden of work (including both paid and unpaid) in developed countries and 51 per cent in developing countries. See generally Floro and Meurs, 'Global trends'; UNDP, *Human Development Report 2007/2008* (New York: Palgrave Macmillan, 2007) at 342, Table 32.

[15] Of men's total work-time in industrial countries, roughly two-thirds is spent on paid activities and one-third on unpaid activities, while the converse is true for women. In developing countries, more than three-quarters of men's work takes place in market activities: UNDP, *Gender Development* at 88. For the more recent figures for the EU, see European Commission, *Equality between Women and Men – 2009*.

[16] Floro and Meurs, 'Global trends' at 6.

unpaid work for middle-income households is to employ domestic workers. Yet domestic workers are themselves predominantly low-paid women, who are particularly vulnerable to exploitation. This solution is not, in any event, available to the vast majority of women, who cannot afford paid domestic help. Instead, women who juggle paid and unpaid work may need to enlist children to perform the work, and these in turn are typically girls, who are removed from school to care for younger children and do domestic work.[17] The specifically gendered nature of disadvantage is therefore replicated through the generations.

2.2 *Gender-based violence*

A further way in which women experience gender-specific disadvantage is in the context of gender-based violence, both physical and psychological. Violence and the threat of violence remain widespread in most countries, from infanticide and selective abortions of girl babies, to childhood sex abuse, forced prostitution, genital mutilation, forced marriage, marital abuse, sexual harassment at work and rape.[18] The persistence of violence against women reflects the absence of fully effective legal systems as well as continued cultural and social power imbalances.

2.3 *Limited agency*

Particularly important is the impact of gender on the power to control important decisions in one's life.[19] Although this lack of agency is also felt by poor men, gender continues to have a specific impact on such power. For example, as Chant notes, '[i]nequitable resource allocation can often lead to "secondary" poverty among women and children in male-headed households, and, as such, for many women the capacity to command and allocate resources may be more important than the actual resource base in

[17] *Ibid.*

[18] UNDP, *Gender Development* at 7. Amnesty International reports that approximately one in three women globally has been a victim of gender-based violence and that gender-based violence 'kills and disables as many women between the ages of 15 and 44 as cancer, and its toll on women's health surpasses that of traffic accidents and malaria combined'. See Amnesty International, *Violence Against Women: A Fact Sheet* (2005), available at: www.amnestyusa.org/sites/default/files/pdfs/vaw_fact_sheet.pdf (last accessed 8 February 2013).

[19] C. Sweetman, 'Editorial' in C. Sweetman (ed.), *Gender and the Millennium Development Goals* (Oxford: Oxfam, 2005) 2–8 at 3.

their households'.[20] In particular, Chant argues that 'women's mounting responsibilities for coping with poverty do not seem to be conferring any leverage in respect of negotiating greater efforts on the part of men'. The result is that 'while responsibilities for dealing with poverty are becoming palpably feminized, there is no corresponding increase in women's rights and rewards. Indeed, the self-same rise in women's burdens seems to have curtailed the resources at their disposal to negotiate gains of any description.'[21]

2.4 *Restricted access to socio-economic goods*

Women's ability to access socio-economic rights, such as housing, education and access to healthcare and protection, is also shaped by the gendered nature of social institutions, including legal, cultural, customary and traditional factors. For example, in respect of housing, Farha argues, 'the gendered nature of social and economic relations within and outside the household means that women experience discrimination and inequality in virtually every aspect of housing.'[22] Women's housing inequality is exacerbated by their exclusion from policy development with respect to housing; by customary practices (that are sometimes enforced by law), which prevent women from inheriting land and housing; and by domestic violence.[23]

A similar argument can be made in respect to the right to education. Barriers to girls' education are frequently specifically gendered. One example is the widespread practice of expelling pregnant girls and child mothers. As Tomasevski, the previous Special Rapporteur on Education, has forcefully argued, schools must be adapted to child parents if the right to education is to be meaningful for many girl children.[24] Similarly, menstruating girls who cannot afford sanitary towels will not go to school if there are no latrines or access to water.[25] Nor will they go to school if their parents regard it as more cost-beneficial for them to do domestic work at

[20] S. Chant, 'Rethinking the "feminization of poverty" in relation to aggregate gender indices', *J. of Human Development* 7:2 (2006) 201–20 at 208.

[21] *Ibid.* at 207–8.

[22] L. Farha, 'Is there a woman in the house? Re/conceiving the human right to housing', *Canadian J. of Women and the Law* 14:1 (2002) 118–41 at 121–2.

[23] *Ibid.* See also Ikdahl, Chapter 9 this volume.

[24] K. Tomasevski, 'Rights-based education as pathway to gender equality' in I. Boerefijn *et al.* (eds.), *Temporary Special Measures* (Antwerp: Intersentia, 2003) 151–72 at 155.

[25] E. Unterhalter, *Gender, Schooling and Global Social Justice* (London: Routledge, 2007).

home.[26] More generally, the benefits of education may be curtailed if other social structures are not changed. 'What girls can do with their education determines the attractiveness of schooling. If women cannot be employed or self-employed, own land, open a bank account, get a bank loan, if they are denied freedom to marry or not to marry, if they are deprived of political representation, education alone will have little effect on their plight.'[27] Thus girl children and women may require different forms of provision to achieve the condition of being educated.[28]

Also specifically affected by gender is access to social protection. Social benefits are frequently only available to those in formal employment and therefore women may have less access to them. The right to social security, if it is to be effective for women, therefore needs to be detached from formal work and made available to workers in the informal sector.[29] The ability to access old-age pensions is also gendered, if this is linked to contributions through paid work. For women who have interrupted working lives, this significantly impedes their access to pensions.[30]

3 From formal to substantive equality

3.1 The limits of formal equality

The above strongly suggests that it is not sufficient simply to extend rights to women. If the gender-specific factors causing women's disadvantage are fully to be addressed, rights must be infused with substantive gender equality. What would this entail? As a start, it is necessary to move away from a concept of equality that simply demands that women be treated in the same way as men. There are several familiar reasons for this.[31] Firstly, such a formal conception of equality expects women

[26] Tomasevski, 'Rights-based education' at 156.

[27] *Ibid.*

[28] Unterhalter, *Gender, Schooling and Global Social Justice* at 49.

[29] See F. Lund, 'A framework for analyzing social protection for workers in the informal economy' in C. Piras (ed.), *Women at Work: Challenges for Latin America* (Washington DC: Inter-American Development Bank, 2005).

[30] European Commission, *Equality between Women and Men – 2009* at 4; European Parliament, Resolution of 3 February 2009 on Non-discrimination Based on Sex and Intergenerational Solidarity (2008/2118(INI)) paras. 5 and 9, available at: www.europarl.europa.eu/oeil/FindByProcnum.do?lang=en&procnum=INI/2008/2118 (last accessed 8 February 2013).

[31] See generally S. Fredman, *Discrimination Law*, 2nd edn (Oxford University Press, 2002) Chapters 1 and 5; C. McCrudden, 'Merit principles', *Oxford J. of Legal Studies* 18:4 (1998) 543–79.

to conform to male-oriented social structures. It does nothing to challenge the structures themselves. For example, women will only be entitled to equal pay or equal treatment to men if they can do the same jobs and work the same hours as their male counterparts. Women with childcare responsibilities will be excluded from equal treatment unless they are able to find other women to look after their children, and the latter are invariably low paid. Formal equality is particularly ill-suited to deal with pregnancy and parenthood: clearly pregnant women are different and should be given specific rights, but to achieve real change requires in addition that fathers are given parental rights in the same way as mothers.

Secondly, formal equality assumes that the aim is to treat everyone on their merits, regardless of their gender. But treating gender as irrelevant merely ignores the ongoing disadvantage experienced by women. The result is to entrench disadvantage. For example, simply extending the right to social security to women on equal terms with men ignores the fact that women have interrupted work patterns and are often engaged in precarious and informal work. Such an approach would not assist those who most need it. This means that equality might demand, not identical treatment, but very different treatment. As Sen has argued: '[e]qual consideration for all may demand very unequal treatment in favour of the disadvantaged. The demands of substantive equality can be particularly exacting and complex when there is a good deal of antecedent inequality to counter.'[32]

Finally, formal equality is a relative concept. It requires only that two similarly situated individuals be treated alike. This means that there is no difference in principle between treating men and women equally badly and treating them equally well. It is here that equality can be no substitute for substantive rights. For example, if women's right to equal pay is based on the pay of men in a very low-paid occupation, equality holds out little promise. Substantive rights to minimum wages are far more valuable. Moreover, because formal equality is agnostic as to the substantive outcome, it can be fulfilled by removing benefits from men rather than extending benefits to women.[33] The result is that women are worse off and men are not better off.

[32] A. Sen, *Inequality Re-examined* (Oxford University Press, 1992) at 1.

[33] S. Fredman, *Women and the Law* (Oxford University Press, 1997) at 356–7.

3.2 *Substantive equality*

Substantive equality goes some way to addressing these problems. Firstly, substantive equality moves beyond the need for a male norm. In its transformative form, substantive equality requires social institutions to change, rather than expecting the individual to conform. Secondly, substantive equality takes into account existing power structures and the role of gender within them. Far from being irrelevant, gender may be highly relevant in addressing inequalities in society. This means that substantive equality does not simply aim at equal treatment. Where equal treatment leads to disadvantage for women, it may be necessary to treat women differently in order to achieve equalities of outcome. Thirdly, substantive equality is not neutral as to the outcome. Equality cannot be achieved by treating all equally badly, or by removing benefits from the advantaged class. It is substantive in the sense that it advances individuals, rather than formal in ensuring only consistency. What that substance is, however, remains controversial. This section considers in more detail what substantive equality might entail in the context of gender, and in particular in relation to engendering socio-economic rights.

There is a temptation to reduce substantive equality to a single dimension, such as dignity,[34] or to redefine equality in terms of equal opportunity or equality of results. Each of these is problematic. While dignity can function as a core rationale for substantive equality, it should not be the central component of its definition. Similarly, equality of opportunity on its own is too vague to function as a legal component of substantive equality. While it is possible to remove barriers at the point of entry, this will not guarantee that women are in a position to make use of these opportunities. Nor will it transform structures that lead to the inequality in the first place. For example, the opportunity to work part-time might

[34] The Canadian Supreme Court and the South African Constitutional Court both understand that equality and the prohibition on discrimination need to be founded on respect for human dignity. See for example *Law* v. *Canada* [1999] 1 SCR 497 (Canadian Supreme Court), para. 51: '[e]quality means that our society cannot tolerate legislative distinctions … that offend fundamental human dignity'; *Hoffmann* v. *South African Airways* 2000 (1) SA 1 (South African Constitutional Court) para. 27: '[a]t the heart of the prohibition of unfair discrimination is the recognition that under our Constitution all human beings, regardless of their position in society, must be accorded equal dignity'. However, the Canadian Supreme Court has recently raised doubts about the use of dignity as the basis of the prohibition on discrimination. See *R* v. *Kapp* [2008] 2 SCR 483 (Canadian Supreme Court), para. 22: 'human dignity is an abstract and subjective notion' and 'it has also proved to be an *additional* burden on equality claimants' (emphasis in original).

make it possible for more women to enter the workforce, and equal pay for equal work for part-time workers might improve their conditions, but the predominance of women in part-time work will not change. Indeed, this might increase their burden of combining paid work with family work, unless the division of labour in the home is changed and men take on equal responsibility for childcare. Equality of results is more quantifiable than equality of opportunity and, correspondingly, more effective. However, on their own, policies aiming simply at results are also insufficiently transformative. 'Feminisation of work' is often associated with decreasing pay and status. For example, in the UK an increase of women in managerial positions in catering coincided with a decrease in pay.

Each of these concepts has its strengths and should not be downgraded. But none can function on its own to constitute the substantive core of equality. I argue instead that substantive equality should be regarded as having four different dimensions.[35]

3.2.1 The redistributive dimension

Firstly, substantive equality concentrates on remedying disadvantage, rather than achieving gender neutrality. Disadvantage is both material and social. As we have seen, gender-based disadvantage includes the lack of empowerment of women within the context of family and social relations. Thus substantive equality aims to redress disadvantage in its specifically gendered context, including women's subordinate position in the family and reproduction, in the paid workforce and in other relationships of power. In particular, substantive equality contemplates different treatment in order to redress disadvantage. This means that affirmative action measures in favour of women do not breach the principle of equality as long as their aim is to redress discriminatory disadvantage.

3.2.2 The recognition dimension

The second dimension is that of respect, recognition and dignity. Including dignity as a facet of substantive equality means that, as well as socio-economic disadvantage and distributive wrongs, account is taken of what Nancy Fraser calls 'recognition' wrongs. The concept of 'recognition' is based in the Hegelian notion that our identity is constructed (at least partially) in terms of the ways in which others regard us. 'Recognition' wrongs consist in 'misrecognition' or inequality in the mutual respect

[35] See S. Fredman, *The Future of Equality in Great Britain*, Working Paper No. 5, Equal Opportunities Commission, Manchester (2002).

and concern that people feel for one another in society.[36] This dimension of substantive inequality includes, in particular, stigma, stereotyping, humiliation and violence on grounds of gender. Such wrongs can be experienced regardless of relative socio-economic disadvantage. Therefore, it is important to recognise the need for respect, recognition and dignity as a separate element of substantive equality, in addition to the first aim of correcting disadvantage. It has the important practical advantage of preventing the right to equality from being fulfilled by treating everyone equally badly, as might be possible under a formal definition of equality. At the same time, recognition, dignity and respect should not be regarded as the sole factor in defining substantive equality.

3.2.3 The transformative dimension

The third dimension of substantive equality is the way it deals with difference. The problem is not so much difference per se, but the detriment that is attached to difference. Substantive equality should therefore aim to respect and accommodate difference, removing the detriment but not the difference itself. Thus instead of requiring women to conform to male norms, substantive equality requires transformation of existing male-oriented institutions and social structures. With this comes the imperative to transcend the public–private divide, recognising the ways in which imbalances in power in the family can reinforce power imbalances in the public sphere and vice versa. Substantive equality also requires the accommodation of differences between women.

3.2.4 The participative dimension

The final dimension of substantive equality is the importance it attaches to women's agency and voice. As has been recognised in several jurisdictions, equality should specifically compensate for the absence of political power of groups 'to whose needs and wishes elected officials have no apparent interest in attending'.[37] Substantive equality requires decision-makers to hear and respond to the voice of women, rather than imposing top-down decisions. The challenges of giving women voice cannot be underestimated. Articulating women's interests from a gendered perspective requires closer attention to the diversity of women's voices,

[36] N. Fraser, 'Social justice in the age of identity politics' in N. Fraser and A. Honneth (eds.), *Redistribution or Recognition? A Philosophical Political Exchange* (London and New York: Verso, 2003) 7–109 at 29.

[37] J. H. Ely, *Democracy and Distrust: A Theory of Judicial Review* (Cambridge, MA: Harvard University Press, 1980) at 46.

to the possible disjuncture between those who speak and those who are affected, and to the need to ensure that the least vocal are nevertheless heard. Moreover, as much as women's voice should be heard in engendering socio-economic rights, so socio-economic rights are necessary to give women the capability of articulating their perspectives. Substantive equality also has the important effect of imposing positive duties on the State, to treat women differently, provide opportunities for participation and restructure institutions appropriately.

4 Engendering socio-economic rights

When interpreted in the light of substantive equality, human rights for women cannot remain untouched. Substantive equality requires a transformation of the right itself. It is helpful in this respect to draw on the capabilities theories developed by Amartya Sen[38] and Martha Nussbaum.[39] The capabilities approach focuses not on an objective formulation of rights as a set of material goods but on whether people are able to be and do what they have reason to value. This is promising in the context of gender equality in that it stresses agency and choice. But it differs from equality of opportunity, because it takes into account the extent to which women are actually able to exercise their choice. For Sen, constraints on freedom include not just political oppression or interference, but also socio-economic and personal circumstances: '[w]hat people can achieve is influenced by economic opportunities, political liberties, social powers and the enabling conditions of good health, basic education, and the encouragement and cultivation of initiatives'.[40] Capabilities refer to valued goals that are feasible for an individual to pursue. It is not enough to have the formal opportunity to pursue one's chosen goals; 'capability' crucially denotes feasible options.[41] This means that for human rights to be meaningful, the State must take positive steps to remove barriers and facilitate the exercise of such rights.[42]

At the same time, to fully engender socio-economic rights, the emphasis on choice in the capabilities approach needs to be tempered by including values, such as caring and responsibility, that are not a matter of choice.[43]

[38] A. Sen, *Development as Freedom* (Oxford University Press, 1999).

[39] M. Nussbaum, *Women and Human Development* (Cambridge University Press, 2000).

[40] Sen, *Development as Freedom* at 5.

[41] *Ibid.* at 75. [42] *Ibid.* at 3.

[43] See further S. Fredman, *Human Rights Transformed: Positive Rights and Positive Duties* (Oxford University Press, 2008) at 15–16.

Sen's normative framework places as its highest value the individual's ability to do or be what she has reason to value. This risks focusing too much attention on what individuals can achieve, giving the impression that the only function of positive duties is to facilitate the ability of individuals to realise their own goals. It is important that this should not eclipse other human rights values, which are not based on choice but on interpersonal relationships and interdependence. Central among these is the value of caring, which comes, not as a matter of choice, but of responsibility. In fact, the needs of the person who is cared for might limit, inevitably and appropriately, the capabilities of the person doing the caring. In the context of gender, it is of great significance that value is attached, not just to choices, but to relationships for themselves. Thus engendering socio-economic rights does not merely require that women looking after children have more childcare options, enabling them to undertake paid work. It also requires that caring activities in themselves are valued and protected, for example through appropriate social security benefits, health services, housing and protection against vulnerability to violence. Giving greater social recognition to caring work might also encourage a fairer division of caring work among men and women.

In the context of gender, the capabilities approach can be developed to take into account the gendered nature of constraints on women. For example, the right to work as it stands is generally equated with paid work. But as we have seen, the right to paid work does not necessarily enhance the range of feasible options open to women. In fact, it might further constrain women. This is because the right to paid work does not take into account the constraints on women due to the interaction between women's work in the paid workforce and their unpaid work in the home. To fully engender the right to work, it is necessary to render unpaid work visible and address the relationship between paid and unpaid work. Otherwise, women are simply required to conform to existing structures. Similarly, the right to social insurance must be transformed so that it no longer privileges those with male patterns of work, who can amass higher levels of contributions than women with broken work histories. In this way, the right is shaped in ways that ensure that women are equally able to access it. The very recognition of non-gainful employment is an important start.[44] A similar analysis can be applied to rights to health, housing and education.

[44] *Report on Equality between Women and Men – 2009*, Report from the European Commission to the European Parliament, the Council, the European Economic and Social Committee, and the Committee of the Regions, Com (2009) 77 Final.

Particularly important in redefining the interface between paid work, unpaid work and childcare is the way in which rights to maternity leave, parental leave and childcare are structured. Women's biological role in reproduction needs to be separated from their social role in parenting. While the former needs to attract rights specific to women, it is essential that the latter yields entitlements and indeed responsibilities for fathers as well as mothers. An ILO review of maternity protection in 2004 showed that 167 countries had some legislation in place.[45] However, it is still rare to have paternity or parental leave. The availability of subsidised childcare is again crucial to women's ability to balance paid and unpaid work, but close attention needs to be paid to the way in which it is set up. In particular, the vast majority of childcare workers may themselves be low-paid women.

5 Socio-economic rights and equality: the ICESCR approach

This section considers the extent to which gender equality is considered as an 'add-on' to existing rights within the ICESCR. As well as a general non-discrimination clause,[46] the ICESCR includes Article 3, which states: '[t]he States Parties to the present Covenant undertake to ensure the equal right of men and women to the enjoyment of all economic, social and cultural rights set forth in the present Covenant'. It should be stressed that equality can enhance socio-economic rights even as an 'add-on'. As the Committee on Economic, Social and Cultural Rights (CESCR) puts it in the General Comment on Non-Discrimination issued in 2009: '[d]iscrimination undermines the fulfilment of economic, social and cultural rights for a significant proportion of the world's population. Economic growth has not, in itself, led to sustainable development and individuals and groups of individuals continue to face socio-economic inequality, often because of entrenched historical and contemporary forms of discrimination.'[47] Moreover, equality can be a powerful partner to socio-economic rights. While the duty of States Parties is only to realise the socio-economic rights in the Covenant progressively and subject to the maximum of its available resources,[48] 'the equal right of men and

[45] ILO, *Maternity at Work*, 2nd edn (Geneva: ILO, 2004), available at: www.ilo.org/wcmsp5/groups/public/@dgreports/@dcomm/@publ/documents/publication/wcms_124442.pdf (last accessed 6 March 2013).

[46] Article 2(2) ICESCR.

[47] CESCR, General Comment No. 20: Non-Discrimination in Economic, Social and Cultural Rights, UN Doc. E/C.12/GC/20 (2009), para. 1.

[48] Article 2(1) ICESCR.

women to the enjoyment of economic, social and cultural rights is a mandatory and immediate obligation of States Parties'.[49] However, it is argued that the ICESCR does not go far enough to engender socio-economic rights in the sense understood above.

5.1 *Equality as an 'add-on'*

In many contexts, equality is regarded as simply extending rights in the ICESCR to women. The *Travaux Préparatoires* state that Article 3 was included in the Covenant to indicate that 'the *same* rights should be expressly recognized for men and women on an equal footing',[50] suggesting a formal and additive approach. But at the same time they refer to the need for 'suitable measures [to] be taken to ensure that women had the opportunity to exercise their rights'.[51] The CESCR claims that it has taken particular note of factors negatively affecting the equal right of men and women to the enjoyment of socio-economic rights in many of its General Comments, including those on the right to adequate housing, the right to adequate food, the right to education, the right to the highest attainable standard of health and the right to water.[52] However, Leilani Farha demonstrates that women's perspectives, particularly on housing, were not reflected in the 'gender neutral documents' being adopted by the UN.[53] This is particularly true of General Comment No. 4 on the Right to Housing,[54] where, she argues, the attempt at gender neutrality has the effect of rendering women's specific experience of housing invisible. For example, although the Comment states that all persons should possess a degree of security of tenure, it fails to capture the particular causes of women's insecure tenure, such as domestic violence and discriminatory inheritance laws, customs and traditions.[55]

The tendency to regard gender equality as an add-on to otherwise neutral rights is also demonstrated through Fleur van Leeuwen's valuable analysis

[49] CESCR, General Comment No. 16: The Equal Right of Men and Women to the Enjoyment of All Economic, Social and Cultural Rights, UN Doc. E/C.12/2005/4 (2005) para. 16; see also CESCR, General Comment No. 3: The Nature of States Parties Obligations, UN Doc. E/1991/23 (1990) para. 1.

[50] Emphasis added.

[51] General Comment No. 16 para. 2.

[52] *Ibid.* para. 4.

[53] Farha, 'Is there a woman in the house?' at 120.

[54] CESCR, General Comment No. 4: The Right to Adequate Housing, UN Doc. E/C.12/1991/4 (1991) para. 6.

[55] Farha, 'Is there a woman in the house?' at 128.

of the practice of the CESCR. She finds that whereas the Committee is sensitive to women's specific experiences, it does not examine whether these are caused by structural discrimination against women. For example, in relation to women's physical security, the Committee has done valuable work in emphasising that abortion should not be prohibited for women who have been raped or whose lives are endangered by the pregnancy. However, it does not go further and insist that abortion services in fact be provided.[56] If the CESCR were to adopt a capabilities approach as advocated here, it would be obvious that merely removing legal prohibitions on abortion would not be sufficient to be sure that women are in fact in a position to choose an abortion. A further step needs to be taken to make these choices feasible. The Committee should formulate appropriate obligations to this effect.

Van Leeuwen concludes that, as a result, the CESCR deals with the symptoms but not the causes of human rights abuses against women. The four-dimensional notion of equality suggested here would take the CESCR further towards truly engendering human rights. In particular, it would require structural changes to healthcare services, such as the provision of proper maternal health and reproductive care, which empower women within their communities and aim at equal respect and concern for women.

5.2 *Traces of substantive equality*

More recently, the CESCR has produced two General Comments, one on equality for women and one on equality more generally.[57] The General Comment on Equality for Women makes it clear that equality should be understood in a substantive way that goes beyond apparent gender neutrality: '[f]ormal equality assumes that equality is achieved if a law or policy treats men and women in a neutral manner. Substantive equality is concerned, in addition, with the effects of laws, policies and practices and with ensuring that they do not maintain, but rather alleviate, the inherent disadvantage that particular groups experience.'[58] However, in the examples it gives of the ways in which Article 3 applies to other rights in the Covenant, so there remains a strong inclination to regard equality as an 'add-on'. This can be seen clearly in respect of Article 6(1), the right

[56] Van Leeuwen, Chapter 8 this volume.
[57] CESCR, General Comment No. 16; CESCR, General Comment No. 20.
[58] CESCR, General Comment No. 16 para. 7.

to work, and Article 7, the right to just and favourable conditions of work. According to the General Comment, '[i]mplementing Article 3 in relation to Article 6 requires inter alia, that, in law and in practice, men and women have equal access to jobs at all levels and all occupations and that vocational training and guidance programmes, in both the public and private sectors, provide men and women with the skills, information and knowledge necessary for them to benefit equally from the right to work'. There is little sense here of the need to modify the structure of work itself to fully engender the right to work as argued above. Similarly, in relation to equal pay and working conditions, the General Comment states, that:

> Article 3 in relation to Article 7 requires, inter alia, that the State party identifies and eliminates the underlying causes of pay differentials, such as gender biased job evaluation or the perception that productivity differences between men and women exist ... The State party should adopt legislation that prescribes equal consideration in promotion, non-wage compensation and equal opportunity and support for vocational or professional development in the workplace.

Here, too, the approach seems simply to attempt to slot women into existing male-dominated structures. Thus, the ICESCR, as interpreted through the General Comments, still stops short of engendering the right to work. This is because it does not address the relationship of unpaid work to market work; nor does it expressly require recognition of such work.

Somewhat more hopeful is the approach to reconciling work and family. The General Comment states that the State Party should reduce the constraints faced by men and women in reconciling professional and family responsibilities by promoting adequate policies for childcare and care of dependent family members. In addition, it regards the right to parental leave as applying to fathers as well as mothers, although it does not specify whether such leave should be paid or not. It is through Article 10, the right to protection for the family, that the Comment comes closest to formulating an engendered approach. Particularly important is the recognition that 'gender based violence is a form of discrimination that inhibits the ability to enjoy rights and freedoms, including economic, social and cultural rights, on a basis of equality'. This enables the Comment to identify the ways in which ICESCR rights should be interpreted so as to protect women's substantive rights to dignity, to widen the range of feasible options open to women, and endorse and value their interrelationships with others.[59]

[59] *Ibid.* para. 27.

It is in the reports of the UN Special Rapporteur on Adequate Housing that the possibility of an engendered approach is particularly evident.[60] His approach to formulating the right incorporates many of the elements of substantive equality set out above. The first element, the need for an asymmetric approach that recognises gender disadvantage, is central to his analysis. Thus he emphasises the inadequacy of formal guarantees of equality to women by demonstrating that, whereas in many countries women's rights are legally protected, in practice women are socially and economically disadvantaged and face de facto discrimination in the areas of housing, land and inheritance rights. In particular, gender-neutral laws are interpreted and implemented in ways that discriminate and disadvantage women.[61]

Particularly important is the fourth element above, namely the commitment to give voice and agency to women. Indeed, it is because he has instituted wide-ranging consultations, and listened to testimonies received from women at grass-roots level, that he has succeeded in formulating the right from a particularly gendered perspective.[62] Women's testimonies also revealed the importance of the second dimension, dignity or recognition, and particularly the central role of violence. The Special Rapporteur emphasises in his reports that the historically unequal power relations between men and women on both individual and societal levels are the root cause of gender-based violence.[63] Indeed, he takes this one step further and concludes that 'persistent poverty, where women and others are forced to live in inadequate and insecure housing and living conditions, is itself a form of violence'. Violence both results from and causes inadequate and insecure housing. Since women have comparatively fewer educational and employment opportunities, they can be disproportionately dependent on family, informal support networks, or a partner or spouse to meet their housing and economic needs. Due to such dependency, fear of homelessness makes many women vulnerable to violence and other forms of exploitation within the family. The need to

[60] See A. Aggarwal, 'UN Special Rapporteur on Adequate Housing: strengthening gendered norms for the right to adequate housing', *Australian J. of Human Rights* 10:1 (2004) 8, available at: www.austlii.edu.au/au/journals/AUJlHRights/2004/8.html (last accessed 8 February 2013).

[61] M. Kothari, *Women and Adequate Housing: Report by the Special Rapporteur on Adequate Housing as a Component of the Right to an Adequate Standard of Living, and on the Right to Non-Discrimination*, UN Doc. E/CN.4/2006/118 (2006) para. 9. See also Ikhdal, Chapter 9 this volume.

[62] Kothari, *Women and Adequate Housing* paras. 8, 12.

[63] *Ibid.* para. 32.

accommodate difference is recognised in the Special Rapporteur's recognition of the role of multiple discrimination, for example against disabled women and Roma women.[64]

It is also important to note that the Special Rapporteur does not necessarily characterise the right to adequate housing as a right to a particular bundle of goods, in this case a house, but as a right to action by the State to protect and expand the range of feasible options available to women, such as the development of gender-sensitive housing policies and legislation, access to affordable utilities such as water, electricity and heating as well as to education, employment and health facilities, and protection against violence.[65] This is a particularly clear example of the way in which engendered socio-economic rights aim to take account of the power relations in which rights are exercised, in order to enhance the set of feasible options open to women, while at the same time valuing and supporting their roles within a complex network of interdependence.[66] Ingunn Ikdahl's research underscores this point:[67] formal rights to property may be meaningless to women because they are overlaid by a web of social, cultural and possibly religious norms.

6 The CEDAW

The CEDAW differs from the ICESCR in that it regards gender equality and socio-economic rights as interdependent, recognising that gender inequality must be addressed at least in part by providing justiciable socio-economic rights. However, on closer inspection it can be seen that the CEDAW speaks with two voices. Parts of the CEDAW, and its interpretation in later General Recommendations, go beyond simply extending given rights to women, and instead reframe the rights themselves in the light of substantive equality. However, other parts of the CEDAW simply extend given socio-economic rights to women.

6.1 *Engendered rights*

The more progressive voice can be heard in some of the salient elements of the CEDAW. As a start, it is expressly asymmetric. Instead of outlawing discrimination on grounds of sex or gender, the CEDAW aims at the

[64] *Ibid.* paras. 47–53. [65] *Ibid.* para. 11.

[66] Aggarwal, 'Strengthening gendered norms'.

[67] Ikdahl, Chapter 9 this volume.

elimination of discrimination specifically against women. According to the CEDAW Committee:

> [t]he Convention goes beyond the concept of discrimination used in many national and international legal standards and norms. While such standards and norms prohibit discrimination on the grounds of sex and protect both men and women from treatment based on arbitrary, unfair and/or unjustifiable distinctions, the Convention focuses on discrimination against women, emphasizing that women have suffered, and continue to suffer from various forms of discrimination because they are women.[68]

Nor is it sufficient to provide formal equality, or to open up opportunities that women are unable to utilise. The emphasis is on ensuring that women are actually in a position to make use of their rights.[69]

This commitment to equality does not merely impose negative duties, or duties of restraint, on the State. Instead, it requires States Parties to take 'all appropriate measures, including legislation, to ensure the full development and advancement of women, for the purpose of guaranteeing them the exercise and enjoyment of human rights and fundamental freedoms on a basis of equality with men'.[70] The State has positive duties to 'protect, promote and fulfil this right to non-discrimination for women and to ensure the development and advancement of women in order to improve their position to one of de jure as well as de facto equality with men'.[71]

Secondly, the CEDAW does not demand conformity as a price for equality. Instead, it demands structural change. Most importantly, the Convention actively addresses the public/private divide, and the social and cultural assumptions and prejudices that keep women in the private sphere. Article 5 is particularly transformative in its approach, requiring States Parties to take all appropriate measures 'to modify the social and cultural patterns of conduct of men and women with a view to achieving the elimination of prejudices and customary and other practices which are based on the idea of the inferiority or superiority of either of the sexes or on stereotyped roles for men and women'. All discrimination against women in matters relating to marriage and family relations must be eliminated, including rights to property, guardianship of children and inheritance.[72]

[68] Committee on the Elimination of Discrimination against Women (CEDAW), General Recommendation No. 25: Temporary Special Measures (Thirtieth Session, 2004), para. 5.

[69] Article 1 CEDAW. [70] Article 3 CEDAW.

[71] CEDAW, General Recommendation No. 25 para. 4.

[72] Article 16 CEDAW.

Thirdly, the CEDAW takes particularly seriously the importance of representation of women in decision-making, the fourth dimension of substantive equality identified above. This includes not just the bare right to vote in elections, but also the right to participate in the formulation of government policy, to hold public office and to participate in non-governmental organisations.[73]

These three elements reflect the CEDAW's commitment to a conception of substantive equality that is sensitive to women's distinct experience of disadvantage. This engendered approach is reflected in many of the socio-economic rights contained in the Convention.

The cluster of rights in respect of reproduction and childcare demonstrate an understanding of rights as enhancing women's feasible options, while at the same time valuing their caring roles. The Preamble sets the tone by stating that 'the role of women in procreation should not be a basis for discrimination'. This is accompanied by a requirement to ensure that family education includes a proper understanding of maternity as a social function and the recognition of the common responsibility of men and women in the upbringing and development of their children.[74] Accordingly, provisions for maternity protection and childcare are proclaimed as essential rights and are incorporated into all areas of the Convention, whether dealing with employment, family law, healthcare or education. Society's obligation extends to offering social services, especially childcare facilities, that allow individuals to combine family responsibilities with work and participation in public life. Special measures for maternity protection are recommended and 'shall not be considered discriminatory'.[75] The Convention also affirms women's right to reproductive choice. Notably, it is the only international human rights treaty to mention family planning. States Parties are obliged to include advice on family planning in the education process[76] and to develop family codes that guarantee women's rights 'to decide freely and responsibly on the number and spacing of their children and to have access to the information, education and means to enable them to exercise these rights'.[77]

An engendered approach to socio-economic rights further requires that violence against women be recognised and addressed within the substance of the rights themselves and not just as an 'add-on'. The absence of direct reference to a prohibition on violence against women in the CEDAW

[73] Article 7 CEDAW. [74] Article 5(b) CEDAW.
[75] Article 4 CEDAW. [76] Article l0(h) CEDAW.
[77] Article 16(e) CEDAW.

itself is startling. Nevertheless, the CEDAW Committee has made it clear that gender-based violence clearly falls within the definition of discrimination in Article 1, since it inevitably impairs or nullifies the enjoyment by women of human rights and fundamental freedoms.[78] In its General Recommendation No. 19 of 1992, the Committee shows how most of the Convention rights must read in a way that addresses gender-based violence, even when not expressly mentioned. Thus States Parties are required by Article 6 to take measures to suppress all forms of traffic in women and exploitation of the prostitution of women. Consistent with the second dimension of substantive equality identified above, the Committee stresses that these practices are incompatible with the equal enjoyment of rights by women and with respect for their rights and dignity.[79] Similarly, gender-specific violence includes sexual harassment at the workplace, which can seriously impair equality for women in the workplace. Violence against women is clearly a breach of the right to equal access to healthcare services, which is part of States' duties under Article 12. The duty of the State extends to the protection of women against violence perpetuated by culture and tradition, such as female circumcision, dietary restrictions for pregnant women and preference for male children.[80]

Also central to an engendered approach is the recognition that equal treatment of men and women may not be sufficient to achieve equality in practice, hence the central importance of mandatory affirmative action in the CEDAW. As originally drafted, however, the reference to 'temporary special measures' in Article 4(1) gave the impression that measures specifically directed at women were an exception to equality, even when they were aimed at redressing previous disadvantage. However, after detailed consultation with women's groups and others,[81] the Committee issued General Recommendation No. 25. In a comprehensive affirmation of substantive equality over formal equality, the Recommendation makes it clear that affirmative action is by no means a breach of equality, but may be necessary to achieve substantive equality. This reaffirms the asymmetry of substantive equality.

The development of substantive equality within the CEDAW has, in some important respects, reshaped the right itself. This can be seen in

[78] CEDAW, General Recommendation No. 19: Violence Against Women (Eleventh Session, 1992) para. 7.

[79] *Ibid.* paras. 13–14.

[80] *Ibid.* paras. 15–16.

[81] See I. Boerefijn *et al.* (eds.) *Temporary Special Measures.*

relation to the right to property. In General Recommendation No. 21, the Committee has recognised that property rights on the break-up of marriage should not depend only on the financial contributions of spouses. This ignores the unpaid work of women. Instead, the right to property should also reflect the contribution of women through their unpaid domestic and reproductive work.[82] Similarly, as Ingunn Ikdahl points out, the CEDAW Committee has required ways to access land that are typical for women to be translated into property rights.[83]

Particularly important is the way in which engendering human rights affects women's right to health. It is not sufficient simply to make health-care services available to women in the same way as they are to men. Instead, States Parties must develop services that are responsive to women's reproductive capacities and particular vulnerabilities, and should recognise barriers that particularly prejudice women, such as the requirement for preliminary authorisation by spouse, parent or hospital authorities, high fees, distance from health facilities and birth clinics, lack of skilled birth attendants and absence of safe public transport.[84] These aspects of the right to health protection are analysed by Henriette Sinding Aasen in Chapter 10 in this volume.

6.2 *Limitations*

In other respects, however, a closer look at the Convention reveals that in key areas it still regards gender equality as an 'add-on' to given socio-economic rights. This is particularly evident from the wording of the major socio-economic rights, namely the rights to work,[85] and credit, benefits and recreation.[86] Both are formulated as if it is sufficient simply to add equality to socio-economic rights, rather than transforming them through the principle of equality. Thus, in each case the State Party is required to 'take all appropriate measures to eliminate discrimination against women … in order to ensure on a basis of equality of men and women, *the same rights*'.[87]

The problems with regarding equality as simply an add-on or extension of a fixed right in this manner can be seen by taking a closer look at the

[82] CEDAW, General Recommendation No. 21: Equality in Marriage and Family Relations (Thirteenth Session, 1994), para. 32; see Ikdahl, Chapter 9 this volume.

[83] Ikdahl, Chapter 9 this volume.

[84] CEDAW, General Recommendation No. 24: Women and Health (Twentieth Session, 1999), para. 21.

[85] Article 11 CEDAW. [86] Article 13 CEDAW. [87] Emphasis added.

rights to work and to education. Article 11(a) refers to 'the right to work as an inalienable right of all human beings'. Article 11(b) gives women the right to the same employment opportunities, including the application of the same criteria for selection in matters of employment. On one level, this could be seen as giving women the right to exit the private sphere and thereby to attain economic independence. On the other hand, it is premised on an intensely male model of work, the assumption being that 'work' equates with paid work outside of the home. As we have seen, for women to be in a position truly to exercise the right to paid work outside of the home, the structure of paid work must itself be transformed, so that both men and women participate in parenting and perform unpaid work in the home. Otherwise, their continuing responsibility for unpaid work in the private sphere will necessarily inhibit their ability to find good-quality paid work.[88] Again, Article 11(e) gives women the equal right to social security, particularly in cases of retirement, unemployment, sickness, invalidity and old age, and other incapacity to work, as well as the right to paid leave. Here, too, women will not achieve de facto equality unless eligibility criteria and contribution requirements are changed to reflect women's interrupted work patterns. Particularly challenging is the application of social security to the numerous women who work in the informal sector.

Similarly, the right to education in Article 10 speaks with two voices. The first is the voice of formal equality. Article 10 gives the right to:

> '(a) [t]he *same* conditions for career and vocational guidance, for access to studies and for the achievement of diplomas ...
> (b) [a]ccess to the *same* curricula, the *same* examinations, teaching staff with qualifications of the same standard and school premises and equipment of the *same* quality ...
> (d) [t]he *same* opportunities to benefit from scholarships ... and
> (e) [t]he *same* opportunities for access to programmes of continuing education, including adult and functional literacy programmes.[89]

On the other hand, the voice of substantive equality, although muted, is nevertheless found in Article 10(c), which requires the 'elimination of any

[88] See further United Nations, *Beijing Declaration and Platform for Action*, Fourth World Conference on Women, UN Doc. A/CONF.177/20 (1995) para. 181: 'Governments [shall] ... [p]romote the equal sharing of responsibilities for the family by men and women'; International Labour Conference, *Gender Equality at the Heart of Decent Work* (Geneva: ILO, 2009) para. 79: 'The achievement of gender equality requires a context in which men and women work together, and work and family responsibilities are shared.'

[89] Emphasis added.

stereotyped concept of the roles of men and women … by encouraging coeducation and … in particular, by the revision of textbooks and school programmes and the adaptation of teaching methods'. Curricula that continue to depict girls in stereotypical household roles will perpetuate fixed roles and limit girls' self-expectations. It is this voice that needs to be developed and strengthened. As we have seen, far more is necessary truly to engender women's rights to education. The same is true for other CEDAW rights, particularly rights to health and housing.

Similarly, despite its assertion that the common responsibility of men and women should be recognised, the CEDAW stops short of full structural change. This is because its emphasis on maternity rights, without corresponding rights for fathers, could reinforce the assumption that it is women who are primarily responsible for childcare. In addition, as Ikdahl concludes, 'while the CEDAW Committee has provided detailed analysis of women's unequal property rights within the family, it has not yet engaged systematically with the effects on women's unequal right to [housing]'.[90]

7 Conclusion

It has been argued here that if socio-economic rights are to have a real effect on achieving equality for women, they need to be infused with substantive equality. This requires a reformulation of the rights themselves, to take into account and address the gender-specific constraints that women experience in exercising these rights. More specifically, it requires greater attention to be paid to the ways in which the rights to respect, protect and fulfil are formulated.

Both the ICESCR and the CEDAW are still in parts wedded to a formal or additive approach to gender equality. However, the CEDAW goes a long way towards embracing an engendered conception of socio-economic rights based on substantive equality, requiring States to transform the underlying power structures that contribute to women's disadvantage. As a result, the CEDAW requires more than merely extending socio-economic rights to women. This is its primary 'added value'. Nevertheless, there remain important parts of the Convention that need continued engagement to ensure that the voice of substantive equality is the dominant one.

[90] Ikdahl, Chapter 9 this volume.

8

'Women's rights are human rights!': the practice of the United Nations Human Rights Committee and the Committee on Economic, Social and Cultural Rights

FLEUR VAN LEEUWEN

1 Introduction

'Women's rights are human rights!' This famous slogan was used by the women's rights movement at the 1993 World Conference on Human Rights in Vienna.[1] The notion may seem self-evident, as the international system for the promotion and the protection of human rights that was installed under the auspices of the United Nations (UN) builds on the idea of equality in dignity and rights of men and women.[2] Yet, as was convincingly shown by critics of this system, it is not. The women's rights caucus present in Vienna in 1993 made it unequivocally clear to the participating states of the World Conference that much of what women experience as everyday abuse in their lives was largely kept outside the realm of *mainstream* international human rights.[3] This despite the fact that it was common knowledge that women were regularly subjected to battery and torture, humiliation, sexual harassment and exploitation,

[1] See for example K. Boyle, 'Stock-taking on human rights: the World Conference on Human Rights, Vienna 1993', *Political Studies* 43:4 (1995) 79–95 at 91.

[2] The notion that men and women should be able to enjoy their human rights on an equal basis is found in the wording of all important international human rights instruments. See Article 1(3) UN Charter; Article 2 UDHR; Article 2(1) and Article 3 ICCPR; Article 2(2) and Article 3 ICESCR; Article 2(1) CRC; and Article 1(1) International Convention on the Protection of the Rights of All Migrant Workers and the Members of Their Families (CMW). See also on the matter M. Pentikäinen, *The Applicability of the Human Rights Model to Address Concerns and the Status of Women* (Helsinki: The Erik Castrén Institute of International Law and Human Rights Research Reports, Publications of the Faculty of Law University of Helsinki, 1999) at 17.

[3] *Mainstream* refers in this context to those human rights treaties that do not focus specifically on the enjoyment of human rights *by women*.

forced marriages and pregnancy – issues that clearly violate internationally recognised human rights norms.[4]

The states represented at the World Conference recognised this deficiency of the international human rights system and laid down in the Vienna Declaration and Programme of Action, the outcome document of the Conference, that human rights of women and of the girl child are an inalienable, integral and indivisible part of universal human rights. Human rights of women, they held, should be integrated into the mainstream of UN system-wide activity, and these issues have to be regularly and systematically addressed throughout relevant UN bodies and mechanisms.[5] In this respect, the World Conference made an important call to the monitoring bodies of the international human rights treaties: in the Vienna Declaration and Programme of Action, they are requested to include the status and human rights of women in their deliberations and findings.[6]

Since the World Conference of 1993, considerable work has been undertaken by various UN bodies to promote the integration of women's rights in the general international human rights framework. The UN General Assembly (GA), the Commission on the Status of Women (CSW), the former UN Commission on Human Rights (UNCHR) and the former UN Sub-Commission on the Promotion and Protection of Human Rights passed resolutions supporting and encouraging the integration of women's rights into the general human rights activities of the UN.[7] The human rights monitoring bodies themselves also showed

[4] C. Bunch, 'Strengthening human rights of women' in M. Nowak (ed.), *World Conference on Human Rights – The Contribution of NGOs Reports and Documents* (Vienna: Manzsche Verlags- und Universitatsbuchhandlung, 1994) 32–41 at 33. See also Boyle, 'Stock-taking on human rights, at 91–2; and E. Friedman, 'Gendering the agenda: the impact of the transnational women's rights movement at the UN conferences of the 1990s', *Women's Studies International Forum* 26:4 (2003) 313–31 at 313–14.

[5] Vienna Declaration and Programme of Action, UN doc. A/CONF.157/23, part I, para. 18, and part II, para. 37. This call was a repetition of the statement made that same year by the former Commission on Human Rights. ECOSOC, Commission on Human Rights, *Integrating the Rights of Women into the Human Rights Mechanisms of the United Nations*, 8 March 1993, UN Doc. E/CN.4/RES/1993/46.

[6] Vienna Declaration and Programme of Action, UN doc. A/CONF.157/23, part II, para. 42.

[7] See for example UNGA, *Implementation of the Nairobi Forward-looking Strategies for the Advancement of Women*, 9 February 1995, UN Doc. A/RES/49/161; ECOSOC, Commission on the Status of Women, *Report of its Thirty-seventh Session*, 9 July 1993, UN Doc. E/1993/27; ECOSOC, *Integrating the Rights of Women into the Human Rights Mechanisms of the United Nations*; ECOSOC, Commission on Human Rights, *Question of Integrating the Human Rights of Women into the Human Rights Mechanisms of the United Nations*, 8 March 1995, UN Doc. E/CN.4/RES/1995/86; ECOSOC, Commission

a willingness to integrate the experiences of women into their work. In response to the appeal of the World Conference in Vienna to include the status and human rights of women in their deliberations and findings, the monitoring bodies addressed the implementation of women's human rights at their meetings of the chairpersons.[8] Moreover, the chairpersons of the human rights bodies showed their commitment to integrating the experiences of women in the work of their committees at their eighth meeting by inviting the UN Division for the Advancement of Women (DAW) to prepare a background paper analysing the measures that had been and should be taken by the human rights monitoring bodies in order to integrate gender perspectives into their work, and by participating in workshops on the integration of gender perspectives.[9]

What remained to be examined was whether the human rights bodies had responded to the request to include the status and human rights of women in their deliberations and findings in their practice. To that end, a study of the work of two mainstream human rights monitoring bodies, the Human Rights Committee (HRC) and the Committee on Economic, Social and Cultural Rights (ICESCR Committee) was conducted. The research question posed was: does the work of the HRC and the ICESCR Committee regarding matters that affect women's physical integrity reflect compliance with the request of the 1993 World Conference on Human Rights, which calls upon these Committees to include the status and human rights of women in their deliberations and findings?

on Human Rights, *Question of Integrating the Human Rights of Women throughout the United Nations System*, 19 April 1996, UN Doc. E/CN.4/RES/1996/48.

[8] See for example UNGA, *Report of the Fifth Meeting of Persons Chairing the Human Rights Treaty Bodies, Effective Implementation of International Instruments on Human Rights, including Reporting Obligations under International Instruments on Human Rights*, 19 October 1994, UN Doc. A/49/537, para. 34; UNGA, *Report of the Seventh Meeting of Persons Chairing the Human Rights Treaty Bodies, Effective Implementation of International Instruments on Human Rights, including Reporting Obligations under International Instruments on Human Rights*, 11 October 1996, UN Doc. A/51/482, paras. 58–61.

[9] See UNGA, *Report of the Eighth Meeting of Persons Chairing the Human Rights Treaty Bodies, Effective Implementation of International Instruments on Human Rights, including Reporting Obligations under International Instruments on Human Rights*, 21 October 1997, UN Doc. A/52/507, para. 62. The UNGA endorsed the request for the study in resolution 52/118. UNGA, *Report of the Third Committee (Part II)*, 4 December 1997, UN Doc. A/52/644/Add.1; and the Commission on Human Rights in Resolution 1998/27. ECOSOC, Commission on Human Rights, *Effective Implementation of International Instruments on Human Rights, including Reporting Obligations under International Instruments on Human Rights*, 17 April 1998, UN doc. E/CN.4/RES/1998/27.

This chapter first provides a brief background to the UN and women's human rights and then explains the critique voiced concerning the international system in this respect. Subsequently, it briefly discusses how the study was conducted and then presents its most important findings. In the last section of this chapter some final remarks and ideas for future action are presented.[10]

2 The UN human rights system and women's rights

> All human beings are born free and equal in dignity and rights.[11]

The Charter of the UN, which was adopted in 1945 by fifty-one states, provides the foundation of the international human rights system as we know it today.[12] The UN Charter and the Universal Declaration of Human Rights (UDHR) that was subsequently drawn up both recognise that *all* human beings have human rights for the simple reason of being human. The Declaration speaks purposefully of *all human beings*, when it holds in Article 1 that all human beings are born free and equal in dignity and rights. The reference to *all men* in the original draft of the document was heavily contested during the negotiations. All parties involved in the drafting process agreed that women were just as much entitled to the rights laid down in the Declaration as men, and some members of the drafting committee argued that the terminology of *all men* could be misleading. The Russian delegate, for example, held that the assumption that *all men* included *all persons* implied a historical reflection on the mastery of men over women. He wanted the wording to be changed so as to make clear that all human beings were included.[13] Agreement amongst the members was found on reference to *all human beings*.[14]

The notion that men and women should be able to enjoy their human rights on an equal basis is part of all the main international human rights instruments. Not only do the documents that compose the so-called Bill

[10] For a full account of this study, the background, the theoretical framework employed, the results and final outcome, see F. van Leeuwen, *Women's Rights are Human Rights – The Practice of the United Nations Human Rights Committee and the Committee on Economic, Social and Cultural Rights* (Antwerp: Intersentia, 2009).

[11] Article 1 UDHR.

[12] The UN Charter was signed on 26 June 1945 in San Francisco, at the conclusion of the UN Conference on International Organization, and came into force on 24 October 1945.

[13] J. Morsink, 'Women's rights in the Universal Declaration', *Human Rights Quarterly* 13:2 (1991) 229–56 at 233.

[14] *Ibid.* at 233–6.

of Human Rights – the UDHR and the two Covenants: the International Covenant on Civil and Political Rights (ICCPR) and the International Covenant on Economic, Social and Cultural Rights (ICESCR) – refer explicitly to the principles of non-discrimination and equality, but also the more specialised human rights treaties hold that States Parties shall respect and ensure the rights as laid down therein without distinction of any kind.[15] These documents thus grant human rights to women on an equal basis with men.

In addition to this *symmetrical* approach to equality, the UN human rights system contains an instrument that focuses solely on the enjoyment of human rights by women: the Convention on the Elimination of All Forms of Discrimination against Women (CEDAW).[16] The CEDAW focuses on the elimination of all forms of discrimination *against women*. Article 1 of the Convention lays down that discrimination is any distinction, exclusion or restriction made on the basis of sex that has the effect or purpose of impairing or nullifying the recognition, enjoyment or exercise *by women*, irrespective of their marital status, on a basis of equality of men and women, of human rights and fundamental freedoms in the political, economic, social, cultural, civil or any other field. In its substantive articles the CEDAW addresses various issues that are characteristic of the lives of women and their enjoyment of human rights.

Consequently, the UN human rights system aims to promote and protect the enjoyment of human rights by women in two ways: through the principles of non-discrimination and equality in its *mainstream* human rights treaties and through these principles in a *women-specific* human rights treaty.

[15] See Article 2(1) and Article 3 ICCPR; and Article 2(2) and Article 3 ICESCR. With regard to the specialised treaties see for example Article 2(1) CRC and Article 1(1) CMW. See also on the matter Pentikäinen, *The Applicability of the Human Rights* at 17.

[16] The CEDAW was adopted on 18 December 1979 and entered into force on 3 September 1981; see UNGA, Convention on the Elimination of All Forms of Discrimination against Women, 18 December 1979, UN Doc. A/RES/34/46. Holtmaat, for example, notes that the CEDAW is asymmetrical in its object and purpose, as it is directed at the elimination of all forms of discrimination against women and not, as is standard in other texts, the elimination of discrimination on the basis of sex. As she observes, the latter all guarantee the right not to be discriminated against on the basis of the mere fact that one is a man or a woman. This means, she holds, that these norms are symmetrical and formal by nature. R. Holtmaat, *Towards Different Law and Public Policy: The Significance of Article 5a CEDAW for the Elimination of Structural Gender Discrimination* (The Hague: Dutch Ministry of Social Affairs and Employment, 2004) at 7.

3 The critique: human rights are men's rights

From its inception in 1945 until the World Conference on Human Rights in 1993, two different strategies can be identified by which the UN sought to address women's enjoyment of human rights: by focusing on the sameness of men and women, thereby employing a strategy of formal equality and, subsequently, by focusing on the (sexual) difference between men and women, thereby choosing a strategy of specialising women's concerns. These ways exemplify the different ideas that exist in terms of addressing women's rights. Parisi refers to this in terms of the *competing feminist agendas* of *non-discrimination* and *special protections*, which, she holds, had long-lasting effects in the women's human rights movement.[17] Eleanor Roosevelt, at that time Chairperson of the UNCHR, for example, pointed out in the 1940s that specialisation of certain issues or rights may lead to marginalisation and stigmatisation of women.[18] At the same time, proponents of the *special protection approach* have argued that addressing women's rights only in a mainstream human rights framework may result in these matters being completely ignored or overlooked.[19]

In the period shortly after the Second World War, when the UN Charter and subsequently the UDHR were adopted, the most important tenet for women's rights proponents was that men and women were the same in rational ability and capacity for autonomy and self-determination. At that

17 For example, Parisi holds that there are a multitude of feminist perspectives that result in a variety of activist strategies with regard to women's human rights. She observes that the central liberal feminist tenet that spilled over to the post-Second World War period is that men and women are the same in rational ability and capacity for autonomy and self-determination and therefore should be afforded full citizenship and its attendant rights, protections and opportunities. Yet there were others who argued that women should be conceptualised as a group marked by sexual difference and that special protection was needed to 'level the playing field'; only in that way could women advance in individual self-determination and self-governance. L. Parisi, 'Feminist praxis and women's human rights', *Journal of Human Rights* 1:4 (2002) 571–85 at 571–2.

18 *Ibid.* at 572–3. The comments were made in regard to the status of the CSW, which was to be either a sub-body to the UNCHR or a separate body. Roosevelt and a number of others felt that the singling out of a group for *special* rights could lead to stigmatisation, backlash and marginalisation. For them, the preferable alternative was to seek inclusion in the primary UN human rights body rather than trying to establish 'separate but equal' human rights institutional mechanisms for women and men. They therefore opposed the idea of the CSW as a separate body in the UN.

19 See for example H. Charlesworth, 'Not waving but drowning: gender mainstreaming and human rights in the United Nations', *Harvard Human Rights Journal* 18:1 (2005) 1–18 at 1; and L. Reanda, 'Human rights and women's rights: the United Nations approach', *Human Rights Quarterly* 3:2 (1981) 11–31 at 12.

time, only thirty of the original fifty-one UN Member States had given women equal voting rights or permitted them to hold public office. The main goal of women's rights proponents was, therefore, to achieve equal legal status, and hence for women to be accorded the same rights as men.[20] Consequently, their position was focused on the concept of *sameness*, rather than on *difference*.[21] This idea of sameness is reflected in all human rights documents that were drawn up after the inception of the UN as they refer to the principles of non-discrimination and equality. These principles, in the formal sense, imply that men and women live similar lives and experience similar abuses and constraints.

This approach failed to ensure enjoyment of human rights by women, for men and women do not live similar lives. From the moment of birth, human beings are differentiated according to sex, being either a boy or a girl. Sex is the first factor that defines a human being in society, and it accordingly places the person in a maze of expectations, customs, practices and constraints that stipulate his or her life. Since the biological and gender-related aspects of men and women differ, so do their lives and their experiences. Consequently, in a system that is based on a concept of sameness that does not exist in practice, rights of men and women are not equally protected. Since the general picture of gender relations throughout the world still portrays an asymmetry of power between men and women, with women generally being subordinate to men, it is men's rights that dictate the international human rights system.[22] Bunch, amongst others, points out that degrading events commonly identified with the lives of men are addressed in the wording and interpretation of the provisions of the mainstream human rights instruments, but experiences common to the lives of many women are not covered by their protection.[23] Thus,

[20] Division for the Advancement of Women, *The Four Global Women's Conferences 1975–1995: Historical Perspective*, available at: www.un.org/womenwatch/daw/followup/session/presskit/hist.htm (last accessed 16 February 2012).

[21] Parisi, 'Feminist praxis and women's human rights' at 572.

[22] See for example C. Bunch, 'Transforming human rights from a feminist perspective' in J. Peter and A. Wolper (eds.), *Women's Rights, Human Rights: International Feminist Perspectives* (London: Routledge, 1995) 11–17 at 13; UN, *The 1999 World Survey on the Role of Women in Development* (New York: UN, 1999) at ix; and J. Marshall, 'Feminist jurisprudence: keeping the subject alive', *Feminist Legal Studies* 14:1 (2006) 27–51 at 42.

[23] Bunch, 'Transforming human rights from a feminist perspective' at 13. See also, for example, U. O'Hare, 'Realizing human rights for women', *Human Rights Quarterly* 21:2 (1999) 364–402 at 368–71; R. Copelon, 'Intimate terror: understanding domestic violence as torture' in R. J. Cook (ed.), *Human Rights of Women: National and International Perspectives* (Philadelphia: University of Pennsylvania Press, 1994) 116–53 at 116–17.

the insertion of the principles of non-discrimination and equality into mainstream international human rights instruments did not necessarily guarantee that human rights of both men *and* women were promoted and protected by the system. In reality, human rights were men's rights: the *male* experience was accepted as the norm, or, as Parisi notes, as the *human* experience.[24] Abuses, exclusions and constraints that are more typical of women's lives were neither recognised nor protected by the human rights instruments.

The adoption of the CEDAW in 1979 was meant to overcome this deficit, but in practice failed to do so. Critics showed that the establishment of mechanisms dealing exclusively with the enjoyment of the human rights of women, including the CEDAW, led to the marginalisation of women's rights.[25] Although the adoption of the CEDAW did mean that women's rights were expressly placed in the ambit of international human rights, critics pointed out that the rights of women were still ignored by the mainstream human rights mechanisms. Mainstream monitoring bodies did not address blatant violations of women's dignity as gross violations of human rights and left these issues up to the specialised CEDAW Committee to deal with.[26] As Charlesworth notes, the existence of special women's institutions such as the CEDAW Committee and the CSW had allowed comparable but male-dominated forums such as the UNCHR and the HRC to claim a general mandate that carried greater prestige and power. The effect of this was that women's interests were ghettoised: the creation of *women's institutions* meant that mainstream human rights bodies and institutions tended to downplay the application of human

[24] Parisi, 'Feminist praxis and women's human rights' at 577; See also, for example, S. Peterson and L. Parisi, 'Are women human? It's not an academic question' in T. Evans (ed.), *Human Rights Fifty Years On: A Reappraisal* (Manchester University Press, 1998) 132–60 at 141.

[25] See for example A. Byrnes, 'Women, feminism and international human rights law – methodological myopia, fundamental flaws or meaningful marginalisation?: some current issues', *Australian Yearbook of International Law* 12 (1992) 205–40 at 205–6; A. Gallagher, 'Ending the marginalization: strategies for incorporating women into the United Nations human rights system', *Human Rights Quarterly* 19:2 (1997) 283–333 at 285; R. Johnstone, 'Feminist influences on the United Nations human rights treaty bodies', *Human Rights Quarterly* 28:1 (2006) 148–85 at 151; Charlesworth, 'Not waving but drowning' at 1; Reanda, 'Human rights and women's rights' at 12.

[26] Reanda speaks of a *ghettoisation* of questions relating to women; the concerns of women will be relegated to mechanisms with generally fewer resources and less power than the mainstream human rights mechanisms. Reanda, 'Human rights and women's rights' at 12.

rights norms to women on the implicit assumption that women's rights were beyond their concern.[27]

In 1993 at the World Conference on Human Rights, 171 states adopted the Vienna Declaration and Programme of Action by consensus, and in doing so acknowledged this criticism of the UN human rights system.

4 The study: are women's rights human rights?

> The concept of human rights, like all vibrant visions, is not static or the property of any group; rather, its meaning expands as people reconceive of their needs and hopes in relation to it. In this spirit, feminists redefine human rights abuses to include the degradation and violation of women. The specific experiences of women must be added to traditional approaches to human rights in order to make women more visible and to transform the concept and practice of human rights in our culture so that it takes better account of women's lives.[28]

This statement made by Bunch sums up the assignment given to the human rights monitoring bodies by the World Conference on Human Rights in Vienna in 1993.

In order to answer the question of whether the work of the HRC and the ICESCR Committee reflects compliance with the request of the 1993 World Conference on Human Rights to include the status and human rights of women in their deliberations and findings, it was pivotal to conduct a preliminary study so as to determine what was asked specifically of the human rights monitoring bodies in the Vienna Declaration and Programme of Action. To obtain a good understanding of this request and what it actually entails for the human rights monitoring bodies, a variety of documents was examined. The starting point was necessarily the Vienna Declaration and Programme of Action of 1993, as well as the Beijing Declaration and Platform for Action of 1995, the outcome document of the Fourth World Conference on Women. In addition, UN reports that follow up on the request of Vienna and its implications for

[27] H. Charlesworth, 'Transforming the United Nations men's club: feminist futures for the United Nations', *Transnational Law and Contemporary Problems* 4:2 (1994), 421–54 at 446. See also O'Hare, 'Realizing human rights for women' at 367–8; H. Charlesworth, 'What are "Women's International Human Rights"?' in R. J. Cook (ed.), *Human Rights of Women: National and International Perspectives* 58–84 at 59.

[28] C. Bunch, 'Women's rights as human rights: toward a re-vision of human rights', *Human Rights Quarterly* 12:4 (1990) 486–98 at 487.

the Committees were studied. These reports and writings contain input from women's rights experts and for that reason also reflect to some extent the criticism of the UN human rights system that was expressed at the 1993 World Conference as well as before. Three documents were of particular importance for the preliminary study: the 1995 report of the expert group meeting on the development of guidelines for the integration of gender perspectives into UN human rights activities and programmes, organised by the former UN Centre for Human Rights and the UN Development Fund for Women (UNIFEM); the 1998 report of the DAW on integrating the gender perspective into the work of UN human rights treaty bodies; and the 1999 report of the workshop on gender integration into the human rights system, organised by the Office of the High Commissioner for Human Rights, the DAW and UNIFEM. Moreover, documents, including many academic writings on women's rights, especially in the context of the UN human rights system, were used to further clarify the request of the 1993 World Conference.

On the basis of the aforementioned documents, four elements of the request of the 1993 World Conference were identified, each of which represents an assignment for the human rights monitoring bodies. In order for the work of the HRC and the ICESCR Committee to reflect compliance with the request from Vienna, it needs to show attention of the two Committees to issues that specifically affect women and their enjoyment of human rights (Element I); to display human rights obligations for States Parties that adequately address these gendered issues, that is, women-inclusive human rights obligations (Element II); to relate these gendered issues to discrimination against women where applicable (Element III); and to address these issues in an integrated manner (Element IV).

Consequently, the request of the World Conference does not only imply an 'add and stir' of women's human rights into mainstream human rights practice – the monitoring bodies are not only asked to pay attention to degrading issues that are common to the lives of women, but they are also requested to change their concept of human rights abuses and their approach to addressing these. In order to comply with the Vienna assignment, they have to move beyond stating mere violations and address their causes.

The four elements mentioned served as a framework for answering the main research question. In order to examine the work of the two Committees, the entire work volume of the HRC and the ICESCR Committee was studied from 1993 until 2010: their Concluding

Observations (COs), General Comments (GCs), Lists of Issues, Reporting Guidelines and Views. Where the statements of the Committees in their COs needed clarification, the Summary Records of the *constructive dialogues* with States Parties were consulted. The following section presents the findings of the study.

5 The findings

5.1 *Element I: issues that specifically affect women*

The HRC and the ICESCR Committee pay attention to a variety of issues that affect women's physical integrity. It is noteworthy that the Committees not only address issues that had already gained general international attention as human rights abuses at the 1993 World Conference on Human Rights, but also discuss issues that are not mentioned in the Vienna Declaration and Programme of Action and were not commonly linked to provisions of their respective mandates.[29] Attention should first of all be drawn to the extensive work of the Committees on manifestations of physical violence against women. In many of their COs, the HRC and the ICESCR Committee pay attention to rape, domestic violence, trafficking in women, sexual harassment and female genital mutilation (FGM).[30] Violence against women, including domestic and sexual violence, has been the focus of human rights forums in the last decades. In 1992 the CEDAW Committee, whose mandate makes no explicit reference to violence against women, adopted General Recommendation 19 on this topic.[31] The UN General Assembly adopted the Declaration on the Elimination of Violence against Women in 1993,[32] and in 1994 the UNCHR adopted Resolution 1994/45, in which it established the mandate

[29] Much attention was paid to violence against women at the 1993 World Conference on Human Rights. Parisi notes that ninety NGOs that were determined to make the slogan 'Women's right are human rights' a success at the World Conference started a campaign to work on making violence against women a special theme at the Conference. Parisi, 'Feminist praxis and women's human rights' at 581. See also for example Y. Ertürk, 'The Due Diligence Standard: what does it entail for women's rights' in C. Benninger-Budel (ed.), *Due Diligence and Its Application to Protect Women from Violence* (Leiden: Martinus Nijhoff Publishers, 2008) 27–46 at 30; Boyle, 'Stock-taking on human rights' at 91–2.

[30] Van Leeuwen, *Women's Rights are Human Rights* at 91–127 and 181–211.

[31] See also Ertürk, 'The Due Diligence Standard' at 29–30; M. van den Brink, 'Het Recht op Lichamelijke Integriteit en het Vrouwenverdrag', *NJCM-Bulletin* 18:6 (1993) 660–73.

[32] UNGA, Declaration on the Elimination of Violence against Women, 20 December 1993, UN doc. A/RES/48/104.

of a Special Rapporteur on violence against women, including its causes and consequences. Moreover, the last decade has seen growing attention to the phenomenon of violence against women from international human rights non-governmental organisations (NGOs) and UN bodies.[33] This international recognition of violence against women as a human rights issue is also reflected in the outcome of this study, which shows that both Committees pay considerable attention to various forms of physical violence against women.

The HRC and the ICESCR Committee also address issues that were in the past generally not considered to be part of the realm of human rights, or at least not of the respective mandates of the two Committees. The HRC pays attention to a variety of reproductive health-related services and programmes. This is remarkable, since the mandate of the HRC and the ICCPR does not make any reference to health or healthcare services.[34] Both the HRC and the ICESCR Committee use their concern about maternal mortality as a basis to address a number of reproductive facilities, services and policies. The HRC links maternal mortality to the right to life and thereby brings the topic of pregnancy within its mandate. The ICESCR Committee links maternal mortality to the right to health. In light of maternal death rates in States Parties, the two bodies address issues such as reproductive information and education, access to contraceptives and unsafe abortions. Their rationale is that States Parties have an obligation to prevent unwanted pregnancies through family planning programmes and services and through sex education, so that women do not have to resort to clandestine abortions, and fewer illegal abortions would reduce the high maternal death rates.[35]

[33] See for example the work of Amnesty International, Human Rights Watch and OMCT, the World Organisation Against Torture, on violence against women.

[34] Former Special Rapporteur on the Right to Health Hunt holds that in light of the right to health, states have an obligation to ensure reproductive health and maternal healthcare services, including appropriate services for women in connection with pregnancy. ECOSOC, Commission on Human Rights, *Report of UN Special Rapporteur Paul Hunt on the Right to the Enjoyment of the Highest Attainable Standard of Physical and Mental Health*, 16 February 2004, UN doc. E/CN.4/2004/49, para. 29.

[35] See for example HRC, *Concluding Observations: Mali*, 16 April 2003, UN Doc. CCPR/CO/77/MLI, para. 14; HRC, *Concluding Observations: Viet Nam*, 26 July 2002, UN Doc. CCPR/CO/75/VNM, para. 15; ICESCR Committee, *Concluding Observation: Nepal*, 21 May 2001, UN Doc. E/C.12/1/Add.59, para. 55; ICESCR Committee, *Concluding Observations: Mauritius*, 28 December 1995, UN Doc. E/C.12/1995/14, para. 15. See also F. van Leeuwen, 'A woman's right to decide? – the UN Human Rights Committee, human rights of women, and matters of human reproduction', *Netherlands Quarterly of Human*

Consequently, the two Committees also address the controversial topic of abortion. The Committees make clear that States Parties should prevent unsafe abortions as they lead to maternal mortality. For that reason, States Parties are requested to allow abortion when pregnancy is the result of rape or when it endangers the life of the pregnant woman. Abortion is not considered to be contrary to human rights per se, as claimed by opponents of the practice. Both the HRC and the ICESCR Committee recommend that States Parties review their *restrictive* abortion laws, for example, when States Parties have high maternal death rates, but never request States Parties to review existing *liberal* abortion laws. Even in States Parties where abortion is often used as a contraceptive method or where many female foetuses are aborted – situations that the Committees identify as human rights concerns – neither the HRC nor the ICESCR Committee challenge the laws on abortion of the States Parties concerned. Instead, they recommend family planning services and information.[36]

The work of the HRC and the ICESCR Committee shows that the two bodies address human rights abuses and constraints that especially affect women. In that regard, their work reflects their compliance with the request of the 1993 World Conference on Human Rights. But there is also room for improvement. As it is clear that maternal mortality is high on the agenda of both Committees and both consider this to be a matter that falls within the ambit of their mandate, it is remarkable that the HRC pays so little attention to the availability of maternal healthcare and abortion services in States Parties, for it is lack of maternal healthcare and unsafe abortions that are the most significant causes of maternal deaths.[37] In light of its reasoning that maternal mortality affects the right to life, the Committee should also address the lack of available or accessible maternal healthcare and abortion services.

The lack of attention from both Committees for so-called *Western beauty practices*, referred to by Special Rapporteurs on Violence against Women Coomaraswamy and Ertürk, for example, is also noteworthy.[38]

Rights 25:1 (2007) 97–116; and van Leeuwen, *Women's Rights are Human Rights* at 43–73 and 149–66.

[36] *Ibid.* [37] See H. Sinding Aasen, this volume, Chapter 10.

[38] ECOSOC, Commission on Human Rights, *Report of the Special Rapporteur on Violence Against Women, its Causes and Consequences, Ms Radhika Coomaraswamy, Cultural Practices in the Family that are Violent Towards Women*, 31 January 2002, UN Doc. E/CN.4/2002/83 at 27; ECOSOC, Commission on Human Rights, *Report of the Special Rapporteur on Violence Against Women, its Causes and Consequences, Yakin Ertürk, Intersections Between Culture and Violence Against Women*, 17 January 2007, UN Doc. A/HRC/4/34, paras. 47–48.

Both Rapporteurs refer to the *beauty myth* of a slim feminine figure that prompts women to undergo cosmetic surgery and develop eating disorders. The ICESCR Committee addresses eating disorders in only one of its COs and the HRC has never referred to any practices relating to the Western beauty myth.[39] Yet it is argued by a number of authors that the practices do fall within the ambit of international human rights law and deserve attention.[40] The statements of the ICESCR Committee on eating disorders in its COs on Norway in 2005 support that interpretation. Consequently, it could be argued that in order for the work of the HRC and the ICESCR Committee to fully reflect compliance with the request of the Vienna Declaration and Programme of Action, it should take into account these Western practices.

On the basis of the aforementioned issues, the conclusion to be drawn with regard to the main research question is that in terms of addressing issues that specifically affect women and their enjoyment of human rights (Element I), the work of the HRC and the ICESCR Committee reflects compliance with the request of the 1993 World Conference on Human Rights, but also leaves room for improvement.[41] It is important that specific experiences that characteristically affect women in their enjoyment of human rights are continuously brought to the attention of the HRC and the ICESCR Committee and that more research be conducted on the relation between these specific experiences and international human rights law. Since the social constructions of man and woman, and of masculinity and femininity, vary not only according to location and culture, but also over time, new situations may emerge that affect the enjoyment of human rights. This means that human rights necessarily have to be interpreted in a dynamic context and that addressing these specific experiences of women is an ongoing assignment that requires the human rights

[39] ICESCR Committee, *Concluding Observations: Norway*, 23 June 2005, UN Doc. E/C.12/1/Add.109, paras. 21 and 41.

[40] See for example B. Winter, D. Thompson and S. Jeffreys, 'The UN approach to harmful traditional practices', *International Feminist Journal of Politics* 4:1 (2002) 72–94 at 87; S. Jeffreys, *Beauty and Misogyny: Harmful Cultural Practices in the West* (London: Routledge, 2005) at 29–30; and R. Howard, 'Health costs of social degradation and female self-mutilation in North America' in K. Mahoney and P. Mahoney (eds.), *Human Rights in the Twenty-First Century: A Global Challenge* (Dordrecht: Martinus Nijhoff Publishers, 1993) 503–16.

[41] For more critical comments on the work of the HRC and the ICESCR Committee in light of their attention to human rights abuses and constraints that typically affect women, see van Leeuwen, *Women's Rights are Human Rights* at 236–9.

monitoring bodies to stay alert to situations that may affect women's human rights.

5.2 *Element II: women-inclusive human rights obligations*

Element II of the request of the Vienna Declaration and Programme of Action dictates that the work of the Committees should display human rights obligations for States Parties that adequately address the gendered issues referred to in Element I. This means that the obligations for States Parties should take into account and address the gender-specific constraints that women experience in exercising their rights.[42] To examine whether the work of the two bodies reflects compliance with this Element, the obligations as discussed in the deliberations and findings of the HRC and the ICESCR Committee were categorised in accordance with the tripartite division of obligations often employed in the human rights discourse: obligations to respect, to protect and to fulfil.[43] The HRC and the ICESCR Committee formulate recommendations and requirements that include obligations for States Parties in all three categories. In doing so, they address the gender-specific circumstances of the issues that affect the enjoyment of human rights by women. States are requested, for example, with respect to matters that affect women's physical integrity, to provide for family planning programmes and services, sex education, shelters for battered women, and telephone hotlines and counselling services for victims of violence. States Parties are also requested to criminalise manifestations of physical violence, such as rape, including marital rape, domestic violence, trafficking and FGM;

[42] Similarly, Fredman argues in this volume that if socio-economic rights are to have a real effect on achieving equality for women, a reformulation of rights is required that takes into account and addresses the gender-specific constraints that women experience in exercising these rights. See S. Fredman, Chapter 7 in this volume.

[43] This division between various types of human rights obligations is employed, for example, by Nowak and by Eide. See M. Nowak, *Introduction to the International Human Rights Regime* (Leiden: Martinus Nijhoff Publishers, 2003) at 49; and A. Eide, 'Economic, social, and cultural rights as human rights' in A. Eide (ed.), *Economic, Social, and Cultural Rights: A Textbook* (Dordrecht: Martinus Nijhoff Publishers, 2001) 9–28 at 23–4. Former Special Rapporteur on the Right to Health Hunt notes in his annual report of 2004 that the analytical framework of obligations to respect, protect and fulfil is very useful as a way of sharpening the legal analysis of, in this case, the right to health: ECOSOC, *Report of UN Special Rapporteur Paul Hunt* paras. 43–44. Moreover, reference to these different types of obligations is, for example, also made in the Montreal Principles on Women's Economic, Social and Cultural Rights. 'Montreal Principles on Women's Economic, Social, and Cultural Rights', *Human Rights Quarterly* 26:3 (2004) 760–80 at 770.

they are also asked to prosecute the perpetrators of these abuses and punish them in accordance with the severity of the crime. The attention that the HRC and the ICESCR Committee have given to the needs of women confronted with various forms of physical violence has been considerable. Also noteworthy are the recommendations of both Committees in which the issue of residence permits for victims of trafficking and FGM are addressed.[44] Although the few recommendations made to States Parties on this matter are still rather mild and States Parties are not required to grant residence permits, they do indicate that the Committees take into account the specific circumstances and consequences of these practices.[45]

Most obligations on physical violence against women as formulated by the Committees, however, focus on the criminalisation, prosecution and punishment of such acts. These obligations are therefore obligations to protect. The same cannot be said for the obligations of States Parties on pregnancy-related matters, which primarily reflect obligations to fulfil. States are requested to provide for various reproductive healthcare services, and under the ICESCR the requirement also includes maternal health-related services and programmes. Considering the fact that the availability of these services is a prerequisite for successfully addressing maternal mortality, it makes sense that the Committees address these issues. However, attention should also be drawn to the fact that the HRC and the ICESCR Committee scarcely formulate any recommendations on pregnancy-related matters that reflect obligations to protect. In general, the work of the two monitoring bodies hardly shows any recommendations that request that States Parties criminalise, prosecute and punish actions of individuals that cause or influence pregnancy-related human rights abuses and constraints. Examples of such abuses and constraints are

[44] See for example HRC, *Concluding Observations: The Netherlands*, 27 August 2001, UN Doc. CCPR/CO/72/NET, para. 11; HRC, *Concluding Observations: Norway*, 21 April 2006, UN Doc. CCPR/C/NOR/CO/5, para. 12; HRC, *Concluding Observations: Belgium*, 16 November 2010, UN Doc. CCPR/C/BEL/CO/5, para. 16; ICESCR Committee, *Concluding Observations: Greece*, 7 June 2004, UN Doc. E/C.12/1/Add.97. Furthermore, attention should be paid to the Views of the HRC in the case of *Diena Kaba* v. *Canada* of 21 May 2010, in which the HRC argued that deportation of Ms Kaba's daughter to Guinea, a country where she runs a real risk of being excised, would constitute a violation of Article 7 and Article 24(1) ICCPR. HRC, *Diena Kaba* v. *Canada*, Communication No. 1465/2006, 21 May 2010, UN Doc. CCPR/C/98/D/1465/2006, para. 10(1)–10(5).

[45] The ICESCR Committee refers in this respect to the double victimisation of victims of trafficking due to the risks and dangers awaiting them upon deportation to their home countries. ICESCR Committee, *Concluding Observations: Germany*, 24 September 2001, UN Doc. E/C.12/1/Add.68, paras. 25 and 43.

forced abortion and forced sterilisation.[46] Only when the gender-specific context of human rights abuses and constraints experienced by women is reflected in the obligations for States Parties can it be argued that the work of the HRC and the ICESCR Committee fully reflects compliance with the second Element of the request of the 1993 World Conference. Therefore, as far as pregnancy-related issues are concerned, more attention should be paid by the Committees to the infringement by other individuals of women's enjoyment of human rights. Recent statements of the HRC in one of its COs regarding the obligation of the State Party concerned to prosecute forced sterilisation indicates the Committee's awareness of the gender specifics of this situation.[47] This may prove to be an indication of future attention to the matter in its COs, which should also be taken up by the ICESCR Committee.

It should further be noted that as far as women's physical integrity is concerned, the obligations of States Parties as formulated by both Committees in regards to various human rights issues lack reference to certain gender-specific constraints that prevent women from exercising their rights. For example, they do not address the issue of the lack of available and accessible abortion and post-abortion services. Although both Committees indicate that States Parties should allow for abortion when a pregnancy is the result of rape or endangers the life of the pregnant woman, the HRC and the ICESCR Committee generally do not question whether these services are actually available, are accessible and are of good quality.[48] Hence, in general, the work of the two Committees does not reflect an obligation for States Parties to ensure that abortion and post-abortion services are actually available and accessible in situations where the abortion is legal.[49] The Committees, however, are aware of the

[46] The HRC requests States Parties in General Comment 28 to prevent forced sterilisation and forced abortion, but scarcely refers to forced sterilisation in its COs and does not address forced abortion at all in these documents. The ICESCR Committee mentions forced sterilisation only in one of its COs and has never addressed the practice of forced abortion. See COs of the ICESCR Committee on Brazil of 2003, paras. 27 and 62. See also van Leeuwen, *Women's Rights are Human Rights* at 165–6.

[47] HRC, *Concluding Observations: Czech Republic*, 9 August 2007, UN Doc. CCPR/C/CZE/CO/2, para. 10.

[48] On the framework of available, accessible and good quality services, see for example ECOSOC, *Report of UN Special Rapporteur Paul Hunt* paras. 41–2. Hunt notes that one framework that is especially useful in the context of policy-making is that healthcare services, goods and facilities, including the underlying determinants of health, shall be available, accessible, acceptable and of good quality.

[49] An exception can arguably be found in the COs of the HRC on Argentina of 2000, where it notes in paragraph 14 that restrictive abortion laws could deter medical professionals

consequences of the lack of these services, for they regularly express their concern about unsafe abortions and the resulting maternal mortality. In light of the request by the 1993 World Conference on Human Rights, which comprises an assignment to formulate obligations for States Parties that take into account the gender-specific forms of the human rights abuses and that especially concern experiences by women, the HRC and the ICESCR Committee should also respond to the above-mentioned issues in their work by formulating appropriate obligations for States Parties on abortion-related services. Steps taken by the ICESCR Committee in 2008 may indicate that the matter will be taken up on a more systematic basis in future reporting procedures.[50]

As noted, the work of the HRC and the ICESCR Committee on physical violence against women mostly reflects obligations to protect human rights. Although the Committees also pay attention to the needs of victims of several types of violence, they do not always take into account the full scope of the gender-specific constraints that women experience in regard to these abuses. This is illustrated by the approach of the Committees in addressing the issue of FGM. The main obligation for States Parties as formulated by the Committees with regard to this practice is to prohibit it in their criminal legislation.[51] Yet what the Committees apparently fail to

from performing the procedure in those cases where it was, in fact, legal. Although these COs could seem to suggest an obligation that States Parties have to ensure in these conditions that abortion facilities are available and accessible, it has never explicitly stated this. Similarly, in its COs on Mexico of 2006, the ICESCR Committee expresses its concern about the obstruction of access to a legal abortion when the pregnancy was the result of rape. However, the Committee did not hold that abortion facilities should be available and accessible when legal, but rather held that the State Party should ensure that *rape victims* be given access to legal abortion. It should be noted, however, that in 2008 the ICESCR Committee recommended that States Parties ensure access to safe abortion in two of its COs. These recommendations, however, focused on abortion services in particular and not on post-abortion care. The context in which the recommendation was made indicates that the ICESCR Committee did not refer to an obligation of States Parties to ensure access to safe abortion in general. See ICESCR Committee, *Concluding Observations: Kenya*, 1 December 2008, UN Doc. E/C.12/KEN/CO/1, para. 33; and ICESCR Committee, *Concluding Observations: UNMIK*, 1 December 2008, UN Doc. E/C.12/UNK/CO/1, paras. 24 and 30.

50 *Ibid.*

51 See for example HRC, *Concluding Observations: Sweden*, 24 April 2002, UN Doc. CCPR/CO/74/SWE, para. 8; HRC, *Concluding Observations: Yemen*, 26 July 2002, UN Doc. CCPR/CO/75/YEM, para. 6; HRC, *Concluding Observations: Benin*, 1 December 2004, UN Doc. CCPR/CO/82/BEN, para. 11; HRC, *Concluding Observations: Yemen*, 9 August 2005, UN Doc. CCPR/CO/84/YEM, para. 11; HRC, *Concluding Observations: Cameroon*, 4 August 2010, UN Doc. CCPR/C/CMR/CO/4, para. 10. See also ICESCR Committee, *Concluding Observations: Cameroon*, 8 December 1999, UN Doc. E/C.12/1/Add.40, para.

take into account is that FGM is usually performed for socio-cultural reasons by predominantly female private actors with the apparent consent of the one to be circumcised or her proxy.[52] This notion raises questions with regard to the prosecution of these acts as well as to the effectiveness of these recommendations in the actual elimination of the custom. Various international organisations that aim to fight FGM on the ground argue that criminalisation of FGM alone is not enough; other measures also need to be taken to combat this phenomenon in an effective manner.[53] The HRC and the ICESCR Committee generally do not consider other means of eliminating FGM and hardly ever formulate recommendations regarding this practice that would denote an obligation to fulfil. The only positive exception to this is found in one of the COs of the ICESCR Committee of 2008.[54]

The final conclusion to be drawn here, as regards the main research question, is that the work of the HRC and the ICESCR Committee in regard to women-inclusive obligations for States Parties (Element II) generally reflects compliance with the request of the 1993 World Conference on Human Rights, but that there is also still more that can be done in order to fully integrate women's rights. On various points, the obligations as formulated by the two Committees could and should be more far-reaching in order to reflect the gender-specific circumstances of the situations that affect women's physical integrity and thereby to effectively address these. Similar to what has been said previously, the characteristics

33; and ICESCR Committee, *Concluding Observations: Benin*, 5 June 2002, UN Doc. E/C.12/1/Add.78, para. 31. See also van Leeuwen, *Women's Rights are Human Rights* at 122–4 and 207–9.

52 L. Obiora, 'Bridges and barricades: rethinking polemics and intransigence in the campaign against female circumcision', *Case Western Reserve Law Review* 47:2 (1997) 275–378 at 284.

53 WHO, *Eliminating Female Genital Mutilation – An Interagency Statement* (Geneva: WHO, 2008) at 13–21; UNICEF, *Changing a Harmful Social Convention: Female Genital Mutilation/Cutting*, 2005 at 23–33, available at: www.unicef-irc.org/publications/396 (last accessed 16 February 2012); UNFPA, *A Holistic Approach to the Abandonment of Female Genital Mutilation/Cutting*, 2007 at 10–12, available at: www.unfpa.org/public/pid/407 (last accessed 12 February 2012); and G. Richardson, 'Ending female genital mutilation? Rights, medicalisation, and the state of ongoing struggles to eliminate the FGM in Kenya', *The Dominion* no. 26 (2005) at 12.

54 The ICESCR Committee in its COs on Kenya of 2008 recommends the State Party to combat FGM amongst other means by continuing to promote alternative rite of passage ceremonies, to educate parents, especially mothers, children and community leaders on the harmful effects of FGM, and to combat traditional beliefs about the usefulness of FGM for the promotion of marriage prospects of girls. ICESCR Committee, *Concluding Observations: Kenya*, 1 December 2008, UN Doc. E/C.12/KEN/CO/1, para. 23.

of these human rights abuses need further clarification; the Committees need to be aware of these; and they should subsequently respond to them by formulating women-inclusive human rights obligations, for example with regard to FGM.

5.3 *Element III: discrimination against women*

Element III of the request of the 1993 World Conference on Human Rights contains an assignment for the human rights monitoring bodies to place the specific human rights issues of women in the context of discrimination against women. The work of the HRC and the ICESCR Committee mostly fails to reflect this point. Although the Committees address many human rights abuses and constraints that characteristically affect women in their respective GCs on equality of men and women, they generally do not label these as symptoms of (structural) discrimination. Reference to these issues in their GCs, as well as reference to Articles 3 of the ICCPR and the ICESCR in the work of the Committees, rather seems to reflect the Committees' awareness of the fact that, as far as the interpretation of human rights is concerned, women may face different hurdles than men in their enjoyment of human rights. Although this understanding is an important first step away from the idea of *sameness*: men and women are the same in rational ability and the capacity for autonomy and self-determination and are therefore entitled to the same rights, this does not mean that the HRC and the ICESCR Committee examine whether these *women-specific* human rights issues are the result of discrimination against women. Occasionally, situations are linked to discrimination, but overall situations such as de facto impunity of rape or sexual exploitation of women and girls are not related to women's unequal status in societies. The only apparent exceptions to this are the statements of both Committees on the abortion of female foetuses and the statements of the ICESCR Committee with regard to sexual harassment and honour crimes.[55]

[55] See HRC, General Comment No. 28, Equality of Rights Between Men and Women (Article 3), UN Doc. CCPR/C/21/Rev.1/Add.10, para. 5; HRC, *Concluding Observations: Republic of Korea*, 1 November 1999, UN Doc. CCPR/C/79/Add.114, para. 10; ICESCR Committee, *Concluding Observations: Republic of Korea*, 21 May 2001, UN Doc. E/C.12/1/Add.59, para. 16; ICESCR Committee, *Concluding Observations: India*, 8 August 2008, UN Doc. E/C.12/IND/CO/5, paras. 17 and 56; ICESCR Committee, *Concluding Observations: Mongolia*, 1 September 2000, UN Doc. E/C.12/1/Add.47, para. 23; ICESCR Committee, *Concluding Observations: Tunisia*, 14 May 1999, UN Doc. E/C.12/1/Add.36, para. 4; ICESCR Committee, *Concluding Observations: Syrian Arab Republic*, 24 September 2001, UN Doc. E/C.12/1/Add.63, para. 14.

The general approach of the HRC and the ICESCR Committee in dealing with various forms of physical violence against women is not to address its root cause, which is often the unequal status of women in society, but rather to call on States Parties to tackle violence against women through criminalisation and prosecution.[56] This means that the Committees request States Parties to address only the manifestations of human rights abuses and constraints and not, for example, the gender ideologies on which they are based.[57] Hence, the work of the HRC and the ICESCR Committee is first and foremost directed toward fighting symptoms, that is manifestations of physical violence against women, rather than the actual disease.[58]

In light of the aforementioned issues, with regard to Element III, the work of the HRC and the ICESCR Committee fails to reflect compliance with the request of the 1993 World Conference on Human Rights. The HRC and the ICESCR Committee need to pay attention to the relationship between the various gendered issues that affect women's enjoyment of human rights and discrimination against women as their possible cause. This attention needs to be reflected in their GCs and COs, both in terms of recognition as well as by way of recommendations that aim to address this.

[56] An exception to this general approach is found in the Concluding Observations from the HRC on Mexico of 2010, in which the Committee recommends the State Party to address violence against women, including by addressing the root causes of the problem, amongst other things, by changing the perception of women's role in society. HRC, *Concluding Observations: Mexico*, 17 May 2010, UN Doc. CCPR/C/MEX/CO/5, para. 8.

[57] It is interesting to refer to the comments of Ertürk, the former UN Special Rapporteur on Violence against Women. In her report of 2006 on due diligence standards with regard to violence against women, Ertürk observes: 'As a general rule, States have sought to discharge their due diligence obligations of prevention of violence against women through the adoption of specific legislation, the development of awareness-raising campaigns and the provision of training for specified professional groups. The forms of violence covered by these interventions include: domestic violence, sexual assault, trafficking, honour crimes and sexual harassment. These programmes tend to view violence against women as a stand-alone issue and there are relatively few examples of linkages being made between violence and other systems of oppression'. ECOSOC, Commission on Human Rights, *Report of the Special Rapporteur on Violence Against Women, its Causes and Consequences, Yakin Ertürk, The Due Diligence Standard as a Tool for the Elimination of Violence Against Women*, 20 January 2006, UN Doc. E/CN.4/2006/61, para. 38.

[58] It is interesting to see that the HRC and the ICESCR Committee do refer to discrimination against women in their COs when it concerns the low representation of women in high-ranking positions.

5.4 *Element IV: an integrated address*

For the work of the HRC and the ICESCR Committee to reflect compliance with Element IV, it is required that the Committees tackle the issues that affect women's physical integrity in an integrated manner. This means that the Committees should not address these issues separately, for example in a section that focuses specifically on issues that affect women, but rather that they pay attention to these issues in all relevant sections of their work. Thus, for example, pregnancy-related matters that impair the right to life are to be addressed together with other 'traditional' human rights issues that affect this right.

The work of the HRC and the ICESCR Committee reflects compliance with Element IV. The issues impairing women's physical integrity are often brought forward in light of the affected substantive provisions and/or with regard to common Article 3 of the Covenants. Thus, for example, pregnancy-related matters are generally addressed in light of Article 6 of the ICCPR and Article 10 of the ICESCR, and female genital mutilation and domestic violence in reference to Article 7 of the ICCPR and Article 10 of the ICESCR, with or without also mentioning common Article 3.[59] On other occasions, where no explicit reference is made to any of the provisions of the ICCPR and the ICESCR, the issues are addressed in different sections, for example in combination with other related human rights issues. For example, the HRC addresses rape during armed conflict together with other human rights abuses that occur under those circumstances, such as extrajudicial killings and disappearances.[60]

[59] See for example HRC, *Concluding Observations: Paraguay*, 24 April 2006, UN Doc. CCPR/C/PRY/CO/2, para. 10; HRC, *Concluding Observations: Senegal*, 19 November 1997, UN Doc. CCPR/C/79/Add.82, para. 12; HRC, *Concluding Observations: Sudan*, 19 November 1997, UN Doc. CCPR/C/79/Add. 85, para. 10; HRC, *Concluding Observations: Sweden*, 24 April 2002, UN Doc. CCPR/CO/74/SWE, para. 8; HRC, *Concluding Observations: Kenya*, 29 April 2005, UN Doc. CCPR/CO/83/KEN, para. 12; HRC, General Comment No. 28, UN Doc. CCPR/C/21/Rev.1/Add.10, para. 11; ICESCR Committee, General Comment No. 14, UN Doc. E/C.12/2005/4, paras. 22, 36 and 51; ICESCR Committee, *Concluding Observations: Nigeria*, 13 May 1998, UN Doc. E/C.12/1/Add.23, para. 20.

[60] See for example HRC, *Concluding Observations: Algeria*, 18 August 1998, UN Doc. CCPR/C/79/Add.95, para. 6; HRC, *Concluding Observations: Russian Federation*, 6 November 2003, UN Doc. CCPR/CO/79/RUS, para. 13; HRC, *Concluding Observations: Democratic Republic of the Congo*, 26 April 2006, UN Doc. CCPR/C/COD/CO/3, para. 13.

Consequently, as the work of the Committees shows attention for issues that affect women's physical integrity in an integrated manner, it reflects compliance with the request of the 1993 World Conference on Human Rights.

5.5 *Conclusion*

Overall, the work of the HRC and the ICESCR Committee regarding matters that affect women's physical integrity reflects compliance with three of the four elements of the request to the human rights monitoring bodies made by the 1993 World Conference on Human Rights. The Committees make good use of the possibilities within their mandates to address issues that affect women's physical integrity; they generally formulate obligations for States Parties that take into account the gender-specific constraints of these human rights abuses; and, moreover, they address these matters in an integrated manner. Overall, however, the work of the HRC and the ICESCR Committee lacks compliance with Element III: the request to link these human rights abuses and constraints to the discrimination against women. Thus, the work of the HRC and the ICESCR Committee shows that both Committees are aware of abuses and constraints that characteristically affect women's physical integrity, but neither addresses the evil that causes them. This deficit must be overcome in order for the Committees to comply with the request of the 1993 World Conference.

6 Final remarks

This study did not look into the actual reasons for the Committees to address human rights concerns and constraints that are characteristic of the lives of women. Yet it appears that the Committees address gender-specific issues only when they have received information on them from States Parties or NGOs, or when a topic has already garnered a lot of international attention. On those occasions where the Committees paid attention to the gender-specific constraints women experience in exercising their rights, they usually received their information from the State Party itself or from NGOs.[61] Similarly, when certain issues

[61] For example, the ICESCR Committee holds in its COs on the Republic of Moldova that the State Party should combat trafficking by improving job possibilities and assistance for women living in poverty. ICESCR Committee, *Concluding Observations: Republic of Moldova*, 12 December 2003, UN Doc. E/C.12/1/Add.91, para. 41 and ICESCR Committee, *Summary Records: Republic of Moldova*, 17 November 2003, UN Doc.

or gender-specific circumstances were systematically dealt with, they often concerned topics that had already received a lot of international attention.[62]

This strengthens the idea that the work of NGOs is very important in the process of making women and their human rights visible within the UN human rights system, for example by producing shadow reports, assisting victims in individual complaints procedures or by participating in general discussion days.[63] The aforementioned also points out the added value of the CEDAW Committee: a body that focuses exclusively on women's rights and, as such, has the capacity to function as a whistle-blower, alerting other monitoring bodies to issues that affect women's enjoyment of human rights and the gender-specific constraints and circumstances that need to be addressed. The findings of the study also expressly show the need for the CEDAW due to the lack of attention the HRC and the ICESCR Committee have shown for Element III of the Vienna request. The CEDAW Committee, with a mandate that explicitly covers an obligation for States Parties to take all appropriate measures to modify the social and cultural patterns of the behaviour of men and women, with a view to achieving the elimination of prejudices, customs and all other practices that are based on the idea of the inferiority or the superiority of either of the sexes or on stereotyped roles of men and women, has the experience and knowledge of how to address gendered human rights abuses as manifestations of deeply rooted discrimination against women.[64]

NGOs and the human rights monitoring bodies clearly have an important role to play in further realising an international human rights system that fully promotes and protects the human rights of both men *and* women. However, more research needs to be conducted into the content of human rights provisions from the perspective of gender. Although

E/C.12/2003/SR.32, para. 65. Also the ICESCR Committee makes recommendations to Kenya as regards addressing FGM in the State Party by means of continuing to promote alternative rite of passage ceremonies. ICESCR Committee, *Concluding Observations: Kenya*, 1 December 2008, UN Doc. E/C.12/KEN/CO/1, para. 23.

62 Section 5.2 of this paper refers to the international attention for violence against women and a number of specific forms of it.

63 On this matter, see also C. Chinkin, 'The role of non-governmental organisations in standard setting, monitoring, and implementation of human rights' in J. Norton *et al.* (eds.), *The Changing World of International Law in the Twenty-first Century: A Tribute to the Late Kenneth R. Simmonds* (The Hague: Kluwer Law International, 1998) 45–66 at 51–65; L. Theytaz-Bergman, 'State reporting and the role of non-governmental organizations' in A. Bayefsky (ed.), *The UN Human Rights Treaty System in the 21st Century* (The Hague: Kluwer Law International, 2000) 45–56.

64 Article 5(a) CEDAW.

literature exists in which provisions of mainstream human rights treaties are linked to issues that are of specific importance to women, the number of publications is still limited and is generally not based on an elaborate study of the content of the provision itself.[65] Studies generally start with looking at the abuses and constraints that are typical of women's lives and subsequently examine how the human rights system deals with, or could address, these matters. Yet if women's rights proponents want to work with the system as it stands now, it is essential that the subsequent step in transforming this system is to address the system itself and the provisions in which it guarantees human rights for all. This is the only way that the system can be changed into an instrument that also promotes and protects the human rights of women in a systematic manner, rather than on an ad hoc basis. Besides the work that has been conducted so far, as represented in publications as well as in the work of the human rights monitoring bodies, this will require further research. This task cannot be performed by the human rights monitoring bodies alone. It is important that human rights scholars, for example, in collaboration with NGOs that work at the grass-roots level, take this up as well.

The aforementioned should culminate in a reformulation of all GCs and reporting guidelines, so as to fully reflect the gender-inclusive content of the human rights provisions and related obligations for States Parties. This should lead to a more structured approach to fully address the promotion and the protection of human rights of women. The reconstructed content of human rights provisions, reflected in these new GCs and reporting guidelines, should allow a more systematic consideration of human rights abuses and constraints that are characteristic of the lives of women, and clarify the way States Parties should address them, taking into account the gender-specific circumstances of the experiences.

[65] Examples of writings in which women's human rights concerns are linked to provisions of the two Covenants include: R. Cook, 'International human rights and women's reproductive health' in J. Peters and A. Wolper (eds.), *Women's Rights, Human Rights: International Feminist Perspectives* 256–75; C. Packer, 'Defining and delineating the right to reproductive choice', *Nordic Journal of International Law* 67:1 (1998) 77–95; R. Cook, 'Women's reproductive rights', *International Journal of Gynaecology and Obstetrics* 46:2 (1994) 215–20; R. Cook, 'International human rights and women's reproductive health', *Studies in Family Planning* 24:2 (1993) 73–86; R. Cook, 'Women's international human rights law: the way forward' in R. J. Cook (ed.), *Human Rights of Women* 12–15; Charlesworth, 'What are "Women's International Human Rights"?'; Copelon, 'Intimate Terror'.

Finally, this study did not only provide answers, it also raised new questions. An important question concerns the motivation of the Committees for addressing certain matters. Although there are strong indications that the work of NGOs in this respect is significant, one of the questions to be raised is, for example, whether the gender or nationality of individual Committee members plays a role in the attention that is paid by the human rights monitoring bodies to issues that affect women's physical integrity, and if so, to what extent. Further research on this matter is required so as to discover the hitches in the process of including the status and human rights of women in the work of the HRC and the ICESCR Committee and to address them effectively. The end of the process of integrating women into the human rights mainstream is not near. It is clear that the request of the 1993 World Conference on Human Rights is not a short-term assignment for the human rights monitoring bodies: it is *not* a matter of adding and stirring women's experiences into the big bowl of international human rights. Rather, it is a process that will be ongoing for as long as gender inequality exists. It is a process that requires the commitment of everyone involved in order to transform the international system so as to ensure that it fully accommodates and responds to human rights abuses and constraints that are typical of women's lives, now and in the future.

9

Property and security: articulating women's rights to their homes

INGUNN IKDAHL

1 Introduction

Since the early 1990s a rapidly expanding body of so-called 'soft law' documents has added to the dynamics and detail of human rights law. These formally non-binding documents have been central for efforts to deepen and expand the understanding of human rights from women's perspectives. By demonstrating how life experiences can be understood and articulated as human rights themes, they have aided in making existing documents relevant for women and other groups whose experiences were not fully considered at the time the treaty texts were drafted.

This chapter seeks to contribute to the understanding of these developments, by exploring how one specific real-life situation has come to be articulated as a human rights theme. Focusing on women's homes, it maps how international human rights institutions have responded to information about situations that are primarily experienced by women. Juxtaposing and comparing the analyses provided by the Convention on the Elimination of All Forms of Discrimination against Women (CEDAW) Committee, the International Covenant on Economic, Social and Cultural Rights (ICESCR) Committee and by the 2000–2008 Commission on Human Rights' (CHR) Special Rapporteur on the Right to Adequate Housing, it identifies two different paths that have been developed for approaching women's rights to their homes, focusing on, respectively, property rights and security.

The chapter starts by describing the housing story of a widow living in an informal settlement in a third-world city (section 2). It proceeds by describing how her situation can be understood firstly as an example of gender bias in the distribution of property rights between spouses (section 3), and secondly as a question of the right to housing (section 4). Finding that soft law documents have been a central tool in making the experiences, threats and vulnerabilities experienced by women legible and visible in the human rights discourse, it proposes that the two approaches are not only overlapping, but also complementary (section 5). Together, they can form the basis for a comprehensive understanding of the situation in terms of human rights, and of the range of measures that can be taken to reduce women's vulnerability.

2 A view from the ground

2.1 Rose's story

As part of the research for my PhD project, I met Rose in her home in the Hanna Nassif settlement, Dar es Salaam, Tanzania.[1] Together with her husband, she had settled in this part of town in 1984. For the first few years they rented a room. But her husband was gainfully employed, and Rose was making money by trading in clothes, and in 1986 they were able to buy a plot in the area. They started construction on the house in 1987 and moved in the following year. In 1990 they had children and decided to expand the building. They added a 'business part', eventually comprising four rooms. Today, three of the rooms in the business part are rented out. Rose uses the fourth for her business of selling beverages.

Rose's life changed when her husband suddenly passed away in 2002. His family blamed her for his death and a conflict ensued. According to Rose, her mother-in-law and sisters-in-law caused her many problems by taking control over the house and other property. They wanted to sell the house, and had even agreed on a price and made arrangements with a buyer. Rose consulted with her own relatives, who saw this as a serious problem. Together, they went to the city and talked to a women's organization, who advised Rose to take the case to court. The court issued an injunction that stopped the sale, and Rose got her house back.

Hanna Nassif was an unplanned settlement and was thus perceived by the inhabitants as vulnerable to state expropriation without compensation as part of development projects in the city. When I met Rose, the area was therefore in the midst of a process of surveying and issuing title deeds for individual plots. Rose was planning to use the name of her three children on the title deed. Due to the circumstances of her husband's death, she feared that the use of her own name would disturb his relatives.

[1] I. Ikdahl, *Securing Women's Homes. The Dynamics of Women's Human Rights at International Level and in Tanzania* (Faculty of Law, University of Oslo, Unipub, 2010).

They would say: 'There, you see, she wanted the property for herself.' Rose believed that the title deed would assure a more peaceful transfer of the property to the children when she passed away. The children could later decide on their own what to do with the house, and if one of the children then passed away, the other two names would still be on the document.

2.2 *Widows and their homes*

Rose's story illustrates that women's use of land, their contributions, and their means of access to land and housing do not translate easily into formal legal ownership. This also has implications for their legal protection in situations such as widowhood, divorce or a husband's decision to sell or mortgage the couple's land and home.

Furthermore, it displays the double vulnerability of women in informal settlements: women are made insecure not only by in-laws refusing to see them as owners upon widowhood; they are also subject to the same vulnerability as men at the hands of a state that does not recognize the legitimacy of the area as a whole. Moreover, even acting and speaking of themselves as owners, as Rose did, does not translate straightforwardly into being named as owner on the title deed. In Rose's situation, the law made her eligible for ownership – but a combination of state and non-state norms and social relations more broadly contributed to her choice of not taking this option.

Her story thus also demonstrates how threats and protection can be influenced by a complex interplay of different norms and institutions. Formal law in Tanzania provides only limited property rights for a widow.[2] However, the local court did rule in favour of Rose in her case against her in-laws. Local norms and practices, as I encountered them during a series of interviews, displayed a mixture of influences: norms of fairness based on the spouses' contribution to acquisition of property, religious norms, and traditional customary law that emphasized the role of male lineage in property ownership and tended to support the view that women who pursued their own individual property rights were selfish or egoistic.

The interaction between local, religious, customary and statutory norms creates a scenario in which not only gender, but also marital status, religion, the bearing of children and social status more generally influence a woman's opportunity to remain in her home in situations such as

[2] M. E. Magoke-Mhoja, *Child-Widows Silenced and Unheard. Human Rights Sufferers in Tanzania* (Milton Keynes: AuthorHouse, 2008).

divorce and widowhood. This story from Tanzania thus corroborates empirical studies from other contexts and countries.

2.3 *Articulating the human rights dimensions*

The present theme aptly illustrates current dynamics in international human rights law. Despite the inclusion of equal rights for women and the principle of non-discrimination in the human rights conventions, women's experiences of insecure housing were chiefly marginalized in human rights debates. In a similar vein, women's rights to land and property, and the insecurity experienced by residents in informal settlements, were low on the agenda of international debates on human rights.

However, various human rights are indeed influenced and could provide the basis for analyses of these types of situations. These include gender equality and the prohibition of discrimination, but also, more specifically, the equal right to enjoyment of property, the right to an adequate livelihood, including the right to housing and the right to food, and equal rights between spouses. Since the early 1990s a range of UN institutions and mechanisms have been involved in developing more detailed human rights analyses of women's rights and access to land, property and housing. Two main approaches emerged: firstly, that this type of situation is a manifestation of a lack of equality in the distribution of *property* rights between husband and wife, and secondly, that it demonstrates the gendered nature of *security* of tenure for one's home. These are presented in the following sections.

3 'Property': equal property rights within the family

3.1 *The equal property rights of wives*

The alleged lack of attention given by international law to the private sphere has been the basis of concern of some feminist lawyers.[3] Nevertheless, the human rights conventions explicitly establish obligations to ensure equality of rights between spouses. Article 23.4 of the International Covenant on Civil and Political Rights (ICCPR) establishes that:

[3] H. Charlesworth and C. Chinkin, *The Boundaries of International Law: A Feminist Analysis* (Manchester University Press, 2000).

> States Parties to the present Covenant shall take appropriate steps to ensure equality of rights and responsibilities of spouses as to marriage, during marriage and at its dissolution.

Furthermore, Article 16.1 of the CEDAW contains both a general call for equal rights and responsibilities of spouses (litra c), and a right to equality in property relations in particular (litra h):

> States Parties shall take all appropriate measures to eliminate discrimination against women in all matters relating to marriage and family relations and in particular shall ensure, on a basis of equality of men and women … (h) The same rights for both spouses in respect of the ownership, acquisition, management, administration, enjoyment and disposition of property, whether free of charge or for a valuable consideration.[4]

The respective treaty bodies have developed more detailed understandings of these provisions. In 1989 the Human Rights Committee (HRC) argued that Article 23 of the ICCPR creates a 'positive duty of States parties' to ensure that spouses have equal rights. Appropriate action may take different forms: legislative, administrative or other types of measures.[5] In its 2000 General Comment No. 28 on *Equality of Rights between Men and Women*, the HRC stated the implications of Article 23.4 for property rights. States must ensure that the matrimonial property regime:

> contains equal rights and obligations for both spouses with regard to … the ownership or administration of property, whether common property or property in the sole ownership of either spouse. States parties should review their legislation to ensure that married women have equal rights in regard to the ownership and administration of such property, where necessary … Equality during marriage implies that husband and wife should participate equally in responsibility and authority within the family.[6]

In 1994 the CEDAW Committee, in its General Recommendation No. 21 on *Equality in Marriage and Family Relations*, discussed Article 16 in detail. The Committee drew attention to ways in which family relations, distribution of work and responsibilities in the household, and gender

[4] Article 16.1(h) CEDAW.

[5] HRC, General Comment No. 18, *Non-Discrimination*, 10 November 1989, UN Doc. HRI/GEN/1/Rev.9 (Vol. I), para. 5. See also HRC, General Comment No. 19, *Protection of the Family, the Right to Marriage and Equality of the Spouses (Article 23)*, 27 July 1990, UN Doc. HRI/GEN/1/Rev.9 (Vol. I), paras. 6–9.

[6] HRC, General Comment No. 28, *Equality of Rights between Men and Women (Article 3)*, UN Doc. CCPR/C/21/Rev.1/Add.10, para. 25.

stereotypes can cause bias in the distribution of property rights between spouses.

A central argument made by the CEDAW Committee was the problematic effect of assigning to the man alone the role of provider and representative of the household. Pointing out the number of single or divorced women who support a family on their own, the Committee argued that the notion that men should have a higher share due to their responsibility to support women and children is based on unrealistic assumptions. Consequently, granting men a greater share of the property in cases of relationship break-up or on the death of a relative is not only discriminatory, but 'will have a serious impact on a woman's practical ability to divorce her husband, to support herself or her family and to live in dignity as an independent person'.[7] The CEDAW Committee thus held that regulation resulting in the husband being accorded 'the status of head of household and primary decision-maker' contravened the Convention.[8]

A second line of reasoning in the CEDAW Committee's General Recommendation No. 21 is that women's proportionately lower contribution, in strictly financial terms, to the family's acquisition of property is frequently intimately linked to gender roles and gendered divisions of work. Women's work is often household-oriented (care for children and the elderly, housework) or small-scale production-oriented (kitchen gardens for subsistence or for small-scale sales). If women have paid employment, they are likely to receive lower wages than men. Building on its earlier attention to women's unpaid and domestic work,[9] the Committee developed an understanding of the implications of gendered patterns of work for women's property rights within the family.[10] It stated its concern that:

[7] CEDAW Committee, General Recommendation No. 21, *Equality in Marriage and Family Relations*, 4 February 1994, UN Doc. HRI/GEN/1/Rev.9 (Vol. II), para. 28.

[8] *Ibid.* para. 17.

[9] CEDAW Committee, General Recommendation No. 13, *Equal Remuneration for Work of Equal Value*, 7 March 1989, UN Doc. HRI/GEN/1/Rev.9 (Vol. II). CEDAW Committee, General Recommendation No. 16, *Unpaid Women Workers in Rural and Urban Family Enterprises*, 2 January 1991, UN Doc. HRI/GEN/1/Rev.9 (Vol. II). CEDAW Committee, General Recommendation No. 17, *Measurement and Quantification of the Unremunerated Domestic Activities of Women and their Recognition in the Gross National Product*, 3 January 1991, UN Doc. HRI/GEN/1/Rev.9 (Vol. II). See also Article 14.1 CEDAW on the obligation of states to consider the unpaid, but economically important work of rural women.

[10] See CEDAW Committee, *Equality in Marriage and Family Relations* paras. 11–12, 15 and 21.

> In some countries, on division of marital property, greater emphasis is placed on financial contributions to property acquired during a marriage, and other contributions, such as raising children, caring for elderly relatives and discharging household duties are diminished. Often, such contributions of a non-financial nature by the wife enable the husband to earn an income and increase the assets.[11]

The Committee concluded that in division of marital property, '[f]inancial and non-financial contributions should be accorded the same weight.'[12]

3.2 *The equal inheritance rights of widows*

While equal property rights of spouses are called for both by the ICCPR and the CEDAW, the absence of explicit calls for equality in *inheritance* matters in treaty texts is noteworthy. Inheritance is not explicitly mentioned in the Covenants, the CEDAW or the Convention on the Rights of the Child (CRC).

The controversial nature of calls for equality in inheritance law is linked to its potential conflict with direct discrimination in customary or religious norms. The tension between calls for equality and religious norms has been a central theme in the context of the high number of reservations made by states during ratification of the CEDAW.[13] At the UN World Conferences during the early 1990s, efforts by women's rights advocates, particularly those from the global south, to place inheritance law on the agenda incited strong protests from some countries.[14]

[11] *Ibid.* para. 32.

[12] *Ibid.* para. 32.

[13] A number of states have made broad reservations to Article 2 CEDAW, limiting its application if it runs counter to Islamic law. Furthermore, Article 16, which established the right to equality in marriage and family relations, has been the most heavily reserved of the substantive Articles of the CEDAW. On reservations to the CEDAW, see R. J. Cook, 'Reservations to the Convention on the Elimination of All Forms of Discrimination against Women', *Virginia Journal of International Law* 30 (1990) 643–716, and A. C. Byrnes, 'The "other" human rights treaty body: the work of the Committee on the Elimination of Discrimination against Women', *The Yale Journal of International Law* 14:1 (1989) 1–67 at 53.

[14] The compromise solution was to carefully avoid placing the word 'equal' immediately before 'inheritance', although the texts committed the states to take steps to promote and strengthen women's rights to inherit. See e.g. *The Programme of Action of the International Conference on Population and Development*, adopted at the UN International Conference on Population and Development, held in Cairo, 5–13 September 1994, UN Doc. A/CONF.171/13, paras. 3.18, 4.6 and 4.17, and *The Beijing Platform for Action*, adopted at the Fourth World Conference on Women, held in Beijing from 4–15 September 1995, UN

However, resistance expressed at world conferences and similar venues does not limit treaty obligations undertaken by States Parties, and the treaty bodies have elaborated on the rights to equal inheritance. In 1994 the CEDAW Committee discussed inheritance in the context of Article 16.1(h) finding that provisions that placed women, whether as widows or daughters, at a disadvantage in relation to inheritance contravened the Convention.[15]

In a similar vein, both the HRC and the ICESCR Committee have drawn attention to the inheritance rights of *widows*. In 2000 the HRC used Article 23 on the equality of rights between spouses as a point of departure for this argument.[16] In 1999 the ICESCR Committee drew attention to women's inheritance rights in the context of the right to food.[17] In 2005 the same Committee argued that the combination of Article 3 (the equal rights of men and women) and Article 10 (according the widest possible protection and assistance to the family) requires that States Parties 'ensure that women have equal rights to marital property and inheritance upon their husband's death'.[18]

The inheritance rights of *daughters* have received less attention from the HRC and the ICESCR Committee.[19] However, the CEDAW Committee's call for equal inheritance rights of daughters was supported by the Committee on the Rights of the Child in 2003.[20]

Doc. A/CONF.177/20, paras. 61(b) 60(f), 165(e) and 274(d). This consensus formulation has later been used in resolutions by the UN General Assembly and the Commission on the Status of Women, and in a series of CHR resolutions on *Women's Equal Ownership of, Access to and Control over Land and the Equal Rights to Own Property* (2000–5, see note 48).

15 CEDAW Committee, *Equality in Marriage and Family Relations* para. 35.

16 Arguing that Article 23 requires that '[w]omen should also have equal inheritance rights to those of men when the dissolution of marriage is caused by the death of one of the spouses'. HRC, *Equality of Rights between Men and Women* para. 26.

17 ICESCR Committee, General Comment No. 12, *The Right to Adequate Food (Art. 11)*, 12 May 1999, UN Doc. E/CN.12/1999/5, para. 26.

18 ICESCR Committee, General Comment No. 16, *The Equal Right of Men and Women to the Enjoyment of All Economic, Social and Cultural Rights (Art. 3 of the ICESCR)*, 11 August 2005, UN Doc. E/DN.12/2005/4, para. 27.

19 When the HRC touched upon discriminatory inheritance law in its General Comment on the rights of the child, the Committee focused on discrimination of children on the basis of their citizenship or whether they were born in or out of wedlock, rather than gender. HRC, General Comment No. 17, *Rights of the Child (Article 24)*, 7 April 1989, UN Doc. HRI/GEN/1/Rev.9 (Vol. I), para. 5.

20 In the context of children orphaned or affected by HIV/AIDS, the CRC Committee reminded states to 'ensure that both law and practice support the inheritance and property rights of orphans, with particular attention to the underlying gender-based discrimination which may interfere with the fulfilment of these rights'. CRC Committee,

3.3 *When some are more equal than others: substantive equality and married women's acquisition of property*

A more detailed understanding of what it takes to realize equality of rights of spouses, as regards property rights in particular, has emerged. I suggest that these developments are best understood on the background of how the analysis of the term 'equality' has moved beyond formal equality and towards exploring the context in which substantive equality shall be realized.

Neither the ICCPR nor the ICESCR defines the concept of discrimination. However, both Committees have adopted definitions similar to that found in Article 1 of the CEDAW.[21] Furthermore, both Committees have adopted rather detailed presentations of their understandings of the concepts of equality and discrimination.[22] Recognizing the need to include both formal and substantive equality, and both direct and indirect discrimination, in the analysis, these suggest approaches resembling those taken by the CEDAW Committee. Nevertheless, the HRC and the ICESCR Committee have been less specific on the implications of these concepts in questions of marital property and inheritance.

The CEDAW Committee has provided the most explicit calls for accommodating difference. Paying attention to how gender roles influence the acquisition and division of property rights, this Committee has focused not only on creating equality by removing notions that men are the proper heads of household, but also by pointing out that differences between the typical 'male' and 'female' life patterns must be accommodated: ways to access land that are typical for women should also translate into property rights, and different types of work and contribution should

General Comment No. 3, *HIV/AIDS and the Rights of the Child*, 17 March 2003, UN Doc. CRC/GC/2003/3, para. 33.

[21] HRC, *Non-Discrimination* paras. 6–7. ICESCR Committee, *The Equal Right of Men and Women* para. 11.

[22] See HRC, *Equality of Rights between Men and Women*; ICESCR Committee, *The Equal Right of Men and Women*; and ICESCR Committee, General Comment No. 20, *Non-Discrimination in Economic, Social and Cultural Rights (Art. 2, Para. 2)*, 2 July 2009, UN Doc. E/C.12/GC/20. For a discussion on the developments leading to the latter document, see D. Otto, '"Gender Comment": why does the UN Committee on Economic, Social and Cultural Rights need a General Comment on women?', *Canadian Journal of Women and the Law/Revue juridique la femme et le droit* 14/1 (2002) 1–52. For a broad presentation of the concepts of non-discrimination and equality as used by the different treaty bodies, see W. Vandenhole, *Non-Discrimination and Equality in the View of the UN Human Rights Treaty Bodies* (Antwerp: Intersentia, 2005).

be considered on equal footing. This discussion thus provides a more 'engendered' interpretation.[23]

4 'Security': the right to secure tenure for one's home

4.1 Analyzing the human right to housing

A second path for articulating the human rights dimensions of Rose's experience is to focus on its consequences for her enjoyment of the human right to housing.[24] The analysis of this right has developed tremendously over the past two decades. By 1990 the lack of analytical work on housing rights was perceived as a problem, as was the lack of normative specificity of economic and social rights more generally.[25]

During the 1990s the right to housing received 'a boost' of attention. While some governments instigated heated debates about the status of housing as a human right, particularly during the preparations for the 1996 World Conference on Human Settlements (Habitat II),[26] UN human rights institutions began to develop a more detailed jurisprudence on the right to housing and the corresponding obligations. Two institutions took the lead in the elaboration of the normative content of the right: the newly established ICESCR Committee and the UN Sub-Commission on Prevention of Discrimination and Protection of Minorities (hereinafter 'the Sub-Commission').[27]

[23] See Fredman, 'Engendering socio-economic rights', this volume.

[24] See, in particular, Article 11.1 ICESCR.

[25] In his 1990 report a Special Rapporteur on the Realization of Economic, Social and Cultural Rights appointed by the UN Sub-Commission on Prevention of Discrimination and Protection of Minorities (hereinafter 'the Sub-Commission') stated that virtually no analytical work had been carried out within the human rights organs of the UN directly concerning housing rights (referred to in Sub-Commission Resolution No. 26/1992, *Promoting the Realization of the Right to Adequate Housing*, 27 August 1992, UN Doc. E/CN.4/Sub.2/1992/L.11/Add.4, at preambular para. 3). In 1996 Philip Alston stated that because of the lack of normative specificity of economic and social rights, 'efforts in the fields over the past few years have focused primarily on developing a more detailed and sophisticated normative framework', P. Alston, 'The US and the right to housing – a funny thing happened on the way to the forum', *European Human Rights Law Review* 2/1 (1996) 120–33 at 122.

[26] Alston, 'The US and the right to housing'.

[27] Furthermore, the outcome documents of the 1996 UN Conference on Human Settlements (Habitat II) recognized key elements of the human right to housing, as well as the multi-faceted relationships between housing and other human rights.

Only two dimensions of these normative developments will be mentioned here: firstly, how attention on forced evictions and the concept of 'legally secure tenure' allowed for an exploration of the role of property rights for housing. Secondly, how discrimination and women's rights to housing were articulated in the emerging analyses.

4.2 Secure tenure: property rights and the right to housing

In 1991 ICESCR Committee General Comment No. 4 provided an analysis of what it takes for housing to be 'adequate'.[28] In its list of criteria for assessing adequacy, it focused not only on the quality of the home, but also on the security against the risk of losing it. This dimension was captured through the concept 'legal security of tenure':

> Legal security of tenure: Tenure takes a variety of forms, including rental (public and private) accommodation, cooperative housing, lease, owner-occupation, emergency housing and informal settlements, including occupation of land or property. Notwithstanding the type of tenure, all persons should possess a degree of security of tenure which guarantees legal protection against forced evictions, harassment and other threats. States parties should consequently take immediate measures aimed at conferring legal security of tenure upon those persons and households currently lacking such protection, in genuine consultation with affected persons and groups.[29]

In 1991 the Sub-Commission appointed a Special Rapporteur on the Realization on the Right to Adequate Housing, Rajindar Sachar.[30] He continued the discussion of vulnerability to being thrown out of one's home as a dimension of the right to housing. In particular, he pointed out the role of illegality and lack of formal property rights, and incorporated this dimension in his proposals for indicators on the right to housing.[31] The Sub-Commission adopted a number of resolutions in response to his work, inter alia urging governments to '[c]onfer legal security of tenure for all persons'.[32]

[28] ICESCR Committee, General Comment No. 4, *The Right to Adequate Housing (Art. 11(1) of the Covenant)*, 13 December 1991, UN Doc. HRI/GEN/1/Rev.9 (Vol. I), para. 7.

[29] *Ibid.* para. 8(a).

[30] Sachar was appointed as Independent Expert in 1991 and as Special Rapporteur in the period 1992–5. Rajindar Sachar, Special Rapporteur, *The Right to Adequate Housing: Final Report*, 12 July 1995, UN Doc. E/CN.4/Sub.2/1995/12.

[31] *Ibid.* paras. 113–14 and 119.

[32] See for example Sub-Commission Resolution No. 29/1995, *Forced Evictions*, UN Doc. E/CN.4/SUB.2/RES/1995/29, paras. 1 and 3.

In 1997 General Comment No. 7 of the ICESCR Committee provided further clarifications on the conditions under which eviction from one's home constitutes a human rights violation.[33] The term 'forced evictions' was defined as:

> the permanent or temporary removal against their will of individuals, families and/or communities from the homes and/or land which they occupy, without the provision of, and access to, appropriate forms of legal and other protection.[34]

General Comment No. 7 further listed examples of instances of forced evictions, including evictions 'resulting from international armed conflicts, internal strife and communal or ethnic violence',[35] and evictions 'carried out in connection with conflict over land rights, development and infrastructure projects, such as the construction of dams or other large-scale energy projects, with land acquisition measures associated with urban renewal, housing renovation, city beautification programmes, the clearing of land for agricultural purposes, unbridled speculation in land, or the holding of major sporting events like the Olympic Games'.[36] Thus, while the definition, as quoted above, included situations where 'individuals, families and/or communities' were evicted, the examples of evictions centred on situations where larger groups or whole communities were influenced.

Overall, these documents established secure tenure and forced evictions as key concepts to describe the relationship between property rights and the human right to housing. As lack of property rights may increase the risk of such evictions, the extension of property rights to informal or illegal settlements emerged as one possible measure for increasing legal security of tenure and thus the adequacy of housing.

4.3 Gender neutrality and non-discrimination in the 1990s documents on the right to housing

The wording of Article 11.1 of the ICESCR itself presents the family, headed by a male breadwinner, as the basic unit for analysis:

[33] ICESCR Committee, General Comment No. 7, *The Right to Adequate Housing (Art. 11.1 of the Covenant): Forced Evictions*, 20 May 1997, UN Doc. HRI/GEN/1/Rev.9 (Vol. I).

[34] *Ibid.* para. 3. [35] *Ibid.* para. 6.

[36] *Ibid.* para. 7.

> The right of everyone to an adequate standard of living for *himself and his family*, including adequate food, clothing and housing.[37]

The underlying stereotype, the presumption that a male breadwinner was providing housing for the family, was debated at a one-day session on the right to housing arranged by the ICESCR Committee in 1990. It was argued that right to housing is not reserved for families, but applies to individuals. Furthermore, home ownership by women should be safeguarded due to the high number of female-headed households.[38] In 1991 General Comment No. 4 brushed aside the term 'himself and his family': this derived from the typical gender roles and economic activity patterns at the time. Given the changes that had taken place since, the term was not found to carry any legal implications.[39]

Furthermore, considerations of equality and non-discrimination were included in the documents. General Comment No. 4 of the ICESCR Committee stated that enjoyment of the right to housing must not be subject to 'any form of discrimination'.[40] It further argued that States Parties must give particular consideration and due priority to social groups living in unfavourable conditions, and that policies and legislation should not be designed to benefit already advantaged groups at the expense of others.[41]

The work of Special Rapporteur Sachar (1991–5) and General Comment No. 7 of the ICESCR Committee (1997) pursued this point by drawing attention to the fact that women in particular suffer from

[37] Article 11.1 ICESCR, emphasis added. See also Article 25.1 Universal Declaration of Human Rights (UDHR). Westendorp has argued: 'The right to housing was formulated in a traditional context; it is the male head of household who is the breadwinner and provider who must be enabled to realize this right for himself, his partner the homemaker, and their children. At the time it was not intended to attribute this right to individual women for the simple reason that they were not supposed (or enabled) to earn the family income and thus could not be burdened with the task of providing housing', I. Westendorp, *Women and Housing: Gender Makes a Difference* (School of Human Rights Research Series Vol. 23; Antwerp: Intersentia, 2007) at 11–12.

[38] Westendorp, *Women and Housing* at 34. M. C. R. Craven, *The International Covenant on Economic, Social, and Cultural Rights. A Perspective on Its Development*, paperback issue (with corrections) (Oxford: Clarendon Press, 1998) at 293 and 334.

[39] ICESCR Committee, *The Right to Adequate Housing* para. 6. See also ICESCR Committee, *The Right to Adequate Food* para. 1. As noted above, the CEDAW Committee has similarly denounced regulation that accords 'the status of head of household and primary decision-maker' to the husband: CEDAW Committee, *Equality in Marriage and Family Relations* paras. 17 and 28.

[40] ICESCR Committee, *The Right to Adequate Housing* para. 6. See also paras. 9 and 17.

[41] *Ibid.* para. 11.

discrimination in the enjoyment of the right to housing.[42] Both pointed out that women suffer disproportionately during and after evictions.[43]

However, the documents' statements of equality and non-discrimination generally lacked concretization and detail on how women's enjoyment of the right to housing may differ from that of men, and how housing needs, experiences and threats are influenced by gender relations.[44] For example, the concept of 'secure tenure' does not in itself answer the question of *which specific* threats such security will protect against.

During the 1990s a rich body of literature provided more grounded and empirically based perspectives on the role of sex and gender relations for housing and property. In particular, as Rose's story illustrates, women may be exposed to additional *types* of evictions and insecurity due to factors such as discriminatory laws, customs and traditions in the field of inheritance and rights to marital property.[45] However, the gender-neutral language of the 1990s documents failed to reflect this. Despite the rejection of the notion of the man as head of household, the ICESCR Committee's work as well as that of Special Rapporteur Sachar largely focused on threats affecting the household as a unit with shared interest, rather than exploring the potential for conflicts and evictions occurring between members of the household.

However, the 1990s soft law documents on the right to housing did not *exclude* such perspectives and arguments. As commented by women's housing rights activist Leilani Farha in 1999: 'At the international level,

[42] Sachar, *The Right to Adequate Housing: Final Report* paras. 44–9, 105 and 169. ICESCR Committee, *Forced Evictions* para. 10.

[43] See Sachar, *The Right to Adequate Housing: Final Report* para. 47; ICESCR Committee, *Forced Evictions* para. 10; and the discussion by L. Farha, 'Is there a woman in the house? Re/conceiving the human right to housing', *Canadian Journal of Women and the Law/ Revue juridique la femme et le droit* 14:1 (2002) 118–41 at 131–6. The disproportionate effect of evictions on women was later discussed by the CHR Special Rapporteur on Adequate Housing in the period 2000–8, Miloon Kothari.

[44] Women's housing rights activist Leilani Farha has made this point repeatedly, in relation to ICESCR Committee General Comment No. 4 (see, e.g., Farha, 'Is there a woman in the house?' at 126–31 and 139) as well as the work of Special Rapporteur Sachar (L. Farha, 'Women and housing' in K. D. Askin and D. M. Koenig (eds.), *Women and International Human Rights Law* (Ardsley, NY: Transnational Publishers, 1999) 483–532 at 505–6.

[45] See also Farha, 'Is there a woman in the house?' at 128 and 137–41, which provides an overview of how each of the 'adequacy' elements listed in the ICESCR Committee's General Comment No. 4 could be reconceptualized in order to ensure women's substantive equality. In a similar vein, the housing NGO COHRE has developed a fact sheet that points out ways in which gender relates to each of the seven aspects of 'adequacy': COHRE, *Fact Sheet on Women's Rights to Adequate Housing, Land and Property* (Centre on Housing Rights and Evictions, not dated) at 2.

there is a dearth of information that details in a substantial or substantive manner the meaning of the international right to housing for women; at the same time, however, the definition of the international right to housing in no way forecloses the possibility of articulating a woman's right to housing.'[46]

4.4 *Unpacking the household: 'family evictions' and the human right to housing*

A rare example of the 1990s' recognition of how women are exposed to distinct types of evictions and insecurity in relation to the human right to housing was found in the final report of Special Rapporteur Sachar. He pointed out that many women do not have *rights* to their homes, neither to the one in which they were born, nor to the home they live in after marriage. While women may have access to a home, they do not have security that they will be able remain in it. He referred to this home-without-rights as 'essential homelessness'.[47]

The interaction between the regulation of property rights between family members and secure tenure was explored further by 2000–8 CHR Special Rapporteur on the Right to Adequate Housing, Miloon Kothari.[48] In his reports, including three studies devoted specifically to the theme of women and adequate housing,[49] he pointed out a range of gender-specific

[46] Farha, 'Women and housing' at 484.

[47] Sachar, *The Right to Adequate Housing: Final Report* para. 46.

[48] While the CHR contributed to the integration of women's rights in the human rights discourse during the 1990s, it was fairly silent on the question of the right to housing. However, at the 2000 session when Miloon Kothari was appointed as Special Rapporteur, the CHR also adopted its first resolution on *Women's Equal Ownership of, Access to and Control over Land and the Equal Rights to Own Property and to Adequate Housing*, CHR Resolution No. 2000/13, 17 April 2000. It was followed by several resolutions on the same theme: CHR Resolution No. 2001/34, 23 April 2001; CHR Resolution No. 2002/49, 23 April 2002; CHR Resolution No. 2003/22, 26 April 2003; CHR Resolution No. 2005/25, 15 April 2005.

[49] M. Kothari, *Women and Adequate Housing. Study by the Special Rapporteur on Adequate Housing as a Component of the Right to an Adequate Standard of Living, and on the Right to Non-Discrimination, Miloon Kothari, in accordance with Commission Resolution 2002/49*, 26 March 2003, UN Doc. E/CN.4/2003/55. M. Kothari, *Women and Adequate Housing. Study by the Special Rapporteur on Adequate Housing as a Component of the Right to an Adequate Standard of Living, Miloon Kothari*, 25 February 2005, UN Doc. E/CN.4/2005/43. M. Kothari, *Women and Adequate Housing. Report by the Special Rapporteur on Adequate Housing as a Component of the Right to an Adequate Standard of Living, and on the Right to Non-Discrimination, Miloon Kothari*, 27 February 2006, UN Doc. E/CN.4/2006/118.

types of evictions and tenure insecurity. These included *family evictions*: situations where a woman faces threats of eviction brought on by family members or other household members. Two types of such situations will be presented here: when families fall apart, and when one family member enacts transactions of the land or house.[50]

The first type of family eviction can occur when family units fall apart, whether through divorce or by death. Special Rapporteur Kothari pointed out that insecurity may be caused by discriminatory inheritance norms, whether grounded in formal law or in religion or custom.[51] He drew attention to instances where widows whose husbands died from HIV/AIDS were evicted from their homes,[52] and argued that housing policies place women's tenure security at risk by not considering marriage separations.[53] The Commission on Human Rights supported this by reaffirming that 'forced relocation and forced eviction from home and land have a disproportionately severe impact on women, *including when these are committed by spouses or in-laws*'.[54]

Thus, women's rights to remain in their homes can be insecure for daughters as well as for wives in cases of family breakdown, whether by divorce or upon the death of a spouse/father. This type of vulnerability frequently hinges on notions that women are family members 'in transit', while land is to remain in the family. Consequently, women's property rights are contingent on their (temporary) membership of the family. When such membership ends, threats of eviction may arise. Viewing such situations as questions of tenure security brings the regulation and practice of property rights within families under the ambit of the right to housing.

[50] Domestic violence is a third example of eviction induced by family members. Kothari has argued that domestic violence can be viewed as a cause of forced eviction, as it makes women unable to stay in their homes. See M Kothari, *Report of the Special Rapporteur on Adequate Housing as a Component of the Right to an Adequate Standard of Living, Miloon Kothari*, 8 March 2004, UN Doc. E/CN.4/2004/48, paras. 41, 56–7. For more on the relationship between domestic violence and the right to housing, see G. Paglione, 'Domestic violence and housing rights: a reinterpretation of the right to housing', *Human Rights Quarterly* (2006) 120–47, and Westendorp, *Women and Housing* at 102–11. This theme will not be discussed in more detail here.

[51] See e.g. Kothari, *Women and Adequate Housing* 2003 para. 41; Kothari, *Women and Adequate Housing* 2005 para. 55; and Kothari, *Women and Adequate Housing* 2006 paras. 38–40 and 44.

[52] Kothari, *Women and Adequate Housing* 2003 para. 30.

[53] Kothari, *Women and Adequate Housing* 2005 para. 55.

[54] CHR Resolution No. 2003/22 preambular para. 7, and CHR Resolution No 2005/25 preambular para. 10 (author's emphasis).

A second type of family eviction identified by Special Rapporteur Kothari includes situations in which women face homelessness because men sell or mortgage the house or property without informing them or asking their consent.[55] A similar observation has been made by the CEDAW Committee, which warned about the problems that may arise when 'there is no legal requirement that a woman be consulted when property owned by the parties during marriage or de facto relationship is sold or otherwise disposed of'.[56]

Such incidents are regulated at the intersection of multiple legal fields, each of which provides possibilities for protection. Firstly, norms and practices in the field of *family law* sometimes place property rights, decision-making and representation of the household in the hands of males. This excludes women from participating in decisions pertaining to sales, mortgages and gifts of the land on which they live, and prevents them from gaining a share of income thereby obtained. Joint ownership regimes in family law may reduce the risks.

Secondly, *contract law and regulation of land markets* have implications here. Regulation of land markets may serve to counteract such dispositions by protecting the rights of users without formal property rights. One example is the requirement of spousal consent to sales or mortgages.[57]

Finally, such situations are influenced by the *regulation of land titling and registration of land rights*, for example when the state seeks to regularize property rights established under traditional or informal tenure systems. The term 'formalization', frequently used in conjunction with titling processes, suggests that the existing relations and interests can be captured on paper and fit in with the property structures of formal law. However, since titling usually means registration of one rights holder only, it will in practice often constitute simplification of complex and overlapping land rights. Thus, titling may change the relationship between the rights of different users of land. When one person is registered as the rights

[55] Kothari, *Women and Adequate Housing* 2003 para. 44.

[56] CEDAW Committee, *Equality in Marriage and Family Relations* para. 31.

[57] 'Spousal consent requirements' are legal measures that make the consent from a non-owning spouse a prerequisite for valid dispositions over property such as the matrimonial home or land used by the spouses. They can also be designed to require consent from other household members, for example adult children, and thus protect a wider range of individuals with interests in the land or house. For an illustration of the controversies such measures can generate, see I. Ikdahl, 'Competing notions of property rights: land rights reform at the intersection of the international and the local' in C. C. Eriksen and M. Emberland (eds.), *The New International Law: An Anthology* (Leiden: Brill Academic Publishers, 2010) 99–113.

holder, he becomes the 'formal owner', while the interests of his family remain informal and invisible to outsiders. They thus experience limited security against transactions in the 'formal market'. Consequently, the frequent gender bias in titling processes is not only a reflection of underlying inequalities, but a manifestation of discrimination. It also makes women more vulnerable to this type of family eviction. Joint titling is an example of a legal measure intended to counteract such risks.[58]

4.5 Bringing women's experiences into the right to housing: mainstreaming, indivisibility and life stories

The right to housing has thus shifted away from the notion of the male-headed household: first to a gender-neutral household threatened from the outside, and then towards taking the individuals within the household as the point of departure. The difference such an individual-centred focus can make is obvious in the context of family evictions. Attention to relations *within* the household facilitates the articulation of a wider range of women's experiences of housing insecurity as human rights themes, in line with the quest for engenderment.[59]

While Kothari's reports during his tenure as CHR Special Rapporteur are seen as having minimal formal weight as a source of international law, his work was significant for this development. The reports demonstrated the impact of unequal property relations within the family on the realization of the right to housing. He established a basis for grounded and gender-sensitive perspectives on how *tenure security* is created, and on the range of situations that can be understood as *forced evictions*. His analyses provide an example of 'gendered' interpretation of the right, in line with the calls for inclusion of women's perspectives in human rights.

Several factors may have contributed to Kothari's focus on the interaction between tenure security and the distribution of property rights between family members. Firstly, his mandate explicitly included the right to non-discrimination, and the CHR requested that he apply a

[58] 'Joint titling' refers to provisions calling for inclusion of both/all spouses when land rights are registered. Rather than establishing only one owner per parcel of landed property, joint titling serves to include several members of a household when rights are registered. For a discussion of challenges in the implementation of such measures, see I. Ikdahl, '"Go home and clear the conflict": human rights perspectives on gender and land in Tanzania' in B. Englert and E. Daley (eds.), *Women's Land Rights and Privatization in Eastern Africa* (Woodbridge/Kampala/Nairobi/Dar es Salaam: James Currey, 2008) 40–60.

[59] See Fredman, 'Engendering socio-economic rights', this volume.

gender perspective in his work.[60] This was in line with the principle of gender mainstreaming, which had been established as a general principle for human rights analysis and activities during the 1990s.[61]

Secondly, he acquired information from a wide range of sources, with a view to increasing the understanding of the types of eviction situations occurring on the ground.[62] Alison Aggarwal, research associate to the CHR Special Rapporteur, has emphasized the importance of this broad approach for his work pertaining to women's rights to housing:

> Working with women's groups has been of critical importance, in light of the limited information on women's rights that is available through the periodic reports by member states to the human rights treaty committees, as well as the lack of data and research available from many national housing groups.[63]

[60] CHR Resolution No. 2000/9, *Question of the Realization in All Countries of the Economic, Social and Cultural Rights Contained in the Universal Declaration of Human Rights and in the International Covenant on Economic, Social and Cultural Rights, and Study of Special Problems Which the Developing Countries Face in Their Efforts to Achieve These Human Rights*, 17 April 2000, paras. 7(c) and 7(d)(iii).

[61] In 1993 the declaration adopted at the World Conference on Human Rights urged the mainstreaming of women's perspectives in all aspects of human rights. *The Vienna Declaration and Programme of Action*, adopted at the UN World Conference on Human Rights, held in Vienna 14–25 June 1993, UN Doc. A/CONF.157/23, section I, para. 18. Similar calls for inclusion were made at the 1995 World Conference on Women, *The Beijing Declaration*, adopted at the Fourth World Conference on Women, held in Beijing 4–15 September 1995, UN Doc. A/CONF.177/20, para. 8. However, the language shifted somehow between these occasions, from 'integration of women's rights' to 'gender mainstreaming'. For a detailed discussion, see S. Kouvo, *Making Just Rights?* (Uppsala: Iustus, 2004).

[62] Kothari cooperated closely with civil society, including through regional consultations. See e.g. M. Kothari, *Report of the Special Rapporteur on Adequate Housing as a Component of the Right to an Adequate Standard of Living, and on the Right to Non-Discrimination in This Context, Miloon Kothari*, 13 February 2008, UN Doc. A/HRC/7/16, para. 37. During these consultations, testimonies from 'grassroots women' were intended to allow the Special Rapporteur to gain 'much of his information on the direct and specific experiences of women from diverse backgrounds': A. G. Aggarwal, 'UN Special Rapporteur on Adequate Housing: strengthening gendered norms for the right to adequate housing', *Australian Journal of Human Rights* 10:1 (2004), available at: www.austlii.edu.au/au/journals/AJHR/2004/8.html (last accessed 13 February 2013).

Furthermore, a questionnaire on women and adequate housing was developed and distributed widely. It was meant to serve multiple purposes: obtaining information with a view to advancing the conceptual understanding of the right to adequate housing; ascertaining gaps in legislation and implementation; and educating states and civil society on women's right to adequate housing. See Kothari, *Women and Adequate Housing* 2008 para. 55. The questionnaire, as amended in 2003, is available at: www2.ohchr.org/english/issues/housing/docs/questionnaireEn.doc (last accessed 6 April 2011).

[63] Aggarwal, 'UN Special Rapporteur on Adequate Housing'.

Finally, the indivisibility of all human rights was a key element of his methodological approach, facilitating studies of the interaction between the right to housing and other rights.[64] Following the end of the Cold War, the divide between civil and political rights on the one hand, and economic, social and cultural rights on the other, had given way to more holistic approaches to human rights. The 1993 Vienna Conference proclaimed that all human rights are 'universal, indivisible, and interdependent, and interrelated'.[65] The emphasis on indivisibility was reflected not only in the Special Rapporteur's argumentation, but also in his efforts to cooperate with the treaty-monitoring Committees, as well as other mandate holders and UN agencies.[66] In particular, his cooperation with the ICESCR Committee was frequently mentioned in the annual reports. In comparison, the reports leave the impression that the contact and cooperation with the CEDAW Committee was more limited.[67]

Thus, methodological approaches to human rights emerging during the 1990s, in particular gender mainstreaming and the indivisibility of rights, facilitated the inclusion of knowledge about social and property relations inside the household and family in the analysis of the right to housing. Ultimately, this allowed for bridging, at least partly, the divide between two debates on property rights: their relevance for the right to adequate housing, as discussed primarily by the ICESCR Committee, and the analysis of equality between the spouses, developed primarily by the CEDAW Committee.

[64] See for example Kothari, *Report of the Special Rapporteur on Adequate Housing* 2008 para. 4.

[65] *The Vienna Declaration and Programme of Action*, section I, para. 5. See also paras. 1, 4 and 32. Over time, this contributed to the progress in the understanding of economic and social rights as binding and justiciable, rather than merely as policy objectives. See e.g. A. Eide, C. Krause and A. Rosas (eds.), *Economic, Social and Cultural Rights*, 2nd edn (Dordrecht: Kluwer Law International, 2001).

[66] See Kothari, *Report of the Special Rapporteur on Adequate Housing* 2008 paras. 56–60, and M. Kothari, *Report of the Special Rapporteur on Adequate Housing as a Component of the Right to an Adequate Standard of Living, Mr. Miloon Kothari*, 1 March 2002, UN Doc. E/CN.4/2002/59, paras. 78–100.

[67] The geographical location of this Committee in New York may have been a factor here: until January 2008 the CEDAW Committee had its meetings and Secretariat in New York, where the Commission on the Status of Women is located, while the other treaty bodies – the CHR and the Office of the High Commissioner on Human Rights – were located in Geneva. Besides, personal connections can also influence such cooperation, and Special Rapporteur Kothari had a background from civil society, with close links to housing NGOs that directed their international lobbying efforts primarily towards the ICESCR Committee.

5 Convergence, complementarity and the way forward

The developments described above shed light on both substantive and institutional aspects of the relationship between equality in the property relations between spouses and the realization of security of tenure.

In the field of substantive rights and obligations, the intimate relationship between the two sets of rights is recognized today. Factors such as discriminatory inheritance norms and marital property regulation that does not recognize women's unpaid work diminish women's enjoyment of their right to secure housing, as well as their right to equal property rights within marriage.

Nevertheless, the specific right taken as the point of departure has implications for the types of measures that are appropriate for improving gender equality. It is significant that the ultimate *objectives* differ between the right to housing and the right to equality in property relations between spouses. As regards the latter, providing women with (equal) property rights to the land and home is the very objective. In contrast, the right to housing regards property rights as only one of several possible legal measures to advance the objective of providing security.

Increasing women's property rights will help the realization of both rights. The principle of equal rights to property between spouses is a powerful argument for land law calling for joint titling, as well as for joint ownership regimes in family law. Furthermore, measures such as sensitization of the bureaucracy and judges, as well as legal aid and awareness campaigns encouraging widows to title land in their own names, can be useful in facilitating women's claims of individual property rights.

However, the supplementary role of the right to secure tenure is demonstrated by the situation of women such as Rose who choose not to pursue individual property rights due to a concern that challenging local norms could jeopardize family relations. Extending the right to secure tenure to this group of women as well requires a dual perspective, considering both the present and the future. Women's right to adequate housing applies *today*, not in an ideal world where stereotypes and discrimination are already abolished. Strategies to increase tenure security need to acknowledge that individual women do not always want to challenge discriminatory norms. In such situations, provisions requiring spousal consent to land transactions may be an important tool. But in addition, the state must consider *tomorrow*, by taking steps to modify discriminatory customs and norms, as well as negative gender stereotypes.[68] A comprehensive approach to the distinct types of evictions and insecurity experienced by women without property rights in their homes is required.

The combination of the 'property' and 'security' approaches thus results in a call for multiple strategies to realize women's rights to their homes, encompassing both immediate and long-term perspectives, and both legal and non-legal measures. For the short-term realization, legislative measures aimed at increasing women's property rights must be designed with a view to accommodating both typically 'male' and 'female' life patterns and ways to access land, along the lines suggested by the CEDAW Committee. Examples of such legal measures include non-discriminatory inheritance law, joint ownership regimes and recognition of unpaid work as basis for property rights. These should be accompanied by measures supporting women who want to claim their property rights. Furthermore, legal regulations protecting against 'family evictions' should be adopted, in order to offer immediate protection of the housing rights of women who do *not* claim property rights in their homes. In a long-term perspective, there is a need for sustained efforts to change customs, norms and stereotypes that obstruct or discourage women from claiming their rights.

Furthermore, the present theme also sheds light on the role of the various institutions participating in the development of human rights law. The soft law documents adopted by the Committees have helped render women's experiences of inequality, suffering and vulnerability pertaining to their rights in their homes visible and tangible in human rights discourse.

However, the two strands of analysis, to a large extent, have remained disconnected. The work of the ICESCR Committee has not fully recognized the issues that unequal property relations within the household raise for specific types of gendered insecurity. Conversely, while the CEDAW Committee has provided a detailed analysis of women's unequal property rights within the family, it has not yet engaged systematically with the effects on women's right to housing – despite the CEDAW's call for rural women's equal enjoyment of '[a]dequate living conditions, particularly in relation to housing'.[69]

In contrast, the work of the CHR Special Rapporteur on the Right to Adequate Housing demonstrates the inherent potential of a combined approach as a means of articulating an engendered understanding of

[68] Articles 2(f) and 5.1 CEDAW. [69] Article 14.2(h) CEDAW.

women's rights in relation to their homes. His work can serve as the basis for recommendations addressed to both Committees regarding their separate work, as well as the cooperation between them.

Firstly, given the development of knowledge and arguments in this field, it would be timely for the Committees to consider these questions explicitly.

The ICESCR Committee could carry this out through a revision of General Comments Nos. 4 and 7. While their current wording does not exclude threats experienced by women in particular, themes such as 'family evictions' are rendered invisible by the dominant perspective on threats affecting the household as a unit with shared interests. An updated interpretation of the right to housing should emphasize that while 'forced evictions, harassment and other threats' (the term used by the Committee in both General Comments) can affect the household or community as a collective, such incidents can also be targeted at individuals. Preferably, it should explicitly draw attention to threats that are predominantly experienced by women, including divorce, widowhood and situations where others sell or mortgage their homes or the land they live on. A reference to the Committee's views on women's equal rights to marital property and inheritance upon their husbands' death, as expressed in General Comment No. 16, could be added to ensure that family law themes are not sidelined in laws, policies and projects focusing on housing and land rights.[70]

As regards the CEDAW Committee, a General Recommendation concerning state obligations pertaining to women's equal right to housing, as established in Article 14 of the CEDAW, would be highly recommendable. This should incorporate an engendered understanding of 'security' for remaining in one's home, and thus supplement the Committee's existing focus on property rights. A systematic analysis of women's equal right to housing would provide guidance for States Parties, as well as facilitate the monitoring of state compliance during the examination of state reports.

Finally, while the normative developments analyzed in this chapter underscore the potential value of interaction and mutual learning between the two treaty bodies, it is also suggested that such interaction remains unsystematic. While it is commendable that CHR Special Rapporteur Kothari sought to cooperate with both bodies, such dialogue should not be left at the level of individuals, but ensured through direct

[70] CESCR GC 16 (2005) para. 27.

and systematic institutional cooperation on themes of shared interest. Arguably, the two complementing paths that have been employed to approach women's rights in their homes demonstrate the ability of the UN human rights system to respond to a complex theme. However, the strengths of a *combined* approach illustrate that cross-fertilization between the various treaty bodies is vital in order to realize substantive equality for women.

10

Maternal mortality and women's right to health

HENRIETTE SINDING AASEN

1 Introduction

Every day around 800 women die from preventable causes related to pregnancy and childbirth. Almost all such maternal deaths (99 per cent) take place in developing countries, most often in poor, rural areas. More than half of maternal deaths occur in sub-Saharan Africa, and one-third in South Asia. Complications during and following pregnancy and childbirth, as well as unsafe abortions, are the major causes, accounting for 80 per cent of all maternal deaths. Most maternal deaths are avoidable, as the healthcare solutions to prevent or manage complications are well known. However, in many developing countries women do not have access to adequate healthcare services and skilled care during pregnancy and childbirth. Poor women in remote areas are the least likely to receive adequate help and services. Factors such as poverty, distance, lack of information, inadequate services and cultural practices prevent women from receiving or seeking adequate care during pregnancy and childbirth.[1]

Despite the fact that maternal deaths happen more often than many human rights violations, it is only recently that the international human rights community has given maternal mortality its attention. In this chapter, the high incidence of maternal mortality and the lack of access to adequate healthcare services in many developing countries is conceptualized as a violation of women's rights to life and health, constituting a particular form of gender-based discrimination and structural disadvantage suffered especially by poor women in low-resource settings (see Articles 1 and 2 of the Convention on the Elimination of All Forms of Discrimination against Women (CEDAW)). In order to secure non-discrimination and substantive equality, the distinct female experience and the needs

[1] World Health Organization (WHO), Fact Sheet No. 348, May 2012.

associated with reproduction must be integrated into human rights norms and principles.[2] Substantive equality requires that more attention be paid to the factual situation of women, acknowledging women's disadvantaged position and the need for structural change.[3] As pointed out by scholars of women's human rights, non-discrimination and substantive equality often require legal analysis based on empirical knowledge of women's situations.[4] Reduction of maternal mortality requires accurate and country-specific information concerning the causes of maternal deaths, women's *de jure* and de facto access to reproductive healthcare services (including abortion services) and the reasons why such services are not accessible. In addition, effective strategies of state accountability for violations of women's rights to life and health, as well as targeted implementation and fulfilment of state obligations in this regard, are imperative in order to ensure adequate maternal healthcare services for women on the ground.

2 Maternal mortality: definition and statistics

A maternal death is defined by the World Health Organization (WHO) as the death of a woman while pregnant or within forty-two days of termination of pregnancy, irrespective of the duration and site of the pregnancy, from any cause related to or aggravated by the pregnancy or its management but not from accidental or incidental causes.[5] In other words, the death must be linked to obstetric complications related to pregnancy.[6] It is estimated that at least 15 per cent of all pregnant women will develop serious obstetric complications that require life-saving access to quality obstetric services.[7] If left untreated, these complications will lead to death or severe disability. Because such obstetric complications often cannot be

[2] See the chapters by Fredman, van Leeuwen and Holtmaat in this volume.

[3] Banda in this volume (Chapter 2, section 7).

[4] T. S. Dahl, *Kvinnerett I* [*Women's Law I*] (Oslo: Universitetsforlaget, 1985) at 74; A. Hellum, *Women's Human Rights and Legal Pluralism in Africa* (Oslo: Tano Aschehoug, 1999) and I. Ikdahl, 'Securing women's homes. The dynamics of women's human rights at the international level and in Tanzania', PhD thesis, University of Oslo, Faculty of Law (2010).

[5] WHO, *Trends in Maternal Mortality: 1990 to 2010 WHO, UNICEF, UNFPA and The World Bank Estimates*, 2012 at 4.

[6] CEDAW Committee, Communication No. 17/2008, 10 August 2011, para. 7.3.

[7] UNICEF, WHO and the United Nations Fund for Population Activities (UNFPA), *Guidelines for Monitoring the Availability and Use of Obstetric Services*, 1997.

predicted or prevented, all pregnant women need access to good-quality emergency obstetric services.[8]

It is estimated that 287,000 maternal deaths occurred worldwide in 2010. Between 1990 and 2010 maternal deaths worldwide dropped 47 per cent, from 543,000 annually.[9] This is a significant reduction. In developing countries the maternal mortality ratio (MMR)[10] is 240 per 100,000 births, while it is 16 per 100,000 births in developed countries.[11] Of these deaths 56 per cent occurred in sub-Saharan Africa, and 29 per cent in Southern Asia. Two countries account for a third of maternal deaths: India (19 per cent, 56,000 maternal deaths in 2010) and Nigeria (14 per cent, 40,000 maternal deaths in 2010).[12] MMRs show greater disparity among countries than any other public health indicator, also within the sub-Saharan region, indicating important differences among countries as well as complex causal relations.[13] Even in relatively prosperous countries the MMR is sometimes very high.[14] For each woman who dies, many more suffer from acute or chronic illness and disability, in addition to the suffering of children and families.

3 Maternal deaths: causes and medical actions

According to WHO, maternal deaths are caused by complications during and following pregnancy and childbirth. Most complications develop during pregnancy, while some complications exist before pregnancy but are worsened during pregnancy. The major complications, accounting for 80 per cent of all maternal deaths, are preventable if specific medical actions are taken:

[8] J. Meyers, S. Lobis and H. Dakkak, 'UN process indicators: key to measuring maternal mortality reduction', *Forced Migration Review* 19 (2004) 16–18, at 16.

[9] WHO, *Trends in Maternal Mortality: 1990 to 2010* at 1.

[10] Number of maternal deaths during a given time period per 100,000 live births during the same time period. See WHO, *Trends in Maternal Mortality: 1990 to 2010* at 6.

[11] WHO, Fact Sheet No. 348, May 2012.

[12] *Ibid.*

[13] J. L. Alvarez, R. Gil, V. Hernández and A. Gil, 'Factors associated with maternal mortality in Sub-Saharan Africa: an ecological study', *BMC Public Health*, 2009, 462ff., available at: www.biomedcentral.com; R. Cook, B. M. Dickens and M. F. Fathalla, *Reproductive Health and Human Rights* (Oxford: Clarendon Press, 2003) at 24.

[14] E. Durojaye, 'Monitoring the right to health and sexual and reproductive health at the national level: some considerations for African governments', *Comparative and International Law Journal of Southern Africa* 42:2 (2009) 227–64 at 228.

(1) Severe bleeding (mostly after childbirth), which can kill a healthy woman within two hours if she is unattended. Injecting oxytocin immediately after childbirth effectively reduces the risk of bleeding.
(2) Infections (usually after childbirth). Good hygiene and treatment of early signs of infection can eliminate this risk.
(3) High blood pressure during pregnancy (pre-eclampsia and eclampsia). Pre-eclampsia should be detected and appropriately managed before the onset of convulsions (eclampsia) and other life-threatening complications. Administering drugs such as magnesium sulphate for pre-eclampsia can lower the risk of developing eclampsia.
(4) Obstructed labour occurs when the head of the baby is too big for the mother's pelvis or if the baby is abnormally positioned for birth. Partography (a graph of the progress of labour and the maternal and fetal condition) is a simple and effective tool for identifying these problems early in labour. Used by skilled practitioners, this tool can identify and manage obstructed labour before the lives of the mother and baby are in danger. If necessary, a caesarean section can be performed.
(5) Unsafe abortion. Many girls and women die due to infections or other damage caused by unsafe abortion procedures. Prevention of unwanted and too-early pregnancies is vital, as well as help in case of unwanted pregnancy. All women, including adolescents, need access to family planning, safe abortion services without risk of social or legal sanctions, and quality post-abortion care.[15]

The remaining deaths (20 per cent) are caused by diseases such as malaria and AIDS during pregnancy.[16] Maternal health and newborn health are closely related. More than three million newborn babies die every year, while an additional 2.6 million babies are stillborn.[17]

Most maternal deaths (80 per cent) are avoidable, since the medical solutions to prevent or manage complications are well documented and well known. All women need access to antenatal care in pregnancy and skilled care during childbirth, as well as care and support in the weeks after childbirth. The main problem is that women do not have access to a functioning health system providing timely and appropriate maternal healthcare, including emergency obstetric care performed by skilled

[15] WHO, Fact Sheet No. 348, May 2012.
[16] *Ibid.*
[17] *Ibid.*

personnel and access to safe abortions.[18] According to WHO, it is particularly important that all births are attended by skilled health professionals, as timely management and treatment can make the difference between life and death.[19] There is also a strong correlation between basic education, public spending on health and access to safe drinking water, and the reduction of maternal mortality.[20]

4 International initiatives, developments and MDGs

In an article entitled 'Maternal mortality: a neglected tragedy. Where is the "M" in MCH?', Rosenfield and Maine drew attention to the 'inherent neglect of women in maternal and child health (MCH) programmes'.[21] In 1987 the International Conference on Safe Motherhood in Nairobi led to the establishment of the Safe Motherhood Initiative, which aimed to find solutions to persistent maternal mortality and morbidity. When the United Nations (UN) International Conference on Population and Development (ICPD) was held in Cairo in 1994, 179 countries agreed on strategies to improve women's reproductive health within a human rights framework. At the Fourth World Conference on Women in Beijing in 1995, the *Beijing Declaration and Platform of Action* was adopted, addressing women's health in a broad human rights framework in which reproductive rights and empowerment of women were central. In 1997 the United Nations International Children's Emergency Fund (UNICEF), WHO and the United Nations Fund for Population Activities (UNFPA) developed a second edition of the *Guidelines for Monitoring the Availability and Use of Obstetric Services*,[22] which focuses on the ability of the health-care system to respond to women's needs for care.

Then, at the Millennium Summit in 2000, called to address serious global concerns, all 189 UN Member States adopted the UN Millennium Declaration on 8 September, stating inter alia that by the year 2015 they intended 'to have reduced maternal mortality by three quarters, and

18 V. Boama and S. Arulkumaran, 'Safer childbirth: a rights-based approach', *International Journal of Gynaecology and Obstetrics* 106:2 (2009) 125–7 at 126.

19 WHO, Fact Sheet No. 348, May 2012.

20 Alvarez *et al.*, 'Factors associated with maternal mortality in Sub-Saharan Africa'.

21 S. Gruskin, J. Cottingham, A. M. Hilber, E. Kismödi, O. Lincetto and M. J. Roseman, 'Using human rights to improve maternal and neonatal health: history, connections and a proposed practical approach', *Bulletin of the World Health Organization* 86:8 (2008) 589–93 at 590.

22 United Nations International Children's Emergency Fund (August 1997).

under-five child mortality by two-thirds, of their current rates' (section 19). This goal is situated in a context of human rights values and principles in that the Declaration also resolves 'to promote gender equality and the empowerment of women as effective ways to combat poverty, hunger and disease and to stimulate development that is truly sustainable' (section 20). The Millennium Declaration as such is based on the values and principles of human dignity, equality and equity, respect for human rights and fundamental freedoms, and respect for the equal rights of all without distinction to race, sex, language or religion (sections 1 and 2). The ambitious goal concerning reduction of maternal mortality by 2015, and other goals (related to poverty, health, peace, security, environment, human rights and democracy), were later encapsulated in the Millennium Development Goals (MDGs), endorsed by the UN General Assembly in 2001. At the 2005 World Summit the goals of universal access to reproductive health, as well as the goal concerning reduction of maternal mortality, were repeated. Specific references to the International Conference on Population and Development (ICPD) and *Beijing Declaration and Platform of Action* were made.[23] The human rights community, that is the Committees of the International Covenant on Economic, Social and Cultural Rights (ICESCR) and the CEDAW, the UN High Commissioner for Human Rights, the Human Rights Council and the UN Special Rapporteur on Health, became involved with the issue of maternal mortality from 2000 onwards.[24] In 2010 the UN Secretary-General launched the *Global Strategy for Women's and Children's Health*[25] in order to mobilize governments, civil society organizations and development partners to accelerate progress towards MDGs 4 and 5 (reduce child mortality and improve maternal health). A high-level Commission on Information and Accountability for Women's and Children's Health was established to determine the most effective international institutional arrangements for global reporting, oversight and accountability on women's and children's health.

[23] Resolution adopted by the General Assembly, 60/1, World Summit Outcome, 24 October 2005, paras. 57(g) and 58.

[24] See overview in R. J. Cook and V. Undurraga, 'Article 12' in M. A. Freeman, C. Chinkin and B. Rudolf (eds.), *The UN Convention on the Elimination of All Forms of Discrimination against Women: A Commentary* (Oxford University Press, 2012) 311–34 at 316–17.

[25] This document was developed under the auspices of the United Nations General-Secretary, Ban Ki-moon, with support and facilitation by The Partnership for Maternal, Newborn and Child Health. The *Global Strategy* was launched at the time of the UN Leaders' Summit for the Millennium Development Goals (MDGs) in 2010.

Despite international campaigns and increased attention, maternal health has been the MDG that has made the least progress.[26] In sub-Saharan Africa, maternal mortality was reported to have decreased by only 0.1 per cent annually, while the number of pregnancy-related complications resulting in extended illness or disability was over 15 million annually.[27] In some sub-Saharan African countries maternal mortality even increased as a result of HIV/AIDS and malaria.[28] The situation is improving, however, and according to WHO, a number of sub-Saharan countries halved their levels of maternal mortality from 1990 to 2010.[29] The UN observes that, despite progress, pregnancy remains a major health risk for women in several regions, in particular sub-Saharan Africa and Southern Asia, where skilled birth attendance is still low.[30] WHO concludes that the global maternal mortality ratio declined by 3.1 per cent per year until 2010, which is far from the annual decline of 5.5 per cent required to achieve MDG 5.[31] Globally, then of the countries with high maternal mortality achieved the MDG 5 of 75 per cent reduction of the maternal mortality ratio by 2010, and nine countries are 'on track'. Fifty countries are 'making progress', fourteen have made 'insufficient progress' (less than 2 per cent annual MMR decline) and eleven countries have made no progress.[32]

5 Maternal mortality and the right to health: instruments and monitoring bodies

5.1 Instruments

Maternal mortality raises several human rights issues, including women's rights to life and health, non-discrimination and participation. The focus here is on the right to health, in particular with regard to state responsibility for provision of healthcare services to women. A key aspect of human rights treaties is that states are made legally responsible and

[26] United Nations, *The Millennium Development Goals Report*, 2009.

[27] Boama and Arulkumaran, 'Safer childbirth'.

[28] D. Shaw, 'Women's right to health and the millennium development goals: promoting partnerships to improve access', *International Journal of Gynaecology and Obstetrics* 93:3 (2006) 207–15; Alvarez *et al.*, 'Factors associated with maternal mortality in Sub-Saharan Africa'.

[29] WHO, Fact Sheet No. 348, May 2012.

[30] UN, *The Millennium Development Goals Report*, 2011 at 29–30.

[31] WHO, Fact Sheet No. 348, May 2012.

[32] WHO, *Trends in Maternal Mortality: 1990 to 2010* at 27.

accountable for their policies and actions, and that principles of accountability, non-discrimination, information and participation are to be implemented into domestic health policies and regulations. As for the normative content of the right to health, the legal starting points are Article 12 of the ICESCR and Article 12 of the CEDAW. Both provisions address important aspects of the right to health, which is further outlined and developed by the ICESCR and CEDAW monitoring bodies (see below). Article 12, paragraph 1 of the ICESCR is the original and general human rights provision on the right to health and state obligations:

1. The States Parties to the present Covenant recognize the right of everyone to the enjoyment of the highest attainable standard of physical and mental health.

Paragraph 2 mentions the steps to be taken by the States Parties in order to achieve the full realization of the right to health, and shall include those necessary for:

(a) the provision for the reduction of the stillbirth rate and of infant mortality and for the healthy development of the child;
(b) the improvement of all aspects of environmental and industrial hygiene;
(c) the prevention, treatment and control of epidemic, endemic, occupational and other diseases; and
(d) the creation of conditions that would ensure all medical service and medical attention in the event of sickness.

Article 10, paragraph 2.1 of the ICESCR states that special protection should be accorded to mothers during a reasonable period before and after childbirth. This provision includes basic maternal healthcare services.

No direct reference is made to women in Article 12 of the ICESCR; only indirect mention is made of the stillbirth rate, infant mortality and the healthy development of the child, and to ensuring all medical service and attention in case of 'sickness'. Maternity is not a disease, however, but a normal condition for women. The provision concerning women and health in Article 12 of the CEDAW is far more specific and women-centred:

1. States Parties shall take all appropriate measures to eliminate discrimination against women in the field of healthcare in order to ensure, on a basis of equality of men and women, access to healthcare services, including those related to family planning.

2. Notwithstanding the provisions of paragraph 1 of this article, States Parties shall ensure to women appropriate services in connection with pregnancy, confinement and the postnatal period, granting free services where necessary, as well as adequate nutrition during pregnancy and lactation.

While paragraph 1 focuses on formal equality in the field of healthcare, paragraph 2 addresses the need of sex-specific healthcare services in order to achieve *substantive* equality for women.

Article 14 of the CEDAW is also important, especially in light of the fact that poor women in rural areas are particularly vulnerable with regard to lack of access to healthcare services:

> States Parties shall take all appropriate measures to eliminate discrimination against women in rural areas … and, in particular, shall ensure to such women the right … [t]o have access to *adequate health care facilities*, including information, counselling and services in family planning … [t]o enjoy adequate living conditions, particularly in relation to housing, sanitation, electricity and water supply, *transport and communication*.[33]

The latter is important in light of the fact that many women die in childbirth because they lack transportation to hospital or even money to pay for such transportation (see below).

The Protocol to the African Charter on Human and People's Rights on the Rights of Women in Africa (Maputo Protocol, 2003) – of particular relevance in the African context – is the first human rights instrument that articulates women's reproductive rights as human rights, and which expressly guarantees women's right to control their fertility. Article 14 contains important provisions for women's sexual and reproductive health, including a provision on a state's duty to take appropriate measures to 'establish and strengthen existing pre-natal, delivery and post-natal health and nutritional services for women during pregnancy and while they are breastfeeding'. The Protocol also protects women's rights in relation to HIV/AIDS. The normative content of this provision is similar to what follows from the CEDAW, but is more elaborate with regard to the particular content of reproductive rights.

5.2 *The role of the monitoring human rights bodies*

In order for human rights to be effective, governments must show sufficient commitment to respect, protect, fulfil and promote them at the

[33] Para. 2(b) and (h), emphasis added.

domestic level. State accountability means that States Parties may be held legally and politically accountable for their health policies, programmes and strategies, in terms of the state report system, individual complaints procedures and political accountability at the national level (being confronted with the state obligations by NGOs, social movements and so on).

An important part of state accountability is the state duty of regular reporting to the monitoring bodies under Article 16 of the ICESCR and Article 18 of the CEDAW. The role of the international monitoring bodies is to assess the efforts of states and thereby contribute to state accountability. Of particular importance are the state reporting procedures in which states periodically submit reports to the monitoring bodies in order for these to review the situation with regard to progress and difficulties, and give recommendations for future state actions ('constructive dialogue'). Many of the countries with high maternal mortality ratios have ratified international or regional human rights instruments and have taken on responsibilities of implementing the right to health for women. Many countries have also adopted measures – both legislative and policy related – to deal with challenges related to women's health. However, it has been questioned whether the steps taken are in line with the obligations imposed by human rights conventions.[34] With regard to maternal deaths, this chapter illustrates the general observation that there is often a great disparity between states' ratification of human rights instruments and the actual implementation of the rights guaranteed. A common problem seems to be the lack of following up on state obligations and commitments at the governmental and domestic levels.[35]

In the following, I will examine key aspects of the right to health for women as this right is interpreted and elaborated by the ICESCR and the CEDAW monitoring bodies. As will be shown, both Committees provide relevant and well-informed comments and recommendations concerning the implementation of the right to health for women, including issues regarding maternal mortality. Both Committees link up and identify with the values and principles laid down in the UN International Conference on Population and Development (ICPD) in Cairo in 1994, and in the Fourth World Conference on Women in Beijing in 1995.[36]

[34] Durojaye, 'Monitoring the right to health' at 229.

[35] *Ibid.* T. Landman, 'Measuring human rights: principles, practice and policy', *Human Rights Quarterly* 26:4 (2004) 906–31 at 906–7.

[36] ICESCR Committee, General Comment No. 14 (2000), para. 2, note 3; CEDAW Committee, General Recommendation No. 24 (1999), para. 3.

The recommendations made by both Committees reflect the examination of many state reports and also the consideration of previous world conferences and programmes of action adopted by the UN. The CEDAW Committee emphasizes its collaboration with non-governmental organizations with special expertise in women's health in the preparation of the General Recommendation on health.[37]

6 Key aspects of the right to health: guidelines from the ICESCR and CEDAW Committees

The ICESCR Committee has in its General Comment No. 14 of 2000 given general and elaborate guidelines for understanding the state obligations following from Article 12. This document is the most comprehensive authoritative interpretation of the right to health at the UN level, although not formally binding.[38] As for the general content, the right to 'a system of health protection which provides equality of opportunity for people to enjoy the highest attainable level of health' and 'timely and appropriate health care' (not a right to be healthy) is emphasized by the Committee, as well as the 'underlying determinants of health' (access to safe and potable water, adequate sanitation, adequate supply of safe food, secure housing, access to health-related information, popular participation in health-related decisions).[39] The right to health is understood as: 'a right to the enjoyment of a variety of facilities, goods, services and conditions necessary for the realization of the highest attainable standard of health'.[40]

This understanding is echoed by the many specific recommendations made by the CEDAW Committee.[41] The right to health is understood by both Committees in broad terms, including medical, physical, environmental and social aspects. Of particular interest concerning the state obligations is the Available, Accessible, Acceptable Services of Good Quality (AAAQ) framework.[42]

[37] CEDAW Committee, General Recommendation No. 24, para. 3.

[38] Articles 31–33 Vienna Convention on the Law of Treaties.

[39] ICESCR Committee, General Comment No. 14, paras. 8, 11.

[40] *Ibid.* at para. 9.

[41] CEDAW Committee, General Recommendation No. 24, paras. 11, 12, 13, 14, 17, 18, 19, 21, 22, 23, 24, 25.

[42] *Ibid.* at para. 12.

6.1 *The AAAQ requirements*

Of great importance concerning maternal health, morbidity and mortality is the AAAQ framework, which is systematically developed by the ICESCR Committee in General Comment No. 14, and on which the CEDAW Committee also draws heavily.[43]

Functioning public health and healthcare facilities, goods and services, as well as underlying determinants of health, must be *available* in sufficient quantity within the State Party, especially for women. The precise nature of facilities, goods and services may vary depending on several factors, including development and resources. In many countries, good-quality reproductive and abortion services are not available at all. From the perspective of women, the requirement of *accessible* reproductive healthcare services and facilities is also urgent. Accessibility means that everyone within the jurisdiction of the State Party must have access to services and facilities. According to General Comment No. 14, paragraph 12, accessibility has four dimensions:

(1) Non-discrimination: healthcare services and facilities must be accessible for all, especially the most vulnerable or marginalized groups, *de jure* and de facto. This is a crucial point in our context: in many countries with high maternal mortality appropriate healthcare services are not accessible for socially disadvantaged women, especially poor and rural women.
(2) Physical accessibility: healthcare services and facilities must be within safe physical reach for all sections of the population, especially for vulnerable or marginalized groups. Healthcare services and underlying determinants of health must also be developed in rural areas. In regard to maternal mortality, many women do not reach maternal healthcare facilities in time due to distance and lack of transportation.
(3) Economic accessibility: services must be affordable for all. Payment for healthcare services, as well as services related to underlying determinants of health, must be based on the principle of equity, ensuring that these services (whether public or private) are affordable for all, including for socially disadvantaged groups. Equity demands that poorer households should not be disproportionately burdened with

[43] See also Cook and Undurraga, 'Article 12'.

health expenses as compared to richer households. Costs are among the main reasons why poor and disadvantaged women do not seek professional healthcare.

(4) Information accessibility: everyone has a right to seek, receive and impart information and ideas concerning health issues. A general problem in many countries is the lack of appropriate information concerning reproductive healthcare issues and rights.

The ICESCR Committee notes that States Parties are to undertake 'actions that create, maintain and restore the health of the population', and that 'public health infrastructures should provide for sexual and reproductive health services, including safe motherhood, particularly in rural areas'.[44]

The CEDAW Committee consistently emphasizes the state's obligation to ensure that policies and laws facilitate equal access to healthcare for women and girls, including sexual and reproductive health services, in a non-discriminatory and gender-sensitive manner.[45] Physical and economic access is highlighted:

> States parties should report on measures taken to eliminate barriers that women face in gaining access to health care services and what measures they have taken to ensure women timely and affordable access to such services. Barriers include requirements or conditions that prejudice women's access such as high fees for health care services, the requirement for preliminary authorization by spouse, parent or hospital authorities, distance from health facilities and absence of convenient and affordable public transport.[46]

The CEDAW Committee stresses the need for free services in order to secure access to necessary services for women, and the duty of the States Parties to ensure to women their right to safe motherhood:

> States parties should include in their reports how they supply free services where necessary to ensure safe pregnancies, childbirth and post-partum periods for women. Many women are at risk of death or disability from pregnancy-related causes because they lack the funds to obtain or access the necessary services, which include ante-natal, maternity and post-natal services. The Committee notes that it is the duty of States parties to ensure women's rights to safe motherhood and emergency obstetric services and they should allocate to these services the maximum extent of available resources.[47]

[44] ICESCR Committee, General Comment No. 14, paras. 37, 36.

[45] CEDAW Committee, General Recommendation No. 24, paras. 11, 12, 13, 14, 17, 18, 19, 21, 22, 23, 24, 25.

[46] *Ibid.* at para. 21. [47] *Ibid.* at para. 27.

According to the CEDAW Committee, studies 'which emphasize the high maternal mortality and morbidity rates worldwide and the large numbers of couples who would like to limit their family size but lack access to or do not use any form of contraception provide an important indication for States parties of possible breaches of their duties to ensure women's access to health care'.[48] The Committee requests States Parties to report on what they have done to address the magnitude of women's ill health, in particular when it arises from preventable conditions.[49] State reports should include what measures States Parties have taken to ensure women appropriate services in connection with pregnancy, confinement and the postnatal period. Information on the rates at which these measures have in fact reduced maternal mortality and morbidity in their countries, in general, and for vulnerable groups, regions and communities, in particular, should also be included.[50]

Another important element in the AAAQ scheme is the requirement for *acceptable* services of good *quality*. Acceptability implies respect for medical ethics, that services are culturally appropriate, sensitive to gender and life-cycle requirements, and that services must be designed to improve the health status of those concerned. The CEDAW Committee elaborates on these requirements with regard to women:

> States parties should also report on measures taken to ensure access to quality health care services, for example, by making them acceptable to women. Acceptable services are those which are delivered in a way that ensures that a woman gives her fully informed consent, respects her dignity, guarantees her confidentiality and is sensitive to her needs and perspectives.[51]

The guidelines provided by both Committees are highly relevant concerning maternal mortality, as many women experience disrespectful and poor-quality treatment, and therefore choose to stay away from public health facilities. When it comes to *quality*, scientifically and medically appropriate services are required, including skilled medical staff, approved drugs and hospital equipment, safe and potable water, and adequate sanitation. Lack of skilled medical attendance in emergency obstetric situations is considered one of the major reasons for the high incidence of maternal mortality.

The CEDAW Committee has raised maternal mortality as a human rights concern several times, for example with regard to Cambodia, Sierra Leone, Peru and Azerbaijan.[52] The state report submitted to the CEDAW

[48] *Ibid.* at para. 17. [49] *Ibid.* [50] *Ibid.* at para. 26.
[51] *Ibid.* at para. 22. [52] Cook and Undurraga, 'Article 12' at 316.

Committee in 2004 by Malawi, which is among the countries with highest maternal mortality in the world, illustrates many of the problems and barriers addressed by the AAAQ framework concerning physical and economic access as well as acceptable care:

> In addition to the insufficient health facilities, women in Malawi face problems to access health facilities, services, and goods. The poor access of women to health care is exacerbated by poor transport network, lack of transport money and time to travel to the health facility ... [T]he attitude of health providers is another reason for people not attending health services. Many health providers are known to be rude, harsh, and discriminatory. In some cases, women are mishandled during childbirth ... Health workers, particularly women, are overworked in health facilities. In maternity wards, patients indicated that men health workers were more caring, possibly because men are summoned only during complications and do not bear as heavy burdens as the women health workers.[53]

The Malawi state report also notes discrimination based on social status: people who are poor, especially women, are discriminated against in favour of those with higher social status including men. In most health centres women have to stand in long queues for treatment.[54] The CEDAW Committee expressed concern about the lack of access for women and girls to adequate healthcare services, particularly in rural areas, and 'is alarmed at the persistent high maternal mortality rate, particularly the number of deaths resulting from unsafe abortions, high fertility rates and inadequate family planning services, especially in rural areas, low rates of contraceptive use and lack of sex education'.[55] The Committee is also concerned that poverty and poor socio-economic conditions are among the causes of the violation of women's human rights and discrimination against women, especial in rural areas and, inter alia, with regard to access to healthcare.[56] The Committee thus:

> urges the State party to continue its efforts to improve the country's health infrastructure and to ensure sufficient budgetary allocations for accessible health services. It calls on the State party to integrate a gender perspective in all health sector reforms, while also ensuring that women's sexual

[53] Combined second, third, fourth and fifth periodic reports of Malawi, 28 June 2004, sections 12.3.3–12.3.4.

[54] *Ibid.* at sections 12.4.1–12.4.2. See also the combined initial, second, third, fourth and fifth periodic reports of Sierra Leone, 14 December 2006, section 19.2.1.

[55] *Concluding Comments of the CEDAW Committee: Malawi*, 3 February 2006, para. 31.

[56] *Ibid.* at para. 33.

> and reproductive health needs are adequately addressed. In particular, the Committee recommends that the State party undertake appropriate measures to improve women's access to health care and health-related services and information, including access for women who live in rural areas. It calls upon the State party to improve the availability of sexual and reproductive health services, including family planning information and services, as well as access to antenatal, post-natal and obstetric services to reduce maternal mortality and to achieve the Millennium Development Goal to reduce maternal mortality.[57]

The Committee did not in this communication directly address the availability of abortion services, but has since made more direct comments on the abortion issue in its communications (see below in 6.2).

The periodic report of Sierra Leone, which is another country with one of the highest maternal mortality ratios in the world, gives information on the following factors that hinder women's access to basic healthcare services and facilities: lack of recognition of the problem in time (10.5 per cent); husband, partner or relatives did not allow the woman to go to hospital (5.3 per cent); no transportation to take women to hospital (21.0 per cent); no competent staff to manage the obstetric problem (21.0 per cent); no blood available for transfusion (10.5 per cent); the women could not afford the cost of treatment (5.3 per cent).[58]

Clearly, a proper implementation of the AAAQ framework described above would contribute to a reduction of maternal mortality.[59] The CEDAW Committee recommends that Sierra Leone assess the actual causes of maternal mortality and set targets and benchmarks within a timeframe for its reduction. It urges the State Party to make every effort to raise awareness of and increase women's access to healthcare facilities and medical assistance by trained personnel, especially in rural areas and particularly in the area of postnatal care. The Committee further

[57] *Concluding Comments of the CEDAW Committee: Malawi* (Thirty-fifth session, 2006), para. 224.

[58] Report to the CEDAW Committee of November 2006 (at 66) with reference to UNICEF. These listed causes of women's lack of access to adequate healthcare services together make up the so-called 'three delays model': delay in making the decision to seek help, delay in arriving at health facilities and delay in receiving treatment. See D. Maine, *Safe Motherhood Programs: Options and Issues* (New York: Center for Population and Family Health, Columbia University, 1991); A. E. Yamin, *Deadly Delays: Maternal Mortality in Peru. A Rights-based Approach to Safe Motherhood* (Cambridge, MA: Physicians for Human Rights, 2007); P. Hunt and J. Bueno de Mesquita, *Reducing Maternal Mortality. The Contribution of the Highest Attainable Standard of Health* (Human Rights Centre, University of Essex, 2007) at 8.

[59] Hunt and Bueno de Mesquita, *Reducing Maternal Mortality.*

recommends that the State Party implements programmes and policies aimed at providing effective access to contraceptives and family planning services.[60]

6.2 *Non-discrimination and substantive equality*

The principle of non-discrimination is an important aspect of the AAAQ framework, as well as an independent human rights principle. As mentioned above, non-discrimination is essential in order to ensure access for everyone to healthcare services. Both Committees address this issue. It is interesting to note that while the text in Article 12 of the ICESCR does not mention women, the ICESCR Committee states that this provision:

> may be understood as requiring measures to improve child and maternal health, sexual and reproductive health services, including access to family planning, pre-and post-natal care, emergency obstetric services and access to information, as well as to resources necessary to act on that information.[61]

This observation is in line with the notion that non-discrimination and substantive equality require reasonable accommodation for differences – between men and women, between urban and rural women, between rich and poor women (e.g. with regard to transportation to health facilities and costs).[62] Thus, the distinct needs of women with regard to maternal healthcare and reproductive services must be taken into account when interpreting and implementing the right to health.

Furthermore, the ICESCR Committee emphasizes that in order to eliminate discrimination against women:

> there is a need to develop and implement a comprehensive national strategy for promoting women's right to health throughout their life span ... A major goal should be reducing women's health risks, particularly lowering rates of maternal mortality and protecting women from domestic violence. The realization of women's right to health requires the removal of all barriers interfering with access to health services, education and information, including in the area of sexual and reproductive health.[63]

Thus, the Committee argues for *transformative* equality in terms of a restructuring of the health service to accommodate the needs of women.

[60] CEDAW/C/SLE/C0/5 (2007), para. 35.
[61] ICESCR Committee, General Comment No. 14, para. 14.
[62] Cook and Undurraga, 'Article 12' at 325.
[63] ICESCR Committee, General Comment No. 14, para. 21.

In line with the CEDAW, this could also include dismantling demeaning stereotypes of women and groups of women in the health sector.[64] In its General Comment No. 16 of 2005,[65] addressing substantive issues arising in the implementation of the ICESCR concerning the equal rights of men and women (Article 3), the Committee gives specific examples of state obligations. With regard to the implementation of Article 3 of the ICESCR in relation to Article 12, a minimum requirement is the removal of legal and other obstacles that prevent men and women from accessing and benefiting from healthcare on a basis of equality, such as the removal of legal restrictions on reproductive health provisions and the provision of adequate training for health workers to deal with women's health issues.[66]

Likewise, the CEDAW Committee points out the obligation of states to 'eliminate discrimination against women in their access to health care services, throughout the life cycle, particularly in the areas of family planning, pregnancy, confinement and during the post-natal period'.[67] The CEDAW Committee specifies the principle of non-discrimination with regard to state obligations, being even more articulate than the ICESCR Committee about the discriminatory nature of refusing certain reproductive healthcare services urgent to women:

> Measures to eliminate discrimination against women are considered to be inappropriate if a health care system lacks services to prevent, detect and treat illnesses specific to women. It is discriminatory for a State party to refuse to legally provide for the performance of certain reproductive health services for women. For instance, if health service providers refuse to perform such services based on conscientious objection, measures should be introduced to ensure that women are referred to alternative health providers.[68]

[64] Cook and Undurraga, 'Article 12' at 325.

[65] E/C.12/2005/4, August 11, 2005.

[66] General Comment No. 16, para. 29.

[67] CEDAW Committee, General Recommendation No. 24, para. 2.

[68] *Ibid.* at para. 11. In Communication No. 17/2008, 10 August 2011, the CEDAW Committee concludes that a woman who was denied appropriate maternal care was discriminated against not only on the basis of her sex, but also on the basis of her African descent and her socio-economic background (para. 7.7). This decision and a recent decision on lack of access to therapeutic abortion is discussed by E. Kismödi, J. B. de Mesquita, X. A. Ibañez, R. Khosla and L. Sepúlveda, 'Human rights accountability for maternal death and failure to provide safe, legal abortion: the significance of two ground-breaking CEDAW decisions', *Reproductive Health Matters* 20:39 (2012) 31–9.

Although abortion is not mentioned explicitly, it is clear that women's access to safe abortion is one of the main concerns, in addition to family planning and contraception. In the recommendations for government action, the CEDAW Committee specifies that the prevention of unwanted pregnancies should be achieved through family planning and sex education, and that maternal mortality should be reduced through safe motherhood services and prenatal assistance. Abortion is also mentioned: 'When possible, legislation criminalizing abortion could be amended to remove punitive provisions imposed on women who undergo abortion.'[69] However, it is not only decriminalization of abortion that is necessary to protect the life and health of women, but also the provision of safe abortion services.[70]

The CEDAW Committee has, however, expressed a bolder attitude to the abortion issue in later communications with States Parties. In the Concluding Observations to Nepal's combined fourth and fifth state report, the Committee expressed inter alia deep concern about the persistence of an extremely high maternal mortality and morbidity rate, in particular among rural, poor and young mothers, the challenges in existing delivery services, especially emergency care, the poor nutrition and the high rate of unsafe abortion *despite the legalization of abortion* in 2002. The State Party was recommended to improve access to abortion services throughout the country.[71] Similarly, Zambia is recommended to provide women with access to good-quality services for the management of complications arising from unsafe abortions, which take place in spite of abortion laws that do not prohibit women from seeking safe abortions in health centres.[72] In another recent decision, the CEDAW Committee urges Peru to establish an appropriate legal framework that allows women to exercise their right to legalized therapeutic abortion under conditions that guarantee the necessary legal security, both for women and for health professionals.[73] As argued by Fredman, if a capabilities approach is adopted, 'it would be obvious that merely removing legal prohibitions

[69] CEDAW Committee, General Recommendation No. 24, para. 31c.

[70] The Human Rights Committee stated in Communication No. 1153/2003, 22 November 2005, that the failure of a hospital in Peru to provide a young girl with a therapeutic abortion amounted to a violation of Articles 7 and 17 of the ICCPR. See van Leeuwen in Chapter 8.

[71] CEDAW/C/NPL/CO/4–5 (2011), paras. 31–32.

[72] CEDAW/C/ZMB/CO/5–6 (2011), paras. 33–34.

[73] CEDAW Committee, Communication No. 22/2009, 25 November 2011, para. 8.17.

on abortion would not be sufficient to be sure that women are in fact in a position to choose an abortion'.[74]

6.3 *Core state obligations of immediate effect*

Article 2.1 of the ICESCR describes the nature of the general legal obligation undertaken by States Parties:

> Each State Party to the present Covenant undertakes to take steps, individually and through international assistance and co-operation ... to the maximum of its available resources, with a view to achieve progressively the full realization of the rights recognized in the present Covenant by all appropriate means, including particularly the adoption of legislative measures.

In General Comment No. 3 of 1990 on the nature of state obligations,[75] the ICESCR Committee has specified that States Parties have obligations of conduct as well as obligations of result, and that some of the obligations are of immediate effect (core obligations): the non-discrimination principle and the duty to take 'deliberate, concrete and targeted' steps 'within a reasonably short time after the Covenant's entry into force for the States concerned', towards the full realization of the right to health.[76]

The CEDAW Committee specifies in General Comment No. 28 of 2010 on the core state obligations under Article 2 of the CEDAW that the obligation to *respect* women's rights requires that States Parties refrain from making laws, policies, regulations, programmes, administrative procedures and institutional structures that directly or indirectly result in the denial of the equal enjoyment by women of their human rights.[77] Health programmes and services that systematically fail to ensure women's rights according to Article 12 of the CEDAW indicate a direct violation of women's core right to health. In a recent case, the CEDAW Committee concluded that the lack of appropriate maternal health services in Brazil, which clearly failed to meet the 'specific, distinctive health needs and interests of women', not only constituted a violation of Article 12.2 of the CEDAW, but also discrimination against women under Article 12.1 and Article 2 of the Convention. The lack of appropriate maternal health

[74] This volume, Chapter 7 (section 5.1).

[75] 14/12/1990.

[76] ICESCR Committee, General Comment No. 3, paras. 1 and 2.

[77] Para. 9.

services was considered to have 'a differential impact on the right to life of women'.[78]

Of special importance in the context of maternal mortality is the notion that 'minimum essential levels of each of the rights is incumbent upon every State party', including essential primary healthcare.[79] In General Comment No. 14 of 2000, the ICESCR Committee gives the supplementary statement that reproductive, maternal (prenatal as well as postnatal) and child healthcare 'are obligations of comparable priority' as those of essential primary healthcare.[80] The CEDAW Committee has pointed out that core obligations with regard to maternal health policies include action- and result-oriented policies that are adequately funded. The policy must ensure strong and focused bodies within the executive branch to implement such policies.[81]

Among the core obligations of each ratifying state is the duty to adopt and implement a national public health strategy and plan of action, on the basis of epidemiological evidence, 'addressing the health concerns of the whole population'.[82] The strategy and plan of action shall be devised, and periodically reviewed, on the basis of a participatory and transparent process. The ICESCR Committee specifies that the principles of *non-discrimination and participation* by individuals and groups in decision-making processes that may affect their development, must be an integral part of policies, programmes and strategies under Article 12.[83] Furthermore, the national strategy and plan of action shall include appropriate methods, 'such as right to health indicators and benchmarks, by which progress can be closely monitored'. Finally, the process by which the strategy and plan of action are devised, as well as their content, 'shall give particular attention to all vulnerable or marginalized groups'.[84]

6.4 *Appropriate indicators and benchmarks*

The ICESCR Committee underlines that in order for States Parties to live up to the Covenant, a national strategy with the formulation of policies,

[78] CEDAW/C/49/D/17/2008, 10 August 2011, para. 7.6.
[79] ICESCR Committee, General Comment No. 3, para. 10.
[80] ICESCR Committee, General Comment No. 14, para. 44.
[81] CEDAW/C/49/D/17/2008, August 2011, para. 7.6; with reference to General Recommendation No. 28, para. 28.
[82] ICESCR Committee, General Comment No. 14, para. 43(f).
[83] *Ibid.* at para. 54. [84] *Ibid.at* para. 43(f).

health indicators and benchmarks are required.[85] States Parties must identify appropriate health indicators, and then set appropriate national benchmarks in relation to each indicator.[86] During the periodic reporting procedure, the Committee will 'engage in a process of scoping with the State party', which involves 'the joint consideration by the State party and the Committee of the indicators and national benchmarks which will then provide the targets to be achieved during the next reporting period'.[87] Thus, the national benchmarks are to be developed together with the state concerned, and according to realistic goals based on the particular circumstances of each state. In the following reporting process, 'the State party and the Committee will consider whether or not the benchmarks have been achieved, and the reasons for any difficulties that may have been encountered'.[88]

The UN and WHO have specified the following reproductive health indicators in developing regions: proportion of deliveries attended by skilled health personnel; proportion of women (15–49 years) attended at least once by skilled health personnel during pregnancy; proportion of women attended four or more times during pregnancy; number of births per 1,000 women aged 15–19; proportion of women who are using any method of contraception and have an unmet need for contraception and for family planning.[89] Sub-Saharan Africa, the region with the highest MMR and among the regions with the least proportion of skilled maternal care, also has the highest birth rate among adolescents and continues to have the lowest level of contraceptive prevalence.[90]

In its Concluding Comments concerning Malawi, a poor country with high maternal mortality, the CEDAW Committee calls for appropriate measures to prevent maternal deaths:

> The Committee urges the State party to continue its efforts to improve the country's health infrastructures and to ensure budgetary allocations for accessible health services. It calls on the State party to integrate a gender perspective in all health sector reforms, while also ensuring that women's sexual and reproductive health needs are adequately addressed. In particular, the Committee recommends that the State party undertake

[85] *Ibid.* at para. 53.

[86] See J. Asher, *The Right to Health: A Resource Manual for NGOs* (Commonwealth Medical Trust, 2004) at 89–97, concerning indicators and benchmarks.

[87] ICESCR Committee, General Comment No. 14, para. 58.

[88] *Ibid.*

[89] UN, *The Millennium Development Goals Report*, 2011 at 29–33.

[90] *Ibid.*

> appropriate measures to improve women's access to health care and health-related services and information, including access for women who live in rural areas. It calls upon the State party to improve the availability of sexual and reproductive health services, including family planning information and services, as well as access to antenatal, post-natal and obstetric services to reduce maternal mortality and to achieve the Millennium Development Goal to reduce maternal mortality.[91]

It seems unrealistic that Malawi will be able to reduce the maternal mortality rate by two-thirds by 2015. However, if the country adopts appropriate and effective measures in line with the UN, WHO and CEDAW Committee recommendations, it could change the devastating situation with regard to maternal mortality. According to WHO and UN estimates, Malawi is not on track, but is making progress.[92]

When considering the periodic report of Sierra Leone, the CEDAW Committee recommends the State Party to 'step up its efforts to reduce the incidence of maternal and infant mortality rates', suggesting assessment of the actual causes of maternal mortality and setting targets and benchmarks within a timeframe for its reduction. It urges the State Party to make every effort to raise awareness of and increase women's access to healthcare facilities and medical assistance by trained personnel, especially in rural areas and particularly in the area of postnatal care.[93] WHO reports that the current progress is insufficient with regard to MDG 5, which means that the annual decline in MMR is less than 2 per cent.[94]

On a positive note, in June 2010 the Delhi High Court issued a groundbreaking decision establishing the right to maternal healthcare as a constitutionally protected right in India. This happened in response to two cases (*Laxmi Mandal* v. *Deen Dayal Harinagar Hospital*[95] and *Jaitun* v. *Maternity Home, MCD, Jangpura*[96]). Both cases were brought by the Delhi-based Human Rights Law Network (HRLN), which, together with the Center for Reproductive Rights, have striven to promote legal accountability for maternal deaths and morbidities.[97] In both cases the Delhi High Court highlights the government's failure to implement public health schemes. In the *Laxmi* case, a poor woman, Laxmi, died shortly

[91] *Concluding Comments of the CEDAW Committee: Malawi*, 3 February 2006, para. 32.

[92] WHO, *Trends in Maternal Mortality: 1990 to 2010* at 27 and 41.

[93] *Concluding Comments of the CEDAW Committee: Sierra Leone*, 11 June 2007, para.35.

[94] WHO, *Trends in Maternal Mortality: 1990 to 2010* at 27 and 43.

[95] Delhi High Court, W.P.(C) 8853/2008.

[96] Delhi High Court, W.P. No. 10700/2009.

[97] Center for Reproductive Rights, http://reproductiverights.org (last accessed 31 May 2012).

after giving birth unattended on a Delhi street. The baby barely survived. This took place despite the fact that maternal health services are supposed to be offered for free to poor women in government hospitals. The Court urged the government of Delhi to immediately create shelters to provide poor pregnant women with food and proper medical care to avoid women being compelled to give birth on the street. At a public hearing in October 2010, the Court ordered the government to establish five professionally managed shelter homes that would provide destitute, pregnant and lactating women with food and medical services twenty-four hours a day. The Delhi government resisted, responding that seven such shelters already existed; these were found not to be government-run. Emphasizing the government of India's obligation to protect the fundamental rights to life and liberty of its people under the Indian Constitution, the Court reacted, saying it cannot be a 'silent spectator … waiting for the government to move like a tortoise and allow destitute and lactating women to die on the streets of Delhi'.[98]

7 Concluding remarks

The unacceptable high maternal mortality ratio in many countries signifies that women's human dignity, basic needs and perspectives are not taken into account, and that public policies, social structures and healthcare services are discriminatory. It reflects the low status of women and provides sensitive indicators of inequality, human rights violations and the powerlessness of women.[99] Effective protection of women's lives and health requires systematic state action in order to correct the social and structural injustices that deprive women of appropriate maternal and reproductive healthcare services. As pointed out by the CEDAW Committee, state policies and executive bodies on maternal health must be targeted as well as action- and result-oriented, and must be adequately funded.[100]

Neither ambitious goals at the highest international level (MDGs) nor engendered rights embedded in treaties and human rights jurisprudence automatically translate into basic healthcare services for women on the ground. There is a huge gap between formal ratification of the ICESCR

[98] Quoted from Center for Reproductive Rights, http://reproductiverights.org (last accessed 31 May 2012).

[99] Cook *et al.*, *Reproductive Health and Human Rights* at 32–3; Alvarez *et al.*, 'Factors associated with maternal mortality in Sub-Saharan Africa'.

[100] CEDAW Committee, Communication No. 17/2008, 10 August 2011, para. 7.6.

and the CEDAW, and appropriate domestic implementation of the right to health for women. With regard to maternal deaths, the main problem is not lack of medical knowledge and international regulation, but rather lack of governmental commitment, follow-up and state accountability for making targeted steps and priorities. Regulations, policies and programmes, including the AAAQ human rights requirements, are not put in place, although they most likely would reduce the sad statistics of women's deaths, morbidity and related suffering. As for the African region, the Maputo Protocol on women's reproductive rights seems to be seriously neglected by many governments.

In general, human rights principles are believed to make a significant contribution to global social reform in several areas, including aid effectiveness in the area of health.[101] A study by Ferguson suggests that the utilization of the human rights framework can strengthen aid effectiveness and improve development outcomes in the health sector. Critical issues such as maternal mortality should, according to the author, be discussed by use of the human rights framework, including international human rights reporting mechanisms. In order to ensure equality and the prioritization of primary healthcare services, health sector budgets should make reallocations on the basis of principles of equality.[102] This is in line with the recommendations of the CEDAW Committee.

According to the South African public health physician Helen de Pinho, 'a rights-based approach does shape how governments respond to the crisis of maternal death in a manner that is fundamentally different to the efficiency-driven neo-liberal approach experienced over the past four decades'.[103] She asserts that this approach requires states to reject the notion of health and healthcare as a commodity to be bought and sold in a market. Rather, a rights-based approach to maternal health requires an acknowledgement of the power dynamics in the structuring of health outcomes (such as maternal deaths). The human rights framework holds governments accountable, exposes rights violations, and defines principles

[101] R. Bösch, 'Human rights and aid effectiveness' in A. Clapham *et al.* (eds.), *Realizing the Right to Health* (Zurich: Rüffer and Rubb, 2009) 446–61 at 459; S. E. Merry, *Human Rights and Gender Violence: Translating International Law into Local Justice* (University of Chicago Press, 2006).

[102] C. Ferguson, *Human Rights and Aid Effectiveness: Inter-linkages and Synergies to Improve Development Outcomes in the Health Sector* (Report for the Human Rights Task Team, OECD/DAC GOVNET, 2008).

[103] H. de Pinho, 'On the "rights" track: the importance of a rights-based approach to reducing maternal deaths' in A. Clapham *et al.* (eds.), *Realizing the Right to Health* 111–20 at 116.

and values for the progressive realization of the right to health. According to de Pinho, the human rights principles of equity, transparency, accountability, participation and non-discrimination provide the values against which maternal health policies should be measured. Contrary to the MDGs, which are not necessarily based on human rights principles, a rights-based approach 'promotes systemic long-term health system planning centred around a functioning health system necessary for sustained maternal mortality reduction'.[104] As pointed out by Kismödi *et al.*, international human rights mechanisms are of particular importance when 'domestic accountability is absent, inaccessible or ineffective'.[105]

The rights-based approach identifies rights-holders and duty-bearers, and make states accountable for the realization of the right to health. A rights-based approach to women's reproductive and sexual health indicates that responsibility does not only fall on individuals, but also on governments and other authorities to ensure availability, accessibility, acceptability and good quality of necessary services.[106] State accountability is an essential strategy in the attempt to reduce maternal mortality and morbidity.[107]

Proper national monitoring systems, including the provision of reliable and disaggregated data, are essential in order to make central and local governments accountable for their policies.[108] Human Rights Watch, in its report *Stop Making Excuses: Accountability for Maternal Health Care in South Africa*,[109] has documented maternity care failures that include abuse of maternity patients by health workers and substandard care, putting women and their newborns at high risk of death or injury. It examines shortcomings in the tools used by health authorities to identify and correct health system failures that contribute to poor maternal health. Other reports document similar lack of accountability for health system failures.[110] The high-level Commission on Information and Accountability

104 *Ibid.*

105 Kismödi *et al.*, 'Human rights accountability for maternal death' at 37.

106 I. Goicolea, M. S. San Sebastián and M. Wulff, 'Women's reproductive rights in the Amazon Basin of Equador: challenges for transforming policy into practice', *Health and Human Rights* 10:2 (2008) 91–103 at 91–2.

107 Kismödi *et al.*, 'Human rights accountability for maternal death' at 37.

108 Bösch, 'Human rights and aid effectiveness' at 458; Goicolea *et al.*, 'Women's reproductive rights in the Amazon Basin of Equador'.

109 Report of 8 August, 2011, available at: www.hrw.org/news/2011/08/08/south-africa-failing-maternity-care (last accessed 1 June 2012).

110 See Center for Reproductive Rights and Women Advocates Research and Documentation Centre (New York, 2008), *Broken Promises: Human Rights, Accountability, and Maternal Death in Nigeria*, and Amnesty International, *Pregnant Women*

for Women's and Children's Health has recommended that, by 2015, all countries take significant steps to establish a system for the registration of births, deaths and causes of death, and have well-functioning health information systems that combine data from facilities, administrative sources and surveys. Today, only a third of countries worldwide have complete civil registration systems with good attribution of cause of death. In order to improve the estimation of maternal mortality, it is imperative that countries take steps to strengthen their registration and information systems.[111]

Authorities need to be held accountable for targets that are realistic and achievable at the level of their responsibility.[112] Ebenezer Durojaye discusses how to measure adherence to human rights in the African context, and recommends the framework developed by an international non-governmental organization, Peoples' Health Movement (PHM) as appropriate for monitoring the right to health including sexual and reproductive rights.[113] He concludes by arguing that civil society groups and human rights institutions need to work together with African governments to ensure proper monitoring of sexual and reproductive rights at the national level. The community-based study performed by Goicolea *et al.* in the province of Orellana in Ecuador concludes that Ecuador's official data of accessibility to pregnancy-related services for women do not accurately represent isolated areas, and that the use of national-level data for monitoring access 'prevents the disclosure of inequalities'.[114] The study indicates that local initiatives for data collection are feasible and may yield information that is more suitable for monitoring and designing interventions. The study also identifies a significant gap between national policies and the reality for women respectively, explained by reference to the lack of targets and inadequate discussions of resources and responsibilities for involved parties. The authors conclude that accountability for sexual and reproductive health and rights in isolated, impoverished areas such as Orellana depends on 'meaningful, accurate, and disaggregated information, and the development of mechanisms to ensure that citizens

in Burkina Faso Dying Because of Discrimination, Report 27 January 2010, available at: www.amnesty.org/en/news-and-updates/report/ (last accessed 1 June 2012).

111 WHO, *Trends in Maternal Mortality: 1990 to 2010* at 1.

112 M. Langford, 'A poverty of rights: six ways to fix the MDGs', *IDS Bulletin* 41:1 (2010) 83–91 at 89.

113 Durojaye, 'Monitoring the right to health'.

114 Goicolea *et al.*, 'Women's reproductive rights in the Amazon Basin of Equador' at 99.

(especially those most vulnerable) can demand that their governments honor stated commitments'.[115] These observations support the CEDAW Committee's recommendations of assessment of actual causes of maternal mortality and give particular attention to rural areas.

Recent research suggests that international treaties 'can play an important role in changing rights outcomes when they impact domestic politics in certain ways'.[116] In fact, an important aspect of the human rights framework is to ensure and stimulate domestic and local participation as well as political and civil society mobilization.[117] In addition, in order for human rights to be effective, they need to be translated into local terms and situated within local contexts of power and meaning. As Sally E. Merry puts it: 'If human rights ideas are to have an impact, they need to become part of the consciousness of ordinary people around the world.'[118] The idea of women's rights to adequate maternal healthcare needs to be part of the general consciousness of women and men, healthcare providers, local governments and health ministries (see Article 5 of the CEDAW).

The recent court cases in India are promising with regard to transformative and substantive equality in the field of maternity protection, as they might have the effect that women's situations and right to necessary healthcare services become part of the public awareness and demands in India. Examining processes of local 'framing' and implementation of global human rights standards is crucial in order to understand the way human rights work in different contexts,[119] and also with regard to women's right to health: how are women's needs and access to maternal healthcare services assessed, understood and handled in different settings, which barriers exist, and how could these barriers most effectively be modified or eliminated in various contexts? Human rights frequently stress *individual* needs, but the health-seeking actions of pregnant women must be understood within the context of their families, communities and society at large, and with regard to the way healthcare services are commonly operated, perceived and evaluated at the local level. Concerning

[115] *Ibid.*

[116] B. Simmons, *Mobilizing for Human Rights: International Law in Domestic Politics* (Cambridge University Press, 2009) at 203.

[117] A. E. Yamin, 'Suffering and powerlessness: the significance of promoting participation in rights-based approaches to health', *Health and Human Rights* 11:1 (2009) 5–22. See also Byrnes, Chapter 1 (section 3) in this volume.

[118] Merry, *Human Rights and Gender Violence* at 3.

[119] *Ibid.* at 1.

public infrastructure, the lack of publicly accessible and good-quality reproductive services for all women, including abortion services, as well as multiple discrimination and economic constraints, are important barriers that States Parties must address properly in order to respect, protect and fulfil women's right to life and health.

PART III

The CEDAW in national law

11

The implementation of the CEDAW in Australia: success, trials, tribulations and continuing struggle

ANDREW BYRNES

1 Introduction

Australia signed the Convention on the Elimination of All Forms of Discrimination against Women (CEDAW) on 17 July 1980 at the mid-decade conference of the United Nations Decade for Women (1976–1985) in Copenhagen, and deposited its instrument of ratification on 28 July 1983; the Convention thus entered into force for Australia on 27 August 1983. Australia acceded to the Optional Protocol to the Convention on 4 December 2008,[1] which entered into force for it three months later.

When it ratified the Convention, the Australian government deposited a declaration describing the country's federal system of government and the division of responsibilities between the Commonwealth and the eight State and Territory governments and stating that the Convention would be implemented in accordance with that federal structure. It also entered two reservations to Article 11 – one relating to the obligation to ensure that paid maternity leave was available throughout the workforce, the other excluding the operation of the Convention in relation to the performance by women in the defence forces of combat-related or combat duties.[2] In

[1] See *Multilateral Treaties Deposited with the Secretary-General*, Chapter IV.8. Australia accepted the Amendment to Article 20, paragraph 1 of the Convention on the Elimination of All Forms of Discrimination against Women, CEDAW/SP/1995/2, on 4 June 1998, although that Amendment has not yet received a sufficient number of ratifications to enter into force.

[2] The reservations are reproduced at Annex A. The government has stated that its aim in relation to reservations is 'to: limit the extent of any reservations to CEDAW; formulate any such reservations as narrowly and precisely as possible; and if appropriate regularly review reservations with a view to withdrawing them'. *Combined Fourth and Fifth Periodic Reports of Australia*, CEDAW/C/AUL/4-5 (2004), para. 18.

2000 it modified the combat duty reservation (limiting it to combat duty only). Since that time the reservations have not been further modified or removed.[3]

Since it became a party to the treaty, the Australian government has submitted a number of reports to the CEDAW Committee – not always on time and on a number of occasions submitting combined reports (the CEDAW Committee having permitted States to combine overdue and due reports in the one document). The government's most recent report under the Convention (its combined sixth and seventh reports) was submitted in 2009,[4] and the Committee reviewed that report at its 46th session in July 2010.[5]

A number of features stand out over the last thirty or so years in terms of the advancement of the human rights of women in Australia, so far as the Convention is concerned. At least five factors may be identified that have been important to the question of ratification and implementation of the Convention:

- the strong women's movement that (re-)emerged in the 1960s, which has consistently pushed for the improvement of laws and policies relating to or with an impact on women and which on many occasions has pushed for the better implementation of the CEDAW Convention;
- the support within government of key political representatives who have been committed to pursuing sexual equality or who have been put in a position in which it was politically difficult to show anything other than support for this goal;
- the presence of feminist civil servants (femocrats)[6] in the bureaucracy and the development of structures (national machinery) to ensure that the voice of the women's office was heard;

[3] In its July 2010 *Concluding Observations on the Combined Sixth and Seventh Reports of Australia*, the CEDAW Committee noted that 'notwithstanding recent developments with regard to women in the armed forces and the adoption of the Paid Parental Leave Act, the State party has not yet withdrawn its two reservations under the Convention' and recommended that it do so 'as soon as possible': CEDAW/C/AUL/CO/7, paras. 18–19 (2010). Given the adoption of a new maternity leave scheme in early 2011, it seems likely that the maternity leave reservation will be lifted in the near future.

[4] *Combined Sixth and Seventh Periodic Reports of Australia*, CEDAW/C/AUL/7 (2009).

[5] See CEDAW/C/SR.935 and 936 (2010) and *Concluding Observations on Australia*, CEDAW/C/AUL/CO/7 (2010).

[6] See M. Sawer, *Femocrats and Ecorats: Women's Policy Machinery in Australia, Canada and New Zealand*, UNRISD, Occasional Paper 6, March 1996, 4–10; L. Chappell, *Gendering Government: Feminist Engagement With the State in Australia and Canada* (Vancouver: UBC Press, 2003).

- the work of the Australian Human Rights Commission and the federal Sex Discrimination Commissioners (as well as their State and Territory counterparts); and
- the use of international reporting procedures, including reporting to the CEDAW Committee, as part of the process of attracting international attention and pressure to the need for change and of adding momentum to domestic efforts to bring about change.

2 Constitutional structure and the place of international law in Australian law

2.1 *The federal system, the powers of the Commonwealth and human rights protection*

Australia is a federal State, comprising the Commonwealth, six States, two mainland Territories (the Australian Capital Territory and the Northern Territory), and a number of external Territories. The Commonwealth Constitution establishes the Commonwealth legislature, executive and judiciary, and provides for the distribution of powers among the Commonwealth and States. The legislative power of the Commonwealth extends to those matters that are specifically listed in the Constitution (in particular in section 51), as well as to other matters incidental to the existence of a national government: a Commonwealth law will only be valid if it is referable to a head of power in the Constitution. The States enjoy legislative power to make laws for the peace, order and good government of their territory (subject to a number of express limitations in the Constitution), and thus share a parallel legislative jurisdiction on many matters within Commonwealth legislative power. A valid Commonwealth law will prevail over an inconsistent law of a State (Constitution, section 109) or Territory. Since Federation (the establishment of the Commonwealth and the States in 1901), there has been a steady accretion of legislative, executive and financial power to the central government.[7]

The Commonwealth Constitution does not contain a comprehensive bill of rights. There are a few rights contained in the text of the Constitution (some of which are either spent, or have been interpreted to be almost meaningless), and the High Court has discovered a number of implied rights, including an implied right of freedom of political

[7] All Australian legislation referred to in this chapter can be found at www.austlii.edu.au.

communication. There is no general constitutional guarantee of equality, or of sex or gender equality, in the Constitution. At the federal level, there is no comprehensive legislative bill of rights; the only bills of rights of reasonably broad coverage (though limited to civil and political rights) are the Human Rights Act 2004 of the Australian Capital Territory and the Victorian Charter of Human Rights and Responsibilities 2006, both ordinary statutes of the legislatures of those jurisdictions. Section 128 of the Commonwealth Constitution provides a procedure for amendment of the document that requires any proposed change to be approved both by a majority of States *and* a majority of voters overall. This makes constitutional change difficult to achieve – generally bipartisan political support from the two major political parties, as well as support from the States is required.[8] A number of efforts to amend the Constitution to add rights protections have been unsuccessful.[9]

An extensive national consultation was held in 2009 on improving human rights protection in Australia. The Report of the National Human Rights Consultation Committee recommended the adoption of a legislative bill of rights (among other measures), an issue on which there has been considerable debate in recent years.[10] In its response to that Report, the Australian government proposed the introduction of the *Australian Human Rights Framework*. While it did not accept the Committee's recommendation supporting the introduction of a statutory charter of rights, the government did take up the Committee's recommendations in relation to the need for enhanced Parliamentary scrutiny of human rights issues.[11] It proposed the establishment of a new Joint Parliamentary Committee on Human Rights, the functions of which would include scrutinising all draft legislation for consistency with human rights standards. These standards were to include the principal UN human rights treaties to which Australia is party, including the CEDAW.[12]

[8] See generally G. Williams and D. Hume, *People Power: The History and the Future of the Referendum in Australia* (Sydney: UNSW Press, 2010).

[9] See A. Byrnes, H. Charlesworth and G. McKinnon, *Bills of Rights in Australia – History, Politics and Law* (Sydney: UNSW Press, 2009) Chapter 2.

[10] *Report of the National Human Rights Consultation Committee*, September 2009.

[11] See generally E. Santow, 'The Act that dares not speak its name: the National Human Rights Consultation Report's parallel roads to human rights reform', *University of New South Wales Law Journal* 33:1 (2010) 8–33, and A. Byrnes, 'Second-class rights yet again? Economic, social and cultural rights in the Report of the National Human Rights Consultation', *University of New South Wales Law Journal* 33:1 (2010) 193–238.

[12] Australian Government, *Australia's Human Rights Framework* (2010).

The legislation to establish this new body was introduced into Parliament in 2010,[13] and was referred to a Senate Committee. The report of that Committee, which by majority supported the Bill, endorsed the use of the United Nations (UN) human rights treaties as appropriate standards, but also recommended that the mandate of the proposed Joint Committee be expanded so that it 'would also have the ability to examine issues raised in the findings of UN treaty bodies (such as concluding observations) ... if considered appropriate'.[14] At Australia's appearance before the UN Human Rights Council as part of the Universal Periodic Review procedure, the government representative undertook to lay treaty body Concluding Observations before the Parliament as a matter of course.[15] The new Parliamentary Joint Committee on Human Rights was established in March 2012, but as of the time of writing had not addressed this issue.[16]

2.2 *Treaty-making and treaty implementation*

Under the Australian Constitution, the executive power of the Commonwealth includes the power to enter into treaties at the international level. As a matter of practice, the Commonwealth generally consults with the States and Territories in the process of treaty negotiation or in the lead-up to ratification, especially where the subject matter of the treaty falls within areas historically regulated by the States. Since the mid 1990s there has also been a procedure for having proposed treaty actions considered by the Parliament, in the form of the tabling of most proposed treaty actions before the Commonwealth Parliamentary Joint Standing Committee on Treaties (JSCOT), which reports to the government on its view of whether ratification is appropriate.[17]

[13] Human Rights (Parliamentary Scrutiny) Bill 2010.

[14] Senate Legal and Constitutional Affairs Legislation Committee, *Report on the Human Rights (Parliamentary Scrutiny) Bill 2010 [Provisions] and Human Rights (Parliamentary Scrutiny) (Consequential Provisions) Bill 2010 [Provisions]*, January 2011, para. 3.116.

[15] Opening and closing remarks at the United Nations Human Rights Council for the Universal Periodic Review – Parliamentary Secretary to the Prime Minister, Senator Hon. Kate Lundy, 28 January 2011, available at: www.geneva.mission.gov.au/gene/Statement158.html (last accessed 13 February 2013).

[16] See www.aph.gov.au/Parliamentary_Business/Committees/Senate_Committees?url=humanrights_ctte/ctte_info/index.htm (last accessed 13 February 2013).

[17] See www.aph.gov.au/Parliamentary_Business/Committees/House_of_Representatives_Committees?url=jsct/index.htm (last accessed 13 February 2013). On the origins and operation of the JSCOT, see H. Charlesworth, M. Chiam, D. Hovell and G. Williams,

So far as the implementation of treaties is concerned, both the Commonwealth and the States/Territories may have a legislative role, depending on the subject matter of the treaty concerned and the specific obligations assumed under it, and any political agreement (or lack thereof) as to the division of responsibility between the Commonwealth and States/Territories in relation to implementation. In some cases a treaty will be implemented only by Commonwealth legislation and other action; in other cases a combination of Commonwealth and State action will be involved.

These constitutional arrangements are reflected in the *Declaration* Australia made when it ratified the CEDAW:

> Australia has a Federal Constitutional System in which Legislative, Executive and Judicial Powers are shared or distributed between the Commonwealth and the Constituent States. The implementation of the Treaty throughout Australia will be effected by the Commonwealth State and Territory Authorities having regard to their respective constitutional powers and arrangements concerning their exercise.

In enacting Commonwealth legislation to implement a treaty, the Commonwealth Parliament may draw on any of the legislative powers it enjoys, for example its power to legislate with respect to corporations, interstate trade and commerce, or banking and insurance, among others. Of particular importance since the early 1970s has been the power of the Commonwealth Parliament to legislate 'with respect to … external affairs'.[18] This provision empowers the Commonwealth to legislate to implement a treaty, even if there is no other relevant source of legislative power. If a law relies for its validity on the fact that it is a treaty-implementation measure under section 51(xxix), then it 'must be reasonably capable of being considered appropriate and adapted to implementing the treaty'. In other words, it must be consistent with the obligations contained in the treaty, and there is a test of proportionality that leaves the legislature some discretion in how it implements the treaty. At the time of Australia's ratification of the CEDAW in 1983, the extent of this power was still in the process of being resolved by the High Court of Australia (the apex constitutional and appellate court).

As a result of the uncertainty about and limited nature of the Commonwealth's legislative power in relation to some treaties,

No Country is an Island: Australia and International Law (Sydney: UNSW Press, 2006) 40–8.

[18] Constitution, section 51(xxix).

implementing statutes will often draw on a number of legislative heads of power, producing an intricately drafted statute that operates in a complex manner. The major piece of Commonwealth legislation implementing the Convention, the Sex Discrimination Act 1984 (Cth), is an example of this and is discussed below.

2.3 International law in the Australian legal system

Under the Australian legal system the rules governing the reception of international law are similar to those that apply in most countries with a common law heritage. In relation to customary international law, the system has a monist flavour, these rules being said to be a source of the common law (though perhaps not 'part of the common law').[19] However, customary international law has been of little practical relevance in relation to gender equality issues under Australian law.

So far as the reception of treaties is concerned, however, the system is dualist – the provisions of a treaty cannot be directly relied on to found a claim under domestic law, unless there is some implementing Act by the legislature or, in certain cases, by the executive government.[20]

This is not to say that an unincorporated treaty can have no impact under domestic law. It can, for example, create a legitimate expectation that a decision-maker will act in accordance with the provisions of the treaty or amount to a relevant consideration that a decision-maker should take into account – and a failure to do either provides grounds for judicial review of the decision under general administrative law principles. Equally, when it comes to the interpretation of statutes, the general rule is that it should be assumed that the legislature (whether Commonwealth or State/Territory) did not intend to legislate in contravention of obligations binding on Australia, and that ambiguous statutes should be read consistently with international obligations where that is reasonably possible. International law obligations have also been accepted as a relevant source for the determination of public policy, or for the development of the common law where that is unclear.[21]

[19] G. Triggs, *International Law: Contemporary Principles and Practices*, 2nd edition (Sydney: LexisNexis Butterworths, 2011) 189–93. See generally Charlesworth *et al.*, *No Country is an Island*, Chapter 2.

[20] Triggs, *International Law* at 178–9.

[21] See Triggs, *International Law* at 180–1; *Royal Women's Hospital* v. *Medical Practitioners Board of Victoria* [2006] VSCA 85, paras. 74–80 (Maxwell P). The Australian cases referred to in this chapter can be found at www.austlii.edu.au.

The upshot is nonetheless that the most effective way of ensuring that treaty obligations, such as those contained in the CEDAW, give rise to directly invocable rights and obligations under Australian law is to implement the treaty by legislation. It is relatively rare for a common-law jurisdiction such as Australia to directly enact the provisions of a human rights treaty as part of domestic law; the more usual practice is to select a number of provisions and either reproduce the treaty language or translate those provisions into the language of domestic law.[22] As will be seen below, it is this last approach that has been taken in relation to legislative implementation of the CEDAW.

3 The background to the ratification of the Convention and its implementation

The ratification of the Convention by Australia and the enactment of the primary implementing legislation at the Commonwealth level,[23] as well as other implementing measures, were controversial and formed a part of the struggle for women's equality that first (re)gathered momentum in the late 1960s and early 1970s and beyond.[24] As Marian Sawer points out,[25] although Australian women achieved some political rights fairly early – in particular the right to vote in the late nineteenth and early twentieth centuries – other efforts to gain constitutional or other recognition of equality and to be free from discrimination on the basis of sex, marital status or pregnancy were long in coming. For example, the marriage bar for women employed in the Commonwealth public service – which

[22] A statute might also provide that a treaty should be taken into account in the exercise of judicial or administrative powers conferred by it or that it is intended to 'give effect' to a treaty, without making the provisions of the treaty directly justiciable. See, for example, the Fair Work Act 2009 (Cth), section 772, which provides that the object of Division 2 of Part 6–4 of the Act (dealing with unlawful grounds for the termination of employment) is to give (further) effect to a number of Conventions, including ILO Conventions Nos. 111 and 156 (though no mention is made of the CEDAW).

[23] This account draws heavily on M. Sawer, *The Commonwealth Sex Discrimination Act: Aspirations and Apprehensions* Forum to mark the 20th Anniversary of the Sex Discrimination Act, The Darlington Centre, University of Sydney, 3 August 2004, and M. Sawer, 'Women's work is never done: the pursuit of equality and the Commonwealth Sex Discrimination Act' in M. Thornton (ed.), *Sex Discrimination in Uncertain Times* (Canberra: ANU E Press, 2010) 75–92 at 75.

[24] There is of course a long history of women's activism for equality in Australia: see Sawer, 'Women's work is never done' at 75–6.

[25] See Sawer, *The Commonwealth Sex Discrimination Act*.

required women to resign from their jobs upon marriage – was abolished only in 1966.

While the struggle for women's rights continued during the first sixty years of the twentieth century, it gained considerable social and political momentum in Australia in the late 1960s, with the rise of the organised women's movement (though this was confronted by a similarly well-organised opposition at various stages). The women's movement over the forty years since then has pursued the goal of equality in many fora and in many different ways, the choice and effectiveness of means depending at least in part on the receptiveness of the Commonwealth and State governments of the day to arguments for more effective legislative and policy measures to address discrimination.

Although it would oversimplify the political history to suggest that, since the Second World War, conservative governments (comprising coalitions of the Liberal Party and Country/National Party) at the Commonwealth level have been largely resistant to demands for action in relation to women's equality and that Labor governments have always been responsive,[26] many of the significant legislative and other advances have come during periods of Labor government. The federal governments since 1972 have been:

1972–1975	Whitlam Labor government (first Labor government since 1949, ending twenty-three years of continuous conservative government)
1975–1983	Fraser Liberal–Country coalition government
1983–1996	Hawke–Keating Labor government
1996–2007	Howard Liberal–National coalition government
2007–2010	Rudd Labor government
2010–	Gillard Labor government.

The Whitlam Labor government that came to power in 1972 had an ambitious reform agenda that included a range of proposed human rights reforms (in which Lionel Murphy, Attorney-General for two of the three years of the Labor government, was a prime mover).[27] The Whitlam government reopened the federal equal pay case immediately when it came to

[26] See J. Ramsay, 'The making of domestic violence policy by the Australian Commonwealth Government and the Government of the State of New South Wales between 1970 and 1985: an analytical narrative of feminist policy activism', PhD thesis, University of Sydney, 2004, Chapter 4.

[27] See Sawer, *The Commonwealth Sex Discrimination Act*, and M. Thornton and T. Luker, 'The Sex Discrimination Act and its rocky rite of passage' in M. Thornton (ed.), *Sex Discrimination in Uncertain Times* 25–45.

office, and ratified International Labour Organization (ILO) Convention No. 111 in 1974. It also ratified the International Convention on the Elimination of All Forms of Racial Discrimination in 1975, and enacted implementing legislation in the form of the Racial Discrimination Act 1975 (Cth), the statute that was to successfully test the boundaries of the Commonwealth's power to implement human rights treaties under the external affairs power.[28] It also drafted a legislative bill of rights that came to naught, though it did not accede to lobbying to include sex discrimination in either of these pieces of legislation. Towards the end of its period of office, urged on by women's groups such as the Women's Electoral Lobby (WEL),[29] it began to focus on the possible enactment of legislation to prohibit discrimination based on sex or marital status, but because of the political turmoil that resulted in the dismissal of the government in November 1975, the proposed legislation was not enacted.[30]

There was some interest in sex discrimination legislation in the Fraser government that came to power at the end of 1975 – in particular on the part of the Minister with Responsibility for Women's Affairs, Robert Ellicott, who was supportive of the adoption of sex discrimination legislation, a goal also supported by leading Liberal women within the Parliamentary party and outside it.[31] However, there was opposition both within the Cabinet and in the broader Liberal constituency, perhaps the most high profile of which was the group called Women Who Want to be Women (WWWW).[32] Notwithstanding the failure by the coalition government to adopt a draft Plan of Action for the UN Decade for Women that contained a commitment to sex discrimination legislation, Australia did sign the Convention at the mid-decade conference in Copenhagen in July 1980. However, ratification did not occur under the Fraser government.

Nonetheless, during this period there were developments on the opposition side of the Parliament that laid the groundwork for the eventual enactment of sex discrimination legislation. In 1981 Labor Senator Susan Ryan, the Shadow Minister for Media, the Arts and Women's Affairs,

[28] *Koowarta* v. *Bjelke-Petersen* [1982] HCA 27; (1982) 153 CLR 168 (upholding the Racial Discrimination Act 1975 as a valid exercise of the external affairs power).

[29] See M. Sawer, *Making Women Count: A History of the Women's Electoral Lobby in Australia* (Sydney: UNSW Press, 2008).

[30] Sawer, 'Women's work is never done' at 79.

[31] *Ibid.* and Thornton and Luker, 'The Sex Discrimination Act' at 28.

[32] Developments had been proceeding at State level, with South Australia (1975), New South Wales (1977) and Victoria (1977) all enacting anti-discrimination/equal opportunity legislation that prohibited discrimination on the basis of sex and marital status (among other grounds).

introduced the Sex Discrimination Bill 1981 into the Senate as a private member's bill.[33] This Bill contained not only non-discrimination provisions, but also affirmative action provisions, and was the precursor to the two pieces of legislation that were ultimately enacted after Labor returned to government in 1983: the Sex Discrimination Act 1984 (Cth) and the Affirmative Action (Equal Opportunity for Women) Act 1986 (Cth). However, Ryan's Bill was not passed by the Parliament.

When Labor was elected to government in 1983, Ryan, now a government Minister (Minister assisting the Prime Minister on the Status of Women), introduced the Sex Discrimination Bill 1983, which contained anti-discrimination provisions but which had had its affirmative action provisions removed. A vigorous and at times bizarre debate over the Bill ensued within and outside Parliament, with some critics arguing that the legislation would destroy the traditional family, produce a 'unisex' society and was a stalking-horse for communism, and making other dire predictions about the likely destructive impact of the Bill on Australian society.[34] After vigorous advocacy and lobbying on both sides of the issue (and with support from some members of the Opposition Liberal Party in the Parliament), the Parliament enacted a much-amended Bill as the Sex Discrimination Act 1984. The Act commenced operation on 1 August 1984. Just over two years later, the Parliament passed the Affirmative Action (Equal Opportunities in Employment) Act 1986, which, despite its title, does not embody obligations to undertake positive action ('reverse discrimination'), but rather established a scheme that required corporations with more than 100 employees to prepare programmes and to report on the steps they have taken to advance equal opportunity for women in the workplace. The Act, which was amended and renamed in 1999,[35] has received mixed reviews so far as its contribution to real change in the workplace is concerned,[36] and since 2009 has been the subject of review

[33] Senate Hansard, Thursday, 26 November 1981, at 2714.

[34] See S. Magarey, 'The Sex Discrimination Act 1984', *Australian Feminist Law Journal* 20 (2004) 127–34; S. Ryan, 'The "Ryan Juggernaut" rolls on', *University of New South Wales Law Journal* 27:3 (2004) 828–32; Thornton and Luker, 'The Sex Discrimination Act'; S. Ryan, 'Opening Address II' in Thornton (ed.), *Sex Discrimination in Uncertain Times* at 11; and S. Magarey, '"To demand equality is to lack ambition": sex discrimination legislation – contexts and contradictions' in Thornton (ed.), *Sex Discrimination in Uncertain Times* 93–106 at 94–6.

[35] The 1986 Act was amended and renamed the Equal Opportunity for Women in the Workplace Amendment Act 1999 (Cth).

[36] See S. Charlesworth, 'The Sex Discrimination Act: advancing gender equality and decent work?' in Thornton (ed.), *Sex Discrimination in Uncertain Times* 133–52 at 136–7; G. Strachan and J. Burgess, 'W(h)ither affirmative action legislation in Australia?', *Journal*

with the goal of improving its effectiveness.[37] Amending legislation was introduced into the Parliament in March 2012.[38]

Of course, the Sex Discrimination Act (SDA) 1984 is not the only legislation implementing the provisions of the Convention: other Commonwealth statutes and the State anti-discrimination legislation,[39] as well as industrial relations laws,[40] do so as well. Even so, neither the Act nor other legislation fully gives effect to all the provisions of the Convention, even those that require merely legislative implementation, such as the inclusion of a general guarantee of equality and non-discrimination in the Constitution or other appropriate legislation.[41] The legislation has also been accompanied by an array of policies and programmes at federal and State level over the years that give effect to various provisions of the Convention (whether

of Interdisciplinary Gender Studies 5:2 (2002) 46–63; G. Strachan, J. Burgess and L. Henderson, 'Equal employment opportunity legislation and policies: the Australian experience', *Equal Opportunities International* 26:6 (2007) 525–40; E. French and G. Strachan, 'Equal opportunity outcomes for women in the finance industry in Australia: merit of EEO plans', *Asia Pacific Journal of Human Resources* 45:3 (2007) 314–32; S. Charlesworth, Submission to the Review of the Equal Opportunity for Women in the Workplace Act (EOWWA) and Agency, 30 October 2009, available at: http://web.archive.org/web/20120411060734/http://mams.rmit.edu.au/isc7fenuga7s1.pdf (last accessed 22 February 2013); and R. Graycar and J. Morgan, 'Equality unmodified?' in Thornton (ed.), *Sex Discrimination in Uncertain Times* 175–96 at 183–6.

[37] See KPMG and Office for Women, Department of Families, Housing, Community Services and Indigenous Affairs, *Review of the Equal Opportunity for Women in the Workplace Act 1999, Consultation Report* (2010) 124–8. In January 2011 the government announced that as part of improving the operation of the Act, it was working with KPMG 'to identify meaningful measures of gender equality in the workplace as well as processes which ease the reporting burden on business', but no timetable or further details were provided. 'Taking action to achieve better gender balance at work', Press release by the Minister for the Status of Women, Kate Ellis, 30 January 2011.

[38] Equal Opportunity for Women in the Workplace Amendment Bill 2012. See Senate Education, Employment and Workplace Relations Committee, *Equal Opportunity for Women in the Workplace Amendment Bill 2012 [Provisions] Report*, May 2012.

[39] Of particular importance are the Anti-Discrimination Act 1977 (NSW); the Anti-Discrimination Act 1991 (Qld); the Equal Opportunity Act 1994 (SA); the Anti-Discrimination Act 1998 (Tas); the Equal Opportunity Act 1995 (Vic); the Equal Opportunity Act 1984 (WA); the Human Rights Act 2004 (ACT); the Anti-Discrimination Act 1992 (NT); the Human Rights Act 2004 (ACT); and the Charter of Human Rights and Responsibilities Act 2006 (Vic).

[40] See Charlesworth, 'The Sex Discrimination Act' at 137–9.

[41] See E. Evatt, 'Falling short on women's rights: mis-matches between SDA and the international regime' in M. Smith (ed.), *Human Rights 2004: The Year in Review*, Castan Centre for Human Rights Law, Monash University, 2005, available at: www.law.monash.edu.au/castancentre/events/2004/evatt-paper1.pdf (last accessed 13 February 2013); and H. Charlesworth and S. Charlesworth, 'The Sex Discrimination Act and international law', *University of New South Wales Law Journal* 27:3 (2004) 858–65.

or not the Convention was explicitly in the minds of the planners). Yet in many ways the battles over the enactment of the Sex Discrimination Act 1984 and over subsequent efforts to improve it or undermine it, have typified the struggle and the objections to equality measures that have had to be overcome in many areas. The Act is viewed by many – with perhaps an excessively optimistic view of the power of law – as a central component of the efforts to address sex discrimination and gender inequality. The willingness of governments to strengthen the SDA and its enforcement mechanisms, or conversely, their preparedness to limit or undermine its effectiveness, have been seen as a touchstone of their commitment to gender equality. The next section gives an overview of the SDA and of its limitations, and the most recent review of its operation.

4 The Sex Discrimination Act 1984 (Cth)

The Sex Discrimination Act[42] had a number of purposes.[43] While motivated primarily by a desire to address discrimination against women and to give effect to the provisions of the CEDAW, it goes beyond this and in effect prohibits discrimination on the ground of sex and marital status against both women and men in many of the areas it covers. To the extent that there was clear Commonwealth power to legislate – for example, in relation to the Territories or to Commonwealth employment – the Act made unlawful all forms of sex discrimination (including pregnancy discrimination), as well as discrimination on the grounds of marital status – both women and men are covered (other than in relation to pregnancy). Discrimination on the ground of family responsibilities was added

[42] See Australian Human Rights Commission, *Short Timeline of the Sex Discrimination Act* (2009), available at: http://humanrights.gov.au/sex_discrimination/sda_25/index.html (last accessed 22 February 2013).

[43] Section 3 of the Act sets out its (current) objects.

The objects of this Act are:

(a) to give effect to certain provisions of the Convention on the Elimination of All Forms of Discrimination against Women; and

(b) to eliminate, so far as is possible, discrimination against persons on the ground of sex, marital status, pregnancy or potential pregnancy in the areas of work, accommodation, education, the provision of goods, facilities and services, the disposal of land, the activities of clubs and the administration of Commonwealth laws and programmes; and

(ba) to eliminate, so far as possible, discrimination involving dismissal of employees on the ground of family responsibilities; and

(c) to eliminate, so far as is possible, discrimination involving sexual harassment in the workplace, in educational institutions and in other areas of public activity; and

(d) to promote recognition and acceptance within the community of the principle of the equality of men and women.

subsequently in reliance on other treaties, as was the ground of potential pregnancy.[44] While sexual harassment is also covered by the protection against discrimination on the ground of sex, the point was put beyond doubt by the inclusion of new sections that made sexual harassment in a range of areas covered by the Act explicitly unlawful.

The Act reaches beyond those areas clearly within other heads of Commonwealth power by relying on the CEDAW, and provides that, in other areas not clearly within Commonwealth legislative competence, the Act applies only to discrimination against women, as legislation giving effect to the Convention.[45] The critical point is that the Act would not have had as broad an application as it did when first enacted if it had not been possible to rely on the Convention as a basis of legislative power. By the end of 2010 the Act had acquired a rather unwieldy and awkward accretion of technical and substantive changes that are the result of political opportunities that presented themselves to improve or expand the Act. Given that the Act coexists at the federal level with a number of other discrimination statutes (disability, age and race discrimination legislation), there is much to be said in favour of the government proposals to rationalise the existing legislation by enacting an equality Act, though concerns have been expressed that symmetrical gender equality legislation may serve to obscure the particular prevalence of discrimination against women.[46]

The Sex Discrimination Act follows the structure of legislation that was in force in a number of States at the time of its enactment. The Act is not a general sex or gender equality statute that states a general principle of equality applicable to all areas of life. Rather it makes unlawful particular discriminatory acts in certain areas, such as employment, education, the provision of goods and services, and the administration of Commonwealth laws and programmes. An unlawful act is a civil wrong. The Act defines two forms of discrimination, direct and indirect discrimination, which are defined in rather complex terms (especially the latter); the Act does

[44] Sex Discrimination Act 1984, section 10A (referring to the ICCPR, ICESCR, Convention on the Rights of the Child and ILO Convention (No. 111) concerning Discrimination in respect of Employment and Occupation 1958). Australia has since also ratified ILO Convention No. 156.

[45] Section 9(10) provides: 'If the Convention is in force in relation to Australia, the prescribed provisions of Part II, and the prescribed provisions of Division 3 of Part II, have effect in relation to discrimination against women, to the extent that the provisions give effect to the Convention.'

[46] Graycar and Morgan, 'Equality unmodified?' at 179–87; S. Rice, 'And which "Equality Act" would that be?' in Thornton (ed.), *Sex Discrimination in Uncertain Times* 197–234.

not import the definition of 'discrimination against women' contained in Article 1 of the CEDAW.[47] It provides that special measures to redress disadvantage are not to be considered discriminatory for the purposes of the Act (tracking Article 4 of the CEDAW); it also has many general and specific exemptions.[48]

Under the system of enforcement provided for by the Sex Discrimination Act, a complainant cannot directly take a complaint of discrimination to court, but must first lodge the complaint with the Australian Human Rights Commission.[49] If the Commission is unable to conciliate the complaint, the complainant may then bring the matter before the courts. The system of conciliation of complaints was intended to ensure that remedies were readily accessible to complainants, given the cost, time and trauma involved in pursuing cases through the courts, the rules of procedure and evidence that apply, and the disparity in power that often exists between complainants and respondents when it comes to marshalling resources for court proceedings.

The current system differs from that originally in place. Under the earlier system, if conciliation of a complaint was unsuccessful, then the matter could be the subject of adjudication by the Commission itself, in proceedings that were meant to be more informal than proceedings before the regular courts (though these tended to become highly judicialised as well). However, in 1995 the High Court held that these arrangements involved an unconstitutional conferral of the judicial power of the Commonwealth on a tribunal that was not a constitutionally recognised court.[50] As a result, the jurisdiction of the Commission to adjudicate complaints no longer exists, though an equivalent jurisdiction exists in some States that are not subject to the same constitutional constraints.

[47] Given that many of the provisions apply to discrimination against men as well as discrimination against women, it would have been necessary to modify the Article 1 definition if this form of definition were to be used. However, the Human Rights Committee adopted such an approach in its General Comment No. 18, so it is a possible approach. The original definition of discrimination in section 9(1) of the Racial Discrimination Act 1975 tracked the definition in the International Convention on the Elimination of All Forms of Racial Discrimination (ICERD). That has now been supplemented by a definition of indirect discrimination, which also uses language drawn from the ICERD.

[48] These include exemptions for religious bodies (s. 37), educational institutions established for religious purposes (s. 38), voluntary bodies (s. 39), sport (s. 42) and combat duties (s. 43). The Australian Human Rights Commission is also given the power under s. 44 of the Act to grant temporary exemptions from the operation of certain provisions of the Act.

[49] Formerly the Human Rights and Equal Opportunity Commission.

[50] *Brandy* v. *Human Rights and Equal Opportunity Commission* [1995] HCA 10; (1995) 183 CLR 24.

A complainant who cannot achieve resolution in conciliation proceedings must now take her complaint to the courts.

The Sex Discrimination Act does not contain a provision providing that it prevails over all other laws (indeed there is a list of laws and general exceptions that it is expressed not to prevail over), though its effect is to make unlawful some acts that might be permitted under State law. This may be contrasted with the Racial Discrimination Act (RDA) 1975 (Cth), which gave effect to provisions of the International Convention on the Elimination of All Forms of Racial Discrimination. By virtue of section 10 of the RDA, where a law discriminatorily denies the enjoyment of a right on the grounds of race, then that law is ineffective in that regard and the person enjoys the right without discrimination.[51]

4.1 Review and reform of the Sex Discrimination Act 1984

The Sex Discrimination Act has been the subject of review on a number of occasions over the past twenty-five years, and improvements made to it as a result.[52] The most recent inquiry was undertaken in 2008 by the Senate Standing Committee on Legal and Constitutional Affairs. In its December 2008 report, the Committee made over forty recommendations for improving the Act and its operation.[53] The government decided to respond to the report in two stages. The first was to amend the Sex Discrimination Act in order to extend protection against discrimination on the ground of family responsibilities, to provide wider protection from sexual harassment for students and workers, and to include breastfeeding

[51] Section 10 provides:

10 Rights to equality before the law

(1) If, by reason of, or of a provision of, a law of the Commonwealth or of a State or Territory, persons of a particular race, colour or national or ethnic origin do not enjoy a right that is enjoyed by persons of another race, colour or national or ethnic origin, or enjoy a right to a more limited extent than persons of another race, colour or national or ethnic origin, then, notwithstanding anything in that law, persons of the first-mentioned race, colour or national or ethnic origin shall, by force of this section, enjoy that right to the same extent as persons of that other race, colour or national or ethnic origin.

(2) A reference in subsection (1) to a right includes a reference to a right of a kind referred to in Article 5 of the Convention.

[52] The major reviews prior to 2008 were House of Representatives Standing Committee on Legal and Constitutional Affairs, *Half Way to Equal: Report of the Inquiry into Equal Opportunity and Equal Status for Women in Australia* (1992), and Australian Law Reform Commission, *Equality before the Law – Women's Equality (Parts I and II)*, ALRC 69 (1994).

[53] Senate Standing Committee on Legal and Constitutional Affairs, *Inquiry into the Effectiveness of the Commonwealth Sex Discrimination Act 1984 in Eliminating Discrimination and Promoting Gender Equality* (2008).

as a separate ground of discrimination.[54] The second stage is the harmonisation and consolidation of Commonwealth discrimination legislation into a single equality Act,[55] in order 'to remove unnecessary regulatory overlap, address inconsistencies across laws and make the system more user-friendly'.[56] Legislation to carry out the first stage was introduced into the Parliament in 2010,[57] and was enacted and commenced operation in mid 2011.[58] The government commenced a public consultation on the consolidation of anti-discrimination laws in September 2011, committing to introduce new protections against sexual orientation and gender identity discrimination.

An exposure draft of a consolidated anti-discrimination statute was published in late 2012.[59] The draft adopted a general definition of discrimination applicable to all protected attributes. Defining discrimination as unfavourable treatment that is not justifiable,[60] the draft moved away from using definitions drawing directly on treaty definitions (as was the case under existing federal sex and racial discrimination legislation), although the implementation of Australia's international obligations relating to equality and non-discrimination is explicitly stated to be an object of the legislation.[61] The exposure draft attracted considerable public discussion, especially in relation to its proposals to expand protection against offensive or insulting conduct and to introduce a shared burden of proof in discrimination cases. The draft was the subject of a major inquiry by a Parliamentary committee,[62] and it was not clear whether the legislation would be passed by the Parliament before the federal election due in 2013.

[54] *Sex and Age Discrimination Legislation Amendment Bill 2010, Explanatory Memorandum* (2010) 1.

[55] *Ibid.*

[56] *Australia's Human Rights Framework*, April 2010, 3.

[57] See *Report of the Senate Committee on Legal and Constitutional Affairs* (February 2011).

[58] See Sex and Age Discrimination Legislation Amendment Act 2011.

[59] Human Rights and Anti-Discrimination Bill 2012 – Exposure Draft Legislation, November 2012, available at: www.aph.gov.au/Parliamentary_Business/Committees/Senate_Committees?url=legcon_ctte/antI_discrimination_2012/index.htm (last accessed 22 February 2013).

[60] *Ibid.*, Chapter 2, Part 2-2. The definition of 'special measures' in clause 21 also departs from the standard international formulation.

[61] *Ibid.*, clause 3.

[62] Senate Constitutional and Legal Affairs Legislation Committee, *Report on the Exposure Draft Human Rights and Anti-Discrimination Bill 2012*, 21 February 2013, available at: www.aph.gov.au/Parliamentary_Business/Committees/Senate_Committees?url=legcon_ctte/antI_discrimination_2012/report/index.htm (last accessed 22 February 2013).

5 The Sex Discrimination Act, the Convention and Australian case law

The Convention and the work of the Committee has been considered in a number of cases decided by Australian courts and tribunals,[63] generally in the context of the interpretation of the Sex Discrimination Act or the corresponding State and Territory legislation. While the Australian courts (in particular the High Court) have been criticised for adopting narrow interpretations of anti-discrimination legislation,[64] where the courts have had the opportunity to draw on the Convention and the work of the Committee to interpret the Sex Discrimination Act or equivalent legislation, they have generally done so in a way that advances the implementation of the Convention (as far as that is possible within the wording and structure of the legislation).[65]

Some cases have involved challenges to the constitutionality of particular provisions of the Sex Discrimination Act on the ground that they exceed the legislative power of the Commonwealth Parliament. Although the High Court has not pronounced on the constitutionality of the Act,[66] these challenges in the lower courts have all failed, and it seems clear in light of the case law of the High Court on the scope of the external affairs power that the provisions of the Act that draw on that power are valid. This underlines the importance of the treaty for the constitutionality of the expansive reach of the Act.

For example, in *Aldridge* v. *Booth*[67] the Federal Court of Australia held that sexual harassment was a form of 'discrimination against women' within the meaning of the Convention and that providing women with

[63] There have been many references to the Convention and to the Concluding Comments of the CEDAW Committee in asylum or refugee cases, where the Committee's output may form part of the material on which an assessment of an asylum seeker's claim may be based. These are not considered here.

[64] See, for example M. Thornton, 'Sex discrimination, courts and corporate power', *Federal Law Review* 36:1 (2008) 31–56; B. Gaze, 'The Sex Discrimination Act after twenty years: achievements, disappointments, disillusionment and alternatives', *University of New South Wales Law Journal* 27:3 (2004) 914–21; B. Smith, 'Rethinking the Sex Discrimination Act: does Canada's experience suggest we should give our judges a greater role?' in Thornton (ed.), *Sex Discrimination in Uncertain Times* 235–60 at 250–5.

[65] See, for example, *Ilian* v. *ABC* [2006] FMCA 1500, [43]–[45].

[66] Though see *Victoria* v. *Commonwealth ('Industrial Relations Act Case')* [1996] HCA 56, in which the Court accepted that the CEDAW and other human rights treaties gave rise to legislative competence on the part of the Commonwealth under s. 51(xxix) of the Constitution.

[67] [1988] FCA 170.

legal protection against sexual harassment in employment gave effect to Australia's obligations under Article 11 of the Convention and was therefore constitutional,[68] a conclusion affirmed by the Full Federal Court in *Hall* v. *A & A Sheiban Pty Ltd*.[69] The cases were decided before the CEDAW Committee adopted its General Recommendation No. 19 (1991), which made it clear that sexual harassment was a form of discrimination against women within the meaning of Article 1 of the Convention.[70]

The most substantial discussions of the Convention have occurred in cases involving the legitimacy of special measures, generally those that make available to women opportunities or services as part of efforts to redress prior disadvantage or other special circumstances. Both the Sex Discrimination Act and the corresponding State statutes contain such provisions. There have been two versions of a special measures provision in the Sex Discrimination Act – the original section 33 and the current section 7D.[71]

The case law got off to something of a false start, but has subsequently corrected itself; the cases demonstrate the difference that taking account of the relevant international standards can make to the outcome of a case. In

[68] [1988] FCA 170, [46]–[60].

[69] [1989] FCA 72.

[70] See also *Johanson* v. *Michael Blackledge Meats* [2001] FMCA 6, [93]–[96].

[71] The current provision relating to special measures is s. 7D:

7D Special measures intended to achieve equality

(1) A person may take special measures for the purpose of achieving substantive equality between:
   (a) men and women; or
   (b) people of different marital status; or
   (c) women who are pregnant and people who are not pregnant; or
   (d) women who are potentially pregnant and people who are not potentially pregnant.

(2) A person does not discriminate against another person under sections 5, 6 or 7 by taking special measures authorised by subsection (1).

(3) A measure is to be treated as being taken for a purpose referred to in subsection (1) if it is taken:
   (a) solely for that purpose; or
   (b) for that purpose as well as other purposes, whether or not that purpose is the dominant or substantial one.

(4) This section does not authorise the taking, or further taking, of special measures for a purpose referred to in subsection (1) that is achieved.

This provision was inserted in 1995 and replaced the original provision on special measures (s. 33), which provided:

> Nothing in Division 1 or 2 renders it unlawful to do an act a purpose of which is to ensure that persons of a particular sex or marital status or persons who

Re Australian Journalists' Association[72] the Australian Industrial Relations Commission refused to permit a change to the rules of the Australian Journalists' Association that was designed to ensure that there was at least one-third representation of women members on the Association's governing body. Boulton J found that the provision was discriminatory and did not fall within section 33 of the Sex Discrimination Act, which permitted measures to be taken that are intended to ensure equality of opportunity.[73] The judge held that women had the same opportunity formally to stand for election and that therefore the section did not apply.

Had the judge looked to Article 4 of the CEDAW (which section 33 was intended to reflect), it is difficult to see how he could have come to any conclusion other than one holding the measure was a permissible temporary special measure and therefore not unlawful. The union subsequently applied for and was granted an exemption under the legislation. In its decision granting the exemption, the Human Rights and Equal Opportunity Commission stated that it did not necessarily agree with the interpretation of Boulton J.[74]

In a later decision of the Australian Industrial Relations Commission, the Commission considered a similar issue and, after considering Article 4 of the Convention and other international cases dealing with the concept of discrimination, took the view – albeit tentatively – that a union rule providing that each union branch must have at least one female vice-president, was covered by section 33 of the Sex Discrimination Act.[75]

Subsequent cases have been more confident in their conclusions about the appropriate standard. The most important of these is *Jacomb v. Australian Municipal Administrative Clerical and Services Union*,[76] in which the Federal Court of Australia discussed in detail, with reference to General Recommendation No. 25 and other sources, the concept of (temporary) special measures under the Convention and implementing

> are pregnant have equal opportunities with other persons in circumstances in relation to which provision is made by this Act.

See generally J. O'Brien, 'Affirmative action, special measures and the Sex Discrimination Act', *University of New South Wales Law Journal* 27:3 (2004) 840–8.

[72] (1988) EOC ¶92–224.

[73] See section 33, *supra* note 66.

[74] *Re an application for an exemption by the Australian Journalists' Association* (1988) EOC 92–236 at 77, 209.

[75] *Re Municipal Officers' Association of Australia: Approval of Submission of Amalgamation to Ballot* (1991) EOC 92–344, (1991) 12 *International Labour Law Reports* 57.

[76] [2004] FCA 1250.

Australian legislation in the context of quotas for women in senior positions in the union.[77] The new section 7D, inserted in 1995, had moved the special measures provision from the part of the Act that dealt with exceptions to the part of the Act that defined discrimination. This was to make clear that special measures were not 'discrimination' that was excused or justified, and were not in fact discrimination at all but a means of achieving substantive equality. The Court examined the history and content of section 7D in light of Articles 4 and 7 of the Convention. Noting that the Act should be interpreted in accordance with the provisions of the Convention,[78] the Court found that the quotas were special measures within the meaning of the Act and the Convention and were therefore not unlawful.[79] There have been a number of similar cases in which the provision of women-only services or facilities has been upheld as special measures within the meaning of the Act and the Convention.[80] There have been similar decisions in relation to State anti-discrimination law as well.[81]

In *McBain* v. *State of Victoria*,[82] the Federal Court of Australia considered a claim that section 8(1) of the Fertility Treatment Act 1995 (Vic), which restricted the availability of IVF treatment to a woman who was married and living with her husband on a genuine domestic basis, or was living with a man in a de facto relationship, was discriminatory on the basis of marital status and inconsistent with the Sex Discrimination Act. The Court held that this was unlawful discrimination in the provision of services, contrary to section 22 of the Commonwealth Act. The Court rejected an argument that section 22 should be construed in light of the Convention on the Rights of the Child and other instruments that a child had a right to be born into a family, to be raised by its mother and

[77] [2004] FCA 1250, [37]–[44].

[78] [2004] FCA 1250, [41].

[79] [2004] FCA 1250, [63]–[66].

[80] See, for example, *Walker* v. *Cormack & Anor* [2010] FMCA 9 (women-only gym sessions a special measure). The issue is discussed more generally in *Lifestyle Communities Ltd (No 3) (Anti-Discrimination)* [2009] VCAT 1869 (special measures under the Victorian Charter of Human Rights and Responsibilities).

[81] For example, in one of the many sex discrimination cases that involve disputes over access to sporting facilities or clubs, *Mangan* v. *Melbourne Cricket Club (Anti Discrimination)* [2006] VCAT 73, the Victorian Civil and Administrative Tribunal construed the 'special measures' provision of the Victorian Equal Opportunity Act (s. 82), in the light of Article 4 of the Convention and the CEDAW Committee's General Recommendation No. 25 on temporary special measures, finding that the measure in question did not satisfy the criteria of a special measure.

[82] [2000] FCA 1009.

father and to know its parents. The Court held that primacy should be given to the CEDAW in this case, since that was the treaty that the Sex Discrimination Act was intended to implement, and found that the denial of access to treatment was discriminatory, and that therefore the State Act was invalid to the extent of the inconsistency.[83]

In *AB* v. *Registrar of Births, Deaths and Marriages*,[84] a person who had been born male, was registered as male on her birth certificate, and was married (though living apart from her spouse), underwent sex affirmation (reassignment) surgery, and sought to have her birth certificate amended to reflect this. The Births, Deaths and Marriages Registration Act 1996 (Vic) provided that the Registrar could consider applications for such changes from persons who were unmarried, and so the Registrar refused AB's application on the basis that she was still married. AB challenged this refusal, arguing it violated section 22 of the Sex Discrimination Act in that it denied persons access to a service (rectification of the register) on the ground of marital status.

The issue was whether the Convention (and the Act) applied to discrimination on the ground of marital status where both married women and men were treated differently in comparison with women and men who were not married, or whether the reference to marital status discrimination applied only in cases where married women were subject to unfavourable treatment in comparison with married men or unmarried women. Resolution of this question was important because, for constitutional reasons, the Sex Discrimination Act would only apply in the context of the case to the extent that it gave effect to the Convention.

The judgments of the trial at first instance, Heerey J, and on appeal of the Full Court of the Federal Court (in particular that of Kenny J), are the most extended discussions to date of the Convention, its drafting history and meaning in the Australian cases. Heerey J dismissed the applicant's case, finding that the Convention and the Sex Discrimination Act did not apply to the present case since all married persons, women or men, were treated the same, and the Convention and the Act only applied to marital status discrimination where married women were treated unfavourably with respect to married men[85] (or unmarried women with respect to unmarried men). A majority of the Full Court dismissed the appeal

[83] The matter came before the High Court of Australia in *Re McBain* [2002] HCA 16, but the case there was decided on procedural grounds and did not reach the merits of the issue.

[84] *AB* v. *Registrar of Births, Deaths and Marriages* [2006] FCA 1071.

[85] *Ibid.*

against this decision, after an extended examination of the meaning of the Convention and the Act.[86]

There are other cases in which there has been reference to the Convention, but less extensive discussion. In *Jordan* v. *North Coast Area Health Service (No 3)*,[87] the New South Wales Anti-Discrimination Tribunal considered whether an award of 75 per cent of legal costs should unusually be made in favour of a successful complainant whose legal costs exceeded the maximum amount that could be awarded under the NSW Act. The Tribunal noted that the rights protected by the Anti-Discrimination Act (ADA) 1977 were 'internationally recognised, fundamental human rights' and that the Act 'reflects, in part [the CEDAW] which commits signatories, such as Australia, to pursue by all appropriate means a policy of eliminating discrimination against women'. The Tribunal concluded that if 'in a particular matter, seeking the ADA's protection of a fundamental human right is undermined by the cost of doing so, then it must be so that that single circumstance could, in the circumstances, justify the making of a costs order'.[88]

The Convention has also been drawn on as representing a clear statement of a public values and benefit, in a case in which the issue was whether the Victorian Women Lawyers' (VWL) Association was a charitable organisation for the purpose of income tax laws.[89] The Court noted that 'the legislation and the Convention to which Australia is a party can be taken as indicative of a now long standing social norm or community value that attaches public benefit to the removal of barriers to the advancement of women, on an equal basis with men, in all fields of human endeavour, including participation in the professions and in public life,'[90] and that as 'VWL's principal purpose was to remove barriers and increase opportunities for participation by and advancement of women in the legal profession in Victoria' and '[h]aving regard to the social norms reflected in the Sex Discrimination Act, cognate State legislation and Australia's membership of the *Convention for the Elimination of All Forms of Discrimination Against Women*', that objective was a purpose 'beneficial to the community'.[91]

[86] *AB* v. *Registrar of Births, Deaths and Marriages* [2007] FCAFC 140 (Kenny and Gyles JJ; Black CJ dissenting).
[87] [2005] NSWADT 296.
[88] [2005] NSWADT 296, [33]–[34]
[89] *Victorian Women Lawyers' Association Inc.* v. *Commissioner of Taxation* [2008] FCA 983.
[90] [2008] FCA 983, [112].
[91] [2008] FCA 983, [147]–[148].

6 The Convention as a framework of reference for law reform

The Convention has also provided a policy framework and specific equality standards for a number of inquiries into law and policy reform. For example, in 1993 the Australian Law Reform Commission (ALRC) was given a reference under which it was to consider whether changes should be made to Australian federal laws or their administration in the light of the obligations of that State under Articles 2 and 26 of the International Covenant on Civil and Political Rights (ICCPR) in relation to the equality of men and women, and in relation to the CEDAW. The inquiry was presided over, for most of its duration, by Justice Elizabeth Evatt, a former member and Chairperson of the CEDAW Committee (1985–92) and subsequently a member of the Human Rights Committee (1993–2000).

The concept of equality and non-discrimination contained in the CEDAW were central to the framework of analysis adopted by the ALRC, and the individual provisions of the Convention provided a list of topics that the Commission drew on in its analysis of substantive law and practice. The Commission affirmed that 'equality in law, as required by CEDAW, needs to be understood in a different and more substantial sense than merely equality before the law. Any understanding of equality must take account of the social and historical disadvantages of women and how that has affected the law.'[92] The Commission made a range of recommendations, some of which specifically referred to the Convention, others of which were intended to implement its substantive obligations. These included a recommendation that the existing federal Sex Discrimination Act contain a general prohibition of discrimination in accordance with CEDAW Article 1,[93] and that any inclusion of temporary special measures in the Act should reflect the CEDAW position that such provisions were not discrimination that could be justified, but rather not discriminatory and a means of achieving substantive equality.[94] Even though not all the recommendations of the Commission were implemented, many were, and the CEDAW framework was important to the framing of the issues and the proposed legislative and policy responses.[95] There have been other

[92] ALRC, *Equality before the Law – Women's Equality (Part I)*, ALRC 69, para. 3.1.

[93] ALRC, *Equality before the Law – Women's Equality (Part II)*, ALRC 69, para. 3.1 and Recommendation 3.1.

[94] *Ibid.* Recommendation 3.7.

[95] *Ibid.* at para. 4.39 and n. 101 (referring to CEDAW's General Recommendation No. 19 on violence against women in relation to the importance of eliminating violence as part of the struggle to achieve equality for women).

inquiries in which CEDAW standards have been considered as relevant to the content of proposals for legislative and policy reform.[96]

7 Activism around the reporting procedure

Australian women's groups and other human rights groups have been active in their use of the reporting procedure under the Convention to advocate for improvements in law and practice relating to women's equality; they have also used the occasion of Australia's reports under other human rights treaties to focus public and international attention on these issues.

A number of features characterise the manner in which this engagement has taken place. First of all, the use of the reporting procedure has been closely linked to existing domestic campaigns of the organisation in question – the CEDAW reporting process has become part of a national advocacy strategy that takes advantage of the attention that such an international event attracts and the opportunities it provides to encourage or pressure government to take action.

The second is the way in which the preparation of an NGO report on the implementation of the Convention has been used as a capacity- and network-building exercise.[97] For example, in the lead-up to the review of Australia's 6th and 7th reports to the CEDAW Committee, an extensive consultation process with women from a variety of groups and backgrounds led to the adoption of a report endorsed by a significant number of groups. This process was led by the Young Women's Christian Association Australia and Women's Legal Services Australia, and contained contributions from other Australian NGOs and was 'endorsed, in whole or in part, by 135 non-government organisations across Australia'.[98] This resulted in a coordinated submission to the CEDAW Committee, in addition to other material that it received. At the same time a report was prepared by

[96] See, for example, the House of Representatives Standing Committee on Employment and Workplace Relations, *Making it Fair: Pay Equity and Associated Issues Related to Increasing Female Participation in the Workforce*, November 2009, paras. 344–379 (reference to the Convention, CEDAW's Concluding Observations and other relevant treaty obligations as part of the framework for assessing policy reform to achieve pay equity).

[97] See A. Cody and A. Pettitt, 'Our rights, our voices: a methodology for engaging women in human rights discourse', *Just Policy* 43 (April 2007) 86–94.

[98] YWCA Australia and Women's Legal Services Australia (with the endorsement of 135 organisations), *NGO Report on the Implementation of the Convention on the Elimination of All Forms of Discrimination against Women (CEDAW) in Australia* (July 2009). The organisations are listed at vii–viii of the Report.

indigenous women's groups in parallel to this report.[99] A similar process had taken place in relation to the hearing before the CEDAW Committee in 2006, and many of the groups involved in that process actively drew on the CEDAW Committee's Concluding Comments as part of their advocacy at the national level.[100]

Australia's approach to the UN human rights bodies and their recommendations and views has generally been supportive and cooperative, with the Commonwealth government prepared to submit reports (though not always on time) and to engage in dialogue with the treaty committees and other procedures. At the same time, governments of both Labor and Liberal/National persuasions have consistently noted that while the pronouncements of the treaty bodies, including their views on communications, deserve due consideration and should be given considerable weight, they are not binding as a matter of international law. Accordingly, the Australian government considers that it is entitled to take a contrary, reasoned view of the meaning of certain provisions of the treaties, or of the application of the relevant provision in the circumstances of a particular case, and that this is consistent with its obligations under the relevant treaties.[101]

Nevertheless, the relationship between the UN human rights system and the Australian government has varied over the years. In particular, during the years of the Howard government (1996–2007), Australia's generally open and cooperative approach to UN human rights bodies took a turn for the worse.[102] A number of hearings before UN committees and findings by special procedures adopted adverse assessments of Australia's record on issues of political importance and sensitivity – in particular, in relation to racial discrimination and indigenous peoples' rights and to the rights of persons seeking asylum or refuge in Australia.

[99] *Aboriginal and Torres Strait Islander Women's CEDAW NGO Report* (2009).

[100] For descriptions of earlier hearings before the CEDAW Committee, see S. Brennan, 'Having our say: Australian women's organisations and the treaty reporting process', *Australian Journal of Human Rights* 5:2 (1999) 94–100, and A. Byrnes, 'Australia and the Women's Discrimination Convention', *Australian Law Journal* 62 (1988) 478–9.

[101] See, for example, the statement in the *Fifth Periodic Report of Australia under the ICCPR*, CCPR/C/AUS/5 (2008), paras. 9–11.

[102] See generally H. Charlesworth, 'Human rights: Australia versus the UN', Discussion Paper 22/06, Democratic Audit of Australia, Canberra, August 2006, and Charlesworth *et al.*, *No Country is an Island* at 82–91. See also D. Kinley and P. Martin, 'International human rights law at home: addressing the politics of denial', *Melbourne University Law Review* 26:2 (2002) 466–77; and S. Zifcak, *The New Anti-Internationalism: Australia and the United Nations Human Rights Treaty System* (Canberra: The Australia Institute, 2003) 24–32.

These triggered a hostile response from the government. This took not only the form of jingoistic assertions of sovereignty, but also, following a review in 2000 of its engagement with the treaty body system, the articulation by the government of a more belligerent ('robust') and less cooperative approach to engagement with the treaty body system.[103] This involved, among other things, slow or no responses to Committee Concluding Observations or Views, failure to publicise Committee findings[104] and a rejection of the substantive findings in a number of cases, and a refusal to sign or ratify the CEDAW Optional Protocol. In some cases these responses reflected ongoing disagreements about the meaning of certain provisions of the treaties,[105] but in others it reflected a more hostile approach to the UN human rights system. This less receptive approach to UN human rights bodies was reflective of the government's

[103] Charlesworth *et al.*, *No Country is an Island* at 87–91.

[104] A number of decisions of treaty bodies decided adversely to Australia from July 2006 have been published on the Attorney-General's Department website, together with (generally undated) responses from the government that set out its understanding of the scope and application of the relevant provisions of the ICCPR where the government's view is different to that of the treaty body. See www.ag.gov.au/RightsAndProtections/HumanRights/Pages/Humanrightscommunications.aspx (last accessed 22 February 2013). The number of violations/communications under the various treaties as of 7 May 2012 was: ICCPR (20/59), CERD (1/9) and the Convention against Torture (CAT) (1/11): see www.bayefsky.com/docs.php/area/jurisprudence/state/9 (last accessed 13 February 2013). For details of Committees' responses to the replies by the Australian government to Committee views, see www.bayefsky.com/docs.php/area/fu-jurisprudence/state/9 (last accessed 13 February 2013).

[105] For example, whether Article 9(1) of the ICCPR provides a substantive guarantee of non-arbitrariness in relation to detention, or merely a guarantee of lawfulness under domestic law. The Human Rights Committee held in *A* v. *Australia* (560/1993), 30 March 1997, UN Doc. CCPR/C/59/D/560/19, and subsequent cases, that the guarantee was substantive, a legal finding the Australian government rejected (response of 16 December 1997, summarised in A/53/40, para. 491 (1998)). The debate continued, with the HRC objecting to this approach (A/55/40, vol. I, paras. 520–1 (2000)) and a riposte by the Australian government:

> Australia is careful to ensure that all communications concerning Australia are responded to in a considered manner. The fact that Australia may on occasion disagree with the Committee does not undermine our recognition and acceptance of the communications mechanism under the Optional Protocol. (*Fifth Periodic Report of Australia under the ICCPR*, CCPR/C/AUS/5, (2008) para. 11).

See also *Response of the Australian Government to the Views of the Committee in Communication No 1324/2004 Shafiq* v. *Australia*, 25 May 2007, and A/63/40 vol. II, 505 (2008) (rejecting Committee's view of scope of ICCPR Article 9(4)). The narrower view of these provisions has been maintained by the subsequent Labor government.

general political approach on human rights issues, including on issues of equality and non-discrimination.[106]

The election of the Rudd Labor government in late November 2007 led to a renewal of a more constructive rhetoric about and engagement with the human rights system, with accession to the CEDAW Optional Protocol, and the ratification of other instruments or the commencement of the steps needed to ratify them. At the same time, in its responses to the Committees on individual communications, the government maintained its different view of the meaning of certain provisions of the treaties,[107] and also continued to emphasise that the views of the treaty bodies on communications were non-binding recommendations.[108]

8 Major issues – the case of paid maternity leave

When Australia ratified the Convention, it entered the following reservation in relation to the obligation under Article 11(2)(b) of the Convention 'to introduce maternity leave with pay or with comparable social benefits without loss of former employment, seniority or social allowances':

> The Government of Australia states that maternity leave with pay is provided in respect of most women employed by the Commonwealth Government and the Governments of New South Wales and Victoria. Unpaid maternity leave is provided in respect of all other women employed in the State of New South Wales and elsewhere to women employed under Federal and some State industrial awards. Social Security benefits subject to income tests are available to women who are sole parents.
>
> The Government of Australia advises that it is not at present in a position to take the measures required by article 11(2) to introduce maternity leave with pay or with comparable social benefits throughout Australia.

106 M. Sawer, 'Australia: the fall of the femocrat' in J. Outshoorn and J. Kantola (eds.), *Changing State Feminism* (Basingstoke: Palgrave Macmillan, 2007) 20–40 at 26, 39–40; L. Chappell, 'Winding back Australian women's rights: conventions, contradictions and conflicts', *Australian Journal of Political Science* 37:3 (2002) 475–88.

107 See, for example, *Response of the Australian Government to the Views of the Committee in Communications 1255/2004 et al., Shams et al.* v. *Australia*, 25 June 2008 (rejecting the Committee's view of the scope of ICCPR Article 9(4)); see also A/63/40 vol. II, 508 (2008).

108 See, for example, the *CEDAW–OP Australian Treaty National Interest Analysis*, tabled before the Parliament's Joint Standing Committee on Treaties, as a prelude to accession to the Optional Protocol: 'The views of the Committee are non-binding, and therefore, while they could guide Australia in its implementation of international law, Australia would not be obliged to conform to the Committee's views if it believes that there is a better way to implement its obligations under CEDAW.' [2008] ATNIA 26, para. 9.

The question of paid maternity leave has been a contentious one in Australia,[109] with the federal Sex Discrimination Commissioners pushing governments of both political complexions to move ahead with a scheme of paid maternity leave for all.[110] There has been a significant measure of public support for this proposal, though support in some sectors such as business (especially among small businesses) has been dependent on the nature of the contributions required from business and likely to be provided by government.

The CEDAW Committee has also pressed Australia on the issue. For example in its 2006 Concluding Comments, the Committee stated:[111]

> 24. [T]he Committee remains concerned about the lack of uniformity in work-related paid maternity leave schemes. It is also concerned that there is no national system of paid maternity leave and that, as a consequence, the State party continues to maintain its reservation to article 11, paragraph 2, of the Convention.
> 25. The Committee urges the State party to take further appropriate measures to introduce maternity leave with pay or with comparable social benefits. It also recommends that the State party evaluate its maternity payment introduced in 2004 in the light of article 11, paragraph 2 (b), of the Convention and to expedite the steps necessary for the withdrawal of its reservation to this article.

In May 2009 the Productivity Commission, to which the government had referred the issue, made public its report.[112] The Commission recommended that the government adopt a taxpayer-funded scheme that would:

[109] See D. Brennan, 'The difficult birth of paid maternity leave: Australia' in S. B. Kamerman, *The Politics of Parental Leave Policies: Children, Parenting, Gender and the Labour Market* (Bristol: The Policy Press, 2009) 15–31; Charlesworth and Charlesworth, 'The Sex Discrimination Act and international law' at 860–3.

[110] See *Pregnant and Productive: It's a Right Not a Privilege to Work While Pregnant*, National Pregnancy and Work Inquiry (1999) Commissioner Susan Halliday (proposing modelling and analysis of possible paid maternity leave schemes); *A Time to Value: Proposal for National Maternity Leave Scheme* (2002) (Commissioner Pru Goward) (proposed as a minimum standard, a fully costed scheme of 14 weeks to be paid by the government at the level of the federal minimum wage); *It's About Time: Women, Men, Work and Family* (2007) (acting Sex Discrimination Commissioner John von Doussa QC). See also Sex Discrimination Commissioner Elizabeth Broderick, Oral evidence, Productivity Commission Inquiry into Paid Maternity, Paternity and Parental Leave, Public Hearing, 20 May 2008.

[111] CEDAW/C/AUL/CO/5, paras. 24–25 (2006).

[112] Productivity Commission, *Paid Parental Leave: Support for Parents with Newborn Children Inquiry Report* (2009).

- provide paid postnatal leave for a total of eighteen weeks that can be shared by eligible parents, with an additional two weeks of paternity leave reserved for the father (or same sex partner) who shares in the daily primary care of the child;
- provide the adult federal minimum wage (currently $543.78) for each week of leave for those eligible, with benefits subject to normal taxation.

The Commission estimated that the government scheme would cost taxpayers around $310 million annually in net terms (with an additional cost of $70 million if superannuation contributions were to be introduced subsequently). This endorsement by the Productivity Commission of the financial feasibility of a scheme (which followed reports by Sex Discrimination Commissioners and others that a scheme was affordable), provided powerful political impetus to the campaign for universal paid maternity leave.

The Australian government indicated its plans in its response to the lists of issues sent to it by the CEDAW Committee in relation to its combined 6th and 7th reports:[113]

> On 10 May 2009 the Government announced its intention to introduce a paid parental leave scheme (Scheme) in January 2011. The Scheme is closely based on the model proposed by the Productivity Commission. It will provide the primary carer with 18 weeks of paid post-natal leave, paid at the federal minimum wage. Eligibility will depend on the primary carer's period of employment with their employer, and whether the carer has an adjusted taxable income of $150,000 or less in the financial year prior to the birth of the child. The Scheme will cover employees, including casual workers, as well as contractors and the self-employed. The Australian Government is currently considering its position on the reservation to article 11(2) (b) of the Convention, particularly in light of its announced intention to introduce paid parental leave throughout Australia in 2011.

This represented a significant advance, though there was criticism of the limitations of the scheme and its perpetuation of gender stereotypes.[114]

The CEDAW Committee welcomed the introduction of the paid parental leave scheme, but noted that 'it does not include superannuation,

[113] *Responses to the List of Issues and Questions with Regard to the Consideration of the Combined Sixth and Seventh Periodic Reports*, CEDAW/C/AUL/Q/7/Add 1, Question 25 at 57 (2010).

[114] YWCA Australia and Women's Legal Services Australia (with the endorsement of 135 organisations), *NGO Report on the Implementation of the Convention on the Elimination of All Forms of Discrimination against Women (CEDAW) in Australia* (July 2009), paras. 12.3–12.6.

which impacts on the major gender gap in retirement savings and economic security between older women and men, that the leave is of limited duration (18 weeks), and that compensation is limited to an amount equal to the federal minimum wage and subject to other conditions'.[115] It called on Australia to ensure that the proposed review of the legislation would address and remedy these aspects of the scheme.[116] The scheme took effect from 1 January 2011, and it seems likely that this will permit Australia to remove its reservation relating to maternity leave.

9 The role of the Convention in the pursuit of equality

The CEDAW has been much more of a focus for advocacy and law-making around women's equality than other international instruments, such as the ICCPR. This is primarily the result of the fact that the main form of gender discrimination that was broadly identified as needing to be addressed at the time of the enactment of the first federal legislation on sex discrimination and around the time of the adoption of the Convention was discrimination against women. Compared with the brief and general non-discrimination guarantees of the ICCPR, the International Covenant on Economic, Social and Cultural Rights (ICESCR), and other treaties, women's rights advocates found the broad-ranging and detailed stipulations of the CEDAW substantively more useful and a more natural basis for political solidarity, emerging as it did from the women's movement in which the advocates of legislative reform in the 1970s and 1980s in Australia also participated. It also provided a firm constitutional basis on which to erect a wide-ranging federal statute.

That said, in a number of areas these other treaties have proved useful, especially as constitutional hooks on which to base federal legislation more firmly, and as the framework for particular administrative schemes of rights protection (ILO 111).[117] The ICCPR also provided an important avenue for advancing activism and law reform around discrimination on

[115] CEDAW/C/AUL/CO/7, para. 38 (2010).

[116] CEDAW/C/AUL/CO/7, para. 39 (2010).

[117] In the 1970s, as part of implementation of ILO Convention No. 111, national and state committees on discrimination in occupation and employment constituted on a tripartite basis were established, with the function of receiving complaints of discrimination in employment on various grounds (including sex). The committees could only conciliate cases and had no power to issue orders; if conciliation failed, under this system the only remedy was a report by the Minister to the Parliament: United Nations, *United Nations Yearbook on Human Rights for 1975–76* (United Nations, 1981) 8. For an example of a case in which ILO Convention No. 111 is discussed in the context of an appeal

the basis of sexuality. In *Toonen* v. *Australia*,[118] the complainant successfully challenged Tasmanian laws that criminalised homosexual conduct before the Human Rights Committee in a complaint lodged under the First Optional Protocol. The Committee found the Tasmanian laws violated Article 17 of the ICCPR,[119] and also noted that discrimination on the basis of 'other status' in Articles 2 and 26 of the Covenant included discrimination on the basis of sexual orientation, although the Committee did not make a finding of violation on this separate ground.[120]

More recently, the revamping of the Equal Opportunity in the Workplace Act 1986 (Cth) – which involved renaming the legislation as the Workplace Gender Equity Act and extending its provisions to men – cites, as the part of its constitutional basis and international reference points, not just the CEDAW, but also Article 26 of the ICCPR and Article 7 of the ICESCR.[121] The Commonwealth Sex Discrimination Act, when initially enacted in 1984, referred specifically only to the CEDAW in so far as it based itself on international treaty obligations to extend the range of the Commonwealth's legislative reach (it applied to men under other legislative powers of the Commonwealth, but its application to women was broader due to the reliance on the Convention). At the time no reference was made to other treaties – it was only in amendments made to the Act in 2011 that other treaties are referred to as providing a substantive basis for the legislation.[122]

10 Conclusion

The following conclusions can be offered in relation to the relevance of the Convention to Australian law and practice relating to gender equality:

against an adverse disciplinary finding, see *Hart* v. *Jacobs* [1981] FCA 223; (1981) 57 FLR 18 (23 December 1981).

118 Communication No. 488/1992, views adopted on 31 March 1994, UN Doc. CCPR/C/50/D/488/1992 (1994). See generally S. Joseph, 'Gay rights under the ICCPR', *University of Tasmania Law Review* 13:2 (1994) 392–411, and W. Morgan, 'Sexuality and human rights: the first communication by an Australian to the Human Rights Committee under the Optional Protocol to the International Covenant on Civil and Political Rights: Comment' 14 (1992) *Australian Year Book of International Law* 277–92.

119 Communication No. 488/1992 at para. 8.6.

120 *Ibid.* at para. 8.7.

121 'Statement of compatibility with human rights', *Equal Opportunity for Women in the Workplace Amendment Bill 2012, Explanatory Memorandum* at 133–4.

122 Sex and Age Discrimination Legislation Amendment Act 2011, s. 4(1) refers to the CEDAW, the two Covenants, the CRC, and ILO Conventions Nos. 100, 111, 156 and 158 – though not the Convention on the Rights of Persons with Disabilities.

- The ratification and continuing efforts to implement the CEDAW have been part of a broader political and social campaign to address discrimination against women and to pursue the goals of gender equality.
- The ratification and implementation of the CEDAW has been both a result of that campaigning and has contributed additional impetus to it – by providing a framework for advocacy and scrutiny of policy and law, and by the reporting procedure providing a stimulus to and opportunities for women's groups to collaborate and coordinate their critiques and to put public pressure on the government nationally and internationally, and by providing material that can be brought back to the domestic debate that has a different form of legitimacy.
- The Convention's requirement to ensure that there are appropriate legislative guarantees and protection of equality and non-discrimination on the ground of sex, although not initially the basis of calls for legislation, subsequently was important to the form and constitutionality of the Sex Discrimination Act 1984 (and other legislation).
- The Sex Discrimination Act has provided some form of remedy for many women who have brought their cases to the Commission, but it suffers from the inherent limitations of individual complaint-based procedures and is not a particularly good vehicle for addressing systemic discrimination, or generating proactive responses.
- Courts have drawn on the Convention and CEDAW Committee output to give CEDAW-consistent interpretations of the Sex Discrimination Act in a number of cases and to produce CEDAW-consistent readings/considerations in other contexts, but given the nature of the Sex Discrimination Act, these cases have not been a major driver of legislative or policy reform.
- The Convention and CEDAW Concluding Observations/Comments and other output have provided a useful substantive framework for policy critique and reform in a number of cases, and have become part of the standard repertoire of argumentation and substantive consideration in policy reform, and appear to carry some, though by no means decisive, weight with legislators and policy-makers.
- Australia's reservations to the CEDAW have admittedly prevented Australian law and policy in the areas they cover from violating Australia's international legal obligations; on the other hand, they have provided a focal point for the exertion of political pressure on the government to review and amend the substantive policies that the reservations seek to immunise, and have led to the modification and removal of some of the reservations.

- The sources of and grounds for resistance to the implementation of the Convention have varied, sometimes depending on the issue. They have included many conservative politicians, socially conservative groups, States rights advocates, some religious groups, the defence establishment (which was able to secure a reservation for its policies but which has engaged in a review and amendment of those policies) and some business groups (depending on the issue – the business community is not monolithic).

There are other areas in which the CEDAW has been important in adding to momentum for legislative and policy change – violence against women and moves towards pay equity are two such areas, but there are many areas in which much remains to be done. The reluctance of the government and others to adopt a more extensive range of temporary special measures (for example, in ensuring the representation of a fixed percentage of women on corporate boards) is something that the CEDAW Committee has consistently urged the government to do.[123]

Notwithstanding the many advances, it has also become clear that one cannot take changes advancing the cause of equality for granted – they are always subject to challenge by countervailing political and social forces, and the forms of discrimination are constantly evolving.[124] Thus, the struggle will continue, and the CEDAW will continue to provide an important frame of reference and resources for that continuing struggle.

Annex A

Australia's declaration and reservations to the Convention on the Elimination of All Forms of Discrimination against Women

Declaration:

Australia has a Federal Constitutional System in which Legislative, Executive and Judicial Powers are shared or distributed between the

[123] Most recently in its 2010 Concluding Observations on Australia: CEDAW/C/AUL/CO/7, paras. 26–27 (2010).

[124] See M. Thornton, 'Auditing the Sex Discrimination Act' in M. Smith (ed.), *Human Rights 2004: The Year in Review* (2005) 21–56 ('the references in the objects clause of the SDA to the *elimination* of discrimination and sexual harassment, which are taken directly from the Convention for the Elimination of Discrimination against Women (CEDAW), are based on a flawed premise. It is naïve to think that we might *eliminate* activity that is ongoing.').

Commonwealth and the Constituent States. The implementation of the Treaty throughout Australia will be effected by the Commonwealth State and Territory Authorities having regard to their respective constitutional powers and arrangements concerning their exercise.

Reservations:

The Government of Australia states that maternity leave with pay is provided in respect of most women employed by the Commonwealth government and the Governments of New South Wales and Victoria. Unpaid maternity leave is provided in respect of all other women employed in the State of New South Wales and elsewhere to women employed under Federal and some State industrial awards. Social Security benefits subject to income tests are available to women who are sole parents.

The Government of Australia advises that it is not at present in a position to take the measures required by article 11(2) to introduce maternity leave with pay or with comparable social benefits throughout Australia.

Reservation [original version July 1983]:

The Government of Australia advises that it does not accept the application of the Convention is so far as it would require alteration of Defence Force policy which excludes women from combat and combat-related duties. The Government of Australia is reviewing this policy so as to more closely define 'combat' and 'combat-related duties'.

Reservation [modified in August 2000]:[125]

The Government of Australia advises that it does not accept the application of the Convention in so far as it would require alteration of Defence Force policy which excludes women from combat duties.

125 The combat-related duties aspect of the reservation was removed in 2000 after review by the Defence Forces, *Combined 4th and 5th Periodic Reports of Australia*, CEDAW/C/AUL/4–5 (2004), paras. 281–2. In its 2009 report the government indicated that, while the range of jobs open to women in the Defence Forces was expanding and it was continuing to review women's roles, it was maintaining the reservation so far as it related to women's direct participation in combat duties: *Combined 6th and 7th Reports of Australia*, CEDAW/C/AUL/6–7 (2009), paras. 9.63–9.65.

12

The Canadian experience with the CEDAW: all women's rights are human rights – a case of treaties synergy

LUCIE LAMARCHE

> *[I]nequality in economic, social and cultural rights undermines women's ability to enjoy their civil and political rights, which then limits their capacity to influence decision and policy-making in public life ... equality in civil and political rights is undermined unless equality in the exercise and enjoyment of economic, social and cultural rights is secured.*
>
> Montreal Principles, 2002[1]

1 Introduction

It is often said that the Convention on the Elimination of All Forms of Discrimination against Women (CEDAW) carries a promise of substantive gender equality as it promotes the elimination of all forms of discrimination against women beyond the enumeration of rights it specifically guarantees. That includes civil and political rights as well as economic, social and cultural ones. In relation to accountability – the corollary proposal to effective rights – the editors of this book suggest that the CEDAW builds the parameters of a gender equality regime over time. We agree with such a proposal.

When it comes to the case of Canada, we believe the situation of the last decade shows that women and women's groups are trying to build such a gender equality regime by using all possible means and protections of rights offered by different international human rights treaties. This chapter wishes to demonstrate the specific synergy between two treaties: the International Covenant on Economic, Social and Cultural Rights (ICESCR) and the CEDAW.

[1] 'Montreal Principles on Women's Economic, Social, and Cultural Rights', 2002 (2004) 26 *HRQ* 760.

The recourse to the practice of shadow reporting to the UN human rights treaty bodies by the Canadian women's movement followed a moment of exuberance where the gender equality seekers relied on the Canadian Charter of Rights and Freedoms and its equality provision to encourage (blame and shame) the Canadian government to comply with international law. Unfortunately, this advocacy exercise revealed that domestic legal gains are influenced by global economic changes that also deeply affect the gender equality regime in relation to economic and social rights. While it is impossible for us to claim that international human rights instruments are by themselves transformative when we consider the quest for gender equality, it is clear they contribute (at least, in regressive times) to the demand for more political accountability.

This chapter is divided into two sections. The first section explores the Canadian constitutional landscape and addresses the particularities of Canada as a dualist federated State of the Americas. In such a context, there always seems to be room to transfer the responsibility for the economic security of women to another level of government. In addition, Canada is also regionally isolated as it is not seriously committed to the positively evolving regime of human rights created over time by the Organization of American States (OAS). It appears, though, that the UN treaty monitoring system recently decided to put an end to the accountability limits of a federated State such as Canada and that the CEDAW Committee contributed to such progress.

The second section, using mostly empirical data and relying on legal-textual analysis, examines the Canadian experience of intertwined reporting and shadow reporting to UN treaty bodies, including the CEDAW Committee. The last decade of such experience reveals that the Canadian women's movement succeeded in crafting a gender equality regime based on different instruments by using all possible synergies between treaties in order to promote an interdependent reading of women's rights and of gender equality. The fight against the increasing poverty of women is an example of this effort as the movement believes that the protection of economic and social rights is an essential component of any human rights accountability system.

We would wish to conclude on a positive note. However, the current political reality dictates more pragmatism. It seems that the better the understanding of substantive gender equality gets on the part of the CEDAW, the less the Canadian government, including provincial and territorial components of the federation, is willing to acknowledge the encompassing scope of its international commitments.

In the meantime, the Canadian women's movement does not appear to intend to change its strategy. It may even export its litigation capacity by presenting before some UN human rights committees, including the CEDAW Committee.

2 Women's rights in context: the Canadian landscape

After a quick survey of Canada's international and regional commitments with regard to women's rights (2.1 and 2.2), this section will summarise the domestic struggle for gender equality that followed the adoption of the Canadian Charter of Rights and Freedoms. After some significant gains, we nevertheless have to conclude that the ambient neoconservative ideology, on top of a wave of budget cuts, is producing diminishing returns for Canadian women (2.3). Finally, the human rights landscape will be examined in the context of federalism. It seems that it is almost always convenient for jurisdictions that are first responsible for social policies to hide behind the veil of the federal treaty-making power (2.4). This dynamic is intimately linked to the decision of the women's movement to move their struggle for equality to the international level.

2.1 International commitments concerning human rights and women's rights: an overview

Canada has ratified the core UN human rights treaties. It became party to the International Convention on the Elimination of All Forms of Racial Discrimination (ICERD) in October 1970; it ratified both the International Covenant on Civil and Political Rights (ICCPR) and the International Covenant on Economic, Social and Cultural Rights (ICESCR) in 1976. It also ratified the CEDAW in 1981 (without reservation), the Convention against Torture (CAT) in 1987 and the Convention on the Rights of the Child (CRC)[2] in 1991. In April 2010 Canada ratified the Convention on the Rights of Persons with Disabilities (CRPD).[3] It does not seem, though, that the Canadian government wishes to become party to the Convention on Migrant Workers (CMW).

[2] In the case of the CRC, Canada registered two reservations. One concerns Article 21 of the treaty and the respect of customary forms of care among Aboriginal people in Canada. The other provides for the protection of domestic policies aimed at separating children from adults when in detention.

[3] In the case of the CRPD, the Canadian government registered a reservation against Article 12(4), promoting an interpretation that provides for the right to continue

Canada ratified the First Optional Protocol to the ICCPR in 1976,[4] but only acceded to the Second Optional Protocol to the ICCPR aiming at the abolition of the death penalty in 2005.[5] In addition, it ratified the Optional Protocol to the CEDAW in 2002[6] and both the Optional Protocol to the CRC on the involvement of children in armed conflict and on the sale of children, child prostitution and child pornography in 2005.[7] The Canadian government states repeatedly that it does not wish to ratify the recent Optional Protocol to the ICESCR,[8] adopted in 2008.

Finally, Canada ratified thirty-two International Labour Organization Conventions. Among them are Convention No. 87 on freedom of association and protection of the right to organise (1948),[9] Convention No. 100 on equal remuneration for men and women workers for work of equal value (1951)[10] and Convention No. 111 concerning discrimination with respect to employment and occupation (1948).[11] Those conventions were ratified in 1972 except for Convention No. 111, which Canada ratified in 1964.

2.2 *Regional commitments*

Canada joined the Organization of American States (OAS) in 1991 and is thereby bound to respect the 1948 Charter of the OAS, as amended by

the use of substitute decision-making arrangements in accordance with the law. Also, the Government of Canada interprets Article 33 (2) of the CRPD as accommodating the situation of federal States where the implementation of the Convention will occur at more than one level of government and through a variety of mechanisms, including existing ones.

4 Optional Protocol to the International Covenant on Civil and Political Rights, 999 UNTS 302, entered into force 23 March 1976.

5 Second Optional Protocol to the International Covenant on Civil and Political Rights, aiming at the abolition of the death penalty, 1642 UNTS 414, entered into force 11 July 1991.

6 Optional Protocol to the Convention on the Elimination of All Forms of Discrimination against Women, 1249 UNTS 13, entered into force 22 December 2000.

7 Optional Protocol to the CRC on the involvement of children in armed conflict, 2133 UNTS 161 and Optional Protocol to the CRC on the sale of children, child prostitution and child pornography, 2171 UNTS 227, entered into force 12 February 2002.

8 Optional Protocol to the International Covenant on Economic, Social and Cultural Rights, UN Doc. A/63/435, 11 December 2008, not yet in force.

9 ILO Convention No. 87 concerning freedom of association and protection of the right to organise, entered into force 4 July 1950.

10 ILO Convention No. 100 concerning equal remuneration for men and women workers for work of equal value, entered into force 23 May 1953.

11 ILO Convention No. 111 concerning discrimination in respect of employment and occupation, entered into force 15 June 1960.

the Protocol of Buenos Aires,[12] as well as the American Declaration on Rights and Duties of Man (1948).[13] Canada did not ratify the American Convention on Human Rights (Pact of San Jose)[14] nor, of course, the Additional Protocol on Human Rights in the Area of Economic, Social and Cultural Rights (Protocol of San Salvador)[15] or the Protocol to Abolish the Death Penalty.[16] Canada also did not ratify the Inter-American Convention to Prevent and Punish Torture,[17] the Inter-American Convention on the Prevention, Punishment and Eradication of Violence Against Women (Convention of Belém do Pará)[18] or the recent Inter-American Convention on the Elimination of All Forms of Discrimination Against Persons with Disabilities.[19] Of this long list of non-ratifications, the most striking abstention concerns the Convention of Belém do Pará, adopted in preparation for the Fourth World Conference on Women of 1995, in which the Canadian government was actively involved.

When joining the OAS, Canada preferred to ratify the 1933 Convention on the Nationality of Women,[20] and both the 1949 Convention of the Granting of Political Rights to Women[21] and the Convention on the Granting of Civil Rights to Women,[22] which entered into force in 1933 and

[12] Charter of the Organization of American States, 119 UNTS 3, entered into force 13 December 1951; amended by the Protocol of Buenos Aires, 721 UNTS 324, entered into force 27 February 1970.

[13] American Declaration on the Rights and Duties of Man, 1948, Basic Documents Pertaining to Human Rights in the Inter-American System, OAS Basic Documents, OEA/Ser.L.V/II.82 doc.6 rev.1 at 17 (1992).

[14] American Convention on Human Rights, 1144 UNTS 123, entered into force 18 July 1978.

[15] Inter-American Convention Additional Protocol in the Area of Economic, Social and Cultural Rights, OAS Treaty Series A-52, entered into force 16 November 1999.

[16] Protocol to the American Convention to Abolish the Death Penalty, OAS Treaty Series A-53, not yet in force.

[17] Inter-American Convention to Prevent and Punish Torture, OAS Treaty Series A-67, entered into force 28 February 1987.

[18] Inter-American Convention on the Prevention, Punishment and Eradication of Violence Against Women, 9 June 1994, I.L.M. No. 1534, Vol. 33, entered into force 5 March 1995.

[19] Inter-American Convention on the Elimination of All Forms of Discrimination Against Persons with Disabilities, OAS Treaty Series A-65, entered into force 14 September 2001.

[20] Convention on the Nationality of Women, OAS, Treaty Series No. 4, 38, entered into force 29 August 1934. The only right granted by this Convention reads as follows: 'Article 1 There shall be no distinction based on sex as regards nationality, in their legislation or in their practice.'

[21] Convention of the Granting of Political Rights to Women, 1438 UNTS 63, entered into force 17 March 1949. Article 1: 'The High Contracting Parties agree that the right to vote and to be elected to national office shall not be denied or abridged by reason of sex.'

[22] Inter-American Convention on the Granting of Civil Rights to Women, 1438 UNTS 51, entered into force 17 March 1949. Article 1: 'The American States agree to grant to women the same civil rights that men enjoy.'

1949, respectively. Those Conventions were adopted by the International Conference of American States, which later became the Organization of American States. They promote an approach of formal equality toward women's rights.

As an OAS Member State, Canada is in the odd position of being needed for contributions and support without being expected to respect the basic human rights treaties adopted by the organisation, as interpreted. For example, Canada claims that it does not have to consider itself bound by the recent Inter-American Court of Human Rights decision in the *Cotton Field* case,[23] also known as the *feminicidas* case or the case of the disappeared women of Ciudad Juárez, Mexico. This decision shows many similarities with the unacceptable reality of the disappearance of indigenous and Aboriginal women in Canada.[24] In the *Cotton Field* case the Inter-American Court of Human Rights concluded that the State has a positive obligation to protect women against violence conducted and committed by private actors. The Court then considered the context of systemic violence against women and of structural discrimination, and found that gender-based violence constitutes gender discrimination. Accordingly, a broad range of remedial measures were ordered by the Court. This decision echoes, contextualises and even enriches General Recommendation No. 19 adopted by the CEDAW Committee in 1992.[25]

2.3 The Canadian standard of equality

The Canadian Constitution was supplemented by new provisions in 1982. Feminists lobbied for the constitutional recognition of women's

[23] *Case of González et al. ('Cotton Field')* v. *Mexico*, 16 November 2009, Inter-Am. Ct. H.R. (Sér. C) No. 205.

[24] In December 2011 the CEDAW Committee decided to conduct an inquiry into the murders and disappearances of Aboriginal women and girls across Canada. The Committee's decision was announced in Canada by Jeannette Corbiere Lavell, President of the Native Women's Association of Canada (NWAC), and Sharon McIvor of the Canadian Feminist Alliance for International Action (FAFIA). See also Amnesty International, Canada, *Stolen Sisters, A Human Rights Response to Discrimination and Violence against Indigenous Women in Canada*, 2004 at 37, available at: www.amnesty.ca/sites/default/files/amr200032004enstolensisters.pdf (last accessed 25 February 2013)

[25] CEDAW Committee, General Recommendation No. 19, Violence against Women, 1992, UN Doc. HRI/GEN/1/Rev.9/ (Vol. II). See para. 24 for a detailed explanation of the State duty to act, which derives from the acknowledgement of the State's positive responsibility toward violence against women.

constitutional rights.[26] As a result, two sex equality provisions, section 15 and section 28, were included in the Canadian Charter of Rights and Freedoms (the 'Charter').[27] Section 15 prohibits discrimination based on enumerated and on analogous grounds, and section 28 deals with sex equality and provides that notwithstanding anything in the Charter, the rights and freedoms referred to are guaranteed equally to male and female persons. Section 35(4) echoes section 28 of the Charter. This section guarantees to male and female persons the Aboriginal and treaty rights provided for by the Charter. As opposed to section 28, section 15 of the Charter is submitted to the limitation of rights provision provided for in section 1.

Although the Canadian feminist campaign for an effective constitutional equality standard gained momentum at almost the same time that the CEDAW was adopted by the UN in 1979, almost no attention was given to this important international development. In fact, Canadian feminists were domestically absorbed by two concerns: the failures of the then Canadian Bill of Rights in relation to women's rights,[28] and the lessons learned from litigating discrimination based on sex in the context of ordinary anti-discrimination and human rights codes adopted at the federal, provincial or territorial levels. In that context, it is important to highlight the connection between the litigating strategy aimed at promoting the adverse impact argument of discrimination and section 15 of the Canadian Charter, which reads as follows: 'every individual is equal before and under the law and has *the right to the equal protection and equal benefit of the law* without discrimination' (author's emphasis).

As the CEDAW is seen as the international legal foundation for a gender equality regime,[29] section 15 of the Canadian Charter was seen until quite recently as the almost exclusive foundation of a domestic women's rights regime in Canada.[30] Bev Baines presents an inventory of the first

[26] P. Kome, *The Taking of Twenty Eight: Women Challenge the Constitution* (Toronto: Women's Educational Press, 1983).

[27] Part I of the Constitution Act, 1982, being Schedule B to the Canada Act, 1982 (UK), c. 11.

[28] Canadian Bill of Rights, S.C. 1960, c. 44.

[29] See L. Farha, 'Committee on the Elimination of Discrimination against Women' in M. Langford (ed.), *Social Rights Jurisprudence: Emerging Trends in International and Comparative Law* (Cambridge University Press, 2009) 553–68, at 553.

[30] The other rights litigated with success by women in Canadian courts are: the right to life, liberty and security of the person, and the right not to be deprived thereof except in accordance with the principles of fundamental justice provided for by section 7 of the Charter. See *Morgentaler* v. *the Queen* [1988] 1 R.C.S. 30.

two decades of women's judicial struggle for equality and organises gains for women in the following categories: athletics, reproduction, crime, family and employment.[31]

A rapid survey of the main constitutional battles for women's rights in Canada indeed shows important victories for women. In *Blainey*,[32] it was decided that the Charter applies to provincial human rights codes, which cannot exclude sex discrimination from complaints against sports organisations. In *Falkiner*,[33] the Ontario Court of Appeal struck down the Ontario government's 'spouse in the house' rule for welfare eligibility as discriminatory. At issue was whether amendments to Ontario's social assistance regulations, which significantly change the definition of 'spouse' for the purpose of receiving social assistance, violated section 7 (security of the person) and section 15 (equality) of the Charter. In *Brooks*,[34] the Supreme Court of Canada broke grounds in deciding that gender equality requires access to an employer's health benefits plan for women who have just given birth. In *Daigle*,[35] the Supreme Court, interpreting the Civil Code of Québec, decided that a woman does not need her husband's permission to be given access to abortion services. In the *Baby R* case,[36] it was decided that a foetus is not a child in need of protection against her mother's behaviour.

Janzen is seen as the leading case for recognising sexual harassment as gender discrimination.[37] In addition, *Lavallée* is the first Canadian case where the battered wife syndrome (when a wife kills her husband) was accepted as a ground of legitimate defence.[38] The *Moge* decision is still relevant today.[39] In *Moge*, the fact that a woman took primary responsibility for child rearing and household work was seen as a long-term economic disadvantage on separation and as a basis for long-term support. In *Seaboyer and Game*,[40] the Supreme Court confirmed that in the course

[31] B. Baines and R. Rubio-Marin, *The Gender of Constitutional Jurisprudence* (Cambridge University Press, 2005) 54–66.

[32] *Re Blainey and Ontario Hockey Association et al.* 58 O.R. (2d) 274 (1986).

[33] *Sandra Falkiner et al.* v. *Director of Income Maintenance Branch of the Ministry of Community and Social Services*, Ontario Court of Appeal, May 2002, Docket C35052, C34983.

[34] *Brooks* v. *Canada Safeway Ltd* [1989] 1 S.C.R. 1219.

[35] *Tremblay* v. *Daigle* [1989] 2 S.C.R. 530.

[36] *Re Baby R* (1988), 15 R.FL. (3d) 225, 53 D.L.R. (4th) 69 (B.C.S.C.)

[37] *Janzen v. Platy Enterprises Ltd* [1989] 1 S.C.R. 1252.

[38] *R.* v. *Lavallée* [1990] 1 S.C.R. 852.

[39] *Moge* v. *Moge* [1992] 3 S.C.R. 813.

[40] *R.* v. *Seaboyer; R.* v. *Gayme* [1991] 2 S.C.R. 577.

of a sexual assault trial, the focus must be kept on the violent acts of the accused, rather than the behaviour of the woman.

To date, the Supreme Court of Canada has rarely explicitly relied on international human rights generally, and the CEDAW in particular, to articulate women's rights to equality in Canada. It did so only in *Ewanchuk* (sexual assault and reference to General Recommendation No. 19 adopted by the CEDAW Committee),[41] *Chan* (refugee claim and risk of forced sterilisation as a form of persecution)[42] and in *Canadian Foundation for Children* (reasonable use of force by way of correction by parents and teachers against children in their care).[43]

Notwithstanding this impressive list of successes, the gender equality standard guaranteed by the Canadian Charter recently suffered from a sustained feminist critique. Margot Young proposes three reasons why Canadian women are experiencing a de facto deficit of equality.[44] First, she says, the courts are unwilling to recognise the full range of norms that pattern sex discrimination. Then, as economic and social rights are not benefitting from explicit constitutional protection in Canada, courts as well as policy-makers promote a restrictive understanding of the government's obligations under rights provisions. Finally, the demand for gender equality finds itself fighting with the discourse of judicial legitimacy in an era of neoconservative ideology and budget cuts.[45] In other words, claims Young, section 15 of the Canadian Charter nowadays promotes a series of uncritical ways of understanding the relationship between equality rights, individuals and the State. As a result, equality law has difficulty dealing with the inequality of those most marginalised and most neglected in society because the further an individual or group sits from what counts as the norm, the more it looks like the inequality complained of is simply idiosyncratic and not a part of the larger patterns of social exclusion.[46]

The increasing level of social exclusion suffered by women who are victims of multiple forms of discrimination sheds a new light on an

[41] *R.* v. *Ewanchuk* [1999] 1 S.C.R. 330.

[42] *Chan v. Canada (Minister of Employment and Immigration)* [1995] 3 S.C.R. 593.

[43] *Canadian Foundation for Children, Youth and the Law* v. *Canada (Attorney General)* [2004] 1 S.C.R. 76.

[44] M. Young, 'Blissed out: section 15 at twenty' in S. McIntyre and S. Rodgers (eds.), *Diminishing Returns Inequality and the Canadian Charter of Rights and Freedoms* (Toronto: LexisNexis Butterworths, 2006) 45–69.

[45] *Ibid.* at 50. [46] *Ibid.* at 63.

old topic: the treaty-making power of the federal government and the implementation of treaties.

2.4 *Canadian federalism and the division of powers in Canada: a closer look at economic, social and cultural rights (ESCR)*

In the *Labour Conventions* case of 1937,[47] the Privy Council of London suggested that a distinction should be made between the federal government's treaty-making power and the implementation process of a treaty in the context of Canadian federalism. Such a distinction respects the equal and distinct jurisdictional powers of provinces (and territories), as provided for by the Constitution Act, that are not subordinated to the Canadian Parliament. Property and private law (the jurisdictional sources of social legislation and of social law) are clearly under provincial jurisdiction. Needless to say, there exists a very strong connection between social spending and the realisation of women's rights.

Social law in Canada is a complex amalgam of cooperation, confrontation, transfer of tax points, debate about national standards and transferring on to the provinces.[48] But as complex as it may be, the current state of social law needs to be assessed against the fact that Canada's ratification of the ICESCR in 1976 proceeded with no provincial opposition. The *Labour Conventions* case then becomes almost irrelevant. What really matters is the systematic and generally resistant attitude of the provinces toward the protection, promotion and implementation of economic and social rights as provided for by international human rights treaties such as the ICESCR.[49]

Against the distinction made between treaty-making and treaty implementation in the *Labour Conventions* case, provincial governments seem to be choosing the opposite approach when confronted with the respect and monitoring of international commitments.[50] In fact, they usually

[47] *Canada (A.G.)* v. *Ontario (A.G.)* [1937] A.C. 326 (hereinafter *Labour Conventions* case).

[48] A useful compilation of the history of social law in Canada can be found in D. Guest, *The Emergence of Social Security in Canada*, 3rd edn (Vancouver: University of British Columbia Press, 1997). See also B. Cameron, 'The social union, executive power and social rights', *Canadian Woman Studies* 23 (2004) 49–56. Also available at: www.srap.ca/.

[49] L. Lamarche, 'Economic and social rights and the era of governance and governance arrangements in Canada: the need to revisit the issue of the implementation of international law of human rights' in C. Carmody and V. Oosterveld (eds.), *Is Our House in Order? Canada's Implementation of International Law* (Montreal: McGill-Queen's University Press, 2010) 116–38.

[50] Article 28 of ICESCR states that the provisions of the Covenant shall extend to *all* parts of federal States, without limitation or exception.

ignore the monitoring process and behave as though treaty-making and treaty implementation with respect to social and economic rights are *both* a federal issue, unless they serve a certain political rhetoric, as in the case of the Province of Québec. Not only is the Province of Québec the land of a distinct society, but it is also the territory that shows a stronger commitment to social rights and to women's rights.

The constitutional imbroglio about the implementation of international human rights standards turned into a domestic cause for concern for Canadian women's groups. Not surprisingly, the CEDAW Committee, as well as other human rights committees, is constantly asked to elucidate upon this issue, without any probing results as yet.

Learning to understand the use of the CEDAW in Canada is a process that has much to do with recognising a growing disenchantment with the Canadian Charter and its equality standard, namely over social rights. After hitting a wall, the women's movement then considered the use of international law of human rights and women's rights as a useful strategy. According to Waldorf and Bazilli,[51] only in 2000 did the political strategy of the Canadian feminist movement become clear. Within the context of budget cuts came a transformation of social laws where the statutory *right to …* became more and more rare, keeping poor women away from claiming and litigating their rights.[52] The UN human rights machinery, including the CEDAW, was then elevated to the rank of the best strategy.

Clearly, by the end of the twentieth century the Canadian women's movement was in search of an effective global women's rights regime. By global, we mean that the recourse to the UN treaty system machinery was based on two assumptions. First, the Canadian women's movement could influence the interpretation of treaties such as the CEDAW or the ICESCR in order for the equality standard to promote substantive equality for women in the context of growing social exclusion. Second, such interaction would increase the level of accountability toward all women's

[51] L. Waldorf and S. Bazilli, *The First CEDAW Impact Study*, International Women's Rights Project (IWRP), 2000 at 35. Also available at: www.iwrp.org/projects/cedaw/. Interestingly, Waldorf and Bazilli recall that the dynamic at the time was more about denouncing government lip service to the CEDAW and to the CEDAW Committee than about *making sense* of the CEDAW at the domestic level.

[52] For an analysis of the *Gosselin* case (this case was about women under 30 years of age being deprived of the basic social assistance unless they subscribe to a workfare (work for welfare) programme. The law was not seen as discriminatory on the basis of age by the Supreme Court of Canada. *Gosselin* v. *Québec (Attorney General)*, [2002] 4 S.C.R. 429), see G. Brodsky, 'Gosselin v. Quebec (Attorney General): autonomy with a vengeance', *Canadian Journal of Women and the Law* 15 (2003) 194–214.

rights (including their economic and social rights) at the domestic level. In order to do so, the movement decided not to privilege the CEDAW as a women's rights instrument but to use all possible ways of reporting about the violations of women's rights in Canada by keeping the focus on the fact that women's poverty is a complex set of rights' violations.

The next section will assess the results of this strategy over a decade (1998–2008), closing with the more recent experience of shadow reporting in front of the Human Rights Council in the context of the Universal Periodic Review (UPR).

3 Using the CEDAW as part of a strategy of shadow reporting in front of UN Human Rights Committees: assessing the first decade

When conducting interviews in 1995, Stienstra and Roberts discovered that, until 1993, there was almost no knowledge of the CEDAW or of international human rights among women's groups in Canada.[53] As they were, between 1993 and 1995, trying to collect from ministries and agencies – federal, provincial and territorial – information about women's rights, implementation of the CEDAW and the Nairobi FLS (Forward Looking Strategy 1995), Stienstra and Roberts realised that government representatives also had trouble tracking and collecting the relevant information. Some women's groups, though, had been aware of the FLS follow-up process, but they clearly represented a small and well-informed minority who attended the Women's Conferences of Copenhagen in 1980 and Nairobi in 1985.

At the domestic level, violence against women has been at the centre of many federal, provincial and territorial governmental strategies and plans of action since the beginning of the 1980s.[54] Not surprisingly,

[53] With the exception of the National Action Committee (NAC – a national women's organisation) 1990 pioneer shadow report in response to Canada 2nd Periodic Report submitted to the CEDAW Committee in 1988. This shadow report was largely inspired by the then recent Supreme Court ruling about the constitutional standard of equality, which focused on impact of discrimination and on adverse effect, thereby departing from the norm of formal equality. See *Andrews* v. *Law Society of British Columbia* [1989] 1 S.C.R. 143. D. Stienstra and B. Roberts, *Strategies for the Year 2000 – A Women's Handbook* (Halifax, NS: Fernwood Publishing, 1995).

[54] See namely Canada, Minister of Supply and Services, *Final Report of the Canadian Panel on Violence Against Women, Changing the Landscape: Ending Violence – Achieving Equality*, 1993; L. Hanvey and D. Kinnon, *The Health Care Sector's Response to Woman Abuse* (Ottawa: National Clearinghouse on Family Violence, Family Violence Prevention

Canada considered that it was well positioned to promote and co-sponsor the 1993 UN General Assembly Resolution 48/104 named the Declaration on the Elimination of Violence against Women.[55]

In 1993 we also saw the beginning of a global campaign claiming that women's rights are human rights.[56] It is in fact in Vienna that a north–south women's global network realised not only its power, but also its capacity to empower itself even more so through human rights instruments such as the CEDAW. In Canada this experience, attended by many, led to an inclusive understanding of the Convention. The Canadian women's movement joined the international network for the interdependence and the indivisibility of all human rights, and discovered through fast-track experimentation the UN system and its mysteries. The fact that the Canadian anti-poverty movement awakened to the international law of economic and social rights as the women's movement was digesting Beijing,[57] created positive conditions of synergy between treaties and between rights. From that perspective, the Vienna Conference has probably been as instrumental for Canadian women as was the Beijing 4th World Conference on Women.

The first UN treaty body to address contemporary and factual women's economic exclusion (although using the term *mothers*) was the ICESCR in its 1993 Concluding Observations.[58] The anti-poverty

Division, Health Programs and Services Branch, Health Canada, 1994); T. Day, *The Health-Related Costs of Violence Against Women in Canada: The Tip of the Iceberg* (London, ON: Centre for Research on Violence against Women and Children, 1995); Statistics Canada, *Family Violence in Canada: A Statistical Profile*, 1998.

[55] Article 2 of UNGA Resolution 48/104 is a benchmark statement as it calls upon States as duty bearers of positive responsibilities in regard to gender and domestic violence eradication.

[56] World Conference on Human Rights, 1993, *Vienna Declaration and Programme of Action*, UN Doc. A/CONF.157/23, 12 July 1993.

[57] This movement developed a sustainable working relation with the ICESCR Committee over time.

[58] UN Doc. E/C.12/1993/5, July 1993, paras. 12 and 13: 'In particular the Committee is concerned about the fact that, according to information available to it, more than half of the single mothers in Canada, as well as a large number of children, live in poverty. The State party has not outlined any new or planned measures to remedy this situation. Of particular concern to the Committee is the fact that the federal Government appears to have reduced the ratio of its contributions to cost-sharing agreements for social assistance.' See also UN Doc. E/C.12/1/Add.31, 10 December 1998, where 15 per cent of the sixty paragraphs of Concluding Observations concern women's rights.

movement, entering the experience of the ICESCR, offered to women an opportunity to become acquainted with the UN system by bringing information about women's poverty to the attention of the Committee. Women's equality-seeking organisations seized this opportunity, which may have been reinforced by a lingering perception that the CEDAW was mainly concerned with domestic violence against women.

More recently, the Canadian feminist movement has been promoting the idea that the CEDAW is also about looking for the causes and the consequences of women's poverty, social exclusion and commodification in a globalised world. In doing so, it departed from a definition of violence restricted to the domestic, to an understanding of violence that includes the negative impact of poor public policies on women. This approach is now understood in Canada as a meaningful way of promoting in front of all human rights treaty bodies the interdependency of all women's rights. Violence against women, as much as indirect and systemic discrimination or poverty, was described as causes and consequences of the violation of all women's rights.

This section focuses on the inputs, that is, the proposals made in the process of shadow reporting by the Canadian women's movement to the CEDAW Committee over the decade 1998–2008 and the outputs – the assessment of the dialogue between Canada and the CEDAW Committee and of the Concluding Comments that followed. Each subsection examines a cycle of reporting (1998, 2003 and 2008) and the last subsection provides information about the new reporting mechanism designed by the Human Rights Council: the Universal Periodic Report (UPR). We conclude by saying that, clearly, this process contributed to the unpacking of the requirements of a gender equality regime in Canada, including with regard to provincial and territorial accountability toward all women's rights. We also conclude that the recourse to the inter-committees synergy, namely between the CEDAW and the ICESCR, contributed to such success as, increasingly, one echoes the other. But we also stress the risk of getting caught by *la saveur du jour*, as there were moments when processes, in relation to accountability namely, mattered more than rights themselves. Sadly though, we come to the conclusion that nowadays neither legal nor political accountability, as components of an international gender equality regime, seem to move the current Conservative government.

3.1 *The 1998 dialogue with the CEDAW Committee: from formal gender equality to gender impact analysis of policies*

The consideration by the CEDAW Committee of the third and fourth Canada Periodic Reports happened in April 1998.[59] The third Report covers the period of 1987–90 and the fourth, the one of 1991–4. The 1998 examination of the Canada Reports by the CEDAW Committee suffered from contextual confusion. On one hand, the Canadian government was promoting, as a follow-up to Beijing, a Federal Plan for Gender Equity,[60] as on the other hand it was implementing an economic austerity strategy aimed at fighting against public deficits.[61] In 1997 a Canadian women's NGO coalition brought to the attention of the CEDAW Committee a shadow report with an introductory statement that reads as follows:

> inequality for women is entrenched in every facet of Canadian life … and the situation for women has been getting progressively worse in all areas of social economic and political life. Every indicator shows that there has been a growth of women's inequality as a direct result of policies and of political choices made by the government of Canada. We want the CEDAW Committee to note the impact on women of the decreasing responsibility and accountability of the Canadian government for social programs and well being and the effects that cuts to social programs … have on women's life.[62]

[59] UN Doc. CEDAW/C/CAN/3, 1992 and UN Doc. CEDAW/C/CAN/4, 1996; UN Doc. CEDAW/C/SR.329 and SR.330, 27 March and 6 April 1998. See also UN Doc. A/52/38/Rev.1 (1997) paras. 306–344 for Concluding Observations. For a critique of the format and of the moment of submission of reports by Canada, see Expert H. B. Schöpp-Schilling's comments, at UN Doc. CEDAW/C/SR.329, para. 27. The Expert reminds the Canadian government that it would have been useful to move from description to impact analysis. See also para. 28 for a request for information from Member Schöpp-Schilling about constitutional relations between federal and provincial and territorial governments. Such critique illustrates the relevance of the 2001 *Guidelines for Reporting* (see UN Doc. HRI/GEN/2/Rev.1, Ch. 5, May 2001, 41ff.). For a general discussion on the evolution of CEDAW reporting guidelines and about the UN Treaty Body Reform and the CEDAW, see H. B. Schöpp-Schilling, 'Treaty body reform: the case of the Committee on the Elimination of Discrimination against Women' 7:1 (2007) *Human Rights Law Review* 201–24.

[60] This Plan, presented at the 4th World Conference on Women in Beijing, promised that the government would embark on a comprehensive strategy to ensure women's economic autonomy and wellbeing, a reduction in violence against women, and the promotion of gender equality for workers in federal departments and agencies.

[61] Canadian Council for Social Development, *Maintaining a National Social Safety Net*, 1996, available at: www.ccsd.ca/pr/pos_chst.html (last accessed 14 February 2013). See also T. Scarth (ed.), *Hell and High Water, An Assessment of Paul Martin's Record and Implications for the Future* (Ottawa: Canadian Centre for Policy Alternatives, 2004).

[62] See paras. 321, 331 and 336 of 1998 CEDAW Concluding Observations in the case of Canada at UN Doc. A/52/38/Rev.1.

In fact, this shadow report was largely a poverty report with an emphasis on the recent Canadian economic and social policies. Violence against women was therein understood and described as including economic (market) violence for which the equality jurisprudence has stopped providing effective answers.

In the context of the examination of Canada's third and fourth Periodic Reports submitted to the CEDAW Committee, twelve of the CEDAW Committee experts took the floor and addressed questions to the Canadian government's delegation. Ms Abaka talked about the need to assess impact of potential privatisation of healthcare; Ms Bustelo Garcia Del Real talked about the need to investigate the reality of women who are victims of violence, prostitution and trafficking. The most inquisitive intervention was the one of the late Ms Schöpp-Schilling, who said categorically to the Canadian delegation that too much information would not compensate for not enough gender impact analysis.[63] In addition, she raised issues that would gain relevancy in relation to State reporting to UN human rights committees in Canada: the binding effect of the CEDAW on provinces and territories and the need for an effective consultation of women's groups. Schöpp-Schilling also expressed strong concern about women's increasing poverty in Canada as a potential consequence of numerous women's rights violations.

In 1998 and 1999 all ICCPR, ICESCR and CEDAW Committees echoed the need for a gender impact economic analysis of Canadian policies.[64] Multiple factors shifted the focus of the 1998 dialogue between the CEDAW Committee and the Canadian government from the requirement of the inclusion of rights in domestic legislation to the need for assessing the impact on women of legal, political and economic transformations and policies, namely the follow-up to the Beijing Platform and the growing significance of results-based management in public administration and the economic reality in Canada. Such a strong departure from the formalistic examination of the legal framework to a gender impact analysis approach of policies on women was promoted and largely crafted by women's interventions and transmission of shadow reports. In fact, the Canadian government's representatives also promoted a more evaluative approach of the exercise in their oral statements. From plans of action

[63] UN Doc. CEDAW/C/SR.330, paras. 325–331.

[64] See, for example, the HRC Concluding Conclusions at UN Doc. CCPR/C/79/Add.105, para. 20, April 1999: 'the Committee is concerned that many of the programme cuts in recent years have exacerbated these inequalities and harmed women and other disadvantaged groups'.

(federal and provincial or territorial and even regional) to planned ministerial gender mainstreaming of policies,[65] to gender-based analysis,[66] and even to budget gender mainstreaming, it would not be very long before the women's movement would claim a domestic participative accountability framework in relation to women's rights.[67]

3.2 The 2003 dialogue: from impact analysis to accountability

The fifth Periodic Report of Canada was submitted to the CEDAW Committee in 2002,[68] a peculiar moment. Indeed, and as acknowledged by government representatives, 2002 witnessed an economic pick-up in Canada. The fifth Report covers the period 1994–8 (the negative period) but is enriched by an update Addendum of 2002 (the so-called positive period).[69]

According to a Canadian government representative, the Report was submitted late because of the complex federal–provincial consultation procedure in Canada managed by the *mysterious*[70] Continuing Committee of Officials on Human Rights.[71] That being said, the Report, again, does not respect the CEDAW Reporting Guidelines adopted in 1996,[72] which

[65] See, for example, UN Doc. CCPR/C/SR.1738, 7 March 1999, where a Canadian government representative (Ms Fry, Canada former Secretary of State of the Department for the Status of Women) affirms that a gender analysis of all policies affecting women's economic status was being carried out. In that regard, Health Canada Gender-Based Analysis was considered a model. Available at www.hc-sc.gc.ca/hl-vs/pubs/women-femmes/gender-sexes-eng.php (last accessed 14 February 2013).

[66] See UN Doc. A/52/38/Rev.1, para. 326: the Committee also noted with satisfaction that Canada continues to strengthen and refine its gender mainstreaming efforts at all levels. See also G. Steinsky-Schwartz, D. Rowan-Campbell and L. Langevin, *Equality for Women – Beyond an Illusion – Expert Panel on Accountability Mechanisms for Gender Equality Final Report*, Status of Women Canada, December 2005.

[67] See as an example the impressive work of FAFIA (Feminist Alliance for International Action) at: http://fafia-afai.org/.

[68] UN Doc. CEDAW/C/CAN/5, April 2002. A majority Liberal government was then governing Canada and would continue to do so until 2006.

[69] UN Doc. CEDAW/C/CAN/5/Add.1, 30 December 2002.

[70] Mysterious, because none of the human rights extended community members ever met a member of this committee. See Senate of Canada, *The Silenced Citizens – Effective Implementation of Canada's International Obligations with Respect to the Right of Children, Final Report of the Standing Senate Committee on Human Rights*, 21 April 2007.

[71] UN Doc. CEDAW/C/SR.603, para. 52, February 2003.

[72] UN Doc. CEDAW/C/7/Rev. 3, July 1996.

were about to be replaced in 2003.[73] The 1996 Guidelines provided for the need to report on progress and difficulties encountered since the consideration by the CEDAW Committee on the previous report.[74]

The first part of the 2002 Report enumerates a list of reports and programmes relating to women's rights including the Statistical Profile 1998–2005 of family violence in Canada; the Statistical Report on women in Canada; the production of the report *Women and Men in Canada – Statistical Glance*; the Federal Plan for Gender Equality 1995, replaced by the 2000 Agenda for Gender Equality (AGE); the Guide for Gender-Based Analysis Policy Making 1996; the Gender Equality Indicators; the Diversity and Justice Gender Perspectives Initiative; the Women's Health Strategy; the creation of CIDA (Canadian International Development Agency) and Foreign Affairs Gender Equality Divisions; the Gender Analysis Initiative adopted by Indian Affairs; and the Social Context Educational Project implemented with the support of the National Justice Institute.[75]

FAFIA (the Canadian Feminist Alliance for International Action) coordinated the production of a very strong and extensive shadow report, positioning itself, from a knowledge-based perspective, as the expert NGO Canadian interlocutor to the CEDAW Committee. But it is the Province of British Columbia CEDAW Group that challenged the seemingly opaque and exclusive federal government's responsiveness at the international level by producing a provincial shadow report.[76] This report strongly emphasises the intersectional reality of discrimination against women and women's exclusion.[77]

The 2003 discussion on the consideration of Canada's fifth Periodic Report led to some difficult exchanges between government representatives and the CEDAW Committee Experts. Schöpp-Schilling came back to the issue of the quality and usefulness of the Report: could Canada present a balanced account of the challenges it faced? Could it present the methods chosen to overcome problems and assess them?[78] And for the first time in the case of Canada, some other experts clearly referred to

[73] UN Doc. CEDAW, A/57/38 (2002), Chapter VI, *Ways and Means of Expediting the Work of the Committee.*

[74] UN Doc. CEDAW/C/7/Rev. 3, Articles 12 and 13.

[75] See also UN Doc. CEDAW/PSWG/2003/I/CPR.2/Add.1, 2 and 3, *Canada List of Issues and Government Responses.*

[76] See *B.C. CEDAW Report: British Columbia Moves Backwards on Women's Equality* (January 2003) available at: http://povertyandhumanrights.org (last accessed 14 February 2013).

[77] *Ibid.* para. 98.

[78] UN Doc. CEDAW/C/SR.603, para. 14.

information received and taken from grass-roots organisations.[79] Many questions expressed deep concern about women's poverty, and even more about Aboriginal women's poverty. Often, issues relating to prostitution, trafficking, violence and family law were introduced in a poverty framework.

On the issue of the federative structure and provincial autonomous jurisdiction over social programmes, the CEDAW Committee decided to offer a lesson of international public law to Canada:

> The Committee recommends that the State party search for innovative ways to strengthen the currently existing consultative federal–provincial–territorial Continuing Committees of Officials for human rights as well as other mechanisms of partnership in order to ensure that coherent and consistent measures in line with the Convention are achieved. The Committee also recommends that the existing mechanisms be used to introduce best practices in order to achieve substantive equality of women with men in the enjoyment of their human rights under all governments.[80]

The output of the 2003 review pushed the idea of public accountability in matters relating to human and women's rights to the forefront of the political agenda in Canada. As a consequence, in 2004 the federal government created the Standing Committee on the Status of Women, which was mandated to review the particular areas of federal policy relating to the status of women. The Committee also has the power to initiate studies without a referral from the House; that is, it may examine and report on all subjects connected to its mandate. The Standing Committee on the Status of Women undertook an extensive consultation with national and regional women's organisations when it was first established in autumn 2004. Up to now, the Committee has adopted twenty very useful reports,[81] which often serve as follow-up material to the CEDAW's Concluding Comments and observations addressed to Canada. Clearly, the Standing Committee (comprising twelve elected MPs) contributes to the repoliticisation of women's rights in Canada when compared to the array of technocratic initiatives that were adopted before.

The 2003 exercise says a lot about the challenge of multileveled accountability claims in the domain of human rights. The precedence of gender mainstreaming strategies adopted by both the federal and

[79] *Ibid.* para. 20 (Ms Shin).

[80] UN Doc. A/58/38 (2003), paras. 349 and 350.

[81] See for example: Report 19 – *Proactive Pay Equity Legislation* (Adopted by the Committee on 10 May 2007; Presented to the House on 16 May 2007); Report 16 – *Restoration of*

provincial governments in Canada stands as an answer to the increased pressure put on them by more efficient UN human rights treaty bodies, including the CEDAW Committee, and domestic civil society. But it also raises interesting questions that resonate with what the critics have said about the Beijing outcome, as sometimes it seems that process matters more than results.[82] Indeed, the Canadian women's movement became frustrated at being offered either more mainstreaming of women's rights or more gender analysis. Although processes and accountability tools are acknowledged as essential to the protection and the promotion of women's rights, it was clear by then that the substance of rights and processes do not always go hand in hand, and that more processes do not necessarily result in better rights or less poverty.

3.3 *The 2008 dialogue: the terms of the equality regime as understood by the CEDAW Committee ... only!*

The year of 2006 was a harsh one for the Canadian feminist movement.[83] The Equality Rights component of the Court Challenges Program was cancelled. Funding for major women's advocacy organisations was reduced or removed and the Status of Women Canada research fund was eliminated. In addition, an estimated eight billion dollars in federal transfers, which benefitted provincial social programmes, was cut between 1995 and 1998 and was never re-established.[84] There was no doubt that the

Court Challenges Program (Adopted by the Committee on 29 March 2007; Presented to the House on 18 April 2007; Concurred in by the House on 1 May 2007); Report 14 – *Eliminating Discrimination against Women in the Employment Insurance Program* (Adopted by the Committee on 1 March 2007; Presented to the House on 21 March 2007); Report 7 – *Matrimonial Real Property Rights on Reserves* (Adopted by the Committee on 20 June 2006; Presented to the House on 21 June 2006); Report 5 – *Interim Report on the Maternity and Parental Benefits Under Employment Insurance: The Exclusion of Self-Employed Workers* (Adopted by the Committee on 24 November 2005; Presented to the House on 28 November 2005), all available at: www.parl.gc.ca/committeebusiness/ReportsResponses.aspx?Cmte=FEWO&Language=E&Mode=1&Parl=39&Ses=1 (last accessed 14 February 2013).

[82] See M. Daly, 'Gender mainstreaming in theory and practice', *Social Politics* 12:3 (2005) 433–50. See also D. Otto, 'The exile of inclusion: reflections on gender issues in international law over the last decade', *Melbourne Journal of International Law* 10 (2009) 11–26.

[83] The Conservative government was elected in January 2006. The election of May 2011 secured its majority in Parliament. It also benefits from a majority in the Senate, a non-elected body.

[84] Council of the Federation, *Reconciling the Irreconcilable? Addressing Canada's Fiscal Imbalance*, 2006, available at: www.councilofthefederation.ca/pdfs/Report_Fiscalim_Mar3106.pdf (last accessed 14 February 2013).

gender-specific consequences of the new neoliberal economic agenda in Canada was prejudicial toward women and even more to some groups of women such as Aboriginal and immigrant women.

With a clearly diminished equality return at home – limited access to justice, social protection and services and decent jobs; increased domestic and economic violence – the women's and the anti-poverty movements decided to maintain the strategy of systematically informing the UN human rights Committees about the Canadian situation.

In this context, the Canadian women's movement found itself confronted with a difficult challenge because fewer resources were available for litigation and for advocacy at the local and international level. The movement was also aware of both the adoption by the CEDAW Committee of General Recommendation No. 25 about Article 4(1) of CEDAW (2004)[85] and of the adoption by the ICESCR Committee of General Comment No. 16 (2005) about Article 3 of the Covenant.[86] Would the understanding of equality between men and women by both Committees echo the Canadian feminist campaign for substantive economic equality? Would women's rights and needs be understood only as requiring temporary special measures? Would women's rights be mainly conceptualised in comparison with men's conditions?

The norm of substantive equality in Canada clearly required an interpretation promoting not only the proactive role of the State, but also the need for specific policies aimed at protecting the rights of a growing percentage of vulnerable women experiencing inter-sectoral forms of discrimination.[87]

Paragraph 28 of CEDAW General Recommendation No. 25 suggests an increased sensitivity of the Committee to the use of different types of measures aimed at guaranteeing women's rights, including specific measures or programmes that would not only be temporary or special:

[85] *Compilation of General Comments Adopted by Human Rights Treaty Bodies, Vol. II*, UN Doc. HRI/GEN/1/Rev.9, 2008, CEDAW General Recommendation No. 25 (2004) about Article 4(1) on temporary special measures, at 365.

[86] *Compilation of General Comments Adopted by Human Rights Treaty Bodies, Vol. I*, UN Doc. HRI/GEN/1/Rev.9, 2008; CESCR General Comment No. 16: The Equal Right of Men and Women to the Enjoyment of all Economic, Social and Cultural Rights (Article 3), 113. See also General Comment No. 20: Non Discrimination in Economic, Social and Cultural Rights (Article 2, para. 2 of the International Covenant on Economic, Social and Cultural Rights), UN Doc. E/C.12/GC/20, July 2009.

[87] For more information, see S. Gavigan and D. E. Chunn (eds.), *The Legal Tender of Gender: Welfare, Law and the Regulation of Women's Poverty* (Oxford: Hart Publishing, 2010).

> States parties should explain the reasons for choosing one type of measure over another; the justification for applying such measures should include a description of the actual life situation of women, including the conditions and influences which shape their lives and opportunities – or that of a specific group of women, suffering from multiple forms of discrimination – and whose position the State party intends to improve in an accelerated manner with the application of such temporary special measures; the relationship between such measures and general measures and efforts to improve the position of women should be clarified.

In 2007 the Canadian women's movement also placed modest hope in the new UN consolidated reporting Guidelines. Would it positively influence the presentation to the CEDAW Committee by Canada of its next Periodic Report if such Guidelines ask for shorter, more-targeted and better-organised information? Would they provide a robust incentive for Canada to abandon the usual format of its Reports, which was a source of great irritation to some members of the CEDAW Committee?[88] Would they emphasise the need for an effective monitoring of all Committee's Concluding Comments?

The 2008 consideration of Canada's sixth and seventh combined Periodic Reports to be submitted to the CEDAW Committee cannot be analysed in a nutshell. In 2005 FAFIA, on behalf of a coalition of women's groups in Canada, submitted to the Human Rights Committee a very detailed brief where the erosion of social programmes and women's poverty were introduced as causes and consequences of the violation of women's rights to equality in Canada.[89] In April 2006 the HRC adopted Concluding Observations with regard to Canada, putting at the forefront the unacceptable situation of Aboriginal women and, maybe surprisingly, considering the usual style and content of HRC Observations, underlying the detrimental effects of cuts in welfare programmes on women and children,[90] especially Aboriginal people and Afro-Canadian women.[91]

[88] See UN Doc. HRI/MC/2006/3, para. E.1.at 68.

[89] FAFIA – Canadian Feminist Alliance for International Action, *Submission to the United Nations Human Rights Committee on the Occasion of its Review of Canada's 5th Report on Compliance with the International Covenant on Civil and Political Rights* (September 2005), paras. 3 and 4 (on file with the author).

[90] UN Doc. CCPR/C/CAN/CO/5, 26 April 2006, paras. 22, 23 and 24.

[91] See also CCPR/C/85/L/Can, List of Issues, 25 July 2005, para. 11: 'What actions have been adopted to assess the situation of the Afro-Canadian community in the areas of employment, habitat, health and education, as recommended by the Special Rapporteur on contemporary forms of racism, racial discrimination, xenophobia and related intolerance?' Also see para. 21 about Aboriginal women.

In 2006 the same coalition submitted a report for the attention of the ICESCR Committee on the occasion of its review of Canada's fourth and fifth Periodic Reports.[92] Following an important consultation, the FAFIA brief focused on social programmes, Aboriginal women, access to justice, abolition of the Court Challenges Program, pay equity, the Live-in Caregiver Program, childcare, employment insurance, welfare assistance and many others areas.

The consultation of the UN High Commissioner for Human Rights Website database reveals twelve identified women's NGOs that submitted a shadow report to the CEDAW Committee in the context of the consideration of Canada's sixth and seventh Reports. It includes associations representing Aboriginal women, immigrant and Afro-Canadian women, and women in prison. In its own submission,[93] FAFIA acknowledged the contributions of a long list of women's groups.

The CEDAW Committee List of Issues was published in March 2008 and contains twenty-nine paragraphs expressing requests for updated and detailed information from the Canadian government.[94] It covers different areas organised according to the sequence of rights guaranteed by the CEDAW: constitutional rights, legislative and institutional frameworks, stereotypes and education, violence against women, trafficking and exploitation, participation in public affairs, employment, health, women in vulnerable situations, minorities, immigrants and refugees. A last section tackles the issue of poverty. Among the list of requests, the Committee shows a sustained preoccupation with Aboriginal women, including the issue of matrimonial property and of Aboriginal women in prisons. Finally, attention is also paid to the dynamic between women and care, including home care and childcare.

It seems to us that the very last paragraph of this List of Issues is worthy of comment. Under the Heading *Marriage and family life*, paragraph 29 reads as follows:

> The Committee on Economic, Social and Cultural Rights, in its concluding observations of 22 May 2006 on the State party's combined fourth and

[92] FAFIA, available at: www2.ohchr.org/english/bodies/cescr/docs/info-ngos/canadian-feminist.pdf (last accessed 25 February 2013).

[93] FAFIA, *Women's Inequality in Canada, Submission to the UN Committee on the Elimination of Discrimination against Women on the Occasion of the Committee's Review of Canada 6th and 7th Reports*, September 2008 at 13, available at: http://socialrightscura.ca/documents/CEDAW/FAFIACanadaCEDAW2008.pdf (last accessed 25 February 2013).

[94] UN Doc. CEDAW/C/CAN/Q/7, 6 March 2008.

> fifth periodic report, noted with concern that single-mothered families were over represented in families whose children were relinquished to foster care. The Committee was also concerned that women continued to be forced to relinquish their children into foster care because of inadequate housing. Please indicate what measures have been taken.

Clearly, this reference to another UN human rights treaty body's assessment of Canada's compliance with human rights instruments shows the capacity of the Canadian women's movement to link different analyses produced by such Committees. Abundantly informed of the Canadian situation by Canadian civil society coalitions, which the women's movement joined or initiated, the CEDAW Committee, now also enriched by the functional Reporting Guidelines and rules of procedure, did not fall short of conclusions that should have alerted Canada in the process of the production of its sixth and seventh Reports.[95]

Paragraph 9 of the CEDAW Committee 2008 Concluding Observations talks about areas requiring Canada's priority attention in the future. This paragraph exhibits an attitude of both confidence and exasperation toward Canada as a State Party. In addition, paragraph 10 of the same document strongly suggests Canada invite provincial and territorial structures to take appropriate steps in order to implement the adopted Observations. This invitation, as we explained before, challenges the status of provinces and territories as being *untouchables* in international human rights law.

The CEDAW Committee was equally confident when it ventured into the land of national minimum social standards as a legal requirement.[96] This has been a constant demand from civil society, excluding Québec (a province where the opting-out of national standards with appropriate compensation is preferred because of the distinctiveness of Québec society), but is also an important domestic issue as on many occasions UN human rights committees, and namely the ICESCR Committee, insisted on the distinction between the protection of rights and the multiple ways of reaching such goals in accordance with domestic traditions. In the present case, the CEDAW Committee clearly decided to support the domestic position of Canadian women's groups.

The CEDAW Committee 2008 Concluding Observations can be grouped into seven main different topics: access to justice (paragraph 22); violence against women and Aboriginal women (paragraphs 30–2); support for

[95] UN Doc. CEDAW/C/CAN/CO/7 and CEDAW/C/CAN/CO/7/Add.1 and Add.1/Corr.1, 7 November 2008.

[96] *Ibid.* paras. 14 and 18.

civil society women's associations (paragraph 28); over-incarceration of Aboriginal women (paragraph 34); participation in public life (paragraph 36); women and the labour market (paragraph 38); and finally, childcare (paragraph 40).

The 2008 consideration of Canada's sixth and seventh Periodic Reports by the CEDAW Committee shows interesting progress from the standpoint of Canadian women's rights and gender equality, as the debate has moved back to substance over processes. But the most interesting point is expressed in paragraph 53 of the 2008 CEDAW Concluding Observations. It requests from Canada a follow-up (one year) report on two specific issues identified as priority issues: national minimum social standards and the investigation of an unacceptable number of murdered and disappeared Aboriginal women.

In February 2010 Canada submitted an answer to this follow-up request to the CEDAW Committee.[97] Canada's answer to the CEDAW Committee is clearer and stronger than on previous occasions, as it raises the point of the alleged limited capacity of the federal government to interfere in fields of provincial jurisdiction, such as in the case of social programmes. Are we back to the *Labour Conventions* case paradigm?[98]

3.4 *And now the Universal Periodic Review (UPR)*

The experience of shadow reporting by the Canadian feminist movement recently expanded as more than fifty associations, representative of civil society, submitted briefs for the attention of the Human Rights Council in the context of the Universal Periodic Review (UPR) procedure in 2009.[99] Again, the more significant submission concerning non-Aboriginal women was the one from FAFIA.[100] This brief covered a wide area of women's rights and violations of such rights including inadequate social assistance, housing, imprisoned women, healthcare, education, civil participation, employment, access to justice, immigration and the trafficking of women.

The Report adopted by the Human Rights Council Working Group carries eighty-eight Conclusions and Recommendations.[101] As far as

[97] UN Doc. CEDAW/C/CAN/CO/7/Add.1, February 2010.

[98] *Supra* note 47.

[99] UN Doc. A/HRC/WG.6/4/CAN/3, 24 November 2008.

[100] FAFIA, *A Failing Grade on Women's Equality – Canada's Human Rights Record on Women*, September 2008, at 13, available at: www2.ohchr.org/english/bodies/cedaw/docs/ngos/FAFIAUPRSeptember8final_3.pdf (last accessed 14 February 2013).

[101] UN Doc. A/HRC/11/17, 9 October 2009.

women's rights are concerned, those Conclusions mostly focus on violence against women, using a language quite close to the 1993 Declaration on the Elimination of Violence against Women.[102] It gets even stronger in the case of Aboriginal women's rights and of women's rights to be protected against all forms of gendered violence. Recommendations 10, 41 and 45 are those in which the Canadian women's movement rests most of their hopes. They concern the justiciability of economic, social and cultural rights and the necessity to provide effective domestic remedies in case of their violation and to integrate the normative content of such rights into poverty reduction strategies. The Canadian government gave clear signals that it does not acknowledge the justiciability of economic and social rights and has refused relevant Recommendations adopted by the HRC.[103]

Such statements raise a point of unresolved tension in Canada. As the Canadian government's answer to the UPR Recommendations echoes the domestic case law about women's social rights, which is not positive, shall we still rely on the equality regime promoted by the CEDAW (the prohibition of all forms of discrimination against women) to indirectly protect those rights? If so, the next logical step will be to rely on the Optional Protocol to the Convention on the Elimination of All Forms of Discrimination against Women that Canada ratified. The synergetic effect of cross-treaty analysis will not work this time as the Canadian federal government does not intend to ratify the Optional Protocol to the International Covenant on Economic, Social and Cultural Rights, which will come into force on 5 May 2013.

4 Conclusion

The analysis of the Canadian experience with the CEDAW confirms one of the hypotheses submitted by the editors of this book. Indeed, the CEDAW contributes to the development of a domestic gender equality regime, at least in a theoretical sense. Interestingly, the transformative effect, analysed over a decade of experimentation by the Canadian women's movement, cannot be measured by the usual standards, which would include constitutional incorporation and judicial interpretation. But it is

[102] *Supra* note 55.

[103] Government of Canada, Canadian Heritage, *Canada's Universal Periodic Review Response to the Recommendations*, June 2009, available at: www.pch.gc.ca/pgm/pdp-hrp/inter/101-eng.cfm (last accessed 14 February 2013).

clear that the CEDAW now belongs to the foundational repertoire of normative thinking on gender equality in Canada.

A decade is a very short period of time in the world of international human rights law. And the point here is not to predict the future. But a decade is enough time to raise the following three questions. The first one brings us back to Margot Young's concern about the need for an understanding of the relationship between gender equality and the State, when the State resists acknowledging the real value of economic and social rights as human rights and women's rights.[104] In that regard, it seems that there is a need in Canada to test the Optional Protocol to the CEDAW in order to promote a comprehensive approach to gender equality that does not avoid the market aspect of discrimination based on gender.

The second question is being raised repeatedly in Canada. As this chapter addressed the synergetic relation between treaties (CEDAW and ICESCR), one can wonder if it is enough to transform the domestic legal landscape. In other words, can the CEDAW serve as a substitute for constitutionally unprotected rights such as social and economic rights? The answer seems to vary according to the ideological standpoint of the government and it shows the relative vulnerability of a comprehensive gender equality regime relying firstly on the CEDAW.

Finally, the Canadian experience with the CEDAW confirms that multiple legal and judicial entry points to gender equality, both domestic and international, complement each other and contribute in different ways to the construction of a gender equality regime. In Canada, it is clear that it is the women's movement, and not the State Party to the CEDAW, that nurtures such a dynamic.

[104] Young, 'Blissed out'. *Supra* note 44.

13

India's CEDAW story

MADHU MEHRA

1 Introduction

This chapter explores the interplay of factors that shaped ratification and domestication of the Convention on the Elimination of All Forms of Discrimination against Women (CEDAW) in India, to understand the complex influences that shape the outcomes of the women question. Although the ratification of the CEDAW was not the consequence of demands from a domestic constituency, there has been considerable activity following ratification. In looking at the events and actors that lent momentum to the work around the CEDAW, and examining the contributions of the judiciary and the legislature in select thematic areas, this chapter contextualizes the possibilities and limitations of domestication of the CEDAW. This chapter is divided into three parts. The first part outlines the formal status of India's obligations under the CEDAW – covering its ratification, the scope of its reservations/declarations and the country reviews held thus. The second part looks at the influences and events that helped ground the CEDAW within India – tracing the domestic and international developments that propelled ratification of the CEDAW, providing an overview of actors and events that popularized the Convention and shaped the contours of the shadow report processes as well. The third part examines CEDAW implementation through judicial pronouncements and related legislative action with respect to three thematic areas – family, sexual violence and sex discrimination in the workplace. The selected

Madhu Mehra is a founding member and Executive Director of Partners for Law in Development (PLD), a legal resource group in India dedicated to the advancement of women's rights and social justice. The author has been part of the national processes on the CEDAW in India, and runs CEDAW programmes that include capacity building, resource production and advocacy. She is also part of CEDAW work in South Asia and in the Asia Pacific region.

themes relate to areas in which India has entered declarations limiting its obligations under the CEDAW, as well as those where no such declarations exist, to allow comparative insight into domestication with respect to both of these categories. The scope of this chapter does not allow for a comprehensive discussion of the select areas covered, let alone the telling of India's full CEDAW story; however, it does provide insights into the complex influences that shape the uneven domestication of treaty obligations.

2 Status of India's ratification, reservations and reporting to the CEDAW Committee

India signed the CEDAW on 30 July 1980 and ratified it on 9 July 1993 with two declarations and one reservation. The reservation to Article 29(1) is of little significance, as it does not touch upon the core obligations under the CEDAW.[1] India's declarations, however, seek to curtail its core obligations under Articles 5(a), 16(1) and 16(2). The two declarations read as follows:[2]

> With regard to articles 5(a) and 16(1) of the Convention on the Elimination of All Discrimination Against Women, the Government of the Republic of India declares that it shall abide by and ensure these provisions in conformity with its policy of non-interference in the personal affairs of any Community without its initiative and consent.
>
> With regard to Article 16(2) of the CEDAW, the Government of the Republic of India declares that though in principle it fully supports the principle of compulsory registration of marriages, it is not practical in a vast country like India with its variety of customs, religions and level of literacy.

These declarations limit India's obligations to eliminate discriminatory cultural stereotypes about women, promote equality in marriage and family relations, and establish the compulsory registration of marriages. The Committee has consistently expressed concern about the obstacle posed by the declarations towards implementation of the CEDAW, urging their withdrawal.[3] Indeed, qualifications that are incompatible with the

[1] The reservation exempts referral of disputes (raised by States Parties) relating to interpretation or application of the Convention by India to arbitration.

[2] *India's Initial Report*, CEDAW/C/IND/1, 10 March 1999, paras. 2–3.

[3] *Concluding Observations: India*, 2 April 2000, A/55/38, paras. 44 and 60; *Concluding Comments: India*, 2 February 2007, CEDAW/C/IND/CO/3, para. 11. The Concluding Comments of 2007 refer to the declarations as reservations.

object and purpose of the treaty are considered impermissible under the law regulating international treaties, regardless of whether such qualification is termed as a declaration or a reservation.[4]

In terms of fulfilling its obligations to report on the progressive implementation of the CEDAW, India has submitted its initial report, a combined second and third periodic report, as well as an exceptional report requested by the Committee; it is in the process of finalizing its combined fourth and fifth periodic reports. The initial report, due in 1994, was submitted in 1999 and reviewed in 2000; the second and third reports, which were due in 1998 and 2002 respectively, were combined and submitted in 2005 and reviewed in 2007; the combined fourth and fifth periodic report is expected to be submitted in 2012. In between the two country reviews of 2000 and 2007, the CEDAW Committee sought information on gender-based violence that was perpetrated during the carnage in Gujarat in 2002, its gendered impact and steps taken to address these issues.[5] The Committee has raised these concerns since 2006, holding a special session on Gujarat in 2010, and intends to pursue the matter in the next periodic review.[6] Although numerically India's reporting has progressed to the fifth periodic report, each of the reviews combined two periodic reports to make up for delayed reporting.

3 Influences and events that grounded the CEDAW in India

3.1 Developments that catalyzed India's ratification

At the time when the CEDAW was adopted in 1979, and later when it came into force in 1981, there were no constitutional impediments for India's ratification of the treaty. The Indian Constitution guaranteed to women equality before the law, while endorsing affirmative action for women.[7] In addition, India had ratified the International Covenant on Civil and Political Rights (ICCPR) and the International Covenant on Economic, Social and Cultural Rights (ICESCR) in 1979, which obligated

[4] Article 19(c) of the Vienna Convention on the Law of Treaties 1969.

[5] The targeting of Muslims in Gujarat in 2002 involved killing, looting, the destruction of property and the use of sexual violence.

[6] *List of Issues and Questions by the Pre-Sessional Working Group: India*, 8 August 2006, CEDAW/C/IND/Q/3, para. 1; *Concluding Observations: India*, 2 February 2007, CEDAW/C/IND/CO/3, paras. 67–8; *Concluding Observations: India*, 22 October 2010, CEDAW/C/IND/CO/SP.1, para. 38.

[7] Articles 14 and 15 of the Constitution of India guarantee equality before the law and non-discrimination on grounds of sex, and mandates affirmative action for women.

the country to prohibit sex discrimination. Yet India did not ratify the Convention until 1993, a little over a decade after it signed the Convention in 1980. The discussion below traces the domestic concerns that made it difficult for India to ratify the CEDAW in the decade of the 1980s, tracing as well the domestic legislative steps, together with the international considerations, that combined to create the momentum for India to ratify the CEDAW in 1993.

3.1.1 Events at the domestic level

Although there was no significant inconsistency between the Constitution of India and the CEDAW, the gap between the constitutional promise of equality and statutory standards was immense in the 1980s. Indeed, the penal and family law regimes reconstituted and entrenched the social and economic inequalities between men and women. Penal provisions relating to violence against women in the matrimonial home were introduced in the mid 1980s, and reform of the anti-rape law came about in the same period. The changes in penal laws came on account of a strong agitation mounted by the women's movements in response to judicial verdicts that showcased the apathy of the law with regard to systemic forms of violence against women. National campaigns against dowry deaths and custodial rape led to a slew of legislative reforms in the mid 1980s, introducing penal provisions on both of these issues.[8] New offences were introduced to address cruelty, abetment to suicide and dowry death relating to women within the matrimonial home.[9] Likewise, amendments to the anti-rape provision followed a nationwide campaign by the women's movement against acquittals in custodial rape.[10] The amendments introduced the concept of custodial rape for the first time, recognizing the disproportionate power exercised by uniformed men in custodial situations.

[8] R. Kumar, *The History of Doing: An Illustrated Account of Movements for Women's Rights and Feminism in India, 1800–1990* (New Delhi: Kali for Women, 1993) at Chapters 7, 8, 9.

[9] The 1983 Amendments introduced: s. 498A of the Indian Penal Code on cruelty within the matrimonial home, and s. 113A in the Indian Evidence Act on presumption of abetment of suicide where a suicide of a woman occurred within seven years of marriage. The 1986 Amendments introduced: s. 304B of Indian Penal Code on dowry death, and s. 113B in the Indian Evidence Act, introducing a presumption that a death of a woman within seven years of marriage was a dowry death.

[10] The offence of custodial rape places upon the accused the burden of proving his innocence. For an account of campaigns relating to custodial rape, see N. Shah and N. Gandhi, *The Issues at Stake: Theory and Practice in the Contemporary Women's Movement in India* (New Delhi: Kali for Women, 1992) 39–42 and 213–16.

The discriminatory citizenship laws saw change, in 1986 and in 1992, notably to allow citizenship to be transmitted by the mother on an equal footing with the father.[11] The amendments in citizenship law, however, were not the result of demands by the women's movement, but rather were a state initiative towards making the law compliant with the Constitution and international standards of equality. A contentious law addressing 'indecent' representation of women was enacted,[12] and amendments to marriage, divorce and succession laws of Parsis were introduced to address some areas of sex discrimination.[13] Nonetheless, the family laws continue, in varying degrees, to be discriminatory against women. Special courts dedicated to family matters and the National Women's Commission were established.[14] Finally, in 1992, a constitutional amendment provided for a reservation of a third of the total seats in elected local governing bodies for women.[15] Consequently, it was not until the 1990s, after the completion of the first phase of law reforms relating to women, that India was able to step into the international arena with evidence of its willingness to pursue gender justice.

3.1.2 Impact of global developments

By the start of the 1990s the global economic environment had changed and these changes came to India's door. In 1991 India initiated structural adjustment programmes to meet the aid conditionality of the World Bank and the IMF. While the main objective of the restructuring involved liberalization of the economy to invite foreign investment,[16] there was

11 An amendment in 1986 reformed the Citizenship Act of 1955 to recognize transmission of citizenship by birth where either parent (as opposed to only the father) was Indian, and the amendment in 1992 similarly recognized citizenship by descent to those born outside the country where either parent was Indian.

12 Despite a growing concern about the stereotyping/objectification of women in the media, the Indecent Representation of Women (Prohibition) Act 1986 lacked support from many sections of the women's movement for arbitrary powers of censorship. See M. Kishwar and R. Vanita, 'Using women as a pretext for repression', *Manushi* 37 (1987) 2–8.

13 The Parsi Marriage and Divorce Act 1936 was amended in 1988 to align it with the Hindu Marriage Act 1955; and the Indian Succession Act 1925 was amended in 1991 to grant equal rights to male and female heirs in interstate succession.

14 The Family Courts Act 1984 has been critiqued for promoting reconciliation rather than women's rights. The National Commission of Women Act 1990 established a national body, following which states gradually enacted laws establishing commissions at the state level.

15 The Constitution (Seventy-Fourth) Amendment Act 1992.

16 Structural Adjustment in India: Independent Evaluation Group, available at: www.worldbank.org.

a growing global pressure by the early 1990s that liberalization must be accompanied by good governance to result in growth and development.[17] The civil society widened its net of alliances within and across regions to address problems emerging from the shared global economic order, pushing the human rights and social justice agendas forward within the international development and poverty reduction frameworks.[18] The women's movements across regions joined forces in this backdrop, to engender world conferences.[19] The participation of women from the different regions at the World Conference on Human Rights in 1993 strongly influenced the *Vienna Declaration and Programme of Action*, which acknowledged for the first time that women's rights are human rights, calling on all countries to ratify the CEDAW and recommending the adoption of an optional protocol.[20] The outcome document also endorsed the call of the UN Human Rights Commission for the creation of the new mandate of the Special Rapporteur on Violence against Women, its Causes and Consequences.

India at this point was not just aligning its economy with the global market, but was also positioning itself as a significant member of the international community – endorsing standards beyond those relating to economic liberalization, including those relating to women's rights.[21]

[17] Responding to reports of the failure of structural adjustment programmes in Africa and Latin America, the International Monetary Fund and the World Bank began to integrate 'good governance' into aid conditionality. According to Shihata, the promotion of social and economic rights of the people (including women) was consistent with the Articles of Agreement and necessary to meet the changing needs of the times. I. F. I. Shihata, 'Human rights, development and international financial institutions', *American University Journal of International Law and Policy* 8:27 (1992) 27–37.

[18] The participation of civil society in every world forum pressed for inclusion of social development in outcome documents of that period. See World Summit for Social Development (Copenhagen, 1995) A/CONF.166/9.

[19] The Tribunal on Violations of Women's Human Rights at Vienna drew attention to violence against women and sought explicit recognition of women's rights as human rights: *Women Testify: A Planning Guide to Popular Tribunals and Hearings*, Centre for Women's Global Leadership (2005). Refer also to the World Conference on Human Rights in 1993 in Vienna and the International Conference on Population and Development in 1994 in Cairo.

[20] A/CONF.157/23, at paras. 18 and 37–44. Notably, para. 39 states: 'The World Conference on Human Rights urges the eradication of all forms of discrimination against women, both hidden and overt. The United Nations should encourage the goal of universal ratification by all States of the Convention on the Elimination of All Forms of Discrimination against Women by the year 2000. Ways and means of addressing the particularly large number of reservations to the Convention should be encouraged.'

[21] The Government of India's initial report to the CEDAW Committee acknowledges the role of the women's movement in ensuring inclusion of violence against women, and

On 9 July 1993, less than a month after the *Vienna Declaration and the Programme of Action* was adopted by 171 states by consensus on 25 June 1993, India demonstrated its commitment to women's human rights before the global community through the ratification of the CEDAW. India's adoption of the outcomes of Vienna was a significant facet of its aspirations in the new global order. In the same vein, India also enacted the Protection of Human Rights Act 1993, under which human rights were defined to mean 'the rights relating to life, liberty, equality and dignity of the individual guaranteed by the constitution or embodied in the International Covenants and enforceable by courts in India'.[22] Under this statute, independent national and state human rights institutions were created, as were human rights courts, for the promotion and protection of human rights. The references to international human rights obligations in the Human Rights Act 1993, following Vienna, stands in contrast to the earlier statutes constituting independent commissions to monitor discrimination relating to women and minorities.[23] The oversight bodies subsequent to Vienna, however, refer to international standards, such as those relating to child rights and disability.[24]

3.2 Events and actors that pushed the CEDAW centre stage

The achievements of women at Vienna in 1993 shaped the ambitious nature and scale of the preparations for the Fourth World Conference on Women in Beijing in 1995. A two-year preparatory process for Beijing was initiated in India to expand participation of women activists in Beijing, to ensure diversity and inclusion of grass-roots constituencies.[25] Through a dedicated national secretariat called the Coordination Unit for Beijing, preparations along several thematic lines, including in relation to women's rights, were

gender-biased perceptions as areas of concern in the Eighth Five-Year Plan (1992–97) for the first time to reflect India's commitments in international forums in national policy. *India: Initial Report*, 10 March 1999, CEDAW/C/IND/1, paras. 71–7.

[22] See section 2(d).

[23] Section 10 of the National Commission for Women Act 1990 and section 9 of the National Commission of Minorities Act 1992 refer only to the constitutional and legal framework.

[24] See Preamble and section 2(b) defining 'child rights' in the Commission for Protection of Child Rights Act, 2005. Similarly, the Persons with Disabilities (Equal Opportunities, Protection of Rights and Full Participation) Act 1995, enacted before the UN Convention, refers to international/regional proclamations.

[25] A coalition of donors, led by Danida, constituted an Inter-Agency Facilitating Committee for Beijing to pool resources for coordinating preparations for the Fourth World Conference on Women in Beijing, led to the establishment of a national secretariat, the Coordination Unit (CU), to undertake preparations through 1994 to 1995.

facilitated from 1994 to 1995.[26] As the CEDAW was relatively unknown at the time, with India having just ratified it in 1993, country-wide orientations and creation of information materials on the CEDAW became integral to the preparations on women's rights, as did a collectively produced shadow report to the CEDAW Committee in anticipation of, rather than in response to, an actual country report.[27] Although this shadow report was eventually not used, since India's initial country report was submitted much later in 1999, it set a precedent of collective report writing for future shadow report processes. Not surprisingly, organizations and activists integral to the Beijing preparatory processes within the country were amongst the first to be mobilized in the CEDAW review process in 1999 when India's initial report was submitted, and they continued to play a significant role in the shadow review processes that followed.[28]

The run-up to Beijing was also marked by alliance building between women's groups and activists in India with regional organizations at the Asia Pacific level. In the context of capacity development and monitoring of the CEDAW, one such organization, the International Women's Rights Action Watch – Asia Pacific (IWRAW-AP) sustained its work in India long after Beijing, contributing significantly to the development of human and institutional resources.[29] With CEDAW compliance by states becoming central to the United Nations Development Fund for Women's (UNIFEM) approach to human rights programming,[30] the UNIFEM South Asia Regional Office played a key role in supporting civil society initiatives, alongside providing technical and facilitation support to

[26] The preparations towards Beijing were along four themes: livelihoods, political participation, health and women's rights, led by a thematic convenor. The women's rights stream was convened by the author of this chapter.

[27] *Indian NGOs Report on the Convention on the Elimination of All Forms of Discrimination against Women* (Coordination Unit for the World Conference on Women, India, 1995).

[28] The National Alliance of Women's Organisations (NAWO) that coordinated the production of shadow reports for both of the country reviews is a network of state-level NGOs that constituted the advisory board to the Coordination Unit during the Beijing preparatory processes. Upon closure of the Coordination Unit after the Beijing conference, the members of this advisory board reconstituted themselves as NAWO. NGOs and individuals that were active during the Beijing process contributed the chapters to the initial shadow report.

[29] IWRAW-AP, which began its Global to Local Programme from 1998, has facilitated preparation of shadow reports and the participation of women's groups from all regions at the country reviews.

[30] See Helen Hintjens, *UNIFEM, CEDAW and the Human Rights-based Approach*, available at: http://repub.eur.nl/res/pub/17998/2DevelopmentChangeGenderRightsUNIFEM.pdf (last accessed 27 February 2013).

governments to enable fulfilment of their CEDAW obligations. The nodal ministry concerned with the CEDAW, the Ministry of Women and Child Development,[31] has partnered with UNIFEM, amongst other things, on capacity development, orientations at the national and South Asia regional levels, as well as issues involving the reporting and reviewing processes.[32]

With the presence of donor aid, regional alliances, technical support and NGOs flushed with the experience of the Beijing conference, the CEDAW appealed to many as an effective forum in which to pursue accountability for women's rights. The CEDAW work grew considerably, corresponding to the diverse strengths of the various actors and their spheres of work. Of these, capacity development, creation of knowledge resources and application of the Convention to thematic issues have evolved as long-term engagements. The CEDAW country review processes have been moments of convergence between women's groups at local, state and national levels, for the collective production of shadow reports, as well as opportunities for simultaneous engagement with the government.

Even as this backdrop conjures up an image of a vibrant community of organizations and activists at the state and national levels working on the CEDAW, many sections of the women's movements have chosen to not engage with CEDAW processes.[33] Likewise, the framing of concerns in activism, or in legal challenges, have not always been with reference to the CEDAW, even if CEDAW review processes have eventually served to reinforce the demands. Of the several forums and methods with which to agitate, engage and advocate for realization of women's rights, the CEDAW review process is just one. Accordingly, some have developed a dedicated organizational interest in the periodic CEDAW reviews, but others have approached CEDAW reviews more selectively, only for pursuing concerns where dialogue with the state was particularly difficult – as, for example, in relation to the Gujarat carnage, and in respect of violence against lesbians and bisexuals.[34] Regardless of the nature of

[31] Formerly, a department under the Ministry of Human Resource Development, it was elevated to the Ministry in 2004.

[32] The South Asian inter-governmental peer learning platforms have been organized periodically by UNIFEM.

[33] Some prefer domestic forums, on account of exclusivity, distance and resource requirements, making international forums beyond the reach of affected constituencies. For others, the scepticism relates to the transformatory capacity of law and human rights discourses in addressing unequal structures of power.

[34] *India: Second and Third NGO Alternative Report on CEDAW* (NAWO, 2006).

engagement with the CEDAW, a growing reliance on international law and mechanisms is evident across human rights sectors.

4 CEDAW implementation and the law

This section examines ways in which judicial pronouncements have advanced women's equality,[35] touching upon legislative action connected with the subject matter of the judgments. The areas covered are limited to family law, sexual assault and sex discrimination in the workplace, for a comparative understanding of domestication where state obligation has been expressly curtailed by India's declarations to the CEDAW, and areas in which no such curtailment exists.

The judicial pronouncements discussed here are those from the Supreme Court of India – that is, the final court of appeal, which exercises writ jurisdiction and has the power of judicial review.[36] Being a federal state, the courts are multi-tiered, with the Supreme Court being the highest in the hierarchy, and the final court of appeal. It is followed by the high courts at the helm in each of the states of India, below which are the district courts. The legal system is based on common law, where both judicial precedents as well as statutes comprise the legal framework, and these are expected to be in compliance with the Constitution, which occupies the highest normative status in the country. While the jurisdiction of lower courts is limited to application of the statutory laws under civil and criminal jurisdictions, the high courts and the Supreme Court exercise judicial review, which allows them to harmoniously interpret a law to achieve compliance with the fundamental rights (that enshrine human rights in the Constitution), or indeed, to strike down an inconsistent law. All three arms of the state – the judiciary, legislature and the executive – are independent of each other.

4.1 Family law

The laws relating to family and marriage, called the personal laws in India, are derived from religion, resulting in community-specific laws for Muslims, Christians, Parsis and Hindus. The Hindus comprise a broad

[35] Full texts of all judgments from India, are available at: www.indiankanoon.org; http://scconline.co.in; www.liiofindia.org/in/cases/cen/INSC/; and www.worldlii.org/in.

[36] Article 13 of the Constitution of India 1949 declares laws inconsistent with or in derogation of the fundamental rights as void.

legal category that includes within its ambit those who are not any of the former groups.[37] While the codification of Hindu law has flattened caste, sect and regional diversities, it allows customs to override the codified law, where these have continued uninterrupted over time. The tribal or the indigenous communities differ widely from each other, and are governed by their community-specific uncodified customary laws.[38] In addition, there is the Special Marriage Act 1956, which facilitates inter-religious marriage without requiring either party to the marriage to change their religion. The family laws across communities are discriminatory to women in different ways. Registration of marriage under Hindu law and those governed by custom is not a necessary requirement under the law. Given the diversity of communities, and the prevalence of uncodified customs and practices, many marriages are not registered.

Article 16(1) of the CEDAW obligates States Parties to eliminate discrimination against women at the point of entering into marriage, during the subsistence of marriage and at its dissolution.[39] Article 5(a) touches upon the ideological origins of discrimination, covering social/cultural/customary norms and practices that contribute to the subordination of women.[40] Article 16(2) calls for compulsory registration of marriages.

[37] Section 2(1) and (3) Hindu Marriage Act 1955.

[38] The Constitution provides for notification of tribes under Article 342; and only those notified are considered as Scheduled Tribes according to Article 366(25). The areas with majority tribal population are notified as Scheduled Areas under 5th Schedule of the Constitution, where application of laws may be curtailed/modified. Section 2(2) of the Hindu Marriage Act 1955 excludes its application to tribal members.

[39] Article 16(1): 'States Parties shall take all appropriate measures to eliminate discrimination against women in all matters relating to marriage and family relations and in particular shall ensure, on a basis of equality of men and women: (a) the same right to enter into marriage; (b) the same right freely to choose a spouse and to enter into marriage only with their free and full consent; (c) the same rights and responsibilities during marriage and at its dissolution; (d) the same rights and responsibilities as parents, irrespective of their marital status, in matters relating to their children; in all cases the interests of the children shall be paramount; (e) the same rights to decide freely and responsibly on the number and spacing of their children and to have access to the information, education and means to enable them to exercise these rights; (f) the same rights and responsibilities with regard to guardianship, wardship, trusteeship and adoption of children, or similar institutions where these concepts exist in national legislation; in all cases the interests of the children shall be paramount; (g) the same personal rights as husband and wife, including the right to choose a family name, a profession and an occupation; (h) the same rights for both spouses in respect of the ownership, acquisition, management, administration, enjoyment and disposition of property, whether free of charge or for a valuable consideration.'

[40] Article 5(a) reads: 'States Parties shall take all appropriate measures: (a) To modify the social and cultural patterns of conduct of men and women, with a view to achieving the

Despite India's declarations to all three Articles, piecemeal legislative action and judicial pronouncements have addressed discrimination in relation to family law. However, the legislative changes relating to areas under Articles 16(1) and 16(2) vary considerably, providing comparative insights into the political complexities that shape the 'reform' related to these two distinct areas.

The declarations are rooted in the politics of patriarchy, cultural identity and electoral gain, in which the women question is embedded in India.[41] Religion-based family law has come to be positioned as an exercise of religious freedom that trumps sex equality, although both are equally placed as constitutionally guaranteed fundamental rights.[42] The Constitution viewed religion-based family law only as an interim arrangement, envisaging the enactment of a 'uniform civil code' in due course as part of a nationalist vision of uniting all communities under one law rather than ensuring gender equality.[43] Given the history of India's partition on lines of religion, and the sentiments attached to religious identities, the debate on the uniform civil code was deferred. By the 1980s, however, liberal secular politics veered towards accommodating the male religious orthodoxy's demands with respect to the family law of minorities. With the emergence of the Hindu Right as a force in national politics in the 1990s, the uniform civil code agenda was resurrected as a test of nationalism for minorities, specifically targeting the Muslim law.[44] With gender equality becoming irrelevant to the national discourse on family law, the women's movement distanced itself from the civil code agenda, focusing instead on possibilities of law reform within the community.[45] The judiciary is

elimination of prejudices and customary and all other practices which are based on the idea of the inferiority or the superiority of either of the sexes or on stereotyped roles for men and women.'

41 For a comprehensive discussion on the political influences in which the women question is framed and negotiated, see R. S. Rajan, *The Scandal of the State: Women, Law, Citizenship in Post Colonial India* (New Delhi: Permanent Black, 2003); F. Agnes, *Law and Gender Inequality: The Politics of Women's Rights in India* (Oxford University Press, 1999).

42 Articles 14 and 15 guarantee equality before the law, and non-discrimination on grounds of sex (including affirmative action for women); Articles 25, 26, 27 and 28 assure freedom of religion; and Article 29 stipulates protection to interests of minorities (defined by language, script or culture).

43 Article 44 of the Indian Constitution states: '*The State shall endeavor to secure for the citizens a uniform civil code throughout the territory of India*' (author's emphasis).

44 For discussion on the uniform civil code, Muslim law and identity politics, see Rajan, *The Scandal of the State* at 147–76 and Agnes, *Law and Gender Inequality* at Chapter 8.

45 Agnes, *Law and Gender Inequality* at Chapter 12.

aware of the pitfalls of striking down family law provisions in this political context, preferring, instead, to harmoniously read the statute with the Constitution to minimize discrimination.

The threat of legislative backlash against judicial rulings upholding women's rights with respect to the family law of minorities was not unfounded in view of the hasty enactment of the Muslim Women's (Protection of Rights on Divorce) Act 1986. The legislation sought to undo the Supreme Court ruling upholding Muslim women's right to claim maintenance from their former husbands under a general law,[46] limiting the husband's obligation to support the divorced wife only for a period of three months following the divorce, and not thereafter.[47] This law was challenged more than once for its inconsistency regarding equality and right to life. The petition by *Maharshi Avadhesh* v. *Union of India* invoked the Hindu Right arguments in favour of a uniform civil code, combined with tangential concerns for Muslim women, to plead for the striking down of the 1986 law and the complete erasure of Muslim law, which was rejected as the reliefs transgressed into legislative ambit.[48] In a subsequent case of *Daniel Latifi and Another* v. *Union of India*[49] that challenged the constitutional validity of the 1986 Act, the Court interpreted the provisions of the law expansively to read the three months to be the period within which all payments and future maintenance was to be completed. Observing that 'a reasonable and fair maintenance for the future of the divorced wife' meant payment for the period beyond the three months, including maintenance, ought to be made within the three months following the divorce, the Court avoided inconsistency with the Constitution and the prospect of striking down the law. Although without reference to the CEDAW, this ruling radically transformed the scope of entitlement available under the controversial law, and finds mention

[46] The *Shah Bano* case [1985 SCC (2) 556] upheld the right of a divorced Muslim woman to claim maintenance from her husband under section 125 of the Criminal Procedure Code that is uniformly available to dependent wives across all religions. Following a backlash by the Muslim orthodoxy against the judgment, the liberal secular Congress Party (then in government) hastily enacted the Muslim Women's (Protection of Rights on Divorce) Act 1986, that sought to exclude divorced Muslim women from recourse to section 125.

[47] The *iddat* period corresponds to three menstrual cycles after divorce where the woman may not marry to ascertain paternity in the event of pregnancy. See section 3(1) of the Muslim Women's Act 1986.

[48] 1994 SCC, Supl. (1) 713.

[49] (2001) 7 SCC 740.

in India's combined second and third periodic reports to the CEDAW as evidence of change within the community.[50]

In *Gita Hariharan and Anr.* v. *Reserve Bank of India*,[51] the Court addressed two separate petitions, both of which challenged the constitutional validity of section 6 of the Hindu Minority and Guardianship Act 1956, and section 19 of the Guardian and Wards Act 1890, for placing the mother in an inferior position with regard to the guardianship of a minor.[52] Both petitioners were women personally affected by this law, one a writer and the other an environmental activist who challenged the law assigning guardianship to the mother only 'after' the father, read literally to mean after the death of the father. Rather than striking down the provision as discriminatory, the Court granted relief to the petitioners by holding that the word 'after' meant 'in the absence of', thereby extending guardianship to mothers while the father was living, or in circumstances where the father was physically absent, had delegated his right or was found unfit. Citing the CEDAW, the *Beijing Declaration* and the Constitution, the Court opted to read the law harmoniously with equality standards, to extend to mothers the right to guardianship of their child in more situations than the law originally intended.[53] By acknowledging mothers as guardians in circumstances during the lifetime of the father, the Court avoided disturbing the legal text declaring the father as the natural first guardian of the child. Yet the same Court had dismissed an earlier petition in 1994, seeking a declaration that the mother also be included as a natural guardian under Hindu guardianship, reportedly terming it 'luxury litigation' by a women's organization. In this case, the petitioner Neela Deshmukh, whose divorced husband challenged her

[50] *Combined Second and Third Periodic Report: India*, 19 October 2005, CEDAW/C/IND/2–3, para. 5.

[51] AIR 1999 SC 1149.

[52] Section 6 (Hindu Minority and Guardianship Act 1956) states: 'natural guardian of a Hindu minor, in respect of the minor's person as well as in respect of the minor's property … are – (a) in the case of a boy or an unmarried girl – the father, and after him, the mother; provided that the custody of a minor who has not completed the age of five years shall ordinarily be with the mother'. Section 19 (Guardian and Wards Act 1890) forbids the court to appoint guardians in certain cases, including 'of a minor whose father is living and is not, in the opinion of the Court, unfit to be guardian of the person of the minor'.

[53] General Recommendation No. 21 at para. 20 states: 'The shared responsibilities enunciated in the Convention should be enforced at law and as appropriate through legal concepts of guardianship, wardship, trusteeship and adoption.'

custody over their children, had approached the Court with Manushi, a women's organization, in 1986.[54]

The Court has consistently sidestepped calls to strike down the family laws. The case of *Ahemdabad Women's Action Group and Others* v. *Union of India* involved several petitions filed by women's groups seeking a declaration that discriminatory provisions in various family laws (Hindu, Muslim and Christian) offended the constitutional provisions of equality and non-discrimination, and were therefore invalid.[55] Observing that the petitions 'wholly involve issues of State policies' for which the relief lay with the Parliament, the Court rejected these.

In *C. Masilmani Mudaliar* v. *Idol of Shri Swaminathaswami Thirukoil and Others*,[56] the Court considered the validity of the right of a woman to sell property that was bequeathed to her for a life term, in lieu of the testator's obligation to maintain her. The sale of the bequeathed property by the woman was challenged by the beneficiary named in the will, to whom the property was to devolve upon the demise of the woman. It was argued that under section 14(2) of the Hindu Succession Act 1956, women do not have complete ownership over property given by a gift, will or any other instrument, or under a decree or order of a civil court or under an award where the terms of the gift, will or other instrument, or the decree, order or award prescribe a restricted estate in such property. The new owners who had purchased the property from the woman rebutted this position, stating that because the woman had a pre-existing absolute right to maintenance irrespective of the will, section 14(2) would not apply. Instead, section 14(1) of the said statute would apply, giving those with a pre-existing right in the 'gift' an absolute title to the bequeathed property. This absolute title allowed the woman to dispose of the property by sale. While the High Court held that the woman could not sell the property, the Supreme Court, on appeal, held that the woman had a pre-exiting right in the property under section 14(1), giving her an absolute title and right to sell it. In determining that section 14(2) did not apply to this case, the Court avoided the question of the woman's 'limited title' to the estate gifted to her. Additionally, the Court referred to several international human rights documents (including the CEDAW) to emphasize

[54] For discussion on the case, see M. Kishwar, 'Public interest litigation: one step forward, two steps backwards', *Manushi* 81 (1994) 11–23. For the text of the petition, see 'Is a father a natural guardian? Hindu Guardianship Act challenged', *Manushi* 35 (1986) 32–6, available at: www.manushi-india.org.

[55] 1997 (3) SCC 573. [56] (1996) 8 SCC 525.

the primacy of sex equality. While referring to India's declaration in relation to Article 5(a) of the CEDAW, the Court noted that India's obligations under Article 2(f) read with Articles 3, 14 and 15 of the CEDAW, denuded the declaration of any effect and made it inconsequential. This case is significant in that sex equality was achieved without reinterpreting or striking down the statutory provision in question, and most importantly, for discounting the legal validity of India's declarations.

In the case of *Madhu Kishwar* v. *State of Bihar*,[57] the majority decision of the Supreme Court concurred with the state-level Tribal Advisory Board holding that discriminatory tribal customary laws of succession were necessary to protect land from alienation and fragmentation, and for the preservation of tribal culture. The editor of a women's magazine and two tribal women who challenged the law in the public interest had argued for women's equal rights to succession to land tenancies, relying upon the constitutional guarantee of equality. They had pleaded that tribal women were not just rendered landless upon the demise of the landholder through whom they enjoyed rights over the land, but also rendered destitute as their livelihood was linked to land. The majority held that the threat of destitution could be tackled through women's right to use of land (without title) to be asserted against the next male successor – offering tribal women survival instead of equality. The Court referred to the Universal Declaration of Human Rights (UDHR) and the CEDAW, along with the Constitution and the Protection of Human Rights Act 1993, to direct the state: 'by appropriate measures including legislation, modify law and abolish gender based discrimination in existing laws, regulations, customs, and practices which constitute discrimination against women'.[58]

The sole dissenting judge, however, also relied upon the CEDAW, the directive principles of state policy[59] and the fundamental rights to hold that there was a need to overturn sex discrimination in succession to tenancy rights.[60] Tribal laws remain unchanged despite proposals by women's groups seeking equal succession with conditions to regulate land alienation.[61]

[57] (1996) 5 SCC 125. [58] *Ibid.* para. 11.

[59] Chapter 4 of the Indian Constitution sets out social and economic guidelines for state policy, which are not justiciable.

[60] Justice Ramaswamy was the sole dissenting judge. See critique of the majority ruling, Kishwar, 'Public interest litigation', *supra* note 54.

[61] M. Mehra and G. Sharma, *Negotiating Gender Justice, Contesting Discrimination: Mapping Strategies that Intersect Culture, Women and Human Rights* (New Delhi: Partners for Law in Development, 2010) at 95–113.

In contrast to the approach of the Supreme Court to challenges relating to substantive aspects of family law, a more radical position was taken in relation to (compulsory) registration of marriages, an area covered by Article 16(2) of the CEDAW, also the subject of India's declaration. The case of *Seema* v. *Ashwani Kumar* pertained to the matter of compulsory registration of marriages, a concern that the Supreme Court framed on its own initiative, in the context of a husband's denial of the marriage to avoid his wife's maintenance claim.[62] The Court inquired into the legislative status of the compulsory registration of marriages in each state to safeguard against such denials by husbands, and sought the opinion of the National Commission for Women, which recommended compulsory registration, attributing to it benefits of preventing child marriage, forced marriages, illegal polygamy and desertion of wives; besides enabling wives to secure residence in the matrimonial home, claim maintenance and inheritance; and deter selling daughters under the guise of marriage.[63]

The Court held that marriages of all persons irrespective of religion should be compulsorily registered in their respective states, and asked the states to report on the status of the law. While about five states had laws on compulsory registration, a few others had laws pertaining to voluntary registration of marriages. Despite India's declaration, the Court laid down guidelines for the states to enact rules with regard to compulsory registration of marriages, with penalties attached to non-registration.[64] Further, the states that had not given specific details regarding their compliance were directed to appraise the Court on the specific measures taken by them. Although projected as a solution to several wrongs, the state laws do not ensure monogamy, are not entirely compulsory or enforceable, and are not an irrefutable proof of marriage.[65]

[62] (2005) 4 SCC 443; (2006) 2 SCC 578; and 2008 (1) SCC 180. This case was a matrimonial suit in the Delhi civil court transferred to the Supreme Court, on its own motion.

[63] These reasons are listed in the affidavit filed by the National Commission for Women before the Supreme Court in *Seema* v. *Ashwani Kumar* (2006) 2 SCC 578. CEDAW General Recommendation No. 21 at 39 requires States Parties to register all marriages – whether contracted civilly, according to custom or religious law – suggesting a linkage between marriage registration and equality between partners in terms of a minimum age for marriage, prohibition of bigamy and polygamy, and the protection of the rights of children.

[64] Most of the states that enacted rules relating to compulsory registration of marriage impose a fine on the party to the marriage (bride and groom, and in one case, guardians of the bride and groom) of up to INR. 1000/- for failure to register within the stipulated period.

[65] Interestingly, some state laws allow registration of multiple marriages of the groom (as marriage is not defined as legal marriage, but includes custom); the proposed rules of

Some women's groups view compulsory registration as counter-productive, in that it potentially excludes many women from staking legal claims, even as it fails to secure claims of women who hold proof of marriage. Linking marriage registration to basic rights arising from cohabitation would hit women in diverse domestic relationships, including 'relationships in the nature of marriage' under the Protection of Women from Domestic Violence Act 2005, and potentially in the future, to same-sex partners.[66] The matrimonial wrongs that compulsory registration seeks to remedy are the result of structurally entrenched gender inequality in society that requires substantive rather than administrative interventions. A better approach might be to broaden the definition of 'wife' to include customary unions, live-in relationships and cohabitations for the purposes of securing rights related to maintenance, as is currently under the consideration of the Supreme Court in *Chanmuniya* v. *V.K. Singh Kushwaha*.[67]

4.2 Sexual assault

This section discusses judicial activism relating to reparative justice, the definition of rape and child sexual abuse – highlighting the pace of legislative responses on areas where the state obligation is not limited by any reservation, or encumbered by considerations of religion or cultural identity.

In *Delhi Domestic Working Women Forum* v. *Union of India and Ors*,[68] an NGO working with migrant domestic workers approached the Supreme Court in the matter of the rape of four tribal girls in a train by army men. Noting the absence of restorative support to rape survivors, the Court framed guidelines mandating provisioning of support services, legal aid,

the state of Rajasthan allow registration of child marriages, and the rules of Bihar state that registration of marriage shall not be an irrefutable proof of marriage. However, to address concerns relating to the prevention of child marriage, polygamy and the wife's right to maintenance through proof of marriage, the rules seem to recognize that they cannot address these issues.

[66] See M. Mehra, *Rights in Intimate Relationships: Towards an Inclusive and Just Framework of Women's Rights and the Family* (New Delhi: Partners for Law in Development, 2010).

[67] 210 INSC 829, dated 7 October 2010. The reference arose from a case involving the husband's rejection of his wife's claim for maintenance on the ground that the marriage was merely a custom and was not legally valid. The custom required a widow to marry her younger brother-in-law upon the death of her husband. While upholding the wife's claim for maintenance, the Supreme Court referred to a larger bench the question of clarifying the definition of the term 'wife'. Partners for Law in Development, together with other organizations, have sought permission to assist the Court in this matter, placing on record its resource book by Mehra, *Rights in Intimate Relationships*.

[68] (1995) 1 SCC 14.

counselling, rehabilitation and compensation to rape survivors – noting that rehabilitation and recovery were essential parts of justice. They called for a compensation scheme and the establishment of a Criminal Injuries Board to dispense compensation regardless of outcome of the rape trial and assigned the responsibility to draft such a scheme to the National Commission for Women. Although the CEDAW was not relied upon in this case, this judgment is important for recognizing reparative aspects of gender justice in the context of sexual assault for the first time.

After several deliberations and draft schemes on compensation for rape victims, the government has framed 'Financial Assistance and Support Services to Victims of Rape – a scheme for restorative justice, 2011' more than fifteen years after the Court's guidelines. The scheme has been approved by the central government, but is not yet functional as it is contingent on state notification, creation of federated boards at the district and state levels, and resource allocation, amongst other things.[69]

The issue of compensation for rape survivors arose again, in the case of *Chairman, Railway Board and Ors* v. *Mrs. Chandrima Das and Ors*,[70] which involved the question of compensation by the state railways to a rape survivor, because the perpetrators were state employees and the crime occurred on state property. The petitioner, a lawyer of the Calcutta High Court, sought compensation for the survivor, a Bangladeshi national. The High Court awarded compensation, holding that the Railway Board was vicariously liable for the rapes perpetrated by its employees in buildings belonging to the railways. On appeal in the Supreme Court, the following questions arose – whether compensation could be awarded for rape as a constitutional rather than a private remedy; whether fundamental rights guaranteed by the Constitution could extend to a foreign national; and finally, whether the railways were vicariously responsible for the private actions of its staff. The Court awarded compensation, holding that the public law remedy for compensation was available for wrongs done by government agents.[71] The Court also relied upon the UDHR and the Declaration on the Elimination of Violence against Women 1993, as well as principles relating to the application and interpretation

[69] The scheme has been critiqued for inadequate compensation, the time limit for applying, the compulsion to pursue criminal prosecution and exclusion of women who 'appear' to be involved in solicitation. See www.indg.in/social-sector/women-and-child-development/financial_assistance_and_support_services_to_victims_of_rape.pdf (last accessed 27 February 2013).

[70] AIR (2000) SC 988.

[71] *Nilabati Behera* v. *State of Orissa* (1993) 2 SCC 746 drew upon the International Covenant on Civil and Political Rights to uphold that compensation was available as part of enforcement of a fundamental right as a public law remedy, as distinct from a private tortious remedy.

of international law set out by several judicial colloquia,[72] to uphold that fundamental rights, particularly the right to life, vest in 'persons' regardless of nationality, and not merely citizens – to uphold the survivor's right to compensation under the Constitution.

The Indian Penal Code has three offences relating to sexual assault and harassment of women – of which only rape is treated as grave in terms of requiring prompt arrest, bail to the accused with permission of the court and substantial punishment. However, rape is narrowly defined to cover penile vaginal penetration, leaving out forms of penetrative sexual assault. Grave sexual offences such as forced nudity and parading fall within the scope of lesser offences.[73] Apart from the inadequate coverage of sexual offences, there are problems with related evidentiary and procedural requirements.[74] Although the women's movement has been campaigning for a comprehensive sexual assault law for more than two decades, and the Committee has urged legal reform relating to sexual harassment, rape and other critical areas within a reasonable time frame,[75] the Criminal Law Amendment Bill 2010[76] falls short of incorporating all the demands.[77] There is no explicit law on child sexual abuse – which has been prosecuted

[72] The proceedings of the judicial colloquia referred to are: Commonwealth Secretariat and Interights, *Developing Human Rights Jurisprudence, Volume 1: First Judicial Colloquium on the Domestic Application of International Human Rights Norms: Bangalore, India, 24–26 February 1988* (London: Commonwealth Secretariat, 1988); A. Byrnes and K. Adams (eds.), *Gender Equality and the Judiciary: Using International Human Rights Standards to Promote the Human Rights of Women and the Girl-child at the National Level* (London: Commonwealth Secretariat, 2000); and A. Byrnes, J. Connors and L. Bik (eds.), *Advancing the Human Rights of Women: Using International Instruments in Domestic Litigation: Papers and Statements from the Asia/South Pacific Regional Judicial Colloquium, Hong Kong, 20–22 May 1996* (London: Commonwealth Secretariat, 1997).

[73] Sections 375, 354 and 509 of the Penal Code relate to rape, outraging the 'modesty' of a woman and sexual harassment by 'indecent' word or gesture, respectively. The latter two are smaller offences that attract smaller sentences – a maximum of two years and one year, respectively. The terminology of 'modesty' and 'indecency' has been critiqued for invoking popular morality to judge women, and is frequently applied as such.

[74] From reporting, to investigation and trial, the rape proceedings have been critiqued as being hostile and demeaning to women. The medico-forensic examination continues to rely upon two finger tests to ascertain rape, and use references such as 'habitual to sex'. With no victim or witness protection, and long, hostile legal procedures, many survivors are unable to continue with the proceedings.

[75] Concluding Observations, 2 April 2000 at paras. 59, 69, 71, 72; and Concluding Comments, 2 February 2007 at paras. 9, 23, 24, 25.

[76] http://mha.nic.in/writereaddata/12700472381_CriminalLaw(Amendment)Bill2010.pdf (last accessed 27 February 2013).

[77] See for example T. K. Rajalakshmi, 'Half measure', *Frontline* 27:4 (2010) 13–26; T. K. Rajalakshmi, 'Bill not comprehensive', *Frontline* 27:13 (19 June–2 July 2010) online.

innovatively through a penal provision on 'unnatural sexual offences', which until recently also criminalized homosexuality.[78]

The issue of the limitations of the penal law relating to sexual assault, and the legislative gap relating to child sexual abuse came before the *Supreme Court in Sakshi* v. *Union of India and Ors.*[79] In that case, the petitioners, a women's organization, raised the issue of the narrow scope of section 375 in terms of the limited definition of penetration. Citing the CEDAW, the CRC, the right to life guaranteed under the Constitution and feminist legal jurisprudence, the petitioners raised concerns arising from the legal vacuum with respect to sexual abuse of children. While emphasizing the urgency for legislation in this regard, the Court set out preliminary guidelines for conducting trials in cases of child sexual abuse. In light of the complex nature of the legislative changes required, the Court highlighted the need for a new law on child sexual abuse. Nearly a decade after the *Sakshi* case, the government has produced a Protection of Children from Sexual Offences Bill 2011, which remains to be enacted.

4.3 *Sex discrimination in the workplace*

Sex discrimination in the workplace is an area where the CEDAW has been invoked most directly to frame guidelines that operate until a law is enacted. Of the three cases discussed in this section, two were initiated by corporations unconnected with women's groups.

In *Vishaka* v. *State of Rajasthan,*[80] a women's organization from Rajasthan drew attention to the risks to and protection gaps for women workers in the absence of a sexual harassment law. This public interest petition backed by the women's movement was triggered in response to a retributive gang rape of a rural social worker in Rajasthan who was working towards stopping child marriages. The Supreme Court referred inter alia to General Recommendation No. 19 on violence against women and Article 11 of the CEDAW, alongside Articles 14, 15, 19(1)(g) and 21 of the Constitution of India,[81] to highlight the need for safe working

[78] On 2 July 2009 the Delhi High Court decriminalized homosexuality in *Naz Foundation* v. *Govt of NCT*, Delhi, 2009 (160) DLT 277. Section 377 of the Penal Code was retained for prosecuting non-consensual homosexual sex and child sexual abuse. See the special issue of the *NUJS Law Review* 2:3 (2009) on the case. Several appeals seeking reversal of the judgment were filed in the Supreme Court, the hearings of which concluded in March 2012. The verdict is awaited.

[79] AIR 2004 SC 3566. [80] (1997) 6 SCC 241.

[81] The Articles pertain to equality before the law, special provisions for women and children, freedom to practise any trade and profession, and the right to life respectively, guaranteed in the chapter on fundamental rights of the Constitution of India.

environments for women as an extension of non-discrimination, the right to practise any profession, as well as the right to life. The Court drew upon the principle of 'legitimate expectation' that flowed from ratification of a treaty[82] and General Recommendation No. 19 to set out guidelines to act as law, thereby plugging the legislative vacuum on sexual harassment in the workplace. Despite the judgment's emphasis on the urgent need for a law on sexual harassment in the workplace, and the Committee's recommendations reinforcing this,[83] problems continue to plague the Bill fifteen years on, and a law remains to be enacted.[84]

In another case pertaining to sexual harassment in the workplace, the *Apparel Export Promotion Council* v. *A.K. Chopra*,[85] the Court noted that '[t]he domestic courts are under an obligation to give due regard to International Conventions and norms for construing domestic laws when there is no inconsistency between them'.[86] In this case, the Court held that 'attempted' molestation was covered by the offence of sexual harassment. Although this judgment relies upon the guidelines set out by the Supreme Court in the *Vishaka* case, it does not refer to terms such as unwelcome conduct or the creation of a hostile workplace that are found in the language of the sexual harassment guidelines. Instead, it describes the conduct in patriarchal terms as being 'wholly against moral sanctions, decency and ... offensive to her modesty', terminology that has often served to discredit the victim. While this case sets positive standards, there remains a need for aligning terminology with international standards, to break away from the language of morality that has historically served to judge women unfairly.

The Court's judgment in *Anuj Garg* v. *Hotel Association of India*[87] elaborates the principle of substantive equality, to strike down a protectionist law that barred women from working in premises where liquor is consumed. The case relates to the validity of a colonial law relating to excise matters that prohibits from employment men below the age of twenty-five years and women absolutely, from premises where liquor or intoxicating drugs are consumed by the public. The respondents, representing the hospitality

[82] The Court invoked the doctrine of legitimate expectation that upholds aspirations for protection of rights set out in treaties ratified by the state, which is to say that citizens may legitimately expect that rights enshrined in a treaty ratified by the state will be protected.

[83] Concluding Observations, 2 April 2000 at paras. 37, 59, 69.

[84] The Protection of Women against Sexual Harassment at Workplace Bill 2010 was referred to a Parliamentary Standing Committee to examine concerns of different constituencies relating to exclusion of domestic workers from the ambit of the Bill, penalty for a false complaint and demand for gender-neutral law. See summary of the Committee's report at www.prsindia.org.

[85] AIR (1999) SC 625. [86] *Ibid.* para. 14.

[87] AIR (2007) SCC 663.

industry, challenged the constitutional validity of this provision on the grounds, inter alia, of sex discrimination, and had the law struck down.

The judgment refers to precedents such as the *Gita Hariharan*, *Vishaka* and *Madhu Kishwar* cases where the CEDAW was relied upon (all discussed in this chapter), and feminist legal texts to elaborate the scope of substantive equality. Highlighting the contradictions between the contemporary social and economic realities, of increasing training and employment opportunities in the hospitality sector with protectionist laws that curb women's freedom to practise a profession, as well as autonomy of choice and equality, the Court noted that: '[i]nstead of prohibiting women employment in the bars altogether the state should focus on factoring in ways through which unequal consequences of sex differences can be eliminated. It is the state's duty to ensure circumstances of safety which inspire confidence in women to discharge the duty freely in accordance to the requirements of the profession they choose to follow.'[88] It further observed that: 'No law in its ultimate effect should end up perpetuating the oppression of women. Personal freedom is a fundamental tenet which cannot be compromised in the name of expediency unless there is a *compelling state purpose*.'[89]

5 Conclusion

The predominant use of the CEDAW in judicial pronouncements has been interpretive, helping to engender constitutional rights to minimize explicit discrimination in the law. While the CEDAW may not be an explicit source of reference in all the cases that have tackled sex discrimination, they nonetheless have aided fulfilment of treaty obligations. There appears to be greater caution with respect to family law of minority communities – which in the case of *Madhu Kishwar* manifested as judicial capitulation to political risks, but in *Daniel Latifi* strikes a fine political balance that entirely transformed the import of the controversial 1986 Act. The state has delegated the responsibility of initiating family law reform with respect to minorities upon the judiciary and the male religious orthodoxy, as is evident from India's second and third periodic reports to the CEDAW.[90] This is despite the Committee pressing the state to recognize women's demands as community initiatives and to work with and support women's groups as members of these communities.[91]

[88] *Ibid.* para. 41. [89] *Ibid.* para. 45 (author's emphasis).

[90] *Combined Second and Third Periodic Report: India*, 19 October 2005, CEDAW/C/IND/2-3, paras. 4–5.

[91] Concluding Observations, 2 April 2000 at paras. 60–61, and Concluding Comments, 2 February 2007 at para. 11.

The difference in the judicial approaches to the two areas covered by India's declarations, family law and marriage registration, provide comparative insights into the two issues: the former involving the substantive rights of women, and the latter involving administrative aspects. The judicial approaches of reading down explicit or *de jure* discrimination in substantive areas of family law contrasts with the proactive directions in the *Ashwani Kumar* case for legislating on compulsory registration of marriage. The approach taken in the *Anuj Garg* case is equally striking, in declaring the offending law void – but it must be distinguished as it involves women's equality within the public domain in the context of globalization, where the hospitality industry and the employment of women are considered a necessary facet of national growth. While the *Ashwani Kumar* judgment stands out for its radical approach, and it seeks only to implement the letter of the CEDAW, in spirit it does not advance or protect women's rights in the context of India.

That the judiciary has played a leadership role in domesticating the CEDAW is demonstrated through the setting out of guidelines for law-making, much more than may be possible through a politically charged legislature. In four cases, guidelines were formulated to plug the legal vacuum, urging legislative reform to follow. The judgments in *Delhi Domestic Working Women Forum*, *Vishaka*, *Sakshi* and *Ashwani Kumar* are illustrative of this trend – covering restorative justice, sexual harassment in the workplace, child sexual offences and compulsory registration of marriage. The promptness of legislative action on registration of marriage contrasts with pending bills relating to sexual assault, areas

Addendum: Since the writing of this chapter, three key legislative reform agendas originating from judgments (pursuant to test cases by women's groups) were finally passed by the parliament. The passage of the Protection of Children from Sexual Offences Act in May 2012 filled a longstanding legislative vacuum (see http://wcd.nic.in/childact/childprotection31072012.pdf). The new law criminalises graded sexual contact, ranging from touching to penetrative sexual assault with and between children, defined as below the age of 18 years, prescribes mandatory reporting and sets out child sensitive procedures. In collapsing all legal minors (i.e. under 18 years) as children, the law disregards the evolving capacities of young persons to engage in consensual sex, thus criminalizing consensual sexual contact between young persons. This does not serve the best interests of young persons, and to this extent, has been critiqued for being inconsistent with international standards. In the backdrop of violent policing of inter-caste/ inter-community relationships in India, the law lends itself as a tool of retribution in the hands of family members, community leaders and vigilante groups (see Geeta Ramaseshan, 'Law and the age of innocence', *The Hindu*, 19 June 2012).

After the dismal offerings of the Criminal Law Amendment Bill, 2010 (discussed in the chapter), a similarly disappointing 2012 version followed which amongst other things, did not account for graded forms of sexual violence that fell between the two ends of the spectrum: penetrative sexual violence and the trivial offence of 'outraging the modesty unencumbered by declarations and where judicial guidelines have existed longer. To that extent, declarations are often political postures necessary to assuage a domestic constituency, but do not imply easier progress in areas where no declaration exists. The story of domestication is a continuing one, involving much more than laws. However, the struggle for norm-setting in law remains a fundamental part of the change, in which the contribution of the courts has been significant, as discussed in this chapter.

of women'. In December 2012, after the homicidal gang rape of a young student in Delhi, widespread public outrage engulfed the streets of Delhi and spread across metros and towns in response to which the government constituted a high level committee headed by retired Supreme Court judge, Justice Verma. In its recommendations, the Committee adopted the demands of the women's groups on changes in the criminal law, covering as well, aspects of prevention, education and accountability beyond the law. With the Verma recommendations being widely welcomed by social movements, the public and lauded internationally, including by the UN High Commissioner on Human Rights (see www.un.org/apps/news/story.asp?NewsID=44000&Cr=india&Cr1=rights#.US8EnKJxS3E), there was pressure for a introducing a new bill that sought to implemented the recommendations. The Criminal Law Amendment Bill, 2013 was enacted against this backdrop of events (see http://164.100.24.219/BillsTexts/LSBillTexts/PassedLoksabha/63C_2013_En_LS.pdf). Its positive features include an expanded definition of rape that goes beyond the penile vaginal penetration; creation of new offences such as stalking, voyeurism, forced disrobing of woman and acid attack; strengthened penal accountability for public servants who disobey the law to the detriment of the victim; and a waiver of the requirement of prior sanction from the government for prosecuting a public servant for sexual offences. In addition, the law stipulates mandatory free medical treatment to victims from public and private medical facilities backed by penalties for failure to do so. Although a significant step forward, the new law does not fully implement the holistic reforms set out by the Verma Committee.

Sixteen years after the *Vishaka* guidelines, the Sexual Harassment of Women at Workplace (Prevention, Prohibition and Redressal) Act 2012 was passed in February 2013 (see http://164.100.24.219/BillsTexts/LSBillTexts/PassedLoksabha/144C_2010_LS_Eng.pdf). The law defines what constitutes sexual harassment, extending its application to the formal and informal sectors, including domestic workers. It requires any organization, which employs more than ten people to set up an internal complaints committee, backed by a penalty for not doing so. Despite these achievements, the bill dilutes rather than builds on *Vishaka* guidelines by allowing conciliation between the complainant and the defendant, even prior to an inquiry. In face of the known power differentials and the hostility against complainants, this can become a channel for coercion. It also prescribes action against the complainant for malicious or false complaints, deterring rather than encouraging women to report harassment.

The recent enactments have followed a long contested legislative journey, coming to fruition just prior to India's next general elections scheduled in 2014, as well as the fifth and sixth periodic review by the CEDAW, expected in the same year. The advances of the Criminal Law Amendment Bill, 2013, are distinct, given the substantial departure it makes from the earlier bills on the subject. This development must be viewed against the backdrop of unrelenting public pressure, international attention and the Verma report, all of which lent force to the demands of women's groups. The need for governments to act, or appear to have acted is of significance for its domestic and international constituencies, which conjoined on the issue of sexual offences against women at a particular historic moment.

14

Judicial education on the Convention on Elimination of Discrimination against Women in Nepal

KABITA PANDEY

The courts have special reason to reject – not reflect – society's irrational prejudices. They can do no less if they are to provide all our citizens a court system which can pride itself on the delivery of quality justice.

Sol Wachtler, Chief Judge, New York Court of Appeals

1 Introduction

The principle of equality is the cornerstone of every democratic society that aspires to social justice and human rights.[1] Article 1 of the Universal Declaration of Human Rights states that all human beings are born free and equal in dignity and rights. Equality means that all people are equal and should be recognized as such without discrimination based on age, caste, class, ethnicity, gender, physical ability, religious or other beliefs, and sexual preference or other such factors. The Convention on the Elimination of All Forms of Discrimination against Women (CEDAW) was ratified by Nepal on 22 April 1991 without reservations. Article 2 of the CEDAW calls on states to "condemn discrimination against women in all its forms" and to "pursue by all appropriate means and without delay a policy of eliminating discrimination against women."[2] Despite the

This chapter is based on a paper presented at the colloquium "From Ratification to Implementation: CEDAW in International and National Law," Oslo, 11–12 March 2010. It was extensively edited for publication by Anne Hellum. I am grateful to Professor Anne Hellum and others for their insightful comments and valuable feedback. I have also benefitted from comments of the anonymous reviewer.

[1] Soli J. Sorabjee, *The World of Gender Justice* (New Delhi: Har Anand Publication, 2001) at 47.

[2] CEDAW Committee, Periodic Report: *International Women's Rights Action Watch (IWRAW): Accessing the Status of Women* (1996).

obligation to proclaim their total opposition to all forms of discrimination against women at all levels and branches of government, the Government of Nepal has failed to take sufficient measures directed at legal and social reforms to address such discrimination.[3] In a situation where the government is reluctant to take steps to modify or abolish existing laws as well as social and religious customs, beliefs and practices that constitute discrimination against women, it is indeed an uphill task for women who seek protection against inequality and violence inflicted on them. Deficits in good governance remain the most significant obstacle to the protection and promotion of women's human rights in Nepal, as in many other South Asian countries.[4]

Nepal's ratification of the CEDAW did not lead to any immediate legal change within the country. In the years following the ratification, laws that defined the status of women in terms of their sex and marital status were reinforced by all branches of government – the legislative and the executive. To make the government accountable, civic organizations such as Pro Public filed a number of petitions that challenged discriminatory laws on the basis of the CEDAW in the Supreme Court.[5] The aim was to empower women to take court action against discriminatory laws on the basis of the CEDAW and the Interim Constitution. The outcome of the court cases indicated that the Supreme Court judges were not conversant with the principles of the CEDAW and provisions of the Nepalese Treaty Act 2047,[6] which provides that the provisions of international conventions take precedence when coming into conflict with domestic law. An example is the judgment of the Supreme Court in the *Meera Dhungana* case from 1994, in which the judges with reference to social norms and value systems refused to provide equal property rights to women.[7] Realizing

[3] Forum for Women, Law and Development on the CEDAW, Initial Report on *Implementation Status of the Outcome Document of Beijing Platform for Action* (Kathmandu, 2003).

[4] O. P. Mishra, *Public Interest Litigation and Our Rights* (Allahabad: Dwivedi Law Agency, 2003); H. M. Seervai, *Constitutional Law of India: A Critical Commentary* (Bombay: N. M. Tripathi Publications, 1991); Laurence H. Tribe, *Constitutional Choices* (Indian Reprint) (New Delhi: Universal Law Publications, 2000); Mahendra P. Singh (ed.), *Comparative Constitutional Law* (Lucknow: Eastern Book Company, 1989).

[5] *Forum For Women, Law and Development* v. *His Majesty's Government*. The Foreign Employment Act 2007 restricted women from going to the Gulf countries for employment and this was challenged. The Supreme Court justified the law, saying it is made for the protection of women; therefore, the government has to implement it.

[6] Section 8 of the Nepal Treaty Act of 1990.

[7] *Meera Dhungana* v. *Ministry of Law and Justice and others, Nepal Law Journal* 9 (1994) at 462–8.

the gap between the CEDAW's formal status in Nepalese law, on the one hand, and the judiciary's lack of knowledge about Nepal's international and national legal obligations, on the other hand, the civic organization Pro Public initiated a judicial education program. The assumption underlying this initiative was that the effectiveness of human rights and rule of law guarantees in the Constitution required extensive education of the judiciary. Since the government had not taken measures to educate members of the judiciary, it was felt that the involvement of civil society in the process of judicial education was critical. This chapter shows how women's rights litigation in combination with judicial human rights education led to legal changes in a situation where both the legislative and executive branches of the Nepalese government disregarded their duty to respect and protect women's rights to protection against discrimination. Analysis of cases decided by the Supreme Court of Nepal between 1991 and 1997 demonstrates how a lack of proper understanding about the principle of equality enshrined in the CEDAW by the members of the judiciary constituted a barrier in the judicial pronouncement. Through examination of cases decided by the same judges after a judicial education program focusing on the CEDAW, this chapter demonstrates how judicial education, under certain circumstances, may lead to significant changes in the legal position of women.

This chapter is based on my own experiences and observations as a program officer working for the Nepalese civic organization Pro Public, which was founded in 1991.[8] Pro Public is a non-profit, non-governmental organization comprising environmental lawyers, journalists, economists and women's rights activists. It focuses on good governance, environmental justice, and consumer control and gender justice. Government accountability is sought through a wide range of methods including advocacy and public interest litigation. Pro Public's mission is to "play the role of a social change agent to empower the Nepalese people through research, advocacy, litigation and capacity building."[9] Its objective is "to act as watchdog in the areas of environment conservation, consumer rights, women rights and child welfare, by way of alternative dispute resolution, negotiations and litigation."[10]

[8] www.propublic.org/index.php (last accessed 2 July 2008).

[9] Mission statement available at: www.propublic.org/index.php (last accessed 2 July 2008).

[10] *Ibid.*

As a program officer, I was involved in public interest litigation and education of judges within a program undertaken by Pro Public under the aegis of the Asia Pacific Advisory Forum on Judicial Education on Equality (APAFEJE). The main target group of this program was the upper level of the judiciary. The overall aim was to make the judges conversant with the judiciary's obligation to protect women against all forms of discrimination under international and national law. The education program was premised on the assumption that the judiciary, when educated about these obligations, would crack down on laws and practices that discriminate against women. Through my work I had a unique opportunity to observe and analyze the performance of the Supreme Court in cases that were decided before and after Pro Public's legal education program. My engagement with legal education and litigation afforded me the opportunity to observe and assess the judiciary's response to education in international law in general and the CEDAW in particular.

To assess the potential of legal education programs directed at high-level judges, I will compare Supreme Court cases concerning the rights of women that were decided before and after a legal education program directed at the judiciary was carried out by Pro Public in cooperation with the Asia Pacific Advisory Forum on Judicial Education on Equality.[11] My research shows that Nepal's ratification of the CEDAW in and of itself had an impact neither on legislation nor on judicial review. It shows how the Supreme Court, after a legal education program carried out by international and regional experts, began to invoke the CEDAW in national law. In a number of cases Nepalese laws and customs that discriminated against women were struck down with reference to the Nepalese Constitution and the CEDAW. In the light of these changes, I argue that if the judiciary is given proper and extensive orientation on women's human rights and the state obligation under the CEDAW, judges will uphold the state obligation to respect, protect and promote women's human rights under international and national law.

This chapter unfolds in five sections. In the section after this introduction, I situate Nepal's ratification of the CEDAW and the state obligation to respect, protect and promote the human rights of women in the broader historical, political and social landscape. The third section describes the national and regional actors and institutions involved in the judicial legal education program initiated by Pro Public. The fourth

[11] The Supreme Court judges who passed the judgments before and after the judicial education program were the same.

section compares cases decided by the Supreme Court of Nepal before and after the judicial education program. The fifth section shows how the Supreme Court rulings have been accepted by both the legislative and executive branches of government.

2 The historical and constitutional context of the CEDAW in Nepal

Nepal ratified the Convention on the Elimination of All Forms of Discrimination against Women (CEDAW) in 1991 without any reservations. The CEDAW thus obliges the Nepalese government to eliminate all forms of discrimination against women as defined by Article 1 and specified in Articles 5–16 of the CEDAW. In accordance with Article 2 of the CEDAW, the Nepalese government has to take all appropriate measures to ensure not only *de jure* but also de facto equality between women and men. Since ratification, the Nepalese government has submitted regular reports to the CEDAW Committee. The Government of Nepal's initial report was presented at the CEDAW Committee's 17th Session in 1999. The combined second and third reports were dealt with at the CEDAW Committee's 30th Session in 2004.[12] The Committee considered the combined fourth and fifth reports of Nepal at its 49th Session in 2011.[13]

The ratification and domestication of the CEDAW must be understood in the light of the political and constitutional changes that took place in Nepal in the 1990s. Before the territorial unification of Nepal in the eighteenth century, the country was divided into a number of independent and separate administrative units, and until 1990 it was ruled by a king. Since the inception of democracy in 1990 and abolition of the monarchy in 2007, Nepal has set out on a political reform process aimed at a federal state governed by a new constitution.

The legal system of Nepal has been strongly influenced by the Hindu religion and customary norms and practices. The Hindu religion is based predominantly on patriarchal norms and values. Before the introduction of the Interim Constitution of 2007, Nepal was constitutionally declared a Hindu Kingdom. Patriarchal values were, and are still, deeply rooted at all levels of law and society. The laws of Nepal have defined the status of women in terms of their sex and marital status, contradictory to the provision of Article 1 of the CEDAW. Despite the ratification of the CEDAW

[12] CEDAW/C/NPL/2–3 and CEDAW/C/SR.630 and 631.

[13] CEDAW/C/NPL/4–5 and CEDAW/C/SR. 989 and 990.

and the constitutional obligation to make it part of national law, a number of discriminatory laws governing marriage, divorce, citizenship and property rights are still in place. Gender-based violence is a serious social problem in Nepal.

Socially and culturally determined gender norms perpetuate gender hierarchies and are embedded in structures such as the family and the local community. They mediate women's access to resources and impact on their status within the family and society. Gender hierarchies within the family constrain women's rights to self-determination and equality in multiple ways. It affects girl-children's rights to education and, in turn, women's access to employment and accumulation of social capital. These factors intersect with rigidly defined and enforced gender norms to create a vicious cycle of discrimination, deprivation and low self-esteem, which constrain women, men and local communities from addressing discrimination and violence against women and girls in Nepal.[14]

Gender has shaped both the legal and cultural landscapes of Nepalese life, and there are many discriminatory laws against women. To date, a predominantly male judiciary interprets laws adopted by the exclusively male legislature to determine issues of male exclusivity.[15] Worse still, women are vulnerable to violent actions and are often abused, usually by male members of society. As stereotypical socio-cultural norms restrain Nepalese women from seeking justice, most of the violence inflicted on them goes unreported. Even those who do report gender-based violence are not treated fairly by the authorities concerned. Officials of the judicial and the quasi-judicial bodies that are in place are more inclined to support the interests of men in cases of violence committed against women and to interpret laws in favor of the male.

During the period between the Government of Nepal's initial report to the CEDAW Committee in 1997 and its current report, Nepal has undergone significant political transformation. The monarchy has been abolished, an Interim Constitution protecting human rights was adopted in 2007 and elections to the Constituent Assembly along multiparty lines were held in 2008. The Interim Constitution is the fundamental law of Nepal providing that any law inconsistent with the provisions of the

[14] *SAATHI Report on the Situation Analysis of Violence Against Women and Girls in Nepal*, Kathmandu (1997).

[15] N. N. Belbase and S. A. Pyakurel, *A Survey on Political Rights and Discriminatory Legal Provisions against Women in Nepal* (Pro Public, 1994).

Constitution shall be void.[16] Section 9 of the Treaty Act of 1991 explicitly states that any law of Nepal that is inconsistent with a treaty or convention acceded to or ratified by Nepal shall not be applicable. In the event of conflict between Nepalese legislation and international treaty obligations, the latter will prevail. Hence, the international instruments acceded to or ratified by Nepal constitute part and parcel of the Nepalese legal system. The Nepalese government is by implication bound to give effect to them as a part of its domestic legal system.

Since Nepal has ratified the CEDAW, the Interim Constitution requires that the state immediately abolish all existing laws that discriminate against women.[17] Through ratification of the CEDAW, the Nepalese state is obliged to take all appropriate measures to modify or abolish social, customary and religious norms and practices that are based in gender stereotypes.[18] This is a mammoth task given the social and cultural fabric of Nepalese society at different levels: the family, the local community and at the national level. To implement the CEDAW at all these levels requires a holistic approach that combines strategies of (1) guaranteeing women's individual rights, (2) giving social support to women, and (3) enhancing social and cultural change.[19]

In spite of these wide-reaching obligations embedded in both the CEDAW and the Interim Constitution, the pace of legislative, administrative and social change has been slow. It is the Ministry of Women, Children and Social Welfare that constitutes the national machinery for the advancement of women. As the coordinating and gender mainstreaming unit of the government, this Ministry has the overall responsibility for the implementation of the national gender equality policies and plans of action. In its comments to Nepal's Combined Second and Third Interim Reports, the CEDAW Committee commended the Nepalese

[16] Article 1, Interim Constitution of Nepal, 2007: "This Constitution is the fundamental law of Nepal. All laws inconsistent with this Constitution shall, to the extent of such inconsistency, be void, (2) It shall be the duty of every person to uphold this Constitution."

[17] Article 2, CEDAW: "States Parties should condemn discrimination against women in all its forms and agree to pursue by all appropriate means and without delay a policy of eliminating discrimination against women. More specifically, Article 2 of the CEDAW:

(a) To embody the principle of the equality of men and women in their national constitutions or other appropriate legislation if not yet incorporated therein and to ensure, through law and other appropriate means, the practical realization of this principle;

(b) To adopt appropriate legislative and other measures, including sanctions where appropriate, prohibiting all discrimination against women."

[18] Articles 2(f) and 5(a) CEDAW.

[19] See Holtmaat's chapter in this book.

government for the National Plan of Action on Gender Equality and Women's Empowerment as it covered the twelve critical areas of concern identified in the *Beijing Platform for Action* 1995.[20] In its comments to Nepal's Combined Fourth and Fifth Periodic Reports, the CEDAW Committee commended Nepal for the Interim Constitution of 2007 and the Supreme Court Decision of December 2007, the Domestic Violence Act of 2009 and the Gender Equality Act of 2006.[21] Appreciating the Nepalese government's efforts to review and revise discriminatory legislation, "the Committee remains concerned at the persistence of a significant number of discriminatory laws and provisions."[22] The inadequate monitoring and poor enforcement of these laws, plans and policies were addressed by the CEDAW Committee in its comments to Nepal's Combined Fourth and Fifth Periodic Reports:

> In accordance with its General Recommendation No. 6 and the guidance provided in the Beijing Platform of Action, the Committee calls on the State Party to provide the national machinery for the empowerment of women at the central and local levels, with the necessary human, financial and technical resources for their effective functioning in all areas of women's empowerment. It also calls on the State Party to strengthen its monitoring mechanism for the implementation of laws and plans of action aimed at achieving de facto equality between women and men.[23]

3 Need for and relevance of judicial education for protection and promotion of women's human rights

The Nepalese Treaty Act[24] and the Interim Constitution provide for an effective remedy and procedure of enforcement of rights in cases of infringements by the government. The extraordinary jurisdiction of the Supreme Court in the Constitution opens avenues for widening the concept of *locus standi* in cases of public interest. However, only an efficient, independent and gender-sensitive judiciary can protect and enforce the fundamental rights of women and other socially excluded people. As a part of the Nepalese democratization process, a number of civil society organizations that set out to empower women through legal literacy, legal

20 CEDAW/C/SR. 630 and 631, para. 191.
21 CEDAW/C/NPL/CO/4–5, para. 4.
22 CEDAW/C/NPL/CO4–5, para. 11.
23 CEDAW/C/NPL/CO4–5, para. 13.
24 In cases of the provisions of a treaty, to which Nepal or Government of Nepal is a party upon its ratification accession, acceptance or approval by the Parliament, are inconsistent with the provisions of prevailing laws (section 9 of the Nepal Treaty Act 1990).

advocacy and public interest litigation have been formed.[25] These organizations see government accountability as key to democracy, good governance, human rights and social justice. Through its work – which involves educating both the grass roots and judiciary about women's rights under the CEDAW and the Interim Constitution – Pro Public has used litigation as a means of domesticating the CEDAW in Nepalese law. In the following section I will show how a legal education program aimed at the Nepalese Supreme Court contributed to what today is referred to as the Court's landmark gender equality jurisprudence.

The Forum for the Protection of the Public Interest (Pro Public) is a Nepalese non-profit, non-governmental organization (NGO) dedicated to the cause of public interest activities. As already mentioned above, it was established in 1991 by a consortium of lawyers, economists, journalists, consumers and women's rights activists. Realizing that public interest litigation often fails because of gender bias and lack of knowledge of Nepal's obligations under the CEDAW, Pro Public embarked on a legal education program teaching law enforcement agencies and judges about Nepal's obligations under the CEDAW and the Nepalese Constitution. The legal education program was carried out in cooperation with the Delhi-based organization Sakshi, which has vast experience in public interest litigation.[26] This legal education program was predicated on the concept of the equality principle as foundational to all human rights and conceived with the view of addressing problems faced by women litigants or victims of violence with regard to the formal justice system. What set this project apart from many others that also deal with women and law was the partnership that it built up between members of the judiciary and NGOs, both nationally and regionally. This resulted in the formation of the Asia Pacific Forum for Judicial Education on Equality Issues (the Forum) in 1997 comprising a network of twenty-four Superior Court Judges and NGO leaders from Bangladesh, India, Nepal, Pakistan, Sri Lanka and the South Pacific, and involving two Senior Court Judges from Canada. So far, the Forum has facilitated judicial education on equality issues (particularly gender equality) at regional and national levels to over 450 judges.

[25] Sapana Pradhan Malla, *Special Measures for Women and their Impact* (Kathmandu: Forum for Women, Law and Development, 2003).

[26] R. Kapur and B. Cossman, *Subversive Sites: Feminist Engagements with Law in India* (New Delhi: Sage Publications, 1996).

The first phase of this initiative began in 1997 under the direction of a core Management Team (MT) composed of committed judicial and NGO educators from each of the five member nations. For the first six years the Forum Secretariat remained in India, under the management of Sakshi. In 2003 the MT agreed that one NGO in rotation should take the Secretariat functions for the Forum, and Pro Public took this responsibility first.[27]

Preliminary studies carried out in India by Sakshi in 1996 and subsequently by Pro Public in Nepal in 1997 confirmed existing fears regarding the gender bias among the judiciary and its subsequent impact on judicial decision-making.[28] These findings emphasized the need for judicial education on equality issues and were instrumental in defining priorities for the work undertaken by the Forum.

Cultural and historical commonalities among the countries of South Asia resulted in the project being conceived along regional lines, and developed with the view to establishing links between judges and selected NGOs. This project also created opportunities and spaces for discussions and activities regarding women's access to justice and judicial education on equality issues. This was ensured by the fact that while overall policy decisions regarding the approach to judicial education were jointly arrived at by the Management Team, responsibility for adaptation of materials to the context of each country lay with the country representatives.

The integration of gender equality in judicial decision-making at multiple levels was seen as a crucial step towards the realization of substantive justice for women. Forum members have taken a strategic approach to ensure outreach to lower courts. As this is the level where the majority of cases involving domestic violence, divorce and custody are dealt with, this is an important development. The fact that senior judges, who act as resource persons in these workshops or meetings, are high in the judicial "pecking order" minimizes or lowers resistance to the idea of gender equality. It also serves to legitimize ideas pertaining to law and gender equality that are often at war with traditionalist views of women's role and place in society. The impact of this work is evidenced in changes in judicial decision-making with regard to gender-based violence led by Forum members. While this is most visible in India, which has a more conducive political environment, the incidence of such judgments in Pakistan, where

[27] Financial support for the project was provided by the United Nations Development Fund for Women (UNIFEM) and the Canadian International Development Agency (CIDA).

[28] Belbase and Pyakurel, *supra* note 15.

retrogressive laws have vitiated the environment since the late 1970s, is a clearer marker of success.[29]

A survey, conducted by Pro Public, found that women lawyers and litigants are usually denied equal treatment and opportunity in the courts.[30] When the verdict is delivered, it will also usually be tainted by prejudice against women because judges do not consider the contextual reality. A woman rarely gets the justice that she deserves. Many judges appear to have difficulty in viewing the merits of cases regarding domestic violence on the basis of criminal evidence. Instead, they often seem to see it as a case of the wife versus the husband, a personal relationship in which the wife's behavior plays a dominant role; that is, "she must have done something to deserve the abuse." The survey also found that judges are exceedingly influenced by traditional beliefs regarding the role and nature of women and that these beliefs affect their decisions involving women's issues.[31] These kinds of attitudes inside the courts are often attributed to the fact that crimes such as rape and domestic abuse, that is wife battering, are underreported.

Judges who participated in the survey opined that the Nepalese social structure is such that it bestows upon a man his wife's guardianship and entitles him to act accordingly.[32] Therefore, if a man slaps his wife when she is at fault, he is only fulfilling his duty as her guardian. While 69 per cent of judges thought that "provocative dressing" can be an invitation to sexual assault, only 3 per cent thought it possible that a husband could commit rape: by the logic of the overwhelming majority of respondents, since the husband has a right over his wife's body, sexual intercourse – even without the consent of the wife – cannot be deemed rape. The survey also revealed the fact that a case generally takes approximately two years to come to the district court level and it might take many more years to resolve it. During the survey it was also found that many judges had not even heard about the CEDAW and, most importantly, most of the judges interviewed were found to be receptive and eager to attend judicial education workshops. To achieve judicial commitment to uphold equality jurisprudence and laws against violence against women, the study recommended that efforts should aim to educate the judges, public prosecutors and other law enforcement

[29] H. T. Thomas, *Gender Equality Judicial Education Project South Asia Program* (Sakshi, 23 June 2006).

[30] Belbase and Pyakurel, *supra* note 15.

[31] An example is the case of *Meera Dhungana* v. *Council of Ministers* 1995.

[32] Belbase and Pyakurel, *supra* note 15.

agencies, stressing not only the seriousness of such crimes, but also of the conscious and unconscious prejudices of judges and other law enforcement agencies. Realizing this, Pro Public, as an active member of the Management Committee of the APAFEJE, organized many one-day and three-day interaction workshops on gender sensitization for judges of the different courts in Nepal with the support from the United Nation Development Program. Similarly, it also organized Regional Protocol Meetings and Management Meetings and provided secretariat services to the APAFEJE.

The Supreme Court, as well as the senior judges of the Appellate Court, served as resource persons for the workshops organized to educate judges on gender equality.[33] The judges from the Southern Asian region served as resource persons in some of the initial training programs. The outcomes of this venture have been visible in the recent Supreme Court deliberation in the issue of marital rape and many other gender equality cases. A number of gender-sensitive judgments were delivered by the judges who had participated in the training workshops.

4 Judicial activism and judicial education: making the CEDAW a part of Nepalese law

The Nepalese judiciary has an obligation to deliver justice based on the established principle of human rights that are universal, indivisible and inalienable. Under the Interim Constitution of Nepal, the courts are obliged to interpret existing laws in the light of the gender equality principle embedded in the CEDAW. Of particular importance regarding the domestication of the CEDAW is the responsibility of the courts, especially the Supreme Court, to declare void such laws that contradict any convention of which Nepal is a party.[34] The implementation of duly ratified international conventions by the national courts as national law is crucial for domestication of women's human rights. The Interim Constitution of 2007 enshrines as its underlying principle the basic human rights of every

[33] Justice Kalyan Shrestha, Key Note Speech on the inaugural session of the Interaction Programme on Gender Equality and Justice, unpublished speech, Halida, West Bengal, 2001. Justice Mr. Kalyan Shrestha, Judge, Supreme Court of Nepal (then judge of the Court of Appeal) from the Judiciary and Mr. Prakash Mani Sharma from Pro Public represented the Management Committee of the Forum, which was constituted to design the courses required for judicial education.

[34] Article 1(a): "This Constitution is the fundamental law of Nepal. All laws inconsistent with it shall, to the extent of such inconsistency, be void."

citizen and lays the foundation for a legal system in line with the concept of the rule of law. The Constitution under the fundamental right chapter recognizes various international and regional instruments including the CEDAW.[35] Under Nepalese law, the human rights of individuals can be enforced through an order of the judiciary, and it the duty of the state to effectively implement international treaties and agreements of which the Nepali state is a party.[36]

The extraordinary jurisdiction of the Supreme Court in the Constitution opens avenues for widening the concept of *locus standi* in cases of public interest, introducing a broader concept of judicial constitutional reform in Nepal. It may be relevant in this context to mention that the Supreme Court has also said in one of its judgments that even though the Directive Principles and policies of the state cannot be enforced by the Court, the Court may take the Directive Principles into consideration.

Only an efficient and independent judiciary can protect and enforce the fundamental rights of the citizens. Even though the Constitution provides an elaborate set of commitments to respect human rights of women and to end all forms of discrimination against women, the Nepalese state has to a great extent failed to take measures to eliminate discriminatory laws and practices. This led lawyers, activists and NGOs to file several petitions in the Supreme Court challenging a number of discriminatory legal provisions prevailing in Nepalese laws. These challenges were based on the CEDAW and the Constitution.[37]

[35] See *Prakash Mani Sharma* v. *Office of the Council of Ministers* (June 2004), *Prakash M. Sharma* v. *Royal Nepal Airline & Others* (May 2004), *Meera Dhungana* v. *Office of the Council of Ministers* (March 2005), *Prakash Mani Sharma* v. *Ministry of Women, Children and Social Welfare* (January 2008), *Sapana P. Malla* v. *Office of the Council of Ministers* (April 2008).

[36] Article 33(M) of the Interim Constitution 2007.

[37] These lawyers and activists were Meera Dhungana (filed case for equal property right), Chanda Bajracharya (filed case for right to equality), Reena Bajracharya (filed case for discriminatory recruitment provision), Sapana Pradhana Malla (filed case against discriminatory provision on citizenship), Kabita Pandey (filed case against discriminatory provision on providing widow allowance on the basis of age), Chandra Kanta Gyawali (filed case against discriminatory citizenship right between men and women) and Prakash Mani Sharma (filed case against discriminatory provision on providing maternity leave to unmarried women). These cases were brought on behalf of the individual petitioner as well as organizations such as Forum for Women Law and Development and Forum for Public Interest Litigation.

4.1 Case law before the judicial education program 1997

Prior to the above-described judicial education program, the Supreme Court upheld gender discriminatory laws and practices in a number of rulings. In a case from 1991,[38] the Court denied citizenship rights to the children born to Nepalese women married to foreign nationals. The Court did not take into consideration Article 9 of the CEDAW that provides that women have the same rights as men to acquire, change or retain their nationality.

In the *Meera Dhungana* case from 1994,[39] the Supreme Court of Nepal declared that the existing provision for inheritance of paternal property being conditional upon daughters remaining unmarried until the age of 35 is discriminatory. The Court issued a directive order to the government to introduce an appropriate bill in the legislature within a year reviewing the laws related to property rights, but it did not declare these provisions void (*ultra vires*). It should be noted that, at that time, many judges had not heard about the CEDAW. The Court further held that any steps towards changing customs and traditions should consider the impact of the changes on Nepalese society and whether Nepalese society could adapt to such changes. In the *Meera Dhungana* case the Court asked the government to take into consideration the patriarchal nature of the society and social harmony while drafting the "bill" that is supposed to introduce "equal protection under law." The Court, in this judgment, was reluctant to introduce change at the cost of social structures. Furthermore, the Court wanted to remain oblivious to the fact that social structures are a result of practices of discrimination built up over many years.

Similarly, in the *Chandra Kanta Gyawali* case from 2002 the Supreme Court stated that the provisions of international conventions cannot prevail over the constitutional and legal provisions of Nepal unless the Parliament has formulated laws to implement such obligations.[40] In *Chanda Bajracharya*[41] and in *Sapana Pradhan*[42] discriminatory legal provisions of the penal law, adoption law, succession law and divorce law were challenged by public-spirited citizens on the grounds of the equality and non-discrimination principle enshrined in the Constitution and in

[38] *Benjamin Peter* v. *Department of Immigration* (December 1991).

[39] *Meera Dhungana* v. *Ministry of Law and Justice and Others* (June 1996).

[40] *Chandra Kanta Gyawali* v. *His Majesty's Government of Nepal* (February 2002).

[41] *Dr. Chanda Bajracharya* v. *Parliament Secretariat and Others* (July 1996).

[42] *Sapana Pradhan* v. *Ministry of Law and Justice* (September 1997).

the CEDAW. In these cases the Court addressed the strong influence of Hindu jurisprudence in the Nepalese legal system, evident from the fact that Article 4 of the Constitution declares Nepal as a Hindu Kingdom. Religious codes, according to the Supreme Court, play a key role in determining matters concerning family and social behavior, culture, tradition, activity and conduct. In these cases the Court concluded that laws and customs, which on the basis of Hindu religion assign different rights and duties to men and women, are a natural part of the social fabric. The Court was of the view that rights and privileges under the Hindu social system should be accepted. Similarly, in *Sabin Shrestha*,[43] the legal provision that requires the consent of the guardian and the approval of the government to be provided in cases of women seeking foreign employment through an employment agency was challenged. The Court, however, quashed the writ petition and justified the provision with the protectionist argument of the government and denied Nepal's obligation under the CEDAW.[44] In most of the abovementioned cases, the petitioners referred to the CEDAW's provisions without success.

4.2 *Case law after the legal education program 1997*

In recent years the very same judges that passed the above-described judgments have issued a number of directive orders for the enactment and amendment of laws that come into conflict with the equality and non-discrimination principles embedded in the CEDAW. The changing jurisprudence of the Supreme Court coincides with the gender-equality education process that started in 1997. My observations as a legal practitioner involved in grass-roots legal education, test case litigation and judicial education over a long period of time demonstrate the mutual interdependence of all these factors.

In the *Reena Bajracharya* case from 2002,[45] the same judges who decided the *Meera Dhungana* case surprisingly declared the recruitment policy of the Royal Nepal Airlines Corporation void (*ultra vires*). Furthermore, the Court reinforced treaty jurisprudence as a national law using the definition of discrimination under Article 1 of the CEDAW. The Court stated that since the human right to equality is inseparably linked

[43] *Sabin Shrestha* v. *Ministry of Law, Justice and Parliament Affairs* (August 2002).

[44] The government argued that preventing women from going to the Gulf countries is aimed at providing protection from the sexual abuses that take place in those countries.

[45] *Reena Bajracharya* v. *His Majesty's Government of Nepal* (May 2001).

to the development of the nation, it is necessary to eradicate gender-based discrimination in the laws and actions based on the law. The Supreme Court stated that gender equality was a concern of the entire humanity and, as such, a matter of everybody's duty and concern. In *Sita Acharya* v. *Public Service Commission* the same judges referred to Articles 3, 4(1) and 4(2) of the CEDAW and the provision in Article 11(3) of the Interim Constitution that obligates the government to implement temporary special measures to achieve de facto equality between men and women.

In *Meera Dhungana* v. *His Majesty's Government et al.* from 2001, the Supreme Court labeled marital rape as heinous sexual crime and endorsed the sexual autonomy of women even within marriage.[46] In a historic verdict,[47] the Supreme Court ordered the government to provide citizenship to every Nepali child born within the country whose parents are unknown. Many children born to women of the Badi community, who are involved in prostitution due to economic and social marginalization, have been deprived of citizenship up until now. The Supreme Court has also asked the government to ensure the overall welfare of Badi women, including social security and provision of alternative employment.

In addition, the Supreme Court has ordered the government to take steps to end the practice of *Chhaupadi*.[48] *Chhaupadi* is a custom that obliges menstruating women to live in makeshift huts outside of the family home. It is still practiced in remote areas in western Nepal. According to another Supreme Court decision, women under the age of thirty-five do not need the consent of their parents or husbands to apply for a passport.[49]

In three recent judgments the Nepalese Supreme Court has ordered the government to improve women's social and economic rights. In one case the government was ordered to provide free medical services to women suffering from uterine prolapse.[50] In another case the Court called for a decent working environment for women working in Cabin and Dance restaurants.[51] In yet another case the government was ordered to provide

[46] *Supreme Court Cases on Gender-related Issues* 2010, Women Law and Development Forum (FWLD), Kathmandu, Nepal.

[47] *Tek Tamrakar and others on behalf of Pro Public* v. *Office of the Council of Ministers* (June 2006).

[48] *Dil Bahadur Biswakarma* v. *His Majesty's Government* (April 2006).

[49] *Punnawati Pathak & others on behalf of Pro Public* v. *Ministry of Foreign Affairs* (November 2006).

[50] *Prakash Mani Sharma & others on behalf of Pro Public v. Government of Nepal* (May 2009).

[51] *Prakash Mani Sharma & others on behalf of Pro Public* v. *Government of Nepal* (November 2009).

a widow's allowance to women from the date of their widowhood.[52] In each of these cases the Court engaged with the state's obligations under the CEDAW, the Treaty Act and the Constitution.

In practice, women-friendly judgments suffer from weak implementation. To ensure that successful judgments are implemented, the petitioners constantly need to monitor and follow up. Similarly, all the beneficiaries of the judgments need to be informed about the outcome of the court case, and their capacity to demand their rights needs to be enhanced. In order to ensure that the judgments are implemented by the concerned government agencies, Pro Public has filed cases in the Supreme Court where it asks the government to implement the Supreme Court judgments.[53]

In one such case the Supreme Court asked the government to report on the implementation status of an earlier court order. Concluding that the court order had not been properly implemented, the Supreme Court ordered the government to implement its decisions with seriousness. In response, the government set up a Judgment Execution Unit in all the Ministries. It also set up a unit in the Law and Human Rights Division of the Office of the Prime Minister to follow up and monitor the activities of all the Ministries regarding the progress made on implementation of the court orders. However, there is still a long way to go to ensure that ordinary women benefit from these legal changes. To make the government accountable, there is a continuous need for legal education directed at grass-roots women, practicing lawyers, judges, public prosecutors and other law enforcement agencies.

The above-described changes in the jurisprudence of the Supreme Court and the breakthrough of the CEDAW into Nepalese law clearly coincide with the gender equality education program that has been carried out since 1997 by Pro Public in cooperation with the APAFEJE.

An important factor regarding the relevance and legitimacy of the program was the contribution made by the then Chief Justice of India to the judges of the Supreme Court of Nepal. In his lectures, Justice A. H. Ahamadi used case law from the Indian Supreme Court to show how the Indian judiciary had used the CEDAW as a source of interpretation of Indian law. He referred to a number of cases where the Hindu law came into conflict with the CEDAW. In this way he played a significant role in creating a realization of the role of the judiciary in the promotion of human rights in general, and women's human rights and gender equality in Nepal in particular.

[52] *Kabita Pandey & others on behalf of Pro Public* v. *Government of Nepal* (February 2010).

[53] *Meera Dhungana* v. *Office of the Prime Minister*, 2004 (Writ No. 1074 decided in 2010).

In Nepal, where the judiciary is empowered to undertake strong judicial review, the CEDAW holds great promise for individual women and women's groups who want to challenge discriminatory laws and customs. Unless the Supreme Court is able and willing to declare Nepalese legislation invalid on the basis of the CEDAW, this legal potential is not realized. As shown by this study, the judges on the bench initially ignored the principle of equality and justice due to the lack of an overall understanding of the CEDAW and the CEDAW's transformative jurisprudence.

The analysis of the judgments made by the Supreme Court before and after the judicial education program took place shows that if the members of the judiciary are sensitized to and informed on the concept of women's human rights, the judiciary can be active in making the state accountable to implement/honor its international obligations under the CEDAW. This underscores the importance and need for continuous judicial education on equality issues and the existence of public interest litigation for the protection and promotion of rights of people who are discriminated against and excluded by the state.

5 Human rights, judicial review, accountability and democracy

It is widely recognized that the status of women in a society is one of the yardsticks by which the ability of a nation to implement instantiating democracy and good governance, participate in the increasingly global economy and redress the condition of a deteriorating environment is measured. The role of the judiciary is particularly important when the legislative and the executive branches of government fail to fulfill their legal duties. As shown in this chapter, this is a frequent occurrence in the case of protection and promotion of women's human rights in Nepal. As the guardian of the Constitution, the role of the judiciary is to keep the law alive and submit itself to the majesty of the law. If the executive branch betrays the people and the Parliament stands paralyzed, some constitutional machinery must move into action.[54] In such situations judges may, as demonstrated in this chapter, play a vital role in ensuring that the constitutional rights of the people are protected and enforced.[55]

[54] V. R. K. Iyar, "The justice manifesto of the human rights judiciary takes over," *Outlook*, New Delhi, March 1996.

[55] P. N. Bhagwati, "Independence of the judiciary in a democracy," *The Economic Times*, New Delhi, 30 July 1995.

This is absolutely essential for maintaining the rule of law and to further the cause of gender justice.[56]

The role of the Supreme Court, while dealing with public interest litigation relating to protection and promotion of women's human rights, is to see that the executive authorities take steps to implement and enforce national and international obligations under the Constitution and international conventions. As such, the Court has to pass orders and give directions for the protection of the fundamental rights of the people. The passing of appropriate orders requiring the implementation of the law in a situation where the legislative and the executive powers are undermining women's rights under national and international law cannot be regarded as the Court having usurped the functions of the legislative or the executive branches of government.[57]

In Nepal the role of the judiciary has been considered pivotal by women's rights activists. The Nepalese government is recognizing its responsibilities as defined by the Court. For example, in Nepal's Combined Fourth and Fifth Periodic Report to the CEDAW Committee, the government states that: "The Supreme Court stands as a very progressive national judicial institution for developing a landmark gender equality jurisprudence treating the rights of women with the utmost respect."[58] The state report describes how the Supreme Court of Nepal has issued a range of directive orders for the enactment and amendment of the laws concerning widows' allowances, women's property rights, marital rape, sexual harassment and discrimination in employment, in the wake of guarantees under the CEDAW.[59]

The Supreme Court and all the branches of the judiciary have been exemplary in promoting and protecting human rights through various judgments that declare a law *void* if it contradicts the rights provision in the Constitution and any convention to which Nepal is a party.[60] This national legal accountability mechanism is in practice strengthened by the state reporting procedure under the CEDAW. How the two supplement and reinforce each other is demonstrated by the Nepalese state's

[56] See *S. P. Gupta* v. *Union of India*, AIR 1982 SC 149.

[57] See www.propublic.org/index.php (last accessed 2 July 2008).

[58] CEDAW/C/NPL/4–5 para. 243.

[59] CEDAW/C/NPL/4–5 paras. 223, 224,225, 226.

[60] Opening remarks by Honorable Sujata Koirala, Deputy Prime Minister and Minister for Foreign Affairs, and leader of the Nepali delegation at the Tenth Session of the Human Rights Council Working Group on Universal Periodic Review, 25 January 2011, Geneva, Switzerland.

Combined Fourth and Fifth Periodic Report of November 2010, where a number of the Supreme Court's judicial directive orders are referred to.[61] Of particular interest is the government's positive response to the Supreme Court's ruling in a case where the Court ordered enactment of legislation.[62]

The Supreme Court has also noted how a woman employee would be subjected to such harassments either with the threat of dismissal from her job or some enticing promises such as promotion, increment in salary or rewards. Such abuses have a drastic negative impact on the victim's work status and morale. Therefore, the Supreme Court ordered enactment of legislation covering all aspects of this issue including proper investigation, adequate penal provisions and relief measures for victims in such cases. The Nepalese government has submitted a bill to the Parliament on "Sexual Harassment at Workplace."[63]

The Nepalese government's decision to follow the decisions of the Court is a positive step towards the government commitment to fulfill its international obligations under the CEDAW. It indicates that the government, when ratifying the CEDAW and incorporating it into the Constitution, seems to have had sincere intentions.

[61] CEDAW/C/NPL/4–5 paras. 223, 224, 225, 226.

[62] *Sarmila Parajuli et al.* v. *Council of Ministers* (February 2006).

[63] Sexual Harassment at Workplace Bill 2010.

15

From ratification to implementation: 'domesticating' the CEDAW in state, government and society. A case study of Pakistan

SHAHEEN SARDAR ALI

1 Introduction

This chapter investigates the extent to which the Convention on the Elimination of All Forms of Discrimination against Women (CEDAW) finds a place in governmental and non-governmental policy documents, legislation, judicial decisions, governance structures and institutions in Pakistan. It poses the question whether the CEDAW's pre- and post-ratification processes and attendant discourse have 'domesticated' it within state, government and society in that jurisdiction. The study suggests that in a country where pluralism is deeply embedded in legal culture as well as in religious and cultural norms, human rights instruments in general and the CEDAW in particular receive an ambivalent and mixed reception as the newest layer of plural legalities.[1]

An initial draft of this chapter was presented at the colloquium 'From Ratification to Implementation: CEDAW in International and National Law', Oslo, 11–12 March 2010; a revised draft was presented at the Centre for the Study of Contemporary Pakistan, SOAS, 19 January 2012. I am grateful to Professors Anne Hellum, Henriette Sinding Aasen, Alan Norrie, Rebecca Probert, Andrew Williams and others for their insightful comments and valuable feedback. I have also benefitted from comments of the anonymous reviewer. I am indebted to Faqir Asfundyar Yousaf, Rukhshanda Naz and Menaal Munshey for their meticulous research assistance.

[1] For a study of cases in the superior courts from 1980 to 2003 where human rights norms and instruments inform judgments, see S. S. Ali, 'Interpretative strategies for women's human rights in a plural legal framework: exploring judicial and state responses to Hudood laws in Pakistan', in A. Hellum, J. E. Stewart, A. Tsanga and S. S. Ali (eds.), *Human Rights, Plural Legalities and Gendered Realities: Paths Are Made by Walking* (Harare: Weaver Books, 2006) 381–406.

This case study draws upon a variety of governmental and non-governmental sources,[2] and surveys of judicial decisions of the high courts and the Supreme Court that have invoked the CEDAW since Pakistan's ratification in 1996, and is informed by the academic literature on the approach of Pakistan and other Muslim states to the CEDAW. The author herself was a participant in the accession process and draws upon those personal experiences in developing the present study. She wrote a comparative study of the CEDAW, Islamic law and the laws of Pakistan, advancing the case for ratification.[3] As a member of the women's and human rights movement, she campaigned for its ratification in seminars and workshops. As a member of the Senate Commission of Inquiry for Women[4] and the Prime Minister's National Consultative Committee, she was privy to discussions leading to the Cabinet's decision to ratify, and she brings this privileged insight to this chapter. In the post-ratification period, she held the post of Cabinet Minister for Health, Population and Women's Development in the government of the North-West Frontier Province[5] (1999–2001) and was the first Chair of the National Commission on the Status of Women (NCSW) (2000–1). This chapter has also benefitted from discussions and personal communications with members of the Pakistani NGO community, in particular those involved in the 38th Session of the CEDAW Committee, in 2007, where Pakistan's country reports were under discussion.

2 The CEDAW within a religious, cultural and socio-legal context

Since its inception as an independent nation in 1947, Pakistan has struggled with multiple strands of its identity (religious, cultural, ethnic and

[2] Including Government of Pakistan (GOP) documents, discussions in the Prime Minister's National Consultative Committee for Women (1994–5), documents relating to the Senate Commission of Inquiry for Women (1995–7), working papers on the GOP's position regarding the CEDAW, Pakistan's country reports to the CEDAW Committee, shadow reports to the CEDAW Committee from NGOs and civil society organisations, and the Concluding Comments of the CEDAW Committee upon consideration of Pakistan country reports.

[3] S. S. Ali, *A Comparative Study of the United Nations Convention on the Elimination of All Forms of Discrimination against Women, Islamic Law and the Laws of Pakistan* (Peshawar: Shaheen Printing Press, 1995).

[4] Leading to the Commission's 1997 *Report of the Commission of Inquiry for Women in Pakistan*.

[5] Now renamed the Khyber Pukhtunkhwa.

linguistic)[6] and the manner in which these inform conceptions of state, government, law and society, as well as the status of women. Pakistan's Islamic identity (and its role in the Constitution and in law-making as well as the broader nation-building project) is the core element in debates on women's rights in that jurisdiction. As Mullally so aptly observes:

> Although the fundamental rights chapter of the Constitution guarantees equality before the law, the pursuit of gender equality has frequently been sacrificed to religious-cultural claims defining and limiting women's status. Yielding to such claims has served the interests of nation-building while at the same time guarding against any serious threat to the modernizing agendas of Pakistan's political élite. Lost within such compromises is the recognition of women as bearers of rights, with equal rights to participate in the definition of religious-cultural norms.[7]

It is pertinent, besides, to highlight the discursive nature of an Islamic legal tradition that is susceptible to multiple interpretations of the Qur'an and Sunna (the primary sources of Islamic law), resulting in a plurality of views regarding authoritative and legitimate formulations of 'Islamic' law:[8] General Zia-ul-Haq's 'Islamisation' of laws and society in Pakistan in the 1970s and 1980s, for example, used the slogan '*chador aur chardewari*' ('women veiled and within the confines of the home') despite its questionable basis in the Islamic tradition;[9] meanwhile, the established right within the Hanafi school of juristic thought (of which most Pakistanis are adherents) of an adult Muslim woman to enter into a contract of marriage without the intervention, presence or consent of her male guardian (*wali*) was challenged in the Saima Waheed case.[10]

The vast majority of Pakistanis are adherents of Sunni Islam, which does not subscribe to an official clergy. This simple but important observation provides a background by which to understand why individuals and

[6] Pakistan is home to some half a dozen major ethnic groups and a similar number of smaller ones including Punjabi, Baluch, Sindhi, Pukhtun and others.

[7] S. Mullally, '"As nearly as may be": debating women's human rights in Pakistan' *Social and Legal Studies* 14 (2005) 341–58.

[8] S. S. Ali, *Gender and Human Rights in Islam and International Law. Equal before Allah, Unequal before Man?* (The Hague: Kluwer Law International, 2000).

[9] For a detailed discussion see K. Mumtaz and F. Shaheed, *Women of Pakistan: Two Steps Forward, One Step Back?* (Lahore: Vanguard, 1987) Chapter 7.

[10] *Abdul Waheed* v. *Asma Jehangir* PLD (1997) Lahore 301. In a similar case the father was convicted for murdering his daughter who had married of her own volition without the consent of the family: see *Muhammad Siddique* v. *State* PLD 449 (2001). The Maliki and Shafai schools, however, hold that a woman's consent must be given through her *wali*: M. A. Mannan (ed.), *D F Mulla's Principles of Mahomedan Law* (Lahore: PLD Publishers, 1995) at 390.

groups vie for authority and legitimacy in the name of Islam and Islamic law. In the sphere of women's rights, this absence of an organised clergy leads to 'forum shopping' for opinions of religious scholars by government and people to advance their rights or undermine them, as the case may be.[11] The potential for using Islam as a socio-economic and political tool in both the public and private spheres is significant and is employed by religious and secular parties as well as by the wider public. The founder of Pakistan did not envisage the nation as a theocracy, a position evident from his public expressions of Pakistan as a modern, democratic state where everyone was equal before and afforded the protection of the law.[12] Yet parallel to such sentiments have always existed religious and conservative forces demanding a clear expression and manifestation of an Islamic identity. Soon after the independence of Pakistan, the liberal, democratic element inside as well as outside of government realised the importance of 'playing the Islamic card'.[13] Aware that multiethnic, multicultural and multilingual Pakistan needed a central theme to bind it together as a nation, religion became the obvious binding force. Consequently, Pakistan's Islamic identity has been highlighted in pronouncements from government, a trend that has found favour with the majority of the population, for whom 'cultural Islam' is an important part of their identity.[14]

In the context of women's rights, Islam has been and continues to be used both for *and* against women's rights and equality, depending on who is deploying the argument and at what forum.[15] Since the inception of

[11] For example, Maulana Fazlullah, a militant clergyman from the Swat valley, has used FM radio to broadcast venomously misogynistic rhetoric, exhorting men to keep women inside the house, declaring them as the cause of all evils in society; while in 2010 Islamabad's Lal Masjid seminary led a vigilante campaign against women of 'loose morals' in the name of an Islamic duty to 'promote virtue and prevent vice'.

[12] See his presidential address of 11 August 1947 in J. Ahmed (ed.), *Speeches and Writings of Mr Jinnah* (Lahore: Sh. Muhammad Ashraf, 1964).

[13] For a detailed discussion with reference to the Constitution, see G. W. Chaudhary, *Constitutional Development in Pakistan* (London: Lowe and Brydone, 1971) and Chaudhary, 'Religious minorities in Pakistan', *Muslim World* 46 (1956) 313–23.

[14] See generally M. Lau, *The Role of Islam in the Legal System of Pakistan* (Leiden: Martinus Nijhoff, 2006); M. Lau, 'Sharia and national law in Pakistan' in J. M. Otto (ed.), *Sharia Incorporated. A Comparative Overview of the Legal Systems of Twelve Muslim Countries in the Past and Present* (Leiden: Leiden University Press, 2010) 373–432; A. M. Weiss, 'Interpreting Islam and women's rights: implementing CEDAW in Pakistan', *International Sociology* 18:3 (2003) 581–601; A. M. Weiss (ed.), *Islamic Reassertion in Pakistan* (Syracuse University Press, 1986); F. Halliday and H. Alavi (eds.), *State and Ideology in the Middle East and Pakistan* (London: Macmillan Educational Ltd, 1988).

[15] See the discussions in F. Rahman, 'Status of women in Islam' in G. Nishat (ed.), *Women and Revolution in Iran* (Boulder: Westview Press, 1983) 37–54; J. L. Esposito, *Women*

Pakistan, this plurality of views has been apparent in the pronouncements of various political and governmental actors as well as the population in general. Jinnah, the founder of Pakistan, advocated women's rights, education and economic empowerment, and was accompanied by his sister Fatima in public engagements to highlight women's presence in the public sphere. Likewise, Ra'ana Liaquat Ali Khan, the wife of Pakistan's first prime minister, founded the All Pakistan Women's Association (APWA) to empower women in the field of education and skill development. But it was during this period that the conservative politician Abul Ala Maududi wrote his famous book *Purdah and the Status of Women in Islam*,[16] which argued for women's complete segregation and a role inside the home prohibiting engagement in the public sphere.[17] The gap between various ideological positions regarding the rights of women in Pakistan became fertile ground for disputes over women's rights in Islam and international law. Last but not least, customary practices, heavily influenced by patriarchal norms, inform perceptions of women's status and undermine women's rights in Islam.[18]

in Muslim Family Law (Syracuse University Press, 1982); A. Al-Hibri, 'Muslim women's rights in the global village: opportunities and challenges', *Journal of Law and Religion* 15 (2001, Fall) 37–66; R. Hassan, 'An Islamic perspective' in J. Belcher (ed.), *Women, Religion and Sexuality* (Geneva: WCC Publications, 1990); F. Mernissi (trans. M. J. Lakeland), *Women and Islam* (Oxford: Basil Blackwell, 1991); L. Ahmed, *Women and Gender in Islam: Historical Roots of a Modern Debate* (New Haven: YUP, 1992); A. Barlas, *'Believing Women': Unreading Patriarchal Interpretations of the Qur'an* (Austin: University of Texas Press, 2002); Z. Mir-Hosseini, *Marriage on Trial: A Study of Islamic Family Law* (London: I. B. Taurus, 1993) and *Islam and Gender, the Religious Debate in Contemporary Islam* (Princeton University Press, 1999); S. Haeri, *Law of Desire: Temporary Marriage in Shi'i Iran* (Syracuse University Press, 1989); H. Afshar, 'Behind the veil' in H. Moghissi (ed.), *Women and Islam: Critical Concepts in Sociology* (London: Routledge, 2004) 71–86.

16 Al-Ash'ari (trans. edn) (Lahore: Islamic Publications, 1972).

17 Maududi typifies the complexity of Pakistani understandings of 'Islamic' law: in various books he argued that women's empowerment through employment in the public sphere is the cause of societal evils and is prohibited in Islam, asking at one point in *Purdah and the Status of Women in Islam*: 'Why should a woman who wins her own bread, supports herself economically and does not depend on anyone for security and maintenance, remain faithfully attached to one man only for the sake of her sexual desire?' In 1966, nevertheless, Maududi and his party turned a political somersault by supporting a female presidential candidate while the 'liberal' opposition parties (and that of the incumbent president) published pamphlets arguing *against* women as heads of state.

18 For instance, Islamic law accords women inheritance rights, yet cultural articulations negate this by denying daughters the right to inherit land; male child preference continues as a cultural norm but has no support in Islam, as the Prophet Muhammad himself had no male offspring to survive him and his preference for his daughter Fatima was

Differing conclusions over women's (in)equality produced by diverse lines of argument based on Islam and Islamic law are evident from the debate on whether Pakistan should become party to the CEDAW. The fifteen-year journey toward final accession in 1996 was difficult and contested, both within official circles as well as within various social constituencies, and reflected the plurality of views regarding what constitutes 'Islamically' and culturally acceptable human rights and whether UN human rights instruments are compatible with human rights in the Islamic legal tradition.[19] The debates also reflected the different 'galleries' (national and international) to which government and society perform, and the various audiences observing these performances. Pakistan's history of participation in human rights treaties (including the CEDAW) has also been influenced by a political history that has oscillated between elected governments and military regimes, both of which have used Islam as a tool of political expediency.

The debate, then, over women's rights and the place of the CEDAW is driven by a range of divergent opinions and viewpoints.[20] In her analysis of plural legalities and their impact on women's rights in Pakistan, Shaheed notes that the intersection of culture with custom, law and politics has direct implications for women's rights.[21] It is the power elite who decide what constitutes 'valid' culture and custom and how these will be applied in the formal and informal realm. Pakistan's discourse of women's rights and of the CEDAW is influenced by the interpretations of those in positions of power (often mitigating *against* women's rights), who are not necessarily those in government.[22] While government may subscribe

exceptional in its explicitness; adult women have the right to marry of their own choice, but societal norms expect women to defer to the spouse chosen by the family.

19 This approach is of course not confined to Muslim countries. There is a rich body of literature on universalism versus relativism in human rights debates, including 'Asian', 'African' and 'Western' concepts of human rights.

20 See e.g. Y. Zaidi, 'The interplay of CEDAW, national laws and customary practices in Pakistan: a literature review' in S. S. Ali (ed.), *Conceptualising Islamic Law, CEDAW and Women's Human Rights in Plural Legal Settings: A Comparative Analysis of Application of CEDAW in Bangladesh, India and Pakistan* (New Delhi: UNIFEM, 2006) 199–263.

21 F. Shaheed, 'Engagements of culture, customs and law: women's lives and activism' in F. Shaheed *et al.* (eds.) *Shaping Women's Lives* (Lahore: Shirkatgah, 1998) 61–79.

22 For instance, in 2008 Baluch tribal senators in the Parliament supported the burying alive of women who had acted against cultural norms. Similarly, at the height of the militancy in the Swat valley in 2007–8, girls' schools were burned down and a 'call' to keep them at home was heeded by parents and families concerned about the safety of their daughters. Students of religious *madrasahs* have been known to harass women who do not cover their head when in public.

to the rhetoric of women's rights, and may desire to be *seen* to subscribe by the international community and by elements of Pakistani civil society, there exists a dissonance between formal laws and governmental policy on the one hand, and practices and beliefs on the other.[23]

3 The arduous journey toward accession

Demands for the ratification of the CEDAW were made by women's NGOs and the human rights movement in Pakistan as soon as it was adopted at the UN in 1981;[24] yet it took fifteen years of consistent lobbying to keep the issue alive until the decision to accede was finally made.[25] On a number of occasions during the mid to late 1980s,[26] the government signalled its intention to sign the Convention, but the issue remained unresolved. It is worthwhile discussing briefly one particular such initiative in 1987, as it reflects the thinking within many sections of state and society regarding

[23] Witness, for instance, the wide gap between enrolment of girls and boys in schools. At a formal level, all children have access to schools but cultural practices hinder girls from going to school.

[24] Pakistan has a robust women's rights and human rights movement dating back to before independence. For an overview see *Women of Pakistan*, *supra* note 9; S. S. Ali, 'Law, Islam and the women's movement in Pakistan' in S. M. Rai (ed.), *Gender and Democratisation: International Perspectives* (London: Routledge, 2000) 41–63.

[25] Prominent among the groups and organisations lobbying for the CEDAW were the Human Rights Commission of Pakistan, the Aurat Foundation, Shirkat Gah Women's Resource Centre, the All Pakistan Women's Association, the All Pakistan Women Lawyers Association, Simorgh Women's Resource and Publication Centre, the Applied Socio-economic Research Resource Centre and the Women's Action Forum.

[26] The government considered the issue in 1984 but no decision was made (see *Working Paper: The Convention on Elimination of All Forms of Discrimination against Women* (Islamabad: Government of Pakistan, Ministry of Foreign Affairs, 1994)). In 1985 the National Commission on the Status of Women, formed to assess the situation and make recommendations for improvement, repeated the demand for accession. However, no action was taken, and in response to the candid views presented in the report by its outspoken female chair, Zari Sarfaraz, the government withheld publication (see *Report of the Pakistan Commission on the Status of Women* (Islamabad: Government of Pakistan Printing Press, 1986)). The *Report* was finally circulated when Benazir Bhutto assumed power in 1988. It is interesting that General Zia-ul-Haq's government, known for its oppressive policies toward women, found it necessary to create a Women's Division in the Cabinet Secretariat that was later formed into a fully-fledged Ministry of Women's Development and Youth Affairs in 1989. It was this Ministry that led the consultation for signing the CEDAW. In 1989 Benazir Bhutto issued a directive to look into the CEDAW with a view to exploring accession. This was done to coincide with the tenth anniversary of the CEDAW and ahead of Bhutto attending a UN-sponsored symposium in New York. Again, no positive outcome came of this initiative. See *Working Paper*, *supra* this note at 3.

the place and position of women and their stereotypical roles in religion, custom and tradition.

In 1987 it was recommended by a committee of federal Ministries that Pakistan sign,[27] but only with a blanket reservation stating that 'The Government of the Islamic Republic of Pakistan agree[s] to ratify the convention to the extent that articles and sub-clauses are not repugnant to the teachings of the Holy Quran and the Government of Pakistan shall be the sole judge of the question whether such repugnancy exists.'[28] This proposal, an example of 'playing the Islamic card' before a conservative domestic audience, would have been unacceptable to the international community, since it would have given Pakistan the right to interpret the CEDAW in accordance not with international norms but with domestic understandings of women's rights. Conversely, such a reservation would no doubt have met with the approval of those significant numbers of Pakistanis who consider Islam to be the overarching normative framework informing their legal and social system.

The Ministry of Foreign Affairs, however, conscious of how such a reservation would be received internationally, opposed this on the grounds that other states would enter objections, the reservation being conceived as contrary to the 'object and purpose of the Convention' under Article 28(2).[29] Despite this, the Ministry's comments on the difficulties encountered by non-Western states in ratifying the CEDAW resonated with the sentiments of the proposed reservation:

> [The CEDAW] was the result of Western women's rights activists and does not take into account the varied socio-economic conditions as well as the diverse customs, values, and religious and ethical perspectives of different societies in various parts of the world … The Convention has been used by Western human rights activists as an instrument to not only criticise the situation in various Islamic countries but also the very fundamentals of the Islamic faith.[30]

The Ministry's statement also reflected the existence and power of popular ideas of gender stereotypes, in that 'diverse customs, values, and religious and ethical perspectives' and 'varied socio-economic conditions' (as quoted above) were taken to inevitably imply a defensible gender *in*-equality and a conflict with ideas of non-discrimination. If anything, of course, it can be argued that it is a government's duty to *remove* 'varied

[27] Including the Ministries of Law and Justice, Religious Affairs, Education, Foreign Affairs, and the Cabinet Secretariat.

[28] See *Working Paper, supra* note 26 at 2.

[29] *Ibid.* [30] *Ibid.*

socio-economic conditions' insofar as they threaten access to basic human rights. Deeply entrenched in the Ministry's comments were popularly held convictions regarding the 'alien-ness' of women's rights emanating from 'Western' forums,[31] regardless of the fact that these rights were being demanded by Pakistani women themselves. A final reason for reluctance to ratify the CEDAW in 1987 was that becoming a party would entail international scrutiny of the position of women in Pakistan, including the compilation of a country report and discussion thereof by the CEDAW Committee, a situation the Ministry of Foreign Affairs did not feel comfortable with. The matter did not progress much further.

During Benazir Bhutto's second tenure as prime minister (October 1993 to November 1996) serious efforts were initiated toward ratification. The government's renewed motivation is apparent from a letter written in August 1993 by the Secretary of the Ministry of Women's Development to the Foreign Secretary, recommending that 'the issue of Pakistan's ratification may be re-examined in view of the fact that women in Pakistan have made substantial progress in improving their status and also as citizens of this country and that *Pakistan's non-ratification was creating international embarrassment*'.[32]

A series of meetings was held in Islamabad, some of which I had the privilege to attend in my capacity as a member of the Prime Minister's Consultative Committee on Women. Four meetings are especially noteworthy,[33] at which representatives from the relevant Ministries (including the Ministry for Religious Affairs, the Interior Ministry and the Council of Islamic Ideology) and NGOs[34] presented their views and comments on possible ratification.[35] The agreed outcome was that a case be prepared

[31] Such popular rhetoric is evident in newspaper and journal articles as well as books authored by, among others, members of Jamaat-e-Islami (the Islamic Party), who frame the West as the morally corrupt 'other' conspiring to undermine a pristine Muslim populace through notions of human rights, liberalism and 'permissive' societal structures. For a detailed discussion see S. A. Cheema, *Problematizing 'Authenticity': A Critical Appraisal of the Jamaat-i-Islami Gender Discourse* (Warwick University PhD thesis, 2011).

[32] *Working Paper, supra* note 26 at 3 (emphasis added).

[33] These meetings were held on 5 October 1994 and 4 January, 31 January and 13 June 1995.

[34] The consensus among NGOs in Pakistan whose views were solicited was that Pakistan should ratify the CEDAW without reservation (the author was personally present at this meeting, held in the Foreign Office on 5 October 1994). NGOs present included the APWA, Aurat Foundation, Shirkat Gah, the HRCP and Behbood.

[35] These views were sought by the Ministry of Foreign Affairs through O.M. No. UN (II)-9/4/94, dated 19 May 1994.

for the government to sign the CEDAW, subject to one specific 'temporary' reservation to Article 2(f), which relates to requiring States Parties to 'take all appropriate measures, including legislation, to modify or abolish existing laws, regulations, customs and practices which constitute discrimination against women'.

Unsurprisingly, the proposal to enter a specific reservation to Article 2(f) met with stiff opposition from the Ministry of Women's Development, backed by legal academics working on the subject, women's groups and human rights activists,[36] who challenged the government's assertion that ratification without reservation was impossible. But, finding itself performing to different galleries, the government was obviously keen to emphasise its Islamic identity, both to the international community and in relation to its Muslim state counterparts. Reserving its position on Article 2(f), on the ground that it was inconsistent with Islamic law, would establish a point regarding the protection of Pakistan's Muslim identity. The fact that other Muslim countries had already entered substantial reservations was highlighted, and it was argued that this much was expected of Pakistan.[37] The hypocrisy of Western governments was also mentioned by the anti-CEDAW lobby, pointing as it did to their reticence to sign without reservations.[38]

Supporters of ratification without reservation (including NGOs, members of civil society, academics and activists, some of whom were represented on the Prime Minister's Consultative Committee) reacted strongly to this proposal, arguing that Iraq, Egypt, Libya and other reserving states did not form the entire spectrum of Muslim countries: Turkey, Tunisia, Senegal, Mali, Indonesia and Yemen were equally 'Islamic' jurisdictions yet had ratified the CEDAW unreservedly. Pakistan, they argued, should come up with its own position regarding the CEDAW and women's rights

[36] The prime minister had constituted a Consultative Committee of concerned individuals and organisations to assist in the ratification process. The author was a member of the Committee as an academic specialising in the CEDAW and Islamic law. The APWA, HRCP, Aurat Foundation, Shirkat Gah, Simorgh, Applied Socio-economic Research and Behbood (being among the best known and reputable in the field of women's rights) were among the NGOs on the Committee (see *Comparative Study* (*supra* note 3) for a comprehensive list).

[37] *Working Paper*, *supra* note 26 at 6.

[38] The CEDAW is the most reserved human rights treaty in the catalogue, with national constitutions and domestic legislation the most-cited reasons for entering reservations. More than a dozen European states have entered reservations on the basis of national laws and constitutions.

and not blindly follow other countries over the specific issue of whether reservations ought to be entered.[39]

It was to assess whether the CEDAW did in fact conflict with 'Islamic' values that, in 1995, I undertook a comparative study of the provisions of the CEDAW alongside the laws of Pakistan and of 'Islamic' law more widely.[40] The study, which was used as a campaign document in NGO seminars and workshops as well as by the government, noted that one-sixth of the CEDAW drafting committee comprised Muslim states, and that it was consequently hard to believe that a 'un-Islamic' document running counter to the spirit of Islamic law could have won their approval. Furthermore, although some Muslim states had entered reservations to certain Articles on the basis of their being repugnant to Islamic law and Shari'a, even these countries were not uniform in their opposition.[41] The Consultative Committee ultimately proposed ratification without reservation.

4 Did the CEDAW conflict with domestic law?

The problem that then arose was how to address the fact that certain laws in force at the time were clearly discriminatory to women.[42] The question was raised in the Prime Minister's Consultative Committee on Women as to whether these laws would require modification or repeal prior to ratification, or whether the process of review of domestic laws could continue thereafter. The view prevailed that the existence of certain provisions of domestic law that were incompatible with the substantive provisions of the CEDAW should not preclude Pakistan from becoming a State Party:[43]

[39] *Comparative Study, supra* note 3 at 131–41.

[40] *Comparative Study, supra* note 3. The study demonstrated that, apart from a few laws informed by a literalist interpretation of the Qur'an and Sunna (including sections of the law of evidence, criminal law and inheritance laws), most laws did not conflict with the CEDAW.

[41] For example, Algeria cited national laws; Indonesia has not entered reservations to the CEDAW's substantive Articles; Turkey's initial reservations (now partially withdrawn) cited the Turkish Civil Code and the Turkish Law of Nationality; Tunisia reserved on the basis of conflict with the Tunisian Nationality Code and Personal Status Code; Mali and Senegal ratified without reservations.

[42] Including the Child Marriages Restraint Act 1929, Offence Against Property (Enforcement of Hudood Ordinance) 1979, Offence of Zina (Enforcement of Hudood Ordinance) 1979, Offence of Qazf (Enforcement of Hudood Ordinance) 1979, Qanoon-i-Shahdat Order 1984, Citizenship Act 1951, Punjab/Sindh/NWFP/Baluchistan Muslim Personal Law (Shariat Application Act) 1962 and the Pakistan Penal Code 1860.

[43] The late Shehla Zia, director of the Aurat Foundation, and the author both advocated this viewpoint at the 4 June 1995 meeting of the Prime Minister's Consultative Committee on Women held in Islamabad.

it was argued that a number of European, African and Asian countries had found themselves in similar situations but were making an effort to overcome the problematic provisions in their respective domestic laws. What was required at that time was for Pakistan to demonstrate goodwill and genuine concern for promoting gender equality by ratifying the CEDAW.

It is uncertain what precise impact the lobbying of human rights groups and academics had on the government's final decision,[44] but one factor stands out clearly in its decision-making: the impending Fourth World Conference on Women, scheduled to be held in Beijing in September 1995, was an incentive to ratify, particularly as Prime Minister Benazir Bhutto was leading the delegation. The Cabinet's decision (less than two weeks before the Beijing Conference) to ratify the CEDAW came at a politically opportune moment and placed Pakistan in a favourable light. Yet contrary to the impression given by government spokespersons that there would be no reservations or declarations, the subsequent instrument of March 1996 included the following declaration: 'The accession by [the] Government of the Islamic Republic of Pakistan to the [said Convention] is subject to the provisions of the Constitution of Pakistan.' A single reservation was also entered to Article 29(1) (dealing with dispute resolution), stating that: 'The Government of the Islamic Republic of Pakistan declares that it does not consider itself bound by paragraph 1 of article 29 of the Convention.'[45]

The declaration led to a number of objections from states,[46] which argued that it undermined the Convention. At the domestic level, NGOs and civil societies, as well as some academics, were of the view that the declaration amounted to creating a hierarchy of laws, with the CEDAW ranked below the Constitution of Pakistan.[47]

[44] In addition to lobbying the government, proponents of the CEDAW also campaigned through seminars and workshops to generate support and raise awareness of the substantive provisions of the Convention. For instance, from April to June of 1995 the Women's Study Centre at the University of Peshawar, of which the author was the director, held a series of seminars at Quaid-i-Azam University Islamabad on the subject; a similar one was held by the Sustainable Development Policy Institute and a third, with the support of the APWA, was held in Lahore in summer 1995.

[45] *Multilateral Treaties Deposited with the Secretary-General*, UN Doc. ST/LEG/SER.E/15 (1997) 175.

[46] Including Austria, Germany, Portugal, the Netherlands, Norway, Denmark and Sweden.

[47] Shirkat Gah, the HRCP, the Aurat Foundation, the Women's Action Forum and others were critical of the declaration and continue to record their disagreement in shadow reports and presentations on the subject. See e.g. *Discrimination Lingers on … A Report*

5 Domesticating the CEDAW in Pakistan

While the pre-accession process presented an opportunity for a critical examination of formal and informal laws, customary practices and religious norms, accession brought its own challenges and highlighted tasks necessary for effective implementation and monitoring. Both the government and NGOs were required to develop a methodology for collaboration as part of the process of monitoring and reporting to the CEDAW Committee. Unfortunately, given economic constraints and limited human resource capacity, the institutional structures that in an ideal world might help domesticate the CEDAW into Pakistani law have not been put in place as part of governmental routine. In fact, since accession the CEDAW has been viewed as a 'project' to be taken up subject to available funding (which is mostly expected to come from foreign donor agencies) without becoming part of mainstream, budgeted government functions. Time and again, and with support from international donors, 'project' proposals have been written and funding received, and consultants have been hired at governmental and NGO levels to write Pakistan's country report as well as shadow reports on behalf of the country's NGOs and civil society.

But this project-like approach toward the CEDAW resulted in Pakistan missing the deadlines for submitting its initial, second and third Periodic Reports, which were finally entered in August 2005 and considered in May 2007.[48] As for NGOs and civil society, two shadow reports have been submitted thus far. The first (*Discrimination Lingers on ... A Report on the Compliance of CEDAW in Pakistan*) was, according to its authors, endorsed by over 900 Pakistani human rights organisations.[49] A second shadow report (*Talibanisation and Poor Governance: Undermining CEDAW in Pakistan*),[50] expressing the views and concerns

on the Compliance of CEDAW in Pakistan (Lahore: National Commission for Justice and Peace, 2007) and *Talibanisation and Poor Governance: Undermining CEDAW in Pakistan* (Lahore: Shirkat Gah Women's Resource Centre, 2007).

[48] The *Fourth Periodic Report* (CEDAW Committee, 11 August 2011, UN Doc. CEDAW/C/PAK/4) was recently submitted and awaits consideration by the CEDAW Committee. The Ministry of Women's Development holds the mandate to prepare Pakistan's country reports, including engaging with civil society and government departments and Ministries in their preparation.

[49] *Supra* note 47. The lead organisations on this report were the National Commission for Justice and Peace and the Democratic Commission for Human Development.

[50] *Supra* note 47. The report was produced by Shirkat Gah with inputs from a number of other NGOs, and responds succinctly to the government's reports and to the prevailing atmosphere of militancy and lack of security in Pakistan at the time.

of twenty-three organisations, was submitted to augment *Discrimination Lingers on* and reviewed questions posed by the CEDAW Committee and the government's responses.

At a most basic level, Pakistan's Constitution requires that an international treaty, on ratification, does not directly become part of the domestic legal system. One of the first steps necessary to domesticate the CEDAW would therefore be to incorporate it into national legislation through an Act of Parliament, a step that the government has not so far taken. Following discussion of the government's *Combined Initial, Second and Third Periodic Report*,[51] and prompted by questions raised by NGOs in Pakistan's two shadow reports, the CEDAW Committee expressed its concern that the Convention had not been incorporated into Pakistani law,[52] to which the government responded in its *Fourth Periodic Report* by stating that: 'An International Convention or Treaty is not directly applicable in Domestic Law on Ratification in Pakistan. However, the provisions of such Treaties and Conventions are taken into consideration in formulating legislation and by Courts when interpreting the law.'[53] Since this is the government's latest position on the matter, it does not appear that any steps are anticipated to domesticate the CEDAW in the near future.

The government's position regarding its reservations to the CEDAW is also under close scrutiny at home and abroad. The position is reiterated in its *Combined Initial, Second and Third Periodic Report* as follows:

> The Declaration facilitated Pakistan's accession to the Convention and represents the legal position on the matter ... The objective was not to go against the object and purpose of the Convention while assuaging the concerns of those who had misgivings about the Convention. Subjecting the implementation of the Convention to the Constitution of Pakistan was a sensible course of action ... Its authors had the benefit of studying [the UDHR, ICERD, ICCPR and ICESCR] the major international human rights instruments then in existence. Many of the principles contained in these documents are reflected in the Constitution. It can therefore be argued that in substance the declaration did not have a negative effect in the implementation of the Convention while at the same time enabling Pakistan to accede to the Convention. In practice also there do not appear to be any legislative, policy or administrative actions taken by the Government, which contravene provisions of the Convention on

[51] CEDAW Committee, 3 August 2005, UN Doc. CEDAW/C/PAK/1–3; CEDAW Committee, 5 October 2006, UN Doc. CEDAW/C/PAK/Q/3; CEDAW Committee, 1 March 2007, UN Doc. CEDAW/C/PAK/Q/3/Add.1.

[52] CEDAW Committee, 11 June 2007, UN Doc. CEDAW/C/PAK/CO/3 at 3.

[53] CEDAW/C/PAK/4, *supra* note 48 at 12.

> basis of the declaration. The short comings in the implementation of the Convention, inevitable in any country, are not directly attributable to the declaration.[54]

In other words, by ratifying the CEDAW but with a declaration and reservation, Pakistan was performing a difficult balancing act before international and domestic audiences demanding very different things of it.

Neither civil society in Pakistan nor the CEDAW Committee was convinced by this statement.[55] Pakistan's delegation was queried on the subject and Pakistan was urged to withdraw its declaration.[56] The Committee also sought clarification over which law would prevail in the event of a conflict of laws, to which the Pakistani delegate responded that: 'the Constitution guaranteed the equality of rights of men and women and banned discrimination based on race, religion, caste or sex. It was also true that no law could stand if it were found to be inconsistent with the basic law in the Koran, which provided the basis for Pakistan's traditional respect for women and protection of their rights.'[57] Another member of the delegation also made the point that Pakistan had ratified the Convention in 1996 but 'its basic law as stipulated in the Constitution remained in force ... There was no need to be concerned about any conflict between the Convention and Muslim principles, as Islamic law provided even more effective protection of women's rights than the Convention.'[58]

Such differing responses offered to the CEDAW Committee by the Pakistani delegates highlight yet again the varying perceptions between and among government circles over where the CEDAW is placed in the legal pluralities of the country. One thing stands out clearly: the government has no intention of modifying its position, stating that the matter is still under review.[59]

6 Legal obstacles to full domestication

Further obstacles in domesticating the CEDAW, and a constant point of issue in country and shadow reports as well as in Committee deliberations,

[54] CEDAW/C/PAK/1–3, *supra* note 51 at 8.

[55] See shadow reports, *supra* note 47.

[56] CEDAW/C/PAK/CO/3, *supra* note 52 at 3.

[57] CEDAW Committee, 19 July 2007, UN Doc. CEDAW/C/SR/781 at 4.

[58] *Ibid.* at 4–5.

[59] The delegation had indicated in its *Combined Initial, Second and Third Periodic Report* as well as at the meeting to consider the country report that the NCSW had been given the mandate to report back on whether Pakistan ought to withdraw the declaration. The *Fourth Periodic Report* does not share the outcome, if any, of the NCSW report.

are those laws that are explicitly discriminatory to women and in direct conflict with the CEDAW. These include the Citizenship Act 1951, the Law of Evidence Act 1984 and the Hudood Ordinance of 1979.[60] The Pakistani delegation at a meeting to consider its reports to the CEDAW Committee in 2007 expressed the government's commitment to abolish 'not only the 1979 Hudood Ordinance but also all discriminatory legislation'.[61] The *Fourth Periodic Report* therefore dealt at length with developments in this area and described the various steps that had been taken to address discrimination. Yet, although some progress was reported, the discriminatory laws remain in force.[62]

Finally, an indicator of domestication would be a level of awareness, discussion and use of the CEDAW's substantive provisions among civil society, academics, communities and individuals as well as the judiciary. In short, how far has its implementation percolated down through Pakistani society?

Although the personal skills and exertions of Salma Waheed, Secretary of the Ministry of Women's Development from 1993 to 1996, were crucial to effective cooperation between the government and wider civil society in the pre-accession process, the relationship between the two regarding the CEDAW is, in general, erratic at best and hostile at times. The first shadow report, *Discrimination Lingers on*, complained of an absence of cooperation post-accession: 'Despite that NGOs were ignored in preparation of the government report, as civil society organisations we pledge ourselves for a meaningful collaboration in the implementation of the human rights standards and commitments in CEDAW.'[63] The government, nevertheless, reiterated its commitment to collaboration with civil organisations, and noted that it had followed the harmonised reporting guidelines and engaged in an inclusive process for preparing the country report.[64]

The processes leading to accession had provided an opportunity for individuals, groups and NGOs to raise the discussion of women's rights, and the CEDAW became the subject of campaigns.[65] In the post-ratification

[60] The Hudood Ordinance sets out punishments for, inter alia, extramarital sex. See the discussion in CEDAW/C/PAK/CO/3, *supra* note 52 at paras. 5, 16 and 17.

[61] CEDAW/C/SR/781, *supra* note 57 at 6. The Women Protection Act 2006 has to an extent 'disabled' the Hudood law on extramarital sex.

[62] See CEDAW/C/PAK/4, *supra* note 48 at paras. 43–64 for details of discriminatory provisions.

[63] *Supra* note 47, at 6.

[64] CEDAW/C/PAK/4, *supra* note 48 at 10–11. The guidelines are set out in Annex I.

[65] Including the 1993–5 campaign for CEDAW ratification (above).

period the CEDAW became part of training programmes run by governmental and non-governmental bodies, and translations of the CEDAW into national and minority languages made its contents more accessible at the grass-roots. The treaty also became a tool for women's rights, forming part of human rights education in NGO advocacy training sessions. Yet the fact remains that indigenising the CEDAW's substantive provisions and taking ownership of this 'bill of women's rights' remains at a superficial level.[66]

7 Using the CEDAW model to advance women's rights in Pakistan

From 1999 to 2001 I held the portfolio of Cabinet Minister for Health, Population Welfare and Women Development in the government of what was then the North-West Frontier Province. As an academic and activist whose training and interest was human rights and Islamic law, my policy initiatives were motivated and informed by the ideas within the CEDAW. In the years after accession, there was a rare opportunity when I, as an academic activist, was able to put research findings into practice and test the CEDAW as a supportive tool and strategy for women's rights in Pakistan. More importantly, as a Cabinet Minister I considered it an obligation to implement Pakistan's CEDAW undertakings. Suffice to say that I encountered stereotypical perceptions of what needs to be done to 'take care' of the 'women question' at play at every level of government, and beyond in civil society.

Yet it is noteworthy that a government then led by a military general (Pervez Musharraf) had a total of 7 women Ministers out of 28 in its provincial and federal Cabinets, while many a democratically elected government has far fewer (this step in itself was in keeping with the spirit of the CEDAW, although the CEDAW was not the motivation behind these appointments). Soon after taking office, all women Ministers met in Islamabad to set up an informal Women Ministers Forum, laying out an agenda, both legislative and at policy and institutional levels, to take up women's issues and address problems confronted by women in the public and private spheres. The Forum's first initiative was, having studied similar bodies in India, South Africa, the UK, Egypt and other countries, to establish a statutory National Commission on the Status

66 As one NGO activist remarked: 'CEDAW has been confined to a module in a human rights training programme; nothing more!' Personal communication.

of Women (NCSW), an autonomous watchdog for policies and actions insofar as they affected women, to monitor implementation of women's rights under national and international law, including the CEDAW.[67] The process of setting up the NCSW (of which the author was appointed first chair), provided a number of lessons in the manner in which the women's rights agenda might be advanced, and in how deep the conviction runs within government.

The first draft produced used the CEDAW and its Optional Protocol as a template,[68] the idea being that there would be the NCSW at the national level and individual complaints mechanisms in the provinces. Women ombudspersons would entertain petitions and provide decisions that would be implemented through government departments and Ministries. This draft met with stiff resistance from officials who felt that the NCSW replicated the role of the Ministry of Women's Development (MWD).[69] The approach of some officials had been to hive off anything to do with 'women's issues' into the MWD's lap, thereby absolving other Ministries of any further obligation. 'What is the need for two Women's Ministries?' one official asked the author. 'We already have one!' Another argument raised against the proposed NCSW and its complaint mechanisms was that we were planning a parallel 'government' for women.[70] But the most potent argument was one of finance: the NCSW as envisaged in our draft was said to be too expensive. The statute that finally won approval from the Cabinet and President was a negotiated document: the Women Ministers Forum had had a choice between a watered-down version without the individual complaints bodies in the provinces, or nothing at all. This is the version that went on the statute book, and the National Commission on the Status of Women came into being in 2000.

[67] The first of these meetings was held in Islamabad on 26 December 1999 with Dr Atiya Inayatullah in the chair. Those present included Zubaida Jalal, Shahida Jameel, Shaheen Atiqurrehman and the author. My ideas on national machineries for women was also informed by the work of Shirin Rai, including S. M. Rai (ed.), *Mainstreaming Gender, Democratising the State. Institutional Mechanisms for the Advancement of Women* (Manchester University Press, 2003).

[68] The 1999 Optional Protocol to CEDAW (OP-CEDAW) created a mechanism whereby a CEDAW Committee could hear complaints and make inquiries into abuses. The adoption of the CEDAW/OP-CEDAW model as a template meant that women would be able to use the NCSW to complain against violations of their rights within a domestic ambit.

[69] The eighteenth constitutional amendment has delegated Ministries of Women's Development to the federating units, i.e. the provinces, and the role of implementing the CEDAW has now been assigned to the Human Rights Ministries in the provinces.

[70] Personal communication with relevant civil servants.

While the NCSW experience was unquestionably informed by the CEDAW/OP-CEDAW model, another major development was not so directly informed: the constitutional amendment creating reserved seats for women at all levels of government and electoral laws facilitating this change. The Women Ministers Forum pressed for one-third representation of women in local bodies as well as in the Parliament (although at the Parliamentary level the proportion was in the end lower). The views within various constituencies were diverse, ranging from approval of women's political rights to complete disapproval on the basis that this would distort and tear the fabric of society. The constitutional amendment leading to women's reserved seats could not have been achieved without the almost unanimous support of male ministerial colleagues and, most of all, General Musharraf himself.

8 Domesticating the CEDAW within the superior judiciary

As touched upon above, one indicator of the CEDAW's domestication would be the use of its provisions in judicial contexts.[71] The judiciary is, of course, potentially an effective vehicle for implementing human rights norms. Yet in the reported case law of Pakistan's superior judiciary (five high courts and the Supreme Court) from accession in 1996 through to 2010, there are only four judgments where the court specifically alluded to the CEDAW, two delivered by the same judge, Justice Tassadaq Hussain Jilani of the Lahore High Court.[72] The third is a judgment of the High Court of Azad Jammu and Kashmir, citing the Jilani judgment, while the fourth is a Federal Shariat Court judgment in 2007 where the court took *suo moto* notice of section 10 of the Pakistan Citizenship Act 1951, declaring it discriminatory as it 'negates gender equality and is in violation of Articles 2-A (Objectives Resolution) and 25 (equality of citizens) of the Constitution, also against international commitments of Pakistan and, most importantly, is repugnant to Holy Quran and Sunnah'.[73]

The most widely cited case is *Mst. Humaira Mehmood* v. *The State*,[74] a case of alleged *zina*[75] and abduction registered by a father (a sitting Member

[71] I draw more widely upon the case law of the superior judiciary where human rights principles and instruments have been invoked, in 'Interpretative strategies', *supra* note 1.

[72] Since elevated to the Supreme Court.

[73] Suo Moto No. 1/K of 2006 at para. 28.

[74] PLD 1999 Lah 494.

[75] Sexual intercourse outside marriage. In 1979 Pakistan adopted six laws through a so-called 'Islamisation' process in which laws were supposedly brought into consonance

of the Punjab Provincial Assembly) against the husband of his daughter, sparked by her having married of her own choice. The father knew, at the time of his complaint, that his daughter and the accused were lawfully married but went ahead and filed a case of *zina* nonetheless, as a result of which they fled. The police took the daughter home against her will, and her family faked a 'suitable' marriage ceremony, which they filmed and later produced in court as evidence of a prior marriage. The judgment against the father was a landmark decision in several ways, drawing as it did on a combination of Islamic law, the Constitution, and human rights instruments emanating from the UN and comparable documents from Islamic forums. The judge emphasised the duty of state institutions to respect, protect and promote the fundamental rights of every person, reminded the parties that Pakistan was a UN Member and a Party to the CEDAW, and drew attention to Article 16, which enjoins all Member States to respect the right of women to family life on a basis of equality with men. Justice Jilani also referred to Article 5 of the Cairo Declaration on Human Rights in Islam to reinforce his argument of women's rights within an Islamic framework. He condemned in no uncertain language the 'alliance' of state, society and family in undermining women's rights.

The second case where the CEDAW was specifically cited is the case of *Mst. Saima and 4 others* v. *The State*,[76] in which a Christian woman contended that she was lawfully wedded to her husband with her full consent and that the marriage had been performed by a Methodist minister. This was challenged by her mother, who argued that the minister did not hold a valid licence. As a consequence, the mother argued that her daughter was committing *zina*, and invoked the Hudood Ordinance 1979. Justice Jilani ruled that where a couple believe themselves to be married, a prima facie case of *zina* does not arise, even within the reading of the Hudood Ordinance. Quoting in particular Article 16 of the CEDAW, he also stated that:

> The Court is also conscious of the protection given to marriage and the institutions of the family under the Constitution of the Islamic Republic of Pakistan and the UN Convention on the Elimination of all Forms of Discrimination Against Women. Article 35 of the Constitution enjoins the State to protect the marriage and the family.[77]

with Islamic law. Of these the Hudood Ordinance 1979 made *zina* an offence punishable with stoning to death and whipping. The Women Protection Act 2006 has disabled its application to some extent but the law remains in force.

[76] PLD 2003 Lah 747.

[77] *Mst. Saima and 4 others* v. *The State* PLD 2003 Lah 747 at 751–2.

In *Mst. Sarwar Jan* v. *Abdur Rehman*,[78] the Court referred to the *Humaira* case approvingly, quoting the Cairo Declaration on Human Rights in Islam and the CEDAW and arguing that the government is under obligations to honour the Qur'an and Sunna and international conventions to ensure the rights of women during marriage and at its dissolution. This case concerned a Muslim wife who applied for dissolution of marriage on the basis of cruel and inhuman behaviour. The Court, discussing women's right to divorce under Islamic law, declared that equality is maintained between the spouses by allowing the wife this right through intervention of the courts.

In the fourth case, Suo Moto No. 1/K of 2006, civil society organisations including the Human Rights Commission of Pakistan (HRCP) and Aurat Foundation, as well as the National Commission on the Status of Women, made submissions and became parties in view of the case's implications for women's rights. The Federal Shariat Court took objection to the Citizenship Act 1951, under which Pakistani men could obtain citizenship for foreign wives but not vice versa, observing that gender inequality violated the Constitution and 'most importantly is repugnant to the Holy Qur'an and Sunnah'.

The Court, invoking its jurisdiction to examine laws regarding their Islamic legitimacy, declared it a basic principle of Islamic law to fulfil obligations and noted that Pakistan had made commitments to the international community by becoming a signatory to the Universal Declaration of Human Rights (UDHR), as well as the Convention on the Nationality of Married Women and the CEDAW.[79] The judgment followed Justice Jilani's style of drawing upon plural legal norms: the Constitution, Islamic law and international human rights law. A fascinating aspect is how its use of both Islamic law and the CEDAW supports a key argument of this chapter – that Islamic law may be used *for* as well as against women's rights to equality and non-discrimination.

Whilst in these cases the CEDAW was specifically cited in arriving at a woman-friendly decision, there is a wider body of case law where human rights in general have been used to support a judgment where women's rights have been threatened and/or violated, but in which no specific

[78] 2004 CLC 17.

[79] Suo Moto No. 1/K of 2006 para. 23. The Court also cited Oppenheim's definition of international law as the 'body of customary and treaty rules which are considered legally binding by civilised States in their intercourse with each other'.

reference has been made to the CEDAW.[80] Why is this? It would appear that judges employ what they perceive as the most relevant laws and legal norms to support their decisions; an invisible 'hierarchy' of laws seems to be at play. Constitutional provisions, Islamic law and other statutory laws are placed above international human rights laws, including the CEDAW. It also appears that using human rights in general, and the CEDAW in particular, is an individual choice dependent upon the values and preferences of any given judge. In the Pakistani judiciary the CEDAW's 'champion' seems to be Justice Jilani, but his decisions, though widely cited abroad in human rights circles,[81] do not find a similarly enthusiastic following at home.

9 The impact of the CEDAW in Pakistan: concluding thoughts

Pakistan's decision to accede to the CEDAW was a complex one politically and legally, dependent upon champions within government as well as among the public. The processes and discourse of CEDAW ratification clearly demonstrate that the Pakistani government found itself having to play simultaneously to two very different 'galleries'. Accession to a women's rights treaty within Pakistan's pluralist Muslim polity was complicated by the plurality of views regarding what constitutes 'Islamically' and culturally acceptable human rights and the question of whether international rights instruments are compatible with rights in the Islamic legal traditions. At a governmental level, acceptance of the CEDAW was a top-down process driven by a conscious desire to acquire a place among the international comity of nations. Striking a balance between the domestic and the international was always going to be a challenge.

The questions of to what extent and at what levels the CEDAW has found a place within national structures and institutions and within civil society are thus difficult ones to answer. The first point to make is that from a governmental level down to the grass-roots, the conflict between Shari'a and international human rights law in general, and the CEDAW in particular, has tended to be overstated. Significantly, there has been little systematic discussion of those Articles of various treaties that clearly fall within

[80] See for instance *Shirin Dokht* v. *Pakistan International Airlines Corporation* 1995 PLC (C.S) 251; *Sameena Masood* v. *Pakistan International Airlines Corporation* PLD 2005 SC 831; *Shrin Munir* v. *Government of Punjab* PLD 1990 SC 295.

[81] For example, The Centre for Women's Research, *CEDAW. A Manual* (Colombo: Cenwor, 2006) at 35; Asia Pacific Forum on Women, Law and Development, *A Digest of Case Law on the Human Rights of Women (Asia Pacific)* (Chiangmai: APWLD, 2006 reprint) at 22.

the *norms* of Islamic law and Shari'a. Education, for example, which is an issue for the CEDAW, is also considered an obligation of every Muslim under interpretations of Islamic law, a Muslim state being in theory accountable for any lapses in providing this right to its entire people. But this theme does not find a place on the government's agenda and it is still not held accountable by those individuals and groups who subscribe to an 'Islamic' human rights agenda. Had those many provisions within the CEDAW that resonated with an 'Islamic' human rights agenda formed the starting point of the ratification debate, and had compliance with these been demanded of the government by Islamists, the outcome for domesticating the CEDAW in Pakistan would have been quite different.

In fact, 'playing the Islamic card' to trump women's rights may be a strategy on the part of those in positions of authority to deflect attention from a range of social and legal shortcomings that have little to do with religion. For example, the government has an obligation to ensure adequate provision for spending on basics that impact on the quality of life of all citizens, male and female. The Qur'an and Sunna demand implementation of these entitlements for all Muslims, but 'cultural Islam', especially in the sphere of the family, tends to undermine the rights of women in respect of health, education and economic empowerment. If women are to be kept from going to school for their own 'protection', the need to provide schools for girls – and the cost of so doing – is removed.

There has also been a process of resistance to ideas of women's rights from some religious-political parties and sections of society who perceived (and still perceive) the CEDAW as an alien, Western imposition. The present socio-political environment in Pakistan is pushing women back into their traditional, disadvantaged roles, and a rising tide of Islamic fundamentalism in recent years has put women's place in the public and private spheres under pressure. Armed conflict in the north-west of the country especially has had as one of its central agendas women's place in an Islamic society, as defined by a literalist, patriarchal reading of religious texts. The burning of girls' schools and threats against health professionals, for example, have led to parts of society demanding of females that they stay at home. Genuine security concerns have meant that even those sections of society who do not subscribe to keeping women at home and restraining their activity in the public sphere have been obliged to do so in the interests of safety. How state and society will respond to this latest challenge to women's rights, and whether the CEDAW is used as a mobilising vehicle, remains to be seen.

More positively, we find individuals and groups at the NGO, academic and civil society levels making robust demands for the use of the CEDAW as a reference point and lobbying to advance the women's rights and development agenda. Unlike India's CEDAW story,[82] demands for accession to the CEDAW were initiated and strongly articulated by civil groups as well as by some governmental and political quarters. The accession process also opened up spaces for mounting challenges to fossilised notions of customary as well as religious laws. Advancing women's rights and the CEDAW at a national level will, however, require a critical mass of dedicated individuals in the right place at the right time. The National Commission on the Status of Women and the Women Ministers Forum may be looked upon as first steps on the road to internalising the equality paradigm in a state and society not naturally inclined to non-discrimination.

In conclusion, there is not in Pakistan at the present time a distinct trend toward effectively domesticating the CEDAW and women's rights instruments more generally. In many ways, the actors are lone persons or groups of persons committed to the CEDAW, playing specific roles at various moments in time. Initiatives by such actors might have made their mark upon the national landscape of women's rights, but the first shoots of equality are yet very fragile. The minimal implementation of the substantive provisions of the CEDAW is as much an issue of governance as it is of divergent ideological, political and socio-economic positions on women's rights and entitlements. The way forward includes a multiple approach of challenging the status quo of male–female inequality in the name of religion, culture and tradition; of accountable and transparent governance where men and women are equally facilitated and empowered; and of the opening up of discursive space to engage with varying interpretations of women's human rights in Islam.

[82] See Madhu Mehra's chapter in this book.

16

Zimbabwe and CEDAW compliance: pursuing women's equality in fits and starts

CHOICE DAMISO AND JULIE STEWART

1 Introduction

This chapter seeks to chart Zimbabwe's history in the utilisation and the implementation of the Convention on the Elimination of All Forms of Discrimination against Women (CEDAW).[1] Progress in implementation over the years since the CEDAW came into effect in 1979 has been slow and, at best, partial. This is despite sporadic state rhetoric recognising the importance of the CEDAW in relation to women's human rights and unfulfilled promises to incorporate all of the CEDAW into domestic law. Zimbabwe signed the CEDAW without any reservations in 1991 and ratification took place in 1997. But this is not sufficient for international treaties and conventions to be incorporated into domestic law: section 111B of the current Constitution requires an Act of Parliament for domestication; this is yet to be accomplished.

2 The political and constitutional situation in Zimbabwe

Zimbabwe is presently in the throes of political and legal change, after twenty-seven years of de facto one-party rule, which brought rampant

[1] This chapter began with a paper presented by Choice Damiso at the colloquium 'From Ratification to Implementation: CEDAW in International and National Law' in Oslo, 11–12 March 2010. After the colloquium, an embellishment and finalisation of the chapter was undertaken by Julie Stewart. The research informing this chapter was predominantly desk research, which involved examining the reporting processes, checking for information from government reports, gender policies and Parliamentary reports of proceedings, and looking for clues as to the role that the CEDAW played in legislative, policy and judicial interventions. Personal experiential data was invoked, and interviews were conducted with women who had been involved in CEDAW advocacy, lobbying and reporting activities in the past.

economic mismanagement and human rights abuses. A Government of National Unity (GNU) is shakily in place.[2] Under regional and international pressure, a Global Political Agreement (GPA) was approved by the three main political parties ZANU (PF), MDC (T) and MDC (M) (as it then was) in September 2008. The GPA took effect on 11 February 2009.[3] According to the GPA, a new Constitution was to be formulated, which would then be followed by free and fair elections. The formulation and drafting of the new Constitution was a protracted, at times acrimonious, and costly affair. The final version was a product of political compromise mainly on the part of ZANU (PF). This draft went to a national referendum on 16 March 2013, although it was only finally released by the Parliamentary Select Committee (COPAC)[4] for publication on 31 January 2013.[5] The nation approved the draft by an overwhelming 93.5% in the referendum. The projected date for the finalizing of the adoption of the new constitution is 8 May 2013.

3 The constitutional and legal position of women in Zimbabwe

The Constitution drafting process has actively addressed the rights of women in Zimbabwe. If the draft approved in the referendum is adopted

[2] In Zimbabwe currently, with an uneasy GNU, the term *government* has to be carefully qualified to single out one specific sector or ministry depending on the governance activities being carried out. A short explanation of the lead-up to this government of so-called National Unity is required. On 21 July 2008 after much political wrangling over the outcomes of the 2008 national and presidential elections, which were alleged to have been grossly manipulated by Zimbabwe African National Union (Patriotic Front) ZANU (PF), the interparty Global Political Agreement (GPA) was entered into by the three main political parties ZANU (PF), Movement for Democratic Change (Tsvangirai) (MDC (T)) and the junior player MDC (Mutambara) (MDC (M)), which is now MDC (Ncube) (MDC (N)). This is a complex power-sharing agreement between the three parties, which left Robert Mugabe as President, with considerable personal power, but created a number of senior political posts for leaders of the other parties, the most significant being the post of prime minister, which went to Morgan Tsvangirai, leader of the MDC (T) faction. The detail of this whole agreement lies beyond the scope of this chapter (a copy can be located at www.copac.org.zw/home/government-of national-unity – last accessed 16 August 2012). The critical point to note is that a nationally inclusive process for creating a new Constitution was one of the key components of this agreement.

[3] The GPA has twenty-five Articles ranging from the composition of the new government to enhancing freedom of the press. However, many of the Articles have not been implemented.

[4] COPAC is the acronym for the Parliamentary Select Committee responsible for coordinating the constitutional review and drafting of a new Constitution.

[5] Available at: www.copac.org.zw/index.php?...copac-draft...31-january-2013...draf... (last accessed 23 February 2013).

by Parliament this will make way for full and unfettered equality for women.[6]

Since colonisation of what is now Zimbabwe by the British in the late nineteenth century, the formal legal and political status of the indigenous population, especially women, has been one of political, legal and social marginalisation. Full political recognition of the indigenous population was only achieved in the Independence Constitution, which came into force on 18 April 1980. Full legal recognition was unequivocally granted to all male Zimbabwean citizens regardless of race. However, for all women equality with men on legal grounds remains incomplete, more so for indigenous women. The reason for this lies embedded in the colonial history of the country and in a chronic case of serial cultural relativism. Granting indigenous women equality rights was seen as politically risky because of assumed cultural resistance from men.

Throughout the colonial period there had been progressive advances for white women such as the right to vote, capacity to enter Parliament, equal status with white men in relation to the public service (at least on paper), and the right to hold and manage their own property. Few of these advances were granted to indigenous women, who continued to be generally perceived at the level of state law and official customary law as minors, trapped in a perceived customary law web of inferiority. Indigenous men also suffered from severe discrimination, but after Independence their legal situation was better than that of women.

Zimbabwe attained formal Independence on 18 April 1980,[7] after a protracted guerrilla war in which both men and women fought

[6] Both the MDC factions accepted the draft without amendment but ZANU (PF) withheld acceptance of the draft, employing delaying and negative tactics until the very last moment. Neither of the other two parties wavered on the content of the draft and ZANU (PF) capitulated. According to the (Zimbabwe) Independent newspaper of 14 August 2012 the main objections relate to presidential powers.

[7] Although there had long been opposition to white minority rule, matters came to a head on 11 November 1965 when the white minority Rhodesia Front government made a Unilateral Declaration of Independence, attempting to avoid the imposition of majority rule that was taking place across the continent at the behest of Britain. This led to sanctions being applied to the country; the white minority-rule Rhodesia Front government ultimately capitulated.

side by side.[8] The Zimbabwe Constitution (1980)[9] was negotiated prior to Independence between the Rhodesia Front Party, the British government (which had temporarily resumed its colonial role), the Zimbabwe African National Union and the Zimbabwe African People's Union. The 1980 constitutional provision on equality, section 23, outlawed discrimination on the grounds of race, tribe, place of origin, political opinions, colour or creed. It made no reference to sex or gender as grounds of unlawful discrimination. As with other 'Westminster' export model post-colonial constitutions, it contained and still contains a provision, section 23(3), that protects customary law and personal law from the application of non-discrimination provisions.[10]

Although the Independence Constitution did not provide adequately for the rights of women, there has been incremental change over the years. Sixteen years after Independence in 1996, gender was added as a further ground on which discrimination was not permitted,[11] but it remained subject to the overriding application of the claw-back clause in matters of personal law and customary law. These are the areas that most affect the pursuit of rights by women. Sex, marital status and disability were added in 2005, as was an affirmative action clause, which mandated that women be treated on an equal basis with men in the land redistribution processes, and this is expressly stated not to be subject to section 23(3).

[8] There had been previous attempts to oust the colonial regime in 1893 and 1896, which were quashed by the superior 'firepower' of the colonial administration. Significant in relation to the situation and status of women is that the most-lauded leader of the early *Chimurenga* (struggles/wars) was Mbuya Nehanda, a spirit medium (*mbuya* meaning literally grandmother, a term of deep respect for a woman in Shona society; one interpretation in her case would be revered grandmother of the nation). At the time of her execution by the colonial authorities for instigating and leading the 'rebellion', she was still a young woman in her mid-thirties.

[9] This Constitution is locally referred to as the Lancaster House Constitution after the British government building in which the negotiations took place.

[10] The Zambian Independence Constitution and the Kenyan Constitution had more or less identical sections, both section 23.

[11] In 1996 one further amendment to section 23 was made to the effect that it was not discriminatory if a law takes due account of physiological differences between persons of different gender. In 2005 sex was added to this proviso, but gender remained in place. This reform emerged from the failed 1999–2000 constitutional reform process, where during debates as to the content of the Constitution, the difference between sex and gender had to be carefully explained to the drafters and their advisers (personal recollection, Julie Stewart). Suffice it to say, at this juncture, that it was differences in physiology based on sex that were being targeted.

Whereas progress and quite significant gains for women have been made on paper, there seems, previously, to have been a point that was regarded as one step too far. This was the crossroads between tradition and culture, and conferring full and unfettered rights on women. Progressively over the years, constitutional reforms, legislation and judicial activism have all led to an improvement of women's legal position, but a final blanket unqualified revocation of the offending provisions of section 23 of the Zimbabwe Constitution is still pending. Yet, over the years there has been recognition by various organs of the government that women's equality needs to be addressed and that Zimbabwe has obligations created by its signing and ratification of international and regional instruments. For example, the National Gender Policy (2004) produced by the then-Gender Department in the Ministry of Youth Development, Gender and Employment Creation, states that one of the strategies to deliver equality to women with men is to:

> incorporate the provisions for [*sic*] international human rights instruments into domestic law; e.g. Convention on the Elimination of All Forms of Discrimination Against Women (Article 6.2.3).

Nothing has been done since this assertion to incorporate the CEDAW wholesale into domestic law.

The Constitution[12] approved in the referendum has among the national objectives that: 'the state must ensure that all international conventions, treaties and agreements to which Zimbabwe is a party and which address gender issues … are incorporated into domestic law'. Although national objectives in the draft Constitution are assumed not to be justiciable, the wording could be used to lobby for incorporation of international, regional and sub-regional instruments addressing the rights of women into Zimbabwean law. These include the CEDAW, the Protocol to the African Charter on Human and People's Rights on the Rights of Women in Africa (African Women's Protocol)[13] and the Southern African Development Community Protocol on Gender and Development[14] (SADC Protocol).[15]

[12] See *supra* note 5 for the access reference. The acronym COPAC does not match the full title of the Committee but it readily identifies the body in Zimbabwe.

[13] Signed in 2003 and ratified in 2008 after a vigorous campaign led by the Zimbabwe Women Lawyers' Association.

[14] Ratified in 2010, after a vigorous women's NGO-led campaign.

[15] Some of the conventions that have been incorporated into Zimbabwean law fairly rapidly and with little contention and no public debate or overt external pressure

Zimbabwe has not signed or ratified the Optional Protocol to the CEDAW, which would enable communications to be presented to the CEDAW Committee where individuals or groups perceive there have been violations of rights conferred by the CEDAW. It is unlikely that the Optional Protocol will be acceded to in the near future. A new Constitution and a change of political power could lead to its ratification. The only current external scrutiny of CEDAW compliance is periodic reporting to the CEDAW Committee and to other human rights bodies.[16]

In response to women's demands and, perhaps, to international pressure, in the current constitutional reform process sex and gender equality are high on the reform agenda.[17] The final draft Constitution includes unequivocal non-discrimination clauses with both vertical and horizontal effect and wide-ranging socio-economic rights.

In the final throes of the drafting process there was constant wrangling over issues related to power, local governance, the role of the defence forces and the powers of the President and executive.[18] The equality and non-discrimination clauses, somewhat surprisingly given past reservations over women's equality, did not seem to be contentious. Women's human rights groups breathed a major sigh of relief when the final draft left the equality clauses and socio-economic rights firmly in place.

What started as a process with promises of openness, transparency and gender equality in participation became a closed operation largely

include the Chemical Weapons Prohibition Act Chapter 11:18 (which incorporates the Convention on the Prohibition of the Development, Production, Stockpiling and Use of Chemical Weapons and on their Destruction, ratified in 1994 and incorporated in 1998) and the Convention on the Prohibition of the Use, Stockpiling, Production and Transfer of Anti-Personnel Mines and on their Destruction, which only came into effect in 1997, and was incorporated in 2001. Neither convention is culturally contentious.

16 These can, however, be influential in stirring government to consider formal change, as will be seen when the two formal CEDAW reporting episodes are discussed.

17 There was a national outreach programme where the views of the population were gathered: to date the results of this exercise remain virtually inaccessible. Whether sex and gender equality were supported by the population at large is unknown.

18 The process by April 2012 ceased to be people-focused and became the purview of an exclusive group, the three main political parties and the traditional leaders.

dominated by males.[19] One of the 'parked'[20] issues in the first COPAC official draft of 2 May 2012[21] was representation of men and women in the Senate and House of Assembly. Initially women hoped that 50/50 representation would be provided for; however, this did not materialise. The final draft provides that proportional representation by province based on party lists in which male and female candidates are listed alternately (zebra pattern) will be the format for directly elected senators. A female candidate must head each list. This would give sixty senators, giving roughly thirty female senators. This would not guarantee equality of representation as there would be twenty-eight other senators who would comprise provincial governors, chiefs and persons representing the disabled, where sex-based ratios are not prescribed and males would probably predominate.

In the House of Assembly the final draft provides that women for 'the life of the first two Parliaments' (Clause 6.9) would have an additional 60 seats in addition to the 210 undifferentiated seats as in the current Parliament. This is less than the 50/50 representation that women had campaigned for, but creates a temporary special block that might help develop women's capacity to engage in the political arena. It also preserves the current number of seats for undifferentiated election, which means that all male sitting members would have a chance to be re-elected, which a 50/50 apportioning of seats based on sex would have precluded.

4 Tracking the influence of the CEDAW in legislative and constitutional reforms

The CEDAW as an influence in improving women's rights in Zimbabwe has until recently not been openly acknowledged by the state. Yet, along with the regional instruments, it seems to have a discernible but not compelling influence on the continued progress towards women's equality.

In tracking progress towards partial equality between men and women in Zimbabwe, three distinct periods can be identified. The first from 1980–91 before the CEDAW was ratified is, arguably, the period when the CEDAW and other human rights instruments and guiding principles

[19] There were two technical expert male drafters and one female drafter. The next tier were from the three main political parties and the Council of Chiefs. The six political representatives (five males and one female) had male constitutional and legal experts as advisers, while the Chiefs had a female lawyer as their adviser, Choice Damiso.

[20] 'Parked' – meaning to be dealt with at a later date.

[21] Can be accessed at the same site as the other drafts – see *supra* note 5.

were most regularly invoked by the courts. Legal reform, short of penetrating constitutional reform, led to significant improvement of women's rights. The second period, from 1992 to around 2000, saw legislative reform benefiting women, but there was a reversion on the part of the Supreme Court to a more restrictive view of indigenous women's rights. Post 2001 there have been constitutional reforms to benefit women, but these remain deeply equivocal, partly because section 23(3) remains in place.

5 Legislative reform and judicial activism: 1980–91

The first and potentially the most-significant piece of legislation in addressing discrimination against women after Independence was the Legal Age of Majority Act (LAMA)[22] enacted in 1982.[23] Prior to this Act, as recorded in the Initial Report to the CEDAW Committee, African women were perceived, arguably erroneously, as perpetual minors:

> [p]assing from the guardianship of their fathers (or brothers, uncles, or such other male relative) to that of their husbands upon marriage. They had no legal status of their own and thus could not contract without the assistance of their guardians, acquire property in their own right, sue or be sued in their own right. In politics and public life they were virtually non-existent. They had very little participation in decision making.[24]

When the Legal Age of Majority Act was formulated, it was intended to confer majority status upon attainment of eighteen years of age on all

22 The Legal Age of Majority Act was repealed in 1996 and its provisions incorporated in section 15 of the General Laws Amendment Act [Chapter 08:07] but it is still referred to as LAMA.

23 The Parliamentary Debates during the passage of LAMA made no reference to any human rights instruments but couched the arguments in terms of women's contributions to the liberation struggle, (Zimbabwe Parliamentary Debates Vol. 5 at 17 June 1982 at 69ff.). Of significance is the clear evidence throughout that debate that there was awareness that the LAMA was designed to have a radical effect on women's rights under customary law. One can confidently argue that the CEDAW and a growing global awareness of women's rights were humming in the background of the deliberations on the LAMA.

24 *Zimbabwe's Initial Combined Report to the CEDAW Committee*, Zimbabwe, CEDAW/C/ZWE/1. But as Jeater notes, this was a distorted and inaccurate view of women's status. See for a more detailed exploration of the creation of these views of indigenous women's status, D. Jeater, *Law, Language and Science: The Invention of the Native Mind in Southern Rhodesia, 1890–1930* (Portsmouth: Heinemann, 2007) at 85. Jeater shows how a version of women's status was cobbled together by Native Commissioners (NCs) from experiences in Natal and from analogies to Old Testament versions of women's subordinate status and from an alien nineteenth-century European jurisprudence:

Zimbabweans regardless of sex or race, thus doing away with the assumed perpetual minority status of African women and progressively removing discrimination against women.[25] Women who were involved in its drafting carefully crafted the wording to provide a strategic base from which to tackle discriminatory practices in all areas of the law, including, as clearly stated in the Act, customary law.

The potential of the Legal Age of Majority Act to radically change the status of women was put to the test with the 1984 case of *Katekwe* v. *Muchabaiwa* 1984 (2) ZLR 112 (Supreme Court), in which the Supreme Court under Justice Enoch Dumbutshena, a noted proponent of the application of international human rights to embellish and develop a national human rights jurisprudence, determined that a father's claim to seduction damages was predicated on the minority status of women and was meant to redress the delict committed against him.[26] Thus a father no longer had a cause of action against the seducer of his major daughter. The

> The NCs believed that they understood much of what they heard because it appeared to have a resonance with things they already knew. For example, the idea that women were 'legal minors' reflected what whites *expected* to see. However, the concept of women's legal minority was part of a specifically European legal system, not really applicable to the local context. The indicators that the NCs used to demonstrate the minority of women would have applied equally to large numbers of men. On the other hand, they would not have applied to senior women, notably the Vatete (father's sister), in decision making about, for example, the distribution of lineage property. The whites didn't see the 'legal minority' of junior men or the legal 'majority' of senior women because they weren't looking for it and didn't ask the right questions. Their assertions about the legal minority of women had been inherited from the codes in Natal, which reflected an attempt to cram fundamentally different systems of power and jurisprudence into a European model that didn't fit.

[25] This conferring of full contractual status on African women on the attainment of majority at the age of eighteen had a mixed reception. Providing that issues related to marriage and the absence of the need for parental consent were not raised, majority status for women was not especially problematic. Suggestions that this new law removed the need for parental or a guardian's consent to the marriage of an African woman caused an outcry. This was soon connected to the issue of payment of both *lobola* (bridewealth) and seduction damages in relation to an African adult woman. For a general discussion of the significance of carefully shaping law reform messages, see A. S. Tsanga, *Taking Law to the People: Gender, Law Reform and Community Legal Education in Zimbabwe* (Harare: Weaver Press, 2003).

[26] Justice Dumbutshena extols the value of both international human rights instruments and the role of regional human rights adjudication bodies in an untitled presentation to the Second Judicial Colloquium on the Domestic Application of International Human Rights Norms, in Harare, 19–22 April, Commonwealth Secretariat, 1989.

daughter could claim such damages on her own behalf under general law. It seemed that progress could be achieved using this legislation, albeit on a case-by-case basis, towards the equality of women with men.

Moving forward in line with this positive interpretation, in 1985 Zimbabwe amended the Matrimonial Causes Act (now Chapter 5:13) to provide for an equitable distribution of matrimonial property upon divorce. This was achieved, at least on paper, by directing the courts to recognise domestic contributions (usually the wife's) to the wellbeing of the family, by making an award based on the value of domestic and caring duties. In practice, wives' contributions remain undervalued, because women tend to make their contributions in terms of the upkeep of the family, provision of food, and covering household and general expenses, while men are free to acquire immovable and movable assets in their own names. It is thus difficult for women to clearly establish the value of their contributions, as the man is usually the one with title deeds, vehicle papers and other documentary evidence of major expenditures, and women have little evidence of substantial contribution through provision of consumables.

6 Making progress: 1991–9 legislative progress and judicial equivocation

In 1996 the legislature amended section 23 of the Constitution to include gender as a ground on which discrimination could not be justified. For women, discrimination vis-à-vis men remained possible, albeit indirectly through the persistence of the claw-back clause section 23(3) that permitted continued discrimination in relation to adoption, marriage, burial, devolution of property on death, or other matters of personal law and customary law.[27] What this amounted to was a ban on discrimination against women and girls in the public weal but licence for its persistence in private arenas.

Despite the retention of the claw-back clause, movements were once again afoot to lay down new approaches to old problems. The Administration of Estates Act Amendment Act 6/97[28] introduced a form of gender-equal inheritance rights subject to the accommodation of the

[27] In the Constitutional Amendment in 2005 this was restyled to read 'personal law', but the effect remained the same and might have even broadened the application of the claw-back clause. So far this has not been judicially determined.

[28] Now incorporated into the Administration of Estates Act (Chapter 6:01).

recognition of polygynous unions. This ushered in a new era for women's and girls' inheritance rights.[29] In simple terms, intestate succession, which had previously been determined by the application of assumed customary law where the parties were African, and which treated the eldest son as the heir and person responsible for the maintenance of the family, was now regulated by legislation that sought to provide more equitably for all potential dependants and beneficiaries of an intestate estate.

A wife or wives in polygynous unions could inherit from a deceased spouse's estate, to the extent of a joint one-third share, the senior wife receiving two shares from the wives' share, in either registered or unregistered polygynous unions. Surviving spouses could take over the former matrimonial home jointly where they occupied it jointly or separately when they occupied separate homes at the death of the husband.[30] Daughters were entitled to inherit on an equal basis to sons.[31]

Women's lobbies on the unfairness of inheritance rights and on abuses perpetrated by uncaring and uninvolved heirs in so-called customary law had led to research initiatives being taken up predominantly by the Women and Law in Southern Africa Research Trust (WLSA). This research revealed that customary law was far more nuanced and flexible than indicated by formal state and colonial versions of its content.[32] This research, and a comprehensive understanding of customary patterns of

[29] For a discussion of the previous situation and a critique of the way in which customary intestate succession was skewed against women and girls, see J. E. Stewart with K. Dengu-Zvobgo, B. Donzwa, J. Kazembe, E. Gwaunza and W. Ncube, *Inheritance in Zimbabwe: Law, Customs and Practice* (Harare: Women and Law in Southern Africa Research Trust (WLSA), 1994, 2nd edn 1995); J. E. Stewart, 'Why I can't teach customary law' in J. Eekelaar and T. Nhlapo (eds.), *The Changing Family: Family Forms and Family Law* (Oxford: Hart Publishing, 1998).

[30] In all monogamous customary law unions, regardless of the legal regime governing the marriage, the Deceased Estates Succession Act (Chapter 6:02) applies, where males and females, be they spouses or children, are treated on an equal basis.

[31] A description of how the law reform process was influenced by the research is discussed in J. Stewart and A. Tsanga, 'The widow's and female child's portion: the twisted path to partial equality for widows and daughters under customary law in Zimbabwe' in A. Hellum, J. E. Stewart, A. Tsanga and S. S. Ali (eds.), *Human Rights, Plural Legalities and Gendered Realities: Paths Are Made by Walking* (Harare: Weaver Press, 2007) 407–36 at 413.

[32] This legislation made the Supreme Court's decision in *Magaya* v. *Magaya* 1999 (1) ZLR 210, discussed below, most surprising. One unfortunate outcome of the *Magaya* judgment has been to confuse lay understanding of the new legislation. It is frequently believed that *Magaya* overturned the new law; it did not. The facts of the case had arisen before the new law came into effect so the previous assumed legal position of African women was relied on.

inheritance and their attendant obligations, was critical in negotiating the final stages of the inheritance law reform. Although women's rights were not directly invoked in this process, they were the background influence that helped drive women lawyers' determination to obtain reform. Based on research and strategic argumentation, formal recognition of women's and all children's rights to inherit from their deceased parents estates was recognised. The key move, when patriarchal and patrilineal arguments were holding sway and likely to derail the reform process, was the capacity of one of the WLSA researchers to ask the then-President of the Council of Chiefs, Chief Mangwende, to explain the purpose behind customary patterns of inheritance. To the great relief of all the women present, he replied that it was to care for and sustain the family of the deceased and that there was no estate until the surviving spouse or spouses died. This led to the Council of Chiefs' acceptance, in principle, of the reform, and the legislation passed through Parliament.

After this progressive legislation came into effect on 1 November 1997, a narrow interpretation of the claw-back provision in section 23(3) of the Constitution in *Magaya* v. *Magaya* 1999 (1) ZLR 100 (S) produced an international and national outcry. The Zimbabwe Supreme Court found that customary law purportedly denied a woman the right to inherit from her deceased father's estate on intestacy. The Court found that customary law was not subject to the operation of the equality provisions in section 23. This was found despite arguments urging the application of non-discrimination principles derived from international instruments including the CEDAW.

The *Magaya* decision gave rise to a fervent invocation of the CEDAW in Parliament in a debate on 18 May 1999. Miss Zindi MP noted that Zimbabwe had ratified the CEDAW and adopted the African Charter on Human and People's Rights (AU Charter). She drew attention to Articles 1, 2, 3, 5, 13, 15 and 16 of the CEDAW and commented:

> Zimbabwe has a duty to ensure and end the discrimination against women in all areas, including law, culture and the family.

She observed that the *Magaya* decision was:

> [a] stark violation of aforementioned international treaties which cannot be part of Zimbabwean laws until Zimbabwe passes a specific act which would make [the] CEDAW part of domestic law in terms of s111B of the Constitution.

She especially noted that Parliament had passed the LAMA:

> But at this moment we are seeing a situation of reversal by our Supreme Court.

She made a general plea for the improvement of the situation of women and girls noting that:

> The AU Charter [sic] Zimbabwe a duty to promote women's rights and *positive* African values [emphasis added].

Still no action was taken to reform section 23(3), and without constitutional reform progressive legislation remains in peril, but further reversals of progressive laws have not taken place.

Implementation of the new inheritance law remains fragmented despite a nationwide campaign to disseminate its contents and its potential to improve the inheritance rights of women and girls.[33]

The Prevention of Discrimination Act, Chapter 8:16 was enacted in 1998 (Act 19/1998). It largely deals with the prohibition of discrimination in the public and commercial arenas and should serve to support the non-discrimination provisions in section 23(1)(a) and (2) of the Constitution.[34] The Act, as with its predecessors, tackles the often-vexatious problem of constitutions only expressly dealing with the prohibition of discrimination in vertical terms, as it directly addresses the often more pernicious problems of horizontal discrimination, and targets discriminatory practices by both real and juristic persons. Measures, albeit limited, were now in place to address many aspects of discrimination in Zimbabwe. However, the legislation is not particularly well known and is used predominantly in relation to racial discrimination. Its potential to deal realistically with gendered discrimination in relation to finance, business and property acquisition is constrained because commercial and financial entities require the individual to have collateral and business plans, as well pre-existing secure and provable employment and a track record. This presents problems for many women.

The 1999–2000 constitutional reform process provided an opportunity for comprehensive reform. During the drafting phase, an attempt was made to expunge section 111B and replace it with automatic incorporation

[33] The campaign was carefully crafted and at a nationwide level. Unfortunately, it came to a premature end with objections from the then-Minister of Information about a logo indicating the involvement of the British Development Agency, DFID. DFID had provided GBP 880,000 and would have provided a further GBP 440,000 for the continuation of the campaign. However, the latter sum was withdrawn during the political wrangle that ensued.

[34] This Act consolidates the provisions of earlier anti-discriminatory legislation such as the Immovable Property (Prevention of Discrimination) Act and the Public Premises (Prevention of Discrimination) Act. In addition, the Act also provides for the right of an aggrieved person to damages.

of signed international instruments into domestic law – it was removed by the oversight committee before that Constitution reached its final draft.[35] Unfettered equality clauses, reflecting the values contained in the CEDAW and other international human rights instruments, were included. In the run-up to the referendum on the Constitution, the failure on the part of feminist lobbyists to understand the formulation of rights clauses helped to fuel campaigns to reject the Constitution because they believed that women's rights were inadequately formulated. This, coupled with weak framing of socio-economic rights as mere objectives, was seen as inadequate appreciation of and attention to women's rights and entitlements.

The rejection of the draft Constitution was hailed as a political triumph for women, but significant rights for women that might have resulted from an affirmative vote, even if it was not the full package sought, were lost. The rejection of the draft Constitution cannot be attributed to any one set of factors,[36] but the heightened and perhaps exaggerated expectations of women certainly had an effect on women's and especially non-law-oriented women's organisations' understanding of what could be covered in a Constitution.[37] The ensuing strong female lobby for the rejection of the draft further fuelled women's dissatisfaction and was probably part of the draft Constitution's ultimate demise. We have no knowledge of how individuals actually voted or why. There are suggestions that the referendum vote was not on the Constitution but on the continuing rule of President Robert Mugabe.

7 More incremental change: 2000–8

This was a period when women's organisations such as Women of Zimbabwe Arise (WOZA), Zimbabwe Women Lawyers' Association (ZWLA) and the Women's Coalition protested against the ongoing curbing of general political rights and the rapidly declining socio-economic situation in the country. WOZA, which protested openly and peacefully, had its key members arrested and held under insanitary and crowded

[35] Personal recollection, Julie Stewart.

[36] It was a straight yes or no vote on the whole draft.

[37] In their deliberations on whether or not to participate in the 2009 constitutional process, and informed by the opportunities for beneficial reform for women through the rejection of the 2000 draft Constitution, ZWLA membership on 3 April 2009, at a meeting at the Crowne Plaza Hotel, Harare, decided that despite the shortcomings of the proposed process:

conditions in police cells, and some WOZA members were spirited away to hidden sites by police.

In response to the protests and the failure of the constitutional reform process, there was increasing repression of civil society by the ZANU (PF) government. Repressive laws on the media and public protest were introduced to legitimise the repression. These were the Public Order and Security Act (POSA) Chapter 11:17 and the Access to Information and Protection of Privacy Act (AIPPA) Chapter 10.27. The law was also used to prevent rallies by the MDC in the run-up to elections. AIPPA was used to close down the only independent daily newspaper and other publications critical of the Mugabe regime.[38] Yet this was a period in which women's rights were further developed, even though the claw-back clause remained firmly in place. In 2000, following the failure of the constitutional reform process, the fast-track land-grab process was launched. In theory, both men and women were supposed to be equal beneficiaries of this process, but, as discussed earlier, this has not, even with constitutional reform, generally benefited women.

The seventeenth Amendment to the Constitution in 2005 expanded the grounds upon which discrimination is prohibited by adding sex, marital status and physical disability. The addition of sex to complement gender as grounds for non-discrimination is significant. Women may be discriminated against based on their ascribed gender roles and the gendered cultural beliefs of what it means to be either male or female. But further, they may be indirectly discriminated against because of failure to appreciate the importance of dealing with sex-based issues such as menstruation, childbirth and breastfeeding, which are exclusively female in nature. Marital status is also particularly important for addressing discrimination of women as some of the disadvantages that women encounter are linked to their marital status. In relation to land, married women may be treated as appendages to their husbands while single women may be discriminated against on the basis that they are not 'traditionally' entitled to access land in their own right.

Amendment No. 17 also introduced provisions to exempt from the general prohibition of discrimination the implementation of affirmative action programmes for the protection and advancement of persons or

> [e]ven though they knew that the process was flawed they would nevertheless strive to ensure their input is taken up ... to ensure women at least got some benefit from the process. The catchphrase was really 'half a loaf is better than none'.

[38] Although two independent weeklies, the *Standard* and the *Zimbabwe Independent*, remained in print.

classes of persons who have been previously disadvantaged by unfair discrimination. Here again, the CEDAW probably informed the legislative process, but not openly.

8 Beyond legislation: the role of the courts in promoting women's rights

Since 1980 the judiciary has taken a start–stop, sometimes a backtracking approach to women's rights. The judiciary at all levels was under attack from the executive. The Chief Justice, Justice Gubbay, was in effect sacked and replaced with a ZANU (PF) sympathiser. Other judges perceived to be averse to manipulation of judicial processes and the impunity of those in power were harassed into resigning.[39] Despite attacks on the judiciary, women's rights have continued to be quite favourably treated. Thus, it can be argued that, with some deviations, there has been slow progress towards a 'women'-sensitive jurisprudence.

It has been difficult to track the direct influence of the CEDAW and other international instruments on the development of women's rights jurisprudence, as there has been reluctance on the part of the Supreme Court to invoke international and regional human rights instruments to achieve equality between individuals. Rather, it seems the principles in these instruments are employed without direct acknowledgement, reliance being placed on local laws and local constitutional provisions to achieve formal equality. This is a strategic approach, as it avoids a direct confrontation with politicians, especially those from the formerly totally dominant ZANU (PF) on issues of national sovereignty.[40]

[39] A. Hellum, B. Derman, G. Feltoe, E. Sithole, J. Stewart and A. Tsanga, 'Rights claiming and rights making in Zimbabwe: a study of three human rights NGOs' in B. A. Andreassen and G. Crawford (eds.). *Human Rights, Power and Non-Governmental Action: Comparative Analyses of Rights-Based Approaches and Civic Struggles in Development Contexts* (London: Routledge, 2012).

[40] Some years ago, I (Julie Stewart) attended a seminar for judges run by the International Association of Women Judges, Justice for Equality Project. The judges present, all of whom were from Zimbabwe, while appreciating the value of the international instruments, were determined to find ways in which local laws could be harnessed for change. This was somewhat to the distress of the organisers and at one point I needed to intervene and point out that how the outcome was achieved was not the issue, provided that the desired sex and gender-based equality was achieved (personal recollection). Yet it was clear that the international instruments were nonetheless a source of inspiration in this quest.

9 Pursuing equality through judicial activism

The period prior to the signing and ratification of the CEDAW was one of the most productive in terms of women's rights within the courts. Following the 1984 case of *Katekwe* v. *Muchabaiwa*, 1987 saw the significant case of *Chihowa* v. *Mangwende* 1987 (1) ZLR 228 (S), in which, relying on the Legal Age of Majority Act, a daughter's right to inherit from her father's intestate estate under customary law was established by the Supreme Court under Chief Justice Dumbutshena. In terms of the development of a jurisprudence of equality in intestate succession under customary law, this was the judicial highpoint.[41] Thereafter the Supreme Court over a period of twelve years under different leadership persistently reduced the rights of female children to inherit from their deceased fathers under customary law. Widows were given no recognition in terms of inheritance rights under customary law in *Chihowa* v. *Mangwende* but had, fortunately, in 1978 been given the right to maintenance from a deceased estate in terms of the Deceased Person's Family Maintenance Act (Chapter 6:03) and this included widows in both registered and unregistered polygynous marriages.[42] Regrettably, this has been a largely underutilised piece of legislation. Notable among its provisions is section 7, which requires that in determining maintenance rights from a deceased's estate, consideration is given to the contribution of surviving spouses in a manner similar to section 7 of the Matrimonial Causes Act.[43]

10 Going both ways at once – judicial contradictions

While the earlier gains around inheritance rights were being slowly eroded by a differently composed Supreme Court, the very same Court

[41] Neither *Katekwe* v. *Muchabaiwa* or *Chihowa* v. *Mangwende* make any reference to the CEDAW or any other international instrument, but the decisions relying on the Legal Age of Majority Act reflect in very strong terms the non-discrimination principles laid out in the CEDAW Article 2.

[42] For a discussion of how research into the customary law of inheritance at an earlier date might have helped the position of widows, see Stewart and Tsanga, 'The widow's and female child's portion'.

[43] In 1997 the legislature passed the groundbreaking Amendment Act to the Administration of Estates Act, which gave surviving spouses rights to inherit from their deceased spouses' estates, even where the estate would have been previously governed by customary law. The history and research behind this reform process are documented in Stewart and Tsanga, 'The widow's and female child's portion', but, as recorded earlier in this chapter, in 1999 the retrogressive decision in *Magaya* v. *Magaya* had muddied the waters of the public's general understanding of inheritance rights.

was pushing the boundaries of women's rights in other areas. Admittedly, these later cases did not touch directly on customary law arenas, the litigants being non-African female Zimbabwe citizens, but the potential for the extension of the decisions to African female citizens was clear.

In 1994 the Supreme Court in *Rattigan & Others* v. *Chief Immigration Officer & Others* 1994 (2) ZLR 54 (SC) used the right of freedom of movement to circumvent patently discriminatory provisions in the Immigration Act Chapter 4:02, based on culture, sex and gender.[44] In the *Rattigan* case, the foreign husband of a Zimbabwean woman was denied a permit to stay permanently in Zimbabwe on the grounds that while the law recognised the right of a foreign wife of a Zimbabwean man to permanent residence in Zimbabwe, the same right was not accorded to the foreign husband of a citizen wife. In the absence of constitutional provisions guaranteeing the right to freedom from sex and gender discrimination, the Supreme Court ruled that the denial of permanent residence to the foreign husband amounted to a violation of the citizen wife's right of freedom of movement, which was guaranteed in section 22 of the Constitution for all Zimbabweans regardless of sex. Parliament attempted to reverse this position by amending section 22 of the Constitution to provide that marriage to a citizen would not prevent a foreigner, regardless of sex, from being denied a permanent residence permit. But in *Kohlhaas* v. *Chief Immigration Officer & Another* 1997 (2) ZLR 441 the Supreme Court, using section 22 of the Constitution regarding freedom of movement for Zimbabwean citizens, circumvented the attempt by the legislature to confer an unfettered power for aliens to be expelled from Zimbabwe. The Supreme Court found that the wife's rights as enunciated in the *Rattigan* decision to choose to reside in Zimbabwe with her 'alien' spouse had not been affected by Constitutional Amendment 14.[45]

It was not only the Supreme Court that was active. The High Court abolished the marital rape exemption in *H* v. *H* 1999 (2) ZLR 358. The import of the decision was adopted by the legislature in the Sexual Offences Act, which was subsequently incorporated into the Criminal Law (Codification

[44] No reference was made to the CEDAW in the *Rattigan* case, but there was supportive reference to a number of human rights instruments in bolstering the approach of the Court, namely Article 7 of the International Covenant on Civil and Political Rights and Article 8 of the European Convention on Human Rights. So there was preparedness to consider such instruments in the legal argument.

[45] Once again, there is no direct reference to international instruments in the judgment, but it would be difficult to refute that the spirit of equality influenced the determination of the Court.

and Reform) Act (Chapter 9:23). Legislation criminalising deliberate HIV/AIDS infection put Zimbabwe at the forefront of reform initiatives in the region, but the laws are rarely used for a variety of reasons, not least among them proof of the source infection. From a women's perspective there is a very real possibility that, although not the original source of the infection within a relationship, the female partner may be the first to discover that she is HIV positive or has AIDS because of antenatal testing during pregnancy. In relation to both these reforms, the 2012 CEDAW State Report indicates that the CEDAW was a stimulus for this reform.[46]

The most recent case where CEDAW compliance arguments were raised is the case of *Margaret Dongo* v. *Registrar General* SC 6/10 (Zimbabwe), where a mother applied for a passport for her minor son but the Registrar General required the consent of the father to be given before issuing the passport. The mother, a politician and women's rights activist, with the assistance of ZWLA, challenged the requirement of the father's consent as guardian. She also challenged the status of the father as the sole guardian of the child. The Court avoided engaging with the human rights arguments raised by the mother. Once again, the matter was determined by creative interpretation of the existing law and it was held that, as obtaining a passport is not an act that changes the status of a child or its relationships, either parent or any other interested individual, such as a grandparent or custodian, could apply for a passport for a minor child.

11 Constitutional reform again? 2008 and onwards

In compliance with the GPA, Zimbabwe is pursuing another attempt at constitutional reform.[47] The constitutional reform process is supposed to be transparent, open, and sex and gender balanced. As discussed earlier, it is impossible to obtain any firm details on the findings from the outreach to the people. Thus political parties, predominantly ZANU (PF), very publicly asserted that clauses they did not like did not reflect the views of the people. Eventually a final draft was settled upon and it now awaits transformation from a constitutional bill into a new national enforceable constitution.

At early public meetings of civil society stakeholders it was indicated that women would constitute 52 per cent of those involved in all stages

[46] Second to Fifth Periodic (combined) Report of Zimbabwe, CEDAW/C/ZWE/2–5.

[47] Constitutional reform processes do create opportunities for national awareness of human rights, governance issues and in particular women's rights; perhaps they also raise expectations to unrealistic levels, as was the case for women's rights in the 1999–2000 constitutional reform exercise.

of the constitutional reform process.[48] By the time of the selection of the various thematic committees and outreach teams, the categories of civil society organisations, political parties, religious and other bodies made it abundantly clear that women would at best form less than 20 per cent of those directly involved with the process of engaging with the people and in deliberating on the new Constitution.[49] In the early stages, cognisant of the opportunity that the new Constitution-making process offered to women, the Women's Coalition organised its own national constitutional meetings drawing on women from all over the country, from rural and urban locations, and from multiple professional and labour realms.[50] Women's organisations mobilised around identifying essential provisions for the advancement and protection of women's rights, and drafts of appropriate clauses were prepared.[51] The CEDAW and the regional instruments were crucial in deciding literally what the bottom line would be in terms of women's demands. The problems lay around channelling these needs into the various thematic committees.[52]

48 Verbal statement – Hon. Paul Mangwana, Joint Chair of the Parliamentary Select Committee presentation at the Crisis Coalition Constitutional Workshop, 3 June 2009, Crowne Plaza Hotel, Harare:

> In the pursuit of the due and proper representation and recognition of women's and the girl child's inherent rights through the development of and lobbying for a new Zimbabwe Constitution, special note is made of the Parliamentary Select Committee's recognition that the constitution making process must reflect and involve in all activities, all committees, all stages and at all levels the national demographic reality and thus that the majority of participants namely 52 per cent must be women.

49 As early as 15 July 2009, the Women's Coalition was expressing concern over the logistics of the First Stakeholders Meeting and the chaos that surrounded Coalition meetings. See http://kubatana.net/html/archive/women/090715wcoz.asp?sector=WOMEN&year=2009&range_start=31 (last accessed 16 August 2012).

50 N. Mushonga, 'Advocacy and lobbying for policy change in Zimbabwe: women's lobbying for a gender-sensitive Constitution', 2011. Available at: www.thephilanthropist.ca/index.php/phil/article/download/889/752 (last accessed 16 August 2012).

51 E. Sithole, *A Critical Assessment of the Sex and Gender Components for Inclusion in the Proposed New Constitution for Zimbabwe*, Occasional Paper, SEARCWL, UZ (Harare, 2009).

52 See zwla.co.zw/index.php?option=com_content&view=article&id=65:zimbabwean-women&catid=35:news-and-media&Itemid=63 (last accessed 16 February 2013) for a copy of the Charter. Constitutional reformers or others interested in women's rights have clear pointers from women on the rights they require as citizens. A shortened version of the Charter is available at www.undp.org.np/constitutionbuilding (last accessed 16 August 2012).

Paradoxically, all the drafts had positive content for women's rights despite the low level of female representation in the bodies that controlled the ongoing Constitution-making process. One unexpected source of support for women's rights are the traditional leaders, who have asserted that they are in a general equality-based alliance with the women's movement. Precisely which clauses in the draft they support is not apparent, but unqualified support for equality for all and in all levels of governance has been promised. Chief Charumbira, President of the Council of Chiefs and a member of the Zimbabwean Senate, made this very clear in a public statement at the launch of G20,[53] on 13 April 2012 in Harare. This approach is not as surprising as one might think. In rural areas where traditional leaders preside, women constitute the largest active constituency, and the traditional leaders are well aware of the latent power of women. An alliance with women also places them in a neutral position between the political parties vying for support. There is also no doubt concern on the part of the Chiefs that they may become irrelevant. Perhaps one ought not to look at this from an entirely cynical perspective as Chiefs in some areas are responding positively and creatively to human rights initiatives and recognising the rights and entitlements of women.[54]

12 Working from the outside in

Zimbabwe has a reputation for signing up to human rights instruments but not pursuing their full implementation or domestication into national law. But from the perspective of women's organisations, this habit is a useful lobbying point. Women's organisations then openly question why the government signs and ignores the human rights obligations contained in the various instruments. In 2003 Zimbabwe signed and subsequently ratified in 2008 the Protocol to the African Charter on Human and People's Rights on the Rights of Women in Africa (African Women's Protocol)

[53] The G20 (Group of 20) is an initiative of the Women's Parliamentary Caucus and the Women's Coalition. Although the G20 had been functional for around fifteen months, a decision was made to officially launch it in April 2012, drawing attention to the women's ongoing scrutiny and vested interests in the constitutional draft that will hopefully emerge. Twenty women with political, legal, civil society and other strategic connections are monitoring the constitutional process, ready to intervene when women's rights need to be protected or asserted in the formulation of the draft Constitution.

[54] A. Matsvayi, 'The role of Chiefs in women's' access to justice: a case study of Chief Makoni, Chief Seke and Chief Chimoyo in Zimbabwe', Masters in Women's Law (MWL) Dissertation (2012), SEARCWL, UZ – forthcoming on www.searcwl.ac.zw (last accessed 25 February 2013).

following a vigorous campaign mounted by women's human rights and legally oriented NGOs. Domestication of this instrument as required by section 111B of the Constitution is yet to take place. A sub-regional document, the Southern African Development Community (SADC) Protocol on Gender and Development (SADC Protocol) was signed, and was ratified on 29 June 2010. Domestication has not as yet taken place. For a more thorough analysis of the formulation and role of the regional and sub-regional instruments in the formulation and pursuit of women's rights, see Musembi's chapter in this volume. Suffice it to say that in the Zimbabwe context, these instruments are used as lobbying tools in conjunction with the CEDAW, and their provisions are used to bolster human rights arguments put to both government and Parliamentarians by various women's groups such as ZWLA, Women in Parliament Support Unit and MUSASA Project.[55]

13 Reporting: fruitful opportunities for prompting change

Since signing the CEDAW in 1991, Zimbabwe has submitted two reports to the CEDAW Committee. The initial report was considered in 1998 and the combined reports for the period between 1998 and 2011 were considered in 2012. In the 2012 report the Minister of Women's Affairs, Gender and Community Development, Dr Olivia Muchena, under whose name the report is published, states that the report was prepared with the participation and support of Civil Society Organisations (CSOs).[56] CSOs are included in the process partly because of their specialist knowledge and skills but also in an attempt to pre-empt a shadow report. However, despite inclusion in the earlier process, ZWLA and the Women's Coalition spearheaded the production of a shadow report in 2011–12, determined to present the other side of the picture.

Producing the periodic reports seems to send government and, to be fair, other bodies into a frenzy of activity. In late 2011, as the time for

[55] MUSASA Project, an NGO that uses the Shona name of a shady sheltering tree for its title, provides legal assistance, counselling and safe houses for women victims of domestic violence.

[56] The preparation of reports to the CEDAW Committee is coordinated by the Inter-ministerial Committee on Human Rights and Humanitarian Law, which is housed in the Ministry of Justice and Legal Affairs and chaired by the Permanent Secretary of that Ministry. The Committee is composed of senior government officers from the Ministries whose portfolios have a human rights component including the following Ministries: Home Affairs, Justice and Legal Affairs, Labour and Social Welfare, Health, Education and Women's Affairs.

the Zimbabwe CEDAW review in February 2012 drew near, civil society bodies found themselves carrying out consultations, research and workshops to produce a comprehensive shadow report. Running parallel with this was a sudden flurry of activity from the Ministry of Women's Affairs, Gender and Community Development to review the National Gender Policy of 2004, which had lain largely dormant for the previous seven years. The target for completing this review and having a new national gender policy was the end of January 2012.[57] Nothing official has emerged as yet in relation to a new policy. Even if a cynical view is taken of the sudden need to review the gender policy, it is indicative of the concern on the part of the government to appear to be responsive to the CEDAW and its imperatives. The careful framing and shaping of state reports demonstrate that the government wants to appear in the best possible light and to be seen as moving towards equal rights for women.

The formulation of Perodic Reports on human rights compliance across a variety of instruments have an interesting similarity: they all carefully outline the positive areas of progress but omit, avoid direct acknowledgement or carefully squirrel areas of non-compliance away in 'back' pages of reports.[58] On the positive side, periodic reporting exercises create opportunities to raise women-specific issues and to press for legal and constitutional reform.

Zimbabwe professes, in the words of Dr Olivia N. Muchena, the Minister of Gender , Women's Affairs and Community Development,[59] as recorded in its 2012 combined report to the CEDAW Committee,[60] to:

> reaffirm its commitment to the implementation of the provisions of this important Convention. CEDAW continues to guide the priorities for gender mainstreaming and promotion of women's rights in Zimbabwe.

[57] Workshop conducted on 6 October 2011 in Harare under the auspices of the Ministry of Women's Affairs, Gender and Community Development to review, revise and begin the reformulation of the National Gender Policy.

[58] See the recent *Zimbabwe Universal Review Report to the United Nations Human Rights Council*, available at: www.ohchr.org/EN/HRBodies/UPR/PAGES/ZWSession12.aspx (last accessed 16 August 2012).

[59] This is more or less the same Ministry but it has regular changes of name.

[60] Combines second to fifth reports. The initial report was made in 1998 and women's NGOs, predominantly led by Zimbabwe Women Lawyers (ZWLA), compiled a shadow report. The official report purports to have been a joint production between the Ministry of Gender, Women's Affairs and Community Development and civil society organisations that are co-opted into a discussion process. However, the views and evidence provided by civil society organisations and NGOs are not always reflected in the final state report.

The introduction to the report records that Zimbabwe amended the Constitution in 2005 to:

> include among other things, prohibition of discrimination on the grounds of sex or marital status, as well as providing for the implementation of affirmative action programmes.

What the introduction fails to point out is that the claw-back clauses in section 23 of the Constitution, which continue to allow discrimination on the grounds of personal law and customary law, remain firmly in place and that the potential for the revival of a *Magaya* v. *Magaya*-like approach to women's rights in these areas remains an ever-present threat.

In its first report to the CEDAW Committee reviewed in 1998, Zimbabwe was commended for its broad-based non-discrimination clause. Unfortunately the Committee had not identified the claw-back provisions that lay buried in section 23(3) of the Constitution.[61] Dr Amy Tsanga has described how the engagement took place with both the state representatives and the shadow report team.[62] Despite the problems of section 23(3) of the Constitution being raised both in the written and the verbal engagements by the shadow report team, the government 'got away' on that occasion with fragmented presentation of the actual legal situation.[63]

In the 2012 government report, the claw-back clause was squirreled away on page 11 and could have remained buried for the less than diligent reader. However, the shadow report prepared by women in CSOs and NGOs, under the auspices of ZWLA, highlighted the presence of the claw-back clause as the very first item in the Executive Summary on page 5 of the shadow report. The presence and effect of the claw-back clause

[61] The CEDAW Committee in its Concluding Observations 132 commented: 'The Committee notes with satisfaction that the Constitution has been amended to prohibit any act of discrimination on the basis of sex.' The Committee failed to note that section 23(3) was still in place. The Committee did raise in Concluding Observations 138 its concern at the continuing influence of customary law and practices, but this was related to social and economic issues not to the content of the law.

[62] Dr Amy Tsanga represented the Zimbabwe Women Lawyers's Association. She had just joined the staff of the Faculty of Law at the University of Zimbabwe. She is now lecturing at the Southern and Eastern African Regional Centre for Women's Law. Her experiences in 1997 informed the shadow reporting process in 2011–12.

[63] This terminology is deliberate as the construction of the state report appeared to be calculated to mask the presence of the claw-back clauses. For an entertaining and instructive analysis of the 1998 reporting exercise, see A. Tsanga, 'The UN Convention on the Elimination of Discrimination against Women (CEDAW) Committee action: notes of a fringe observer', *Legal Forum* 10:1 (1998) 41–8.

was reiterated at every possible opportunity throughout the report.[64] The adverse effects of the claw-back clauses are raised prominently throughout the shadow report and were central in the presentations made by the shadow reporting team in their engagement with CEDAW Committee members in Geneva.[65]

Scrutiny of both the state report and the shadow report in 1998 indicates that although the shadow report raised the problems with the claw-back clause, this was not taken up by the Committee. Admittedly, the problems created by section 23(3) were treated in a somewhat muted manner in the shadow report, and the opportunities for dialogue between the Committee and the proponents of the shadow report were not at that time formalised. Dr Amy Tsanga – who was part of the shadow reporting process and was present when the state report was presented to the Committee – points out that in 1998 the NGO observers had to grab any available opportunities to engage Committee members on critical issues. This required both guile and bravado:

> Of course the fringe observers, now turned lobbyist and activist, also learn not to be a pain. Timing is important. A Committee member who has sat through the proceedings may indeed make a bee-line for the 'ladies' to use a euphemism and may not be in the frame of mind for winding dialogue or being besieged by a group of over-zealous observers dying to exercise their vocal chords after hours of silence. Fortunately most members of the Committee take the initiative in seeking out the NGO representatives for clarification.[66]

[64] Available at: www2.ohchr.org/english/bodies/cedaw/docs/ngos/ZCS_Zimbabwe51.pdf (last accessed 16 August 2012).

[65] It is clear from the Committee's Concluding Observations that it was alive to the existence of the claw-back clause from the Concluding Observation that:

> While noting that Section 23 of the Constitution of the State party prohibits discrimination on the basis of race, tribe, place of origin, political opinions, colour, creed, sex, gender, marital status or physical disability, the Committee expresses its concern at the absence of a specific prohibition of discrimination against women as defined in article 1 of the Convention. The Committee is also concerned that Section 23(3) of the State Party's Constitution represents a 'claw back clause', which allows for the application of discriminatory customary law in respect of personal laws. The Committee notes the State party's willingness expressed in the report and during the dialogue to review its Constitution; however, it remains concerned at the fact that no action has been taken to repeal the discriminatory provisions from the Constitution, even as the constitutional review process is awaited.

See www2.ohchr.org/english/bodies/cedaw/docs/co/CEDAW-C-ZWE-CO-2–5.pdf (last accessed 16 August 2012).

[66] Tsanga, 'Notes of a fringe observer'.

The recognition of the adverse impact of the claw-back clauses in the 2012 review process reveals the extent to which the role of the Committee and their direct, albeit brief, engagement with the proponents of the shadow reports has altered the impact of the reporting processes on States Parties. In addition, the shadow reporting team who attended the Committee sessions were alert to the intervention opportunities that were now available in a way that was not possible in 1998. The use of Facebook, emails and cellphones during the review of the Zimbabwe State Report in February 2012 transformed a remote and distant activity into one with a sense of immediacy for those following the process in Zimbabwe. Adding to the efficacy of this engagement were the contributions and clarifications that could be made on the day even from 10,000 kilometres away. The Zimbabwe Women Lawyers' Association in conjunction with the Women's Coalition ran a full-day online communication process with those from among their number who were in Geneva. During the day, answers to queries on information contained in the state report on the government's financial provisions and implementation in relation to key areas of interventions stated to have been carried out in favour of women were sought. For example, there was a query on the number of shelters provided by the government for victims of domestic violence. An answer was immediately provided by the main NGO working in this area, MUSASA Project, indicating that the government had not provided the requisite number of shelters and that where there were shelters, these were run by NGOs. In Paragraph 23 of the Concluding Observations of the Committee it is observed that:

> While noting the adoption of the new Domestic Violence Act the committee expresses its concern at the high level of violence against women in the state Party … the State Party has not availed the required monetary and human resources to implement the provisions of the Domestic Violence, especially the effective setting up of the Domestic Violence Council.[67]

Further the Committee stated that it is:

> again concerned that only one shelter for women victims of violence has been established by the State Party in the country (the other two shelters were established by NGOs).[68]

[67] www2.ohchr.org/english/bodies/cedaw/docs/co/CEDAW-C-ZWE-CO-2–5.pdf (last accessed 16 August 2012).

[68] *Concluding Observations 24 and 44 of the CEDAW Committee on the Zimbabwe State Report 2012*, available at: www2.ohchr.org/english/bodies/cedaw/docs/co/CEDAW-C-ZWE-CO-2–5.pdf (last accessed 16 August 2012).

The 2012 state report to the CEDAW Committee refers to the banning of harmful cultural practices in the Domestic Violence Act Chapter 5:16 and the Criminal Law (Codification and Reform) Act Chapter 9:23. The Committee, through the shadow report, was informed that implementation remains a problem. The Committee's Concluding Observations draw specific attention to harmful cultural practices and the need for measures to be accelerated to curb them. Of special note is that although Zimbabwe is only required to report again in 2016 on measures to address harmful customary practices and domestic violence, an interim report on progress is required in 2014.

14 Making nothing look like something: why now?

Compliance with the CEDAW and the regional instruments would appear to be a matter of concern for the Ministry of Women's Affairs,[69] as indicated by the release of a draft of the National Women's Council and Elimination of Discrimination Against Women Bill, 2012 (third draft dated 6 July 2012) during the last stages of the constitutional review process. The release of the Bill is puzzling because there is a Gender Commission proposed in the new Constitution, and there would be significant overlaps between the two bodies. More specifically the draft Constitution seeks to remove all forms of discrimination against women, and mandates and would facilitate wholescale legislative reforms giving effect to sex and gender equality in the law. The proposed Bill, which is being dealt with in the same general timeframe despite purporting to:

> [i]ncorporate certain regional, continental and international instruments bearing on women's rights into the domestic law of Zimbabwe,[70]

only incorporates those provisions that would not conflict with section 23(3) of the current Constitution.

Is this a response to the CEDAW Committee's observations? The draft Women's Council Bill appears, like the National Gender Policies and the state reports to the CEDAW Committee, to be attempting to create a veneer of compliance without articulating or tackling the deep-seated

[69] The Minister being Dr Olivia Muchena, from ZANU (PF).

[70] According to the Preamble, the draft further seeks to put in place a National Women's Council that would investigate issues of discrimination against women, making recommendations on the removal of barriers to the attainment of full equality by women, but this lies beyond the scope of this chapter.

legal and constitutional roots of discrimination against women. Why the urgency with far-reaching reforms potentially coming to fruition in the near future?

15 By way of not concluding

A conclusion seems inappropriate for this chapter as so much is pending. Zimbabwe could be on the path to a fairer, more equal and equitable future for all. However, paper provisions alone will not achieve this; political will in large amounts, active implementation strategies and cooperation across all sectors in the country will be required. Continued pressure from bodies such as the CEDAW Committee will be important in producing both new legislation and implementation of the provisions in the proposed Constitution if it comes into force. Despite the stop–start process of developing a new Constitution, there does seem to be room for optimism, and perhaps new allies have been made along the way. We can but wait and see.

Addendum: On 22 May 2013, after this chapter was finalized, Zimbabwe acquired the new Constitution which is discussed in this chapter. Despite latent fears that it might be altered or adulterated during its passage through Parliament it cleared the final hurdles unscathed. In a public signing ceremony President Robert Mugabe signified his assent. Immediately thereafter the Constitution was published in the Government Gazette.

The transition period between the old and new orders will be protracted as only some of the provisions of the new Constitution came into effect immediately. In relation to this chapter the important provisions that are already in effect are the Declaration of Rights, the provisions on citizenship and the composition of Parliament. Section 23(3), the claw-back clause which exempted personal law and customary law from being subject to section 23(2), the non-discrimination clause of the old Constitution, was swept away. Readers will recall that section 23(3) received trenchant criticism throughout the chapter.

Law reform will be required to bring many areas of current law into line with the new Constitution but many of the laws discussed in the chapter which were at risk of restricted application to women have been broken free of their fetters, as at least on paper have women. Implementation will be a long, hard road but the way is now open.

17

THE CEDAW after all these years: firmly rooted in Dutch clay?

MARJOLEIN VAN DEN BRINK

1 Introduction

The Netherlands[1] has a reputation to maintain where human rights are at stake. And yet it was not until 1991 that the Netherlands ratified the Convention on the Elimination of All Forms of Discrimination against Women (CEDAW). The delay was at least partly compensated by a unique provision included in the Act approving ratification, that required the government to periodically report to Parliament on the implementation of the Convention. This has led to more political attention and public exposure than other international human rights treaties have received. Other than that, the Convention's impact has been limited, even in the courts, despite the Dutch (moderately) monist system. A major exception is the case of a religiously orthodox political party that refused to grant women full membership. This case has centred primarily on the obligations of the state to eliminate sex-based discrimination under the CEDAW, although the applicants based their claim on other human rights instruments as well (see section 6.1 below). However, even though the highest Dutch court ordered the government no longer to condone the party's discriminatory policy, the government decided to await the decision of the European Court of Human Rights (ECtHR). This political choice to await the Court's decision seems illustrative of a decreasing feeling of urgency regarding gender equality, but also reflects the government's dwindling willingness to conform to decisions of human

The author thanks Rikki Holtmaat and Wendy van der Tol for their useful comments on an earlier draft.

[1] The Netherlands Antilles form part of the Kingdom of the Netherlands. Presentations to the CEDAW Committee are always combined presentations by the Netherlands and the Netherlands Antilles. This contribution is limited to the situation in the Netherlands.

rights bodies, including, for that matter, the ECtHR.[2] Still, the impact of ECtHR decisions and EU law exceeds that of international human rights treaties, and the CEDAW in particular. In this contribution the impact of the CEDAW in the Netherlands is explored by tracing its influence in legislation, case law, policy-making, and in education and legal training. Some tentative explanations will be offered for its limited and possibly even waning influence. The conclusion is not too optimistic, but there is no reason to despair, at least not yet.

2 History of the ratification process

The CEDAW was opened for signature on 1 March 1980. The Netherlands, together with many other states, signed the document on 17 July of that same year, at the occasion of the Second United Nations World Conference on Women in Copenhagen. Ratification, however, took considerably more time: eleven years and six days to be precise. A rather remarkable delay, given the Dutch reputation as a human rights defender. The main reason for this time lapse rests in the initial idea of the government that the Dutch situation, upon accession, should be fully in compliance with the demands of the Convention. The government, perhaps, had some reason to be wary of over-hasty ratification. The optimism regarding the Dutch human rights record had, by that time, been dampened somewhat by the critical findings of other human rights bodies.

In 1984 a Ms Broeks filed a complaint against the Netherlands under the individual complaints procedure of the International Covenant on Civil and Political Rights (ICCPR). At that time, married women who lost their jobs were only granted unemployment benefits if they could show that they were the breadwinner. The Human Rights Committee found a violation of Article 26 of the ICCPR.[3] Because the Dutch social security system was largely based on the breadwinner principle, the government feared huge costs and even considered withdrawing from the ICCPR.

In 1988 the Netherlands had the dubious honour of being the first state to be found to have acted in violation of the International Convention on the Elimination of All Forms of Racial Discrimination (ICERD), in

[2] In office at the time was a minority government of the Liberal Party (VVD) and the Christian Democrats (CDA), with the 'support' of the populist Party for Freedom (PVV), under Prime Minister Mark Rutte (VVD). This government was replaced on 5 November 2012 by a government of the VVD and the Labour Party (PvdA) again under Prime Minister Rutte.

[3] HRC, *S.W.M. Broeks* v. *the Netherlands*, Communication 172/1984, 9 April 1987, UN Doc. CCPR/C/29/D/172/1984.

an individual complaints procedure.[4] Ms Yilmaz-Dogan, pregnant at the time, had been dismissed by her employer because 'when a Dutch girl marries and has a baby, she stops working. Our women workers of foreign descent,[5] on the other hand, take the child to the neighbours or family and at the slightest setback disappear on sick leave.' The Cantonal Court accepted the argument and approved the dismissal. The Advocate-General at the Supreme Court rejected Yilmaz-Dogan's request to seek annulment of the Cantonal Court's decision, and the Prosecutor of the District Court refused to prosecute Yilmaz-Dogan's former employer under the Dutch Penal Code. This led the CERD Committee to the conclusion that the Netherlands had failed to redress her dismissal. Such experiences do not tend to encourage the ratification of new human rights treaties.

The government[6] felt that full compliance with the CEDAW required that the Algemene wet gelijke behandeling,[7] the Equal Treatment Act that was being drafted at the time and that included sex as a protected ground, should have entered into force. The length of the drafting process of this Act was not caused by any major conflicts regarding the prohibition of sex discrimination, although there were some, of course. The most-heated debates involved sexual orientation as a protected ground. Fortunately, the government eventually changed its mind and decided that ratification did not have to be postponed until the full implementation of the CEDAW had been accomplished. The responsible Ministers declared in Parliament that 'the meaning of treaty obligations is not determined, let alone fixated by the views of the national legislature at the time of ratification'.[8] Thereafter, the Parliamentary approbation process accelerated and the Convention

[4] CERD Committee, *Yilmaz-Dogan* v. *the Netherlands*, Communication 1/1984, 10 August 1988, CERD/C/36/D/1/1984.

[5] Yilmaz-Dogan was of Turkish descent.

[6] During the whole national ratification process – that is, from 1977 to 1994 – the Dutch government was led by the Christian Democratic Party (CDA) in varying coalitions with the Liberal Party (VVD) or the Labour Party (PvdA) and/or the Democrats (D66). These were the Cabinets Van Agt I, II and III, and Lubbers I, II and III.

[7] General Act on Equal Treatment of 2 March 1994, prohibiting discrimination on the grounds of religion, belief, political opinion, race, sex, nationality, hetero- or homosexual orientation or civil status. Most recent version *Staatsblad*, 2007, 321. All Dutch legislation enacted since 1 May 2002 is available at: www.overheid.nl. An English translation of the Dutch Equal Treatment Act is available at the website of the International Labour Organization: www.ilo.org/dyn/natlex/natlex_browse.details?p_lang=en&p_country=NLD&p_classification=05.01&p_origin=SUBJECT (last accessed 25 February 2013).

[8] 'De betekenis van verdragsverplichtingen wordt immers niet bepaald, laat staan gefixeerd door de opvattingen van de nationale wetgever ten tijde van een verdragsgoedkeuring.' [The meaning of treaty obligations is after all not determined let alone

was ratified on 23 July 1991.[9] Had ratification still been dependent on the entry into force of the Equal Treatment Act, ratification would have been delayed for another three years. Rumour has it that the government's change of mind was to a large extent thanks to the unremitting efforts of one or two civil servants who strongly supported ratification.

The occasion of the ratification of the CEDAW was reason for the Dutch government to withdraw from the Convention on the Nationality of Married Women 1957.[10] According to the government, Article 3 of this Convention was not in accordance with the CEDAW's Article 9, because the former is based on a presumption of *un*equal legal positions of men and women, whereas the CEDAW is based on the equality principle.[11]

Ratification of the Complaints Protocol[12] was a far quicker process, although it still took a good two and a half years before the Protocol was ratified on 22 May 2002. The Netherlands played a prominent role in the drafting of the text. A Dutch proposal, drawn up by national and international experts at the initiative of the University of Maastricht, served as the basis for the international negotiations, in which Dutch representatives were equally active.[13]

The Netherlands ratified the amendment to Article 20, paragraph 1 of the Convention on 10 December 1997.[14] The amendment is meant to

fixated by the views of the national legislator at the time of ratification.] *Tweede Kamer* 1988–1989, 18950 (R 1281), nr. 9 at 4. See also: *Tweede Kamer* 1984–1985, 18950, no. 3 at 7; *Tweede Kamer* 1986–1987, no. 6 at 14; and 1988–1989, no. 9 at 3. More extensively: J. H. J. de Wildt, 'Het Internationaal Verdrag inzake de Uitbanning van Alle Vormen van Discriminatie van Vrouwen' [The International Convention on the Elimination of All Forms of Discrimination against Women], *Ars Aequi* 41:5 (1992) 259–66.

9 Rijkswet van 3 juli 1991 inzake goedkeuring van het Verdrag inzake de uitbanning van alle vormen van discriminatie van vrouwen [CEDAW Approbation Act 1991], *Staatblad* 1991, 355.

10 4468 UNTS 66, entered into force 11 August 1958.

11 See: *Tweede Kamer* 1988–1989, 18950 (R 1281), no. 9 at 15; see also CEDAW Committee, *Initial State Party Report: the Netherlands*, 17 April 1993, UN Doc. CEDAW/C/NET/1 at 171–2.

12 Optional Protocol to the Convention on the Elimination of All Forms of Discrimination against Women, 2131 UNTS 83, entered into force 22 December 2000.

13 *Staten-Generaal* 2001–2002, 28253 (R 1714), nos. 252 and 1, Facultatief Protocol bij het Verdrag inzake de uitbanning van alle vormen van discriminatie van vrouwen, 6 October 1999 [Letter of Minister regarding tacit approval of the Protocol, with an explanatory note].

14 So far, the ratification has not helped much: on 20 January 2011 only 60 states had ratified the amendment. To enter into force, ratification by two-thirds of all States Parties, at the time of writing 124 ratifications, is required.

lift the restriction on the number of annual meetings for the CEDAW Committee.

2.1 Reservations and declarations

The Netherlands did consider a number of reservations, among these a reservation to Article 11(1)(e) of the CEDAW on social security.[15] However, it was decided that such a reservation would be useless, since the Dutch courts had already shown their willingness – in the aftermath of Ms Broeks' victory as mentioned above – to fully apply the ICCPR non-discrimination clause contained in Article 26 to social security issues. Other suggested reservations, such as with regard to compulsory military service, were likewise rejected. In the end, no reservations were made. The government did, however, make a declaration on two paragraphs in the Preamble: paragraph 10 on apartheid and (neo)colonialism and paragraph 11 on disarmament, territorial integrity and state sovereignty. The government felt that 'it was not desirable to introduce political considerations such as those contained in paragraphs 10 and 11 of the preamble in a legal instrument of this nature. Moreover, the considerations are not directly related to the achievement of total equality between men and women.'[16]

The Netherlands has retained a consistent policy regarding reservations by other states that, according to the Dutch government, are incompatible with the object and purpose of the Convention. It has, however, never precluded the entry into force of the Convention between itself and the states making these reservations (see UN treaty collection). This commendable alertness seems to be characteristic of the active interest taken by the Ministry of Foreign Affairs in the position of women and women's human rights, albeit mostly abroad. Generally speaking, the CEDAW seems to play a much bigger role in Dutch foreign policy than it does at home.[17]

[15] De Wildt, 'Het Internationaal Verdrag inzake de Uitbanning van Alle Vormen van Discriminatie van Vrouwen' at 265.

[16] C.N.161.1991.TREATIES-5 (*Depositary Notification*), available at: http://treaties.un.org/doc/publication/mtdsg/volume%20i/chapter%20iv/iv-8.en.pdf (last accessed 18 February 2013).

[17] See Hellum on Norway in this volume.

3 Parliamentary approbation of ratification: national reports

In the Netherlands the Parliamentary approbation of proposals to ratify international treaties may occur either tacitly or explicitly. In the case of the CEDAW, the approbation was given explicitly, and subject to a remarkable condition that has not been repeated since.[18] Article 3 of the Approbation Act 1991 requires the Minister of Social Affairs and Employment to report to Parliament every four years on the implementation of the Convention in the Netherlands. This exceptional clause was included after a proposal thereto by three Members of Parliament, who were not fully confident that the periodic reports to the CEDAW Committee would provide a sufficiently reliable picture of the situation in the Netherlands.[19] This amendment lies at the heart of a number of detailed, comprehensive and critical reports dealing with the implementation of the CEDAW in the Netherlands. These national reports are commonly known as 'NIRV' (Nationale implementatie rapportage vrouwenverdrag) or as '*Kalsbeek-rapportage*', after Member of Parliament Ella Kalsbeek, the primary sponsor of the amendment.

In 1996 a preliminary report was published outlining the major issues involved in the implementation of the CEDAW in the Netherlands.[20] This was followed by an exploration into the character of the obligations imposed by the Convention. The Groenman Commission – named after its chairperson, former Parliamentarian Louise Groenman – concluded on the basis of its analysis that the Convention requires implementation at three levels: direct discrimination and legal inequalities must be eliminated, the position of women must be improved and dominant gender ideology must be combated.[21] This distinction was taken up by the Dutch government in its second report to the CEDAW Committee, by discussing the progress made regarding the implementation of all topics covered by the Convention at these three levels. This is a really helpful approach because it

[18] CEDAW Approbation Act 1991.

[19] *Tweede Kamer* 1989–1990, 18950 (R 1281), no. 11, Goedkeuring van het verdrag inzake de uitbanning van alle vormen van discriminatie van vrouwen [Ratification process of CEDAW] (New York, 18 December 1979).

[20] J. C. Hes and C. E. van Vleuten, *Het Vrouwenverdrag in de Nederlandse Rechtsorde* [The Women's Convention in the Dutch Legal Order] (The Hague: Vuga/SZW, 1996).

[21] L. S. Groenman *et al.*, *Het Vrouwenverdrag in Nederland Anno 1997* [The Women's Convention in the Netherlands in 1997] (The Hague: Vuga/SZW, 1997) at 19. See also Holtmaat on the CEDAW's holistic approach in this volume.

makes immediately clear that implementation in some fields has seen far more progress and success than in other fields. The Committee accepted the structure of the report, and later endorsed this approach in its General Comment No. 25 on temporary special measures.[22] Unfortunately, the Dutch government discontinued this three-level analysis after its third report to the CEDAW Committee. The Groenman Report concluded with sixty-five recommendations for concrete actions to enhance implementation. As a result, a major national women's conference was held in 1997 in Nijmegen where public policy makers, NGO representatives and academics discussed ways to ensure the observance of the Convention.

After these first general reports, the government has commissioned both 'regular' national reports,[23] as well as several detailed studies on specific topics, all drafted by independent experts. Specific topics that have been dealt with include health, parenting and labour market participation, violence against women, and structural gender discrimination (Article 5(a)).[24] Moreover, many 'working documents', that is research reports that for one reason or another have not been officially published, have been produced. In 2003 the government decided to stop the production of general national reports altogether and focus instead on one theme at the time, thus radically changing the character of the national reports.[25]

[22] The Committee states the object and purpose of the Convention is (1) to ensure full equality of women before the law and protection against discrimination in the public as well as the private sphere, (2) to improve the de facto position of women, and (3) to address prevailing gender relations and the persistence of gender-based stereotypes. See GA, 59th Session, *Report of the CEDAW Committee on its 30th and 31st Session*, 2004, UN Doc. A/59/38, Annex I.

[23] For example, M. H. Marchand, *Emancipatie op een Zijspoor? Tweede Nationale Rapportage Inzake de Implementatie van het VN Vrouwenverdrag* [Emancipation Being Side-Tracked? Second National Report on the Implementation of the UN Women's Convention] (Amsterdam: UvA, 2003).

[24] N. Holtrust, A. C. Hendriks and D. M. J. Bauduin, *De Betekenis van Artikel 12 Vrouwenverdrag voor Nederland: gezondheid als recht* [The Significance of Article 12 of the Women's Convention for the Netherlands: Health as a Right] (The Hague: Vuga/SZW, 1996); W. C. Monster, E. Cremers and L. Willems, *Vrouwenverdrag, Moederschap, Ouderschap en Arbeid* [Women's Convention, Motherhood, Parenthood and Employment] (The Hague: Vuga/SZW, 1998); I. Boerefijn, M. M. van der Liet-Senders and T. Loenen, *Het Voorkomen en Bestrijden van Geweld tegen Vrouwen* [The Prevention and Combating of Violence against Women] (The Hague: Vuga/SZW, 2000); R. Holtmaat, *Naar Ander Recht en Beleid* [Towards Different Law and Public Policy] (The Hague: Vuga/SZW, 2004).

[25] Written replies to the list of issues regarding the Convention on the Elimination of All Forms of Discrimination against Women (CEDAW) raised in connection with the fifth periodic report of the Netherlands (CEDAW/C/NLD/5), Annex 2: *Letter to the House of Representatives of the States General* (10 December 2008). The latest report published

The importance and value of the knowledge and awareness generated by the special clause in the Approbation Act can hardly be underestimated. However, it is uncertain how long the government will keep up the good work. Aversion to what is perceived as 'international meddling in domestic business' is increasing. This aversion is primarily directed at the ECtHR, which is considered to be too activist, systematically overstepping its authority. Although the international treaty bodies are not yet 'targeted' by these critics because they are perceived as less of a nuisance than the binding decisions of the ECtHR, that may be just a matter of time.[26]

4 Reporting to the CEDAW Committee

By the end of 2010 the Netherlands had submitted five reports to the CEDAW Committee. Unfortunately, not all reports were submitted on time, and the Committee has made critical remarks about this. The Dutch

in this series is: M. Keizer and S. Keuzenkamp, *Moeilijk Werken. Gezondheid en de Arbeidsdeelname van Migrantenvrouwen* [Difficult Employment. Health and Labour Market Participation of Migrant Women] (The Hague: SCP, 2011).

[26] The government under Prime Minister Mark Rutte (a minority Cabinet composed of the Liberal VVD and Christian Democrat CDA, 'supported' by the right-wing populist PVV) stated in its policy document on human rights in foreign policy that the antiquated European treaties (that is of the Council of Europe, not the EU) are an obstacle for necessary reforms, in particular in the area of migration policy, and that the ECtHR 'should not undermine its authority by pronouncing on issues that are only marginally related to human rights'. *Tweede Kamer* 2010/11, 31735, no. 1, *Verantwoordelijk voor Vrijheid. Mensenrechten in het Buitenlands Beleid*' [Responsible for Freedom. Human Rights in Foreign Policy]. This triggered a heated debate between supporters of this stance, who regard human rights as a leftist hobby, and defenders of human rights and their mechanisms. In the meantime, the government backed down a little (after the First Chamber of Parliament adopted a motion urging the government to continue doing its best to realise human rights in conformity with its international obligations: *Eerste Kamer*, 2010/2011, 32502B, 19 April 2011, Motie van het Lid Bemelmans-Videc c.s.). See 'Mensenrechten in Discussie: Linkse Hobby, rechts Liberaal Gedachtengoed, of van Ons Allemaal?' [Human rights in debate: left-wing hobby, right-wing liberal legacy, or belonging to all of us?], editorial, *NJCM-Bulletin* 36:4 (2011) 429–32; 'Het Kabinet-Rutte en de Europese Mensenrechten: Een Kwestie van Contrasten' [The Rutte-Administration and European human rights: an issue of contrasts], editorial, *NJCM-Bulletin* 36: 6–7 (2011) 617–21; J. Gerards, 'De Waarde van een Europees Mensenrechtenhof' [The significance of a European Court of Human Rights], *Recht der Werkelijkheid* [Law in Reality] 32:2 (2011) 65–73; Thierry Baudet, 'Dik of Dun' [Fat or thin], *Recht der Werkelijkheid* [Law in Reality] 32:2 (2011) 74–9. For an analysis and many more references: T. Spijkerboer, 'Het Debat over het Europese Hof voor de Rechten van de Mens' [The debate on the European Court of Human Rights], *Nederland Juristenblad* 87:4 (2012) 254–62.

reports have met with varying enthusiasm. The first report, for instance, was fairly well received. One of the CEDAW Committee members even commented on 'the wonderful way they are dealing with women in the Netherlands'.[27] The second and third reports, in which the government applied the three-level analysis as developed in the Groenman Report (see section 3 above) to analyse its own progress in implementing the CEDAW, also met with approval, despite the fact that the second report had been handed in two years late. This positive reception may have been due to the fact that, by its analysis, the government showed that it had listened to the Committee's critique that the first report was too descriptive and lacked analysis. This is not to say, however, that there was no critique. The (married) husband's 'right to veto' regarding the children's family name was critically questioned. Another major point of criticism concerned a Dutch political party.[28] This national Calvinist party, the SGP, refused full membership to women, in particular withholding them from administrative and public offices. Thus, although the SGP allowed women (if only since 24 June 2006) to become members, they were excluded from representational positions, for instance in Parliament, but presumably in greater numbers at the local level.[29] The Dutch government has quite firmly dismissed both concerns, at the national level when reporting back to Parliament, and at the international level at the occasion of the presentation of the fourth Dutch report to the CEDAW Committee. On the issue of the SGP, the government told the CEDAW Committee that '[t]he State had appealed the [lower court's] judgment on the ground that caution should be exercised in intervening in the constitution of political parties, because a variety of fundamental rights and freedoms were at stake. The right to stand for election and the prohibition of discrimination must be balanced against the freedom of assembly of a political party.'[30] The Committee's

[27] M. van den Brink and M. Jacobs, '"The wonderful way they are dealing with women in the Netherlands". Nederland en het Vrouwenverdrag' ['The wonderful way they are dealing with women in the Netherlands'. The Netherlands and the Women's Convention], *NJCM-Bulletin* 19:6 (1994) 742–50.

[28] CEDAW Committee, *Concluding Observations: the Netherlands*, A/56/38(SUP), 20 July 2001, paras. 185–231. See also M. van den Brink, 'VN-Vrouwenverdrag: De Eerste Tandjes Komen Door. Kroniek 1999–2001' [UN Women's Convention: its first teeth appear], *NJCM-Bulletin* 26:8 (2001) 1069–78.

[29] T. Loenen, 'De SGP-Discussie *Revisted*' [The SGP debate *revisited*], *Nederlands Juristenblad* 85:36 (2010) 2269–74 at 2273.

[30] CEDAW Committee, summary record 767th meeting, 24 January 2007, CEDAW/C/SR.767 (B), 5 March 2007, Consideration of reports submitted by States Parties under Article 18 of the Convention (*continued*), *Fourth Periodic Report of the Netherlands*, at 3. See also CEDAW Committee, Consideration of reports submitted by States Parties under

criticism of the Dutch law on surnames was dismissed with reference to a decision of the ECtHR,[31] in which the Court concluded that states enjoy a wide margin of appreciation in this area, because national law tends to be 'strongly determined by national traditions', thus brushing aside the specific expertise of the CEDAW Committee, as well as the fact that it is oftentimes precisely those traditions that stand in the way of women's emancipation.[32] The candid way in which the government dismissed these comments is surprising and does raise questions regarding the willingness of the Dutch government to really engage in a constructive dialogue. The Committee raised both issues – family names and the issue of the SGP, in particular – again on the occasion of the presentation of the fourth and fifth reports, but so far to no avail. A third point of concern of the CEDAW Committee that the Dutch government seems unwilling to accept is in regard to the direct effect of the Convention provisions in the Dutch legal system. I will return to some of these issues in section 6 where the role of the CEDAW in the national courts and legal practice is discussed.

4.1 *The role of NGOs in the reporting procedure*

On the occasion of the presentation of the first report to the CEDAW Committee, the Committee expressed its surprise that Dutch women's NGOs were not involved in the drafting of the report. The Dutch government explained that this is standard practice in all human rights reporting procedures, and is meant to prevent confusion as well as the entangling of responsibilities and interests. If Dutch NGOs were to participate in the drafting of Dutch State Party reports, they would become an accomplice to the act, so to speak, and it would be much more difficult for them to fulfil the critical role expected of NGOs. Instead, the government offers NGOs financial support to draw up their own shadow reports.[33] That is very welcome, of course, given the considerable effort, expertise and time required for the drafting of shadow reports, as well as for their presentation to the CEDAW Committee. So far, every governmental report has been followed by a shadow report endorsed by a great number of Dutch human and

Article 18 of the Convention on the Elimination of All Forms of Discrimination against Women, *Fifth Periodic Reports of States Parties: the Netherlands*, CEDAW/C/NLD/5, 24 November 2008, at 66–7.

[31] *Bijleveld* v. *the Netherlands*, appl. no. 42973/98, ECtHR 27 April 2000.

[32] CEDAW/C/NLD/5, 24 November 2008 at 77–8.

[33] See CEDAW Committee, *Consideration of the Initial Report on the Netherlands*, A/4938(supp), 4 February 1994, paras. 245–317 at 54, para. 253.

women's rights organisations. Occasionally, other shadow reports have been presented on specific topics if these were not addressed in the general report. An example is the report by the former Dutch Emancipation Council on the issue of family law and lesbian women, an issue on which the Dutch women's movement at the time was either divided or lacked expertise. That such things may sometimes change very quickly is shown by the fifth Dutch shadow report that was co-sponsored by the Federation of Dutch Associations for the Integration of Homosexuality (COC), as well as by the Dutch Transgender Network.[34]

Both the government and NGOs are happy with this practice of 'independent' NGO participation, because it allows for a more critical involvement in reporting back to the CEDAW Committee. In the Dutch CEDAW Network (Netwerk VN-Vrouwenverdrag), a number of women's and human rights NGOs cooperate in collecting information to be included in the shadow reports to the CEDAW Committee, in the drafting and lobbying of the reports, and in reporting back to civil society in the Netherlands on the outcome of the constructive dialogue. The subsidies offered by the government are primarily used to pay one or two independent experts to draft the reports and present them to the CEDAW Committee. Also of importance is the participation of 'mainstream' (that is, not specifically women's) human rights organisations in the network. These organisations do not only contribute to the quality and expertise of the shadow reports, their participation is also a means to bring knowledge about women's and gender issues to mainstream human rights NGOs.

5 The legal status of the CEDAW

The Dutch legal system can be characterised as moderately monist. Transformation into national law is not necessary for a treaty to become effective in the national legal order. Article 93 of the Dutch Constitution provides that 'provisions of treaties and of resolutions by international institutions, which may be binding on all persons by virtue of their contents shall become binding after they have been published'. Article 94 of the Constitution states that national provisions that conflict with treaty provisions that are binding on all persons, shall not be applicable.

[34] Dutch CEDAW Network, *Women's Rights – Some Progress, Many Gaps. Shadow Report by Dutch NGOs; An Examination of the Fifth Report by the Government of The Netherlands on Implementation of the UN Convention on the Elimination of All Forms of Discrimination against Women (CEDAW), 2005–2008* (Utrecht: Aim for Human Rights, 2009).

It is up to the courts to decide whether a treaty provision has direct effect, that is whether it has a general purpose and is sufficiently concrete to be applied without any administrative interference. If it is, the provision may be invoked in the courts. No equivalent national provision is needed. Generally speaking, civil and political human rights, such as religious freedom or the right to vote, tend to be regarded as sufficiently concrete to be binding on all. On the other hand, social, economic and cultural rights, such as the right to work or to a decent standard of living, are mostly considered in need of elaboration before they can be applied by the courts.

In the wake of the fourth Dutch government report to the CEDAW Committee, a heated debate on the legal status of the CEDAW and on the direct effect of its provisions flared up. The debate was incited by NGOs, who were appalled that the government in its fourth report had brushed aside recommendations on issues such as the all-male SGP Party and had merely repeated that sex equality was not the only fundamental concern at issue. Criticism of the law on surnames was confronted equally briefly by merely repeating what the government had already stated before (see section 4 above). This made the NGOs suspicious about the status accorded to the CEDAW by the Dutch government. To make things worse, the government representative told the Committee that it was not possible to say anything in general about the direct effect of the Convention. She stated that:

> '[D]irect effect' means that a stipulation is legally enforceable by an individual. Article 93 of the Dutch Constitution stipulates that stipulations in Conventions have binding force if they can bind all individuals through their content. The more generally stipulations are formulated and the more active action on the part of the state they require, the less the question of direct effect. The question whether a stipulation binds everyone and therefore has direct effect is, in the final instance, determined by the Dutch courts in individual cases.[35]

Moreover, Dutch civil servants present suggested that, although the Convention was an important document, it was not a legal document, thus referring implementation entirely to the sphere of public policy. The Dutch CEDAW Network (see section 4 above) made sure questions were asked in Parliament about these negations of the CEDAW's legal status. The Minister responsible replied that a distinction must be made between the legally binding nature of the document for the state and any direct

[35] See CEDAW/C/NLD/5, 24 November 2008 at 10–11.

effect of the Convention, that is whether it can be invoked by individuals in court.[36] The Netherlands has felt bound to the Convention since its ratification. Still, the Minister continued, the question whether a specific provision has direct effect can only be answered by courts in concrete cases. The Minister promised to explain everything to the CEDAW Committee in the fifth report. However, the fifth report is disappointing in that the Minister's words are merely repeated.[37] And although this statement is correct in itself, it does not convey the impression that the government is intent on taking away the concerns of the CEDAW Committee, Parliament and NGOs on the legal status accorded to the Convention. Rather curious also was the terminology used by the Minister when referring to the constructive dialogue with the Committee: he promised Parliament to keep them posted 'on the *defense* of the fifth implementation report'.[38]

It is hard to say where all this leaves the CEDAW. On the one hand, the Convention's position does not differ from that of other human rights treaties ratified by the Netherlands. On the other hand, there seems to be some reason to fear that the government's attitude is a consequence of a 'two-spheres' conception of the nature of women's human rights, that is a conception of women's human rights as belonging to the policy sphere of international cooperation instead of as an integral part of the legal human rights framework. It would be very unfortunate if this phenomenon – that is finally disappearing at the UN level, albeit slowly –now took root in the Netherlands.

6 The CEDAW in the Dutch courts

The International Law Association concluded in 2004 that '[w]hile provisions of UN human rights treaties are often referred to [by the Dutch courts], reference to the products of the supervisory bodies is haphazard and extremely limited in comparison to the products of the European

[36] Letter of 5 November 2007 of the Minister of OCW (Onderwijs, Cultuur en Wetenschap/ Education, Culture and Science) on the legal scope of the CEDAW, DE/RV/07/42724.

[37] See *4th and 5th Dutch Periodic Reports to the CEDAW Committee*, UN Doc. CEDAW/C/ NLD/4, 10 February 2005, and UN Doc. CEDAW/C/NLD/5, 24 November 2008. CEDAW Committee, *Concluding Observations: the Netherlands*, UN Doc. CEDAW/C/NLD/CO/5, 1 March 2010, para. 13.

[38] *Tweede Kamer* 2009–2010, 30420, no. 141, 'Emancipatiebeleid, Brief van de Minister van Onderwijs, Cultuur en Wetenschap' [Emancipation policy, letter of the Minister of Education, Culture and Science].

Court of Human Rights'.[39] This impression was confirmed by an exploratory small-scale survey in 2009. Janse and Tigchelaar did a quick scan of the digital databases containing the major Dutch legal journals. Although their findings are probably not fully accurate, the emerging picture leaves little room for doubt regarding the situation in general. The research showed that in the ten years since 1999, the CEDAW was referred to only ten times in Dutch case law.[40] The Appellate Court in The Hague even dismissed a claim regarding the exclusion of women of 75 years and older from the nationwide preventive breast cancer screening, without discussing the relevance of the CEDAW, or any other human rights provision for that matter, on which the plaintiffs and the women's test-case fund (Stichting Proefprocessenfonds Clara Wichmann) had based their claim that this was a violation of women's right to self-determination.[41] References to the Committee – and thus its interpretations and recommendations – were even more scarce: four references were found. The same effect – more references to Conventions than to their monitoring bodies – was found for both the ICCPR and the Convention on the Rights of the Child (CRC): the ICCPR was referred to 454 times, the Human Rights Committee only 65 times; the CRC was referred to 266 times as opposed to only 10 references to its supervising Committee.

The absence of the CEDAW in legal practice is striking, in particular when compared to the more recent CRC, which, even prior to its ratification, was invoked in the courts in the so-called *Valkenhorst* cases. These cases evolved around the claims of a number of children who had been born in an institution for unmarried pregnant girls who were promised eternal secrecy. These children, when they became adults, sued the institution because it refused to provide them with information concerning their biological fathers. The Dutch Supreme Court relied on the CRC to construct a right to information regarding biological descent.[42] However, the ICCPR and the CRC also become insignificant documents in the Dutch courts when compared to the

[39] International Law Association, 'Final report on the impact of findings of the United Nations human rights treaty bodies', *Report of the Seventy-First Conference* (London: ILA, 2004) at 682.

[40] R. Janse and J. Tigchelaar, 'Het Vrouwenrechtencomité: Niet Bekend en Niet Geacht?' [The Women's Rights Committee: not known and not considered?] in N. Doornbos, N. Huls and W. van Rossum (eds.), *Rechtspraak van Buiten* [The Administration of Justice from the Outside] (Deventer: Kluwer, 2010) 309–16.

[41] Hof Den Haag, 9 February 2010, *LJN*: BL3061.

[42] Hoge Raad, 15 April 1994, *NJ* 1994, 608.

European Convention on Human Rights (ECHR) and the work of the Human Rights Court in Strasbourg. Janse and Tigchelaar found 7,678 references to the Convention and 1,120 references to the case law of the Strasbourg Court. The existence of the ECHR, not to speak of the EC sex equality Directives, explains at least some of the absence of the CEDAW in the Dutch courts, but hardly all of it.

6.1 *The male-dominated political party*

Of the very few cases involving the CEDAW, four concerned the issue of the male-dominated political party, the SGP. And the good news is that the news coverage was such that it was difficult not to know about it. Not only is the issue highly controversial – as is any question regarding orthodox religious faiths in the early years of the twenty-first century – it also led to a remarkable difference of opinion among the courts. In 2005 the Court in The Hague found that the SGP refusal to accept women as (full) members was in violation of Article 7 of the CEDAW.[43] It therefore ordered the state to stop state subsidies to the Party. Thus, at the end of the year, when the SGP applied for the yearly financial support for political parties, the request was rejected. The SGP then went to the Administrative Court and asked for a revision of that decision.[44] This Court rejected the claim, and the SGP appealed.[45] The Raad van State, the highest administrative court in the Netherlands, was asked by the SGP to order the Dutch state to revise its decision to terminate financial support – paid to all political parties represented in Parliament in the Netherlands – to the SGP. The state had terminated financial support earlier, to comply with the prior court decision that the SGP's refusal to admit women as members was a violation of Article 7 of the CEDAW. In appeal, the Raad van State took the desirability of a diverse society as its starting point. Subsidies granted to political parties must be regarded as being in the interest of society generally. Article 7 of the CEDAW is, according to the Court, a balanced provision, offering space for minority views such as those of the SGP and – apparently of some importance – there are sufficient numbers of other political parties that do allow female membership. In addition women have the possibility to found their own political parties. Excluding the SGP from government funding in these circumstances would undermine the legitimacy of the

[43] Rechtbank Den Haag, 7 September 2005, *LJN*: AU2091.
[44] Rechtbank Den Haag, 19 February 2007, *LNJ*: AZ5393.
[45] Raad van State (AVRvS), 5 December 2007, *LJN*: BB9493.

outcome of Parliamentary debates. Thus, the Raad van State ordered the state to revise its rejection of the SGP's demand for subsidies.

Meanwhile, both the SGP and the state had appealed the initial court's decision in 2005 to the Court of Appeal in The Hague.[46] The manoeuvring space for the Court of Appeal was limited by the very speedy decision of the Raad van State, published only fifteen days before the Court of Appeal issued its decision. The Raad van State clearly was not willing to wait for the Appellate Court's decision. The Court of Appeal could not do much else than confirm the Raad van State's decision regarding the revision of the rejection of the demand for subsidies. However, contrary to the Raad's finding that the SGP was allowed to exclude women from its membership, the Court of Appeal concluded that such discrimination against women, even if following from sincere religious beliefs, is not protected by the constitutional right to religious freedom. Peters and Bleeker, commenting on these cases, conclude that the legal situation is chaotic:

> The legislature must do something about the SGP; subsidies must continue to be paid to the SGP; the SGP does not have to be prohibited; the SGP is no longer allowed to withhold the right to be eligible to women in principle, however it is in practice.[47]

On 9 April 2010 the Supreme Court finally cut the knot, after having first postponed its decision that was originally foreseen at the end of February 2010.[48] The Court established that, in so far as enjoyment of the right to stand for election, as provided for by Article 7(a) of the CEDAW, is conditional on participating in a political party, the direct effect of Article 7(a) of the CEDAW entails the direct effect of Article 7(c) of the CEDAW, that provides for the right to participate in NGOs and associations that are active in the field of the country's public life. The Court further established that Article 7(a) of the CEDAW requires the state to effectively ensure women's right to stand for election and it further stated that the Convention leaves no room for a margin of appreciation regarding active and passive voting rights for women. The Court found that, in this particular case, the prohibition of discrimination must be given precedence over the SGP's fundamental rights. The Court argued:

[46] Hof Den Haag, 20 December 2007, *LJN*: BC0619.

[47] J. Peters and K. Bleeker, 'Staat Moet SGP Aanpakken Maar Ook Subsidiëren. Over Botsende Competenties en Grondrechten' [State should tackle SGP but also subsidise the party. On conflicting competences and constitutional rights], *Nederlands Juristenblad* (2008) 556–63.

[48] Hoge Raad, 9 April 2010, *LJN*: BK4549.

> Article 4 of the Constitution, Articles 25 and 2 of the ICCPR and, for women, Article 7 of the CEDAW, guarantee everyone regardless of sex the right to elect members for representational bodies as well as the right to be elected into those bodies. These provisions all mention active and passive voting rights in one breath, thus expressing that these rights are each other's essential counterpart in a democracy, because voters must have the right to determine who among them will be elected. Because thus the exercise of the passive right to vote affects the core of the democratic functioning of the state, it is unacceptable that a political group violates a fundamental right that guarantees the voting rights of all citizens, when drafting their list of candidates, even when the violation finds its basis in a principle grounded in a religious conviction or other belief.[49]

The Court concluded:

> The Court of Appeal ... has concluded rightly that the state must take measures that will ensure that the SGP will grant women passive voting rights and that the state must apply a measure that is effective but that at the same time infringes the fundamental rights of the (members of the) SGP as little as possible.
>
> This, however, does not mean that the court is qualified or able to order the state to take specific measures to end the discrimination by the SGP with regard to the passive voting rights of her female members ... [T]he choice of measures to be made by the state requires a balancing of interests that coincide to a large extent with deliberations of a political nature that such a decision can't be demanded of the court. This is also true for the [lower court's] order that the state stops granting subsidies to the SGP.[50]

Thus, the Dutch state must take effective measures to ensure women's right to stand for election. The state should be careful, however, to select measures that respect the SGP's fundamental rights as much as possible. Because the Supreme Court cannot order the state to make law, nor order the state to take other measures to comply with Article 7 of the CEDAW, it was left up to the state to come up with a solution.

On 6 October 2010, however, the SGP lodged a complaint with the ECtHR that the Dutch Supreme Court had deprived the SGP and its members of their right to freedom of assembly and association, their right to freedom of expression and their right to freedom of religion (Articles 11, 10 and 9 of the ECHR respectively).[51] The government

[49] *Ibid.*, paras. 4.5.4–4.5.5.

[50] *Ibid.*, paras. 4.6.1–4.6.2.

[51] Application no. 58369/10 by Staatkundig Gereformeerde Partij against the Netherlands, 6 October 2010, para. 59.

then decided to await the ECtHR's decision before deciding on further action.[52]

It is ironic that a government that was so clearly reluctant to redress the SGP situation had to defend the Supreme Court's decision in Strasbourg. The decision to postpone left two possibilities, one of which would be that the ECtHR agreed with the SGP that their rights have been violated. In that case, the Dutch state is no longer obliged to take measures, although of course the CEDAW Committee might still see things differently. However, equally possible was that the Court would judge the SGP's discriminatory policy regarding its female members to be unacceptable. In that case, the Dutch state would have to take steps after all. However, the responsible Minister (Home Office), notified Parliament that he was going to 'consider the necessity and desirability of further action after the European Court has reached a decision'.[53]

That time came on 10 July 2012, when the ECtHR found the SGP's application manifestly ill-founded.[54] The Court does not address the question of whether the SGP really is a 'victim' of the alleged violations in the absence of any government action, because 'the application is in any event inadmissible on other grounds'.[55] The Court recalls that political parties may pursue their political aims on condition that the means used are legal and democratic, and that the changes proposed by that party are compatible with fundamental democratic principles.[56] It further emphasises that the advancement of sex equality prevents states from 'lending its support to views of the man's role as primordial and women's as secondary', referring to its previous judgments in Űnal Tekeli and in Konstantin Markin.[57] The fact that no women have expressed the wish to stand for election is not decisive, nor is the fact that the bye-laws of the SGP do not contain any formal impediment to the possibility of women being elected,[58] a fact that – remarkably enough – had been considered relevant by the Minister of the Home Office.[59] The Court then concludes:

[52] Brief van de Minister van Binnenlandse Zaken en Koninkrijksrelaties aan de Voorzitter van de Tweede Kamer der Staten-Generaal inzake HR-uitspraak SGP [Letter of the Minister of the Home Office on the Supreme Court's decision on the SGP], 8 April 2011.

[53] *Ibid.* See also C. Flinterman and I. Lintel, 'Vrouwen verkiesbaar bij de SGP: een kwestie van tijd en politiek?' [Women eligible in the SGP: a matter of time and politics?], *Nederlands Juristenblad* 86:30 (2011), 2029–30.

[54] ECtHR Staatkundig Gereformeerde Partij against the Netherlands, Application no. 58369/10, 10 July 2012.

[55] *Ibid.*, para. 67. [56] *Ibid.*, para. 71.

[57] *Ibid.*, para. 73. [58] *Ibid.*, para. 76.

[59] *Ibid.*, paras. 56–8.

> The Supreme Court ... concluded from Article 7 of the Convention on the Elimination of All Forms of Discrimination against Women and from Articles 2 and 25 of the International Covenant on Civil and Political Rights taken together that the SGP's position is unacceptable regardless of the deeply held religious conviction on which it is based ... For its part, and having regard to the Preamble to the Convention and the case-law cited ... the Court takes the view that in terms of the Convention the same conclusion flows naturally from Article 3 of Protocol No. 1 taken together with Article 14.[60]

The ball had been kicked back to the Dutch government.[61]

6.2 *Income insurance for the pregnant self-employed*

The second issue in which the CEDAW played a role, though less prominent than in the SGP cases, concerned loss of income during pregnancy and maternity for the self-employed. In 2001 legislation regarding this issue was revised. The financial safety net that had granted self-employed women a benefit at minimum level was revoked and women were referred to private insurance. Most private insurances only insured against the risk of this specific loss of income on condition that the self-employed would take the general loss of income insurance as well. Moreover, in most cases women were only eligible for payment if they had been insured for a minimum of two years. Quite a number of law suits followed. Some women asked the Commissie gelijke behandeling, the Dutch equality body, to give its opinion while others went to court. The CEDAW was not invoked before the Commissie gelijke behandeling, because this body is only competent to interpret equal treatment legislation. However, Article 11(2)(b) of the CEDAW was invoked before the lower court in The Hague in a collective action instigated by a number of self-employed women, a trade union and a women's test-case fund. The Court found that Article 11(2)(b) 'contains no direct, clear-cut prescriptions on how to realise its purported aim, thus leaving scope for national policy making'. Therefore, the provision was to be regarded as an instruction norm, that is an instruction to the state to achieve a certain purpose as opposed to a concrete obligation to take a specific measure, and thus lacked direct effect.[62] It concluded that other

[60] *Ibid.*, para. 77.

[61] In March 2013 the SGP decided to insert in its regulations that the 'sex of a candidate cannot be an objection'. This became effective on 1 April 2013. The Minister of Internal Affairs informed Parliament by letter on 26 March 2013 that the case had ended (Brief inzake tenuitvoerlegging arrest Hoge Road in SGP Zaak, 2013–0000171386).

[62] Rechtbank Den Haag, 25 July 2007, *LJN*: BB0334.

national or international provisions did not also oblige the government to take action.[63]

In conclusion, one can say that the CEDAW plays a very small role in the Dutch courts. Given the existing strong provisions in both the European Human Rights Convention and EU sex equality Directives, this is not really surprising. However, in a few cases at least, the CEDAW's specific gender focus has been relied upon, albeit not always with success. Maybe the CEDAW can be employed more fruitfully in the future if more use is made of the CEDAW's unique provision on the elimination of gender ideology as contained in Article 5(a).[64] However, in order to get the Dutch courts to acknowledge the direct applicability of this provision, lawyers in the Netherlands will have to do some serious thinking.

7 Complaints under the Optional Protocol

By October 2009 three complaints against the Netherlands had been lodged under the Optional Protocol. In two cases the Committee has given its opinion. The first complaint concerned the complex situation of a woman working part-time and being simultaneously a co-working spouse, resulting, according to the plaintiff, in a discriminatory loss of income during pregnancy and maternity.[65] The Committee found, however, that the situation was not due to direct or indirect sex discrimination, because the loss of income was due to her special employment situation, and not because the relevant legislation had been applied in any discriminatory manner. The second plaintiff, a victim of trafficking invoking Article 6 of the CEDAW, did not fare much better.[66] The Committee ruled that the complaint was inadmissible, because she had failed to exhaust the available domestic remedies. A third complaint has been discontinued.

[63] This, as well as related issues, have been dealt with by different courts, but all cases have finally failed, if not in the lower courts, then in the Supreme Court, including the cases that were argued on the basis of EU Directives, such as Directive 86/613 on the self-employed or the pregnancy Directive 2004/113/EC. See Hoge Raad, 11 July 2008, *LJN*: BD1850 and Hoge Raad, 11 April 2011, *LJN*: BP3044.

[64] Holtmaat, *Naar Ander Recht en Beleid*; R. Holtmaat and C. Tobler, 'CEDAW and the European Union's policy in the field of combating gender discrimination', *Maastricht Journal of European and Comparative Law* 12:4 (2005) 399–424; see also Holtmaat in this volume.

[65] CEDAW Committee, *Ms. Dung Thi Thuy Nguyen* v. *the Netherlands*, Communication 3/2004, 14 August 2006, UN Doc. CEDAW/C/36/D/3/2004.

[66] CEDAW Committee, *Ms. Zhen Zhen Zheng* v. *the Netherlands*, Communication 15/2007, 27 October 2008, UN Doc. CEDAW/C/42/D/15/2007.

Three complaints is not an impressive number. Nevertheless, the Minister responsible for the implementation of the CEDAW may have been right when he remarked:

> The Netherlands so far has only received three complaints under the Optional Protocol. In absolute figures that is a small number, however nevertheless significant when compared to the very few individual complaints that have been lodged with the Committee thus far. I feel this says something about the visibility of the CEDAW in the Netherlands.[67]

And it just might indicate that Dutch lawyers have more faith in the CEDAW Committee than the small number of references in the national courts would make us believe.

8 The impact of the CEDAW on legislation

A quick search on 'women's convention' in the Dutch database Opmaat, containing all official government documents published since 1995, including the notes of Parliamentary debates, explanatory memoranda accompanying bills and the like, resulted in a mere 207 hits. A very disappointing result and, I assume, an indicator of the lack of significance attached to the CEDAW.[68] In a few instances questions were asked in Parliament, following recommendations of the CEDAW Committee. Issues referred to included the law regarding family names, already briefly discussed above, and sexual and domestic violence as grounds for residence permits in asylum procedures. Following up on a recommendation of the CEDAW Committee after the second government report, two Members of Parliament asked the government to oblige each Ministry to subject at least one new legislative proposal a year to a Gender Impact Assessment.[69] The proposal was not successful. The majority of references were less closely linked to the work of the Committee.

Ministerial proposals for the annual women's emancipation plans usually include rather general references to the CEDAW. A positive exception is the Ministry of Foreign Affairs, which tends to conduct a very active human rights policy. Gender is a specific point of attention in the

[67] Letter of 5 November 2008 on the legal scope of CEDAW at 2.

[68] The lack of references stands in stark contrast with EU Directives. See for instance J. H. Gerards, 'Implementation of the Article 13 Directives in Dutch equal treatment legislation', *Maastricht Journal of European and Comparative Law* 13:3 (2006) 291–309.

[69] *Tweede Kamer* 2003–2004, 27061, no. 24, Meerjarennota emancipatiebeleid, Motie van de leden Stuurman en Tonkens [Several year note on emancipation policy, Motion of Members of Parliament Stuurman and Tonkens]. On the Gender Impact Assessment see M.

work of the Department for International Development Cooperation. Although this is obviously to be applauded, the gender expertise available for the international arena seems to make Dutch NGOs more sharply aware of the perceived lack of expertise on women's human rights issues regarding the position of Dutch women. Civil servants responsible for the implementation of the CEDAW in the Netherlands apparently are mostly unaware of the legal character of the document. According to the NGO representatives who presented the fourth Dutch shadow report to the CEDAW Committee, the civil servants in the Dutch delegation valued the Committee's recommendations and comments as something of an expert opinion, not as legal interpretations of the competent body.[70] The CEDAW Committee's Concluding Observations on the fifth Dutch report show that the Committee's recommendations in this regard so far have had no effect. The Committee regrets that:

> the Netherlands has argued in court the non-direct applicability of substantive provisions of the Convention … and … reiterates its concern that as a consequence of the position of the State Party, the judiciary is left with the responsibility of determining whether a particular provision is directly applicable. CEDAW urges the Netherlands to reconsider its position and to ensure that substantive provisions of the Convention are fully applicable in the domestic legal order … and to provide for domestic remedies for alleged violations of any rights guaranteed to individuals by the Convention.[71]

A specific issue where the CEDAW popped up concerned the lack of a financial safety net for loss of income due to pregnancy and childbirth for the self-employed, which has already been mentioned. Thanks to a strong lobby, supported by women's NGOs, politicians, trade unions, as well as decisions and an advisory report of the national equality body, the issue did not disappear after the disappointing court decision. In 2008 the government presented a bill to Parliament proposing the reinstallation of a minimum financial safety net for the self-employed. The proposal was adopted and entered into force in June 2008.[72] However, self-employed

Verloo and C. Roggeband *Emancipatie-Effectrapportage: Theoretisch Kader, Methodiek en Voorbeeldrapportages* [Gender Impact Assessment: Theoretical Framework, Method and Examples] (The Hague: Vuga/SZW 1994).

70 See the diary of Marjan Wijers and Margreet de Boer at www.vrouwenverdrag.nl (last accessed 18 February 2013).

71 CEDAW Committee, *Concluding Observations: the Netherlands*, CEDAW/C/NLD/CO/5, 5 February 2010, paras. 12–13.

72 Wet van 29 mei 2008 tot wijziging van de Wet arbeid en zorg in verband met een uitkering aan zelfstandigen bij zwangerschap en bevalling en een verruiming van de periode

women who suffered loss of income due to pregnancy between 2001 and 2008 were left without any compensation. It is important and telling that even though the CEDAW was mentioned, the government explicitly stated that it did not feel there was any international obligation for the enactment of this legislation.

The absence of the CEDAW in political and legislative debates may be explained in part by the existence of substantial domestic sex equality legislation, resulting from the implementation of EU Directives. However, this cannot explain why the CEDAW does not play a more prominent role in debates on issues regarding women's human rights outside the equality framework. In three recent debates, all dealing with topics that may have significant consequences in terms of women's human rights, the CEDAW was not mentioned once. These issues included legislative changes in the Act on the termination of pregnancies,[73] a bill on the possibility to evict perpetrators of domestic violence temporarily from their own homes[74] and the introduction of the obligation to agree on a 'parental plan' as a condition to obtain a divorce.[75] In the discussions regarding the parental plan the CRC was mentioned; however, the CEDAW was not. Rather remarkable, moreover, is that the explanatory memorandum to the bill on the restraining order in case of domestic violence was formulated entirely in neutral terms, not once referring to either men or women.

From these findings it may be concluded that, even though it is not to be ruled out that the CEDAW in a very general sense informs political debates on important gender-biased issues, its role or influence is certainly not very prominent or influential. Ways will have to be found to encourage politicians to make more use of the concrete recommendations and suggestions regarding implementation of women's human rights, and to insist that the government takes the CEDAW Committee's comments seriously.

voor deelname aan een vrijwillige verzekering in enkele socialezekerheidswetten [Act on Employment and Care with Regard to a Pregnancy Benefit for the Self-Employed], *Staatsblad* 2008, 192.

[73] Besluit van 18 mei 2009, houdende wijziging van het Besluit afbreking zwangerschap [Decision Changing the Decision on the Termination of Pregnancy], *Staatsblad* 2009, 230.

[74] Wet van 9 oktober 2008, houdende regels strekkende tot het opleggen van een tijdelijk huisverbod aan personen van wie een ernstige dreiging van huiselijk geweld uitgaat [Act on a Temporary Eviction from Home of Perpetrators of Domestic Violence], *Staatsblad* 2008, 421.

[75] Wet van 27 november 2008 tot wijziging van Boek 1 van het Burgerlijk Wetboek en het Wetboek van Burgerlijke Rechtsvordering in verband met het bevorderen van voortgezet

9 Research, education, training and awareness-raising

Both in the period prior to and following the Dutch ratification of the CEDAW, there was ample attention for the Convention. This was the heyday of Dutch feminist scholarship, and an impressive number of feminist expertise centres and women's organisations were subsidised by the government. In anticipation of the Dutch ratification, two volumes were published on 'International Law and Women', highlighting among others the expected added value of the CEDAW.[76] *Nemesis*, an academic journal on women and law, published a special issue on the CEDAW on the occasion of the Dutch ratification in 1991, and many contributions on the CEDAW in the following years until the journal was discontinued in 2003. In 1994 a volume was published containing a detailed analysis of all provisions in the Convention.[77] A human rights NGO published a low-cost practical guide explaining the treaty on an article-by-article basis, illustrated with many concrete examples.[78] Studies were commissioned on such issues as the significance of the CEDAW for Dutch aliens law, and on the multicultural society.[79] Shortly after the Optional Protocol was ratified, the Clara Wichmann Institute, an independent (though subsidised) expert institute on women and law, published a guidebook on how to use the complaints

ouderschap na scheiding en het afschaffen van de mogelijkheid tot het omzetten van een huwelijk in een geregistreerd partnerschap [Act on the Advancement of Continued Parenting after Divorce ...] *Staatsblad* 2008, 500.

[76] H. van Maarseveen, D. Pessers and M. Gunning (eds.), *Internationaal Recht en Vrouwen. De Betekenis van het Internationale Recht voor Vrouwen in Nederland. Part I: Commentaren & Part II: Teksten van Verdragen, Resoluties, Statuten en Andere Internationale Documenten*, [International Law and Women. The Significance of International Law for Women in the Netherlands. Part I: Comments & Part II: Texts of Treaties, Resolutions, Charters and Other International Documents] (Zwolle: W. E. J. Tjeenk Willink, 1987).

[77] A. W. Heringa, J. Hes and L. Lijnzaad (eds.), *Het Vrouwenverdrag: Een Beeld van een Verdrag ...* [The Women's Convention: Picture of a Convention ...] (Antwerp/Apeldoorn: Maklu Uitgevers, 1994).

[78] W. Evenhuis and E. van Dijk, *Met Recht een Vrouw. Het VN-Vrouwenverdrag Toegelicht* [A Woman by Rights. An Explanation of the UN Women's Convention] (Amsterdam: Greber Uitgever & Distributeur, 2001).

[79] S. van Walsum, *Het VN-Vrouwenverdrag en het Nederlands Vreemdelingenrecht* [The UN-Women's Convention and Dutch Aliens Law] (Amsterdam: Clara Wichmann Instituut, 1995); R. Holtmaat (ed.), *Een Verdrag voor Alle Vrouwen. Verkenningen van de Betekenis van het VN-Vrouwenverdrag voor de Multiculturele Samenleving* [A Treaty for All Women. Explorations of the Significance of the UN-Women's Convention for the Multicultural Society] (The Hague: E-Quality, 2002).

procedure.[80] In fact, so much was being written that the Institute had to publish a revised edition of its bibliography on the CEDAW.[81] In 2004 the Clara Wichmann Institute had to close its doors, due to lack of income.[82] Fortunately, the archive function of the Institute has been taken over by the Dutch Institute for Emancipation and Women's History, Atria (formerly known as the IIAV, thereafter as Aletta). Many publications have been made accessible on the Internet.[83] It is possible to study other publications at the Institute or order hard copies.

Now that the heyday of the second feminist wave seems to be over, the number of publications on the CEDAW is decreasing. A special site dedicated to the CEDAW was opened by an ardent supporter of the Convention, Jeroen de Wildt, a civil servant who had previously been involved in the ratification process.[84] However, because no funding whatsoever has been made available to support the work involved in keeping this very informative site up to date, of late the site seems to have slowed down, which, although understandable, is nevertheless a great pity.

In Dutch primary and secondary schools courses are taught on 'citizenship', religion and on what is called 'philosophy of life' (*levensbeschouwing*). Depending on the orientation of schools and teachers, in such courses attention may be paid to human rights or at least human rights issues. It is highly unlikely, though, that specific attention will be paid to the CEDAW.

At the university level, in particular in the law schools, the picture is a little different. In the last decades of the twentieth century, almost every Dutch law school had a specific 'women and law' department, however small. These were mostly established in the wake of the second feminist wave. The existence of such departments is a good guarantee that courses will be offered that focus on women's rights issues, although not necessarily on human rights. Most of these departments, unfortunately, have

80 F. van Leeuwen, *Het Facultatief Protocol bij het VN-Vrouwenverdrag; Klagen over Vrouwendiscriminatie* [The Optional Protocol to the UN Women's Convention; Complaining about Women's Discrimination] (Amsterdam: Clara Wichmann Instituut, 2004).

81 M. Kruizinga, *VN-Vrouwenverdrag. Een Geannoteerde Bibliografie* [UN Women's Convention. An Annotated Bibliography], 2nd revised edition (Amsterdam: Clara Wichmann Instituut, 2002).

82 In October 2009 a volume commemorating the fifth anniversary of the closure of the Clara Wichmann Institute was published: M. de Boer and M. Wijers, *Vrouw & Recht. De beweging, de mensen, de issues* [Women & Law. The Movement, the People, the Issues] (Amsterdam University Press/Pallas Publications, 2009).

83 www.atria-kennisinstitut.nl/aletta/atria (last accessed 18 February 2013).

84 www.vrouwenverdrag.nl (last accessed 18 February 2013).

disappeared again. Moreover, severe budget cuts at the universities, in combination with revised curricula in many law schools, have led to a strong reduction in the number of optional courses offered. The result is that many courses on women or gender and (human rights) law have disappeared. However, specific courses on gender and human rights have survived in a few law schools. Attention is also paid to the CEDAW in some more general human rights courses, but there is no guarantee that this will continue to be the case. It is interesting to note that foreign students in particular are interested in such courses, provided they are taught in English.

A special education institute exists for the judiciary and other legal professionals (SSR).[85] The brochure for judges and prosecutors for the year 2010 mentions no courses on human rights, let alone on the CEDAW, although there are possibilities for internships in Strasbourg or Luxembourg. Future judges, the judiciary in training, follow a compulsory programme. In a few courses in this curriculum specific attention is paid to human rights, according to the course summaries. Among these, courses on immigration law seem to be overrepresented. In the commercial market, many other training institutes and universities offer post-academic programmes. Presumably in some of the human rights courses offered, attention will be paid to the CEDAW.

A number of women's and feminist organisations and institutions were discontinued or had to merge with other organisations in these last years, partly because of new rules regarding government subsidies whereby many subsidies were made contingent on specific projects, thus undermining any long-term perspective. Nevertheless, others survived, such as the previously mentioned Aletta, and some took a new form, such as E-Quality, initially a 'proper' women's institute, nowadays a 'knowledge centre for emancipation, family and diversity'. In 2012 a new reduction in the number of women's organisations took place, when Aletta and E-Quality merged into a 'knowledge centre for emancipation and women's history' (Atria).

What has helped to keep the CEDAW alive is that between 2003 and 2010 one of the CEDAW Committee members was Dutch. Cees Flinterman – Member of the Human Rights Commission (HRC) since 1 January 2011 – was always ready to discuss what happened during the latest session and the improvements that had been made. Debriefing lunches

[85] www.ssr.nl (last accessed 18 February 2013).

were organised on a regular basis at his university (Utrecht), both in the human rights department and for a more general public. Flinterman also regularly met with the Dutch section of the Committee on Feminism and International Law, one of the standing committees of the International Law Association. In May 2009 a topical colloquium on 'Women's Human Rights *versus* Religion/Culture/Tradition'[86] was organised in the Peace Palace in The Hague, with the help of Flinterman. Several CEDAW Committee members attended. It is quite likely that it would have been impossible to organise a prestigious event such as this, if there had not been an esteemed CEDAW Committee member to back it up.

The picture, as it arises from this overview, seems to indicate that the general public is hardly likely to be aware of the CEDAW. However, in all probability, people know very little about law and human rights generally, except maybe for some very vague ideas. Arguably, we should not expect a thorough knowledge of human rights. It might be a more realistic goal to make sure that women know where to go when they feel treated badly and that they have access to expert legal counselling.

From this perspective, it is more troubling that even legal professionals seem to receive little information on the CEDAW. If they have to deal with issues of sex equality and women's rights, they tend to stick to provisions that have already proven to be successful, such as Article 26 of the ICCPR and Article 8 of the ECHR. As long as they are successful, that is not a real problem. However, it would seem that the most gender-specific provisions of the CEDAW, including its obligation to combat gendered stereotypes and ideologies, do remain underused in this way.

10 In conclusion

Drawing conclusions on the embeddedness of the CEDAW in Dutch society as well as in the legal clay is not easy. The picture emerging is ambivalent. On the one hand, there is the unique and extremely helpful Article 3 of the Dutch Approbation Act, instructing the government to report periodically to Parliament about the 'real state of affairs'. This provision has

[86] As was to be expected, the use of the word 'versus' raised many critical comments, as well as lively debate. For the results of the conference see: R. Holtmaat and I. Boerefijn (eds.), *Women's Human Rights and Culture/Religion/Tradition: International Standards as Guidelines for Discussion? Proceedings of the Colloquim Peace Palace, The Hague 12 May 2009* (Utrecht: Sim Specials, 2010). See also R. Holtmaat and J. Naber, *Women's Human Rights and Culture: From Deadlock to Dialogue* (Antwerp: Intersentia 2011).

been the source of some beautifully detailed and thorough analyses of the way the CEDAW should and could be implemented in the Netherlands. On the other hand, there are signs that civil servants involved in the implementation process know less and less about the treaty obligations. This is at least partly due to the fact that the staff are expected to be internally (or externally) mobile, which means that they change jobs every so many years. However, it may also be that it is not the most experienced and knowledgeable employees who are assigned to the CEDAW file.

The impact of the CEDAW in legal practice is lagging behind that of other conventions, the ICCPR and the ECHR in particular, not to speak of EU law. Still, the one case to which the CEDAW is core, the SGP case, caused unprecedented controversy between the national courts and could count on a high media profile. So, I would recommend that we continue to rely on successful provisions such as Article 26 of the ICCPR and Articles 8 and 14 of the ECHR, and try to focus, in our work on the CEDAW, on the most gender-specific elements of that document. It is here that the CEDAW will arguably have the most added value, both in the courts as well as in developing new policies and legislation.[87] An impressive amount of information on the CEDAW has been published, and expert knowledge on the Convention is available both in mainstream human rights organisations and among women's organisations. However, in order to make it work, we have to make sure that Dutch politicians and policy makers understand the legal character of the CEDAW and turn back to their conception of the CEDAW as a dynamic instrument: implementation is a progressive process and the constructive dialogue with the CEDAW Committee is an instrument to help that process along. That means that reporting to the CEDAW Committee on the situation in the Netherlands should be regarded as an opportunity to improve that situation, not as an opportunity to 'defend' it, as the responsible Minister apparently thinks.[88] Whether the CEDAW Committee can do anything to stimulate such a change in perception is a difficult question to answer. Possibly it could by offering more concrete and feasible advice

[87] For suggestions on how to use the CEDAW to enhance gender sensitivity in the interpretation of other important legal regimes, see Holtmaat and Tobler, 'CEDAW and the European Union's policy in the field of combating gender discrimination'. Compare also Fredman on the CEDAW in the UK in this volume.

[88] In a similar vein, J. Morijn, 'Reforming United Nations human rights treaty monitoring reform', *Netherlands International Law Review* (2011) 295–333 at 312.

that may be implemented right away. That, however, is a very complex task for an international body. Moreover, past experiences, such as the SGP issue, are not encouraging. Arguably, the strategy that the CEDAW Committee is currently trying out – that is teaming up with other treaty bodies in dealing with provisions and topics that the Convention shares with other human rights treaties – may prove to be more fruitful, even if only because it may ease the increasingly burdensome task of reporting to and complying with a steadily expanding human rights monitoring system.[89]

[89] For an example, see the CEDAW Committee's project in cooperation with the Children's Rights Committee to draft a joint General Recommendation on harmful practices, 2011, available at: www2.ohchr.org/english/bodies/cedaw/JointCEDAW-CRC-GeneralRecommendation.htm (last accessed 18 February 2013).

18

The CEDAW in the UK

SANDRA FREDMAN

1 Introduction

Although the United Kingdom (UK) signed the Convention on the Elimination of All Forms of Discrimination against Women (CEDAW) in July 1981, it was not ratified until April 1986. This lack of interest in the substance of the Convention has marked the attitude of successive governments ever since. The CEDAW is little known and little used in the UK, even among women activists. Although the government duly goes through the motions of preparing reports and responding to questions, it does not regard the CEDAW as normative, in the sense of shaping policy or providing direction. To the extent that existing practices and policies happen to comply with the CEDAW, it is happy to report compliance; where there is a challenge or a shortfall, however, it generally finds a means to justify its reluctance to change. Thus, even when there has been significant progress on the legislative and policy front in pursuing equality for women, this cannot be attributed to the CEDAW. Correspondingly, the CEDAW on its own is not capable of evincing change where the UK falls short of its obligations. It is argued here that this is in part because of the lack of visibility and 'belief' in the CEDAW in the UK. But it is also in part because the CEDAW Committee itself has not been sufficiently incisive, either in highlighting some of the issues that are most problematic in the UK, or in identifying clear breaches of rights. The pay gap and the fact that women remain primarily responsible for childcare are the foremost examples of this. Instead of the CEDAW, of course, it is the EU that has been the strongest influence on gender equality law in the UK in recent decades. Paying more attention to the CEDAW in EU law, to the extent

The author would like to thank Natasa Mavronicola for her help in gathering statistics for this paper; and Chris McConnachie for his help in editing the final draft.

that the CEDAW lies within its competence, would give greater leverage to the CEDAW in the UK.

2 The legal status of the CEDAW in the UK

Since the UK has a dualist system of international law, treaties are not binding unless incorporated by legislation. Successive UK governments have consistently refused to incorporate the CEDAW into domestic law. This is despite the CEDAW Committee's persistent urging of it to do so. Thus, both in 1999[1] and again in 2008,[2] the Committee recommended that the UK fully incorporate the CEDAW. In its 1999 Concluding Observations, the Committee emphasised that the incorporation of the European Convention on Human Rights (ECHR) in the Human Rights Act 1998 was not sufficient, since it did not provide for the full range of women's human rights in the CEDAW or for temporary special measures. In its most recent report, in 2008, the CEDAW Committee once again urged the government to utilise the opportunity presented by the proposed introduction of a new Equality Bill to ensure the incorporation of the Convention.

The UK government has flatly rejected this recommendation on both these occasions. In particular, it refused to regard the Equality Bill as an opportunity to incorporate the CEDAW. In its response to the 2008 Concluding Observations, the UK stated: '[t]he UK rejects this recommendation on the basis that such an approach would create a separate, parallel regime within the Equality Bill that incorporates all the elements of CEDAW that are, to the extent that the UK is obliged to comply with them, already covered by or present in other areas of UK law'.[3] It justifies this by arguing that, whereas the Equality Bill prohibits discrimination in specific fields only (work, the provision of goods, facilities and services, education, premises, associations and the exercise of public functions), the CEDAW covers all fields including in particular

[1] See Committee on the Elimination of Discrimination against Women (CEDAW), *Concluding Observations, Third and Fourth Periodic Reports: United Kingdom of Great Britain and Northern Ireland*, UN Doc. A/54/38/Rev.1 (1999), part two, paras. 278–318.

[2] CEDAW, *Concluding Observations, Fifth and Sixth Periodic Reports: United Kingdom of Great Britain and Northern Ireland*, UN Doc. A/63/38 (2008), para. 248 *et seq.*

[3] CEDAW, *Response by the United Kingdom (UK) and Northern Ireland (NI) to Select Recommendations of the United Nations Committee on the Elimination of All Forms of Discrimination against Women following the Examination of the UK and NI's 5th and 6th Periodic Reports on July 10 2008*, UN Doc. CEDAW/C/UK/CO/6/Add.1 (2009), para. 5.

social and cultural fields. Moreover, the UK does not regard many of the Convention's obligations as conferring rights on people, as the Equality Bill does. An example is the obligation to 'ensure that family education includes a proper understanding of maternity as a social function and the recognition of the common responsibility of men and women in the upbringing and development of their children, it being understood that the interest of the children is the primordial consideration in all cases'. According to the UK government, it is neither appropriate nor possible for legislation to address such obligations. Rather, it justifies the lack of incorporation by pointing to Article 3 of the CEDAW, which recognises that non-legislative measures can be the right way to address some of the Convention's obligations.

This approach to the CEDAW is typical of the general resistance of UK governments to incorporation of international treaties, and in particular of its resistance to the notion that socio-economic rights are human rights. A major breakthrough in this philosophy can be detected in its recent Green Paper on a new 'Bill of Rights and Responsibilities', where the previous Labour government recognised that socio-economic rights are fundamental human rights. However, even here it did not regard socio-economic rights as appropriate for judicial enforcement. Moreover, with the change of government in 2010, the more positive attitude to socio-economic rights was not sustained. The Conservative Party has made it clear that it is not only opposed to socio-economic rights as human rights, but it may well repeal the Human Rights Act 1998, which incorporates the ECHR itself. The presence of the Liberal Democrats in the Coalition government is likely to restrain such a drastic move, but the economic policy of severe cutbacks means that socio-economic rights will inevitably be deeply damaged. There is therefore, in my view, no prospect of incorporation of the CEDAW into UK law.

The approach to the CEDAW is, to be fair, no different from the UK's approach to international human rights commitments more generally. A clear dividing line is drawn between international and domestic law, and claims that the UK has breached its international commitments under the International Covenant on Civil and Political Rights (ICCPR), the International Covenant on Economic, Social and Cultural Rights (ICESCR) or the International Convention on the Elimination of All Forms of Racial Discrimination (ICERD) are also unlikely to have much political traction, let alone legal persuasiveness. This is particularly so with the International Labour Organization (ILO), where the UK has regularly ignored decisions by the ILO Committee of Experts that the UK is in breach of ILO Conventions.[4] The situation is radically different if the UK has chosen to incorporate international commitments into domestic law, as it has done with the EU and the ECHR.

More optimistic would be an approach that attempted to bring the CEDAW before the courts as an interpretive source in respect of either interpretation of existing legislation or of the ECHR, particularly in respect of the non-discrimination provision in Article 14. It is only very recently that some reliance has been placed on the CEDAW as an interpretive aid, but even here the references are made almost in passing. Thus in *Yemshaw* v. *London Borough of Hounslow*,[5] Baroness Hale briefly referred to the CEDAW Committee's definition of gender-based violence in General Recommendation 19, in interpreting a statutory provision deeming persons to be homeless where they are exposed to violence in the home. In *Quila*,[6] the Article 16(1) right to marry and to freely choose a spouse in the CEDAW was briefly mentioned in the process of finding that an immigration rule imposing age-based restrictions on foreign spouses of British citizens was in violation of the Article 8 right to respect for family life under the ECHR. Also constructive would be a greater emphasis on the CEDAW within the EU, either through direct incorporation or as an interpretive device in European Court of Justice (ECJ) judgments, which would then filter back into UK domestic law. This in turn requires greater awareness of the CEDAW among litigators and women's groups, which is lacking at present.

3 Reservations

The CEDAW Committee has also urged the UK government to reconsider its reservations to the CEDAW. In its response to the 2008 report, the UK government assured the CEDAW Committee it was reviewing its

[4] See for example ILO Committee of Experts on the Application of Conventions and Recommendations (CEACR) Individual Observation Concerning Right to Organise and Collective Bargaining Convention, 1949 (No. 98), United Kingdom (2007); see further K. Ewing, *Britain and the ILO*, 2nd edn (London: Institute of Employment Rights, 1994); T. Novitz, 'International promises and domestic pragmatism: to what extent will the Employment Relations Act 1999 implement international labour standards relating to freedom of association?' *MLR* 63:3 (2000) 379–93; R. Dukes, 'The Statutory Recognition Procedure 1999: no bias in favour of recognition?' *Industrial L. J.* 37:3 (2008) 236–67 at 260–4.

[5] [2011] 1 WLR 433, para. 20.

[6] *R (on the Application of Quila and Another)* v. *Secretary of State* [2011] 3 WLR 836, para. 66.

reservations. Its 2009 report contains no further information. However, it has been argued convincingly that several of the UK's reservations are in any event inconsistent with its obligations under the ECHR.[7] For example, the UK has entered a comprehensive reservation to the CEDAW permitting it to apply all UK legislation and rules of pension schemes affecting retirement pensions, survivor's benefits and other benefits in relation to death or retirement (including retirement on grounds of redundancy). It has also entered reservations in relation to certain social security benefits. This contrasts with the position under the ECHR. Not only has the UK no equivalent reservations under the ECHR, but in addition such reservations are clearly inconsistent with ECHR jurisprudence, which has held that social security benefits, including survivors' benefits, must be applied without discrimination on grounds of sex.[8]

The UK has also entered reservations in respect of 'succession to, or possession and enjoyment of, the Throne, the peerage, titles of honour, social precedence or armorial bearings, or as extending to the affairs of religious denominations or orders or to the admission into or service in the Armed Forces of the Crown'.[9] Particularly problematic is the reservation in respect of persons subject to immigration control:

> [t]he United Kingdom reserves the right to continue to apply such immigration legislation governing entry into, stay in, and departure from, the UK as it may deem necessary from time to time, and, accordingly, its acceptance of Article 15(4) ('States Parties shall accord to men and women the same rights with regard to the law relating to the movement of persons and the freedom to choose their residence and domicile') and of the other provisions of the Convention is subject to the provisions of any such legislation as regards persons not at the time having the right under the law of the UK to enter and remain in the UK.[10]

As JUSTICE (a UK-based NGO) argues, this is an unnecessary reservation. Article 15(4) does not confer a right to remain in the UK; rather it requires that men and women should have the same rights, whatever they may be. Indeed, it could be argued that any reservation permitting the

[7] JUSTICE, *Review of the UK's Reservations to International Human Rights Treaty Obligations* (2002), available at: www.liberty-human-rights.org.uk/pdfs/policy02/interventions-dec-2002.pdf (last accessed 19 February 2013).

[8] See *Stec* v. *United Kingdom* (Appl. No. 65731/01 and 65900/01), Judgment (Grand Chamber), 12 April 2006, ECHR 2005-X.

[9] See http://www.un.org/womenwatch/daw/cedaw/reservations-country.htm (Note 59) (last accessed 6 March 2013).

[10] *Ibid.*

state to continue to discriminate breaches the basic principle that human rights are universal. As JUSTICE puts it, '[d]iscriminatory reservations undermine the core values of equality and non-discrimination which uphold the very objects and purposes of human rights treaties'.[11]

4 Presence and visibility of the Convention and Optional Protocol

The most salient aspect of the Convention in the UK is its lack of visibility. The provisions of the Convention and the views of the Committee are virtually unknown among the general public and possibly across branches of government too. The result is that they are not utilised by women to any great extent or operationalised by government. In its 2008 Concluding Observations, the Committee requested the UK to undertake public awareness and training programmes and to raise awareness among women of their rights under the Convention and the Optional Protocol, as well as the Committee's General Recommendations. It also requested the UK to ensure that the Convention, the Protocol, the Committee's General Recommendations and its views on individual communications are made an integral part of educational curricula, including for legal education and the training of judicial officers, judges, lawyers and prosecutors.

The response has, however, been in the opposite direction. The Coalition government in power since 2010 has cut back on public support for the very bodies that had previously created 'opportunity structures' for women's organisations to utilise the CEDAW.[12] A major victim of the cuts was the Women's National Commission (WNC), a publicly funded umbrella body that was set up in 1969 with the remit 'to make known to Government, by all possible means, the informed opinion of women'.[13] At the time of its abolition in 2010, the WNC had over 670 partners from organisations working to promote women's equality, representing the voices of an estimated 8 million women. A major part of its remit was to produce shadow reports to the CEDAW Committee in consultation with its partner organisations. The WNC has been criticised for its weakness in engaging government on behalf of women, and even its supporters have

[11] *Ibid.*

[12] L. Predelli, 'Women's movements: constructions of sisterhood, dispute and resonance: the case of the United Kingdom', FEMCIT Working Paper No. 2 (2008) at 150, available at: www.femcit.org/publications.xpl (last accessed 19 February 2013).

[13] Baroness Joyce Gould, Chair of the Women's National Commission, press statement on 14 October 2010, available at: http://wnc.equalities.gov.uk/ (last accessed 6 March 2013).

pointed to the fact that its limited budget put real constraints on what it could be expected to achieve.[14] Nevertheless, its abolition removes the main forum within which engagement with the CEDAW has so far taken place in the UK. Other bodies, such as the Women's Resource Centre, have been actively engaged in writing their own independent shadow reports, in the attempt to raise concerns in relation to issues not covered in the WNC's 'official' shadow reports. However, like many organisations, the Women's Resource Centre is severely constrained by budgetary and capacity limitations. There have also been independent shadow reports from the UK on violence against women. However, the consultation process for these reports was facilitated by the WNC.[15] Without the extra budgetary support, it is difficult to see how this process can be maintained.

The government recognises that abolishing the WNC will change the way the UK women's NGO sector liaises with the United Nations. It argues, however, the role of submitting a shadow report will now lie with the Equality and Human Rights Commission (EHRC), and that other leading NGOs are well placed to submit shadow reports.[16] However, this ignores the fact that the EHRC has simultaneously been subject to deep funding cuts. Ministers are also considering the scope for transferring some of the EHRC's functions and services to government departments or contracting with private or voluntary sector bodies to undertake them.

Predelli found that women's organisations regarded the CEDAW as an important instrument. However, while some regarded the CEDAW as a valuable lobbying tool, others pointed out that it did not have much influence on policy-making.[17] The reporting process clearly has some traction in drawing ministerial attention to the issues, but there is little evidence of real change as a result of the CEDAW Committee's comments.

Overall, however, the CEDAW remains conspicuous by its absence within the equality community in the UK. During the whole of its lifetime, the Equal Opportunities Commission, which was dedicated to gender equality, paid no attention to the CEDAW. Because the new Equality and Human Rights Commission now has an express human rights remit, more formal attention has been paid to the Convention, including the preparation of a shadow report in the last reporting round. However, the CEDAW still has no real dynamic energy behind it. A major reason for

[14] Predelli, 'Women's movements', *supra* note 12 at 153.

[15] *Ibid.* at 195–6.

[16] Government Equalities Office, *WNC Equality Impact Assessment* www.equalities.gov.uk/news/changes_announced_to_geos_non.aspx.

[17] Predelli, 'Women's movements' at 195–200.

this is that the actors in the field do not perceive the CEDAW as including hard-edged rights, which could be used to take matters further than existing domestic law, augmented as it already is by the EU and the ECHR. This is an issue that the CEDAW Committee should take seriously if the CEDAW is to be a real presence in the UK. Its recommendations, for example, should be much more specific as to where and in what terms the UK has been in violation of the Convention. It is also true to say that there has been little engagement with the CEDAW at an academic level. The alliances forged between academic researchers and NGOs in other countries has therefore been absent.

5 The Optional Protocol

The Optional Protocol is even less visible than the Convention itself. The UK acceded to the Protocol on 17 December 2004, and it entered into force on 17 March 2005. In its most recent report the UK acknowledged that the communications and inquiry procedures provided by the Optional Protocol and the views of the Committee were not widely known, nor sufficiently utilised by women.[18] Certainly, there is no readily accessible government guidance on the use of the Protocol, nor any public information on the rights contained in the CEDAW.[19] There have only been two cases against the UK since it acceded to the Optional Protocol. The first was brought by a woman who complained that UK law had prevented her from passing on her British nationality to her Colombian-born son (by then 52 years old).[20] On 7 March 2007 the Committee declared her application inadmissible on the grounds that the facts of the case occurred before the CEDAW Optional Protocol entered into force in the UK, and because the applicant had not exhausted all domestic means of pursuing her complaint. The second was by a woman who complained that her proposed deportation to Pakistan put her at risk from her violent husband.[21]

[18] CEDAW, *Concluding Observations, Fifth and Sixth Periodic Reports: United Kingdom of Great Britain and Northern Ireland* at para. 262.

[19] See Equality and Human Rights Commission, *Submission on the Sixth Periodic Report of the United Kingdom to the United Nations Committee on the Elimination of All Forms of Discrimination against Women* (2008), para. 12, available at: www2.ohchr.org/english/bodies/cedaw/docs/ngos/EHRC_UK41.pdf (last accessed 19 February 2013).

[20] *Salgado* v. *UK*, CEDAW/C/37/D/11/2006, 22 January 2007.

[21] *NSF* v. *UK*, CEDAW/C/38/D/10/2005, 12 June 2007.

On 6 June 2007 the Committee declared her application inadmissible on the grounds that the applicant had not exhausted all domestic means of pursuing her complaint.

A review by Jim Murdoch for the government into the workings of the CEDAW Optional Protocol, published in December 2009,[22] concluded that it was difficult to identify any real benefits from the UK's recognition of the Protocol. He argues that the Protocol has had no impact on policy-making; it has not been used to highlight systemic problems of discrimination against women; it has not resulted in the advancement of women's rights, nor has it resulted in their mainstreaming. It had been expected that the Protocol would galvanise NGOs to engage with the Convention and the Committee, but this has not happened. In Murdoch's view, this was not coincidental. In his view:

> the near-absence of engagement by NGOs may not unreasonably be considered to reflect a lack of trust or confidence in the efficacy of the right of communication. If the CEDAW Committee were to adopt more progressive and demanding standards than the European Court of Human Rights, for example, individuals would make more use of this alternative machinery. In turn, regional (and domestic) bodies would in time be likely to reflect this emerging case-law in their own determinations.[23]

It is true that in its early years the results of cases brought under the Optional Protocol were disappointing. In 2009 of the thirteen cases in total submitted against any State Party under the Protocol since it came into effect, eight were declared inadmissible. In only five cases was a violation found. However, it may be that Murdoch's judgement was premature. All five cases dealt with in 2010 and 2011 were successful. Moreover, a relatively robust jurisprudence is developing, particularly in relation to domestic violence against women, and reproductive and maternal healthcare. At the same time, the number of cases declared inadmissible for failure to exhaust domestic remedies is worrying. Arguably, the difficulty faced by women in pursuing domestic remedies should be taken into account.

[22] J. Murdoch, *The Optional Protocol to the United Nations Convention for the Elimination of All Forms of Discrimination against Women (CEDAW): The Experience of the United Kingdom* (London: Ministry of Justice, 2009) at 27.

[23] *Ibid.* at 25.

6 The principle of equality

Turning to the substance of the Convention, it is of great importance that the CEDAW Committee has challenged the principle of equality used in the UK, arguing that it focuses too much on gender neutrality, as well as same treatment and equality of opportunity. The CEDAW, by contrast, requires an emphasis on substantive equality and the pursuit of equality in practice for women. The Committee pointed to three areas in which the UK focus on equality of opportunity and gender neutrality are most apparent. The first can be seen in the statutory 'gender duty', which is a duty on all public bodies to pay due regard, in the exercise of all their functions, to the elimination of unlawful discrimination and the promotion of equality of opportunity on grounds of gender.[24] Here the Committee, while welcoming the introduction of the duty, expresses concern that 'varying levels of public understanding of the concept of substantive equality have resulted only in the promotion of equality of opportunity and of same treatment, as well as of gender-neutrality, in the interpretation and implementation of the Gender Equality Duty'.[25]

Secondly, the CEDAW Committee expressed the concern that new institutional structures might lose their focus on discrimination against women by including in their remit multiple grounds of discrimination. The Women and Equality Unit has now become the Government Equalities Office; and the Equal Opportunities Commission, previously dedicated to gender equality, has now been incorporated into the new Equality and Human Rights Commission, which is responsible for discrimination on grounds of race, age, disability, sexual orientation, religion and belief, as well as gender.

A third area of concern relates to affirmative action. The UK has consistently taken a symmetric or gender-neutral stand to discrimination, so that discrimination on grounds of gender is always unlawful (subject to limited exceptions) even if it aims to redress previous disadvantage or discrimination against women. In its 2008 Concluding Observations the Committee once again expressed concerns that 'although temporary special measures are provided for in some legislation, they are not systematically employed as a method of accelerating the achievement of

[24] See section 76A of the now repealed Sex Discrimination Act 1975. The 'due regard' standard is retained in section 149(1) of the new Equality Act 2010, discussed below.

[25] CEDAW, *Concluding Observations, Fifth and Sixth Periodic Reports: United Kingdom of Great Britain and Northern Ireland* at para. 264.

de facto or substantive equality between women and men in all areas of the Convention'.[26] It therefore recommended 'further implementation of temporary special measures, including through legislative and administrative measures, outreach and support programmes, the allocation of resources and the creation of incentives, targeted recruitment and the setting of time-bound goals and quotas'.[27]

There has been some movement on these points in the Equality Act 2010, although not, it should be stressed, as a response to the CEDAW Committee. The Gender Duty has now been incorporated into a 'single equality duty' that covers all the protected grounds (race, gender, disability, age, sexual orientation and religion or belief). Although the duty now covers multiple 'protected grounds', risking dilution of the gender dimension, and although the duty is still primarily formulated in terms of equality of opportunity, a new section elaborating the duty has several distinctly substantive elements. Thus, the Act states that 'paying due regard' to the need to advance equality of opportunity, involves having due regard in particular to the need to:

(i) remove or minimise disadvantages connected to a protected characteristic (which includes gender);
(ii) meet the needs of persons with the protected characteristic which are different from the needs of others; and
(iii) encourage persons who share a protected characteristic to participate in public life or any other activity where participation by such persons is disproportionately low.[28]

This directly reflected submissions by the author and Sarah Spencer during the consultation period, to the effect that the duty should specify the aims of substantive equality by reference to a four-dimensional approach: namely, reducing disadvantage; accommodating difference; facilitating participation; and recognising individual dignity.[29] These recommendations were accepted by the government's review body in

[26] *Ibid.* para. 268. [27] *Ibid.* para. 269.
[28] Equality Act 2010, section 149(1).
[29] S. Fredman and S. Spencer, 'Beyond discrimination: it's time for enforceable duties on public bodies to promote equality outcomes', *EHRLR* (2006) 598–606; S. Fredman and S. Spencer, 'Equality: towards an outcome-focused duty', *Equal Opportunities Review* 156 (2006) 14–19; S. Fredman and S. Spencer, *Delivering Equality*, Submission to the Cabinet Office Review (2006).

the run-up to the legislation, and substantially incorporated into the legislation.[30]

The Committee's second concern, in relation to the new institutional structure, and particularly the Equality and Human Rights Commission, is well founded. In its shadow report to the Committee, the EHRC represented the merger of the Gender, Race and Disability Commissions in a positive light. It argued that it had taken on the Gender Agenda from the Equal Opportunities Commission (EOC), which includes issues of equal pay and pensions, reconciliation of work and family life, violence against women and the caring agenda.[31] It also informed the Committee that these critical areas had been integrated into the Commission's first full business plan of 2008–9. The track record on gender issues is, however, mixed. On the one hand, one of its more prominent activities in the first years of its existence was to conduct an inquiry into sex discrimination and the gender pay gap in financial services. This yielded some stark evidence of gender discrimination, and the Commission made some important recommendations.[32] The Commission has also been active in investigating the failure of local authorities to provide support services for women who have been victims of violence. In its 2007 report, *Map of Gaps*, the Commission found that almost a third of local authorities provided no specialised support services.[33] By 2009 specialised services were still absent in over a quarter of local authorities.[34] The Commission has since written to all offending local authorities and has indicated that all have responded satisfactorily.[35] On the other hand, when it comes to enforcement activity, the Commission has paid significantly less attention

[30] Discrimination Law Review, *A Framework for Fairness: Proposals for a Single Equality Bill for Great Britain* (2007), paras. 5.28–5.30; *Equality Bill Government Response to the Consultation* (Cm 7454, July 2008), para. 2.25.

[31] EHRC, *Shadow Report to CEDAW Committee*, (2008), para. 6, available at: www2.ohchr.org/english/bodies/cedaw/docs/ngos/EHRC_UK41.pdf (last accessed 19 February 2013).

[32] See EHRC, *Financial Services Inquiry* (2009), available at: www.equalityhumanrights.com/legislative-framework/formal-inquiries/inquiry-into-sex-discrimination-in-the-finance-sector/ (last accessed 19 February 2013).

[33] EHRC, *Map of Gaps: The Postcode Lottery of Violence Against Women Support Services in Britain* (2007), available at: www.equalityhumanrights.com/uploaded_files/research/map_of_gaps1.pdf (last accessed 19 February 2013).

[34] EHRC, *Map of Gaps 2* (2009), available at: www.equalityhumanrights.com/uploaded_files/research/map_of_gaps2.pdf (last accessed 19 February 2013).

[35] EHRC, *Map of Gaps: Enforcement under the Gender Equality Duty* (2011), available at: www.equalityhumanrights.com/key-projects/map-of-gaps/enforcement-under-the-gender-equality-duty/ (last accessed 19 February 2013).

to gender than to other strands. This is particularly true in respect of supporting litigants to take cases to court. Between October 2007 and 31 March 2009 the Commission undertook 203 completed cases on behalf of individuals, of which only 10 concerned sex discrimination, as against 179 in relation to disability discrimination. A similar pattern can be seen in relation to more general enforcement powers, where gender formed a significantly smaller proportion of cases than disability or race. Gender does, however, feature more prominently than the three 'new' strands of sexual orientation: age and religion and belief.[36] The EHRC has also been bedevilled by serious leadership problems, which has made it difficult for it to achieve the kind of focus that might be desirable.

There has also been some progress in relation to the Committee's third concern, namely temporary special measures. Although the new equality duty does not in itself authorise temporary special measures, and there is still no comprehensive set of such measures, there was some attempt made in the Equality Act 2010 to include limited provision for positive measures. Thus, section 158 of the Act applies to situations in which a person reasonably thinks that women (or others with a protected characteristic) are at a disadvantage, or have different needs from others, or their participation in any activity is disproportionately low. In such circumstances, proportionate action may be taken to address these issues. This will, for example, allow measures to be targeted at women, including training to enable them to gain employment, or health services to address their needs. Charities are also permitted to provide benefits to persons with the same protected characteristic (apart from colour) to prevent or compensate for disadvantage.[37] The Act also expressly permits more favourable treatment for women in recruitment and promotion if their participation is disproportionately low, or they suffer disadvantage connected to that characteristic.[38] However, this provision is hedged about with limitations. It only applies to those who are equally well qualified. It cannot be part of a general preference policy. Instead, individual assessments are required. It is permissive rather than mandatory. In addition, it must be proportionate to the aim of enabling or encouraging women to

[36] See EHRC, *A Legal Enforcement Update from the Equality and Human Rights Commission* (2009) and EHRC, *Legal Enforcement: Update from the Equality and Human Rights Commission* (2010), both available at: www.equalityhumanrights.com/legal-and-policy/enforcement/ (last accessed 19 February 2013).

[37] Provided that this is permitted by their charitable instrument: Equality Act 2010, section 193.

[38] Equality Act 2010, section 159.

overcome or minimise that disadvantage, or participate in that activity. Even in this limited form, however, it went sufficiently against the grain for the newly elected Coalition government in 2010 to have delayed its implementation indefinitely.

7 Employment

There is not sufficient space to deal with all the Articles of the CEDAW in this chapter. Instead, I shall focus on the right to work in Article 11. In this context, as in others, the CEDAW has had little impact on the formulation of policy or legislation. However, I would suggest that even if the recommendations of the CEDAW Committee had been followed, this would not be sufficient to achieve real change. This is because Article 11 itself is not sufficiently incisive; and the recommendations of the Committee are too muted to address the complex and deep-seated causes of women's inequality in the UK workforce.

In its Concluding Observations in 2008, the Committee noted the measures taken to narrow the gender pay gap and the various measures taken to facilitate participation in the labour market and the reconciliation of family and work life.[39] This included the adoption of flexible working arrangements, and the extension of the statutory maternity pay and maternity allowance from 26 to 39 weeks. However, the Committee expressed its concern at the persistence of occupational segregation between women and men in the labour market and the continuing pay gap. It was also concerned about the lack of available and affordable childcare. It urged the UK to ensure equal opportunities for women and men in the labour market, including through the use of temporary special measures, and to continue to take proactive and concrete measures to eliminate occupational segregation and to close the pay gap between women and men, including through the introduction of mandatory pay audits. It also recommended that the UK continue its efforts to assist women and men to reconcile family and professional responsibilities and to share family responsibilities by providing, inter alia, more and improved childcare facilities. Lastly, it recommended that the UK encourage men to share responsibility for childcare, including through awareness-raising activities and through the provision of parental leave.[40]

[39] CEDAW, *Concluding Observations, Fifth and Sixth Periodic Reports: United Kingdom of Great Britain and Northern Ireland* at para. 286.

[40] *Ibid.* paras. 286–7.

However, it is submitted that its recommendations do not go far enough to fully address this issue. This can be seen in four respects. Firstly, although it urges the UK to encourage men to share responsibility for childcare, it does not give sufficient emphasis to this crucial issue. Until men do in fact share responsibility for childcare equally with women, there will not be true equality in the labour market. Increasing paid maternity leave without ensuring that equal rights are provided for fathers will entrench the expectation that it is mothers who take paid leave. Conversely, providing more paid childcare facilities, while important, also reinforces the view that women should conform to male working patterns, rather than that paid work and family work should be reconciled. While the UK has taken some small steps in this direction, they are not sufficient.

The insufficiency of these steps can be seen by considering the right to request flexible working arrangements. The Committee referred with approval to the flexible working arrangements in the Work and Families Act 2006.[41] This permits an employee to request the employer to change her working conditions in order to care for a child or adult. However, this is not a right. The employer may refuse the request for a variety of reasons, such as the burden of additional costs, the detrimental effect on the ability to meet customer demand, inability to reorganise work among existing staff, inability to recruit additional staff, detrimental impact on quality, detrimental impact on performance, insufficiency of work during the periods the employee proposes to work or planned structural changes. This provision has had some success. New research from the Government Equalities Office shows that of those employees making requests, 81 per cent had been granted. However, only 30 per cent of working parents have made such a request, meaning that only 24.3 per cent have in fact benefited from the right. This might be because they are not aware of the right: one-third of working parents are not aware that they are entitled to request flexible working, and only 12 per cent are aware that the right has been extended to all parents of children up to the age of 16. Of even more concern is the fact that parents perceive the request as potentially having negative effects, with as many as 33 per cent concerned that they would appear to be lacking in commitment to the job if they made such a request.[42] But particularly problematic is the absence of figures as to the uptake by fathers as against mothers. It is submitted that the CEDAW

[41] *Ibid.*

[42] Department of Work and Pensions, *Building Britain's Recovery: Achieving Full Employment* (Cm 7751, The Stationery Office, 2009) at 96.

Committee should have insisted that figures be provided for fathers' take-up, and that proper targets and benchmarks be provided by the UK to show progress in this direction.

The second problematic aspect of the Committee's recommendations under Article 11 is that, having challenged the UK government over its understanding of equality as limited to equal opportunities, the Committee reverts to the notion of equal opportunities. Although it also calls for special measures and concrete measures, this dilution of the notion of substantive equality is worrying. Here too, the Committee should require proper targets and benchmarks, to prevent States Parties from making vague and general assertions about progress.

The third problematic aspect of the Committee's response is its approach to the pay gap. Although the Committee noted with concern that the pay gap in the UK was one of the highest in Europe, it relied on figures showing that the average hourly earnings of full-time women employees amount to approximately 83 per cent of men's earnings. However, this fails to highlight the true extent of the problem. Headline statistics on the current extent of the gender pay gap tend to take the most optimistic figure available, namely the median pay gap for full-time workers, based on hourly pay excluding overtime. *Framework for Fairness*, the report of the Discrimination Law Review on which the new Equalities Bill is based, states with some pride that the gap narrowed to its lowest value since records began, reaching 12.6 per cent in 2007.[43] According to the Office for National Statistics, the gap narrowed to 10.2 per cent in 2010.[44] But this figure vastly understates the true extent of the problem. As a start, official usage has shifted to the median instead of the customary mean. Reverting to the mean reveals a significantly higher gap, namely 15.5 per cent in 2010.[45] This means that the mean pay gap has narrowed by approximately 20 per cent since 1975, the year in which the Equal Pay Act of 1970 was brought into force.[46] The Office for National Statistics explains that the median is now used because high earners tend to skew the earnings distribution, raising the mean. It is not clear, however, why the fact that high

[43] Discrimination Law Review, *A Framework for Fairness* at 53.

[44] R. Pike, 'Patterns of pay: results of the Annual Survey of Hours and Earnings 1997–2010', *Economic & Labour Market Review* 4:3 (2010) 14–40 at 14.

[45] *Ibid.* at 21. This is a slight reduction on the mean pay gap of 16.4 per cent reported in 2009. See C. Halsworth, 'Patterns of pay: results of the Annual Survey of Hours and Earnings 1997–2009', *Economic & Labour Market Review* 4:3 (2010) 59–70 at 62.

[46] D. Perfect, *Gender Pay Gaps*, Briefing Paper 2, EHRC (2011) at 7, available at: www.equalityhumanrights.com/uploaded_files/research/gender_pay_gap_briefing_paper2.pdf (last accessed 19 February 2013).

earners are predominantly male should not be reflected in the overall figure. This is all the more so since the overall figure masks wide differences in the gender pay gap in respect of different types of jobs. In 2010 the mean gap in skilled trades was 26 per cent, compared with the smaller gap of 4.2 per cent for professional occupations.[47]

Moreover, to gain a full picture of the true gender gap, it is necessary to look well beyond hourly pay of full-time workers excluding overtime. Full-time male employees consistently earn a greater proportion of additional payments than their female counterparts. Particularly disturbing are the figures for part-time workers, where the median gap between part-time women's pay and full-time men's pay was a scandalous 39.4 per cent in 2009, a gap which seems to have widened since 2007 when it was 39.1 per cent.[48] While the earnings of full-time women have been rising relative to men's earnings, recent research points out that the gap between full-time women and their part-time counterparts (the 'part-time pay penalty') has widened since 1975.[49] The part-time pay penalty was 31.1 per cent in 2008.[50] Given that 74 per cent of all part-time employees are women, and that approximately 43 per cent of women workers in the UK work part-time (as against only 12 per cent of men), any measure tackling the pay gap must pay particular attention to part-time workers.[51]

Nor is women's pay inequality limited to their time in the paid workforce. It extends into retirement. Only 30 per cent of women reaching state pension age are entitled to a full basic state pension, compared with 85 per cent of men.[52] But the widest gender gap in retirement income is caused by differential access to private and occupational pensions. According to

[47] Pike, 'Patterns of pay' at 29.

[48] Office for National Statistics, 'Annual Survey of Hours and Earnings' (2009) at 4, available at: www.ons.gov.uk/ons/rel/ashe/annual-survey-of-hours-and-earnings/2009-revised/index.html (last accessed 19 February 2013). The Office for National Statistics no longer presents statistics on the median pay gap between part-time women's pay and full-time men's pay; see Pike, 'Patterns of pay' at 19.

[49] A. Manning and B. Petrongolo, 'The part-time pay penalty for women in Britain', *Economic Journal* 118:526 (2008) F28 –F51 at F35.

[50] C. Dobbs, 'Patterns of pay: results of the Annual Survey of Hours and Earnings, 1997 to 2008' *Economic & Labour Market Review* 3:3 (2009) 24–32.

[51] Statistics derived from the UK Labour Market Statistics, January 2012, see Office for National Statistics, 'Labour Market Statistics' (2012) at 7, available at: www.ons.gov.uk/ons/dcp171778_250593.pdf (last accessed 19 February 2013). See further S. Connolly and M. Gregory, 'The part-time pay penalty: earnings trajectories of British women', *Oxford Economic Papers* 61:1 (2008) i76 –i97 at i76.

[52] M. Sargeant, 'Gender equality and the Pensions Acts 2007–2008', *Industrial L. J.* 38:1 (2009) 143–8 at 143.

new figures from the Prudential Class of 2010 retirement survey, women planning to retire in 2010 expect to receive an average annual pension of £12,169, a mere 62 per cent of the average pension of their male counterparts, who expect to collect an average pension of £19,593. And the pension income gender gap has widened by £782 since 2009 when the difference between men's and women's pensions was £6,642.[53] Women working part-time are at the greatest risk of having an employer who does not offer a pension scheme.[54] And many women are left out of the pension system altogether, among them a disproportionate number of ethnic minority women.[55]

The causes of the pay gap are complex. As the Committee itself noted, occupational segregation is a major factor. Women are still concentrated in lower-paying occupations, with nearly two-thirds of women employed in twelve occupation groups, most of which are related to women's traditional roles in the family – caring, cashiering, catering, cleaning and clerical occupations, as well as teaching, health associate professionals (including nurses), and 'functional' managers, such as financial managers, marketing and sales managers, and personnel managers.[56] Other structural factors include the gender skills gap, particularly for older women, because there is less access to training in the lower-paid sectors where more women than men tend to work.[57] But most important is the fact that women remain primarily responsible for childcare. Taking time out of the labour market, amassing less experience, limitations in respect of travel to work, and part-time working, all extract a severe wage penalty.

[53] Prudential, *Pension Gap Between Men and Women Grows* (2010), available at: www.pru.co.uk/pdf/presscenter/pension_gap_grows.pdf (last accessed 19 February 2013).

[54] Department for Work and Pensions, *Women and Pensions: The Evidence* (2005) at 9, available at: www.dwp.gov.uk/docs/women-pensions.pdf (last accessed 19 February 2013). Excluding part-time employees from occupational pension schemes may result in indirect discrimination on the basis of gender; see Pension Advisory Service, *Women and Pensions* (2008) at 25, available at: www.pensionsadvisoryservice.org.uk/media/109/women%20pensions%20-%20september%202009.pdf (last accessed 19 February 2013). A reform is currently in the works under the Pensions Act 2008, which will involve automatic contributions for employees between the age of 22 and retirement age and earning more than £5,035 a year (this figure will increase in time); see Department for Work and Pensions, *Automatic Saving: Changing Workplace Pensions* (2009), available at: www.dwp.gov.uk/docs/automatic-savings-changing-workplace-pensions-nov09.pdf (last accessed 19 February 2013).

[55] *Ibid.* at 10.

[56] Women and Work Commission, *Shaping a Fairer Future* (2006), para. 8.

[57] *Ibid.* paras. 3–27. See further National Skills Forum, *Closing the Gender Skills Gap* (2009), http://www.policyconnect.org.uk/fckimages/Closing%20the%20Gender%20Skills%20Gap.pdf (last accessed 6 March 2013).

The limitations of the Committee's report, however, go beyond its underestimation of the true extent of the wage gap. They extend too to its recommendations. As we have seen, it recommended that the state take proactive and concrete measures to eliminate occupational segregation and to close the pay gap between women and men, in particular through the introduction of mandatory pay audits. Here too the Committee might have been more effective had it been more prescriptive, requiring the UK to set targets and benchmarks. Particularly helpful would have been a recommendation that the UK put in place more effective equal pay legislation, going well beyond mandatory pay audits. The current legislative framework, which depends on individuals enforcing an individual right to equal pay for work of equal value, has not delivered equal pay for various well-chronicled reasons. The new Equality Act does little to improve matters. As a result of pressure from trade unions and activists, the Labour government in power until 2010 did make a small gesture towards mandatory pay audits, but only for employers with over 250 employees. Thus the Equality Act includes a provision giving the Secretary of State power to produce regulations requiring employers with more than 250 employees to publish information about the pay gap in their enterprises.[58] However, the current Coalition government has refused to bring this provision into force, arguing that 'it is working with business on how to best support increased transparency on a voluntary basis'.[59] The result is that the only innovation in the Equality Act is a provision making it unlawful for an employer to prevent employees from discussing their pay with each other where this relates to the gender pay gap.[60] Also problematic is the fact that even the lightweight Gender Equality Duty is being rolled back. Under the Gender Equality Duty, a public employer was required, 'in formulating its gender equality objectives, to consider the need to have objectives to address the causes of any gender pay gap'.[61] However, the Coalition government has decided to remove these specific duties and replace them with no more than a general transparency requirement. Under the new regulation, public bodies will simply have to publish information showing

[58] Equality Act 2010, section 78.

[59] EHRC, *What is the Equality Act?* (2011), available at: www.equalityhumanrights.com/legal-and-policy/equality-act/what-is-the-equality-act/ (last accessed 19 February 2013).

[60] Equality Act 2010, section 77.

[61] Sex Discrimination Act 1975 (Public Authorities) (Statutory Duties) Order 2006, para. 2(5).

how they have complied with their general duty to pay due regard to the need to eliminate discrimination, including pay discrimination.[62]

8 Conclusion

There seems little prospect in the UK of the CEDAW emerging from the shadows. While the UK has, of its own initiative, taken important steps towards gender equality, these have been taken without any genuine normative input from the CEDAW. Real change in the role of the CEDAW in the UK requires the CEDAW Committee to take a more incisive position, both in its Concluding Observations and in its developing jurisprudence under the Optional Protocol. The need for such an approach has added urgency since 2010, with the election of a government determined to make swingeing cuts in public provision and with little commitment to advancing equality legislation. Budget cuts have already had a particularly deleterious effect on women in the UK, and the government has unilaterally decided not to bring into force key aspects of the new equality legislation. This is despite the fact that such legislation was duly passed by Parliament. It is in such a climate that international human rights law, and particularly the CEDAW, should be in a position to play a central role.

[62] Equality Act, section 149(1); Equality Act 2010 (Statutory Duties) Regulations 2011, section 2.

19

Domestication of the CEDAW in France: from paradoxes to ambivalences and back again

HÉLÈNE RUIZ FABRI AND ANDREA HAMANN

1 Introduction

Who knows about the Convention on the Elimination of All Forms of Discrimination against Women (CEDAW) in France? Very few people.[1] Who uses the CEDAW in France? Even fewer. And yet France has been a party to the Convention for almost thirty years, after a rather smooth ratification process involving both Houses of Parliament and the executive branch. During the Parliamentary discussion of the draft legislation to authorize the ratification of the Convention by the president,[2] a member of the National Assembly in strong support of the ratification even firmly stated that the time had indeed come for France, home country of human rights, to also become the home country of women's rights. The double meaning of this seemingly positive statement is revealed when considered in its original French,[3] where the notion of 'human rights' translates into 'droits de l'homme' and where 'homme' means in general 'human', but also and more commonly 'man'. The French language, including that of human rights, thus uncovers the first and original bias against women. French grammar and vocabulary are indeed strongly gendered, and it remains common that job titles for most positions of power are

[1] Quite significantly, both on the notoriety of the Convention and present-day vectors of communication, see the Facebook group 'Savez-vous ce qu'est la CEDAW?' ('Do you know what the CEDAW is?') – which counted one member. See www.facebook.com/topic.php?uid=122179016387&topic=9918 (last accessed 30 August 2011).

[2] These Acts of Parliament do not amount in themselves to ratification acts of international instruments, but authorize the executive branch to ratify (president) or approve (government) the relevant instrument.

[3] '... pour que la France, après avoir été le pays des droits de l'homme, devienne aussi, enfin, celui des droits de la femme'. See Yvette Roudy, Minister Delegate for Women's Rights, Assemblée nationale, 1st meeting of 27 June 1983, at 3257.

expressed in their masculine versions, even when a woman occupies the position. Opting for the feminine wording of professional titles very often provokes reactions and comments on the lack of elegance or the strangeness these feminized titles supposedly carry. This original bias is so deeply entrenched in minds and mentalities that it takes not only legislation and other policy measures, but also no less than a soft revolution of mindsets to overrule or erase ancient stereotypes and to succeed in conceiving a truly equal notion of equality.

However, assessing the CEDAW's formal and real status in French law and practice raises methodological questions. Putting the issue into context indeed requires taking into account what is often referred to as French 'exceptionalism' or 'specificity', understood as the influence of republicanism, universalism and even anti-Americanism.[4] The claim of specificity should not and must not become a systematic explanation in order to justify being exempted from providing any kind of argument, but, at the same time, one cannot ignore and disregard that this specificity does indeed exist and must therefore be adequately acknowledged as part and parcel of the dominant French legal culture.

This specificity is one of the multiple sources of the equally multiple layers of paradoxes and ambivalences that characterize the French perception and understanding of and dealing with the issue of women's rights, which inevitably reverberates on the perception and understanding of and dealing with (i.e. domesticating) the CEDAW.

It is therefore useful to begin by reflecting on the general context – social, cultural, political and legal – in France, in order to grasp more comprehensively the paradoxes and ambivalences at stake, and to perceive the slow process of persuasion that is at work in order to impose the legitimacy of a gendered discourse on the domestic scene (section 2). This more fine-tuned perception and assessment will in turn provide useful guidance in understanding the current status of the domestication of the CEDAW in France. First, it sheds a tinted light on a complete and smooth ratification process, coupled with long-standing and sometimes puzzling reservations (section 3). Moreover, even if the theme of equality between women and men is increasingly present on the political and legal scene,

[4] Significantly, even in academia the common and widespread reaction when feminist approaches to law are mentioned is to consider these to be typically Anglo-Saxon themes and concerns, thereby conveying the impression that France is shielded against these issues. For comments from the French side, see H. Ruiz Fabri and E. Jouannet (eds.), *Féminisme et droit international* (Paris: Collection de l'UMR de droit comparé, Edn. SLC, forthcoming).

regarding domestic implementation the overriding observation is, quite simply, that of a quasi-invisibility of the instrument in the domestic legal sphere (section 4). It goes without saying that the invisibility of an international instrument strongly suggests that the provisions it contains do not reach the individuals it is designed for, and thus points to a general lack of direct effect in the domestic legal order.

2 Contextualization: a troubled process of 'persuasion'

France is a developed Western country whose global social context is not necessarily one of the most problematic towards the CEDAW, a factual observation from which one should nevertheless be careful not to deduce that the situation regarding women and their equal rights is satisfactory in general. But whatever is done – or not done – is not only difficult to connect to the CEDAW, whose implementation tracks require a rather voluntaristic investigation (see below), but is also difficult to place in a common framework. This is to say, that if and when policies aimed at dealing with women's rights are designed and implemented, they nevertheless do not belong to any kind of policy conceived in a unified way, and especially not to an approach based on the idea of gender mainstreaming.[5]

It is noteworthy in this regard that gender mainstreaming is absent from the discourse in France and, probably even more significantly, that the very notion does not translate into French.[6] This is not to say, however,

[5] As understood, for instance, by the UN Economic and Social Council: 'Mainstreaming a gender perspective is the process of assessing the implications for women and men of any planned action, including legislation, policies and programmes, in all areas and at all levels. It is a strategy for making women's as well as men's concerns and experiences an integral part of the design, implementation, monitoring and evaluation of policies and programmes in all political, economic and societal spheres so that women and men benefit equally and inequality is not perpetuated. The ultimate goal is to achieve gender equality' (*Report of the UN Economic and Social Council for 1997*, A/52/3, 18 September 1997, Chapter IV). See also Council of Europe, *Gender Mainstreaming: Conceptual Framework, Methodology and Presentation of Good Practices*, Final Report of the Group of Specialists on Mainstreaming 1998 EG-S-MS (98) 2 rev., available at: www.coe.int/t/dghl/standard-setting/equality/03themes/gender-mainstreaming/EG_S_MS_98_2_rev_En.pdf (last accessed 19 February 2013). Article 8 of the Treaty on the Functioning of the European Union provides that 'In all its activities, the Union shall eliminate inequalities, and promote equality, between men and women.'

[6] The most common translation is through a long expression: 'intégration des politiques d'égalité entre hommes et femmes' or 'intégration de la dimension de genre'. These expressions are not very meaningful at first sight and require further explanation. They have not reached everyday language. Significantly, *Eurovoc*, the Multilingual Thesaurus of Europe, does not provide any proper translation.

that gender mainstreaming does not occur or is not implemented. At the very least, it is sometimes referred to by government officials when justifying certain policies, especially at the international level where the notion operates as a buzzword and an inescapable part of its vocabulary. But from there to deducing that it might have become a leading idea or a clear political and policy-building choice is a very big step, and currently still too big a step. Therefore, depending on the issue at stake, there can be discrepancies and interferences. It is for this reason that we focus so insistently on paradoxes and ambivalences, neither pretending that a similar situation does not exist elsewhere but simply that it is distinctly perceivable in France, nor providing a full and exhaustive account of this situation, but rather some revealing insights.

First, it is noteworthy that the early 1980s saw the creation of a Ministry specifically devoted to women's rights.[7] This was a spectacular initiative; however, it did not take place in a vacuum since, especially since the mid 1970s, several structures dedicated to policies concerning women had already been set up. However, the permanency of such structures goes together with the instability of their status and the variability of their prominence on the political agenda. In this regard, a major aspect of context lies in the observation that structures and policies strongly depend on the political majority in power and, if it is obvious that the right wing cannot repudiate a cause such as the advancement of women's rights, it is also just as obvious that their enthusiasm for and commitment to this issue is less than that of the left wing,[8] and that the approach taken is much more conservative.

More generally speaking, however, the cultural environment is not particularly favourable for, on the one hand, an approach centred around issues regarding women – there has been long-standing resistance to such issues and the acknowledgment of the legitimacy of the related discourse

[7] Until May 2012 it was to be compared to a situation where, among the institutional mechanisms in charge of promoting women's rights and equality was the Minister delegated to Social Cohesion and Parity, attached to the Ministry of Employment, Social Cohesion and Housing. In order to fulfil her mission, the Minister has at her disposal a Service of Women's Rights and Equality. This Service was the only (amputated) remainder of the former Ministry of Women's Rights. This Ministry was set up again in May 2012.

[8] It has been observed that out of the twelve major reforms implemented between 1967 (legislation on birth control, which can be taken as a starting point) and 2001, eleven were supported by the left wing while the right wing only supported two. See J. Mossuz-Lavau, *Les lois de l'amour: les politiques de la sexualité en France 1950–2002* (Paris: Payot, 2002) at 409. Also see G. Allwood and K. Wadia (eds.), *Gender and Policy in France* (Basingstoke: Palgrave Macmillan, 2010) at 16.

is only very recent – and, on the other hand, an approach centred around the issue of non-discrimination or discrimination. There is indeed strong resistance in France to any notion of affirmative action as well as of positive discrimination, which is to be linked to the French idea of equality, an idea that, incidentally, does not necessarily match the sociology of a society that continues to dwell on a logic of privileges.

The French legal and political culture is indeed not spontaneously favourable to pushing to the foreground specific issues related to women, especially when these issues are raised in terms of rights. This is intrinsically related or even due to the French approach to universalism, which has led to the construction of a 'universal subject', regardless of gender or any other factor marking a specific social identity. The result of this approach is a strongly anchored resistance to any notion of affirmative action.[9] This does not mean that affirmative action does not exist. It means, however, that the very idea struggles to impose and establish its legitimacy. This might account for the somewhat original path chosen in France and consisting of translating equality into parity, as the meeting point between the necessity to develop the presence of women in powerful or decision-making positions in particular and the French understanding of equality. This path might even appear as being more radical than many affirmative action devices, unless one pays attention to how it is actually implemented. Thus, one must perforce acknowledge that the French discourse on parity promises much more than what the implementation of the parity devices brings about concretely. For instance, as regards political representation, parity concerns candidacy but not the actual positions after election. To this must be added that the sanctions for non-compliance seem not to be particularly dissuasive, especially for big political factions. In any event, the idea of parity – like that of affirmative action – provokes deaf resistance focused on the view that gender should be irrelevant. The reason is not only that the notions of affirmative

[9] Compare this to the situation in Germany, where the positions regarding affirmative action remain contrasted due to the unclear interpretation of Article 3 of the Basic Law, as amended in 1994 (some arguing that this Article allows for affirmative action, others arguing against this view). For an insightful presentation of the German approach to affirmative action (notably the private sector/public sector divide), see A. J. Stock, 'Affirmative action: a German perspective on the promotion of women's rights with regard to employment', *Journal of Law and Society* 33:1 (2006) 59–73; and M. Zuleeg, 'Gender equality and affirmative action under the law of the European Union', *Columbia Journal of European Law* 5 (1998–1999) 319–28. Also see the two European Court of Justice cases *Kalanke* v. *Freie Hansestadt Bremen* 17 October 1995, C-450/93, 1995 ECR I-3051 and *Marschall* v. *Land Nordrhein-Westphalen* 11 November 1997, C-409/95, 1997 ECR I-6363.

action or parity conflict with the alleged neutrality of universalism in terms of gender, but also the fact, largely and easily demonstrated, that this neutrality is biased, if only because women remain very largely underrepresented in decision-making spheres and processes. Suffice it to mention that despite the legislation on parity, for which, spectacularly, a constitutional amendment was necessary,[10] France remains at the 63rd rank regarding the proportion of women in Parliament (18.9 per cent in the House of Representatives and 21.9 per cent in the Senate).[11]

Moreover, the reactions are split into two major trends. On the one hand, some try to accommodate the French political culture with a gendered approach by promoting the idea that the gender-based difference is different from other differences and would be the only one compatible with the traditional universalism. But others denounce this kind of thought as being based on essentialism and, more practically, as leading to a victimizing approach on women's issues. In fact, depending on the issue at stake, the approach could vary deeply, or at least there can be two competing approaches. For instance, abortion could be analyzed from the angle of the right of women over their bodies (in other words, women's right to choose), but could also be presented as a necessary answer to an important and costly social need due to the still-high number of unwanted pregnancies. Multiple, simultaneous and overlapping approaches are not necessarily incompatible, but at the same time they do not imply the same degree of involvement in the given answer. The approach to domestic violence, for example, can differ greatly depending on whether the aim is to reduce such violence on the basis of the human and social cost it generates, or whether the aim is not only to eradicate domestic violence to the largest extent possible but to purely and simply render it inconceivable. In all these regards, France appears to stand on the minimalistic side, although this does not mean to say that nothing is being done.

Indeed, a feminist influence definitely does exist. But, then again, it is important to grasp its springs and specificities. Although there have been feminist actions or claims with wide media coverage in order to boost or achieve certain reforms, media action remains overall relatively rare and occurs only in waves. The common perception tends to associate

[10] See Constitutional Act No. 99–569 of 8 July 1999 on equality between men and women, which adds a paragraph to Article 3 of the 1958 Constitution according to which the law promotes equal access of women and men to electoral mandates and elective functions.

[11] See Inter-Parliamentary Union (2011), *Women in National Parliaments: Situation as of 31 January 2011*, available at: www.ipu.org/wmn-e/classif.htm (last accessed 19 February 2013).

feminism with hysteria, and the very notion of 'feminism' is not promoted in France.[12] In truth, it even has a negative connotation. This state of things cannot but provide a feedback on the modes of action embraced by feminist movements. Several tendencies need to be signalled in this respect. The first is that, in order to allow the cause to gain ground, French feminist movements have not necessarily deemed it efficient to formulate questions in properly feminist terms; as if it were more operative, in certain situations, to proceed in a manner, if not exactly concealed, at least not openly admitted by incorporating the issue into a more global perspective[13] or a different approach (see above). The result is the absence of a felt need to point out and deal with the issue in 'feminist' terms. This can at least partly explain why there are so few shadow reports on the CEDAW in France.[14] Another tendency is that of a State-centred feminism or even a 'State feminism'. Two factors nurture this trend: one is that, although it is well known that legal changes largely depend on changes in mindsets, feminist movements partly turn their claims towards the State and law-making processes. The other is that it is for the State to face and bear the commitments resulting from European and international law and to implement them at the domestic level. But one could easily get the impression that the pressure is generated more by a necessity not to lose face at the international level rather than by internal pressures to confront and abide by international obligations.[15]

Ultimately, these observations point back to the initial and overarching one, that is that the CEDAW is little known, if at all. One last contextual aspect relating to the legal culture and system must nevertheless be emphasized, considering that it largely contributes to accounting for the lack of visibility or recourse to the Convention in France. Indeed, the openness of the French legal culture and system to international law in general, and especially to a 'global' law, is very limited, although the situation has evolved progressively. The priority is systematically given to domestic law and to the French Constitution, which are thus the primary

[12] In 'Quel féminisme aujourd'hui?', *Le Monde*, 16 July 2011, Joy Sorman states: 'le mot "féminisme" sent désormais la naphtaline ou … est assimilé à un mot d'ordre agressif', meaning that the word is felt either to be outdated or aggressive. See also the Introduction in C. Guionnet and E. Neveu, *Féminins/masculins, sociologie du genre*, 2nd edn (Paris: Armand Colin, 2009) at 12–30.

[13] Allwood and Wadia, *Gender and Policy in France* at 15.

[14] The only one available online is: *Coordination française pour le Lobby européen des femmes, Rapport alternatif 2007 sur la France*, available at: www2.ohchr.org/english/bodies/cedaw/docs/ngos/CLEF_fr.pdf (last accessed 26 February 2013).

[15] See section 4 below.

legal tools used by a domestic court. And although the legal system has progressively opened up to international law – a recent phenomenon qualified very positively as *Völkerrechtsfreundlichkeit* in Germany (i.e. friendliness to international law) and more neutrally as 'openness to international law' in France – preference and priority are given to general instruments. This, in turn, must also be related to the phenomenon of European law, which plays a predominant role and gives an important impetus in all European Union (EU) countries, and which explains the priority of European texts over global instruments. European law thus creates a 'shield' against general international law, which has to be related to the relative efficiency and accessibility of safeguard mechanisms. Moreover, considering specifically international law instruments, the purpose of a specific instrument targeting specific issues falls short because of the preference given to more general but better-known instruments. The added efficiency in human rights protection that the CEDAW could bring about is clearly not obvious, although the CEDAW could be considered as providing a more extended protection – at least in normative terms – in fields such as protection against violence, gender stereotyping or family name.

In this context, one cannot but notice several discrepancies. The first can be observed between what is officially presented and how it is presented to the CEDAW Committee,[16] and the actual visibility of the CEDAW on the domestic political and legal scene. In this regard, it is for instance noteworthy that there has never been a Committee decision against France based on the communications procedure provided for by Article 2 of the 1999 Optional Protocol, which speaks to the absence of transparency of the CEDAW as an accessible legal tool in France,[17] although this is not a major specificity if one notices the very low number of cases submitted to the Committee in general. But, more importantly, there is a sharp discrepancy between the highly developed and ample legal arsenal in France and its (lack of) practical efficiency, which might generally be accounted for by the lack of means allocated to the adopted policies.

[16] See periodical reports to the Committee and auditions of France before the Committee (see section 4 below).

[17] There has been one case against France, which has been considered inadmissible. See Communication 12/2007, *SOS Sexisme c/ France*, CEDAW/C/44/D/12/2007 about the legal impossibility for married women to transmit their name to their children.

3 Ratification and reservations: wavering between 'sense and sensibility'

The ratification of the CEDAW by France occurred relatively soon after its adoption and entry into force, which, significantly, coincided with a political shift bringing the Socialist Party to the forefront. In this new political context, historical in the trajectory of the Fifth Republic, the ratification of the CEDAW in itself has not raised any difficulties, but must, at the same time, be put into perspective to take due note of the underlying sensibilities. Assessing the smooth ratification of the CEDAW is indeed not an easy task and reveals ambivalent postures vis-à-vis the Convention. On the one hand, the most positive interpretation of the fluent ratification process is the general lack of reluctance towards the Convention. On the other hand, another plausible path is the relative indifference of France towards the instrument. This relative indifference can be explained on several grounds, one being the general perception that the Convention does not impose any direct obligations on France other than that of submitting periodical reports to the CEDAW Committee, and another being the fact that the overall context in France is certainly not hostile towards the issue of women's rights. However, amidst this relative indifference, the perception is that the main interest of being a party to the Convention lies in the pull effect the CEDAW could trigger for future policy measures even if, ultimately, the general understanding remains that the instrument is first and foremost directed at developing countries.[18] And yet it is also precisely this understanding that prompts an almost virtuous cycle, the underlying idea being that of exemplarity, of a duty for developed countries to participate in the system in order to give the necessary impulses and keep it alive.

A new layer of paradoxes, a wavering between making sense and protecting domestic sensibilities, thus reveals itself when one examines

[18] The debates in the French Parliament in relation to the ratification by France of the CEDAW exemplify perfectly this perception. See Draft Legislation No. 1514 authorizing the ratification of the Convention on the Elimination of All Forms of Discrimination against Women – Senate (1st reading), No. 225 (1982–1983), submitted on 12 April 1983 by M. Pierre Mauroy, Prime Minister, Return to the Commission of Foreign Affairs, Defense and Armed Forces, Rapporteur: M. Gérard Gaud, Report No. 254 (1982–1983) (20 April 1983), Discussion on 17 May 1983, Adoption on 17 May 1983; and Draft Legislation No. 104 (1982–1983) – Assemblée nationale (1st reading), No. 1514, submitted on 18 May 1983, Return to the Commission of Foreign Affairs, Rapporteur: Mme Paulette Nevoux (19 May 1983), Report No. 1565 (9 June 1983), Discussion on 27 June 1983, Adoption on 27 June 1983.

France's ratification of the CEDAW. The ratification process, indeed, appears to have been quick, fluent and smooth, but the attached reservations already shed a tinted light on the approach to and the perception of the Convention.

3.1 *Constitutional context and ratification process*

Article 55 of the French Constitution draws rather clear lines regarding international treaties and traces a monist frame regarding their integration into the domestic legal order. According to this provision, and under the condition that they are introduced into the domestic legal order in accordance with the necessary formalities, international treaties and agreements acquire a normative force superior to that of Acts of Parliament. Despite the long-standing resistance of some courts, notably the Conseil d'État, Acts of Parliament can be subject to judicial review regarding their compatibility with international treaties, at any given time and during any given case.[19] The tricky issue, however, remains whether the judge considers the Convention to be directly invocable by individuals. In this regard, one cannot but be struck by the insistence, during the Parliamentary debates relating to the ratification of the CEDAW, on the absence of direct obligations imposed by the Convention,[20] which is another way to emphasize its non self-executing character. Obviously, this

[19] However, this applies only to civil and administrative jurisdictions (see for instance Conseil d'État, 5 January 2005, *Mlle Deprez et M. Baillard*). Indeed, the Constitutional Court has, in a famous 1975 decision, refused to review the compatibility of Acts of Parliament with international treaty provisions, passing over this task to civil and administrative courts (see Conseil constitutionnel, *Interruption volontaire de grossesse*, Decision No. 74–54 DC, 15 January 1975). The recent introduction of the procedure of priority preliminary rulings on the issue of constitutionality (*question prioritaire de constitutionnalité* – introduced by the constitutional reform of 23 July 2008, which entered into force on this particular aspect on 1 March 2010) provoked debates and hesitations on a possible change of attitude by the Constitutional Council, but the constitutional judges have strongly reaffirmed and confirmed their position of refusal to exercise a 'conventionality review' (*contrôle de conventionnalité*) in the case *Loi relative à l'ouverture à la concurrence et à la regulation du secteur des jeux d'argent et de hasard en ligne* (Conseil constitutionnel, Decision No. 2010–605 DC, 12 May 2010).

[20] This aspect was emphasized by both Houses during the discussions: see Assemblée nationale, 1st session of 27 June 1983, at 3256 ('certains ont pu regretter que la générosité de ses dispositions puisse être compromise par l'absence d'obligation directe pour les Etats membres' – some may regret that the generosity of its provisions might be compromised by the lack of direct obligations for States Parties); Sénat, session of 17 May 1983, at 837 ('les Etats n'ont pas d'obligations directes et immédiates du fait de la Convention' – States have no direct and immediate obligations imposed by the Convention).

posture does not force the judge to refuse the invocation of CEDAW provisions by individuals. However, it does not contribute to encouraging the judge to accept such invocation easily. The resulting case law thus appears rather chaotic, inconsistent and, in some instances, even plainly open to criticism.[21]

France signed the Convention on 17 July 1980, but the subsequent ratification of international treaties and agreements is submitted to the rules laid out by Articles 52–5 of the Constitution. If the ratification in itself remains a presidential prerogative, certain treaties nevertheless require a prior authorization by the Parliament. Article 53 thus provides that certain categories of treaties, including those relating to the status of persons, may be ratified only by virtue of an Act of Parliament. A draft legislation was therefore elaborated and subsequently discussed in both Houses of Parliament, the National Assembly and the Senate.[22] Both Houses unproblematically approved the draft, although the approaches diverged and the discussions had different orientations. The Act of Parliament authorizing the president to ratify the CEDAW, adopted on 27 June 1983, was promulgated on 1 July 1983,[23] and the president subsequently ratified the Convention on 14 December 1983. Consistent with Article 27(2) of the Convention, the CEDAW entered into force for France on 13 January 1984, and consistent with Article 55 of the French Constitution, henceforth supersedes Acts of Parliament but is superseded by constitutional provisions.[24]

This smooth ratification process, all the more noticeable since France was the first EU country to ratify the CEDAW, must, however, not overshadow the fact that France took several precautions at the time of

[21] See below subsection 4.1.

[22] See Draft Legislation No. 1514 authorizing the ratification of the Convention on the Elimination of All Forms of Discrimination against Women – Senate (1st reading), No. 225 (1982–1983), submitted on 12 April 1983 by M. Pierre Mauroy, Prime Minister, Return to the Commission of Foreign Affairs, Defense and Armed Forces, Rapporteur: M. Gérard Gaud, Report No. 254 (1982–1983) (20 April 1983), Discussion on 17 May 1983, Adoption on 17 May 1983; and Draft Legislation No. 104 (1982–1983) – Assemblée nationale (1st reading), No. 1514, submitted on 18 May 1983, Return to the Commission of Foreign Affairs, Rapporteur: Mme Paulette Nevoux (19 May 1983), Report No. 1565 (9 June 1983), Discussion on 27 June 1983, Adoption on 27 June 1983.

[23] Act of Parliament No. 83–561 of 1 July 1983, published in the *Journal officiel de la République française* (*JORF*) on 2 July 1983 (at 2011).

[24] See for instance Conseil d'État, Assemblée, *Sarran, Levacher et autres*, 30 October 1998; Cour de cassation, Assemblée plénière, *Me Pauline Fraisse*, 2 June 2000. Both Courts laid down the now well-established and uncontested principle that the supremacy of international treaties and agreements in the domestic legal order does not extend to constitutional provisions.

ratification, by introducing a certain number of declarations and reservations to the Convention. These declarations and reservations were smoothed over by the justification that the Convention should not be allowed to undo certain more favourable policy measures that were already in place in France. It is noteworthy in this respect that most reservations have since then been withdrawn, once the adjustment reforms were completed. In other words, certain reservations were unquestionably motivated by reasons of political opportunism, which, however and importantly, were not intended to cover up inaction.

3.2 *Declarations and reservations*

Although Article 28 of the Convention allows States to make reservations as long as they are compatible with the object and purpose of the instrument, a large number of States including France have made reservations going against the very object of the Convention, thereby depriving certain provisions of their intended efficiency. France's declarations and reservations nevertheless appear for the most part unproblematic – even if they can be puzzling – but they nevertheless require explanation and contextualization.

3.2.1 Declarations

The Government of France has, for instance, declared that 'the preamble to the Convention in particular the eleventh preambular paragraph contains debatable elements which are definitely out of place in this text'.[25] To understand this declaration, one must realize that this paragraph contains all the buzzwords (nuclear disarmament, colonial domination and so on)[26] that are likely to spark off strong reactions in the French political

[25] CEDAW, Meeting of States Parties to the CEDAW, 14th Meeting, 23 June 2006, Item 6 on the provisional agenda: 'Declarations, reservations, objections and notifications of withdrawal of reservations relating to the Convention on the Elimination of All Forms of Discrimination against Women', CEDAW/SP/2006/2 at 12–13. English version available at: http://daccess-dds-ny.un.org/doc/UNDOC/GEN/N06/309/97/PDF/N0630997.pdf?OpenElement (last accessed 26 February 2013).

[26] In the eleventh paragraph of the Preamble, the States Parties '[affirm] that the strengthening of international peace and security, the relaxation of international tension, mutual co-operation among all States irrespective of their social and economic systems, general and complete disarmament, in particular nuclear disarmament under strict and effective international control, the affirmation of the principles of justice, equality and mutual benefit in relations among countries and the realization of the right of peoples under alien and colonial domination and foreign occupation to self-determination and independence, as well as respect for national sovereignty and territorial integrity, will

sphere and media, regardless of the substantial issue at the core of the Convention. These are, in general, sensitive issues for France, and their appearance in an international instrument is therefore highly likely to provoke reluctance. Furthermore, '[t]he Government of the French Republic declares that the term "family education" in Article 5(b) of the Convention must be interpreted as meaning public education concerning the family and that, in any event, Article 5 will be applied subject to respect for Article 17 of the International Covenant on Civil and Political Rights and Article 8 of the European Convention for the Protection of Human Rights and Fundamental Freedoms',[27] and that 'no provision of the Convention must be interpreted as prevailing over provisions of French legislation which are more favourable to women than to men'.[28] This latter declaration particularly emphasizes the express wish of France to protect discriminations more favourable to women that had already been established by policy measures. However, several of these more favourable discriminations, especially those related to maternal status, have been progressively challenged under the impetus of European law.[29]

3.2.2 Reservations

Regarding reservations, these initially concerned a certain number of provisions but can, as at the time of writing, be separated into two categories given that a large number of these provisions have since then been

promote social progress and development and as a consequence will contribute to the attainment of full equality between men and women'.

27 CEDAW, Meeting of States Parties to the CEDAW, 14th Meeting at 12–13. Both Articles enshrine the right to respect for one's private and family life, home and correspondence. Article 17 of the International Covenant on Civil and Political Rights thus provides that:
1. No one shall be subjected to arbitrary or unlawful interference with his privacy, family, home or correspondence, nor to unlawful attacks on his honour and reputation;
2. Everyone has the right to the protection of the law against such interference or attacks;

while Article 8 of the European Convention on Human Rights provides that:
1. Everyone has the right to respect for his private and family life, his home and his correspondence;
2. There shall be no interference by a public authority with the exercise of this right except such as is in accordance with the law and is necessary in a democratic society in the interests of national security, public safety or the economic wellbeing of the country, for the prevention of disorder or crime, for the protection of health or morals, or for the protection of the rights and freedoms of others.

28 *Ibid.*

29 A particularly interesting investigation into the theme of maternal status has been carried out by Elisabeth Badinter, *Le conflit – La femme et la mère* (Paris: Flammarion, 2010).

withdrawn. This withdrawal indicates that they were mainly introduced for conjuncture and policy adjustment reasons.[30] Most reservations were thus withdrawn very shortly after the ratification of the Convention.

The reservation to Article 7, for instance, was withdrawn only two months after the Convention entered into force for France,[31] and reservations to Articles 15(2) and (3) and 16(1)(c) and (h)[32] were withdrawn in 1986.[33] Finally, reservations to Articles 5(b) and 16(1)(d) were withdrawn in 2003,[34] and the withdrawal of the reservation to Article 14(2)(c)[35] was announced in 2008.[36]

[30] It was explained, during the Parliamentary debates prior to the adoption of the Act of Parliament authorizing the ratification of the CEDAW, that the reservations that were made by France at the time of signature of the Convention were generally due to the fact that an important number of the CEDAW's provisions are ill-adapted to industrialized countries and concern issues that are more characteristic to developing countries. However, the question was also raised – but not explicitly answered – whether all of these reservations truly resulted from positive discriminations more favourable to women. See Assemblée nationale, 1st meeting of 27 June 1983, at 3256.

[31] On 26 March 1984 the French government notified the Secretary-General of the decision to withdraw the reservation to Article 7, a withdrawal that was explained to have been rendered possible by the entry into force of Act of Parliament No. 83–1096 of 20 December 1983, which abrogates Article LO 128 of the Electoral Code, relating to the temporary disqualification of individuals who were granted French citizenship. In this particular case it is obvious that the reservation introduced at the time of ratification was purely short term: the legislation that would render French law consistent with the CEDAW had not yet entered into force, while elections were scheduled to take place during the intermediate time. Therefore, the reservation was necessary to cover an incompatibility, but was never intended to remain in place. As a matter of fact, the French notification was published in the *JORF* only on 31 January 1985, but the withdrawal of the reservation was effective as of 26 March 1984.

[32] Those Articles must not prevent application of the provisions contained in Book III, Title V, Chapter II of the Civil Code, which concern the matrimonial regime of community of property (*régime en communauté*).

[33] On 21 July 1986 the French government notified the Secretary-General of the decision to withdraw these particular reservations, considering that Act of Parliament No. 85–1372 of 23 December 1985, relating to equality of spouses concerning property rights arising during marriage and equality of parents concerning property of underage children, which entered into force on 1st July 1986, had abrogated the previous discriminatory provisions governing these issues. Once again, the reservation had clearly been introduced pending a legislative reform that was already on the political agenda at the time of ratification.

[34] The Secretary-General was notified of this decision by the French government on 22 December 2003.

[35] 'The Government of the French Republic declares that Article 14, paragraph 2(c), should be interpreted as guaranteeing that women who fulfil the conditions relating to family or employment required by French legislation for personal participation shall acquire their own rights within the framework of social security.' CEDAW, Meeting of States Parties to the CEDAW, 14th Meeting at 13.

[36] Consistent with France's conception and implementation of the welfare system, the country has a strong and densely developed social security system, with the consequence

Three reservations nevertheless subsist as at the time of writing, regarding Articles 14(2)(h), 16(1)(g)[37] and 29. The reservation to Article 29[38] is probably the most classical one since it concerns the almost traditional refusal of France to be subjected to the compulsory jurisdiction of the International Court of Justice.[39]

Concerning the reservation to Article 14(2)(h), which states that:

> States Parties shall take all appropriate measures to eliminate discrimination against women in rural areas in order to ensure, on a basis of equality of men and women, that they participate in and benefit from rural development and, in particular, shall ensure to such women the right:
>
> ...
>
> (h) To enjoy adequate living conditions, particularly in relation to housing, sanitation, electricity and water supply, transport and communications[40]

the situation seems to be at a standstill. Following the 2008 audition, the Committee recommended to France to schedule, as soon as possible, the withdrawal of this particular reservation, which the Committee incidentally considers to be an interpretative declaration rather than a reservation. As of this date, however, the reservation has not yet been

that almost the entire population enjoys insurance coverage. Yet what was lacking and had justified the reservation in the first place was a specific provision concerning women in rural areas, especially farm workers, and their self-standing right to autonomous social security benefits. After implementation of important measures enacting the 1999 legislation (Act of Parliament No. 99–574), which has considerably extended the rights of farmers' spouses, the reservation withdrawal procedure was announced during France's 2008 audition before the CEDAW Committee.

37 'The Government of the French Republic enters a reservation concerning the right to choose a family name mentioned in Article 16, paragraph 1(g), of the Convention.' CEDAW, Meeting of States Parties to the CEDAW, 14th Meeting at 13.

38 'The Government of the French Republic declares, in pursuance of Article 29, paragraph 2, of the Convention, that it will not be bound by the provisions of Article 29, paragraph 1.' *Ibid.*

39 Although France has looked for ways of getting back to the forum of the ICJ, including by accepting to be defendant on the basis of Article 38, para. 5 of the International Court of Justice (ICJ) Statute, its willingness has not yet reached the point of removing the various reservations made regarding compromissory clauses referring to the ICJ, and especially its compulsory jurisdiction, in international treaties.

40 'The Government of the French Republic declares that Article 14, paragraph 2(h), of the Convention should not be interpreted as implying the actual provision, free of charge, of the services mentioned in that paragraph.' CEDAW, Meeting of States Parties to the CEDAW, 14th Meeting at 13. As a matter of fact, France is the only country that made a reservation to Article 14(2)(h).

withdrawn, although no obvious obstacle seems to stand in the way of such withdrawal.

The most problematic reservation still in place is probably the one to Article 16, but it might also be the least surprising one. Article 16 concerns marriage and family life and is undoubtedly the most controversial provision of the CEDAW, and therefore the one that has the highest number of reservations from States Parties.[41] The Committee has expressed a long-standing concern over reservations to Article 16,[42] and has recently once more emphatically expressed its doubts and concerns regarding the manner in which States Parties take into account and comply with this provision. Article 16 aims at guaranteeing equality between men and women in marriage and family relations, and the Committee has declared that '[n]either traditional, religious or cultural practice nor incompatible domestic laws and policies can justify violations of the Convention. The Committee also remains convinced that reservations to Article 16, whether lodged for national, traditional, religious or cultural reasons, are incompatible with the Convention and therefore impermissible and should be reviewed and modified or withdrawn.'[43] Concerning France in particular, the Committee has expressly requested the withdrawal of its reservation after the 2008 examination, during which the State Secretary for Solidarity and head of the inter-ministerial delegation indicated the issue would be submitted to the competent Ministries. The issue seems to be one of detail, but reveals surprising facets and intricacies of the French legislation. The law on family name remains firmly rooted in a Revolutionary legislation adopted in 1794,[44] whose cornerstone principles have over time become inconsistent with European and international law and with the 1958 French Constitution, but certain provisions of which are still in

[41] Fifty per cent of States that have made reservations have made one to Article 16.

[42] 'The Committee has noted with alarm the number of States parties which have entered reservations to the whole or part of Article 16, especially when a reservation has also been entered to Article 2, claiming that compliance may conflict with a commonly held vision of the family based, inter alia, on cultural or religious beliefs or on the country's economic or political status.' See CEDAW Committee, General Recommendation 21, 13th Session, 1994, available at: www.un.org/womenwatch/daw/cedaw/recommendations/recomm.htm (last accessed 19 February 2013).

[43] See www.un.org/womenwatch/daw/cedaw/reservations.htm (last accessed 19 February 2013).

[44] Loi du 6 Fructidor An II, according to the Republican calendar established during the French Revolution and used between 1792 and 1806 (23 August 1794 on the Gregorian calendar).

force.[45] In order to bring it into conformity with those latter instruments, especially the principle of non-discrimination, the legislation was significantly amended in 2002,[46] and even further in 2005.[47] It is still not entirely consistent with Article 16(1)(g) in the sense that, in the case that maternal and paternal filiation are simultaneously established, absent explicit declaration by both parents, the child will automatically be given the sole name of the father. This reservation is therefore the only one made to a substantial provision and which, evidently, was not made to protect positive discriminations contained in the French law that are more favourable to women, nor was it made for incidental reasons pending a legislative adjustment already scheduled. On the contrary, this reservation simply mirrors a legal necessity, considering the discrimination – pertaining to one single hypothesis and therefore in a way almost 'minimal', but discrimination nonetheless – still anchored in the French legislation on family name, and that the French system, in spite of numerous amendments, has not yet succeeded to bring into conformity with the principle of non-discrimination dictated by the Constitution, and European and international law, including the CEDAW.[48]

4 Domestic implementation of the CEDAW: displaying 'pride and prejudice'

Formally, there is no doubt: France is party to the CEDAW and satisfies the formal requirements of the Convention in the sense that what has been presented during the Parliamentary debates as the sole direct obligation imposed on States by the Convention, that is producing periodical reports on implementation, is in fact realized with considerable care. This is, undoubtedly, an aspect concerning which France does not wish to

[45] For a general overview on the legal rules governing transmission of family name to a child in France, see N. Baillon-Wirtz *et al.*, *L'enfant sujet de droits* (Paris: Editions Lamy, 2010) 104–12.

[46] Act of Parliament No. 2002–304 of 4 March 2002 (as amended by Act of Parliament No. 2003–516 of 18 June 2003). Only by this legislation was the possibility introduced into French law for a mother to transmit her family name to her child, but it remains discriminatory considering that the father was given the right to veto such transmission of the mother's name.

[47] Ordinance No. 2005–759 of 4 July 2005 reforming the law on filiation, ratified by Act of Parliament No. 2009–61 of 16 January 2009.

[48] During its 2008 audition before the Committee, France indicated, however, that withdrawal, or at least reducing the scope, of the reservation seems possible.

lose face, even less so considering that the CEDAW has been presented, again during the debates prior to its ratification, as an instrument mainly designed and intended for developing countries.

But the fact remains, precisely, that producing periodical reports also implies that they must be given concrete content and, henceforth, be linked to a certain number of actions and policy measures in the CEDAW. But do these actions and policy measures result from the CEDAW? Is it the Convention that provokes them? Providing an unequivocal answer to these questions is not an easy task, in light of the almost proud French State reports presented at the international level, which are tempered by the hesitant and prejudiced approach displayed at the domestic level.

Indeed, France is standing in a very paradoxical place as regards domestic implementation of the CEDAW. Paradoxical because, as has been shown in the previous section, on the one hand, while there has been and still is resistance, the context in France is no way hostile to tackling the issue of discrimination against women. But on the other hand, the fact remains that the CEDAW, although ratified by France almost thirty years ago, is still almost absent from the legal panorama. Upon closer scrutiny, the status of domestic implementation of the Convention can be approached from two different perspectives, the first being a 'defensive' one and the second an 'offensive' perspective. In both cases, however, the findings converge and lead back, in a seemingly closed circle, to the opening observations of invisibility, paradox and ambivalence.

4.1 'Defensive' perspective: timid recourse to the CEDAW before courts and by specialized agencies

From the defensive perspective, one could expect an international convention such as the CEDAW to be invoked as a legal tool during proceedings before domestic courts and referred to by various other bodies dealing with the issue of discrimination against women. Yet an inquiry into such use of the Convention reveals a quasi void, in the sense that there is almost no trace of recourse or reference to the CEDAW, whose use accordingly seems to remain in essence confined to an exceptionally small circle of specialists.[49]

[49] This circle involves the few NGOs specialized in the area, some academics – mainly sociologists and political scientists (for the first time in 2011, the Centre national de la recherche scientifique (CNRS) launched an inventory of the researchers working on gender) and the officials working for the *Observatoire de la parité* and the HALDE.

Concerning the 'appearance' of the CEDAW before domestic courts, a comprehensive examination of the case law distinctly reflects the paradoxes and ambivalences identified in the previous developments and, more generally, mirrors the hesitant approach to the notions of discrimination and women's rights. On one hand, the principle of equality is guaranteed by the Constitution in its Preamble,[50] a principle that thus has constitutional value and can be invoked before a domestic court. On the other hand, however, the principle is phrased in very broad and vague words, leaving ample room for additional measures to give it a specific content. This is precisely where the CEDAW could step in, with its detailed approach to the notion of discrimination and precise requests directed at States Parties. And yet, surprisingly, the case law relating to the CEDAW is substantially disappointing, and at the very best minimalistic and inconsistent. In fact, both the highest French judicial court, Cour de cassation, and the French constitutional court, Conseil constitutionnel, have to this date not decided a single case based on or even merely with reference to the CEDAW. The Conseil d'État, the highest French administrative court, is the only higher jurisdiction whose case law exhibits rare traces of the CEDAW. In fact, the Conseil d'État has to this date issued a total of five rulings where the CEDAW was used as the basis for the plaintiff's claim, or was at least referred to (of course among other international agreements, particularly the European Convention on Human Rights and EU Directives). A brief overview of the available case law sheds clearer light on the wavering, cautious but also inexperienced approach to the CEDAW by this Court.

The first case,[51] occurring almost 15 years after the ratification of the Convention by France, was unusual in the context of the discrimination against women in the sense that it mainly concerned the rights of unwed or divorced fathers regarding their children and, therefore, in fact, dealt with 'reverse discrimination'. In this case an association defending the rights of children attacked the governmental decree creating the Observatory on parity between women and men,[52] claiming the decree created an instance of discrimination and thus violated the equality principle enshrined in the French Constitution and several international

[50] The Preamble of the 1958 Constitution refers to the Preamble of 1946, which provides that the law guarantees, in all fields, equal rights to women (para. 3, 'La loi garantit à la femme, dans tous les domaines, des droits égaux à ceux de l'homme').

[51] Conseil d'État, case no. 176205, 30 April 1997.

[52] Decree no. 95–1114 of 18 October 1995, *JORF* 19 October 1995, at 15249.

Table 19.1 *Reference to the CEDAW in French case law*

Jurisdiction	Date of issue	Reference to the CEDAW ('visa')	Articles	Findings
Conseil d'État	30 April 1997	x	Art. 23	Plaintiff's argument dismissed
Conseil d'État	27 Nov 2000	x	None	None involving the CEDAW
Conseil d'État	7 Nov 2001	x	Arts. 2(e), 3 and 15	CEDAW not directly invocable by individuals before domestic courts
Conseil d'État	15 Oct 2004	x	Arts. 9, 15(4) and 16(1)(c)	No discrimination found
Conseil d'État	20 April 2005	x	Arts. 2(d) and 11(1)(e)	No discrimination found

obligations undertaken by France, including the ECHR and the CEDAW. The Conseil d'État found that, contrary to what the plaintiff argued, the CEDAW does not prevent States Parties from adopting measures aiming at establishing a de facto equality between women and men, and that Article 23 provides that the Convention shall not affect 'any provisions that are more conducive to the achievement of equality between men and women' that may be contained in the legislation of a State Party, thus concluding that the plaintiff's argument was to be dismissed.

The second case[53] is minor for the purpose of this study in the sense that the CEDAW was merely mentioned by the plaintiff to back her argument while the actual case was decided exclusively on the basis of domestic legislation and therefore without any reference to the Convention. The actual argument of discrimination was indeed never brought before the Court.

The third case was decided less than a year later,[54] and the Conseil d'État seized the opportunity to make a significant statement on the status of the CEDAW in the French legal order and before domestic courts. This case dealt with the administrative decision to escort the plaintiff back to the border while she claimed that this expulsion violated Articles 2(e), 3 and 15 of the CEDAW. Article 2 concerns domestic policy measures, enjoining States Parties to condemn discrimination against women in all its forms and, more specifically regarding point (e), to 'take all appropriate measures to eliminate discrimination against women by any person, organization or enterprise'. Article 3 enjoins States Parties to 'take in all fields, in particular in the political, social, economic and cultural fields, all appropriate measures, including legislation, to ensure the full development and advancement of women, for the purpose of guaranteeing them the exercise and enjoyment of human rights and fundamental freedoms on a basis of equality with men'. And Article 15 provides that States Parties shall guarantee women equality with men before the law. Having assessed these articles, the Conseil d'État found that they could not usefully be invoked by the plaintiff before a domestic court considering their inter-State nature. The Court concluded that Articles 2(e), 3 and 15 of the CEDAW only create obligations between States Parties, but that they under no circumstance create rights for individuals that those individuals could henceforth claim before a court of law. In other terms, the Conseil d'État denied any direct effect to the provisions at stake in the

[53] Conseil d'État, case no. 219375, 27 November 2000.

[54] Conseil d'État, case no. 230324, 7 November 2001.

case, a position which is in line with the overall case law regarding direct effect of international conventions.[55]

The fourth ruling[56] rejected the plaintiff's claim for annulment of the withdrawal of her residence permit, which was granted to her on the grounds of family reunification. The plaintiff invoked Articles 9, 15(4) and 16(1)(c). These provisions enjoin States Parties to respectively guarantee equality as regards the acquisition, change or conservation of nationality; equality before the law and, more specifically, equality with regard to the law relating to the movement of persons and the freedom to choose their residence and domicile; and the same rights and responsibilities during the marriage and at its dissolution. The Court found that no discrimination such as that prohibited by these Articles was created by the withdrawal decision, which was taken on the basis of an Ordinance of 1945 whose Articles apply without any discrimination based on gender, and therefore no discrimination in the sense of the CEDAW either.

Finally, the last ruling to the time of writing[57] was a case of discrimination in the field of employment brought to the Court by a labour union, which ended with the plaintiff's withdrawal from the case. It is noticeable, however, that in this instance the CEDAW was invoked by the plaintiff as the main (international) foundation for his claim. The Court found that while the principle of equality entails equal treatment for individuals in the same situation, it does not provide for different treatment for individuals in different situations. Based on this statement the Court ruled that, even though women are in a different situation than men considering the necessity to cease their professional activity during maternity, the French agreement on unemployment insurance could, without violating the principle of equality, refrain from defining an accounting regime specific to women that would factor in their different situation. Thus, the Court found that the contentious agreement on unemployment insurance did not create an instance of discrimination such as that prohibited by Articles 2(d)[58] and 11(1)(e)[59] of the CEDAW.

[55] Although the case law has very recently evolved, relaxing the conditions under which a direct effect can be acknowledged. Conseil d'État, Assemblée, 11 avril 2012, *Gisti*, decision no. 322326.

[56] Conseil d'État, case no. 241661, 15 October 2004.

[57] Conseil d'État, case no. 264348, 20 April 2005.

[58] States Parties commit 'to refrain from engaging in any act or practice of discrimination against women and to ensure that public authorities and institutions shall act in conformity with this obligation'.

[59] 'States Parties shall take all appropriate measures to eliminate discrimination against women in the field of employment in order to ensure, on a basis of equality of men and

As already mentioned, what is striking in these rulings is the Court's obviously hesitant and even reluctant approach to the UN Convention. In all of them, the CEDAW is only incidentally referred to, European instruments being given clear priority (which is evident even when looking at the order in which the relevant legal texts are listed in the decisions). This is not surprising as such, considering that the fully integrated normative EU system takes obvious precedence over global legal instruments, but also, on the other hand (but related to this first aspect), considering that domestic judges are clearly more at ease with these already well-known and much-practiced European instruments. What is even more striking, though, is the manifest inconsistency that appears in the case law of the Conseil d'État, when confronting the three last CEDAW cases. In 2001 the Conseil d'État ruled that Articles 2(e), 3 and 15 of the CEDAW do not create rights for individuals and that individuals can therefore not invoke these provisions before a domestic court. However, the next CEDAW case before the Conseil d'État (2004) again concerned Article 15, and Article 2 was invoked in the 2005 case regarding its point (d).[60] Yet in both the 2004 and 2005 cases the Conseil d'État seems to have departed from its 2001 findings, that is that these Articles do not create rights for individuals: instead of dismissing the arguments on the same grounds as in the 2001 case, it carried out a substantial examination in order to determine whether the relevant measure did or did not create an instance of discrimination prohibited by these very CEDAW provisions. It is true that French courts, including the Conseil d'État, are not bound by a doctrine of precedent as it prevails in common law courts, but one could nevertheless expect it to be familiar with its own rulings and therefore to adopt a substantially consistent line of reasoning when confronted with provisions of a legal instrument on which it has already ruled. By the same token, there is nothing in the 2004 and 2005 decisions that would indicate that the Conseil d'État has deliberately decided to overrule its 2001 position regarding the invocability of CEDAW provisions by individuals. The most likely explanation for the observed inconsistencies is therefore also the least flattering one, namely that the wavering case law simply reflects the unease of French judges when confronted with the CEDAW, their lack

women, the same rights, in particular: the right to work as an inalienable right of all human beings.'

[60] The 2001 previous case concerned its point (e), which is nevertheless formulated in exactly the same way as point (d): 'State Parties undertake to refrain from .../State Parties undertake to take all appropriate measures ...'

of understanding of the instrument, but also, and probably most significantly, their lack of interest in it.

The same lack of interest or even lack of knowledge can also be observed when looking at other domestic (non-judicial) bodies dealing with women's rights or discrimination issues. In fact, the only bodies that refer to the CEDAW or even merely quote it are specialized agencies such as the Observatoire de la parité and non-governmental organizations, mainly because they investigate the issue for the purpose of establishing shadow reports. But apart from these rare exceptions, the CEDAW's notoriety hardly ever reaches beyond these specialized and closed circles. In other words, the CEDAW is and remains a matter for and of specialists. And even when these specialized agencies refer to the CEDAW, such reference seems to be, in most cases, a mere formality. The only body regularly referring to the UN Convention and remaining updated on the domestic status of the CEDAW is the Commission nationale consultative des droits de l'homme (CNCDH – National Advisory Commission on Human Rights). Even the Haute autorité de lutte contre les discriminations et pour l'égalité (HALDE – High Authority to Combat Discrimination and Promote Equality) does not refer to the CEDAW (which is only marginally mentioned on its website), although, significantly and paradoxically, the CEDAW Committee regards this agency as a crucial tool to ensuring that CEDAW obligations are implemented in France. In sum, the Convention is extensively and properly dealt with neither by the judiciary, who prefer to circumvent the instrument when possible, nor by the vast majority of organizations that are active in the field of discrimination against women. This 'default' attitude does not contribute to enhancing the visibility of the CEDAW in the domestic political and legal scene, and henceforth its effectiveness for those for whom it was designed.

4.2 'Offensive' perspective: the CEDAW as ex ante *impetus or* ex post *justification?*

From the 'offensive' perspective, again the findings are, if not exactly negative, at least nuanced. As was observed earlier, although there has been resistance to the notions tackled here, one cannot but be struck by the vast legal arsenal, and might therefore conclude that France has taken many measures in order to generally implement the Convention. But, upon closer scrutiny and especially when looking at the national reports submitted by France to the Committee, it becomes difficult to identify what prompts what, and what justifies what. In other words, does France's commitment to the CEDAW serve as an initial and genuine impetus for gender policies, or merely as a subsequent justification? The official discourse is obviously that the Convention contains certain obligations to which France is firmly committed, and that certain domestic measures were therefore taken to comply. However, this rather seems to be a discourse of *ex post* justification while the true chain of events seems more to be that these measures would have been taken anyway – simply because the evolving socio-political context (and European law) demands it – but that, since the CEDAW requires certain programmatic domestication steps, they are officially justified by precisely these requirements. In the end, it therefore seems difficult to consider that it is the Convention in itself that creates an incentive for French policy measures, or even that the CEDAW has a relevant effect of impetus on domestic policy measures at all. The reality seems more to be that gender-related domestic measures are linked to the Convention subsequently, rather than it being the Convention that inspires the measures in the first place. At best, the obligation under which France is, like all States Parties to the CEDAW, required to submit reports on the status of implementation to the CEDAW Committee at four-year intervals,[61] can have the effect of prompting certain reforms or emphasizing the necessary ones, and of encouraging the government to commit to achieve them.

5 Conclusion

The distinctive 'positive' feature of French policies on discrimination and women's rights is the extensiveness of legislative devices regarding issues of equality, notably since the 1980s but even more increasingly since 2000 (twenty-two new laws relating to women's rights have been adopted between 2002 and 2007). However, and without great surprise, the 'negative' feature of these same policies is their imperfect translation into social reality. The impact of a law inevitably depends on its application, but many of the adopted laws have suffered delays in their implementation, others have almost not been implemented at all, others yet need to be completed by

[61] The first two reports were submitted as a joint report in 1991, the 3rd and 4th reports were submitted in 1999, the 5th report in April 2002 and the 6th report in 2006. Following the 6th report, the audition for France before the CEDAW Committee was held on 18 January 2008 in Geneva. The 7th report was announced for the beginning of 2009 but the CEDAW Committee requested that both the 7th and 8th reports be submitted jointly in January 2013. The Committee therefore does not seem to consider the French reports to be urgent.

regulatory or financial measures that are delayed, and others again are not followed up on, which prevents one making a realistic assessment. Furthermore, and this is one of the major concerns emphasized by NGOs in their shadow reports, in spite of a seemingly very complete legal arsenal, what is mainly lacking is transparent and accessible information on the CEDAW, and of course mainly and most notably transparent to and accessible by the individuals whom the Convention seeks to protect. In the end, the main flaw thus remains – and this is an almost trivial observation as far as human rights treaties are concerned – a distortion between the formal law and its effective implementation, and the major issue does not seem to be the actual domestication measures taken by France, but rather the transparency of and information about the CEDAW and about the legal tools created by French policies to comply with its obligations under the CEDAW.

20

Rise and fall of the CEDAW in Finland: time to reclaim its impetus

KEVÄT NOUSIAINEN AND MERJA PENTIKÄINEN

1 Introduction

This chapter is premised on considering the Convention on the Elimination of All Forms of Discrimination against Women (CEDAW) as one of the most interesting human rights treaties due to its several special characteristics: its broad approach to equality (and non-discrimination), its broad, substantive coverage calling for specific actions to overcome discrimination against women in a number of spheres of life, and the Convention's reach beyond the public–private divide in human rights norms. It is the only human rights treaty that directly addresses the dimension of human reproduction by touching upon family planning (the right to decide freely on the number and spacing of children).[1] Additionally, the CEDAW appears to be the only human rights treaty that targets culture and tradition as influential forces shaping gender roles and family relations as well as restricting women's enjoyment of their fundamental rights. This aspect of the Convention deserves our attention, and these structural forms of discrimination should be addressed. Altogether, the CEDAW provides a comprehensive framework for challenging the various forces that have created and sustained discrimination against women.

This chapter considers the impact of the CEDAW on Finnish law and practices.[2] After its ratification, the CEDAW influenced Finnish equality

[1] The *Beijing Declaration and Platform for Action* 1995 (*Beijing Document*) is a particularly important international instrument elaborating the issue of reproductive rights, but as this instrument is not made in a treaty format, it is not legally binding.

[2] The analyses of the significance of the CEDAW and the work of the CEDAW Committee included in this chapter are partly based on a number of interviews conducted in 2009 by the authors. The interviewed experts were: Pia Puu Oksanen and Maarit Pihkala (Finnish branch of Amnesty International), Paula Havu (Finnish UN Association), Tanja Auvinen

law to a great extent. Finland did not use sweeping reservations, and has not neglected its reporting duties under the Convention. After the end of the Cold War, Finland's membership the Council of Europe in 1989 and accession to the EU in 1995 brought a new type of 'rights discourse' to Finland. A reform of the Finnish Constitution introduced the stronger protection of constitutional rights, and allowed the courts to refer to human rights instruments. It would seem safe to assume that the new constitutional constellation gave an opening to even more extensive use of the potential of the CEDAW. Yet quite the opposite seems to be the case. The CEDAW seems to have become marginalised as a source of Finnish legal reform and in court praxis. The stronger emphasis on constitutional and human rights did not enhance the role of the Women's Rights Convention.

The aim of this chapter is to explain this paradox, by considering the political and legal trajectories of human rights and gender equality policies in Finland. The explanation is sought in the specific political and social circumstances of the country during the Cold War period and in the following decades. The turn in the national tide of the CEDAW seems to have taken place around 1990. Attention here is focused on showing how changing geopolitical circumstances have played a role in this. This chapter illuminates social and political factors behind the historical rise and decline of the national reception of the Convention in Finland.

The specific features of the Finnish women's movement and equality policies are used to explain why certain issues, especially those related to equality in the labour market, take pride of place in national politics, and why other issues covered by the CEDAW tend to be left aside. Both the initial success at ratification, which led to the adoption of the first piece of anti-discrimination law in Finland, and the weaker interest and impact of the Convention later on, are understood in the light of features of 'state feminism' typical for the Nordic societies.

Due to the paucity of references to the CEDAW in both Finnish legislative work and court practice after 1990, the main focus of this chapter is on Finnish periodical reports to the CEDAW Committee in the post-Cold War period. The very 'state feminism' that eased the adoption of equality

(Coalition of Finnish Women's Associations (NYTKIS)), Pirkko Mäkinen (Finnish Ombudsman on Gender Equality), Sinikka Mustakallio (expert on gender equality, World of Management (WoM)), Leena Ruusuvuori (National Council of Women of Finland), Milla Aaltonen and Johanna Lampinen (Finnish League for Human Rights), Kati Kivistö (Ministry of Justice), Pasi Mustonen (Ministry of Social Affairs and Health) and Riitta Martikainen (Ministry of Social Affairs and Health).

legislation in the context of ratification of the CEDAW has made later civil society engagement with the Convention ambiguous. Women's organisations are invited by the government to participate in the national reporting procedure to the CEDAW Committee, but cooperation with state officials seems to curtail, to some extent, independent activities by NGOs. This chapter shows that the Finnish reports concentrate on issues that are largely outside the scope of mandatory EU equality law, such as violence against women. The Committee hearings have opened a channel to Finnish women's organisations to stress the national shortcomings in combating violence against women. Because a recent European Council Convention also concentrates on violence against women, the combined pressure towards due diligence may lead to better recognition of violence against women as discrimination. Reclaiming the significance of the CEDAW may hopefully take place through a coincidence of European and United Nations (UN) instruments addressing the same issues that are problematic in the Finnish human rights discourse.

2 Ratification of the CEDAW: legal and political background

2.1 *Gender equality in Finland prior to the CEDAW*

Finnish women were politically emancipated quite early, when general suffrage in Parliamentary elections was introduced in 1906. Political rights provided the 'first-wave' feminists with an opening for legislative reform, but the number of women in Parliament remained limited for decades.[3] Political parties in the first half of the twentieth century were based on civic activism, and women could present their political agendas through independent women's organisations within each party.[4] Cooperation across party lines between women in Parliament became and has remained a feature of Finnish politics even after the number of

[3] In the first Parliament of the independent state of Finland of 1917, the number of women MPs was 18. In the subsequent Parliament, this figure was reduced. See I. Sulkunen, M. Lähteenmäki and A. Korppi-Tommola, *Naiset eduskunnassa* [Women in Parliament] (Helsinki: Edita, 2007). In 2012 the Finnish Parliament had 85 women Members (out of 200).

[4] T. Skard and E. Haavio-Mannila, 'Naiset parlamenteissa' [Women in the Parliament] in E. Haavio-Mannila *et al.* (eds.), *Keskeneräinen kansanvalta. Naiset Pohjoismaiden politiikassa* [Unfinished Democracy. Women in Nordic Politics] (Oslo: Nordic Council of Ministers, 1983) 87–129 at 87; R. Ruusala, *Vasemmiston naisjärjestöjen tavoitteet ja toimintamenetelmät* [Aims and Working Methods of Left-Wing Women's Organisations] (Tampere: Tampereen yliopiston politiikan tutkimuksen laitos, 1967).

women Parliamentarians has risen. Formally, equal rights for women were largely achieved by 1960.

Finnish women were required to perform heavy tasks in agriculture and industry both before and during the Second World War and in the post-war era. Finland differed from its Nordic neighbours by having a strong presence of women in the labour market. In this respect Finland resembled its eastern neighbour, the Soviet Union, more than its western neighbour, Sweden.[5] Accordingly, the ideal of breadwinner–homemaker nuclear families was a realistic option in Finland, less often than in most Western societies. Rapid socio-economic changes since the 1960s brought issues related to social and economic rights to the fore in Finland.[6] The shift from agriculture to an industrial and service-based economy accelerated, and women were at least as eager as men to move to urban areas. 'Second-wave' feminist activism rose at this period of structural change.[7]

The Scandinavian models of social welfare, modestly introduced in the pre-Second World War period, were now appearing in Finland on a larger scale. Due to both political and economic reasons and losses caused by the war, welfare state development in Finland lagged behind in comparison with Sweden and other Nordic states. From the 1960s onwards both economic and political conditions existed for adopting Nordic welfare state institutions. These changes introduced a corporatist type of governance, based on cooperation between the central administration, trade unions and business, with a range of councils, boards and committees.[8] This

[5] E. Haavio-Mannila and R. Jallinoja, *Changes in the Life Patterns of Families in Finland: National Report based on Statistics and Earlier Studies* (Department of Sociology, Helsinki University, 1980).

[6] R. Julkunen, 'Suomalainen sukupuolimalli – 1960-luku käänteenä' [The Finnish gender model – with 1960s as a turning-point] in A. Anttonen, L. Henriksson and R. Nätkin (eds.), *Naisten hyvinvointivaltio* [Women's Welfare State] (Tampere: Vastapaino, 1994) 179–201.

[7] In political terms, feminism in Europe and the USA is often divided into three 'waves': the first occurring in the late nineteenth and early twentieth centuries, with a focus on women's legal equality; the second taking place from the 1960s to the 1990s and focusing on women's actual position in the private and public spheres; and the third, beginning in the 1990s, with a focus on differences among women and their identities. For the first-and second-wave feminism, see R. Jallinoja, *Suomalaisen naisliikkeen taistelukaudet. naisasialiike naisten elämäntilanteen muutoksen ja yhteiskunnallis-aatteellisen murroksen heijastajana* [The Fighting Periods of the Finnish Women's Movement. Women's Movement as the Reflection of the Changing Life Conditions of Women and Societal–Ideological Break] (Porvoo: WSOY, 1983).

[8] L. Karvonen, 'Trade unions and the feminization of the labour market' in L. Karvonen and P. Selle (eds.), *Women in Nordic Politics: Closing the Gap* (Aldershot: Dartmouth, 1995) 133–53.

kind of corporatist governance had little constitutional foundation, as it evolved through agreements between major institutions. Women found this corporatist system more difficult to access than the Parliament.[9] In 1964 the so-called 'incomes policy' was introduced – a centralised settlement under which wages rose in line with the growth of gross national income – which resulted in the institutionalisation of negotiation authorities and statistics production.[10] When party machinery became more professional and the corporatist machinery developed, the losers in the power game were representatives of civic activism, including women's organisations. Because formal equality of women was already largely achieved, the women's movement had also lost its former common goal.

In this new setting, interest turned to issues of de facto equality. Gender equality goals concentrated on women's efficient participation in the labour market. The new focus was on social and economic issues rather than formal rights, which had been the target of many 'first-wave feminists'. Culture, social issues, health, family and education policies had earlier been areas where women politicians had been considered to be 'at home', and thus there was continuity with first-wave policies. Grievances connected to gender segregation and lower pay for women in the labour market, difficulties with childcare and other issues important for working mothers became the core of new gender equality politics.[11]

In 1966 the Finnish government set up a committee to consider the position of women, and the committee report was published in 1970.[12] The committee emphasised a gender-neutral approach and paid special attention to the obstacles that blocked women's full participation in the labour market as well as the promotion of dual-breadwinner families.

[9] H. M. Hernes and E. Hänninen-Salmelin, 'Women in the corporate system' in E. Haavio-Mannila *et al.* (eds.), *Unfinished Democracy: Women in Nordic Politics* (Oxford: Pergamon Press, 1985) 106–33 at 118–20.

[10] The first national incomes policy agreement, where a collective agreement between the main national-level labour market organisations was linked to government promises on price and taxation policies, was established in 1968.

[11] S. Sinkkonen and E. Haavio-Mannila, 'Naisliikkeen heijastuminen kansanedustajien lainsäädäntötoiminnassa. Mies- ja naiskansanedustajien 1907–1977 valtiopäivillä tekemien aloitteiden vertailu' [The impact of women's movement to the legislative work of MPs. Comparison of legislative initiatives by male and female MPs], *Politiikka* 22:2 (1980) 101–17.

[12] *Committee Report on the Position of Women* (1970). As to the contents, see Julkunen 'Suomalainen sukupuolimalli' at 179–201 and K. Nousiainen, 'Utility-based equality and disparate diversities' in D. Schiek and V. Chege (eds.), *European Non-Discrimination Law: Comparative Perspectives on Multidimensional Equality Law* (London: Routledge, 2008) 187–214 at 188.

Measures for these aims were individual taxation, childcare services and other social welfare strategies. Gender equality was considered useful for national prosperity, rather than as an end in itself.[13] Anti-discrimination laws and policies held no special place on the agenda presented by the committee. One of the few references to anti-discrimination measures was to the UN Declaration on the Elimination of Discrimination against Women of 1967.[14]

2.2 *Towards the ratification of the CEDAW*

Finland's international position during the Cold War after the Second World War era was precarious.[15] The country's international orientation was limited by the imperative to remain as neutral as possible to the divisions caused by the Cold War. The situation encouraged a political orientation associated with Western values under international commitments that were neutral to global bipolarisation. Accordingly, Finland did not join the Council of Europe and remained outside the European Community (EC), but did join the European Free Trade Association (EFTA). In the post-Second World War period, Finland became internationally active through two channels particularly – the UN and Nordic institutions, especially the Nordic Council.[16] The emphasis on Nordic cooperation influenced the manner of implementation of the UN conventions. From 1975 onwards, Finland played an active role in setting up the détente between Cold War parties through the so-called Helsinki Process, which also introduced human rights into the East–West dialogue.[17]

[13] Nousiainen, 'Utility-based equality and disparate diversities'.

[14] *Committee Report on the Position of Women* (1970) at 65–70.

[15] While not *de jure* one of the Axis powers, Finland fought against the Soviet Union on the side of Nazi Germany, and was classified as a co-belligerent by the Paris Peace Treaty of 1947. The country remained unoccupied and retained its democratic rule through the war period, and did not become a part of the Socialist Bloc. Yet Finland tried to avoid any disagreements with the Soviets during the Cold War, which limited the country's international options considerably, as the Soviet Union opposed Finland's Western commitments.

[16] In 1955 Finland joined both the UN and the Nordic Council, which had been established in 1952 as a tool for inter-Parliamentary cooperation and consultation among the Nordic states (including Denmark, Finland, Iceland, Norway and Sweden). The Nordic Council of Ministers and a number of Nordic conventions, as well as various more or less formal institutions of cooperation, were active especially during the Cold War era. See B. Sundelius, *Managing Transnationalism in Northern Europe* (Boulder: Westview Press, 1978).

[17] The Conference on Security and Co-operation in Europe (CSCE) was established by the adoption of the Helsinki Final Act in 1975. The CSCE was renamed as the Organization

Finland's general international orientation was also important for gender equality politics. Because Finland did not join the European Convention on Human Rights (ECHR), and was not bound by the EC gender equality law, the UN instruments became the major international influence on Finnish national legislation and practices. Finnish women's organisations took advantage of the governments' international politics. These organisations, as well as public opinion in general, seem to have believed that the level of gender equality in Finland was already high. The UN policies for the advancement of women thus offered an opportunity for the Finnish government to highlight the country's achievements in equality internationally. These governmental strivings gave women's organisations an opening for requiring further national equality reforms by claiming that they were needed for maintaining the country's international image.

At the UN level, Finnish protagonists for women's rights had a forerunner, Ms Helvi Sipilä. An advocate by training, Sipilä was an activist in the International Council of Women and International Federation of Women Lawyers, and she represented Finland in various UN functions and meetings. She played a prominent role in promoting women's rights at the UN as Deputy Secretary-General, and was an important figure in the efforts that led to both the establishment of the UN Development Fund for Women (UNIFEM) and the adoption of the CEDAW, as well as in putting into effect the 1975 (International Women's Year) World Action Plan.[18] Sipilä and other Finnish activists for women's rights may have seen a greater need for promoting women's rights outside Finland rather than within, but Sipilä's prominent position was useful for feminists at home who wished to refer to the UN gender equality instruments in Finnish national policies.

Nordic orientation was, as already stated, favoured in the post-Second World War period for reasons of international politics, but rapid economic growth and urbanisation also made Nordic welfare state ideology both

for Security and Co-operation in Europe (OSCE) as of the beginning of 1995. The 1975 Helsinki Final Act remains its founding document.

[18] Helvi Sipilä represented Finland in a number of UN organisations between 1960 and 1972. She became a member of the Commission on the Status of Women in 1960, and she continued her career as a Rapporteur and finally as the Deputy Secretary-General of the UN in 1972. Issues related to the position of women, such as the preparation of the UN Women's Year and the Mexico Conference 1975, were delegated to Sipilä. See A. Winter-Mäkinen, *Naisjuristien vuosisata: Poimintoja naisjuristien historiasta* [Century of Women Lawyers: Excerpts from the History of Women Lawyers] (Helsinki: Lakimiesliitto, 1995) 135–6.

feasible and desirable. Considerable Nordic cooperation in many matters, including law preparation, was already common in the pre-Second World War era, but this cooperation intensified during the Cold War. From the 1960s on, welfare state institutions developed quickly. In 1978 cooperation on gender equality issues at the Nordic level was formalised when the Nordic Council of Ministers approved an Action Programme for Nordic cooperation. Nordic Ministers responsible for gender equality issues were to meet regularly, and a committee was established to prepare equality issues. The main areas of cooperation were working life, social and family policies, education, housing and social planning, and political participation.[19] In the 1970s two-breadwinner families became an acceptable goal rather than a necessity in all Nordic states. Women also gained political power, as their number in the Nordic Parliaments grew and formed the 'critical mass' needed for political initiative.[20] This orientation strengthened a new type of feminism, known as 'state feminism'.

The term 'state feminism' refers to cooperation between women's movements and state authorities, especially through specialised bodies to promote gender equality.[21] The rise of bodies devoted to national equality increased rapidly in the UN Member States, since the UN International Women's Year 1975 delegates had recommended that such bodies be established.[22] The Nordic states were forerunners in setting up such bodies. In the 1970s, equality councils or delegations were set up in all Nordic states (in 1972 in Finland,[23] Norway and Sweden; in 1975 in Denmark; and

[19] E. Haavio-Mannila, 'Convergences between East and West: tradition and modernity in sex roles in Sweden, Finland and the Soviet Union', *Acta Sociologica* 14 (1971) 114–25.

[20] D. Dahlerup, *The New Women's Movement: Feminism and Political Power in Europe and the USA* (London: Sage Publications, 1986).

[21] The idea of 'state feminism' and the idea that the Scandinavian welfare states may be 'women friendly' was introduced by Norwegian political scientist Helga Hernes in 1987. See H. Hernes, *Welfare State and Woman Power. Essays in State Feminism* (London: Norwegian University Press, 1987).

[22] This launched what is described as 'state feminism' in many UN Member States. See J. Lovenduski, 'Introduction: state feminism and the political representation of women' in J. Lovenduski (ed.), *State Feminism and Political Representation* (Cambridge University Press, 2005) 1–19.

[23] The Council for Equality between Women and Men still exists, but other equality bodies have been established and have overtaken some of its old functions. The office of the Ombudsman for Equality and the Equality Board was established in 1986 to monitor the Act on Equality between Women and Men. It is situated at the Ministry of Social Affairs and Health, which has since then housed all Finnish gender equality bodies. An Equality Unit was established to prepare the government's equality policies. For the time being, the Council for Equality functions as a consultative body for equality politics with mem-

in 1976 in Iceland). A Nordic Gender Equality Programme was adopted in 1982, and a central task presented to national equality councils was to draft gender equality legislation.[24]

The Finnish Council for Equality between Women and Men was established in the Prime Minister's Office to propose and prepare reforms for gender equality. The Council was a permanent government advisory body 'with a secretariat and a small budget', consisting of politically nominated members.[25] In spite of its scarce resources, the Council became an important activist force pushing for legislative changes and political action, able to channel the traditional cooperation among women politicians to new challenges and activities. In 1973 it established a labour market subcommittee to prepare an assessment of gender discrimination in Finland and to make a proposal on how discrimination in the labour market was to be prevented.[26] The subcommittee report, delivered in 1975, contained an analysis of different forms of discrimination in working life.[27] The Council in its report to the Ministry of Justice insisted that such discrimination was to be prohibited in law.[28] Thus, the Council became a forum

bers who represent parties in the Parliament, and thus are capable of policy and opinion building on a wider political basis than those represented in the government.

24 M. Eduards, B. Halsaa and H. Skjeie, 'Equality: how equal' in E. Haavio-Mannila *et al.* (eds.), *Unfinished Democracy* 134–60 at 138–45.

25 A. Holli and J. Kantola, 'A politics for presence: state feminism, women's movements and political representation in Finland' in J. Lovenduski (ed.), *State Feminism and Political Representation* 62–84 at 67.

26 In a sense, the CEDAW is conceptually connected to two terms, sex and gender, as the Convention presupposes both that certain biological features of women are to be given consideration, and requires policies to eradicate cultural and social practices that put women as a gender at disadvantage. In this chapter the terms sex and gender are used interchangeably, where the choice of term has no special relevance. The choice reflects the fact that the distinction sex/gender is difficult to make in Finnish, as the language lacks grammatical gender. Consequently, the Finnish term *sukupuoli* is translated, often rather haphazardly, either as sex or as gender.

27 The majority of the members of the subcommittee were representatives of the labour market organisations. Discrimination was considered in the light of the definitions of discrimination in ILO Conventions No. 100 (concerning Equal Remuneration for Men and Women Workers for the Work of Equal Value) and No. 111 (concerning Discrimination in Employment and Occupation), the International Convention on the Elimination of All Forms of Racial Discrimination (ICERD) and the UNESCO Convention Against Discrimination in Education. See *Sukupuoleen kohdistuva syrjintä työmarkkinoilla* [Discrimination against Women in the Labour Market],Tasa-arvoasiain neuvottelukunta, työmarkkinajaosto, valtioneuvoston kanslian julkaisuja [Publications of the Prime Minister's Office] 3 (1974) 21–3.

28 *Sosiaali- ja terveysministeriön selonteko Suomen hallituksen tasa-arvo-ohjelman toteuttamisesta vuosina 1980–86 ja sen jälkeisistä tasa-arvon edistämistoimenpiteistä*

for claims regarding gender inequality that were otherwise difficult to present in the corporatist regime, where women were underrepresented in decision-making bodies.

The Council for Equality between Women and Men also played an important role in the ratification of the CEDAW in Finland. In 1972, its first year of operation, when the Council considered legislation against gender discrimination, it also discussed the plans in the UN for a Women's Rights Convention. An official Finnish delegation took part in the World Conference on the Status of Women held in 1975 in Mexico. The publicity that the conference received in Finland was 'uncertain and confused', as it was difficult for the public to conceive that relatively independent, working Finnish women could be discriminated against.[29] The activists in the Council for Equality thought otherwise. In 1977 the Council stated that it was important that the CEDAW be accepted by the UN and ratified by Finland as soon as possible. Typically for the Nordic type of 'state feminism', Finnish women's organisations promoted this agenda in cooperation with the state equality body. Women's sections in the political parties remained important feminist political players, as feminist groups in civil society had little visibility and impact.[30] Altogether, a sharp distinction between state and society was not made in the Finnish welfare context.

The first real Gender Equality Programme of the Government of Finland was presented in May 1980,[31] as part of the UN Decade for Women and as preparation for the World Conference on the UN Decade for Women held in 1980 in Copenhagen.[32] This government programme targeted state administration, which was obliged to take measures

[Report by the Ministry of Social Affairs and Health on the Implementation of the Government's Gender Equality Programme in 1980–86 and on Later Equality Policy] sarja B: Tiedotteita 1/1987, Ministry of Social Affairs and Health, 48–55.

29 Winter-Mäkinen, *Naisjuristien vuosisata* at 166.

30 R. Jallinoja, *Suomalaisen naisliikkeen taistelukaudet. naisasialiike naisten elämäntilanteen muutoksen ja yhteiskunnallis-aatteellisen murroksen heijastajana* [The Fighting Periods of the Finnish Women's Movement. Women's Movement as the Reflection of the Changing Life Conditions of Women and Societal-Ideological Break] (Porvoo: WSOY, 1983).

31 A very modest programme for gender equality policies had already been adopted in the Prime Minister's Office Programme for the UN Decade for Women for 1978–79, but the 1980 Government Programme was the first one to contain comprehensive aims and measures for such policies.

32 *Suomen hallituksen ohjelma sukupuolten tasa-arvon edistämiseksi YK:n naisten vuosikymmenen jälkipuoliskolla 1980–1985* [The Finnish Goverment's Programme for Promoting Gender Equality at the Latter Half of the UN Decade for Women] 29 April 1980, Valtioneuvoston kanslia [Prime Minister's Office] 1980:2.

concerning education, working life, women's positions in state administration, family law, social policies, community policies, participation in society and international cooperation. Two points were considered crucial: the commitment that Finland would sign the CEDAW and start the reforms needed for its ratification, and that anti-discrimination law would be developed to combat discrimination in working life. The two points were intertwined, because an Act on gender equality was presented as a *conditio sine qua non* for the ratification of the CEDAW.[33] The 'state feminists', or women's organisations and the equality body in cooperation, saw the CEDAW as a means to push for an Act prohibiting gender discrimination.

Most Finnish governments since 1980 have had a Gender Equality Programme and many programmes have referred to issues related to the UN instruments. While government programmes as such have contained relatively short texts on gender equality policies, a more detailed equality programme has often been prepared by the Ministry responsible for gender equality.[34] The government Gender Equality Programme adopted in 1980 was explicitly named as a programme for the UN Decade for Women. A detailed government programme adopted in 1997 was named *From Beijing to Finland* (*Pekingistä Suomeen*), in reference to the *Beijing Declaration and Platform for Action* of 1995.

In all Nordic states gender equality and discrimination against women were focuses of interest earlier than other forms of discrimination-related inequalities. Consequently, no other inequalities associated with discrimination were given much attention in Finland at the time that gender equality was brought to the agenda. All Nordic states had signed the International Convention on the Elimination of All Forms of Racial Discrimination (ICERD) in 1966 and ratified it by 1972. The ratification of ICERD in 1970 in Finland was considered to require few measures, especially in terms of legislation.[35] The CEDAW had a much deeper

[33] *Ibid.*, Chapter 2.6.

[34] Up until 1987 the Prime Minister's Office was responsible for preparing these more detailed programmes, and since then they have been prepared by the Ministry of Social Affairs and Health.

[35] In 1970 an amendment to the Penal Code, motivated by ICERD, criminalised ethnic agitation. A provision that obligated employers to treat employees equally irrespective of a number of grounds was included in the Employment Contracts Act of 1970. This provision was also motivated by ILO Conventions Nos. 100 and 111. Criminalisation of work-related discrimination on several grounds was also considered necessary by a committee in 1973, but again the main motivation was the ratification of ILO Convention No. 111.

impact on Finnish society, not least in the form of the first piece of anti-discrimination law in Finland – the Act on Equality between Women and Men. This is discussed in more detail below.

3 Reception of the CEDAW in the Finnish legal system

3.1 Ratification in the context of Nordic 'state feminism'

Finland signed the CEDAW in July 1980, together with fifty other states, in connection with the World Conference on the UN Decade for Women held in Copenhagen. The Council for Equality between Women and Men was given the task of assessing what kinds of legal measures were required for ratification. In its report in 1981, the Council divided these measures into those that were to be fulfilled before ratification and others that could be performed afterwards. Modifications to certain family law provisions and the enactment of a new Anti-discrimination Act were considered necessary before ratification could take place.[36]

Left-wing politics and corporatism for the fair distribution and redistribution of resources was characteristic for Finland as well as the Nordic welfare states of the time.[37] The Nordic legal systems did not allow direct reference to human rights treaties by the courts. Rights were more or less subordinated to concerns regarding representative democracy and state-centred ideas of the common good, and authorities had no strong commitment to legally protected individual and minority rights.[38] The Nordic states were agnostic towards 'high-voltage constitutionalist rights talk' and judicial activism.[39] They adhered to the dualist model of international law, and the impact of human rights treaties was largely based on what the government and legislature considered necessary at ratification.

[36] *Syrjintäsopimustyöryhmän selvitys YK:n naisten syrjinnän poistamista koskevan yleissopimuksen ratifioinnin edellytyksistä ja tarvittavista lainsäädännöllisistä ja muista toimenpiteistä* [The Report of the Working Group on Discrimination on the Conditions of Ratification of the UN CEDAW Convention, and on Legislative and Other Action Needed] (Helsinki: Valtioneuvoston kanslia, tasa-arvoasiain neuvottelukunta [Prime Minister's Office, Council for Equality], 1981).

[37] D. Bradley *et al.*, 'Distribution and redistribution in post-industrial democracies', *World Politics* 55:2 (2003) 193–228.

[38] J. Lavapuro, T. Ojanen and M. Scheinin, 'Rights-based constitutionalism in Finland and the development of pluralist constitutional review', *International Journal of Constitutional Law* 9:2 (2011) 505–31 at 506.

[39] R. Hirshl, 'The Nordic counter-narrative: democracy, human development and judicial review', *International Journal of Constitutional Law* 9:2 (2011) 449–69.

Rights under ratified international human rights instruments were not given constitutional protection, and the Finnish Constitution at that point did not even allow judicial review. The Constitution was protected through Parliamentary preview by the Parliament's Constitutional Committee, and civil rights protection relied on the principle of legality, overseen by ombudsman-type authorities.

Thus, legislative measures undertaken prior to ratification of the CEDAW were crucial to its impact at the Finnish national level. The legislation held to be contrary to the CEDAW, and thus in need of amendment, included norms regarding custody, citizenship and choice of family name.[40] The provisions on child custody were altered by the Act on Custody of and Access to Children, which repealed norms on custody that privileged fathers in representing the child legally. Under the Act on Citizenship, mothers were not able to transmit their citizenship to their children, and the reform gave equal rights to both parents. A new Act on Family Names was also passed. It repealed the earlier family name provisions that had forced women to adopt the name of their husbands upon marriage, either as such or as a part of a double name. Somewhat surprisingly, repealing family name provisions caused much political controversy. In spite of the fact that wives had been obliged to assume their husband's name as the mutual family name relatively late in history in Finland, the opponents to the amendment lamented the loss of a tradition and suspected that allowing the wife to retain her family name would ruin family unity and lead to the dissolution of family life. Despite such reservations, amendments were introduced enabling the wife to retain her family name and allowing the spouses to choose the family name of either of them as the mutual family name.

The Act on Equality between Women and Men (*tasa-arvolaki*) 1986 was the most important and visible legislative outcome of the ratification of the CEDAW. Thereby, the CEDAW also became the catalyst for the introduction of the first piece of anti-discrimination law to Finnish society – the former few prohibitions of discrimination had been added to existing labour and penal law. The Council for Equality between Women and Men claimed that a separate Act on gender equality, containing prohibitions against discrimination, was a prerequisite for the ratification

[40] The working group that assessed the preconditions on ratification proposed a provision on gender equality in the Constitution. Such a provision was not introduced before ratification, but later, when the provisions on fundamental rights in the Constitution were amended as a part of constitutional reform in 1995.

of the CEDAW. In March 1982 the Prime Minister's Office nominated a committee to prepare such an Act. The committee presented a report in October that year, and after further preparatory work, a Government Bill for an Act was presented to the Parliament.[41] The preparatory work refers to various human rights instruments, including the CEDAW.[42] The Act on Equality prohibited discrimination on the grounds of sex and set positive duties for authorities and employers to promote equality. The Articles on the prohibition of discrimination in general and in working life in particular were drafted in relation to Articles 2 and 11 of the CEDAW.

Among the main features of the Act were that it prohibited discrimination against both women and men, especially in working life. The CEDAW is literally concerned with discrimination against women, but it was not considered appropriate in Finland to single out women or men in legislation. Rather, gender-neutral formulations had gained ground for a long time. Most second-wave feminists in Finland[43] were also committed to gender-neutral policies.[44] Perhaps even more than in most countries, the Finnish prohibition of discrimination on the grounds of sex/gender was conceived from the beginning as a symmetrical prohibition, needed by both women and men. Finnish gender equality policies reflected a persistent feature of Finnish gender relations, an emphasis on marginalisation and alleged discrimination of men as a counterweight to promoting the position of women.

It has been claimed that the CEDAW accelerated the adoption of equality legislation in Finland. However, since all women's organisations had demanded such legislation and all other Nordic states had already adopted equality acts, the Finnish Act on Equality between Women and Men would probably have been enacted, irrespective of the CEDAW. There was much reluctance to adopt anti-discrimination policies. Employers' organisations opposed non-discrimination law in general and tried to overturn all

[41] *Committee Report Containing a Draft Proposal for an Act on Equality between Women and Men* (1982). The committee report was severely criticised by labour market organisations. Provisions against discrimination were held to go against the right to regulate labour issues by means of collective agreements. The preparatory work was finalised by a small working group. *Prime Minister's Office Working Group Report on a Draft Proposal for an Act on Equality between Women and Men* (1982).

[42] Other international instruments mentioned include ILO Convention No. 100 and Article 4 of the European Social Charter.

[43] See the remarks in *supra* note 7.

[44] R. Jallinoja, *Suomalaisen naisliikkeen taistelukaudet* and R. Jallinoja, 'Independence or integration: the women's movement and political parties in Finland' in D. Dahlerup (ed.), *The New Women's Movement* 158–78.

legal proposals to that end. Small employers in particular were set against an Anti-discrimination Act on gender discrimination, and even launched media campaigns against it. However, in the 1980s, Finnish political actors were acutely aware of the aim of creating a positive international image of the country in the UN, and a coalition of women's organisations and other equality actors could benefit from referring to the UN conventions in promoting their aims. Thus, the CEDAW offered important support for the proponents of the Act on Equality between Women and Men.[45]

The fact that the CEDAW motivated the Act on Equality also had a profound impact on the formulation of the Act. The material scope of the Finnish Act on Equality was broad from the beginning. The approach is based on the CEDAW, which clearly differs from, for example, the narrower scope of the EC equality law. The broad scope of the prohibition of discrimination was offset by the fact that remedies and sanctions were offered mainly against discrimination in employment.[46] Positive duties and measures introduced by the Act also reflect the impact of the CEDAW. The provisions of the Act on Equality between Women and Men obligating employers, authorities and educational institutions to promote equality by positive measures were 'programmatic', however, and not backed by sanctions. The Finnish implementation thus shows a limited willingness to introduce justiciable rights to combat discrimination, or mandatory positive duties or measures monitored by authorities.

The strong emphasis on discrimination in the labour market may be understood against the background of the work done by the Labour Market Subcommittee of the Council for Equality and the state feminists' attempts to find remedies for gender segregation in the labour market, pay and other forms of discrimination neglected by the corporatist decision-making. In spite of the general scepticism regarding individual rights, combating discrimination against working women was considered necessary.

While gender equality matters were organised somewhat similarly under Nordic 'state feminism', the Equality Acts passed at that time differed from country to country. In Denmark, Norway and Sweden, national legislation on gender equality was enacted before these states ratified the CEDAW. The Danish legislation was enacted to transpose EC law, since

[45] N. Bruun and P. K. Koskinen, *Tasa-arvolaki* (Act on Equality between Women and Men), 2nd revised edn (Helsinki: Lakimiesliiton Kustannus, 1997) at 31.

[46] N. Bruun and P. K. Koskinen, *Tasa-arvolaki* (Act on Equality between Women and Men), 1st edn (Helsinki: Lakimiesliiton Kustannus, 1986).

Denmark, as a European Economic Communities (EEC) Member State, was obligated to implement the EC Directives on equal pay and equal treatment, which were limited to working life in their material scope.[47] The Swedish Act on Equality between Women and Men at Work of 1979 was limited to employment issues, but it contained positive duties for employers.[48] The Norwegian Act on Equal Status of 1978 prohibited discrimination on the grounds of sex with a wider scope. Like the later Finnish Act on Equality, the Norwegian Act had a broad material scope, but both made exceptions regarding family life and religious communities. Under Norwegian law, 'private' discrimination was not excluded as such, but the sanctions could not be applied to such discrimination. The Finnish solution was to exclude relations in private life altogether from the material scope of the Act on Equality. The criticism of the feminists towards a gender-neutral formulation of the Norwegian Act on Equal Status was known in Finland, but unlike in Norway, a gender-neutral approach had wide approval, even by feminists.[49] Although the Norwegian and Swedish Equality Acts were used as models when the Finnish Act on Equality was drafted (as regards the structure of the Act, the concepts used and solutions adopted), the Finnish Act of 1986 differed from its Nordic counterparts in many ways.[50]

When the Finnish Parliament decided on the ratification of the CEDAW in the summer of 1986, Finland was the last Nordic state to ratify this Convention.[51] While the CEDAW has been the target of numerous (sometimes even sweeping) reservations by the States Parties to it, Finland ratified it without reservations. This was possible due to the above-mentioned changes introduced to the Finnish legislation, supported by 'state feminist' activists.

The orientation of Finland, both to the UN and towards the Nordic Council during the Cold War era, was important in shaping the manner in which Finland joined and implemented the CEDAW. The Nordic point of reference from which the CEDAW was presented to Finnish politics was important, partly in terms of the type of provisions introduced on the

[47] The pertinent EC Directives were those on equal pay (75/117/EEC) and equal treatment (76/207/EEC).

[48] M. Eduards *et al.*, 'Equality: how equal' at 144–7.

[49] H. Ellilä *et al.*, 'Meillekin tasa-arvolaki?' [An Equality Act also for Finland], *Oikeus* 2 (1983) 115–19.

[50] Bruun and Koskinen, *Tasa-arvolaki*, 1st edn at 43.

[51] Sweden submitted the instrument of ratification in July 1980; Norway in May 1981; Denmark in April 1983; Iceland in June 1985; and Finland in September 1986.

basis of the Convention, but also because all the other Nordic states had introduced gender equality laws before Finland, and prior to Finland's ratification of the CEDAW. References to Nordic solutions that paid attention to working life in particular were important for framing the Finnish legislative solutions politically.

Over the years, all Nordic pieces of legislation on gender equality have undergone extensive amendments, and at present are being reformed in the context of a wider development in Europe. Due to the increasing number of grounds to be protected against discrimination, and the requirement to establish equality bodies to monitor these prohibitions, a pan-European tendency to unify equality law and these bodies has been influencing Nordic equality policies.[52]

3.2 *The CEDAW and the arrival of 'rights discourse' in Finland*

The end of the Cold War had strong impact on the development of Finnish law in general, including gender equality law. Finland joined the Council of Europe in 1989 and ratified the European Convention on Human Rights (ECHR) in 1990. The ratification of this Convention was a turning point in legal attitudes to human rights instruments in Finland. It was only after this time that human rights conventions accepted by Finland gained more concrete attention, for example in Finnish law schools. The ECHR had an impact on the reform of the Finnish Constitution[53] and it also introduced the first judicial review of any kind to the Finnish legal tradition.

The Finnish Constitution underwent a complete reform in the 1990s. First, a new chapter on basic rights and liberties entered into force in 1995, and at the overall reform of the Constitution in 2000, a stronger protection of rights was introduced. Constitutional rights were drafted to reflect international development in the area of human rights and European constitutional development after the Second World War. International human rights norms binding Finland were taken as a starting point. Finland's adherence to EC/EU law had an even more fundamental impact

[52] J. Kantola and K. Nousiainen, 'Institutionalising intersectionality in Europe: introducing the themes', *International Journal of Feminist Politics* 11:4 (2009) 459–77.

[53] Issues related to fair trial and freedom of speech in particular have been brought to the fore. M. Pellonpää, 'Euroopan ihmisoikeustuomioistuimen ja EY:n tuomioistuimen vaikutuksista Suomen valtiosäännön kannalta' [On the impact of the European Court of Human Rights and EC-Court in the light of the Finnish Constitution] in H. Kanninen *et al.* (eds.), *Puhuri käy* [Strong Wind Blowing] (Helsinki: Edita, 2009) 103–27.

on Finnish law. During the accession period in the early 1990s, and since EU membership in 1995, Finnish constitutional law has been influenced greatly by European law.[54]

Both the European Court of Human Rights and the EU Court assert judicial protection of a pan-European set of rights in the Member States.[55] The adoption of a modest form of judicial review in the constitutional reform of 2000 further boosted the 'rights discourse' in Finland. Stronger protection of constitutional rights has met with criticism in all Nordic states, including Finland.[56] Increasing emphasis on rights is criticised as detrimental to popular sovereignty. They are seen to go hand in hand with globalisation and economic liberalisation, and also as an ideological veil over increasing social differentiation and poverty. Interestingly, criticism has emerged in the context of defining the position of the CEDAW in the Nordic setting. In a Norwegian Parliamentary power inquiry, the granting of special legal standing to the CEDAW above ordinary legislation was especially criticised.[57]

In Finland there has been no open questioning of the relevance of the CEDAW. International development has otherwise deflected its influence. Here, the Finnish accession to the EU had a fundamental impact. Since the early 1990s Finnish non-discrimination law has been deeply influenced by the *acquis communautaire* in the field. As early as 1994, the preparations to join the European Economic Area (EEA)[58] brought a need to strengthen protection against discrimination on the grounds of sex.

The history of outlawing discrimination on grounds other than gender by a separate Act of anti-discrimination law is quite recent in Finland and has been strongly influenced by European non-discrimination law. Since Article 13 of the 1997 Treaty of Amsterdam gave the EU powers to combat discrimination on the grounds of gender, race, ethnicity, religion, belief,

[54] T. Ojanen, 'The impact of EU membership on Finnish constitutional law', *European Public Law* 9:2 (2004) 449–69.

[55] A. Follesdal and M. Wind, 'Introduction – Nordic reluctance towards judicial review under siege', *Nordisk Tidskrift for menneskerettigheter* 27:2 (2009) 131–41.

[56] K. Tuori, 'Judicial review as a last resort' in T. Campbell, K. D. Ewing and A. Tomkins (eds.), *The Legal Protection of Human Rights: Sceptical Essays* (Oxford University Press, 2011) 365–91.

[57] See the chapter by A. Hellum in this book.

[58] The EEA was created in 1994 to allow the EFTA countries to participate in the European Single Market without joining the European Community. The EFTA countries were to adopt EC law. Of the Nordic states that joined the EEA Treaty, Iceland and Norway remain bound by it, but since Finland and Sweden joined the EU in 1995, they became bound by EU law directly and not through the EEA obligations.

age, disability and sexual orientation, the European anti-discrimination law could move beyond discrimination grounds of Member State nationality and sex.[59] Legislative measures were soon undertaken against discrimination on the grounds mentioned in the Amsterdam Treaty. In many EU Member States, including Finland,[60] national anti-discrimination law and monitoring bodies needed to be levelled out.[61] Unifying equality legislation into a single piece of legislation, and establishing a single equality body became a European trend.[62] In Finland a committee was nominated in 2008 to propose a reform of anti-discrimination and equality law, including both the Act on Equality between Women and Men and the Non-Discrimination Act (*yhdenvertaisuuslaki*), which prohibits discrimination on other grounds.[63] Since the unification of the Act on Equality with anti-discrimination law on other grounds was criticised by the labour market and women's organisations, gender equality law was left outside the reform.[64]

While the CEDAW was given particular attention at the time of its ratification in Finland, it has received less attention in the legislative field in the era of strong European influences from the 1990s on, despite its impact in the context of the constitutional rights reform of 1995. The basic rights provisions of the Constitution came to include a revised provision (section 6) on equality, which was expanded to cover not only formal equality before the law, but also a general prohibition of discrimination (including a reference to sex as a prohibited ground), a provision on the equal rights

59 M. Bell, *Anti-Discrimination Law and the European Union* (Oxford University Press, 2000) at 157.

60 Finland became a member of the EU in 1995, together with Austria and Sweden.

61 Two Directives based on Article 13 of the Amsterdam Treaty, the Council Directive (2000/43/EC) on equal treatment between persons irrespective of racial or ethnic origin and the Council Directive (2000/78/EC) establishing a general framework for equal treatment in employment and occupation (which bans discrimination on several grounds), were implemented in Finland by a single piece of legislation, the Non-Discrimination Act of 2004.

62 K. Nousiainen, 'Unification (or not) of equality bodies and legislation', *European Gender Equality Law Review* 2 (2008) 24–33; Kantola and Nousiainen, 'Institutionalising intersectionality in Europe'.

63 J. Kantola and K. Nousiainen, 'Pussauskoppiin: Tasa-arvo- ja yhdenvertaisuuslakien yhdistämisestä' [Into the kissing booth? Working toward uniformity in the Finnish Gender Equality and Non-Discrimination Acts], *Naistutkimus* 2 (2008) 6–20.

64 J. Kantola and K. Nousiainen, *Institutionalising Intersectionality with a Separate Strands Approach: The Case of Finland*, paper presented in the European Consortium for Political Research (ECPR), Joint Sessions 14–18 April 2009, Workshop 14, Institutionalising Intersectionality: Comparative Analyses.

of children and a provision on the promotion of equality of the sexes.[65] The aim of the amended provision was to guarantee not merely formal but also substantive equality. The preparatory work refers to the CEDAW as a 'special convention against discrimination' that was taken into account as a motivation for the constitutional provision on discrimination.[66] The constitutional provision on the promotion of gender equality was also motivated by a reference to Article 2(a) of the CEDAW, which obligates the States Parties to include the principle of equality between men and women in their legislation.

While, according to its preparatory work, the Finnish Act on Equality between Women and Men has similar aims to those of the Constitution, the constitutional provision does not refer to any single act, but contains a general obligation to develop legislation. The means of promoting equality are not limited by the Constitution, but are to be chosen by the legislature. Legislation enacted to fulfil the obligation is open to judicial review, and, in principle, its interpretation should take into account the obligations under the CEDAW. Yet references to the CEDAW in case law have remained few. Two possible explanations for this may be offered. First, judicial review is very seldom used in practice, and second, the Finnish case law since the 1990s concerning gender equality mainly concerns issues related to EU law.

The CEDAW has been a point of reference in Finnish post-1990 legal discourse at times in the Parliamentary preview of Government Bills, especially concerning section 6 of the Constitution (on equality). Nevertheless, the Parliament's Constitutional Committee seems to refer to other human rights instruments rather than the CEDAW in its opinions on section 6. For example, in 2006 a Government Bill proposed a higher parental leave benefit for fathers than for mothers, with the motivation that this would encourage fathers to use their right to parental leave, which would eventually lead to a more-balanced sharing of parental leave. The Parliament's Constitutional Committee was asked for an assessment of the constitutionality of the proposal. The Committee heard a number of experts, who referred to international human rights instruments including the CEDAW, and who held that the amendment violated section 6 of the Constitution.[67] The Parliament's Constitutional Committee merely

[65] Section 6(4) of constitutional rights reads as follows: 'Equality of the sexes is promoted in societal activity and working life, especially in the determination of pay and other terms of employment, as provided in more detail by an Act.'

[66] See *Preparatory Works for the Constitution*, in Government Bill (HE) 309/1993, 43.

[67] Government Bill (HE) 112/2006 vp.

referred to Article 26 of the International Covenant on Civil and Political Rights (ICCPR) and to ECHR Protocol 12, but not to the CEDAW, as a motivation for its assessment that the amendment needed to be passed by qualified majority procedure.[68]

4 The CEDAW supervisory process and Finland

The most visible supervision of the implementation of the CEDAW takes place in the context of the reporting procedure established within the framework of the Convention. The Optional Protocol to the CEDAW adopted in 1999, introducing the individual communication procedure and allowing the CEDAW Committee to receive communications from individuals or groups of individuals, was ratified by Finland, among the first states to do so, in 2000 when the Protocol also entered into force. At the time of writing no communications have been filed against Finland. To a large extent, this can be explained by the general lack of information on this communication procedure in Finland. Furthermore, the Finnish 'state feminism' discussed above has engaged major women's organisations in close cooperation with the government, which has clearly diminished the interest of these organisations in resorting to this supervisory mechanism.

4.1 National reports

At the time of writing, the CEDAW Committee had considered six governmental (state) reports of the Finnish government. The first report was submitted in 1988 and the sixth report in 2007.[69] The Committee

[68] *Report of the Parliament's Constitutional Standing Committee* 38/2006 vp.

[69] *Suomen ensimmäinen raportti kaikkinaisen naisten syrjinnän poistamista koskevan yleissopimuksen toteuttamisesta*, sosiaali- ja terveysministeriö, tasa-arvojulkaisuja, Helsinki 1/1988 [Initial Report of the Government of Finland on the Implementation of the CEDAW, Ministry of Social Affairs and Health]; *Suomen toinen raportti YK:n naisten oikeuksien sopimuksen toteuttamisesta*, ulkoasiainministeriön julkaisuja, 26/1992, Helsinki 1992 [Second Report of the Government of Finland on the Implementation of the CEDAW, Ministry for Foreign Affairs, 1992]; *Suomen kolmas raportti YK:n naisten oikeuksien sopimuksen toteuttamisesta*, ulkoasiainministeriön julkaisuja, 6/1997, Helsinki 1997 [Third Report of the Government of Finland on the Implementation of the CEDAW, Ministry for Foreign Affairs, 1997]; *Fourth Periodic Report by Finland to the Convention on the Elimination of All Forms of Discrimination against Women*, February 2000, available at: www.formin.fi/public/default.aspx?contentId=67770&nodeId=31460 (last accessed 1 February 2012); *Fifth Periodic Report of the Government of Finland on the Implementation of the Convention on the Elimination of All Forms of Discrimination*

considered Finland's fifth and sixth reports jointly in 2008. While the Committee requested Finland to respond to the concerns expressed in the Concluding Observations in its seventh periodic report due in 2011,[70] it also asked Finland to provide, within two years, detailed written information on the implementation of the recommendations the Committee had made on the problem of violence against women. This separate special report on violence against women was submitted in 2010.[71] Despite the delayed submission of the most recent report, in general the Finnish government has followed the reporting timetable set for governmental reports quite well. It has also responded to the requests of the CEDAW Committee to provide further information on specified topics.

Regarding the substance of the governmental reports, in its first report the Finnish government provided some basic information under each Article of the CEDAW and shed light on the legislative changes made in the national ratification process of the Convention. In the subsequent reports, the government has focused on reporting on certain issues, for example those on which the CEDAW Committee had requested additional information. Information is provided especially on violence against women, women belonging to certain minority groups (Sámi and Roma women, women with disabilities and women of immigrant background), trafficking in human beings and exploitation of prostitution of women, women in political and public life, women's position in the labour market and discrimination in employment (including difficulties in combining work and family life and the wage difference between women and men) and women's health. In the sixth report information was also given on the legislative reform that aimed at consolidating the Act on Equality between Women and Men and the Non-Discrimination Act,[72]

against Women, October 2003, available at: www.formin.fi/public/default.aspx?contentId=67770&nodeId=31460 (visited on 1 February 2012); *Sixth Periodic Report of the Government of Finland on the Implementation of the Convention on the Elimination of All Forms of Discrimination against Women*, October 2007, available at: www.formin.fi/public/default.aspx?contentId=67770&nodeId=31460 (last accessed 1 February 2012); *Seventh Periodic Report of the Government of Finland*, May 2012, available at: http://formin.finland.fi/public/default.aspx?contentid=67770 (last accessed 9 June 2012).

[70] The seventh report was submitted to the CEDAW Committee in May 2012. It was not possible to include references to its substance in this chapter.

[71] *Response by Finland to the Recommendations Contained in the Concluding Observations of the Committee Following the Examination of the Fifth and Sixth Reports of Finland on 9 July 2008*, CEDAW/C/FIN/CO/6/Add1.

[72] See also the remarks on this above.

mainstreaming gender equality into the Finnish state administration, promoting equality in the media and equality in education.

The increase of the number of substantive issues addressed in the reports over the years has rendered governmental reports quite lengthy. Since the second report, the reports have also included an annex with useful statistical information on the situation of women in Finland. The more recent reports are loaded with information that makes them rather burdensome to read. Finland's seventh periodic report was prepared by taking into account the CEDAW Committee's new reporting guidelines setting a maximum length to the report and requiring that the information in the report address the Committee's observations point by point.[73] Thus, the seventh governmental report by Finland should include more precise information on both legislative and other measures and should be more concise, thereby enhancing the readability of the report.

It may be observed that while the first Finnish governmental reports were rather self-critical, in the subsequent reports the government's self-criticism has decreased to some extent. Despite this, the Finnish government may be credited for being somewhat frank and open with regard to the problems existing in Finland. It neither denies the existence of the problems nor exercises the kind of window-dressing that is sometimes typical of governmental reporting.

A notable change in the Finnish government's reports to the CEDAW Committee took place in the mid 1990s, that is at the time when Finland joined the EU. The reports submitted after 1995 include remarks on the effects of EU policies and EC legislation in Finland. They also contain references to the implementation of the *Beijing Declaration and Platform for Action* (*Beijing Document*) adopted at the Fourth World Conference on the Status of Women held in 1995.[74] These references to a variety of

[73] HRI/GEN/2/Rev.6.

[74] It is notable that the CEDAW Committee has asked the States Parties to the CEDAW to also report on their implementation of the *Beijing Document*, which the Committee considers to reinforce the provisions of the CEDAW. In this way, the CEDAW Committee has made the implementation review of the *Beijing Document* part of its review work. In fact, this echoes the practice of the Committee on the Elimination of Racial Discrimination, which has made the follow-up to the Declaration and Programme of Action of the World Conference against Racism, Racial Discrimination, Xenophobia and Related Intolerance held in 2001 in Durban as part of its review work. See also M. Pentikäinen, *Creating an Integrated Society and Recognising Differences: The Role and Limits of Human Rights, with Special Reference to* Europe (Rovaniemi: Acta Universitatis Lapponiensis 140, Lapland University Press, 2008) at 127. Additionally, the CEDAW Committee has also referred to the importance of the Millennium Development Goals in its implementation review.

international sources in the reports have made it increasingly difficult to distinguish the role of both the CEDAW and the remarks of the CEDAW Committee in the national-level developments in Finland. The very fact that nowadays the governmental reports of Finland to the CEDAW Committee also contain remarks on these other developments – not merely those relating to the CEDAW – in fact calls for an increasingly analytical approach in reports. Although reporting broadly on the effects of various international norms on the Finnish legislation and practices is very useful for getting an overall picture of the state of affairs, the reports to the CEDAW Committee would benefit from focusing on the implementation requirements stemming from the CEDAW, that is reporting on the measures linked particularly to the obligations under this Convention.

4.2 *Involvement of civil society in the supervisory process*

In Finland, actors in civil society participate in the CEDAW reporting procedure in two visible ways: the government has involved non-governmental organisations (NGOs) in the process of compiling governmental reports, in addition to which NGOs prepare their own reports ('shadow reports') to the CEDAW Committee. At the time of initiating the preparation of a governmental report, NGOs are consulted about the themes that should be included in the governmental report. NGOs are also invited to a discussion on the draft governmental report before the final report is submitted to the CEDAW Committee. In these NGO hearings, organisations have both voiced their concerns for the issues falling within the scope of the CEDAW and have reported on their own activities in promoting equality between women and men.[75] While this process has been generally welcomed by NGOs, it has also resulted in including remarks on the NGO activities on advancing equality between women and men in the governmental reports. This reporting method is not unproblematic, since it is not always clearly indicated which of the activities reported are solely those of NGOs and which NGO activities are supported by the government (by public funds). In practice, this reporting strategy has blurred the primary role and responsibility of the government with respect to the implementation of the CEDAW.

[75] In practice, these hearings are organised by the Ministry for Foreign Affairs, which is responsible for the national coordination of the governmental report. In this process the Ministry for Foreign Affairs consults a number of authorities, NGOs and individual experts on whether the CEDAW Committee's observations and recommendations have been addressed by the Finnish government.

The compiling of 'shadow reports' by NGOs has been supported by the increased positive attitude of the CEDAW Committee to include civil society actors in information gathering on actual situations in the States Parties to the CEDAW. The NGO reports are considered by the Committee together with the governmental reports, and the particular added value of these NGO reports has been linked to their role of creating dialogue in the Committee.[76] Finnish NGOs have prepared their own (joint) reports for the CEDAW Committee on two occasions when the periodical state report has been considered by the Committee. The first NGO report was prepared in 2004, not only as a reaction to the Finnish government's fifth report to the CEDAW Committee and including civil society actors' views on the implementation problems in Finland, but also to draw particular attention to the twenty-fifth anniversary of the CEDAW. The second joint NGO report was prepared in 2008 to be considered together with the Finnish government's sixth report to the CEDAW Committee.[77] Finnish NGOs also submitted their views in the process of the consideration of the Finnish government's special report on violence against women in 2010.[78] Compared to the Finnish governmental reports, the Finnish NGO reports are much more concise with a clearer focus on reporting on the problems of implementation. NGOs have raised concern particularly for the following problems: violence against women, trafficking in women and exploitation of women within prostitution, increased pornographic visualisations in the media, advertising and culture in general, inequality in working life as well as in political and public life, insufficiency of resources channelled to the promotion of equality, legislation and particularly gender equality in legislative reform, women belonging to minorities,[79] equality planning in educational establishments and gender-sensitive budgeting. The NGOs have also drawn attention to the narrow interpretation of the govern-

[76] C. Flinterman, Professor of Human Rights, Utrecht University, member of the CEDAW Committee, Panel discussion on the CEDAW Committee at the Workshop on Human Rights Treaties and Treaty Bodies, University of Helsinki, 22 April 2009.

[77] The preparation of the first joint NGO report involved eighteen different organisations, including the major Finnish women's organisations. The second joint NGO report combined the views of eleven organisations.

[78] Finnish NGOs' parallel report to the UN Committee monitoring the Convention on the Elimination of All Forms of Discrimination against Women, July 2010. The report is on file with the authors.

[79] This concerns the proposals of consolidating the Act on Equality between Women and Men and the Non-Discrimination Act (discussed in section 3.2) in which the NGOs see the danger of the loss of visibility of the issue of discrimination against women.

mental obligations under the CEDAW in Finland that has led to insufficient national implementation of the Convention.

The Finnish NGOs that have participated in the processing of the Finnish government's reports to the CEDAW Committee have commended the procedure of involving NGOs in the supervisory work. According to them, the Committee also appears to pay special attention to the views of and concerns raised by NGOs. A look at the remarks put forth by the Committee in its Concluding Observations on Finland supports this: the Committee often echoes the concerns of NGOs.

4.3 *The CEDAW Committee's observations on Finland*

The CEDAW Committee's observations and comments on state reports have become increasingly concrete over the years, and thereby also more helpful in the efforts to improve the implementation of the provisions of the CEDAW. In its Concluding Observations on Finland, since the beginning of and throughout the review process the Committee has mostly voiced its concern for violence against women, the situation of women belonging to various groups (immigrant women, Roma and Sámi women, women with disabilities), discrimination of women in working life (including the wage gap between men and women) and unequal participation of women in political and public life. In its most recent Concluding Observations on Finland (based on the fifth and sixth governmental reports), the CEDAW Committee also drew attention to the following issues as principal areas of concern and recommendation: gender equality in legislative reform, gender mainstreaming, invisibility of the CEDAW and its Optional Protocol in Finland, trafficking and exploitation of women in prostitution, stereotypes in media and advertising, education (concern, for example, for the overall gender neutrality of the educational curriculum and teaching materials) and the health of girls (for example, alcohol abuse).

Of various concerns raised by the CEDAW Committee with respect to Finland, violence against women appears to be a serious and persistent problem. Violence against women was already being discussed by Finnish feminists in the late 1970s, thus prior to Finland's ratification of the CEDAW, but it was only in the 1990s that it was recognised as a problem by official Finnish equality bodies. The attention of the CEDAW Committee and other UN (as well as Council of Europe) bodies and instruments to this violence prompted the Finnish Council for Equality between Women and Men to put this problem on its agenda.

One of the major challenges to addressing the problem of violence against women in Finland is that in the Finnish context this has not been considered as a form of discrimination, as defined under the CEDAW in accordance with the CEDAW Committee's General Recommendation No. 19 on violence against women. In Finland, this kind of violence is usually discussed under some other heading, such as domestic violence or violence in intimate-partner relations. Resources earmarked for anti-violence policies and especially for the actors who are important in crime prevention in the field are highly insufficient.[80] The CEDAW Committee has drawn attention to several problematic aspects in Finnish policies, such as insufficient services to victims (including the lack of shelters for victims) and the use of mediation in the context of violence against women.[81]

The attention of the international supervisory bodies, including the CEDAW Committee, to the problem of violence against women has had a decisive impact on the inclusion of this issue on the broader political agenda and activating discussions on this problem at the Finnish domestic level. It was this attention that resulted in the compilation of the first studies on the issue and initiating the debate on the prevalence of the general culture of violence, including violence against women, in Finland. After the 1995 Beijing Conference on the Status of Women, the Finnish government adopted a strategy against violence against women, and since then different aspects of violence against women have been on the governmental agenda.

Despite this, the consideration of the problem of violence against women remains highly insufficient in Finland and the political programmes adopted have had only a limited impact on the actual situation. The special report on violence against women requested from Finland by the CEDAW Committee in 2008 was an important signal of concern from the international level. This report and the CEDAW Committee's observations on the shortcomings of the Finnish government's measures to combat violence against women helped to introduce new national initiatives in the area, including a new *Action Plan to Reduce Violence against*

[80] This was raised by the Finnish NGOs, for example, in their joint report of 2008 to the CEDAW Committee.

[81] *Concluding Observations of the Committee on the Elimination of Discrimination against Women: Finland*, United Nations, Convention on the Elimination of All Forms of Discrimination against Women, Advanced unedited version, 18 July 2008, CEDAW/C/FIN/CO/6, paras. 15 and 16.

Women.[82] The Action Plan is comprehensive and based on cooperation of authorities, but – again – the actual resources allocated to it are very limited. The coordination among authorities continues to be in the hands of social welfare and health authorities. The emphasis is on preventive measures. Legislative measures, such as amendment of the Penal Code, take a secondary place in the Action Plan.

It is still too early to say whether the more recent international attention to violence against women has had more concrete effects on the Finnish national practices. There is room for some optimism, however, since the adoption of the Council of Europe Convention on Preventing and Combating Violence against Women and Domestic Violence in May 2011 and the ongoing ratification process in Finland now keeps the issue firmly on the agenda of the Finnish domestic authorities.

Another issue that has been repeatedly raised by the CEDAW Committee and that deserves be noted in this context is the situation of minority women. As discussed above, Finland has been a latecomer in addressing discrimination on grounds other than gender. Multiple and intersectional discrimination has received very little attention in Finland, and CEDAW reporting has been an important channel for voicing the problems met by women belonging to older minorities (such as Roma and Sámi women) and the increasing number of immigrant women. The Finnish reform and unification of equality law and equality bodies that began in 2008 (discussed above) was partly motivated by the assumption that such a reform would make it easier to address multiple discrimination. Although the CEDAW Committee has emphasised the need to take the problems of minority women seriously, the Committee has also taken the side of Finnish NGOs in that it has warned about the danger of marginalisation of gender issues, if equality law and bodies were unified to encompass all grounds of discrimination, with gender merely as one among them.[83] Thus, on this account the CEDAW Committee has clearly adhered to the concerns raised by the civil society actors. Anti-discrimination law reform now proceeds on a two-track model, consisting of two separate Acts and separate bodies for gender and other equality strands. It remains unclear if this outcome improves protection against intersectional discrimination.[84]

[82] *Action Plan to Reduce Violence against Women*, Ministry of Social Affairs and Health, Helsinki 2011.

[83] *Concluding Observations*, paras. 9 and 10.

[84] Many EU Member States have opted for unification of equality law and bodies. See Kantola and Nousiainen, *Institutionalising Intersectionality with a Separate Strands Approach*.

5 Concluding remarks

Ratification of the CEDAW was used effectively by Finnish women's organisations in pushing for anti-discrimination and equality legislation. However, Finnish equality policies of the 1980s were already inherent in the Nordic political climate of the time. The wide scope covered by the CEDAW parallels similar ambitions by Finnish activists in the 1970s. Yet the most visible piece of national legislation adopted at the time of the ratification of the CEDAW, that is the Act on Equality between Women and Men, concentrated on working life, especially when remedies and sanctions are considered. This emphasis written into this Act has contributed to a highly limited understanding of the significance of the CEDAW in Finland and has tended to blur the wide coverage of the CEDAW incorporating a broad principle of equality.

The Finnish corporatist type of governance has channelled the labour market and related issues to a tripartite cooperation between labour market organisations and the government. This tradition has promoted a definition of equal pay, reconciliation of work and family life, and similar issues as matters to be negotiated rather than as areas involving discrimination to be combated. It has also resulted in the blurring of the human rights relevance of these questions. For instance, the issue of unequal pay is not usually seen as a human rights issue in Finland. Furthermore, the strong nexus between the agendas of gender and social equality, the latter understood in terms of social and economic utility, may also make it difficult to introduce issues that are important to minority women, if such issues are not seen to enhance employment or other utilitarian goals.[85]

The general problem today is the loss of focus in anti-discrimination work. Finnish gender equality policies in the 1990s concentrated on the issues specified by the *Beijing Document*. It introduced gender mainstreaming, which in many ways resembled the Nordic approach to gender equality. But, as the report on the Government Gender Equality Programme 1997–9 remarked, monitoring and assessment were not a part of the original Nordic model.[86] Violence against women received

In general, addressing multiple discrimination is challenging due to the functioning of non-discrimination law, which makes it difficult to deal with the cases in which various grounds of discrimination cumulate. See Pentikäinen, *Creating an Integrated Society* at 170.

[85] Nousiainen, 'Utility-based equality'.

[86] Report on the Government Gender Equality Programme, *Tasa-arvo valtavirtaan. Sukupuolten tasa-arvon tila vuosituhannen kynnyksellä*. Sosiaali- ja terveysministeriö, työryhmämuistioita [Equality Against the Stream: The State of Gender Equality at the

attention in the 1990s in Finland due the developments at the international level and the criticism Finland received from international bodies and actors. However, the problem was not defined domestically in terms of discrimination as interpreted by the CEDAW Committee. What is particularly important is that, while the Finnish Act on Equality between Women and Men has a broad material scope, it is limited by two important exceptions: family and other private life, and religious practices of religious communities are excluded from its scope of application. Since no similar exceptions are made to the scope of the CEDAW, the Convention provides an extremely useful tool for addressing these legal lacunae. The importance of the nexus between religions and human rights, including the human rights of women, has acquired unprecedented reference in modern societies that are becoming increasingly diverse in terms of religious differences. In this context, the provisions of the CEDAW deserve special attention.

In Finland the CEDAW and human rights in general have been emphasised more in the context of Finnish foreign policies and international cooperation rather than as matters of relevance at home. It is quite telling that in the area of state administration, the CEDAW appears particularly in the work of the Ministry for Foreign Affairs. The visibility given to the CEDAW in the work of this Ministry is explained by the foreign policy emphases of the Finnish government in the area of human rights highlighting the rights of women. The text of the CEDAW as well as some information on the work of the CEDAW Committee have been placed on the website of the Ministry for Foreign Affairs.[87] The Ministry of Social Affairs and Health, which bears the main responsibility for gender equality issues internally in Finland, also pays some attention to the CEDAW in its work. It is noteworthy that the visibility given to the CEDAW on the website of this Ministry is more limited than that on the website of the Ministry for Foreign Affairs.[88]

It may be said that the human rights culture has been and still is quite thin at the domestic level in Finland and is waiting to be rooted firmly in national practices. The Finnish paradox is that gender equality is considered a self-evident value and a goal already achieved. This attitude makes it difficult to efficiently address gendered practices that are disadvantageous

Turn of the Millennium, Working Group Report No. 33 of the Ministry of Social Affairs and Health, 1999] (Helsinki: Edita, 1999) at 7.

[87] See www.formin.fi (last accessed 9 June 2012).

[88] See www.stm.fi (last accessed 9 June 2012).

to women, let alone to define them as discrimination, even where such practices are rather obvious.[89] The potential of the CEDAW has remained underused, both by the Finnish government and civil society actors, including NGOs. The cooperation between state equality bodies and women's organisations has been a mixed blessing, as it seems to preclude forms of independent NGO activism, for example, in the form of individual communications. The government also partly relies on civil society organisations to carry out tasks for which the government is responsible. However, many measures required by the Convention can only be taken up by the government and executed by governmental actions. From the viewpoint of the state obligations under the CEDAW, it may be said that domestic actions by the Finnish government clearly remain insufficient. The implementation of the CEDAW requires both long-term work on gender equality and combating discrimination against women, as well as sufficient resources. All this has been lacking in Finland.

Promotion of equality in Finland has been further complicated and rendered increasingly unclear by the nature of the contemporary debate on equality and non-discrimination at the domestic level. On the one hand, all possible problems are easily labelled as equality and non-discrimination issues in Finnish public debate. On the other hand, the experts on equality issues wrestle with detailed anti-discrimination legislation (e.g. EU legislation), and there is little questioning of the real impact, effectiveness and flaws of this legislation. The 'big picture' has been lost. Drawing attention to the CEDAW, and putting this Convention in the limelight, may help us to see this 'big picture' again. This requires taking the CEDAW from the margins to the centre of human rights work.

[89] See also the report on the Government Gender Equality Programme, *Tasa-arvo valtavirtaan* at 8.

21

Making space and giving voice: the CEDAW in Norwegian law

ANNE HELLUM

1 Introduction

Norway, like other nation-states in Northern Europe, is in the throes of rapid and uneven social, political and legal change. Faced with accumulating international legal obligations, unprecedented cultural diversity and increasing transnationalism, a revitalization of traditional nationalism is taking place in Norway, as elsewhere in Northern Europe.[1] Matters related to ratification and domestication of international human rights conventions have in the course of the last twenty years become a site of political and legal contestation, and have challenged privileged positions of identity, status and power.[2] The controversial status of human rights in general and the Convention on the Elimination of All Forms of Discrimination against Women (CEDAW) in particular, which is a key theme in this chapter, illustrates the ambiguous relationship between Norway's identity as an international champion of human rights and gender equality on the one hand, and the growing concern for protection of national sovereignty and representative democracy on the other.

The research for this chapter started in 2010 when I was granted a six-month research fellowship within the research project 'Should states ratify human rights convention?', led by Andreas Føllesdal and Geir Ulfstein at the Centre for Advanced Study at the Norwegian Academy of Science. I am grateful to research assistant Anniken Sørlie for assistance with data collection and to Ingunn Ikdahl, Beatrice Halsaa, Vibeke Blaker Strand, Lene Løvdal, Else McClimans, Geir Ulfstein and Henriette Sinding Aasen for comments on earlier drafts.

[1] S. Algashi, T. H. Eriksen and H. Gorashi (eds.), 'Introduction' in *Paradoxes of Cultural Recognition. Perspectives from Northern Europe* (Farnham: Ashgate, 2010) 1–18.

[2] For an overview of these debates from a Nordic perspective, see A. Føllesdal and M. Wind, 'Nordic reluctance towards judicial review under siege', *Nordic Journal of Human Rights* 27 (2009) 131–42.

Through the Human Rights Act of 1999, the European Convention for the Protection of Human Rights and Fundamental Freedoms of 1950 (ECHR), the International Covenant on Civil and Political Rights (ICCPR) of 1966 and the International Covenant on Economic, Social and Cultural Rights (ICESCR) of 1966 were incorporated into Norwegian law so as to take precedence when coming into conflict with other Norwegian law.[3] The exclusion of the CEDAW, the Convention on the Rights of the Child (CRC) and the International Convention on the Elimination of All Forms of Racial Discrimination (ICERD) gave rise to claims from politicians, women's rights organizations, human rights organizations and independent experts that these conventions should be given the same status as other conventions. These claims sparked political and legal debates about the justiciability of the CEDAW, the CRC and the ICERD, and how their incorporation would affect representative democracy and national sovereignty.[4]

Taking the CEDAW as the starting point, the aim of this chapter is to show how the prevailing tension between international and national law as well as between gender-neutral and gender-specific law is played out in the context of Norway, which is a modern Western welfare state. Unlike EU law, the ECHR and the ICCPR, which address discrimination on the basis of sex (female and male), the CEDAW is premised on the assumption that a symmetrical approach covering discrimination on the basis of sex does not sufficiently recognize the pervasive discrimination against women on the basis of their gender, and that an asymmetric and gender-specific guarantee is needed.[5] As such the Norwegian CEDAW

[3] The European Convention of 4 November 1950 for the Protection of Human Rights and Fundamental Freedoms (ECHR), the International Covenant of 16 December 1966 on Civil and Political Rights (ICCPR) and the International Covenant of 16 December 1966 on Economic, Social and Cultural Rights (ICESCR) were incorporated by Act of 21 May 1999, No. 30. The UN Convention on the Rights of the Child (CRC) was incorporated into the Human Rights Act by Act of 1 August 2003, No. 86. The UN Convention on the Elimination of All Forms of Discrimination against Women was incorporated into the Human Rights Act by Act of 19 June 2009, No. 80. The Race Convention was incorporated into the Discrimination Act of 3 June 2005, No. 33.

[4] H. Skjeie, 'Policy views on the incorporation of human rights conventions: CEDAW in Norwegian law', *Nordic Journal of Human Rights* 27 (2009) 260–71; A. Hellum, 'The Global Equality Standard meets Norwegian sameness' in A. Hellum, S. S. Ali and A. Griffiths (eds.), *From Transnational Relations to Transnational Laws* (Farnham: Ashgate, 2011) 71–93.

[5] The main view of the framers of the Women's Convention is described in A. Byrnes, 'Article 1' in M. Freeman, C. Chinkin and B. Rudolf (eds.), *The UN Convention on the Elimination*

controversy speaks to the broader debate about the added value of the CEDAW in comparison to other treaties.

With the overall focus on law reform, judicial review and state report review, this chapter describes and analyzes the relationship between the Women's Convention and Norwegian laws, policies and practices. Through a textual approach, legislative debates, court cases and administrative practices are reviewed with a view to determining whether, by whom and with what effect the CEDAW has been invoked. To understand the process whereby the CEDAW has been adopted or resisted, an actor perspective focusing contestations within and between different state and non-state actors is adopted. In line with a polycentric conception of law, the state is seen as a body of different centres with different legal cultures and different perceptions of the relationship between international and Norwegian law.[6] The most significant state actors in this respect are the Ministry of Children and Equality,[7] the Ministry of Foreign Affairs, the Ministry of Justice and the State Legal Counsel. To situate the process of domestication in a broader historical and political terrain, the chapter draws on interdisciplinary women's and gender studies and interviews with key actors in government, politics and civil society. I also make use of my own observations as a legal expert where I, as Director of the Institute of Women's Law, Child Law, Anti-Discrimination and Equality Law, have provided advice to state and non-state actors regarding the incorporation and implementation of the CEDAW in Norwegian law.[8]

2 Norway 2012: gender-neutral laws and gendered realities

Gender equality, welfare and democracy are established Norwegian values. Yet the Norwegian Constitution does not explicitly prohibit discrimination.[9] The Gender Equality Act and the Human Rights Act constitute the main vehicles for domestication of the CEDAW in Norwegian law. The first National Action Plan on Gender Equality (2011–14), which specifically addresses the CEDAW, was adopted in 2011. The Norwegian

of All Forms of Discrimination against Women: A Commentary (Oxford University Press, 2012) 51–70 at 52.

[6] H. Petersen and H. Zahle, *Legal Polycentricity in Law* (Aldershot: Dartmouth, 1995).

[7] Since 2010, the Ministry of Children, Equality and Social Inclusion.

[8] Since 2008, The Institute of Women's Law, Child Law, Discrimination and Equality Law.

[9] A special article proclaiming that Norwegian authorities should respect and protect human rights was included in the Norwegian Constitution in 1994, section 110c(1) of the Constitution.

Storting's Human Rights Commission in their Report of 2011 recommends a prohibition against unfair or disproportionate discrimination.[10]

In spite of formal equality between the sexes, statistics show that there are significant social, political and economic differences between women and men, and between different groups of women.[11] While roughly as many women as men today have higher education, women's and men's choice of study is highly gendered. Women tend to choose teaching, health and care services and men tend to choose technical subjects and natural sciences. These choices are reflected in a gender-segregated labour market where women's monthly pay is 85 per cent of men's. Although there are almost as many women as men in paid work, women are much more likely than men to work part-time. Fourteen per cent of employed men and 41 per cent of employed women work part-time. As a consequence, 9 out of 10 people with minimum pensions are women. Women are not equally represented in Parliament, where 6 out of 10 representatives are men. Forty per cent of board members in public limited companies are women, while 83 per cent of the board representatives in private limited companies are men.

Immigration patterns are highly gendered. Eighty per cent of labour immigrants are men while 66 per cent of family immigrants are women. Men are in the majority (60 per cent) among refugees, while 60 per cent of immigrants moving to Norway to study, including au pairs, are women. Access to justice is marked by significant gender and race differences. The majority of gender discrimination cases handled by the Equality and Anti-Discrimination Ombud are filed by professional Norwegian women while the majority of complaints regarding ethnic discrimination are filed by men from minority backgrounds.[12]

[10] In 2009 the Storting's Human Rights Commission was appointed to prepare and put forward recommendations for a limited revision of the Constitution with the object of 'strengthening the position of human rights in Norwegian law'. Their report, Document 16 (2011–12) *Report to the Presidium of the Storting by the Human Rights Commission Concerning Human Rights in the Constitution*, suggests a new article 98: 'All people are equal under the law. No person must be exposed to unfair or disproportionate discrimination.'

[11] Statistics Norway, 2011, available at: www.ssb.no/likestilling_en/ (last accessed 1 September 2012).

[12] T. Nordstrøm, 'Diskriminering på tvers – rapport fra et oppsøkende rettighetsinformasjonsprosjekt' [Intersectional discrimination – report from an outreach programme directed at immigrant women], *Studies in Women's Law*, No. 83.2010 (Institute of Women's Law, University of Oslo, 2010).

It was against this background that The Equality and Anti-Discrimination Ombud in her supplementary report to Norway's eighth periodic report to the CEDAW Committee in 2012 called for systematic review of gender-neutral law texts 'in order to ensure that they do not in practice exclude or hinder gender-specific measures that are necessary to address specific problems of women and girls'.[13] There is a growing concern that gender-neutral legislation, policies and programmes provide inadequate protection of women from different age groups, social groups or ethnic groups from direct, indirect and intersectional discrimination; and as such hinder the achievement of substantive equality.

3 Ratification of the CEDAW and the Optional Protocol in a changing economic, political and legal landscape

Gender equality legislation was already in place when Norway ratified the CEDAW in 1981.[14] The Equal Pay Council and the Gender Equality Council were established in the early 1970s and followed by the Gender Equality Act in 1978.[15] In 1975 the Faculty of Law at the University of Oslo, on the basis of a proposal from female lecturers and students working in the student legal aid scheme, Free Legal Advice for Women (JURK), introduced women's law as an elective subject, setting out to describe, understand and improve the position of women in law and society.[16] Changes in Norwegian laws and policies were stimulated by international participation such as the Nordic initiatives in the UN Commission on Women in 1972, to speed up the process of transforming the Declaration on the Elimination of Discrimination against Women into a binding human rights convention.[17] The political structure for women's rights and gender equality proponents in Norway in the 1970s was, with the discovery of oil reserves in the North Sea and the introduction of new labour market

[13] *The Equality and Anti-Discrimination Ombud's Report to the Pre-session of the CEDAW, a Supplementary Report to the CEDAW Committee* (Oslo: The Equality and Discrimination Ombud, 2012).

[14] Norway ratified the CEDAW on 21 May 1981.

[15] Lov 9. juni 1978 nr 45 om likestilling mellom kjønnene [the Gender Equality Act].

[16] T. S. Dahl, *Women's Law: An Introduction to Feminist Jurisprudence* (Oslo: Norwegian University Press, 1987).

[17] B. Halsaa, 'No bed of roses? Academic feminism 1880–1990' in H. R. Christensen, B. Halsaa and A. Saarinen (eds.), *Crossing Borders: Re-mapping Women's Movements at the Turn of the 21st Century* (Odense: University Press of Southern Denmark, 2004) 81–99 at 93 and K. Nousiainen and M. Pentikäinen's chapter in this book.

policies implicating new roles for women in paid work and politics, extremely favourable.[18]

It was against this background that the Norwegian Labour Party in its ten-point programme promised to present a bill prohibiting discrimination against women. In 1974 a White Paper proposing an Act on gender equality was circulated in a public hearing.[19] The White Paper was surrounded by two major controversies related to the purpose and scope of the proposed legislation.[20] Should it adopt a gender-specific approach prohibiting discrimination against women or a gender-neutral approach prohibiting gender discrimination? Should it apply in both the public and the private space, or make exemptions for the private and religious sphere? In 1976 two proposals representing these opposing strands were debated in the Norwegian Parliament. Neither the Labour Party's proposal of a Gender Equality Act nor the Socialist Left Party's proposal of an Act against discrimination of women got a majority vote. In 1978 Parliament passed the Gender Equality Act, which was a compromise between the two strands. The Act prohibits gender discrimination, but allows differential treatment that promotes gender equality in conformity with the purpose of the Act, which is to improve the position of women. In spite of fierce criticism from most of the women's organizations, the Act exempted religion from its scope.[21] Family life was included but was not to be enforced by the Gender Equality Ombud and the Gender Equality Tribunal.[22]

Three years later, in 1981, Norway ratified the CEDAW without any reservations.[23]

The Convention was welcomed by all the political parties in Parliament and by the women's organizations, who wanted an Act that prohibited

[18] B. Halsaa, 'No bed of roses?' at 93.

[19] *Utkast til Lov om likestilling mellom kjønnene* [White Paper, Gender Equality Bill from the Ministry of Government Administration and Consumer Affairs]. Notat fra Forbruker og administrasjonsdepartementet [Oslo: Ministry of Government Administration and Consumer Affairs, July 1974].

[20] The legal and political controversies surrounding the Act are described in T. S. Dahl, K. Graver, A. Hellum and A. Robberstad, *Juss og Juks* [Law and Deceit] (Oslo: Pax, 1976); Sosialistisk Opplysningsforbund (written by T. Skard), *Hvorfor nei til likestillingslova?* [Why Reject the Gender Equality Act?] (Temahefte sosialistisk opplysningsforbund, 1976).

[21] According to section 2.1 in the Gender Equality Act of 1978, the Act shall 'apply to all areas, except for the internal affairs of religious communities'.

[22] According to Article 2.2 of the Gender Equality Act of 1978: 'With regard to family life and purely personal matters, this Act shall not be enforced by the bodies mentioned in section 9 of this Act.'

[23] Ratification of 21 May 1981.

discrimination against women in all spheres of life.[24] In the light of the Gender Equality Act, which was passed in 1978, it was assumed that Norwegian law was in consonance with the CEDAW. The ratification was, in Norway as in Finland, to a large extent seen as an act of solidarity with women in developing countries.[25]

The Norwegian state's ratification of the Optional Protocol to the Convention on the Elimination of All Forms of Discrimination against Women, which took place on 5 March 2002, was not plain sailing.[26] The objections, which were raised by the Government Legal Counsel, marked a growing resistance to judicial review.[27] The Government Legal Counsel argued that the CEDAW, due to the vague character of its standards, particularly the social and economic rights embedded in the Convention, could not be made the subject of judicial review in a Norwegian court of law.[28] The Ministry of Foreign Affairs, on the other hand, was of the view that the CEDAW's non-discrimination standard, in as far as it extended into the sphere of social and economic rights, was justiciable. This line of argument, which was adopted by the government and approved by Parliament, lent itself to the Norwegian Human Rights Law Commission's general view that there is no watertight division between civil, political, social and economic rights.[29]

[24] T. Skar, 'Milepeler i norsk kvinnebevegelse' [Milestones in the Norwegian women's movement], Seminar series, available at: http://kilden.forskningsradet.no/artikkel/vis.html?tid=45836 (last accessed 1 September 2012).

[25] See K. Nousiainen and M. Pentikäinen's chapter in this book.

[26] Optional Protocol to the Convention on the Elimination of All Forms of Discrimination against Women, A/RES/54/4.

[27] The government at the time of writing (Stoltenberg II) has, on the basis of advice from the State Legal Counsel, decided not to ratify the Optional Protocol to the Convention on the Rights of the Child A/RES/54/263, the Optional Protocol to the International Covenant on Economic, Social and Cultural Rights A/RES/63/117, and Protocol No. 12 to the Convention for the Protection of Human Rights and Freedoms (on discrimination), which entered into force 1 April 2005. The prevailing view of the State Legal Counsel is that conferral of legal power to international treaty bodies leads to erosion of representative democracy. See Letter of 22 October 2009 from the State Legal Counsel to the Ministry of Foreign Affairs 2009–0646 THS/-.

[28] H. F. Ervik, *Individuell klage som instrument for kvinners menneskerettigheter* [Individual Complaint Procedure as a Tool for Women's Rights], Kvinnerettslige studier nr. 41, Department of Public and International Law's Publication Series No. 5/1998 (Department of Public and International Law, University of Oslo, 1998).

[29] Menneskerettighetslovutvalgets innstilling NOU 1993: 18, *Lovgivning om menneskerettigheter* [Human Rights Legislation], 110. Arguing that there was no watertight division between civil, political, social and economic rights, the Norwegian Human Rights Law Commission suggested that the Convention on Social, Economic and Cultural Rights

4 Incorporation of the CEDAW into the Human Rights Act in 2009

On 19 June 2009, almost thirty years after ratification, the Women's Convention and the Optional Protocol to the Convention were incorporated into the Human Rights Act, so as to take precedence when coming into conflict with other Norwegian law. This long journey, which will be described below, illustrates the contested status of international human rights treaties in Norwegian law in general, and the long-standing controversy regarding the relationship between a gender-specific and a gender-neutral approach to gender equality in particular.

The story goes back to 1989, when the government, to strengthen and clarify the status of human rights in Norwegian law, appointed a Human Rights Law Commission to assess how central human rights conventions could be incorporated into Norwegian law.[30] The Norwegian legal system is, in spite of the increasing inflow of international law, seen as dualist. It is held, in line with the dualist doctrine, that a special Act is necessary to make binding international treaties a part of Norwegian law. On the basis of the recommendation from the Norwegian Human Rights Law Commission, a special Article proclaiming that Norwegian authorities should respect and protect human rights was included in the Norwegian Constitution in 1994.[31] Further incorporation of human rights conventions into Norwegian law was, in accordance with this new constitutional provision, to take place through legislation.[32]

In 1993 the Human Rights Law Commission suggested that a limited number of human rights conventions be incorporated into the Human Rights Act so as to take precedence when coming into conflict with other Norwegian law.[33] To distinguish between those conventions that were suited for this form of incorporation and those that were not, the

be incorporated into the Human Rights Act, so as to take precedence when coming into conflict with other Norwegian law.

30 Menneskerettighetslovutvalget [the Human Rights Law Commission] was appointed in 1989. Its recommendations are found in NOU 1993: 18, *Lovgivning om menneskerettigheter* [Human Rights Legislation].

31 Section 110c(1) of the Constitution.

32 Section 110c(2) of the Constitution.

33 For an overview of the debate about the CEDAW in Norwegian law up to 2002, see V. Blaker, *Kvinnekonvensjonens status i norsk rett* [The Status of the CEDAW in Norwegian Law], Institutt for offentlig retts skriftserie [Department of Public and International Law's Publication Series] No. 1 (Department of Public and International Law, University of Oslo, 2003).

Commission introduced a distinction between 'main conventions' and 'special conventions'.[34] According to the Commission, the three 'main' international conventions that were suited for incorporation were the ECHR, the ICCPR and the ICESCR. The Commission recommended that 'special' conventions, such as the CEDAW, the CRC, the ICERD and the Convention against Torture and Other Cruel, Inhuman or Degrading Treatment or Punishment (CAT), should not be incorporated into the Human Rights Act. An important reason why the latter instruments were seen as unsuitable for incorporation was, according to the Commission, their lack of individual complaint mechanisms that could establish and clarify the content and scope of their provisions.

The Human Rights Law Commission's recommendations were followed up through the Stoltenberg I government's proposition on the Human Rights Act.[35] In the public hearing following the proposal, the Gender Equality Ombud argued that the CEDAW, dealing with the rights of half of the world's population, should be seen as a 'main' convention.[36] The Ministry of Education and the Ministry of Children and Family were also of the view that the CEDAW should be incorporated into the Human Rights Act.[37] The Ministry of Justice was of the view that 'it was not natural to see the Women's Convention as a "main" convention, although it was central and important to eliminate discrimination against women'.[38]

The distinction between 'main' conventions and 'special' conventions was not accepted by Parliament, where a majority was of the view that the CEDAW and the CRC, because of their basic character, should be incorporated into the Human Rights Act. When passing the Human Rights Act, a majority in Parliament requested the Stoltenberg I government to incorporate the CEDAW and the CRC into Norwegian law 'within reasonable time'.[39]

[34] *Hovedkonvensjoner* and *særkonvensjoner.*

[35] Proposition to the Odelsting No. 3 (1998–9).

[36] Proposition to the Odelsting No. 38 (1998–9), 29 and E. A. Grannes, 'Lovgivning om likestilling – bør FNs kvinnekonvensjon inkorporeres i norsk rett' [Equality legislation – should the CEDAW be incorporated into Norwegian law], *Mennesker og rettigheter* [Humans and Rights] 2 (2001).

[37] Proposition to the Odelsting No. 38 (1998–9), 30.

[38] *Ibid.*

[39] Recommendation No. 51 (1998–9) to the Odelsting, para. 1. See A. Hellum, 'Maktutredningens påstander settes ut i live – en knekk for demokratiet? [The Power and Democracy Commission's assertions: a democratic problem] *Krititisk juss* [Critical Legal Studies] 30 (2004) 115–17.

On 20 January 2003 the CEDAW Committee considered Norway's fifth and sixth periodic reports.[40] In its Concluding Comments, the Committee recommended that:

> the State party amend section 2 of the Human Rights Act (1999) to include the Convention and its Optional Protocol, which will ensure that the provisions of the Convention prevail over any conflicting statutes and that its provisions can be invoked in domestic courts.[41]

In 2003 a White Paper outlining the strengths and weaknesses of alternative ways of incorporating the CEDAW was issued by the Ministry of Children and Equality, which did not take a position. The White Paper referred to the CEDAW Committee's recommendation. It was circulated through a broad public hearing. Of the twenty-nine consultative bodies that expressed their opinion, twenty-two were of the view that the Convention should be incorporated into Norwegian law so as to take precedence over other Norwegian legislation in the event of conflict.[42] Of the bodies that were in favour of incorporation into the Human Rights Act, thirteen referred explicitly to the CEDAW Committee's recommendation.[43] Only two of the consultative bodies, namely the Ministry of Justice (Legislation Department) and the Office of the Norwegian Government's Legal Counsel, argued against incorporation into the Human Rights Act. The Ministry of Justice and the Government Legal Counsel argued that the standards set out in the CEDAW, due to their vague and unclear character, were unsuitable for application in Norwegian courts of law. With reference to the dualist character of the Norwegian legal system, the Ministry of Justice argued that most of the standards embedded in the CEDAW, due to their lack of clarity, were not self-executive. With reference to the majority in the Norwegian Commission of Power and Democracy Report (see below), submitted to the government in 2003, both the Ministry of Justice and the State Legal Counsel argued that

40 CEDAW/C/NOR/5 and CEDAW/C/NOR/6.

41 *Ibid.*

42 Proposition to the Odelsting, No. 35 (2004–5), 75 and 79–80.

43 Among these were Akademikerne [the Academicians], Den norske kirke (Oslo biskop) [The Church of Norway, Oslo Bishop], Forsvarsdepartementet [Ministry of Defence], Juridisk rådgivning for kvinner [Free Legal Advice for Women], Likestillingsombudet [Ombud for Equal Status], Oslo kvinnesaksforening [Oslo Association for Women's Rights], Avdeling for kvinnerett [The Institute of Women's Law], Norsk senter for menneskerettigheter [Norwegian Centre for Human Rights], Senter for kvinne- og kjønnsforskning, Universitetet i Tromsø [Centre for Women's and Gender Research, University of Tromsø], Utenriksdepartementet [Ministry of Foreign Affairs] and Yrkesorganisasjonenes Sentralforbund [Confederation of Vocational Unions].

incorporation of the CEDAW into the Human Rights Act would skew the balance between the judiciary and the Parliament and as such undermine representative democracy.[44] The Ministry of Children and Equality, however, was of the view that the CEDAW should be incorporated into the Gender Equality Act and not be given precedence in the case of conflict with other Norwegian law.[45]

The CEDAW Committee's recommendation was not adopted by the Bondevik II government. On the basis of advice from the Ministry of Justice and the Government Legal Counsel, the government decided to look closely into the Official Report submitted by the majority in the Commission of Power and Democracy before making any decision regarding the legal status of the CEDAW.[46] The majority in the Commission was concerned that Parliament's scope of action – and thus the Norwegian system of representative government – was being curtailed by the growing number of international treaties that had been ratified by the Norwegian state. The minority in the Commission argued that international human rights instruments such as the CEDAW, by challenging structural power relations, were a tool for a fairer distribution of power and resources between women and men and as such a means of achieving greater democracy.[47] Adopting the majority view, the Bondevik II government's report to Parliament concluded that the rule of precedence, embedded in the Human Rights Act, should for the future be restricted to very special cases in relation to incorporation of international conventions:

> As regards incorporation the main rule should be that the incorporated rule is given status as ordinary law, and that general national principles regarding interpretation are applied. In this way the Government wishes to increase the predictability and clarity of the legal system, and thereby avoid a development to the effect that power is transferred from the legislative to the executive branch of government. In the light of certain international bodies' dynamic interpretation of international law – going in directions beyond the scope of what the legislative branch of government at the time of incorporation reasonably could foresee – it is ample reason to emphasise the need to be as consistent as possible as regards incorporation of international treaties that have a binding effect. The Government

[44] Norwegian Official Report NOU 2003:19 *Makt og demokrati* [Power and Democracy].

[45] Proposition to the Odelsting, No. 35 (2004–5), 80.

[46] Norwegian Official Report (Flertallets rapport) [Majority report] NOU 2003: 19 *Makt- og demokratiutredningen* [Power and Democracy Report].

[47] H. Skjeie, Mindretallsuttalelse [Minority view] NOU 2003: 19.

> is of the view that rules giving international law precedence in the event of conflict with other Norwegian law should be used restrictively.[48]

These views were echoed in the debate in Parliament about the Bondevik II government's proposal to incorporate the CEDAW into the Gender Equality Act. The proposal, which was passed by Parliament, implied that the CEDAW and its Optional Protocol 'shall apply as Norwegian law'.[49] However, in the event of conflict with other Norwegian legislation, the CEDAW and its Optional Protocol would not, like the Conventions that were incorporated into the Human Rights Act, enjoy statutory precedence over other Norwegian legislation. Like human rights and women's rights organizations, the opposition parties (Labour, the Socialist Left Party and the Centre Party) were of the view that the CEDAW should be incorporated into the Human Rights Act so as to take precedence when coming into conflict with other Norwegian legislation.[50]

When coming into power after the elections in 2005, the Stoltenberg II government, in its political statement for the governing period of 2005–2009 (The Soria Moria Declaration), pledged to 'incorporate the UN Convention on the Elimination of All Forms of Discrimination against Women into the Human Rights Act'.[51] In March 2007 the Minister of Justice, however, said that the government would reconsider the Soria Moria position on the CEDAW.[52] It was, according to the Minister of Justice, a general need to consider what consequences incorporation of conventions embodying vague and imprecise provisions, such as the CEDAW, the ICERD and the CAT, in the Human Rights Act would have for the nature of the Norwegian legal order.

The proponents of incorporation into the Human Rights Act, particularly the women's organizations, the Anti-Discrimination and Equality Ombud and experts from the Institute of Women's Law at the University of Oslo, argued that the Convention constituted a necessary safeguard against the rapidly increasing body of gender-blind laws and policies that

48 Report No. 17 (2004–5) to the Storting, 74–5.

49 The Gender Equality Act, section 1b.

50 From the newspaper debates see C. Holst and H. Skjeie 'Vikeplikt' [commentary], *Dagbladet*, 23 April 2005; N. Høstmælingen 'Annenrangs menneskerettigheter' [commentary], *Morgenbladet*, 15 April 2005.

51 The Soria Moria Declaration of 13 October 2005, Chapters 17 and 71.

52 See debate between A. Hellum, 'Politisk spydspiss med sviktende legitimitet' [Political spearhead with faltering legality], *Dagbladet*, 8 March 2007 and Minister of Justice, K. Storberget, 'Politisk kritikk med sviktende legitimitet' [Political criticism with faltering legality], *Dagbladet*, 19 March 2007.

in practice fail to adequately address the specific concerns of women and girls.[53] Norwegian state actors such as the Ministry of Justice and the State Legal Counsel were, however, of the view that it was unnecessary to incorporate the CEDAW into the Human Rights Act since the ECHR, the ICCPR and the ICESCR already prohibited sex discrimination.

In response to Norway's seventh periodic report, which gave account of the arguments for and against incorporation into the Human Rights Act, the CEDAW Committee recommended that:

> the state party take all necessary steps to incorporate the Convention on the Elimination of All Forms of Discrimination against Women into the Human Rights Act so as to ensure that elimination of discrimination against women is addressed as a core human rights obligation.[54]

The shadow report by the women's organizations emphasized the need to address the negative impact of the Human Rights Act's gender hierarchy:

> The present situation is giving rise to a wide range of legal controversies as to the status of CEDAW in Norwegian law, which in turn is having an adverse effect on the interpretation of the Gender Equality Act and the use of CEDAW in Norwegian courts. The hierarchic ranking of human rights instruments is also having a negative effect on the authority and status of the Discrimination and Equality Ombud and the efforts to promote gender equality, as equality considerations have to yield to other laws.[55]

The women's organizations' claim was also prompted by the need for a safeguard against the rapidly increasing body of gender-blind laws and policies that in practice fail to adequately address the specific concerns of women and girls.

In spring 2009 the Ministry of Justice and the Government Legal Counsel were publicly criticized for their political resistance to the

[53] To discuss the implication of incorporating the CEDAW into the Human Rights Act, the Institute of Women's Law, Free Legal Advice for Women (JURK) and the Norwegian Women's Rights Organization organized a seminar on the CEDAW at the Institute of Women's Law at the University of Oslo on 4 December 2008. A report from the seminar, 'Er Norge i utakt med FNs kvinnekonvensjon' [Is Norway out of step with the UN's Convention on Women] is found at the Norwegian Women's Rights Organization's home page: http://kvinnesak.no/?p=418 (last accessed December 2010).

[54] CEDAW/C/NOR/CO/7, para. 14.

[55] Shadow report by women's organizations in Norway to Norway's seventh periodic report on the implementation of the CEDAW, FOKUS (Forum for Women and Development) Secretariat, Oslo, 19 June 2007 at 11. A submission to the CEDAW Committee was also made by the Norwegian Centre for Human Rights, submission of 17 July.

Stoltenberg II government's policy regarding the incorporation of the CEDAW.[56] In the aftermath of this newspaper debate, the Minister of Justice and the Minister of Children and Equality, in June 2008, announced that the government had decided to put forward a proposal to incorporate the CEDAW into the Human Rights Act. In November 2009 the Ministry of Justice sent out a White Paper suggesting incorporation of the CEDAW into the Human Rights Act.[57] The White Paper was circulated in a broad public hearing. Among the thirty-four bodies (state and non-state actors) that expressed their view, only the Government Legal Counsel opposed incorporation into the Human Rights Act.

Assuming that Norwegian law, by and large, was in consonance with the CEDAW, the Ministry of Justice concluded that incorporation of the CEDAW would not skew the balance between the legislative and judicial branches of government.[58] In Parliament, all the political parties with the exception of Fremskrittspartiet (Progress Party) voted for the proposal.[59] It was generally agreed that the gender equality principle's centrality as a national value should be reflected in the Human Rights Act. In his address to Parliament, the Minister of Justice, however, emphasized that this was the very last convention that would be incorporated into the Human Rights Act so as to take precedence over other Norwegian law.[60]

The incorporation of the CEDAW into the Human Rights Act was a breakthrough for the claim that the CEDAW as a gender-specific instrument added value to the ECHR, the ICCPR and the ICESR, which took a gender-neutral approach. The CEDAW controversy shows how several democratically elected governments were effectively disempowered by the technical legal arguments mobilized by legal experts in the Ministry of Justice and the Government Legal Counsel. In terms of democracy and transparency, civil society played a key role in promoting accountability vis-à-vis the executive branch of government through public debate.

[56] Interview in *Klassekampen* with Professor Mads Andenæs (Director of the Norwegian Centre of Human Rights) 8 June 2008; 'Konvensjonell Sexisme' [Conventional sexism], article by Professor Anne Hellum in *Dagbladet*, 12 June 2008; 'Om å holde ord' [About keeping promises], opinion by Professor Anne Hellum, Professor Hege Skjeie and senior researcher at PRIO Helga Hernes in *Dagbladet*, 28 May 2009.

[57] *Høyring – inkorporering av kvinnediskrimineringskonvensjonen i menneskerettsloven* [Hearing – Incorporation of the CEDAW in the Human Rights Act] Ministry of Justice, 7 November 2008.

[58] Proposition to the Odelsting No. 93 (2008–9), 36.

[59] Populist right-wing party.

[60] Innst. O. [Recommendation to the Odelsting] nr. 115 (2008–9).

5 The state report review process: state–civil society

An important function of the CEDAW Committee is to create a forum for holding governments accountable for their international undertakings, and for the engagement of civil society as part of national and transnational struggles to achieve women's rights and gender equality.[61] To ensure that the review of a state report is linked to domestic law and policy-making processes, the Committee has made provisions for civil society and national human rights institutions to make formal and informal contributions to the work of the Committee. A key question, in this section, is how the Norwegian government in its international and national gender policies has responded to the Committee's initiatives aimed at a participatory, balanced and transparent state report review process.

5.1 The CEDAW in Norwegian international gender policy

Norway's smooth ratification of the CEDAW speaks to the strong political commitment to women's rights and gender equality as a global development issue in the 1970s.[62] The CEDAW has, since its enactment, been a basic reference point for Norwegian development policy.[63] In the *Action Plan for Women's Rights and Gender Equality in Development Cooperation* from 2007, Norway's rights-based approach to development is anchored in the CEDAW.[64] In the foreword to the Action Plan, the Minister of Development Erik Solheim stated:

> The Government wants Norway to be a fearless champion of women's rights and gender equality. Accordingly, the rights, participation and influence of women will be at the core of Norway's development cooperation efforts. Our aim is to ensure the realization of the rights of women that are set out in international human rights conventions.

Seeing human rights and democracy as mutually constitutive, the Action Plan will use the CEDAW Committee's Concluding Comments to Norway's partner countries in development cooperation as the point of departure for dialogue and priority-setting. Ratification of the CEDAW

[61] See Andrew Byrnes' chapter in this book.
[62] See Skar, 'Milepeler i norsk kvinnebevegelse'.
[63] *Action Plan for Women's Rights and Gender Equality in Development Cooperation 2007–2009*, Norwegian Ministry of Foreign Affairs.
[64] *Ibid.*

is seen in the Action Plan as an expression of the partner countries' own development targets and commitments. According to the Action Plan:

> Most of Norway's partner countries have acceded to CEDAW, and are required to report every four years to the CEDAW Committee. After its analysis of the report and subsequent dialogue with the authorities, the Committee draws up concluding comments with recommendations for follow-up in the country in question. These concluding comments form a good basis for cooperation on the target country's own terms and should be used actively in development cooperation.[65]

Civil society, particularly women's organizations, are seen as key actors in development and democracy building. With reference to the situation in Norway, the Action Plan states:

> In Norway, civil society has played an important role in shaping democratic development, including the position of women and the realization of women's rights. The establishment of women's networks and interest groups and the participation of women in organizations in general have influenced the national agenda.[66]

By strengthening civil society in the global south, the Action Plan sets out to promote democracy in terms of accountability vis-à-vis national authorities. Democratic values such as democracy, good governance, accountability, equal rights and development are seen as closely interlinked. The Action Plan states:

> measures to strengthen the competence and capacity of civil society to play such a role will be given high priority. Women's organizations and networks in developing countries will be supported directly through Norwegian embassies, national and regional umbrellas and trust funds.[67]

5.2 *The CEDAW in Norwegian gender policy*

In national gender policy measures to strengthen the competence and capacity of women's organizations' ability to use the state reporting procedure as an accountability mechanism were for a long time absent. The Ministry of Children and Equality has, since ratification in 1981, produced eight periodic reports to the United Nations on Norway's implementation of the CEDAW. The Ministry regularly invites women's organizations

[65] *Ibid.*
[66] *Ibid.*
[67] *Ibid.*

and the Anti-Discrimination Ombud to make comments on the state reports. Draft reports have been circulated, and public hearings have been held. A recent study based on women's organizations' participation in the CEDAW and the ICERD state reporting process between 1982 and 2008, however, shows that the participation of non-governmental women's organizations in these processes has been severely limited.[68] In most instances, the comments from the women's organizations, according to the study, had not been included as separate attachments to the state report but were incorporated without any reference to the statements made by the actual organizations.[69]

In 2007 the women's organizations presented their first shadow report to the CEDAW Committee.[70] Due to lack of funding, the women's organizations were unable to attend the Committee's preparatory meeting. The CEDAW Committee, in its Concluding Comments to Norway's seventh periodic report, took notice of 'the absence of Norwegian NGOs at the session, apparently for lack of funding'.[71] In 2011 thirty-two women's organizations coordinated by FOKUS submitted an NGO shadow report to the CEDAW Committee.[72] In its Concluding Comments to the Norwegian eighth periodic report, the Committee commended 'the State party for its financial support of women's organizations (NGOs) for the finalization of a shadow report and for travelling expenses to both the pre-session working group and the session'.[73]

The FEMCIT study on women's movements in Norway challenges established wisdoms regarding the influence of women's networks and

[68] B. Halsaa and C. Thun, *Partnering with the State? The Role of Women's Organizations in Governmental, CEDAW and CERD Consultation Processes*, FEMCIT Working Paper No. 4 (Centre for Gender Research, University of Oslo, 2010) at 131. The study was carried out by the EU project 'Gendered citizenship in multicultural Europe: the impact of contemporary women's movements' (FEMCIT). It was based on NGO comments that have been included in the national reports and on shadow reports.

[69] Norway's fifth periodic report, where comments from the Gender Equality Ombud, the Centre for Gender Equality, the MIRA Resource Centre for Black, Immigrant and Refugee Women and the Women's Front were attached as an appendix, makes an exception.

[70] The report was a cooperation between FOKUS, Kompetanse- og ressurssenter i internasjonale kvinnespørsmål [the Competence and Resource Centre for International Women's Issues], Kvinnesaksforeningen [the Norwegian Association for Women's Rights], Kvinnefronten [the Women's Front] and Internasjonal kvinneliga for fred og frihet [the Women's International League for Peace and Freedom].

[71] CEDAW/C/NOR/CO/7, para. 5.

[72] Among the organizations that contributed to the report were The Norwegian Association for Women's Rights, The Norwegian LGBT Organization, the MiRA Resource Centre for Black, Immigrant and Refugee Women and the foundation Stop the Discrimination.

[73] CEDAW/C/NOR/CO/8, para. 3.

interest groups on national law and policy making.[74] It shows how the increasing amount of complicated national and international law and policy documents, and lack of sufficient funding have weakened majority and minority voluntary membership organizations' ability to formulate claims and exert influence on Norwegian law and policy making. Among the approximately 200 organizations that were included in the FEMCIT study, only six organizations had been involved in the CEDAW reporting procedure, and none in the CERD reporting procedure. The women's organizations that participated in the study were of the view that participation in the CEDAW reporting procedure required extensive professional and economic resources of which ordinary membership organizations not were in command.

The CEDAW Committee's Concluding Comments to Norway's most recent state report has, however, prompted the Ministry of Children, Equality and Social Inclusion to take economic measures to facilitate NGO shadow reporting.[75] The NGO shadow report from 2011, in which women from majority and minority organizations cooperated, indicates that the state reporting procedure gradually is becoming an arena where claims addressing discrimination attributed to the intersection of gender, ethnicity, sexuality, age or religion are discussed and coordinated.

5.3 *National human rights institutions and Parliament*

To broaden the participation in the state report review, the CEDAW Committee has made specific provisions for national human rights institutions (NHRIs) to contribute formally to its work. The Committee adopted a statement on NHRIs in 2008, in which it underlined the importance of NHRIs to the domestic implementation of the Convention, and welcomed the submission of written information for the pre-sessional working groups and the session, and undertook to make

[74] B. Halsaa, C. Thun and L. N. Predelli, *Women's Movements: Constructions of Sisterhood, Dispute and Resonance: The Case of Norway: Feminist Citizenship in Multicultural Europe: The Impact of Contemporary Women's Movements (FEMCIT)*, FEMCIT Working Paper No. 4. (Centre for Gender Research, University of Oslo, and Department of Social Science and Centre of Research in Social Policy, Southborough University, 2008)

[75] The need of a national gender policy that takes measures to fortify the capacity of membership-based Norwegian women's organizations to articulate claims is in the context of the increasingly complex political and legal landscape emphasized by the FEMCIT research. See Halsaa et al., *Women's Movements* at 270.

time available for oral interventions by NHRIs at the public sessions of the Committee.[76]

The Norwegian Centre of Human Rights (NCHR), which is a multidisciplinary research centre at the Faculty of Law at the University of Oslo, was granted status as Norway's national institution for human rights by royal decree in 2001.[77] The Anti-Discrimination Act mandates the Equality and Anti-Discrimination Ombud to ensure that the CEDAW and the ICERD are complied with in law and practice.[78] The NCHR made a submission to the CEDAW Committee's consideration of Norway's fifth, sixth and seventh periodic reports with focus on the incorporation of the CEDAW into the Human Rights Act. In 2011 the Equality and Anti-Discrimination Ombud made a written supplementary report to Norway's eighth periodic report to the CEDAW Committee.

Unlike in the Netherlands,[79] the Norwegian Parliament is not involved in the state reporting procedure. To broaden democratic participation, the CEDAW Committee has in its Concluding Comments to Norway emphasized that:

> the Convention is binding on all branches of Government, and invites the state party to encourage the Parliament, in line with its procedures, where appropriate, to take the necessary steps with regard to the implementation of the present concluding observations and the Government's next reporting process under the Convention.[80]

5.4 *Towards a more democratic and transparent review process*

The CEDAW Committee's call for a more participatory, balanced and transparent state reporting process involving civil society, national

[76] Kongelig Resolusjon 21. September 2001, 'Etablering av og mandat for nasjonal institusjon for menneskerettigheter ved Institutt for menneskerettigheter' [Establishment and mandate for a National Institution for Human Rights at the Institute for Human Rights].

[77] For a description of the complex architecture of the national supervisory human rights mechanisms in Norway, see *Protecting and Promoting Human Rights in Norway: Review of the Norwegian Centre for Human Rights in its Capacity as Norway's National Human Rights Institution*, by the Norwegian Ministry of Foreign Affairs team for the review of the existing national institution: N. Sveaass, B. Kofod Olsen, K. Lund and G. M. Ekekløve-Slydal (Oslo: NCHR, 2011).

[78] The Anti-Discrimination Act (ADA).

[79] See van den Brink's chapter in this book.

[80] CEDAW/C/NOR/CO/8, para. 8.

human rights institutions and democratically elected Parliamentarians is slowly prompting change. Through its contribution to a more democratic and transparent review process, the CEDAW adds value in comparison to both EU law and the ECHR, which are based on a top-down model.[81]

6 The CEDAW in national legislation

The equal status of women in law and society has been an important part of law and policy making since the enactment of the Gender Equality Act in 1978. The Norwegian state's obligation to incorporate the principle of gender equality and non-discrimination in existing legislation derives from a wide range of international and regional international treaties that in practice reinforce and supplement Norwegian gender equality policy. The rapid and uneven development in the field of gender equality is characterized by a situation where Norwegian law is both ahead of and behind its obligations under international law. By passing an Act requiring that 40 per cent of all company board members should be women, the Norwegian Parliament made international headlines.[82] So did the marriage law reform, which put lesbian and homosexual couples on an equal footing with heterosexual couples.[83] An increasing number of reforms are, however, a response to Norway's international legal obligations, particularly European Union law and the CEDAW.

6.1 *In the shadow of European Union law*

Norway is not a member of the EU, but has been a member of the European Free Trade Association (EFTA) since 1994. It is bound by the European Economic Area (EEA) agreement, which guarantees equal rights and obligations within the 'Internal Market' for citizens.[84] The EU Gender Equality

[81] Since 1984 the EU Commission has been assisted by the European Network of Legal Experts in the Field of Gender Equality in order to help monitor the implementation of the EU *acquis* related to the principle of equal treatment between men and women and to develop new legal initiatives in this field. Publications from the Commission's Network of Legal Experts is found at http://ec.europa.eu/justice/gender-equality/tools/legal-experts/index_en.htm (last accessed 1 September 2012).

[82] Article 6–11a of the Norwegian Companies Act. Amended by Act of 19 December 2003, No. 120. Following this law reform, the share of women on corporate boards increased from 25 per cent in 2004 to 42 per cent in 2009.

[83] By Act of 27 June 2008, No. 53, section 1 of the Marriage Act allows same-sex marriage.

[84] www.efta.int/eea/eea-agreement.aspx (last accessed 1 September 2012).

Directive is directly binding in Norwegian law through the EEA agreement.[85] The Court of Justice of the European Union (ECJ) has through its case law in the 1970s, 1980s and 1990s, been way ahead of the CEDAW Committee in its development of women's protection against direct and indirect discrimination in the labour market.[86] Through a dynamic interpretation of EU law, the ECJ has significantly strengthened women's protection against pregnancy and part-time work-related discrimination.[87] This body of case law, which today is codified in the Recast Gender Equality Directive, is reflected in a series of changes in the Norwegian Gender Equality Act.[88]

In 2002 the Gender Equality Act underwent extensive revisions in the light of Norway's obligations under EU law and the CEDAW.[89] A duty for public authorities and employers to make active, targeted and systematic efforts to promote gender equality was included.[90] A new provision providing protection against sexual harassment was introduced.[91] The protection against direct and indirect discrimination was strengthened.[92] The principle of equal pay for work of equal value was extended to work connected with different trades and professions.[93] The rules concerning burden of proof were changed in the favour of victims of discrimination.[94] Liability for damages regardless of the fault of the employer was introduced.[95] Giving an account of Norway's international legal obligations, the Proposition to the Odelsting, which was worked out by the Ministry of Children and Equality, makes systematic reference to both EU law and the CEDAW.[96] While the obligations under the CEDAW serve as a general point of reference in the Proposition, the actual changes in the text of the Gender Equality Act are made with direct reference to the Equal Pay Directive, the Gender Equality Directive and the Burden of Proof

[85] The Equal Treatment for Men and Women Directive (2002/73/EØF), which now is replaced by the Recast Gender Equality Directive (2006/54).

[86] R. Nielsen, 'The impact of EU law on Scandinavian law in matters of gender equality' in R. Nielsen and C. Tvarnø, *Scandinavian Women's Law in the 21st Century* (Copenhagen: DJØF Publishing, 2012) 63–91.

[87] Case 170/84 *Bilka*; C-109/00 *Tele Danmark*; C-177/88 *Dekker*; C-171/88 *Rinner-Kuhn*; C-109/88 *Danfoss*.

[88] Proposition to the Odelsting No. 77 (2000–1); Proposition to the Odelsting No. 35 (2004–5).

[89] Act of 14 June 2002, No. 21.

[90] GEA section 1a. [91] GEA section 8a.

[92] GEA section 3. [93] GEA section 5.

[94] GEA section 16. [95] GEA section 17.

[96] Proposition to the Odelsting No. 77 (2000–1).

Directive.[97] As shown above, the substantive inputs to these reforms came from EU law, which has taken a more incisive position than the CEDAW. Yet in the public hearing, state and non-state actors such as the Ministry of Foreign Affairs, the women's organization Kvinnefronten (Women's Front) and the National Union (LO) invoked the CEDAW, and not EU law, in support of the reform.[98]

6.2 *The actual added value of the CEDAW*

In recent years the CEDAW has clearly emerged from the shadows. In the following examples of how it has been invoked in legislative matters concerning protection against discrimination in family and religious affairs, the needs for gender-specific legislation and protection against intersectional discrimination are presented.

6.2.1 Exemptions for religion and family in the Gender Equality Act

Recognizing that gender stereotypes embedded in social, cultural and religious structures are a *root cause* of discrimination against women, the CEDAW Committee has, in its General Recommendations and Concluding Comments, systematically addressed discrimination in the private sphere, the family sphere and the religious sphere. It has, in its Concluding Comments to Norway's periodic reports, addressed the Gender Equality Act's exemptions for religion and family life on a number of occasions. Dealing with Norway's third and fourth periodic reports in 1995, the Committee expressed a concern for provisions in the Gender Equality Act to exempt certain religious communities from compliance with the equal rights law. Since women often face greater discrimination in family and personal affairs in certain communities and in religion, they asked the Norwegian government to amend the Gender Equality Act to eliminate exceptions based on religion.

The CEDAW Committee's recommendation was not followed up by the Bondevik II government's revision of the Gender Equality Act in 2002, which was carried out to ensure compliance with Norway's international legal obligations.[99] In 2007 the Stoltenberg II government appointed the Commission to Propose a Comprehensive Anti-Discrimination

[97] 75/117/EØF; 76/207/EØF; 97/80/EØF.

[98] Proposition to the Odelsting No. 77 (2000–1), 45.

[99] Report to the Odelsting No. 77 (2000–1).

Legislation (Discrimination Law Commission). A part of its mandate was to consider whether the special exemptions for religious communities from the prohibition against discrimination on the basis of gender or homosexual cohabitation in the Gender Equality Act and the Working Environment Act should be abolished. In 2008 the Discrimination Law Commission, in a partial report mainly looking into Norway's obligations under the ECHR, concluded that the existing exemptions for religion in the Gender Equality Act and the Working Environment Act were too wide.[100] In 2009 a specialist report, looking into Norway's international legal obligations embedded in the ICCPR, ICESCR, CEDAW, CRC, ECHR and EU law recommended a more wide-reaching prohibition against religious discrimination in the Gender Equality Act than the Discrimination Law Commission had made.[101] In 2010 the Gender Equality Act and the Working Environment Act were changed accordingly.[102]

In its consideration of Norway's third periodic report, the CEDAW Committee asked why the Gender Equality Act applied to, but was not enforced by, the Ombud and Tribunal in relation to family matters.[103] In 2009 the Discrimination Law Commission, without any discussion of the Committee's previous comments, suggested exempting family life from the scope of the proposed unified discrimination legislation (see below).[104] The majority in the Commission was of the view that the proposed change was in consonance with the protection of the right to privacy in Article 8 of the ECHR. The minority in the Commission argued that since unequal family relations constitute one of the root causes of discrimination against women, family life not should be exempted.[105] In their comments to the proposal, a number of women's organizations were of the same view as the minority.[106] Experts in the field of discrimination and equality

[100] Official Report NOU 2008: 1 *Kvinner og homofile i trossamfunn* [Women and Homosexuals in Religious Communities].

[101] V. B. Strand, 'Report commissioned by the Ministry of Children and Equality of January 2009' *Studies in Women's Law* 80 (2001); V. B. Strand, *Diskrimineringsvernets rekkevidde i møte med religionsfrihet* [Balancing Protection against Discrimination and Religious Freedom] (Oslo: Gyldendal, 2012).

[102] Act of 9 April 2010, No. 12.

[103] With regard to family life and purely personal matters, the Gender Equality Act 'shall not be enforced by the bodies mentioned in section 9 of this Act'.

[104] Official Report NOU 2009: 14 *Et helhetlig diskrimineringsvern* [Comprehensive Anti-Discrimination Legislation].

[105] Professor Dr Juris Hege Brækhus, Faculty of Law, University of Tromsø, is a former member of the Tribunal and teaches anti-discrimination and equality law.

[106] *Høringsuttalelsefra Norsk kvinnesaksforening* [Statement from the Norwegian Rights Association], December 2001.

law referred to the CEDAW Committee's Concluding Comments and argued that Article 8 of the ECHR should be interpreted in the light of the CEDAW.[107] The government has not yet decided what weight the CEDAW Convention and the CEDAW Committee's Concluding Observations should be given in the proposed revision of the Gender Equality Act, which will be put before Parliament in the course of 2013.

6.2.2 Gender-specific or gender-neutral anti-discrimination law

What distinguishes the CEDAW from other international human rights treaties and European Union law is, as already pointed out, its explicit recognition that it is mostly women who suffer from discrimination on the ground of their sex, as well as from a range of other discrimination grounds resulting in intersectional discrimination.[108] The CEDAW Committee has, on a number of occasions, addressed the consequences for attention to women's rights issues of the establishment of unified legal and institutional structures and mechanisms with the responsibility for promoting equality issues more generally, and for addressing multiple grounds of discrimination.

In its Concluding Comments to Norway's seventh periodic report, the Committee noted the reorganization of the Norwegian gender equality machinery. The Centre for Gender Equality was closed down in 2005 and replaced by a new organ: the Equality and Anti-Discrimination Ombud. The Ombud was, as a result of the reform, mandated to monitor the Gender Equality Act, the Discrimination Act and the Anti-Discrimination and Accessibility Act. In addition, she was mandated to promote equality, mainly on the basis of gender, ethnicity and disability.[109] The CEDAW Committee stated:

> While appreciating that the State party has a long-standing policy of gender mainstreaming in all fields covered by its central administration, the Committee notes with some concern that the new scope of action of the Anti-Discrimination Equality Ombud may result in insufficient focus being given to discrimination against women.[110]

107 *Høringsuttalelse, Avdeling for kvinnerett, barnerett, likestillings og diskrimineringsrett* [Statement from the Institute of Women's Law, Discrimination Law and Child Law] of 3 December 2009.

108 See R. Holtmaat's chapter in this book.

109 The Anti-Discrimination and Equality Ombud and the Anti-Discrimination Tribunal Act (ADA) of 10 June 2005, No. 40.

110 CEDAW/C/NOR/CO/7, para. 15.

The reorganization of the national gender equality machinery was a controversial issue, which was addressed in the Norwegian women's organizations' shadow report to Norway's seventh periodic report. In the shadow report, the women's organizations stated that they strongly regretted the government's decision to close down the Centre for Gender Equality:

> The earlier Centre for Gender equality played an important role in developing and influencing Norwegian policy-making, keeping gender equality clearly in focus. The Centre's independent role – given to the Centre by Parliament – allowed the Centre for Gender Equality to be a reprimanding and correcting mechanism for the Government's priorities and policies … The Centre played an important liaison role between the women's organizations in promoting women's rights.[111]

Following up the procedural reform mandating the Ombud to monitor the Gender Equality Act, the Anti-Discrimination Act and the Anti-Discrimination and Accessibility Act, the Discrimination Law Commission in 2009 submitted its proposal for a new comprehensive Anti-Discrimination Act. The Commission suggested that the Gender Equality Act, which in accordance with section 1 in the Act 'shall promote equality and aims in particular at improving the position of women' be abolished. The Commission did not consider the CEDAW Committee's concerns regarding the establishment of unified legal and institutional structures and mechanisms. In the NGO shadow report commenting on Norway's eighth periodic report, the women's organizations were of the view that the suggested amendment:

> would be contrary to the obligation under the CEDAW, which requires dynamic action. Another consequence would be that differential treatment aimed at improving the status of women would be put on par with differential treatment aimed at improving the status of men.[112]

The Anti-Discrimination Ombud in her Supplementary Report to Norway's eighth periodic report to the CEDAW Committee commented:

> If protection against discrimination on grounds of gender is incorporated in a new comprehensive Act without retaining the 'statement of purpose', the Ombud sees a danger that the work against discrimination of women

[111] *Shadow Report by Women's Organizations in Norway to Norway's Seventh Periodic Report on the Implementation of CEDAW.*

[112] *NGO Shadow Report to CEDAW 2011, Supplementing and Commenting on Norway's Eighth Periodic Report on the Implementation of CEDAW* at 10.

> can be weakened. A neutral statement of purpose in a comprehensive Act will obscure the fact that, as a society, Norway has not achieved full gender equality, and that discrimination has a gender perspective that still requires targeted efforts and measures aimed at improving the position of women in particular.[113]

In its Concluding Comments to Norway's eighth periodic report, the Committee noted the Discrimination Law Commission's proposal and expressed concern:

> that the use of gender-neutral legislation, policies and programs ... might lead to inadequate protection of women against direct and indirect discrimination and hinder the achievement of substantive equality of women and men.[114]

In response to criticisms from the Ombud and the women's organizations, the Ministry of Children, Equality and Inclusion in a press statement of 2 September 2011 informed the public that the government had decided not to propose a comprehensive Anti-Discrimination Act. According to the Minister, a proposition to revise the Gender Equality Act, the Anti-Discrimination Act, the Anti-Discrimination and Accessibility Act and a Bill protecting lesbian, gay, transsexual and intersex persons against discrimination would be presented to Parliament in 2012–13.[115] This indicates that the women's organizations' mobilization of the CEDAW is having an impact on the law reform process.

6.2.3 Intersectional discrimination

Although the Women's Convention does not explicitly refer to intersectional discrimination suffered by women by virtue of their sex and other status, it recognizes that different groups of women, such as elderly women, rural women and migrant women may be subject to intersectional discrimination based on both their sex and other characteristics.[116] The Committee has addressed the concept of intersectional discrimination in its General Recommendation 28 and in its General Recommendations concerning disabled women, elderly women and migrant women workers.[117]

113 *The Equality and Anti-Discrimination Ombud's Report to the Pre-session of the CEDAW. A Supplementary Report on Norway's Eighth Official Report to the CEDAW Committee* at 7.

114 CEDAW/C/NOR/CO8, para. 8.

115 www.regjeringen.no/nb/dep/bld/aktuelt/nyheter/2011/arbeidet-med-ny-diskriminerin gslovgivnin.html?id=653933 (last accessed 1 September 2012).

116 Byrnes, 'Article 1' at 68.

117 CEDAW GR 24, para. 6; CEDAW GR 25, para. 12; CEDAW GR 26, paras. 6 and 7.

In Norway, the quest for an intersectional approach to gender discrimination has come from both immigrant women's organizations and international human rights treaty bodies. In 2001 the MIRA Resource Centre for Immigrant and Refugee Women expressed concern that the Norwegian Gender Equality Act did not take their problems and experiences into account. In the government's proposed revision of the Act, they commented:

> We are of the view that the new proposal to the Gender Equality Act does not represent the multiplicity of diversity that exists in contemporary Norway. We wish that the Ministry of Children and Family would take the living conditions of immigrant and refugee women in Norway into account so as to enhance equality for women from the minority population.[118]

The CEDAW Committee has in its Concluding Comments to Norway's fifth, sixth, seventh and eighth periodic reports expressed concern about the particular forms of discrimination faced by refugee, minority and migrant women, particularly multiple discrimination.[119] The Equality Tribunal has addressed multiple discrimination in several cases.[120] With reference to these cases, the Discrimination Law Commission concludes that intersectional discrimination is covered by existing legislation and sees no need for a legal provision that explicitly addresses the issue. A different view was presented by the Gender Equality Commission, which was appointed in 2011 by the government to assess existing gender policies.[121] With reference to General Recommendation 28, paragraph 18, the Gender Equality Commission proposes a separate legal provision that would address intersectional discrimination. In her supplementary report to Norway's eighth periodic report, the Anti-Discrimination Ombud emphasizes the need to strengthen the legal protection against intersectional discrimination:

> The Ombud believes that this is unfortunate seen in light of Norway's obligations under the CEDAW Convention, including the obligation to

[118] Proposition to the Odelsting No. 77 2001–2022.

[119] CEDAW/CNOR/CO/7, paras. 24, 27, 34 and 39; CEDAW/C/NOR/CO/8, paras. 32, 35, 36; CEDAW GR 28, para. 18.

[120] See the Equality Tribunal case 1/2008 and the Equality Tribunal case 8/2008. Case 09–136827TVI-OSFI. Øst Finnmark Court Judgment of 17 March also addresses intersectional discrimination.

[121] Norwegian Official Report NOU 2011: 18 *Struktur for likestilling* [Structure for Equality] at 22.

> ensure the legal recognition of (and policies and programmes addressing) intersecting forms of discrimination and its compounded negative impact on women concerned (GR 28, Para. 18). The explicit inclusion of a prohibition on intersectional and multiple discrimination in the statutory framework will remove any doubts about the legal basis for considering the grounds together when enforcing the Act.[122]

The CEDAW Committee, in its Concluding Comments to Norway's eighth periodic report, expresses 'concern at the lack of attention, in some laws and policies, to the specific needs of minority groups of women, including women with ethnic minority backgrounds and women with disabilities, often leading to intersectional discrimination'.[123] Whether and to what extent these concerns will be taken into consideration in the proposed revision of the Gender Equality Act will be decided in the revision of that Act, which will be presented in 2013.

6.2.4 A gender-neutral or gender-specific crisis centre Act?

Crisis centres run by women's NGOs are in Norway, as elsewhere in the world, the most important lifeline for women living in violent relationships. In the Soria Moria Declaration, the Stoltenberg II government promised to make the crisis centres that are run by women's NGOs a public responsibility. As a follow-up, the Ministry of Children and Equality presented a White Paper introducing a Crisis Centre Bill in 2008.[124] The Bill, which was gender-neutral, defined the right holders as 'persons that have been exposed to violence in intimate relationships'. The White Paper made no reference to the CEDAW, although the government at that point in time was tabling a proposal to incorporate the CEDAW into the Human Rights Act. A consequence of the gender-neutral wording of the proposed legislation was that women would be denied a right to a separate shelter.[125] For this reason, its gender-neutral character was criticized by most of the crisis centres for women and women's organizations that were included in the hearing. In their critique of the White Paper, Oslo Crisis Centre, The Equality and Anti-Discrimination Ombud and the Institute of

122 *The Equality and Anti-Discrimination Ombud's Report to the Pre-session of the CEDAW. A Supplementary Report to Norway's Eighth Official Report to the CEDAW Committee* (Oslo: The Equality and Anti-Discrimination Ombud, 2011).

123 CEDAW/C/NOR/CO/8, para. 8.

124 White Paper, *Forslag til lovfesting av krisesentertilbudet* [The Crisis Centre Bill], 30 October 2008.

125 R. Hennum, 'Kjønnslikestilling på ville veier – kan kjønnsnøytrale krisesentre forsvares' [Can gender-neutral crisis centers be defended?] in B. Halsaa and A. Hellum (eds.), *Rettferdighet* [Justice] (Oslo: Universitetsforlaget, 2010).

Women's Law invoked the CEDAW, with particular reference to General Recommendation 19 concerning violence against women. In response to this critique, the final proposal, which was put forward to Parliament by the Ministry of Children and Equality, referred to Norway's international obligations, particularly the ECHR and the CEDAW. Both the Ministry of Justice and the Ministry of Children and Equality were, however, of the view that a gender-specific Crisis Centre Act would be a contravention of Norway's obligations under the ECHR.[126] Their attention was primarily drawn to the ECHR's gender-neutral approach without any consideration of how it should be balanced against the CEDAW's emphasis on the need for measures that take into consideration the gendered character of domestic violence. Under the gender-neutral Act, which was passed by Parliament, shelters were instructed to offer separate departments for women and men.[127]

The Equality and Anti-Discrimination Ombud, who has monitored the implementation of the Act, reports that some crisis centres offer accommodation for women and men at the same address.[128] The Ombud, in her supplementary report to Norway's eighth periodic report, expresses a concern that the gender-neutral character of the offer may have detrimental consequences for women and girls with immigrant backgrounds. She is also concerned that in 2009 fewer than half of the Norwegian crisis centres were adapted to the needs of women with disabilities. Similar concerns were raised in the NGO shadow report.[129] The CEDAW Committee in its Concluding Comments to Norway's eighth periodic report encouraged Norway to:

> Provide adequate assistance to and protection to women victims of violence, including women with disabilities, by strengthening the capacity of shelters and crisis centres, and ensure that the need to help men victims of violence is addressed without detriment to the needs of women victims of violence.[130]

The government's decision to evaluate the Crisis Centre Act indicates that interventions by the Ombud, civil society and experts from the Institute

126 Proposition to the Odelsting No. 96 (2008–9).

127 Lov om kommunale krisesentertilbud, 15 May 2009, section 2 [The Crisis Centre Act, section 2].

128 *The Equality and Anti-Discrimination Ombud's Report to the Pre-session of the CEDAW. A Supplementary Report to Norway's Eighth Official Report to the CEDAW Committee* (Oslo: The Equality and Anti-Discrimination Ombud, 2011) at 6.

129 *NGO Shadow Report to CEDAW* 2011 at 27.

130 CEDAW/C/NOR/CO/8, para. 26d.

of Women's Law are taken into consideration by law and policy makers in the field of domestic violence.

6.3 *Slowly but surely*

After initially appearing to be in the shadow of EU law, the CEDAW's actual value has, as demonstrated above, become more apparent in recent years. Between 2006 and 2010 the Anti-Discrimination and Equality Ombud invoked the CEDAW nine times in public hearings on law and policy reform.[131] In the same period the Institute of Women's Law at the University of Oslo invoked the CEDAW six times in public hearings.[132] The women's organizations use the CEDAW and not EU law or the ECHR to support their claims. This suggests that the CEDAW is better known and enjoys greater socio-political legitimacy than EU law and the ECHR. An area of potential added value is family and marriage law, where existing legislation, as demonstrated by the CEDAW Committee's comment to Norway's eighth periodic report, leaves much to be desired:

> The Committee is concerned that the State party's current law on property distribution upon divorce (Norwegian Marriage Act) does not adequately address gender-based economic disparities between spouses resulting from traditional work and family life patterns. This often leads to enhanced human capital and earning potential of men while women may experience the opposite, so that spouses currently do not equitably share in the economic consequences of the marriage and its dissolution.[133]

7 The CEDAW in judicial review

The CEDAW requires effective judicial and other protection of women's entitlement to enjoy rights on an equal basis with men. 'Effective' protection of women's human rights under national law means providing for both legally binding and practically available protection.[134] In Norway,

131 An overview of the Anti-Discrimination and Equality Ombud's reference to the CEDAW in public hearings is found in A. Hellum and E. McClimans, 'Kartlegging av Likestillings- og diskrimineringsombudets tilsyn med FNs kvinnediskrimineringskonvensjon og FNs rasediskrimineringskonvensjon' [A mapping of the Anti-Discrimination Ombuds supervision of state compliance with the CEDAW and the ICERD], *Kvinnerettslig skriftserie* [Studies in Women's Law] No. 87 (2011).

132 An overview of inputs to public hearings and evaluation reports conducted by the Institute of Women's Law is found at: www.jus.uio.no/ior/forskning/omrader/kvinnerett/evalueringer_utredninger_horingsuttalelser/ (last accessed 1 September 2012).

133 CEDAW/C/NOR/CO/8, para. 37.

134 Byrnes, 'Article 1' at 84–5.

discrimination cases can be dealt with by the courts or the Equality and Anti-Discrimination Ombud and its appeals board,[135] the Equality and Anti-Discrimination Tribunal.[136]

7.1 The CEDAW in international and national judicial review

No individual cases have so far been lodged and decided under the Optional Protocol.[137]

The Norwegian state invoked the CEDAW in the University of Oslo case in which the EFTA Court handed down a judgment against Norway for breaching the European Union's Equal Treatment Directive of 2006.[138] The EFTA Court found that earmarking of research fellowships and professorships for women was a contravention of the EU Equal Treatment Directive of 2006.[139] The EFTA Court did not apply the revised EU Equal Treatment Directive of 2002, which refers to the CEDAW, since it had not yet entered into force.[140]

In 2009 the CEDAW was invoked in a Supreme Court case concerning the right to freely choose one's defence counsel.[141] With reference to Article 11, the appellant argued that his right to freely choose his defence counsel had not been respected, because the appeals court case was dealt with while his lawyer was on pregnancy leave. The Supreme Court turned the appeal down with reference to the need for speedy conduct of the legal process. The same year, the CEDAW was invoked in an appeal court case concerning adoptive parents' right to parental benefits pursuant to section

[135] Until 2006, the Gender Equality Appeal Board.

[136] An overview and analyses of the cases decided by the courts and the Anti-Discrimination Tribunal up to 2009 is found in H. Aune, 'Kvinnekonvensjonen og kvinnerettslig teoris betydning for norsk rettsanvendelse og rettsvitenskapelig analyser' [The impact of CEDAW and feminist jurisprudence on application of the law and legal analysis in Norway], *Retferd* [Nordic Journal of Law and Practice] 2:129 (2010) 51–71. For an overview of case law up to 2012 and academic articles dealing with the CEDAW in Norwegian law, see I. Ikdahl, 'Kommentar til FNs Konvensjon om avskaffelse av alle former for diskriminering av kvinner' [Commentary to the Convention on the Elimination of All Forms of Discrimination against Women], *Norsk lovkommentar- Lovdata* [Norwegian Law Commentary – Lawdata], August 2012 (online).

[137] There is no readily accessible government guidance on the CEDAW or the use of the Protocol. The Equality and Anti-Discrimination Ombud has since 2011 provided information about the Convention and the Optional Protocol on her website.

[138] E-1/102. [139] 76/207/EØF.

[140] 2002/73/EF. [141] Rt. 2009, 1389.

14–6 of the National Insurance Act.[142] In this case the Agder Court of Appeal in its interpretation of the National Insurance Act referred to the Gender Equality Act and Articles 11, 15 and 16 of the CEDAW. The Court ruled that a practice where the adoptive father could accumulate benefits right until paternity leave, while the adoptive mother had her application turned down on the ground that adoptive mothers must meet the benefit entitlement criteria on the date of assumption of care, constituted direct gender discrimination.

7.2 *The CEDAW in the practice of the Ombud and the Equality and Anti-Discrimination Tribunal*

In Norway, the overwhelming majority of discrimination cases are channelled through the administrative route: the Equality and Anti-Discrimination Ombud and the Equality and Anti-Discrimination Tribunal.[143] Unlike the courts, these law enforcement agencies do not have the power to award damages.

7.2.1 The Ombud

The mandate of the Equality and Anti-Discrimination Ombud is to oppose discrimination and promote equality regardless of gender, ethnicity, functional ability, language, religion, sexual orientation and sex.[144] The Ombud is professionally independent, while administratively placed under the Ministry of Children, Equality and Social Inclusion.

As a law enforcer, the Ombud is mandated to issue opinions on complaints concerning breaches of the Gender Equality Act, the Anti-Discrimination Act and the Anti-Discrimination and Accessibility Act.[145] The Ombud has invoked Article 5a of the CEDAW in several cases concerning advertisement based on stereotypical gender roles.[146] The CEDAW has also been invoked in three ongoing cases concerning gender

[142] Agder Court of Appeal, 12 February 2009. Two other cases make brief mention of the CEDAW.

[143] Between 2007 and 2010 the Ombud handled 273 complaints concerning gender discrimination. Between 2008 and 2011 the Tribunal handled 43 appeal cases.

[144] The Anti-Discrimination and Equality Ombud and the Anti-Discrimination Tribunal Act (ADA) of 10 June 2005, No. 40.

[145] ADA section 1.2.

[146] Gender Equality Ombud Case 2002/381 and Gender Equality Ombud Case 2003/083.

violence.[147] In a case concerning a Roma woman, who alleged that the police had not given her adequate protection against her violent husband, the Ombud invoked General Recommendation 19 from the CEDAW Committee and Article 14 of the ECHR with particular reference to *Opus* v. *Turkey*, where the Court referred to the CEDAW.[148]

As a national supervisory human rights body, the Ombud is mandated to ensure that the CEDAW and the ICERD are complied with in law and practice.[149] So far, the Ombud has not issued any formal report to the Ministry of Children, Equality and Social Inclusion on breaches of the CEDAW and the ICERD in law and practice.[150]

7.2.2 The Equality and Anti-Discrimination Tribunal

The Ombud's decisions can be appealed to the Equality and Anti-Discrimination Tribunal. Since the ratification of the CEDAW in 1981 and up to the time of writing, the CEDAW has been referred to in less than ten appeal cases decided by the Tribunal. In the following, a selection of cases demonstrates how the Tribunal, through cases concerning the power of the Tribunal, the right to equality in relation to education, day care, insurance and health, has interpreted the Gender Equality Act in the light of the Convention and the CEDAW Committee's General Recommendations and Concluding Comments. A significant trend in the Tribunal's jurisprudence is the use of Article 5a in the CEDAW to strengthen the Gender Equality Act's protection against discrimination.

A key case concerning the legal powers of the Tribunal was dealt with in 2006. Whether or not the Gender Equality Ombud and the Tribunal have the power to assess whether an Act passed by Parliament is in consonance with the Gender Equality Act or Norway's obligations under international law has been a long-standing controversy between the Ministry of Justice and the Ombud. In the Egg Donation Case, the Tribunal concluded that it has the power to deal with concrete situations where the Gender Equality Act comes into conflict with other Norwegian laws.[151] In such matters,

[147] Anti-Discrimination and Equality Ombud Case 10/1147, Anti-Discrimination and Equality Ombud Case 10/1153, and Anti-Discrimination and Equality Ombud Case 10/1004.

[148] *Opus* v. *Turkey*, para. 76.

[149] ADA section 1.3.

[150] A description and assessment of the Ombud's role as a national supervisory body in the field of gender and race discrimination is found in Hellum and McClimans, 'Kartlegging av Likestillings- og diskrimineringsombudets tilsyn'.

[151] Egg Donation Case. The Equality and Anti-Discrimination Tribunal LKN 2006–09. The Tribunal's decision has not been appealed.

it elaborated, it is empowered to make a decision on the basis of general interpretative principles, including the presumption that Norwegian law is in consonance with its obligations under international law and section 2 of the EEA Act, concerning conflicts between Norwegian law and legal obligations pertaining to the EEA agreement. This view was affirmed by the Ministry of Justice and confirmed by Parliament when the CEDAW was incorporated into the Human Rights Act in 2009.[152]

In 2001 the Gender Equality Appeal Board, for the first time, invoked the CEDAW. The Board had to rule whether the teaching materials used by the ACE (Accelerated Christian Education) schools in Norway constituted a contravention of the right to equal education embedded in section 7 of the Gender Equality Act.[153] The Ombud, who initiated the case, concluded that the ACE schools' teaching materials, portraying women and girls as subordinate to men, were in contravention of the Act. The ACE schools invoked section 2 of the Gender Equality Act, which at that point in time exempted internal religious affairs. To support its view, the schools argued that the principle of religious freedom embedded in the Constitution should take precedence over the gender equality principle, which does not enjoy constitutional protection. The majority of the Gender Equality Appeal Board disagreed with the schools. In its decision, the majority interpreted the Gender Equality Act in the light of Article 5a in the CEDAW and referred to the CEDAW Committee's comment to Norway's third and fourth periodic reports, where Norway was asked to 'amend the Norwegian Equal Status Act to eliminate exceptions based on religion'. The exemption for internal religious affairs did not, according to the majority, apply in relation to education, which is a civil and not a religious matter. The curriculum was, according to the majority, based on a stereotypical notion of gender roles that clearly undermined women's right to equal education both under the Gender Equality Act and the CEDAW. The general exemption for internal religious affairs has, as described above, been abolished.[154]

In an appeals case from 2005 concerning temporary special measures, the Board interpreted Article 3 of the Gender Equality Act in the light of Article 5a in the Women's Convention.[155] The Board unanimously ruled that the Frognerbekken Day Care Centre's decision to offer three

152 Proposition to the Odelsting No. 93 (2008–9) at 3.

153 The ACE Case. Gender Equality Appeal Board Case LDN 2001–1.

154 Act of 9 April 2010, No. 12.

155 Frognerbekken Day Care Centre Case. Gender Equality Appeal Board Case LDN 12–2005.

vacancies to one boy and two girls instead of the three boys who were first on the waiting list was not a contravention of the Gender Equality Act. Had they not given the two girls preference, all the children in the day care centre would have been boys. In its interpretation of Article 3 in the Gender Equality Act, the Board stated that:

> Article 5a of the CEDAW imposes on states an obligation to take all appropriate measures in order to modify gender-stereotyped gender roles. In addition, ensuing from the Gender Equality Act, the state's duty to promote equality in day care centres is also expressed in the Government's Action Plan for gender equality in kindergartens and basic education.

The CEDAW Convention was also invoked in a case where the Tribunal ruled that the use of gender as a factor used in calculating premiums for accident and sickness insurance constituted a contravention of the Gender Equality Act.[156] The decision, which also referred to the revised EU Gender Equality Directive, which had not then entered into force, was appealed by the insurance company and struck down by the appeals court without any discussion of Article 5a in the CEDAW. The ECJ has later ruled that the use of statistical gender differences in calculation of insurance premiums constitutes a contravention of the right to an individual assessment and, as such, direct gender discrimination under EU law.[157]

In 2003 the Board had to rule whether, pursuant to the Gender Equality Act, it is permitted to charge a higher user co-payment for the sterilization of women than for the sterilization of men.[158] After the introduction of different rates for women and men, the number of women undergoing sterilization in public hospitals dropped by 77 per cent. The Ombud was of the view that differential pricing was a contravention of Article 3 in the Gender Equality Act. The health authorities appealed the Ombud's decision. In its decision, the majority of the Board interpreted the Gender Equality Act's prohibition against direct discrimination in section 3 in the light of Article 12.1 of the Woman's Convention. The majority ruled that different pricing of the same health service for women and men, regardless of biological differences, constituted direct discrimination under the Gender Equality Act. The minority of the Board was of the view that sterilization of women and men constituted different medical interventions and therefore constituted neither direct nor indirect discrimination. The

[156] Insurance Case. Gender Equality Appeal Board Case LDN 2004–1.

[157] C-236/09 *Association Belge des Consommateurs Test-Achats and Others.*

[158] The Sterilization Case. Gender Equality Appeal Board Case LDN 2003–4.

Ministry of Health has not appealed the case, and has in the same vein refused to change its practice.

7.3 *The effectiveness and legitimacy of the CEDAW in judicial review*

Most Norwegian gender discrimination cases are, as we have seen, dealt with by the Ombud and the Tribunal, which are administrative agencies with specialist competence in the field of women, gender and the law. These agencies are, through the use of international legal sources such as the CEDAW, EU law and the ECHR, making their mark on the development of the standards in the Gender Equality Act.[159] A number of their decisions have, as demonstrated above, paved the way for legal reform. There have, however, been incidents where the executive branch of government, instead of appealing the Tribunal's decision to the courts, has flatly refused to comply.[160] Such incidents, which undermine the Tribunal's authority, have prompted a broader discussion about the Tribunal's effectiveness and legitimacy. To strengthen the Tribunal's effectiveness, the Equality Commission in NOU 2011:18 suggests that the Tribunal be awarded power to award financial compensation in discrimination cases. In its Concluding Comments to Norway's eighth periodic report, the CEDAW Committee welcomed the appointment of the Equality Commission, mandated to strengthen the Ombud's and the Tribunal's mandate for promoting equality and the advancement of women.[161]

8 Making space and giving voice

The incorporation of the CEDAW into the Human Rights Act put the gender-specific prohibition against sex discrimination in the CEDAW on an equal footing with the gender-neutral prohibitions against sex discrimination in the ICCPR, the ICESCR and the ECHR. The controversies surrounding the gender-neutral Anti-Discrimination Bill and the gender-neutral Crisis Centre Act show how the CEDAW is, slowly but surely, making its mark on the prevailing tension between gender-specific and gender-neutral law. The jurisprudence of the Ombud and the Tribunal show how Article 5a, with its focus on stereotypes that reflect subordinate

159 The Faculty of Law at the University of Oslo and the Faculty of Law at the University of Tromsø offer optional courses in discrimination and equality law and women's law and human rights.

160 The Sterilization Case. Gender Equality Appeal Board Case LDN 2003–4.

161 CEDAW/C/NOR/CO/8, para. 13.

and unequal roles for women, is being used to strengthen women's and girls' protection against discrimination in cases concerning advertisement, education, work and insurance. The relatively frequent use of Article 5a in matters concerning direct, indirect and structural discrimination points to the actual added value of the CEDAW, in comparison to other regional and international instruments in a modern, Western welfare state. The Anti-Discrimination Tribunal's lack of power to award damages in conjunction with lack of case law from national and international courts is, however, a factor that affects the legal legitimacy and the effectiveness of both the Gender Equality Act and the CEDAW.

The role of non-state actors in promoting accountability vis-à-vis Norwegian authorities is key, both in relation to law reform and judicial review. The lack of legal aid in discrimination cases and insufficient funding of membership-based organizations clearly hampers the women's organizations' ability to use the CEDAW in litigation and as a means to exert influence on Norwegian law and policy making.[162] In a similar vein, the lack of legal literacy programmes addressing immigrant women may partly explain why the majority of the gender discrimination complaints handled by the Ombud and the Tribunal are filed by ethnic Norwegian women, while the majority of those regarding ethnic discrimination are filed by men with ethnic minority backgrounds. While the CEDAW Committee's contribution to enhancing the status and power of the Tribunal has so far been modest, the Committee's call for a more participatory, balanced and transparent state reporting process involving both majority and minority civil society organization, national human rights institutions and democratically elected Parliamentarians is, slowly but surely, prompting change. This is indeed promising with a view to strengthening the legitimacy and effectiveness of the CEDAW in a changing social, political and legal landscape. See addendum.

[162] The Legal Aid Act does not include discrimination cases in prioritized cases without financial means-testing.

Addendum: In March 2013, a Proposition to the Storting (2012–13) Prop. 88 L on Discrimination Law was put forward by the Ministry of Children, Equality and Inclusion. With reference to the interventions made by the women's organizations and the Anti-Discrimination Ombud it suggests that the provision in the Gender Equality Act stating that the Act shall 'promote equality with the aim of improiving the position of women' be upheld and not abolished as suggested by the Discrimination Law Committee in 2009. The Proposition, however, turns down the longstanding quest from the women's organizations, the Anti-Discrimination Ombud and the Gender Equality Commission to strengthen the Equality Tribunal's effectiveness by awarding the Tribunal power to award compensation in discrimination cases. The proposition thus fails to provide for effective protection of women's human rights under national law in terms of legally binding as well as practically available protection.

Conclusions

ANNE HELLUM AND HENRIETTE SINDING AASEN

1 General reflections

A common aim of all human rights conventions is the protection of human equality, freedom and dignity. All human rights regimes belong to the same normative family and are based on the same values and principles. As shown by the chapters in this book, much can be learned from comparing the interpretation and implementation of different international, regional and national anti-discrimination and equality regimes. A common thread running through all the chapters is the potential and actual added value of the CEDAW's *transformative, holistic and gender-specific* approaches to gender equality and its relationship to other human rights regimes. All in all, the chapters show how the jurisprudence of the CEDAW Committee has gradually evolved in response to a wide range of challenges in a diverse, increasingly complex and rapidly changing world. They provide a window into the twists and turns of the processes whereby international and national lawmakers, the CEDAW Committee, courts, legal scholars and civic organizations have contributed through their work to the development of the Convention's normative content and how it is put into practice.

The rich and nuanced insights provided by the chapters in this volume offer a unique opportunity for further reflection on the options and limits of the Convention and the Committee in comparison and interaction with other instruments. The diverse and complex perspectives of the authors, each speaking with a distinct voice and giving particular insight into fundamental issues related to the interpretation and implementation of the CEDAW, have made it a challenge to arrive at general conclusions. There are, however, some patterns or lines of arguments that can be extracted from the various parts of the book. Focusing on the CEDAW's transformative approach to equality, section 2 addresses the

We would like to thank Andrew Byrnes, Ingunn Ikdahl and Geir Ulfstein for insightful comments on the concluding chapter.

strengths and weaknesses of the CEDAW with regard to the realization of the CEDAW's potential added value. In section 3 the Convention's holistic approach, which links civil, political, social and economic rights, is discussed in light of other human rights regimes and the demand for substantive equality and engenderment. Section 4 analyzes the potential and actual added value of the CEDAW regime in light of national case studies from South Asia, Southern Africa, Australia, Canada and Northern Europe.

2 From potential to actual added value: the transformative approach (Part I)

The chapters in Part I call for careful consideration of the basic values that are to be protected through human rights instruments in general and the CEDAW in particular. Rikki Holtmaat, with reference to Martha Nussbaum, points to participation, autonomy and freedom as key elements in all human rights protection. The autonomy and capacity of each human being to make his/her own life plan come true is the fundamental idea of human rights across all societies and cultures. At the same time, equal respect for all individuals requires due respect and protection of individual diversity.[1] Today, the CEDAW Convention has been ratified by almost all countries in the world (although with extensive reservations), and the Committee seeks to apply a universal standard of equality and non-discrimination to various categories of women in legal, political, social, cultural and economic contexts. All cultures, as changing and contested bodies of perception, have the potential to protect individual dignity, autonomy and diversity. In light of the domestic studies presented in Part III of this book, it is clear, however, that gender stereotypes embedded in social and cultural perceptions and practices represent strong barriers to gender equality throughout the world.

In line with the demand for substantive equality, the purpose of the CEDAW is threefold: (1) to guarantee women's individual rights, (2) to give social support to women and (3) to enhance social and cultural change.[2] This triple approach to gender equality, which moves beyond formal and symmetric gender equality, distinguishes the CEDAW from other international anti-discrimination and equal rights regimes. The Convention acknowledges that to achieve substantive equality, biologically, socially

[1] R. Holtmaat, Chapter 3 (Introduction and section 9).

[2] General Recommendation No. 25.

and culturally constructed differences between women and men must be taken into account. Assuming that discrimination against women is created and upheld through unequal constructions of gender relations embedded in social and cultural perceptions, norms and practices, States Parties are obliged to take legislative as well as other measures to address and overcome harmful gender stereotypes in their respective countries. While Article 2(f) of the CEDAW addresses discriminatory laws, regulations, customs and practices, Article 5(a) obligates States Parties to take all appropriate measures 'to modify the social and cultural patterns of conduct of men and women, with a view to achieving the elimination of prejudices and customary and all other practices which are based on the idea of the inferiority or the superiority of either of the sexes or on stereotyped roles for men and women'.

Several of the authors in this volume emphasize the potential added value of Article 5(a) of the CEDAW.[3] As pointed out by Fleur van Leeuwen in her analysis of women's reproductive rights, a problem of other human rights regimes and monitoring bodies is that they do not address the core causes of human rights violations that affect women's rights to life and health, for example, but only the manifestations or symptoms of these.[4] Rikki Holtmaat is of the view that '[t]hanks to the existence of Article 5, the Women's Convention is a revolutionary instrument that addresses the root causes of discrimination against women'.[5]

To what extent, then, has the Committee been a driving force for the advancement of the CEDAW's transformative approach to substantive equality in general and elimination of gender stereotypes in particular? Simone Cusack observes that attempts to hold States Parties accountable for wrongful gender stereotyping have been successful in the majority of individual communications considered by the Committee.[6] In the same vein she points to the lack of clarity surrounding States Parties' obligations regarding gender stereotyping. Applying the tripartite framework of state obligations – the obligations to respect, protect and fulfil – Cusack's analysis seeks to sharpen the understanding of content and meaning of the obligations in Articles 2(f) and 5(a). Addressing the realization of the normative potential of Article 5(a), Cusack emphasizes that:

[3] R. Holtmaat, Chapter 3; S. Cusack, Chapter 4; C. M. Bailliet, Chapter 5; C. N. Musembi, Chapter 6.

[4] F. van Leeuwen, Chapter 8 (section 5.3).

[5] R. Holtmaat, Chapter 3 (Concluding remarks).

[6] S. Cusack, Chapter 4 (section 3.1.5).

> [s]trong leadership from the CEDAW Committee on these issues will not only help to guide States Parties in the implementation of their obligations under CEDAW, but will also influence the thinking and decision-making of other human rights treaty bodies as well as domestic courts. If the Committee is successful in this endeavour, it may change forever – and for the better – the way we think about discrimination and inequality.[7]

Andrew Byrnes articulates the role of the Committee as being 'a forum for holding governments accountable for their international undertakings, for the engagement of civil society as part of national and transnational struggles to achieve women's equality, and as a site for the generation and interpretation of legal norms'.[8] The primary method of the Committee, as described by Byrnes, is to consider reports submitted by States Parties on the steps that they have taken to implement the CEDAW, and to engage in a 'constructive dialogue' with States Parties. Regarding the Convention's approach to Article 5(a), which obliges States Parties to modify and eliminate gender stereotypes, Byrnes characterizes the CEDAW Committee as a:

> vigorous actor in the cause of universal standards of human rights, and has engaged in advocacy for a norm of equality that transcends and prevails over national laws, practices, religions, customs and traditions that are inconsistent with that norm. This is not to say that the Committee (or the Convention) is antagonistic to religion or traditional cultures and customary laws and practices as such – indeed it sees the centrality of these to women's sense of themselves and their place in the world – but that it is resolute in being critical of those harmful practices that deny women's agency, violate their dignity or their persons, and exclude them from full participation in the life of their communities and societies.[9]

In relation to Article 5(a), the CEDAW Committee is thus faced with the problem of striking an appropriate balance between respect for diverse conditions of life on the one hand, and effective human rights protection on the other.[10] Addressing the challenges the realization of Article 5(a)'s potential brings about at the national and local levels, all the authors in this section of the book are concerned with factors that affect the legitimacy

[7] S. Cusack, Chapter 4 (Conclusion). See also R. Holtmaat, who points out the need for a new General Recommendation from the CEDAW Committee on Article 5 (Chapter 3, section 6).

[8] Chapter 1 (Introduction).

[9] A. Byrnes, Chapter 1 (Conclusion).

[10] H. Keller and G. Ulfstein, 'Conclusions' in H. Keller and G. Ulfstein (eds.), *UN Human Rights Treaty Bodies: Law and Legitimacy* (Cambridge University Press, 2012) at 414–55 at 425.

and the effectiveness of the CEDAW. As pointed out by Rikki Holtmaat, state resistance is often linked to the close relationship between national identity and religious and customary gender stereotypes protected by statutory and constitutional law. In order to achieve a higher level of social and cultural acceptance of the norm of women's equality, Holtmaat, with reference to the growing body of cross-cultural human rights scholarship, emphasizes the need to promote and enhance a dialogue between the state and the main internal stakeholders, that is religious leaders, community leaders and (women) NGOs. On the basis of review of the CEDAW Committee's Concluding Comments, Holtmaat shows how the Committee often stresses the necessity of engaging in dialogue with civil society about social and cultural changes that need to take place in order to put an end to discrimination against women. She also documents how the Committee, in its Concluding Comments, encourages States Parties to see culture as something that can be changed. As an example she refers to a Concluding Observation on Jordan of 2007, where the Committee 'urges the State party to view culture as a dynamic aspect of the country's social fabric and life and therefore subject to change'.[11] Holtmaat thus disagrees with legal anthropologist Sally Engle Merry, who claims that the CEDAW Committee has 'an old vision of culture as fixed, static, bounded … juxtaposed to a more modern understanding of culture as a process of continually creating new meanings and practices that are products of power relationships and open to contestation among members of the group and by outsiders'.[12]

Addressing the tensions between the equality and anti-discrimination standards in the CEDAW on the one hand and the formal and informal customary and religious norms on the other, Andrew Byrnes shows how the CEDAW Committee 'sees the tensions that can exist between particular interpretations of culture and the Convention, and rejects those aspects of cultural practices that mean that women are discriminated against'.[13] Documenting how the Committee addresses gender stereotypes in all parts of the world, he notes in relation to Sally Engle Merry's claim that when 'the drafters of the convention thought about culture, they used … culture to describe other worlds, not their own',[14] this may

[11] CEDAW Committee, *Concluding Observations: Jordan*, 2007, CEDAW/C/EST/JOR/CO/4, para. 20.

[12] S. E. Merry, 'Gender Justice and CEDAW' (2011), quoted from A. Byrnes in this volume, Chapter 1 (section 7).

[13] A. Byrnes, Chapter 1 (section 7).

[14] Merry, 'Gender Justice and CEDAW'.

fail to adequately reflect the role of prominent women from non-Western countries who were involved in the drafting of the Convention, and who saw it as an important vehicle for engaging with the discriminatory aspects of their own cultures. Pointing to recent communications by the CEDAW Committee, Rikki Holtmaat shows that the current understanding of gender stereotypes does not refer only to non-Western 'exotic' or 'backward' traditions, but encompasses gender stereotyping in all parts of the world.[15] Anne Hellum's study of the CEDAW in Norwegian law underscores Holtmaat's and Byrnes' views. She shows how in cases concerning education and advertisement, the Norwegian Equality and Anti-Discrimination Ombud and Tribunal refer to Article 5(a) and the Committee's Concluding Comments to the Norwegian state reports.[16] According to Hellum, the relatively frequent use of Article 5(a) in matters concerning direct, indirect and structural discrimination of women and girls from the ethnic Norwegian majority points to the actual added value of the CEDAW, in comparison to other regional and international instruments in a modern, Western welfare state.

In their analysis of state resistance to human rights, several of the authors in this book show how the dominant national legal culture often serves as a shield against international legal influence. An interesting example is Hélène Ruiz Fabri and Andrea Hamann's analysis of the CEDAW in French law. The authors argue that the CEDAW's lack of impact on French law must be understood in the light of the dominant French legal culture's emphasis on French 'exceptionalism' or 'specificity'. According to the authors: 'the common and widespread [academic] reaction when feminist approaches to law are mentioned is to consider these to be typically Anglo-Saxon themes and concerns, thereby conveying the impression that France is shielded against these issues'.[17] To understand the CEDAW's invisibility in French law, the authors argue: 'The claim of specificity should not and must not become a systematic explanation in order to justify being exempted from providing any kind of argument but, at the same time, one cannot ignore and disregard that this specificity does indeed exist and must therefore be adequately acknowledged as part and parcel of the dominant French legal culture.'[18]

[15] R. Holtmaat, Chapter 3 (section 9) and R. Holtmaat, 'Article 5' in M. Freeman, C. Chinkin and B. Rudolf (eds.), *The UN Convention on the Elimination of All Forms of Discrimination against Women: A Commentary* (Oxford University Press, 2012) 141–68.

[16] A. Hellum, Chapter 21 (section 7).

[17] H. Ruiz Fabri and A. Hamann, Chapter 19 (section 1).

[18] *Ibid.*

Addressing challenges faced by both the newly appointed Working Group on Laws that Discriminate against Women and the CEDAW Committee, Fareda Banda asks how intervening in socio-cultural issues that could discredit the entire work of the particular human rights treaty body, such as sexual orientation discrimination, should be handled: 'Can a Working Group on laws that discriminate based on a human rights mandate take such an approach [sacrifice the rights of lesbian women for 'the greater good'] – what about non-discrimination being a binding norm of immediate enforceability without exception?'[19] Her clear answer is no. Banda refers to the decision in the Indian *Naz Foundation* case, which led to the repeal of a section of the Penal Code that criminalized sexual activity between two people of the same sex. In this case, the Court emphasized that the ban was based on British colonial laws that did not reflect Indian traditions and values. According to Banda, this Indian case could serve as an example of good practice in engagement with states.[20]

The requirement of substantive equality, however, calls for careful consideration of what should be treated equally and what should be treated differently under various historical and social circumstances. In situations where women's family roles have not changed, measures for the continued protection of women living under marriage laws that are in conflict with the CEDAW may be necessary in the short term. Celestine Nyamu Musembi adds an important dimension to this discussion when she asks if the CEDAW Committee is too inflexible in its approach to the different ways States Parties deal with discriminatory practices. With reference to the CEDAW Committee's communication with several African States Parties, she claims that the Committee fails to appreciate differentiated efforts in various countries to deal with, for example, polygamy. According to Nyamu Musembi:

> States that have taken no steps at all to address the issue, as well as states that have made some attempts – legislative, administrative or aimed at social education – are equally rebuked in stylized language contained in a standard stern paragraph that is administered to all with the slightest variation. Nothing in this stylized language suggests appreciation of the differentiated circumstances of each state, nor the varying levels of effort at reform. It only reinforces the conclusion that, in the view of the CEDAW Committee, nothing short of immediate legislative prohibition will do, an attitude that narrows the scope of possible actions envisioned in Article 5(a).[21]

[19] F. Banda, Chapter 2 (section 8). [20] *Ibid.*
[21] C. N. Musembi, Chapter 6 (section 2.2).

Nyamu Musembi gives voice to the concern that the preferred long-term solution (abolishing polygamy) is often not attainable in a short-term perspective, without running the risk of women losing the little protection they have in existing legal and social arrangements. She asks 'What is the appropriate feminist response in situations where measures are undertaken that confer tangible and immediate benefits on women, but that rest on a stereotyped understanding of gender roles and therefore pose long-term negative consequences?'[22] She contrasts the position of the CEDAW Committee with the position of the Maputo Protocol and the solutions in several African states, which aim at a gradual phasing out of polygamy, and at the same time extend equal protection of the law to all women. According to Nyamu Musembi, the CEDAW Committee can draw inspiration from the Maputo Protocol's approach in order to engage African states in a more constructive and productive dialogue that reflects an in-depth understanding of each country's context and milestones on the way forward towards transformed gender relations.[23]

A similar line of argument is pursued by Cecilia Bailliet, who argues that looking at women's diverse and individual needs, abilities, priorities and circumstances is an essential part of preventing gender stereotyping and upholding individual dignity and equality.[24] Addressing the relationship between provisions (a) and (b) in Article 5 of the CEDAW concerning gender stereotyping and recognition of maternity, respectively, Bailliet's chapter complements Cusack's chapter on wrongful gender stereotyping. Bailliet argues that the CEDAW Committee's jurisprudence gives more weight to issues of equality (the extension of existing human rights to women on equal terms with men) than to equal worth and the female experience of motherhood (the issue of difference). Seeing maternal identity as an important manifestation of human dignity, Bailliet asserts that the CEDAW regime has had a limited or too-narrow approach to the recognition and protection of maternal identity. She compares the CEDAW approach with that taken by the Inter-American Court of Human Rights, which in its approach uses narratives 'to flesh out our understanding of non-discrimination and the scope of harm to marginalized groups'.[25] Bailliet suggests that this approach reflects a higher level of legitimacy in the Latin American context compared to the CEDAW regime, and that

[22] C. N. Musembi, Chapter 6 (Conclusion).

[23] *Ibid.* See also F. Banda on polygyny in this volume, Chapter 2 (section 8).

[24] C. M. Bailliet, Chapter 5 (section 6); S. Cusack, Chapter 4.

[25] C. M. Bailliet, Chapter 5 (section 3).

it offers an interpretation of human rights that is more inclusive of the actual women concerned. She concludes that the CEDAW Committee, which has supported the Inter-American human rights system as a partner in the protection of women's rights, should take more advantage in future of the method of narratives in order to give voice to individual women's experiences of human rights violations.[26]

Overall, Part I of the volume contributes to the perspective that the CEDAW has added significant value to the international, regional and national discourses on the rights of women. An important observation made by Byrnes, which is underscored in several of the national case studies in Part III, is that only when the process of preparation, consideration and evaluation of a report by the Committee is linked into domestic processes of policy-making and NGO advocacy, is the reporting procedure likely to have any significant impact at the domestic level. The realization of CEDAW's normative potential, however, encounters a number of problems. A critical factor is the nature of the CEDAW state obligations, which vary from being quite general (take 'appropriate' or 'necessary' steps or measures) to more specific (replace discriminatory laws, ensure women's right to vote). In complex situations it can be difficult for an external body such as the CEDAW Committee to assess whether or not the State Party has in fact lived up to its obligations, since there may be a range of options available for the State Party, and the Committee does not necessarily have the complete picture of the complex relationship between the customary and religious laws embedded in state law and in the existing customary and religious norms.[27] Fareda Banda points out the additional problem of international and regional differences in interpretation of basic concepts, for example the relationship between equality and equity.[28] As demonstrated by Nyamu Musembi and Bailliet, this is where dialogue between international and regional human rights regimes is needed, in particular with regard to how to balance gender equality and gender differences, and what constitutes appropriate measures to achieve substantive equality in different cultural and social contexts.

While the prescribed 'constructive dialogue' between the Committee and the States Parties appears to take place in most cases, there are significant exceptions. Many States Parties exercise considerable resistance to change and give little attention to the Committee's General

[26] C. M. Bailliet, Chapter 5 (Conclusion).

[27] A. Byrnes, Chapter 1 (sections 6 and 7); C. Damiso and J. Stewart, Chapter 16.

[28] F. Banda, Chapter 2 (section 8).

Recommendations and Concluding Observations (and may in fact not be scheduled to appear again before the Committee for many years).[29] As pointed out by Fareda Banda, it is clear that state accountability for violations of women's rights and effective implementation of state obligations are serious challenges. Ratification of the CEDAW, as emphasized by Banda, does not necessarily mean loyalty and commitment to its objectives from all States Parties. In light of the CEDAW's transformative ambition, this is a serious problem for its credibility, legitimacy and effectiveness in those countries where there is little or no progress in areas of great concern for many women. This point is underscored in Banda's analysis of how the limited resources of the CEDAW Committee to follow up communications with States Parties that have discriminatory laws and practices and problematic reservations to the CEDAW led to the establishment of the new UN Working Group on the Issue of Discrimination against Women in Law and Practice on 8 October 2010.

3 The actual added value of the CEDAW: engenderment of socio-economic rights (Part II)

For poor and marginalized women and girls, social and economic rights, such as the right to food, water, housing and education, are key in addressing marginalization and the absence of substantive equality.[30] As already pointed out, optimistic feminist legal scholars argue that the CEDAW's recognition of the interdependence and indivisibility of civil, political, social and economic rights makes it the instrument with the greatest potential to address the close relationship between women's marginalization, social rights and inequality.[31] As underscored by all the authors in Part II of this book, the holistic approach, embedded in the CEDAW and developed through the jurisprudence of the CEDAW Committee, is a necessary and essential condition for transforming social and economic rights in light of women's lived experiences, constraints and social realities. Two key questions regarding the realization of this normative potential are central: if and in what way has the CEDAW contributed

[29] A. Byrnes, Chapter 1 (Conclusion); F. Banda, Chapter 2 (sections 4.1 and 8).

[30] 'Montreal Principles on Women's Economic, Social, and Cultural Rights', *Human Rights Quarterly* 26:4 (1991).

[31] L. Farha, 'Committee on the Elimination of Discrimination against Women: women claiming economic, social and cultural rights – the CEDAW potential' in M. Langford (ed.), *Social Rights Jurisprudence: Emerging Trends in International and Comparative Law* (Cambridge University Press, 2008) 553–68.

to the transformation of existing social and economic rights in light of women's lived experiences, and how does the CEDAW Committee's jurisprudence interact and intersect with the jurisprudence of other UN bodies that address social and economic rights without discrimination? Does the CEDAW Committee's jurisprudence influence the rapidly developing social rights jurisprudence, or is it operating in isolation and thereby contributing to fragmentation and marginalization of international law's protection against sex and gender discrimination?

3.1 From the margins to the centre: gender mainstreaming

The failure of the UN human rights system to provide effective protection of women's human rights was acknowledged by the 171 states that adopted the Vienna Declaration and Programme of Action by consensus in 1993. This requires that the status and rights of women be integrated into the mainstream UN human rights monitoring mechanisms and bodies. It was requested that the mainstream UN human rights system add the experiences of women to its traditional human rights approaches, in order to make women more visible and to transform the concept and practice of human rights so that it takes better account of women's lives.[32] This was affirmed in the 1995 *Beijing Declaration*,[33] and in 1997 the UN Economic and Social Council formally adopted the principle of gender mainstreaming:

> Mainstreaming a gender perspective is the process of assessing the implications for women and men of any planned action, including legislation, policies and programmes, in all areas and at all levels. It is a strategy for making women's as well as men's concerns and experiences an integral dimension of the design, implementation, monitoring and evaluation of policies and programmes in all political, economic and societal spheres so that women and men benefit equally and inequality is not perpetuated. The ultimate goal is to achieve gender equality.[34]

The chapters in Part II of this book demonstrate the many synergies between the UN gender mainstreaming strategy, the CEDAW regime and other international human rights regimes that protect and promote

[32] F. Van Leeuwen, Chapter 8 (section 4), with reference to C. Bunch, 'Women's rights as human rights: toward a re-vision of human rights', *Human Rights Quarterly* 12:4 (1990) 486–98.

[33] *Beijing Declaration and Platform for Action* (adopted 15 September 1995), Fourth World Conference on Women, UN Doc. A/CONF.177/20 (1995).

[34] UN Economic and Social Council (UN 1997, 28).

women's social and economic rights.[35] In her study of the normative development of women's right to secure housing, Ingunn Ikdahl describes and analyzes the various strategies and normative synergies in General Recommendations and reports of the CEDAW Committee, the ICESCR Committee and the UN Special Rapporteur on Adequate Housing. She documents how the approaches of the CEDAW regime and the ICESCR regime are overlapping and complementary, and have at least in part been combined by the Special Rapporteur through reliance on the principles of gender mainstreaming and indivisibility of rights. Together, they form the basis for a comprehensive understanding of the right to safe housing, and of the range of legal and institutional measures to be taken to reduce women's vulnerability. Addressing maternal mortality as a violation of women's rights to life and health and a particular form of structural and gender-based discrimination, Henriette Sinding Aasen describes the interplay and normative synergies between the CEDAW and the ICESCR regimes with regard to the content and implementation of the right to health for poor women in low-resource settings. Fleur van Leeuwen shows how, after 1993, the Human Rights Committee (HRC) and the ICESCR Committee began to address issues that traditionally were not seen as human rights issues, such as maternal mortality, access to contraceptives, reproductive and sexual information, education and abortion.

Rather than a conflicting jurisprudence, these chapters illustrate how, through a dynamic approach and by drawing inspiration from each other, the various treaty bodies are extending and gradually transforming socio-economic rights so that they become more inclusive of women. In addition to the CEDAW and its Committee, other human rights regimes, such as the UN Special Rapporteur on Adequate Housing, and regional instruments and bodies, have also contributed to the advancement and engenderment of women's rights. This trend points not to fragmentation, but to a development towards more similarities and greater unification of different human rights regimes.

3.2 *From gender mainstreaming to engenderment?*

Despite the clear trend of greater integration of women's human rights after 1993, the question of if and to what extent these normative synergies

[35] An overview of the measures that were taken by the UN to mainstream gender into the different human rights treaty bodies is found in A. Gallagher, 'Ending the marginalization: strategies for incorporating women into the United Nations human rights system', *Human Rights Quarterly* 19:2 (1997) 283–333.

have contributed to substantive equality for women remains a key question. The chapters in Part II of this book address this question and provide nuanced answers to it. The notion of *engenderment*, elaborated by Sandra Fredman in Chapter 7, is in our view a fruitful analytical tool to assess the legal development from a gender perspective. Exploring how the CEDAW's normative potential has been translated by the CEDAW Committee and other treaty bodies, Fredman suggests that it is not sufficient to extend existing human rights to women on equal terms with men. Instead, the rights themselves need to be recast in light of the specific needs and disadvantaged situations of women.

Considering the gendered nature of the current social disadvantages of women, Fredman points out the limitations of formal equality, which require women to conform to male-oriented social structures rather than challenging the unfairness of existing structures.[36] Fredman argues that if the gender-specific factors that cause disadvantages for women are to be fully addressed, 'rights must be infused with substantive gender equality'.[37] This means moving beyond the need for a male norm with which to compare women, and requiring that existing social norms change. Where equal treatment leads to a disadvantage for women, it may be necessary to treat women differently (e.g. with regard to education, work and healthcare). However, the definition of the *substance* of substantive equality remains controversial. According to Fredman, the conceptions of dignity, equal opportunity and equality of result are all too limited to function on their own to constitute the substantive core of equality. She proposes that the concept of substantive equality has four different and complementary dimensions: redistribution, recognition (including respect and dignity), transformation and participation.[38]

Fredman concludes that the CEDAW regime has a significant added value in terms of engenderment and substantive equality. She points out three factors that, in her view, reflect the CEDAW's commitment to a conception of substantive equality that requires more than merely extending socio-economic rights to women: the asymmetric approach and focus on women's disadvantaged positions, the demand for structural change (Article 5), the emphasis on women's representation and participation. This engendered approach is reflected in many of the socio-economic rights contained in the Convention. However, according to Fredman, despite these positive aspects of the CEDAW, it also speaks with another

[36] S. Fredman, Chapter 7 (section 3.1).

[37] *Ibid.* [38] S. Fredman, Chapter 7 (section 3.2).

voice, which simply extends existing socio-economic rights to women, rather than reframing them. In particular, this is evident from the wording of the right to work and work-related benefits (Article 11), which in her view is premised on a male model of work and the assumption that 'work' equates to paid work outside the home. The right to education in Article 10 also speaks to a great extent with the voice of formal equality between men and women (same conditions, same curricula and examinations) and does not address common barriers for girls to access educational institutions. Thus, according to Fredman, important parts of the Convention are still in need of continued engagement to ensure that feminist jurisprudence continues to develop the CEDAW in the direction of engendered human rights, particularly through the medium of General Recommendations and the developing jurisprudence under the Optional Protocol.[39]

Fredman argues that the ICESCR does not go far enough to engender socio-economic rights, and that a gender-neutral approach to equality often does not recognize the particular experiences of women. She asserts that the approach of the ICESCR Committee to a great extent has been to slot women into existing male-dominated structures, for example with regard to the right to work and favourable working conditions. This observation is partly supported by Ingunn Ikdahl, who describes how women's experiences of a lack of secure housing were initially marginalized in mainstream (male) human rights discourses.[40] Ikdahl, however, draws attention to the cumulative effect of the different entry points of various bodies in the UN system that over time have strengthened women's right to secure tenure. Ikdahl has shown that through a focus on equal distribution of property between husband and wife during marriage and in the event of divorce and death, the CEDAW Committee has contributed to human rights analysis of the gendered nature of security of tenure for one's home. In addition, the reports of the Special Rapporteur of the Right to Adequate Housing have had significant impact on adding women's perspectives to the ICESCR Committee's understanding of adequate and secure housing. As forced eviction from the home was identified as

[39] S. Fredman, Chapter 7 (Conclusion and Introduction). Another area that calls for engagement from a grounded women's perspective is the human right to water, which is embedded in the CEDAW, the CRC and the ICESCR. See A. Hellum 'Engendering the human right to water: taking the lived realities of women and girls as starting point' in M. Langford and A. Russell (eds.) *The Right to Water: Theory, Prospects and Practice* (Cambridge University Press, 2013).

[40] I. Ikdahl, Chapter 9 (section 4).

a human rights issue, women's experiences of being evicted from their homes upon divorce or widowhood (family evictions) were conceptualized as a violation of the right to secure housing.

Both Ikdahl and Fredman emphasize the significant impact of the UN Special Rapporteur on Adequate Housing on the engenderment of the right to secure housing for women. Ikdahl shows how the reports of the Special Rapporteur have been central in making the experiences, threats and vulnerabilities experienced by women visible in the human rights discourse on the right to safe housing according to Article 11.1 of the ICESCR.[41] Fredman points out that the approach of the Special Rapporteur incorporates many of the elements of substantive equality, in particular the fourth dimension of giving women voice, agency and participation: 'Indeed, it is because he has instituted wide-ranging consultations, and listened to testimonies received from women at grass-roots level, that he has succeeded in formulating the right from a particularly gendered perspective.'[42] The use of women's testimonies seems to have brought attention to the experiences and vulnerabilities of women and paved the way for a renewed understanding of the right to adequate housing, one that is more inclusive of women and sensitive to their situation of dependency and lack of power. This focus on individual testimonies and stories is in line with Bailliet's view that individual narratives are necessary in order to acknowledge the nature of the human rights violations and to restore the dignity of the individual woman.

Van Leeuwen examines whether or not the work of the HRC and ICESCR Committee reflects compliance with the request of the 1993 World Conference on Human Rights to add the experiences of women to existing approaches in order to transform the concept and practice of human rights so that they take better account of women's lives.[43] In her analysis of the practices of these treaty bodies, van Leeuwen concludes that the recommendations and guidelines are often too limited in their formulation of specific state obligations. While the gender-specific constraints experienced by women in exercising their rights are addressed by the HRC and ICESCR Committee, formulations of state obligations to *fulfil* the right to health (e.g. with regard to accessible pregnancy-related and maternal services) are not spelled out. In general, the Committees do not question whether or not abortion services are available to women, even though they indicate that States Parties should allow abortion when

[41] *Ibid.* (section 4.4). [42] S. Fredman, Chapter 7 (section 5.2).
[43] F. van Leeuwen, Chapter 8.

pregnancy is the result of rape or endangers the life of the woman, and despite the fact that they regularly express concern about unsafe abortions.[44] Van Leeuwen concludes that the work of the two Committees needs to be more far-reaching in order to reflect the gender-specific circumstances that affect women's rights, and to formulate adequate women-inclusive human rights obligations that can effectively address the constraints experienced by women.[45] Another criticism is that the Committees mostly fail to place the specific human rights issues of women in the context of gender-based and structural discrimination:

> Although the Committees address many human rights abuses and constraints that characteristically affect women in their respective GCs on equality of men and women, they generally do not label these as symptoms of (structural) discrimination. Reference to these issues in their GCs, as well as reference to Articles 3 of the ICCPR and the ICESCR in the work of the Committees, rather seems to reflect the Committee's awareness of the fact that … women may face different hurdles than men in their enjoyment of human rights. Although this understanding is an important first step away from the idea of *sameness* … this does not mean that the HRC and the ICESCR Committee examine whether these *women-specific* human rights issues are the result of discrimination against women.[46]

Henriette Sinding Aasen addresses the high prevalence of preventable maternal deaths as a violation of women's rights to life and health, and as a form of gender-based discrimination caused by structural disadvantage suffered by poor women.[47] Although high-level international campaigns by the UN and WHO have focused on strategies in order to reduce the alarmingly high maternal mortality in many developing countries, it still constitutes a major challenge to women's rights to life and health. Both Article 12 of the ICESCR and Article 12 of the CEDAW contain provisions concerning the right to health. While Article 12 of the ICESCR is written in gender-neutral terms, Article 12 of the CEDAW is formulated in gender-specific terms, granting women adequate maternal healthcare services. Aasen examines the jurisprudence of the ICESCR and CEDAW Committees with regard to maternal mortality, women's reproductive rights and access to maternal healthcare services. She finds the Available, Accessible, Acceptable Services of Good Quality (AAAQ) framework developed by the ICESCR Committee particularly well suited to address the lack of services. This framework is also utilized by the

[44] F. van Leeuwen, Chapter 8 (section 5.2).
[45] *Ibid.* [46] F. van Leeuwen, Chapter 8 (section 5.3).
[47] H. S. Aasen, Chapter 10.

CEDAW Committee in its dialogue with States Parties. Both monitoring bodies, according to Aasen, provide relevant guidelines that address maternal deaths, and recognize that non-discrimination and substantive equality require reasonable accommodation for social differences, between men and women, between urban and rural women, and between rich and poor women. However, the engendered, diverse and inclusive understanding of women's right to health that has been developed at the international level, in particular the recognition of the need for appropriate, women-specific and accessible maternal healthcare services, has not yet materialized on the ground in countries with high maternal mortality. Thus, there is an urgent need for new, radical and structural strategies to implement women's rights to life and health, including proper national reproductive health indicators and monitoring systems.

4 Making space and giving voice: from international to national law (Part III)

The case studies from Southern Asia, Southern Africa, Northern Europe, Canada and Australia provide a window into the process whereby the CEDAW is making its mark on national law, policy-making and judicial decision-making. The most striking similarity between these studies is the women's organizations' increasing use of the CEDAW's state reporting procedure as a means of holding national governments accountable for their duty to respect, protect and fulfil the human rights of women. As already pointed out, the most striking difference regarding the CEDAW's effect on national law is between those states that have acceded to regional mechanisms that provide protection against sex and gender discrimination, those that do not have that option and those that have acceded regional instruments with weak enforcement mechanisms.[48]

There are, however, significant variations between and within these broad categories, pointing to an uneven and complex process of legal development, which in our view must be understood in light of each country's historical, political, legal and economic contexts. To better understand these variations, we will highlight the following factors and how

[48] Beth Simmons' study of international law in domestic politics suggests that the nature of the legal system generally has a consistent effect on governments' commitment patterns. According to Simmons' study, governments in common-law settings are systematically more reluctant to ratify human rights treaties and tend to enter far more reservations than governments in civil-law jurisdictions. B. A Simmons, *Mobilizing for Human Rights: International Law in Domestic Politics* (Cambridge University Press, 2009) at 109.

they play out in different political, legal, economic and cultural contexts: the degree of democracy, the nature of the legal system and the dominant legal culture, the availability of other international and regional mechanisms, the states' motivations for ratification, the democratic elements in the processes of ratification and monitoring, the extent of legal education of duty-bearers and rights-holders, and the strength of civil society.[49] Our concluding comments focus on the state reporting procedure and how the CEDAW features in national law and policy reform and in national judicial review.

4.1 The state reporting procedure and democratic involvement

Looking into more or less democratic, liberal and autocratic states that have or have not become parties to regional human rights mechanisms, the domestic studies in this volume confirm the assumption that the introduction of a new monitoring mechanism dealing with discrimination against women has given women a stronger stake in organizing demands of equality and non-discrimination under both international and national law.[50] Yet the extent to which the international and national dialogue facilitated and monitored by the CEDAW Committee has led to change varies significantly. The discussion below focuses on the role of democratic elements in the ratification and monitoring process.

The process whereby a treaty is ratified and monitored is a factor that is likely to have a bearing on the level of state commitment and as such on the domestication process. The political legitimacy and effectiveness of the actual treaty obligations is from this perspective seen as being linked to the democratic elements in the domestic ratification and monitoring

[49] With the exception of ratification of regional treaties, these factors are pointed out by Simmons, *Mobilizing for Human Rights.*

[50] This assumption is clearly spelt out in K. Knop, 'Why rethinking the sovereign state is important for women's human rights law' in R. Cook (ed.), *Human Rights of Women. National and International Perspectives* (Philadelphia: University of Pennsylvania Press, 1994). Recent empirical evidence confirms that membership in women's NGOs tends to grow in the first and second years after CEDAW ratification, the assumption being that ratification will contribute to the empowerment of women's rights organizations. See Simmons, *Mobilizing for Human Rights* at 212. A recent study on contemporary women's movements in the UK, Spain and Norway show that various uploading processes related to the CEDAW, EU law and other international instruments are regarded as important opportunity structures for women's organizations. See L. N. Predelli and B. Halsaa (eds.), *Majority–Minority Relations in Contemporary Women's Movement: Strategic Sisterhood* (Basingstoke: Palgrave MacMillan, 2012) at 266.

process, including the degree of involvement of the Parliament and civic organizations. Andrew Byrnes demonstrates in this volume how the CEDAW Committee has made provisions for civil society, national human rights institutions and Parliaments to make formal and informal contributions to the work of the Committee in order to ensure that the review of a state report is linked to domestic law and policy-making processes.[51]

In regard to political legitimacy, the studies uncover variations regarding Parliamentary involvement in the ratification and monitoring processes. Van den Brink describes that in the Netherlands, where ratification requires approval by a Parliamentary majority, the responsible Ministry is required by law to report to the Parliament every four years on the implementation of the CEDAW.[52] The Dutch study shows how this procedure has enhanced the political legitimacy of the CEDAW and facilitated democratic control of the executive power regarding the fulfilment of the treaty obligations. The Norwegian study reflects the CEDAW Committee's call for a more democratic and participatory monitoring process, not only involving civil society but also national human rights institutions and Parliamentarians.[53]

While the CEDAW Committee has clearly provided space for and given voice to women's claims, there are significant variations regarding NGOs' involvement in the state reporting procedure. In some countries the state agency in charge of the reporting procedure consults NGOs in the drafting of the state report. In other countries the NGOs are offered state support to produce independent shadow reports, and funding to present these to the Committee. The Dutch study shows how the government has offered NGOs economic support to write shadow reports in order to assist NGOs in fulfilling the critical role assumed by the human rights system.[54] In Finland and Norway, 'state feminism'[55] diminished for a long time the possibility for women's organizations to make full use of the Convention's communications procedure as independent actors.[56]

51 A. Byrnes, Chapter 1.

52 M. van den Brink, Chapter 17 (section 3).

53 A. Hellum, Chapter 21 (section 5.3).

54 M. van den Brink, Chapter 17 (section 4).

55 'State feminism' was defined by Helga M. Hernes in *Welfare State and Woman Power. Essays in State Feminism* (Oslo: Norwegian University Press, 1987) at 15 as 'a state where injustice on the basis of gender would be largely eliminated without an increase in other forms of inequality, such as among groups of women'.

56 K. Nousiainen and M. Pentikäinen, Chapter 20 (section 4.2); A. Hellum, Chapter 21 (section 5.2).

The Norwegian study shows how the CEDAW Committee's interventions have prompted the state to make funds available for NGO shadow reporting, and in this way has contributed to greater civil society mobilization. In the UK, many women's organizations regard the CEDAW as a valuable lobbying tool that draws ministerial attention to women's rights issues. Although the CEDAW Committee has requested that the UK ensure that the Convention and the Protocol are made an integral part of legal education of rights-holders and duty-bearers, the UK Coalition government, in power since 2010, has cut back on public support for the very bodies that had previously created 'opportunity structures' for women's organizations to utilize the CEDAW, such as the Women's National Commission (WNC).[57]

According to political theorists, the state's motivation for ratification of international treaties is a factor that is likely to affect whether and to what extent the obligations arising from treaty obligations are loyally implemented.[58] The studies in this volume illustrate this point. For example, the Pakistani case indicates that the ratification of the CEDAW has had little effect in the context of an autocratic state that ratified the CEDAW in pursuit of increased international political and economic goodwill.[59] The Zimbabwean study, on the other hand, demonstrates how the gamble of the ZANU PF government, which ratified the CEDAW without any intent to put the principle of gender equality on an equal footing with the protection of customary law, has backfired. As shown by Damiso and Stewart, Zimbabwe's ratification of the Maputo Protocol in 2008 is used by various women's groups as a lobbying tool in conjunction with the CEDAW in the ongoing debates on legal and constitutional reform.[60] In the present political climate, where the Zimbabwean Unity government seeks to appear in the best possible light and to be seen as moving towards equal rights for women, the state reporting process is clearly a factor that strengthens the legitimacy of women's rights organizations' demands for gender equality.

In political theory, domestic ownership is seen as important for the reception of international human rights standards in national law. In

[57] S. Fredman, Chapter 18 (section 4).

[58] Political theory assumes that states have different motives for ratification of international treaties, and that information about the state's motivation is important to understanding whether and to what extent the obligations arising from treaty obligations are loyally implemented. See Simmons, *Mobilizing for Human Rights* at 354.

[59] S. S. Ali, Chapter 15 (section 5).

[60] C. Damiso and J. Stewart, Chapter 16 (section 12).

many countries both state and non-state actors rely on technical or economic support from international or regional human rights networks or international donors. The studies in this part of the book illustrate the complex relationship between domestic ownership and the increasing involvement of international consultants and experts in the national reporting processes. The Indian, Nepalese, Pakistani and Zimbabwean studies highlight how the presence of donor aid, regional alliances and technical support may strengthen the capacity of women's organizations to use the state reporting procedure as an arena of convergence between themselves and engagement with the government.[61] In the Pakistani study, Shaheen Sardar Ali describes how the government's use of external consultants and experts may negatively affect the sense of domestic ownership, which may in turn undermine the political legitimacy of the treaty obligations. According to Ali:

> Unfortunately, given economic constraints and limited human resource capacity, the institutional structures that in an ideal world might help domesticate the CEDAW into Pakistani law have not been put in place as part of governmental routine. In fact, since accession the CEDAW has been viewed a 'project' to be taken up subject to available funding (which is mostly expected to come from foreign donor agencies) without becoming part of mainstream, budgeted government functions. Time and again, and with support from international donors, 'project' proposals have been written and funding received, and consultants have been hired at governmental and NGO levels to write Pakistan's country report as well as shadow reports on behalf of the country's NGOs and civil society.[62]

In Ali's view, the lack of steps to incorporate the CEDAW into national legislation through an Act of Parliament, as required by the Constitution and the Convention, should be seen as a reflection of the absence of national institutional commitment in the state reporting process.

Despite these variations, the studies indicate that the involvement of women's organizations, as emphasized by Byrnes' analysis of the work of the CEDAW Committee, is a key factor in the social and political legitimacy and the effectiveness of the state reporting procedure at the national level.[63]

4.2 *The CEDAW in national law and policy-making*

Whether or not the CEDAW and the work of the CEDAW Committee has had any effect on national law and policy-making, and if so to what

[61] Chapters 13–16. [62] S. S. Ali Chapter 15 (section 5).
[63] A. Byrnes, Chapter 1.

extent, is difficult to assess since debates on ratification and domestication are often a continuation of women's rights struggles that predate the CEDAW, and which must be described and understood in the context of national and local histories and timescales.

The clearest effect of ratification is demonstrated by the Australian and the Finnish studies. The Australian Sex Discrimination Act (SDA) of 1984 was motivated primarily by a long-standing claim for an Act that addresses discrimination against women, and to give effect to the provisions of the CEDAW, which Australia ratified in 1983.[64] Unlike the CEDAW, the SDA prohibits discrimination of both women and men on the ground of sex and marital status in many of the areas it covers. Yet the recommendation of the Australian Law Reform Commission (ALRC), that the SDA contain a general prohibition of discrimination as defined in Article 1 of the CEDAW, has gone unheeded. In the same vein, Finland's ratification of the CEDAW in 1986 prompted reform of legislation held to be contrary to the CEDAW. The Act on Equality between Women and Men was the most visible legislative outcome of the ratification.[65] Unlike the CEDAW, the Equality Act adopted a symmetric and gender-neutral approach with the overall focus on discrimination in the labour market.

According to Mehra, ratification of the CEDAW in India in 1993 took place after an extensive law reform that narrowed the gap between the constitutional promise of equality and the statutory standards that were in place in the 1980s.[66] According to Mehra, reservations to Articles 5(a), 16(1) and 16(2) have hampered reform relating to community-specific family and marriage laws for Muslims, Christians, Parsis and Hindus. Mehra's analysis of the political contestations related to the Supreme Court judgments concerning sexual violence show that implementing normative changes in areas free of reservations, despite NGO presence and a wide variety of actors heavily involved in the implementation process, is also an uphill battle.[67] In Nepal, which ratified the CEDAW in 1991 without reservations, the pace of legislative change in the first ten years after ratification was very slow in spite of the Interim Constitution and the Nepalese Treaty Act, which provided that ratified conventions take precedence when in conflict with other Nepalese law.[68] Both in India

[64] A. Byrnes, Chapter 11 (section 1).
[65] K. Nousiainen and M. Pentikäinen, Chapter 20 (section 2).
[66] M. Mehra, Chapter 13 (section 2).
[67] M. Mehra, Chapter 13 (section 3.2).
[68] K. Pandey, Chapter 14.

and Nepal, state resistance to legal reform has been countered by judicial review making extensive reference to the CEDAW (see the next section).

The Northern European studies describe how the CEDAW has operated in the shadow of the more-effectively sanctioned EU law, particularly in the field of labour law. The Dutch study shows that the CEDAW is largely absent in national political and legislative debates compared to the EU Directives, in spite of the high degree of involvement of Parliamentarians, women's organizations, and experts in the field of women's law and anti-discrimination law in the state reporting procedure.[69] In France, the twenty-two new laws relating to women's rights adopted between 2002 and 2007 were prompted by EU law. One area where the CEDAW does have a potential added value in comparison to EU law is in the right of French women to give their family names to their children. Yet France's reservation to Article 16(1)(g) of the CEDAW has, along with the lack of transparency, served as a shield against law reform in this area.[70] In the UK, successive Conservative and Labour governments have resisted the CEDAW Committee's persistent urging that it incorporate the Convention into the Human Rights Act of 1998. Most reforms strengthening women's protection against discrimination in the labour market are a result of the UK's obligations under EU law.[71] Even in Finland, where the Constitution makes human rights instruments part of national law, references to the CEDAW in law reform have, since the ratification of the CEDAW, been few in comparison to references to EU law.[72] The Norwegian study shows that the most recent reforms of the Gender Equality Act make reference to Norway's obligations under both EU law and the CEDAW. According to Hellum, the CEDAW has been of particular importance in relation to law reform providing protection against structural discrimination and discrimination on religious grounds.[73] It has also served as a safeguard against gender-neutral laws that overlook the specific situation of various groups of women. The Norwegian study demonstrates the actual added value of the CEDAW, and how the realization of its potential is linked to increased participation and networking involving women's organizations, national human rights institutions, and experts in the fields of women's

[69] M. van den Brink, Chapter 17 (section 8).

[70] H. Ruiz Fabri and A. Hamann, Chapter 19 (section 3.2).

[71] S. Fredman, Chapter 18 (section 5).

[72] K. Nousiainen and M. Pentikäinen, Chapter 20 (section 3).

[73] A. Hellum, Chapter 21 (section 6.1).

law, anti-discrimination and equality law, in relation to law reform at the national level.

The Canadian, UK and Dutch studies demonstrate how the political opportunities for women's rights and gender equality proponents has become more unfavourable under conservative neoliberal governments. As already mentioned, the UK Coalition government, in power since 2010, has cut back on public support for the organizational structure that has facilitated the capacity for women's organizations such as the Women's National Commission (WNC) to utilize the CEDAW.[74] Due to budget cuts under the conservative government, many of the established study centres for gender and the law in the Netherlands have lost their funding.[75] In Canada, where economic and social rights do not benefit from explicit constitutional protection, and the courts promote a restrictive understanding of the state's social and economic rights obligations, women's organizations have turned to the international human rights arena in order to make the conservative government accountable for the increase in women's poverty and inequality resulting from its neoliberal policies.[76] The Canadian study demonstrates the normative potential of a claims-making strategy involving both the CEDAW Committee and the ICESCR Committee. It also demonstrates this strategy's lack of transformative power in the context of a national government that, in line with its neoliberal economic politics, refuses to comply.

In autocratic states such as Pakistan and Zimbabwe, where national identity is closely linked to a constitutional gender hierarchy embedded in religion and custom, the CEDAW has had little direct impact on law reform. It should, however, be borne in mind that in order to have an impact, women's rights experts and organizations in these countries often couch their equal rights claims in religious or customary terms. In Pakistan, according to Ali, a comparative study emphasizing the similarities between the basic principles underlying the CEDAW and Islam influenced the Pakistani government's decision to ratify the CEDAW.[77] In a similar vein, the Zimbabwean study shows how a research project carried out by the Women and Law in Southern African Research Trust (WLSA), documenting that the customary norms on the ground were changing so

[74] S. Fredman, Chapter 18 (section 4).

[75] M. van den Brink, Chapter 17 (section 9).

[76] L. Lamarche, Chapter 12 (section 3).

[77] S. S. Ali, Chapter 15 (section 3) and S. S. Ali, *A Comparative Study of the United Nations Convention on the Elimination of All Forms of Discrimination against Women, Islamic Law and the Laws of Pakistan* (Peshawar: Shaheen Printing Press, 1995).

as to allow widows to inherit their husbands, led to legal reform recognizing women's right to inherit from their spouses on an equal footing with men.[78]

Although many women's organizations regard the CEDAW as a valuable lobbying tool that draws public attention to women's rights issues, the record of legislative change as a result of the Convention and the Committee's interventions is mixed. The studies show how state resistance to human rights in general and to the CEDAW in particular is prevalent in both democratic and autocratic states in both the north and the south. As demonstrated by the Indian, Nepalese, Pakistani and Zimbabwean studies, ethnic and religious identity politics is a factor that hampers law reform in various ways. In Canada, where the Convention is relatively well known by both rights-holders and duty-bearers through research and action, the growing state resistance is ascribed to the neoliberal politics of the existing government. In Northern Europe, EU law, with its more concise legal standards and strong enforcement machinery, has been a more effective tool for legal change than both the CEDAW and the ECHR. The Northern European studies indicate that the extent to which the CEDAW's normative potential in areas not covered by EU law is realized depends on factors such as the degree of transparency, existence of national research addressing the CEDAW and the strength of the women's organizations.

4.3 *The CEDAW in judicial decision-making*

The domestic studies demonstrate that judicial review is an important safeguard in situations where the executive branch of government refuses to comply with existing human rights obligations. In the studies included in this volume, the Convention is most frequently referred to in case law in Southern Asian countries, where no regional instruments are in place. Yet in later years the CEDAW has gained ground in Northern European case law as well, and is slowly starting to make its mark on case law from the ECtHR.

Comparisons between the countries indicate that the effect of domestication through judicial review is greatest in relatively democratic South

[78] See J. Stewart and A. Tsanga, 'The widows' and female child's portion: the twisted path to partial equality for widows and daughters under customary law in Zimbabwe' in A. Hellum, J. E. Stewart, A. Tsanga and S. S. Ali (eds.), *Human Rights, Plural Legalities and Gendered Realities: Paths Are Made by Walking* (Harare: Weaver Press, 2007) 407–37.

Asian states such as India and Nepal. Madhu Mehra analyzes how the Indian judiciary, in the context of a volatile political terrain marked by ethnic and religious identity politics, has played a leadership role in domesticating the CEDAW.[79] Being a federal state, with a legal system based on common law, the Supreme Court and the high courts are, through the exercise of judicial review, empowered to harmoniously interpret a law to achieve compliance with the fundamental rights (that encompass human rights) in the Constitution. In a series of landmark cases covering restorative justice, sexual harassment in the workplace, child sexual offences and compulsory registration of marriage, the Indian Supreme Court has formulated guidelines, urging legislative reform to follow. Through its decisions and in spite of reservations, the Supreme Court has to a certain degree initiated family law reform with respect to minority women. The Indian state's passivity in relation to minority women, which must be understood in light of the volatile political situation regarding ethnic and religious minorities, has been criticized by the CEDAW Committee. Pointing to the political contestations related to the Supreme Court judgments concerning sexual violence against women, Mehra, however, shows that implementation of the CEDAW is also resisted in areas free of reservation and despite strong NGO presence.

The Nepalese study demonstrates the close relationships between legal literacy, legal aid, judicial education and judicial review.[80] Kabita Pandey compares judgments handed down by the Nepalese Supreme Court before and after the civic organization Pro Public's judicial training programme focusing on the CEDAW. In the light of the Supreme Court's changing jurisprudence, Pandey argues that the judiciary, when given training on women's human rights and the state obligation under the CEDAW, upholds the state obligation to protect and promote women's human rights in its judgments. It appears that an important factor regarding the legitimacy and effectiveness of this legal education programme was the systematic use of regional legal resources, including the contributions of the then-Chief Justice of India, showing how the Indian judiciary handled cases where Hindu law came into conflict with the CEDAW. Furthermore, the Nepalese study indicates that the Court's directive orders for the enactment and amendment of discriminatory laws concerning widow allowances, women's property rights, marital rape and sexual harassment have to a large extent been followed up by the executive branch of government.

[79] M. Mehra, Chapter 13 (section 3.1 and section 3.2).

[80] K. Pandey, Chapter 14 (section 4).

As shown by Byrnes, Australian courts have drawn on the Convention and CEDAW Committee output to give CEDAW-consistent interpretations of the SDA in a number of cases.[81] A comprehensive overview of the main constitutional battles for women's rights in Canada shows that the Supreme Court of Canada rarely relies explicitly on human rights in general or the CEDAW in particular.[82] It did so, however, in the *Ewanchuk* case concerning sexual assault, and in the *Chan* case, where the risk of forced sterilization was seen as a form of persecution.

The CEDAW is also making a modest mark on judicial review in autocratic states such as Pakistan. In the reported case law of Pakistan's superior judiciary (five high courts and the Supreme Court) from accession in 1996 through to 2010, there are four judgments where the court specifically alluded to the CEDAW. While these judgments are widely quoted abroad and in human rights circles, they are rarely quoted in the reported case law from the five high courts and the Supreme Court in Pakistan. According to Ali, this reflects a situation where using human rights in general and the CEDAW in particular is out of tune with the dominant legal argumentation culture. The analysis of reported Supreme Court cases from Zimbabwe shows that the CEDAW has been invoked in two cases. It also shows how the judiciary, in the context of an undemocratic and violent regime where human rights lawyers are subject to threats, violence, torture and unlawful arrest, have contributed to piecemeal legal change through dynamic interpretation of national statutory law. While not explicitly referred to in most judgments, according to the authors the CEDAW often informs the work of practising lawyers and judges.

While initially situated in the shadow of the dynamic case law from the European Court of Justice (ECJ), the CEDAW has become more visible in Northern European case law in recent years. This is reflected in the relatively high number of complaints under the Optional Protocol to the CEDAW lodged against the states. By October 2009 three complaints against the Netherlands had been lodged under the Optional Protocol, one unsuccessful, one dismissed and one pending. There have been two cases against the UK and two against France, all of which were declared admissible by the CEDAW Committee. No complaints have thus far been lodged against the Norwegian or the Finnish states. The number of court cases in Northern European national courts that refer to the CEDAW is also increasing. A prominent case involving the CEDAW is that concerning

[81] A. Byrnes, Chapter 11 (section 5).

[82] L. Lamarche, Chapter 12 (section 2.3).

the Dutch SGP Party's refusal to accept women as (full) members. In 2010 the Dutch Supreme Court established that Article 7(a) of the CEDAW requires the state to effectively ensure the right of women to stand for election. On 10 July 2012 the ECtHR, with reference to the CEDAW, the ICCPR and the ECHR, concluded that the SGP's position is unacceptable regardless of the deeply-held religious conviction on which it is based.[83] Also, in the UK, increasing reliance has been paid to the CEDAW as an interpretative aid in cases before the courts. In the *Yemshaw* case the CEDAW Committee's definition of gender-based violence in General Recommendation 19 was invoked when interpreting a statutory provision deeming persons to be homeless when they are exposed to violence in the home.[84]

In Norway, the CEDAW has, since 2009, been referred to in only one Supreme Court case and in one Court of Appeals case.[85] According to Hellum, the low number of court cases where the CEDAW is referred to can be explained in part by the low number of discrimination cases handled by the courts in general. In Norway, most discrimination cases are dealt with by the specialist administrative agencies, the Equality and Anti-Discrimination Ombud, and the Equality and Anti-Discrimination Tribunal. These cases demonstrate how the Tribunal has interpreted the Gender Equality Act in light of the Convention and the Committee's General Recommendations and Concluding Comments. A significant trend in both the Ombud's and the Tribunal's jurisprudence is the use of Article 5(a) in the CEDAW to strengthen the Gender Equality Act's protection against discrimination. Looking into the background of the Tribunal members, Hellum shows that in most of the cases in which the CEDAW is referred to, it was invoked by female Tribunal members with a specialist background in women's law, anti-discrimination and equality law.

As demonstrated by these studies, the judiciary does not operate in a legal vacuum but is receptive to the legal, political and cultural contexts in which it operates. How elite legal education, carried out at a certain historical moment, may have an effect on both judicial review and law reform is demonstrated by the Nepalese case. The Dutch and Norwegian studies suggest that the increasing attention given to the CEDAW through a combination of research, civic action and state reporting makes a difference

[83] M. van den Brink, Chapter 17 (section 6.1).
[84] S. Fredman, Chapter 18 (section 2).
[85] A. Hellum, Chapter 21 (section 7.2).

in comparison to countries where the CEDAW has been given little attention in research and action, such as France and the UK. While these are important factors, the dominant culture of legal argumentation may, as demonstrated by the Canadian, French and UK studies, constitute an additional barrier. Yet even in situations with fierce state resistance, the Pakistani and Zimbabwe studies demonstrate that individual judges are taking the Convention itself or its spirit into consideration.

5 Future prospects and research needs

Through a comparative and interactive perspective, the chapters in this book show how the CEDAW slowly but surely is making its mark on international, regional and national legal developments. From different angles and perspectives the authors describe and analyze the development of the CEDAW's *transformative, holistic and gender-specific* approaches to gender equality and non-discrimination as the outcome of a multiplicity of interactive and overlapping international, regional and national processes. Uncovering synergies and tensions, the various chapters point to the CEDAW regime's significance as a framework and an international legal arena where women's NGO's, governments and women's rights scholars from various parts of the world frame their diverging claims and arguments.

The chapters in Part I show how the CEDAW regime's potential added value is translated into actual added value. Through 'constructive dialogue' and individual communications from the Committee, the CEDAW's transformative approach is linked to domestic processes of law-making, litigation and NGO advocacy in different political, legal and economic contexts. Addressing the options and limits of the CEDAW regime's transformative capacity, the chapters in this part of the book point to the tensions between the quest for concise concepts and effective sanctions on the one hand, and the Convention's method of 'constructive dialogue' on the other. A critical factor in all parts of the world is the complex nature of the demand for substantive equality and appropriate measures, which, in the context of complex plural legal situations, makes it difficult for an external body such as the CEDAW Committee to strike a balance between equality and difference, and to assess the various short- and long-term measures available for the State Party.

Focusing on if and to what extent the CEDAW Committee, the ICESCR Committee and the HRC interpret social and economic rights in the light of women's lived realities, the authors in Part II address the relationship between the CEDAW regime's potential and actual added value in comparison to other regimes. Showing how the regimes learn and draw inspiration from each other through a synergetic process, most authors conclude that the CEDAW regime has contributed to engendering social and economic rights to a greater extent than the HRC or ICESCR Committee. This is ascribed to the asymmetric approach and specific focus on women's disadvantaged positions, the demand for structural change (Article 5), and the emphasis on women's representation and participation. However, important parts of the Convention, such as the right to work and the right to water, still need continued engagement to ensure that the Committee continues to develop the CEDAW in the direction of more engendered social and economic human rights.

Despite significant variations regarding the realization of women's right to equality and non-discrimination in various historical, political, legal and economic settings, the national case studies presented in Part III clearly indicate that the involvement of women's organizations is a key factor in the social and political legitimacy and the effectiveness of the state reporting procedure at the national level. The case studies show that the CEDAW has had greater impact on judicial review and legislation in South Asian countries where no regional instrument is in place, than in Northern Europe where the CEDAW operates side by side with EU law and the ECHR. As pointed out by the Northern European authors, the CEDAW's potential added value in areas not developed in EU law and the ECHR, such as protection against structural discrimination, religious discrimination and sexual violence, should be given more attention in academic work as well as by state and non-state actors.

As a normative and institutional framework in which similarities and differences between international, regional and national conceptions of discrimination, equality and difference are discussed and resolved, the CEDAW regime has clearly had a catalytic effect on the multiple levels on which it operates. The findings that emerge from the chapters in this book thus point in the same direction as the international legal scholar Bruno Simma's optimistic view that the establishment of separate epistemic communities 'contribute[s] to a growing and ever more dense corpus of law which responds to the needs of the specific regime. In a positive light, these sub-systems of international law, more densely integrated and more technically coherent, may show the way forward for general international law, as both laboratories and boosters for further progressive development at the global level.'[86]

At a theoretical and methodological level, the CEDAW regime has provided space for the development of an interdisciplinary, interregional and transnational human rights jurisprudence focusing on the relationship between substantive equality and engenderment. The CEDAW's context-sensitive human rights approach, which includes a grounded understanding of the circumstances that affect women's lives and enjoyment of rights, is clearly a factor that constitutes both potential and actual added value in comparison to other international and regional regimes. In order to contribute to the further realization of the CEDAW's transformative potential, as well as continued engenderment and effective implementation of women's human rights, further research is needed. The chapters in this book demonstrate that in particular interdisciplinary analysis of the interaction between international and national law, and between state and non-state actors, at the international, national and local levels, is of particular importance. Such research can provide important knowledge about the legal, political, social and cultural factors that affect the legitimacy and effectiveness of the CEDAW, the various processes of domestication and engenderment, and the potential and limitations of the work of the CEDAW Committee in different contexts and settings. Only on the basis of such in-depth analysis can the full realization of the added value of the CEDAW be ensured.

[86] B. Simma, 'Universality of international law from the perspective of a practitioner', *European Journal of International Law* 20:2 (2009) 265–97.

INDEX

AAAQ (Available, Accessible, Acceptable Services of Good Quality) framework, 303–8, 640–1
Aasen, Henriette Sinding, 11, 13, 239, 636, 640–1
AB v. *Registrar of Births, Deaths and Marriages*, 344–5
Abaka, C., 373
Aboriginal women, 380, 381–2, 383
abortion, 89, 254, 258–9, 309–11
Act on Equal Status, Norway, 572
Act on Equality between Women and Men, Finland, 22, 569–71, 575, 576, 578–9, 581n.79, 585, 646
Act on Family Names, Finland, 569
Administration of Estates Act Amendment Act, Zimbabwe, 463–6, 470n.43
affirmative action, 238, 520–1, 523–4, 534–6
Affirmative Action (Equal Opportunities in Employment) Act, Australia, 333–4
Afghanistan, 89–90
Africa
  culture as source of rights, 204–12
  gender stereotypes, 186
  maternal mortality, 294, 298, 313
  pluralism in constitutional reforms, 197–204
  polygamy, 188–94
  women's employment, 219
African Charter on Human and People's Rights on the Rights of Women in Africa Protocol, *see* Maputo Protocol
age of majority, 461–3
agency, 221–2, 227–8, 234
Aggarwal, Alison, 234–5, 286
Ahamadi, A. H., 426
Ahemdabad Women's Action Group and Others v. *Union of India*, 399
Ahrens, R. Z., 162–3
aid effectiveness, 316
Aldridge v. *Booth*, 340–1
Aletta, Dutch Institute for Women's History, 506, 507
Ali, Shaheen Sardar, 19, 431, 438, 440n.43, 446, 447n.67, 645, 648, 651
All Pakistan Women's Association (APWA), 434
Alston, Philip, 277n.25
American Convention on Human Rights, 16, 174–5, 362
American Declaration on Rights and Duties of Man, 361–2
Anti-Discrimination Act, Norway, 606, 611, 613, 619, 623
Anti-Discrimination and Accessibility Act, Norway, 611, 613, 619
Anuj Garg v. *Hotel Association of India*, 406, 408
Apparel Export Promotion Council v. *A. K. Chopra*, 406–7
Arab Charter on Human Rights, 90–1
Arbour, Louise, 77
Argentina, 179–80, 258–9n.49
Asia, 294, 298
Asia Pacific Advisory Forum on Judicial Education on Equality (APAFEJE/FORUM), 413, 418–9, 426

A. T. v. *Hungary*, 138, 139
Attar, Abdul Wahab, 79
Aurat Foundation, 440n.43, 450
Australia and the CEDAW
  case law, 340–5, 355, 651
  constitutional structure, 325–7
  equality, 330–5, 353–4
  human rights, 325–7, 348–50
  implementation of the CEDAW, 16–17, 323–5, 330–5, 354–7
  international law, 329–30
  law reform, 346–7, 355, 356
  national law, 329–30, 646
  reporting, 324, 347–50, 351–3, 355
  reservations to, 323–4, 356–7
  Sex Discrimination Act, 16–17, 332–45, 354, 355, 646
  treaty implementation, 327–9
  women's rights, 330–5
Australian Human Rights Commission, 337–8
Australian Industrial Relations Commission, 342
Austria, 47, 139
autonomy, 112–16

Bailliet, Cecilia, 6, 8, 632–3, 639
Banda, Fareda, 6, 7, 631, 633, 634
Banda Report on Laws that Discriminate against Women, 69–77, 631
Bangladesh, 418–19
Bazilli, S., 368
Beate-Schöpp-Schilling, Hanna, 42n.54
Beijing Declaration and Platform for Action, 296, 297
Beijing Fourth World Conference on Women
  Canada, 370
  discrimination, 62, 63–9
  Finland, 567, 579, 583
  gender mainstreaming, 635
  health, 296, 301
  India, 391–3
  Pakistan, 441
Bentzon, A. W., 211
Beslan massacre, 179
Bhutto, Benazir, 436n.26, 438, 441
bigamy, 188n.18
Bill of Human Rights, 245–6
births, registration of, 317–18
Bleeker, K., 497
Botswana, 193, 199–200
Brazil, 311–12
Brink, Marjolein van den, 20–1, 643
Brooks v. *Canada Safeway Ltd*, 365
Bulgaria, 148–49
Bunch, C., 248, 250
Burrows, N., 103, 140
Burundi, 61, 109
Bustelo García del Real, C., 373
Butler, J., 115n.94
Byrnes, Andrew, 6–7, 16–17, 140–1, 628, 629–30, 633, 643, 645, 651

C. Masilmani Mudaliar v. *Idol of Shri Swaminathaswami Thirukoil and Others*, 399–400
Canada and the CEDAW
  case law, 365–6, 651, 653
  dignity, 225n.34
  economic, social and cultural rights, 367–9
  equality, 363–7
  implementation of the CEDAW, 17, 45, 48, 358–60, 383–4
  international instruments, 360–1
  judicial education, 418–19
  maternal identity of refugees, 176–7
  Montreal Principles, 358
  national law, 648, 649
  ratification, 360
  regional instruments, 16, 361–3
  shadow reporting, 358–60, 368–83
  Standing Committee on the Status of Women, 376
  women's rights in Canada, 360–9
Canadian Charter of Rights and Freedoms ('the Charter'), 17, 363–5
Canadian Foundation for Children, Youth and the Law v. *Canada*, 366

Cancado Trindade J, 166–7, 169, 170, 171–3, 174–5, 177
Cantoral-Huamaní and García-Santa Cruz v. *Peru*, 178
capabilities approach, 218, 228–30
case law
  Australia, 340–5, 355, 651
  Canada, 365–6, 651, 653
  CEDAW in, 649–53
  France, 548–54, 652–3
  India, 394–407, 407–9, 650
  Inter-American Court of Human Rights, 180–1
  Nepal, 423–7, 650
  Netherlands, 494–501, 651–3
  Pakistan, 448–51, 651, 653
  UK, 652–3
  Zimbabwe, 462–3, 465–6, 469–72, 651, 653
CEDAW (Convention on the Elimination of All Forms of Discrimination against Women)
  added value of, 102–5, 626–34, 653–5
  adoption of, 1–2
  autonomy, 112–16
  criticisms, 102–5
  culture in, 56–9, 111–12, 120–2, 196, 628–32
  dialogue, role of, 121–2
  discrimination, 71, 99–102, 108–10
  diversity, 112–16
  effects of, 625–626, 653–5
  employment, 524–30
  engendered socio-economic rights, 10, 235–41
  engenderment of human rights, 217–18, 636–41
  equality, 105–8, 235–41
  freedom, 112–16
  further research, 655
  gender-specific approach, 2, 3
  gender stereotypes, 106–8, 110, 116–20, 128
  gender stereotyping, 7–8, 124–6, 128, 131–9, 156–7
  gender stereotyping limitations, 140–5, 152–6
  gender stereotyping, states' obligations, 119, 129–31, 136–9, 140–2, 146–52
  health, right to, 299–300, 640–1
  holistic approach, 2, 3, 7, 9–13, 95–7, 122–3, 557, 634–41
  human rights values, 97–9
  judicial decision-making, 641–2, 649–53
  laws discriminating against women, 74–6, 77–8, 85, 86–7
  limitation of rights, 152–6
  marginalization of women's rights, 249–50
  marriage, 196–7
  maternal identity, 172
  maternal mortality, 299–300, 302–15, 636
  maternity, 158, 161–3
  national law, 13–23, 641–2, 645–9
  and other international regimes, 5, 180–2, 514, 634–41, 653–4
  parental gender roles, 106–8, 110
  pluralism under, 8–9, 183–94, 204–5, 213
  polygamy, 9, 187–94, 196–7, 631–2
  Preamble, 2–4, 97–9
  property rights of women, 238–9, 272
  purpose, 4–5, 105–8
  ratification, 65, 119, 642–5
  reservations to, 56–7, 79–80, 87–8, 323–4, 356–7
  States Parties, resistance from, 51–9, 348–50, 356, 649
  substantive equality, 4–9, 86, 106, 110, 235–41, 626–34
  terminology, 1n.1
  transformative approach, 2, 3, 4–9, 86, 106–8, 111–12, 185–6, 626–634, 653
  as 'Western' instrument, 437–8, 452
  women's human rights, 246
  see also Australia and the CEDAW; Canada and the CEDAW; Finland

and the CEDAW; France and the CEDAW; India and the CEDAW; Nepal and the CEDAW; Netherlands and the CEDAW; Norway and the CEDAW; Optional Protocol to the CEDAW; Pakistan and the CEDAW; United Kingdom (UK) and the CEDAW; Zimbabwe and the CEDAW
CEDAW Committee
Australia, 324, 347–50, 351–3
Canada, 359–60, 368–83
civil society organizations, 32, 35, 642–5
composition, 28–31
Concluding Observations, 121–2
efficacy of, 519
Finland, 558–9, 582–4
France, 138, 545–6
gender impact analysis, 373–4
gender stereotyping, 129, 136–9, 141–2
General Recommendations, 39–45, 50, 141–2, 186–8, 197, 238, 272–4
General Statements, 41
health rights guidelines, 302–15
housing, right to, 290
impact of, 60–1
India, 386–7, 404–5, 406, 407
inheritance rights, 275
laws discriminating against women, 66–8, 86–7
location, 30–1
maternal mortality, 297, 319
maternal rights, 180–2
members, 346
monitoring role, 27–8, 301–2
Nepal, 310, 414, 416–17, 428–9
Netherlands, 143, 487–8, 489–92, 503, 507–8, 509–10, 643
norms in conflict with, 55–9
Norway, 597, 600, 602–7, 609–17, 643–4
and other treaty bodies, 509–10
Pakistan, 442–4, 445
pluralism, approach to, 8–9, 186–94, 204–5, 213
polygamy, 187–94, 196–7
property rights of women, 272–4, 275, 276–7, 284, 289, 290
reporting procedure, 31–8, 60–1, 347–50, 642–5
reservations, 56–7, 87–8, 546
role, 6–7, 48–55, 59–61, 265, 627–9, 633–4
and the Special Rapporteur, 287
States Parties, resistance from, 51–9, 348–50, 356, 649
substantive equality, 627–34
UK, 512, 516, 520–30
violence against women, 46, 168, 252, 518–19
Zimbabwe, 475–80
Centre for Human Rights, 251
Chairman, Railway Board and Ors v. *Mrs. Chandrima Das and Ors*, 403–4
Chamallas, M., 170n.38
Chan v. *Canada*, 366, 651
Chandra Kanta Gyawali v. *His Majesty's Government of Nepal*, 423
Chanmuniya v. *V. K. Singh Kushwaha*, 402
Chant, S., 221–2
Charlesworth, H., 102–3, 249–50
Chhaupadi, 425
Chihowa v. *Mangwende*, 470
child guardianship, 398–9, 472, 569
child sexual abuse, 404
childcare, 219–22, 237, 525–6, 621–2
China, 80
Chinkin, C., 102–3, 104n.48
citizenship rights, 19, 389, 423, 425, 445, 450, 471, 518, 552, 569
Ciudad Juárez Inquiry, 143
civil society organizations
Australia, 347–8
Canada, 368–83
Finland, 564–5, 577, 580–2, 587
France, 554
judicial education, 411–13, 417–21
Nepal, 18, 411–13, 418–21, 426
Netherlands, 491–2, 493, 507

civil society organizations (*cont.*)
Norway, 597, 599–600, 601, 603–5, 612, 642n.50
Optional Protocol, 519
Pakistan, 438–9, 441, 442–3, 445–6, 453
reporting to CEDAW Committee, 32, 35, 642–5
Special Rapporteur on laws that discriminate against women, 76
UK, 516–18, 642n.50
women's human rights role, 264–7
Working Group on Laws that Discriminate against Women (WG), 62, 65–6, 94
Zimbabwe, 467–8, 474–80, 476n. 60
Clara Wichmann Institute, 505–6
COHRE, 281n.45
Cold War, 562–3
combat duties, 323–4, 357
Commission nationale consultative des droits de l'homme (CNCDH – National Advisory Commission on Human Rights), France, 554
Commission on Human Rights, 243, *see also* Human Rights Council
Commission on Information and Accountability for Women's and Children's Health, 297, 317–18
Commission on the Status of Women (CSW), 65–6, 67–9, 83, 85, 243, 247n.18
Committee on Economic, Social and Cultural Rights (CESCR), *see* ICESCR Committee
Committee on the Elimination of Racial Discrimination, 27–8, 483–4, *see also* International Convention on the Elimination of All Forms of Racial Discrimination (ICERD)
compounded stereotyping, 127n.6, 142–3
control, *see* agency
Convention against Torture (CAT), 360, 596, 599
Convention of Belém do Pará (Inter-American Convention on the Prevention, Punishment and Eradication of Violence against Women), 174–5, 181, 362
Convention on the Elimination of All Forms of Discrimination against Women, *see* CEDAW
Convention on the Nationality of Married Women, 450, 485
Convention on the Rights of Persons with Disabilities, 142, 360
Convention on the Rights of the Child (CRC), 343–4, 360, 361, 495–6, 589, 594n.27, 596, 610
Cook, Rebecca, 104n.46, 107, 113–14, 131, 154, 166, 173–4
Coomaraswamy, Radhika, 254–5
Cotton Field case (*González et al.* v. *Mexico)*, 178, 363
Council for Equality between Women and Men, Finland, 564–5n.23, 565–6, 568
Council of Europe, 562, 584
courts, pluralism in, 204–12
Criminal Law Amendment Bill, India, 404–5
crisis centres, 615–7, 623
Cristina Muñoz-Vargas y Sainz de Vicuña v. *Spain*, 139
cultural feminism, 162–3
culture
and the CEDAW, 56–9, 111–12, 120–2, 196, 628–32
dialogue, role of, 120–2
France, 534–5, 630
gender stereotypes, 116–20
Maputo Protocol, 196
Pakistan, 431–6
as source of rights, 204–12
and women's rights, 204n.65
Zimbabwe, 465, 474
Cusack, Simone, 6, 7–8, 104n.46, 113–14, 131, 154, 160, 166, 173–4, 627–8
customary law, 202–3, 210–12, 457–8, 463–5, 474, 477–8
customary practices, 56–9, 202–3, 435–6

Dairiam, Shanthi, 60–1
Damiso, Choice, 19–20, 644
Daniel Latifi and Another v. *Union of India*, 397–8, 407
data collection, 51
daughters, inheritance rights of, 275
De Beer, M., 165
de facto equality, 4–5, 66–7, 98n.11, 106
De Pinho, Helen, 316–7
death of spouse, 195, 269–271, 274–5, 283
deaths, registration of, 317–18
Deceased Person's Family Maintenance Act, Zimbabwe, 470
Declaration on Social Progress and Development, 161n.8
Declaration on the Elimination of Discrimination against Women, 562
Declaration on the Elimination of Violence against Women, 175, 403–4
Delhi Domestic Working Women Forum v. *Union of India and Ors*, 402–3, 408–9
democracy, 49–50, 53–5
Denmark, 161, 162, 571–2, 572n.51
dignity, 98–9, 225, 226–7, 234–5
discrimination
  in the CEDAW, 71, 99–102, 108–10
  gender discrimination, 457, 463, 466, 468, 522, 611–17
  gender stereotypes, 108–9
  healthcare, 308–11, 312
  housing, 279–82
  in the HRC, 261–2
  in the ICESCR, 261–262
  non-discrimination principle, 99–102, 237, 308–11, 312
  property rights, 276
  sex discrimination, 99–102, 389, 405–7, 408–9, 468
diversity, 112–16
Division for the Advancement of Women (DAW), 244, 251
divorce, 90, 283, 397–8, 463
domestic violence, 263, 283n.50, 420–1, 425, 479–80, 504, 615–17, 619–20
domestic work, 219–22
dowry death, 388
Dr. Chanda Bajracharya v. *Parliament Secretariat and Others*, 423–4
Durojaye, Ebenezer, 318
Dutch Emancipation Council, 492

eating disorders, 255
economic participation, 218–21
Ecuador, 318–19
education, 151–2, 222–3, 240–1, 452, 618, 621, 638
Egypt, 90, 439
elderly women, 196
Ellicott, Robert, 332
employment, 219, 424, 524–30
engenderment
  CEDAW, 235–41
  formal equality, limitations of, 223–4
  gendered disadvantage, 218–23
  housing, right to, 234–5, 285–6, 636, 638–9
  of human rights, 10, 217–18, 228, 636–41
  ICESCR, 230–5, 638–9
  of socio-economic rights, 11–12, 218, 228–30, 241, 634–5, 636–41
  substantive equality, 223–8, 636–41
Entity for Gender Equality and the Empowerment of Women (UN Women), 68–9
Equal Opportunities Commission, UK, 517, 520, 522
Equal Opportunity in the Workplace Act, Australia, 354
equality
  Australia, 330–5, 353–4
  Canada, 363–7
  CEDAW, 235–41
  engenderment of socio-economic rights, 223–8, 241
  Finland, 559–68
  France, 535–6
  ICESCR, 230–5

equality (*cont.*)
judicial education, 419–21
and maternity, 158–60
meaning of, 90–1, 98–9
vs. non-discrimination principle, 99–102
Norway, 571–2, 590–2
of opportunity, 225–6
property rights, 276–7
of results, 226
UK, 52–3, 520–4
of women and men, 160n.7
E-Quality, Netherlands, 507
Equality Act, UK, 52–3, 512–13, 521–2, 523–4, 529–30
Equality and Anti-Discrimination Ombud, Norway, 591, 599–600, 603–4, 606, 610, 611–13, 614–17, 618n.137, 619–20, 623–4, 652
Equality and Anti-Discrimination Tribunal, Norway, 620–4, 652
Equality and Human Rights Commission, UK, 517, 520, 522–3
Equality Now, 62n.2, 64, 65–6, 70, 86
Ertürk, Yakin, 116, 254–5, 262n.57
European Convention on Human Rights (ECHR)
and the CEDAW, 5
Finland, 20, 563, 573–4
France, 20, 543
Netherlands, 20, 495–6, 508, 509
Norway, 20, 589, 596, 600, 601, 610, 616, 623
review process, 607
UK, 20, 512, 515
Zimbabwe, 471n. 44
European Court of Human Rights (ECtHR), 21, 482–3, 489, 490–1, 494–6, 498–500, 652
European Court of Justice (ECJ), 607–8, 622
European Economic Area (EEA), 607–8, 620–1
European Free Trade Association (EFTA), 20, 562, 607–8, 618
European Union (EU)
and the CEDAW, 514
Denmark, 571–2
Finland, 558, 562, 563, 574–7, 579
France, 538, 553
Gender Equality Directive, 23
membership, 20
national law, influence on, 571–2, 647–8, 649
reporting, 607n.81
review process, 607
women's employment, 219
European Union Directive on Gender Equality, 5
Evatt, Elizabeth, 346
eviction from the home, 278–9, 282–5

fair trial, right to, 133
family, 233, 237, 282–5
family law, 284, 389, 394–402, 407–9, 617
family life, 609–11
family names, 490–1, 538n.17, 546–7, 569
Farha, Lielani, 222, 231, 281–2
Fazlullah, Maulana, 433n.11
female genital mutilation (FGM), 195, 259–60, 263, 264–5n.61
feminism, 162–3, 212–13, 536–7, 559–60
Feminist Alliance for International Action (FAFIA), Canada, 375, 379–80, 382
Ferguson, C., 316
Fineman, Martha, 159, 170–1
Finland and the CEDAW
civil society organizations, 564–5, 577, 580–2, 587
constitution, 558, 568–9, 573–4, 575–7
equality, 559–568
European influence on, 573–7, 579, 647
implementation of the CEDAW, 20, 22, 557–9, 585–7, 651
maternity, 161
national law, 569–72, 646, 647

ratification, 568–73, 572n.51
reporting, 558–9, 577–84
reservations, 558, 572
shadow reporting, 581–2
state feminism, 564–5, 577, 587, 643–4
fixed parental gender roles
in the CEDAW, 106–8, 110
dialogue, role of, 120–2
discrimination, 108–10
diversity, principle of, 112–16
states' obligations, 116–20
transformative equality, 111–12
flexible working arrangements, 525–6
Flinterman, Cees, 507–8
Floro, M. S., 219
forced eviction, 278–9, 282–5
forced sterilization, 258
formal equality, 97–9, 106, 110, 223–4
Foster, D., 165
France and the CEDAW
case law, 548–54, 652–3
civil society organizations, 554
constitutional background, 540–2
cultural environment, 534–5, 630
declarations, 542–3
gender stereotyping, 138
implementation of the CEDAW, 20, 21–2, 531–3, 539–40, 547–56, 630, 651
international law, 537–8
language, role of, 531–2
national law, 647
ratification, 539–42
reservations, 541–2, 543–7
socio-political context, 533–8
Fraser, Nancy, 226–7
Fredman, Sandra, 10, 11–12, 21, 256n.42, 310–11, 521–2, 637–9
freedom, 112–16
Freud, Sigmund, 160n.7
fulfilment of rights, 150–2, 256–61
full equality, 106

G20 (women's rights group), Zimbabwe, 474
gender, meaning of, 1n.1
gender discrimination, 457, 463, 466, 468, 522, 611–17
gender equality, *see* equality
Gender Equality Act, Norway, 22–3, 590–1, 592, 593–4, 600, 608–11, 612–13, 619, 620–3, 624
Gender Equality Duty, UK, 520, 521–2, 529–30
gender impact analysis, 373–4
gender mainstreaming, 72, 285–7, 376–7, 533–4, 635–6
gender relations, 106–9
gender stereotypes
African countries, 186
in the CEDAW, 106–8, 110, 116–20, 128
dialogue, role of, 120–2
discrimination, 108–10
diversity, principle of, 112–16
equality, 105–8
institutionalization of, 144–5
and maternity, 160, 173–9, 632–3
meaning of, 126–8
rape conviction rates, 88–9
states' obligations, 116–20
transformative equality, 111–12, 627–30
gender stereotyping
CEDAW, 7–8, 124–6, 128, 131–9, 156–7
compounded stereotyping, 142–3
housing, right to, 279–82, 288–9
human rights, 128–31
limitations, 140–5, 152–6
meaning of, 126–8
and pluralism, 183–4
States Parties, 119, 129–31, 136–9, 140–2, 146–52
Germany, 162, 535n.9
Ghana, 199–200, 201
Gita Hariharan and Anr. v. *Reserve Bank of India*, 398–9
Goicolea, I., 318–19
González et al. ('Cotton Field') v. *Mexico*, 178, 363

Goodmark, L., 164
Goonesekere, Savitri, 61
government, role of, 606
Government of National Unity (GNU), Zimbabwe, 455, 455n.2
Groenman Commission, 104–6, 111–12, 487–8
Gross, A. M., 115n.94
Guardian and Wards Act, India, 398–9

H v. *H*, 471–2
Hall v. *A & A Sheiban Pty Ltd*, 340–1
Halperin-Kaddari, Ruth, 42n.54
Hamann, Andrea, 21–2, 630
Haupt, P., 165
Haute autorité de lutte contre les discriminations et pour l'égalité (HALDE – High Authority to Combat Discrimination and Promote Equality), France, 554
health, right to, 51, 239, 299–300, 640–1
healthcare
  AAAQ framework, 303–8, 640–1
  CEDAW Committee, 302–15
  human rights of women, 13, 292–3, 315–20, 495
  ICESCR Committee, 302–15
  indicators, 312–15
  international instruments, 298–300
  monitoring bodies, 300–2
  non-discrimination, 308–11, 312
  Norway, 622–3
  States Parties' obligations, 311–12
Hellum, Anne, 22–3, 117n.106, 590, 630, 652
Helsinki Process, 562
Hernandez, Berta, 165
Hernes, Helga, 564n.21
Hindu law, India, 394–5
Hindu Minority and Guardianship Act, India, 398–399
Hindu Succession Act, India, 399
Hinduism, Nepal, 414–15, 423–4, 426
Holtmaat, Rikki, 4, 6, 7, 59, 626, 627, 629, 630
homes
  equality improvement measures, 288–91
  human rights, 268–9, 271
  property rights of women, 12–13, 271–7
  'Rose' case study, 269–71
  security of tenure, 277–87
  soft law, role of, 268–9
  see also property rights
home work, 219–22
housing
  engendered rights, 234–5, 285–6, 636, 638–9
  equality improvement measures, 288–91
  gendered disadvantage, 222
  human rights, 271, 277–8
  property rights of women, 12–13, 271–7
  'Rose' case study, 269–71
  security of tenure, 277–87
  soft law, role of, 268–9
  see also property rights
Hudood Ordinance, Pakistan, 19, 445, 448–9n.75, 449
human rights
  Australia, 325–7, 348–50
  CEDAW Preamble, 97–99
  conflict over support for, 489n.26
  discrimination approach, 99–102
  engenderment of, 217–18, 228
  gender stereotyping, 128–31
  healthcare, 13, 292–293, 315–320, 495
  homes, women's rights to, 268–9, 271
  housing, right to, 271, 277–8
  indivisibility of, 287
  life plan, recognition of, 166–7
  maternal mortality, 13, 292–3, 315–20
  maternity and life plan, 8, 168–73
  men's rights as, 247–50
  narrative, use of, 164–6, 179–80, 632–3, 639
  soft law, 268–9
  women's experiences added to, 252–64
  women's rights as, 12, 242–5, 250–2, 264–7

Human Rights Act, Norway, 589, 590–1, 595–601
Human Rights Committee (HRC)
  and Australia, 349n.105, 354
  Canada, 373, 379
  gender impact analysis, 373
  gender stereotypes, 108
  inheritance rights, 275
  Netherlands, 483, 495
  polygamy, 187, 188–9n.19
  property rights of women, 272, 275
  reproductive health, 253–4, 257–9
  role of, 27–8
  women's experiences, 252–64, 639–40
  women's human rights, 244–245, 264–7, 636, 653–4
  World Conference request regarding women's experiences, 250–2
Human Rights Council, 62–3, 77–81, 93, 327, 382–3
Human Rights Law Network (HRLN), 314
Human Rights Watch, 317
Hungary, 138, 139
Hunt, Paul, 253n.34, 256n.43, 258n.48

ICCPR (International Covenant on Civil and Political Rights)
  Australia, 17, 346–7, 349n.105, 353–4
  Canada, 360, 361
  Finland, 576–7
  France, 543
  gender impact analysis, 373
  India, 387–8, 403–4n.71
  Netherlands, 483, 495, 508, 509
  Norway, 589, 596, 600, 601, 610, 623
  Optional Protocols, 361
  property rights, 271–2, 276
  UK, 513
  women's human rights, 1–2, 5, 245–6
  Zimbabwe, 471n. 44
ICERD (International Convention on the Elimination of All Forms of Racial Discrimination), 332, 337n.47, 338, 360, 483–4, 513, 567, 589, 596, 599, 620
ICESCR (International Covenant on Economic, Social and Cultural Rights)
  Australia, 17, 353, 354
  Canada, 360, 367–8, 370–1, 378, 648
  engendered socio-economic rights, 230–5, 638–9
  gender impact analysis, 373
  health, right to, 299–300, 640–1
  housing, right to, 279–80, 636
  India, 387–8
  inheritance rights, 275
  maternal mortality, 253–4, 257–9, 297, 299–300, 302–15, 636
  maternity, 170n.39
  Norway, 589, 594n.27, 594–5n.29, 596, 600, 601, 610, 623
  political systems, 53n.90
  property rights, 275, 276
  UK, 513
  women's experiences, 252–64, 264–5n.61, 639–40
  women's human rights, 1–2, 5, 244–6, 250–2, 264–7, 636, 653–4
  World Conference compliance, 250–2
ICESCR Committee
  Canada, 380, 381
  gender stereotyping, 108
  health rights guidelines, 253–4, 257–9, 302–15
  housing, right to, 277, 278, 279, 280–2, 289, 290
  limitation of rights, 153–4n.113
  monitoring role, 301–2
  property rights, 290
  and the Special Rapporteur, 287
  substantive equality, 232–5, 281n.45
  women's rights, 244–5
Ikdahl, Ingunn, 11, 12–13, 235, 239, 241, 636, 638–9
immigration, 176–7, 515–16

India and the CEDAW
  case law, 394–407, 407–9, 650
  constitutional framework, 394
  Gujarat exceptional report, 387
  implementation of the CEDAW, 17–18, 60–1, 385–6, 407–9, 426, 631
  international influence on, 389–91
  judicial education, 418–20
  maternal mortality, 294, 314–15, 319
  national law, 388–9, 394–407, 646, 649
  ratification, 386–91
  regional instruments, 16
  reporting, 386–7, 645
  reservations, 386–7
  sexual orientation, 93, 631
  shadow reporting, 392
  women's groups activism, 391–4
individual rights strategy (IRS) to eliminate discrimination, 110
inheritance rights, 274–5, 423, 463–6, 470
Institute of Women's Law, Norway, 590, 599–600, 615–16, 617
insurance, 622
Inter-American Commission on Human Rights, 166, 180–1
Inter-American Convention on the Prevention, Punishment and Eradication of Violence against Women (Convention of Belém do Pará), 174–5, 181, 362
Inter-American Court of Human Rights
  Canada, 363
  and the CEDAW, 180–2
  life plan, recognition of, 166–7
  maternal identity, 8, 158–9, 173–9
  maternity and life plan, 168–73
  narrative, use of, 165–6, 632–3
International Conference on Population and Development (ICPD), 296, 297, 301
International Convention on the Elimination of All Forms of Racial Discrimination (ICERD), *see* ICERD
International Court of Justice (ICJ), 545
International Covenant on Civil and Political Rights, *see* ICCPR
International Covenant on Economic, Social and Cultural Rights, *see* ICESCR
International Criminal Tribunals, 169
international instruments, 298–300, 329–30
International Labour Organization (ILO), 331–2, 353, 361, 513–14
International Law Association, 494–5, 508
International Women's Rights Action Watch – Asia Pacific (IWRAW-AP), 392
intersectional discrimination, 613–15
Ireland, 118, 129n.17
Irigaray, Luce, 160n.7
Islam, 57, 431–6, 437–8, 439–40, 444, 451–2

Jacomb v. *Australian Municipal Administrative Clerical and Services Union*, 342–3
Jamaat-e-Islami, 438n.31
Janse, R., 495–6
Janzen v. Platy Enterprises Ltd, 365
Jeater, D., 461–2
Jilani J, 448, 449, 451
Jinnah, Muhammad Ali, 434
Jordan v. *North Coast Area Health Service (No 3)*, 345
judicial decision-making, 641–2, 649–53
judicial education, 151–2, 411–13, 417–421, 507, 508, 650, 652
judiciary, 147–9, 469
JUSTICE, 515–16

Kadhi courts, 202–3
Kang, J. M., 113n.89
Karen Tayag Vertido v. *The Philippines*, 133, 135–6n.42, 138–9, 141, 147–8, 152, 156

Katekwe v. *Muchabaiwa*, 462–3, 470
Kenya
  bigamy, 188n.18
  constitution, 457n. 10
  female genital mutilation (FGM), 260n.54, 264–5n.61
  judiciary, 89
  personal law, 198–200, 200–1n.61, 202–3
  polygamy, 189–91
  property rights, 189–90, 211–12
  woman-to-woman marriage, 205–10
Kismödi, E., 317
Kohlhaas v. *Chief Immigration Officer & Another*, 471
Kothari, Miloon, 282–4, 285–7

Labour Conventions (*Canada* v. *Ontario*) case, 367–8
labour market, 218–21, 571
labour rights, 91–2
Lal Masjid seminary, 433n.11
Lamarche, Lucie, 17
land rights, 284–5
language, role of, 531–2, 565n.26
Law of Evidence Act, Pakistan, 19, 445
laws discriminating against women, *see* Working Group on Laws that Discriminate against Women (WG)
Laxmi Mandal v. *Deen Dayal Harinagar Hospital*, 314–15
L. C. v. *Peru*, 137–8
Leeuwen, Fleur van, 11, 12, 231–2, 627, 636, 639–40
Legal Age of Majority Act (LAMA), Zimbabwe, 461–3, 470
legal pluralism, 184n.2, *see also* pluralism
lesbian women, 92–3, 114–16
Lesotho, 193, 199–200
Levit, Nancy, 136
L'Heureux-Dubé, Claire, 131
Libya, 80, 439
life plan
  and gender stereotypes, 173–9
  and maternity rights, 8, 168–73
  recognition of, 166–7
Lijnzaad, L., 103
Lippmann, Walter, 128
Loayza Tamayo v. *Peru*, 166–7

Maarseveen, Henc van, 101
MacKinnon, Catherine, 76
Madhu Kishwar v. *State of Bihar*, 400, 407
Magaya v. *Magaya*, 200–1n.61, 464n. 32, 465–6, 470n. 43
Maharshi Avadhesh v. *Union of India*, 397
Maine, Deborah, 296
Malawi, 192, 199–200, 201–2, 305–7, 313–14
Mangwana, Paul, 473n. 48
Maputo Protocol
  and the CEDAW, 5
  culture in, 196
  equality, meaning of, 90
  marriage, 196–7
  pluralism under, 194–7
  polygamy, 9, 91, 196–7, 632
  ratification, 15–16
  reproductive rights, 300, 316
  Zimbabwe, 458, 474–5, 644
Margaret Dongo v. *Registrar General*, 472
marital rape, 420, 425, 471–2
marriage, 196–7, 271–4, 284, 386–7, 401–2, 408–9, 432, 468, 617
maternal mortality
  AAAQ framework, 303–8, 640–1
  causes, 294–6
  CEDAW, 299–300, 302–15, 636
  definition, 293
  engendered rights to health, 640–1
  HRC, 253–4, 257–9
  human rights of women, 13, 292–3, 315–20
  ICESCR, 253–4, 257–9, 297, 299–300, 302–15, 636
  indicators, 312–15
  international initiatives, 296–8
  international instruments, 298–300

maternal mortality (*cont.*)
maternal mortality ratio (MMR), 294, 313, 314
medical solutions, 295–6
monitoring bodies, 300–2
non-discrimination, 308–11, 312
States Parties' obligations, 311–12
statistics, 292, 293–4, 298
maternity
adoptive parents, 618–19
CEDAW, 158, 161–3, 180–2
and equality, 158–160
and feminism, 162–3
gender stereotypes, 160, 173–9, 632–3
income insurance, 500–1, 503–4
and life plan, 8, 168–73
narrative, use of, 164–6, 171–3, 179–80
paid maternity leave, 350–3, 357, 501
Maududi, Abul Ala, 434
McBain v. *State of Victoria*, 343–4
McCarthy, M., 160n.7
Meera Dhungana v. *His Majesty's Government et al.*, 425
Meera Dhungana v. *Ministry of Law and Justice and others*, 411, 423
Mehra, Madhu, 17–18, 646, 650
men, 135–6, 247–50
menstruation, 425
mental harm, 175–9
Meron, T., 155n.124
Merry, Sally Engle, 57–8, 103n.43, 104n.47, 121n.125, 319, 629
Meurs, M., 219
Mexico, 48, 79, 80–1, 162, 258–9n.49, 262n.56
migrants, 515–16, 551–2, 584, 613–15
Miguel Castro-Castro Prison v. *Peru*, 8, 158–9, 168–73, 174–5, 176
Millennium Declaration, 296–7
Millennium Development Goals (MDGs), 78, 84, 297–8, 317
minority women, 72, 277, 278, 584, 613–15
MiRA Resource Centre for Immigrant and Refugee Women, 614
Moge v. *Moge*, 365
Moldova, 264–5n.61
Monica Jesang Katam v. *Jackson Chepkwony & another*, 205–10
Morocco, 60–1, 162n.12
mortality, *see* maternal mortality
Mothers of the Plaza de Mayo, Argentina, 179–80
Movement for Democratic Change (Tsvangirai) (MDC(T)), 455, 455n.2
Mst. Humaira Mehmood v. *The State*, 448–9
Mst. Saima and 4 others v. *The State*, 449
Mst. Sarwar Jan v. *Abdur Rehman*, 450
Mugabe, Robert, 455n.2, 467
Mullally, S., 432
Murdoch, Jim, 519
Murphy, Lionel, 331
MUSASA Project, Zimbabwe, 475, 479
Musharraf, Pervez, 446, 448
Muslim law, 202–3, 397–8
Muslim Women's (Protection of Rights on Divorce) Act, India, 397–8

Narayan, Uma, 82n.76
narrative
in human rights, 164–6, 179–80, 632–3, 639
life plan, recognition of, 166–7
maternity rights, 164–6, 171–3, 179–80
National Commission on the Status of Women (NCSW), Pakistan, 436n.26, 446–8, 450, 453
national human rights institutions (NHRIs), 35–6, 605–6
national law
Australia, 329–30, 646
Canada, 648, 649
CEDAW in, 13–23, 641–2, 645–9
Finland, 569–72, 646, 647
France, 647
India, 388–9, 394–407, 646, 649

Nepal, 414–17, 646–7, 649
Netherlands, 502–4, 647, 648
Norway, 607–17, 647–8
Pakistan, 440, 444–6, 648–9
UK, 647, 648
Zimbabwe, 648–9
National Women's Council and Elimination of Discrimination Against Women Bill (draft), Zimbabwe, 480–1
Naz Foundation v. *Government of NCT of Delhi*, 93, 631
Nehanda, Mbuya, 457n. 8
Nepal and the CEDAW
case law, 423–7, 650
constitutional background, 414–16, 421–2
gender norms, 414–15
implementation of the CEDAW, 16, 18, 60–1, 410–14, 415–17, 427–9
judicial education, effects of, 421–7, 650, 652
judicial education, need for, 411–13, 417–21, 427–9
maternal mortality, 310
national law, 414–17, 646–7, 649
ratification, 410, 414
reporting, 310, 414, 416–17, 428–9, 645
Supreme Court, 411–413, 417–18, 421–7, 428–9
women in Nepal, 414–17
Nepalese Treaty Act, 411, 416, 417
Netherlands and the CEDAW
awareness of the CEDAW, 505–8
case law, 494–501, 651–3
gender stereotyping, 143
Groenman Commission, 104–6, 111–12, 487–8
implementation of the CEDAW, 20–1, 482–3, 508–10, 651
judicial education, 507, 508
legal status of the CEDAW, 492–4
maternity, 161
national law, 502–4, 647, 648
national reports, 487–9, 643
ratification, 483–6, 643
reporting, 487–8, 489–92, 503, 643
reservations, 486
scholarship, 505–7
shadow reporting, 491–2
Nigeria, 294
Nilabati Behera v. *State of Orissa*, 403–4n.71
non-discrimination principle, 99–102, 237, 308–11, 312
non-governmental organizations (NGOs), *see* civil society organizations
Nordic Council, 562, 564
norms, 55–9, 270–1, 288–9
Norway and the CEDAW
civil society organizations, 597, 599–600, 601, 603–5, 612, 642n.50
Constitution, 595
equality, 571–2, 590–2
European influence on, 607–9
Human Rights Act, 589, 590–1, 595–601
implementation of the CEDAW, 20, 22–3, 588–90, 623–4, 630, 651
judicial review, 617–23, 652–3
maternity, 161, 162
national law, 607–17, 647–8
ratification, 572n.51, 592–4
reporting, 597, 600, 602–7, 643–4
reservations, 593
shadow reporting, 600, 604–5, 612
Norwegian Centre of Human Rights (NCHR), 606
Nousiainen, Kevät, 22
Nussbaum, Martha, 218, 228–30, 626
Nyamu Musembi, Celestine, 6, 8–9, 102n.36, 121, 631–2, 633

Odgaard, R., 211
Office of the High Commissioner for Human Rights (OHCHR)
Banda Report, 69–77
and the CEDAW, 30, 31

Office of the High Commissioner for Human Rights (OHCHR) (*cont.*)
  laws discriminating against women, 62–3, 67–9, 77, 78–9
  women's human rights, 251, 252–3, 297
  see also Human Rights Council
Oppenheim, L. F. L., 450n.79
oppression, 99–100
Optional Protocol to the CEDAW
  accession, 323–4
  Australia, 349–50, 350n.108
  Canada, 45, 48, 361, 383, 384
  civil society organizations, 519
  complaints, 651
  Finland, 577, 651
  France, 538, 651
  gender stereotyping, 136–7
  jurisprudence, 45–8
  Netherlands, 485–6, 501–2, 651
  Norway, 594, 618, 651
  UK, 48, 518–19, 651
  Zimbabwe, 459
Optional Protocols to the ICCPR, 361
Organization of American States (OAS), 16, 359, 361–3
Otto, Dianne, 144, 170

Pakistan and the CEDAW
  case law, 448–51, 651, 653
  constitutional position, 443–4
  implementation of the CEDAW, 16, 19, 80, 430–1, 442–8, 451–3, 645
  Islamic identity and women's rights, 431–6, 437–8, 439–40, 444, 451–2
  judicial education, 418–20
  national law, 440, 444–6, 648–9
  pre-accession debates, 435–40
  ratification, 440–1, 644
  reporting, 442–4, 445
  reservations, 437–40, 441
  shadow reporting, 442–3
  women's groups activism, 445–6, 453
  women's rights advanced using the CEDAW, 446–8
Pandey, Kabita, 18, 650
parental gender roles, *see* fixed parental gender roles
Parisi, L., 247, 249, 252n.29
parity, 535–6
part-time work, 527–8
pay, 88, 233, 526–30
pensions, 527–8
Pentikäinen, Merja, 22
Peoples' Health Movement (PHM), 318
personal law, 197–204
Peru, 137–8, 165, 166–7, 310, 310n.70
Peters, J., 497
Peters, J. S., 164
Philippines, 45, 48, 133, 135–6n.42, 138–9, 141, 147–8, 152, 162
physical integrity, 263–4
pluralism
  CEDAW Committee, 8–9, 183–94, 204–5, 213
  constitutional reforms in Africa, 197–204
  culture as source of rights, 204–12
  definition, 184n.2
  feminist response, 212–13
  Maputo Protocol, 194–7
Poland, 89
political participation, 496–500
political representation, 459–60
political systems, 53–5
polygamy
  CEDAW, 9, 187–94, 196–7, 631–2
  inheritance rights, 463–4
  Maputo Protocol, 9, 91, 196–7, 632
polygyny, 91, 463–4
Portugal, 162
poverty, 218–21
Predelli, L., 517
pregnancy, 263
President of the Republic of South Africa v. *Hugo*, 213n.91
Preston, R. C., 162–3
Prevention of Discrimination Act, Zimbabwe, 466
Pro Public (Forum for the Protection of the Public Interest), 18, 411–13, 418–21, 426

property rights
  in the CEDAW, 238–9, 272
  CEDAW Committee, 272–4, 275, 276–7, 284, 289, 290
  customary recognition of, 210–12
  disposal of bequeathed property, 399–400
  equality improvement measures, 288–91
  human rights, 271
  inheritance rights, 423
  Kenya, 189–90, 211–12
  'Rose' case study, 269–71
  security of tenure, 12–13, 277–87, 288–91
  soft law, role of, 268–9
  of women, 12–13, 271–7, 288–91
  Zimbabwe, 211, 457, 463
  see also homes; housing
prostitution, 144–5
protection obligation, 149–50, 256–61
Protection of Human Rights Act, India, 391, 400
Protection of Women from Domestic Violence Act, India, 402
psychological harm, 175–9

Quila (R (on the Application of Quila and Another) v. *Secretary of State)*, 514

R. v. *Ewanchuk*, 366, 651
R. v. *Gayme*, 365–6
R. v. *Lavallée*, 365
R. v. *Seaboyer*, 365–6
Ra'ana Liaquat Ali Khan, 434
Racial Discrimination Act, Australia, 338
Rai, Shirin, 447n.67
rape, 88–9, 263, 388, 402–6, 420, 425, 471–2
Rattigan & Others v. *Chief Immigration Officer & Others*, 471
Re Australian Journalists' Association, 341–2
Re Baby R, 365
Re Blainey and Ontario Hockey Association et el., 365
Reanda, L., 249n.26
Reena Bajracharya v. *His Majesty's Government of Nepal*, 424–5
refugees, 176–7
religion
  and the CEDAW, 56–9
  equality, meaning of, 90–1
  India, 394–402
  inheritance rights, 274
  Nepal, 414–15
  Norway, 593, 609–11, 621
  Pakistan, 431–6, 437–8, 439–40, 444, 451–2
  woman-to-woman marriage, 207
remuneration, 88, 233, 526–30
reproductive health
  AAAQ framework, 303–8
  CEDAW Committee, 302–15
  HRC, 253–4, 257–9
  ICESCR Committee, 253–4, 257–9, 302–15
  indicators, 312–15
  Maputo Protocol, 300, 316
  monitoring bodies, 300–2
  non-discrimination, 237, 308–11, 312
  Norway, 622–3
  States Parties' obligations, 311–12
respect, 146–9, 256–61
retirement, 527–8
R. K. B. v. *Turkey*, 150, 156
Roberts, B., 369
Roosevelt, Eleanor, 247
Rosenblum, Darren, 100–1, 103n.43, 104n.47, 116n.99, 145
Rosenfield, Allan, 296
Ruiz Fabri, Hélène, 21–2, 630
Russia, 161–2, 179, 245
Ryan, Susan, 332–3

Sabin Shrestha v. *Ministry of Law, Justice and Parliament Affairs*, 424
Sachar, Rajindar, 278, 280–1, 282
Safe Motherhood Initiative (SMI), 296
Şahide Goekce (deceased) v. *Austria*, 47
Sakshi, 418–19
Sakshi v. *Union of India and Ors*, 405, 408–9

Sandra Falkiner et al. v. *Director of Income Maintenance Branch of the Ministry of Community and Social Services*, 365
Sapana Pradhan v. *Ministry of Law and Justice*, 423–4
Sarfaraz, Zari, 436n.26
Saudi Arabia, 65, 79–81
Sawer, Marian, 330–1
scarification, 195
Schaffer, K., 171
Schöpp-Schilling, H. B., 372n.59, 373, 375–6
Second World War, 560
security of tenure, 12–13, 277–87, 288–91
Seema v. *Ashwani Kumar*, 401, 408–9
Sen, Amartya, 218, 224, 228–30
sex, 1n.1, 448–9
sex discrimination, 99–102, 389, 405–7, 408–9, 468
Sex Discrimination Act, Australia, 16–17, 332–45, 354, 355, 646
sex equality, *see* equality
sex industry, 144–5
sex stereotypes, 127n.6
sex-role stereotypes, 127n.6
sexual assault, 388, 402–5, 408–9
sexual harassment, 405–6, 429
sexual orientation, 92–3, 631
sexual stereotypes, 127n.6
SGP (Staatkundig Gereformeerde Partij/ The Reformed Political Party), 21, 490–1, 496–500, 509, 651–2
Shah Bano case (*Mohd. Ahmed Khan* v. *Shah Bano Begum & Ors*), 397n.46
Shaheed, Farida, 116–17, 435
Shari'a, 440, 448, 450, 451–2
Shihata, I. F. I., 390n.17
Sierra Leone, 307–8, 314
Simma, Bruno, 654–5
Simmons, Beth, 641n.48
Sipilä, Helvi, 563
Sita Acharya v. *Public Service Commission*, 425
Smith, S., 171
social and cultural change strategy (SSCC) to eliminate discrimination, 110
social security/benefits, 223, 240, 527–8, 544–5n.36
social standards, 381–2
social support strategy (SSS) to eliminate discrimination, 110
socio-economic rights
  CEDAW, 10, 235–41
  engenderment of, 11–12, 218, 228–30, 241, 634–41
  formal equality, limitations of, 223–4
  gendered disadvantage, 218–23
  ICESCR, 230–5, 638–9
  resistance to, 513
  substantive equality, 225–8
Solheim, Erik, 602
Sorman, Joy, 537n.12
South Africa, 203, 225n.34
Southern African Development Community Protocol on Gender and Development (SADC Protocol), 458, 475
Special Marriage Act, India, 395
Special Rapporteurs
  Banda Report, 69–77
  economic, social and cultural rights, 277n.25
  health, 72, 253n.34, 256n.43, 258n.48, 297
  housing, 72, 234–5, 278, 280–1, 282–4, 285–7, 289–90, 638–9
  indigenous people, 72
  laws discriminating against women, 66, 67–9, 74–6, 77–8
  minorities, 72
  promotion and protection of human rights and fundamental freedoms while countering terrorism, 92
  violence against women, 254–5
Spencer, Sarah, 521–2
state feminism, 564–5, 577, 587

States Parties
  CEDAW Committee's role, 48–55, 627–9, 633–4
  customs and beliefs, conflict with, 435–6
  dialogue, role of, 120–2
  gender relations, 97
  gender stereotyping, 129–31, 136–9, 140–2, 146–52
  health obligations, 311–12
  healthcare benchmarks, 312–20
  resistance to the CEDAW, 51–9, 348–50, 356, 649
  women, issues specifically affecting, 252–6
  women-inclusive human rights obligations, 256–61
  Working Group on Laws that Discriminate against Women (WG), 87–94
sterilization, 622–3
Stewart, Julie, 19–20, 211, 644
Stienstra, D., 369
Sub-Commission on Prevention of Discrimination and Protection of Minorities, 277, 278
substantive equality
  Australia, 346–7
  in the CEDAW, 4–9, 86, 106, 110, 235–41, 626–34
  engendered rights, 223–8, 636–41
  vs. formal equality, 223–4
  gender stereotyping, 133–4
  healthcare, 308–11
  in ICESCR, 232–5, 281n.45
  India, 406
  meaning of, 98n.11
  property rights, 276–7
  UK, 520, 521–2, 523–4, 526
succession, laws of, 400
Sweden, 161, 571–2, 572n.51

Tanzania, 192, 211, 269–71
Tigchelaar, J., 495–6
Timmer, Alexandra, 153
Tomasevski, K., 222
traditional practices, *see* culture
trafficking, 264–5n.61, 501
transformative equality
  in the CEDAW, 2, 3, 4–9, 86, 106–8, 111–12, 185–6, 626–34, 653
  healthcare, 308–9
  meaning of, 111, 227
  strategies in the CEDAW, 110
Tremblay v. *Daigle*, 365
Tsanga, A., 211, 477, 478
Tsvangirai, Morgan, 455n.2
Tysiac v. *Poland*, 89

Uganda, 191, 199–200, 201
UN High Commissioner for Human Rights, 77, 297
unemployment insurance, 552
United Kingdom (UK) and the CEDAW
  case law, 652–3
  employment, 524–30
  equality, 52–3, 520–4
  implementation of the CEDAW, 20, 21, 48, 511–12, 518–19, 530, 651
  legal status of the CEDAW, 512–14
  managers, women as, 226
  maternity, 162
  national law, 647, 648
  pay gap, 88
  reservations, 514–16
  shadow reporting, 516–18
  visibility of the CEDAW, 516–18, 642n.50, 644
United Nations (UN)
  Charter, 97–9, 245, 247–9
  Decade for Women, 566, 567
  and Finland, 562–3
  General Assembly, 243, 252
  human rights system, 245–6
  International Women's Year, 563
  Secretary General, 297
  Security Council, 169
  see also bodies, conferences and conventions listed by name

United Nations Children's Fund (UNICEF), 296
United Nations Development Fund for Women (UNIFEM), 251, 392–3, 563
United Nations Population Fund (UNFPA), 296
United States (US), 162
Universal Declaration of Human Rights (UDHR), 1–2, 97–9, 170, 245–6, 247–9, 400, 403–4, 410, 450
Universal Periodic Review (UPR) procedure, 382–3

Valkenhorst cases, 495
Victoria v. *Commonwealth ('Industrial Relations Act case')*, 340n.66
Victorian Women Lawyers' (VWL) Association, Australia, 345
Vienna Declaration and Programme of Action, 242–5, 250–2
Vienna World Conference on Human Rights, 242–5, 250–2, 287, 370, 390–1, 635
violence against women
  Canada, 369–71, 372–3
  CEDAW Committee, 46, 252, 518–19
  elimination strategies, 110
  engendered rights, 234–5, 237–8
  Finland, 559, 578, 582–4, 585–6
  gendered disadvantage, 221
  HRC, 252–3, 256–7, 262
  ICESCR, 252–3, 256–7, 262
  India, 388
  integrated human rights approach, 263
  Maputo Protocol, 195
  Nepal, 415, 420–1, 425
  security of tenure, 283n.50
  UK, 522
  World Conference on Human Rights, 252n.29
  Zimbabwe, 89
Vishaka v. *State of Rajasthan*, 405–6, 408–9
V. K. v. *Bulgaria*, 148–9
voice, 227–8, 234

Wachtler, Sol, 410
Waheed, Salma, 445
Waldorf, L., 368
welfare state, 560–1
welfare system, 223, 240, 527–8, 544–5n.36
West, Robin, 159–60, 177–8
Westendorp, I., 280n.37
Western beauty practices, 254–5
westoxification, 82
widowhood, 195, 269–71, 274–5, 283
Wildt, Jeroen de, 506
Winston, M., 99n.19
woman-to-woman marriage, 205–10
Women and Law in Southern Africa Research Trust (WLSA), 464–5, 648–9
Women Ministers Forum, Pakistan, 446–7, 453
Women of Zimbabwe Arise (WOZA), 467–8
Women Who Want to be Women (WWWW), Australia, 332
Women's Coalition, Zimbabwe, 467–8, 473, 473n. 49, 475, 479
Women's National Commission (WNC), UK, 516–17
Women's Resource Centre, UK, 517
women's rights
  Australia, 330–5
  and culture, 204n.65
  discrimination against women, 261–2
  HRC, 252–64, 639–40
  as human rights, 12, 242–6, 250–2, 264–7, 636, 653–4
  ICESCR, 252–64, 264–5n.61, 639–40
  integrated approach, 263–4
  issues specifically affecting women, 252–6
  maternal mortality, 13, 292–3, 315–20
  men's rights as human rights, 247–50
  property rights, 12–13, 271–7, 288–91
  security of tenure, 12–13, 277–87, 288–91

women-inclusive human rights obligations, 256–61
work, 232–3, 239–40, 524–30, 636–41
Work and Families Act, UK, 525–6
Working Group on Laws that Discriminate against Women (WG)
Banda Report, 69–77, 631
challenges, 87–94
focus areas, 84–5
formation of, 7, 62–3, 81–5
history, 63–9
mandate, 82
members, 83–4
opportunities, 86–7
proposal, 77–81
World Conference on Human Rights, Vienna, *see* Vienna World Conference on Human Rights
World Conference on Women (Beijing), *see* Beijing Fourth World Conference on Women
World Health Organization (WHO), 296, 313, 314
Wright, S., 103

Yemshaw v. *London Borough of Hounslow*, 21, 514, 652
Young, Iris Marion, 99–100
Young, Margot, 366, 384

Zambia, 192, 199–200, 310, 457n. 10
ZANU (PF) (Zimbabwe African National Union (Patriotic Front)), 455, 455n.2, 456n. 6, 457, 459n. 17, 468, 469, 472
Zhen Zhen Zheng v. *The Netherlands*, 179n. 57
Zia, Shehla, 440n.43
Zia-ul-Haq, Muhammad, 432
Zimbabwe and the CEDAW
case law, 462–3, 465–6, 469–72, 651, 653
Chiefs, role of, 465, 474
constitution, 454–60, 466–7, 468–9, 472–4, 477–8, 480–1
implementation of the CEDAW, 16, 19–20, 454, 480–1
judiciary, 469
legal reform, 460–9, 474–5
national law, 648–9
personal law, 199–200, 200–1n.61
property rights, 211, 457, 463
ratification, 454, 644
reporting, 459, 475–80, 645
violence against women, 89
women's groups activism, 467–8, 472, 473, 474–80, 476n. 60
women's rights, 455–60
Zimbabwe Women Lawyers' Association (ZWLA), 467–8, 472, 475, 476n. 60, 477, 479
zina (extramarital sex), 448–9
Zuloga, P. P., 169–70, 171–2, 175–6

For EU product safety concerns, contact us at Calle de José Abascal, 56–1°,
28003 Madrid, Spain or eugpsr@cambridge.org.

www.ingramcontent.com/pod-product-compliance
Lightning Source LLC
LaVergne TN
LVHW011534200926
848484LV00001B/263
* 9 7 8 1 1 0 7 0 3 4 6 2 4 *